Managing Your Personal Finances

4th Edition

Joan S. Ryan, M.B.A., Ph.D., C.M.A.

Clackamas Community College

Oregon City, Oregon

SOUTH-WESTERN

THOMSON LEARNING

Australia • Canada • Mexico • Singapore • Spain • United Kingdom • United States

SOUTH-WESTERN
THOMSON LEARNING

Managing Your Personal Finances, 4th Edition
Joan S. Ryan

Vice President/
Executive Publisher
Dave Shaut
Team Leader
Karen Schmohe
Executive Editor
Eve Lewis
Project Manager
Carol Sturzenberger
Channel Manager
Nancy A. Long

Marketing Coordinator
Yvonne Patton-Beard
Production Manager
Patricia Matthews Boies
Manufacturing
Coordinator
Kevin Kluck
Editorial Assistant
Stephanie White
Production Assistant
Nancy Stamper

Design Coordinator
Tippy McIntosh
Consulting Editor
Cinci Stowell,
Stowell Editorial Services
Composition/Prepress
Lachina Publishing
Services, Inc.
Printer
R. R. Donnelley
Willard, OH

For more information,
contact South-Western,
5191 Natorp Boulevard,
Mason, OH 45040; or you
can visit our Internet site at
http://www.swep.com

For permission to use
material from this text or
product, contact us by
Tel (800) 730-2214
Fax (800) 730-2215
www.thomsonrights.com

This book is printed on
acid-free paper.

About the Author:

Joan Ryan, M.B.A., Ph.D., C.M.A., has taught personal finance for over 20 years. She began at Willamette High School in Eugene, Oregon, where this textbook was initially developed and tested. After four years there, she taught in the business department at Lane Community College (also in Eugene) for 12 years. After 8 years at Clackamas Community College, she is currently business department chair and teaches accounting, personal finance, and business law. She also is a C.M.A. (certified management accountant), a state-certified mediator, and adjunct faculty at Portland State University in accounting.

Reviewers:

Rosella Bannister
Ann Arbor, MI
Cynthia Bertrand
Baton Rouge, LA
Margaret Girouard
Biloxi, MI

Claudia M. Kerbel
Warwick, RI
Gemelia Tyler
Hillsboro, OH
Gary G. Vink
Chambersburg, PA
Julie M. Werner
Warner Robins, GA

YOUR COURSE PLANNING JUST GOT EASIER!

- **NEW! Managing Your Personal Finances by Ryan**

  Firmly rooted in proven personal financial management techniques, this text features a conversational writing style that is highly readable and understandable. 75+ hours completion time.

Student Workbook	0-538-69961-2
Student CD	0-538-69963-9
Printed Tests	0-538-69962-0
Video Package	0-538-69960-4

- **NEW! Security First Bank: A Banking Customer Simulation by Sargent and Ward**

  Students receive hands-on practice in important life and personal finances skills. This simulation is designed to help users succeed in banking. 15+ hours completion time.

Simulation	0-538-43187-3

- **NEW! Investing in Your Future by NAIC**

  This text teaches users every step of the way toward smart saving and investing. 30+ hours completion time.

Student Edition (includes Stock Selection guide Software)	0-538-68607-3

- **NEW! Fundamentals of Insurance by Crews**

  This text gives an overview of insurance including an industry review, various types of insurance, rates and claims, and career opportunities. It covers basic competencies required in introductory insurance courses. 30+ hours completion time.

Student Edition	0-538-43201-2
Video	0-538-43250-0

- **Skills for Consumer Success by Donnelly**

  This text enables students and others who are learning their roles in the marketplace to sharpen their consumer skills. 30+ hours completion time.

Text with Windows Data Disk	0-538-68612-X
Tests	0-538-68614-6

- **Family Financial Management by Roman and Finch**

  This comprehensive money-management simulation allows students to calculate net worth, plan monthly budgets, complete banking transactions, make rent and mortgage payments, and reconcile monthly bank statements. 20+ hours completion time.

Simulation	0-538-67501-2

- **On Your Own by Donnelly**

  Students use a simulated checkbook, expense report, and personal financial record folder to learn how to open a checking account, rent an apartment, apply for credit, look for a job, buy a car, and pay taxes. 20+ hours completion time.

Simulation	0-538-62328-4

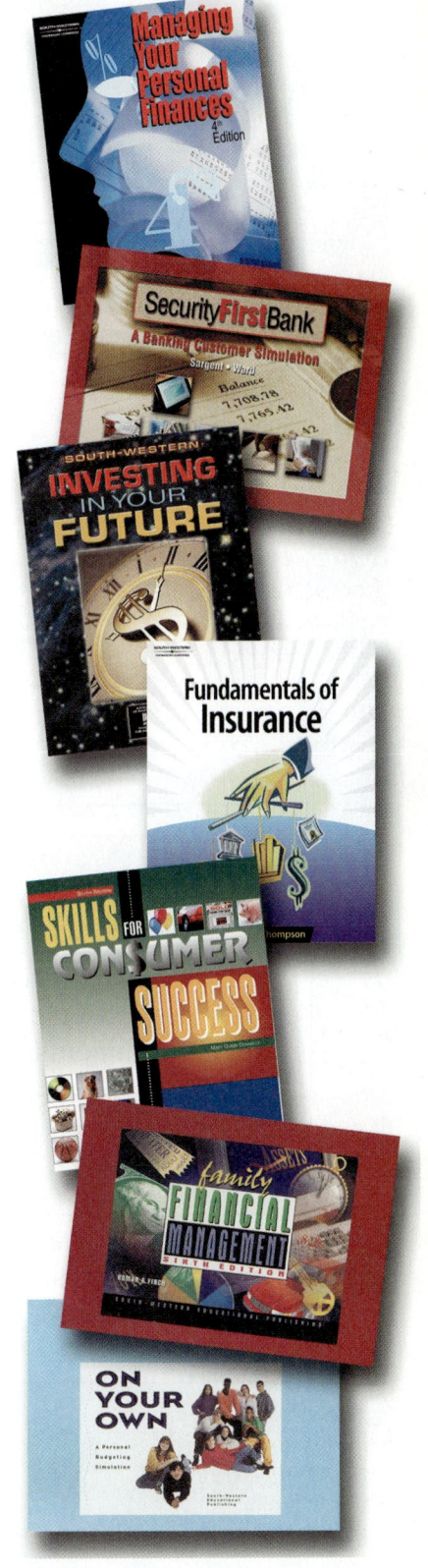

Join Us on the Internet
www.swep.com

SOUTH-WESTERN ™

THOMSON LEARNING

HOW TO USE THIS BOOK

Engage Student Interest

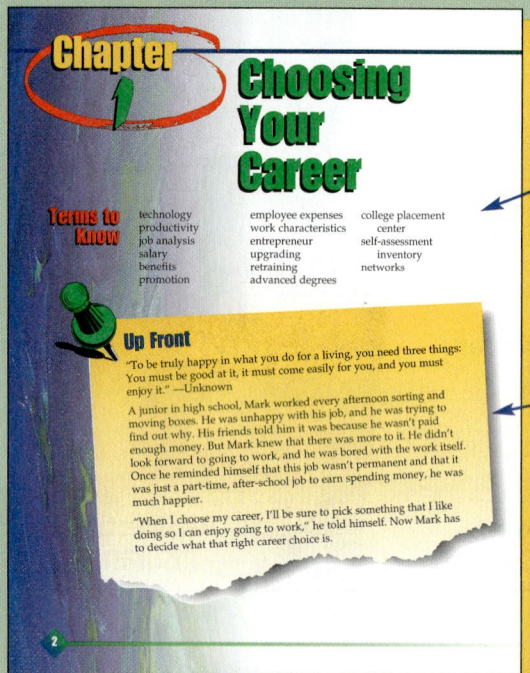

Terms to Know are vocabulary words defined within the chapter.

Up Front presents a story that's tailored to the chapter's contents. By reading the story, you'll have an overview of the chapter's main topics.

Lessons make the text easy to use in all classroom environments.

Goals are clearly stated learning objectives. Each goal represents a section of the chapter.

Special Features Enhance Learning

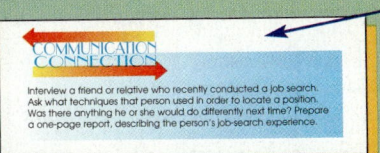

Communication Connection offers speaking and writing activities related to the chapter content.

Did You Know? provides interesting facts about chapter topics.

Career Links presents information on a career related to the chapter's topics.

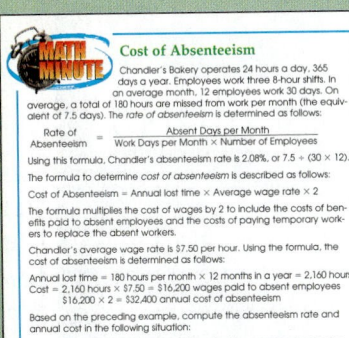

Pros and Cons provides an opportunity for you to think critically about issues that have no clear-cut answers.

Net Notes points you to Web sites that will help you learn more about the chapter's content.

Around the Globe supplies international connections relevant to personal finance topics.

Math Minute presents review and practice in basic math skills linked to chapter topics.

Personal Perspective is a full-page feature that will extend your knowledge by acquainting you with real-world issues.

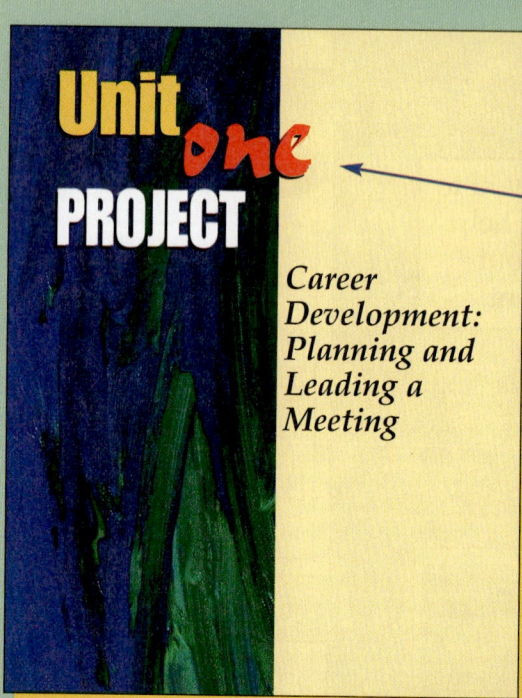

PERSONAL PERSPECTIVE

A Career in Computers . . . or Not?

Computer-related careers are among the most rapidly growing. Perhaps you are interested in the "hard sciences." If so, your future may lie in computer programming, computer systems design, or computer maintenance. Or maybe your interests lie with the "soft sciences." If so, you might look into information management, data entry and retrieval, or computer-aided decision-making, which includes marketing and management. No matter what your interests, computer-related fields offer numerous opportunities for employment, training, and advancement.

According to the U.S. Census Bureau, the electronic economy has three primary components—the supporting infrastructure, electronic business processes (how business is conducted), and electronic commerce transactions (buying and selling).

★ E-business infrastructure is the hardware, software, and telecommunication networks. It is also the human support services needed in electronic business.

★ E-business processes are the methods used to conduct business over a computer network. These processes include production, customer service, and internal and external management.

★ E-commerce is any transaction completed over a computer network that involves the transfer of ownership or rights to use goods and services. For example, when you buy a product over the Internet, you have participated in e-commerce. Businesses must consider how and when to include the Internet in their sales and marketing strategy.

In the fall of 1999, the Census Bureau began measuring e-commerce activities and use. The electronic economy is here, and the Census Bureau is preparing to collect the data and identify the future for potential careers in e-commerce.

Think Critically

1. What computer skills do you have?
2. Are you interested in one of the three fields of e-commerce? If so, which one and why?
3. What are some resources you might use to help you gain knowledge and experience in e-commerce?

18 Career Decisions

Unit *one* PROJECT

Career Development: Planning and Leading a Meeting

A **Project** ends each unit. It's an opportunity for you to apply and extend your knowledge.

Review and Assessment

Check Your Understanding contains end-of-lesson activities to review terms and concepts.

Check Your Understanding

Review Terms
1. technology
2. productivity
3. job analysis
4. salary
5. benefits
6. promotion
7. employee expenses
8. work characteristics
9. entrepreneur

Review Concepts
1. Why are terms such as "information age" and "electronic era" used to describe today's occupations and career environment?
2. What are some U.S. government publications you could use to research careers?

Chapter Review gives you the opportunity to tie your learning together. *Summary* is a bulleted list of chapter concepts for quick review. *Review Terms* helps you acquire a vocabulary of personal finance terms. *Review Facts and Ideas* tests your recall of the chapter's main points. *Apply Your Knowledge* and *Solve Problems* challenge you to dig deeper into issues.

Chapter Review
Summary

10.1 Savings Goals and Institutions

- Savings provide money to meet short-term needs. Some of these needs, such as vacations and major purchases, you can anticipate and include in your budgeted savings. Others, such as emergencies and special social events, you may not foresee but need to save for anyway.

Apply Your Knowledge

1. Describe some new technology that has been introduced in the past few months.
2. Describe some technological advance made just a year or two ago that is now obsolete.
3. What is the role of information in many of today's careers?
4. How has world interdependence changed our lives as Americans?
5. What are some positive features of employment that you have observed in the work of your parents or others?

Review Terms

Directions: Can you find the definition for each of the following terms used in Chapter 10?

annual percentage yield (APY)
certificate of deposit (CD)
compound interest
discretionary income
interest
liquidity
maturity date
money market account
principal
securities
share account
stockbroker

1. Ability of an asset to be converted into cash quickly without loss of value.
2. The date on which an investment becomes due for payment.
3. Money paid by a financial institution for the use of the saver's money.
4. A savings account at a credit union.
5. A sum of money in a savings account on which interest accrues.

Review Facts and Ideas

1. What do most occupations center on today?
2. What is one of the largest career groups today?
3. List three publications of the U.S. government that will assist you with career choices.
4. Describe the types of information that would be listed on a job analysis.
5. List some employee expenses that you might expect to pay in your first occupation choice.

Solve Problems

1. If you buy a house for $125,000, how much down payment will you have to make if the lender requires a down payment of (a) 10 percent, (b) 15 percent, (c) 20 percent, (d) 25 percent?
2. You bought your home last year for $130,000. You made a down payment of 20 percent. Through your mortgage payments, you have reduced your debt by $2,000. The annual appreciation rate for homes in your area has averaged 3 percent.
   a. What was the amount of your down payment?
   b. What was your initial loan amount?
   c. How much do you owe now?
   d. What is the current market value of your home?
   e. What is your equity in the home now?
3. Suppose your local taxing authority requires you to pay property taxes at the rate of $16 per thousand. Your house is assessed at $210,000. How much property tax will you owe each year?
4. Make a list of the features you want in a home. Be sure to include features of the location where you would like to live as well as features of the house and property. Then prioritize your list in order of importance to you. Select a moderate price range for homes in your area. Then search the newspaper classified ads or online listings for houses in that price range that meet your criteria. Clip or print out the listings for three houses that you would like to tour if you were in the market for a home. Which of your criteria do these houses meet and which do they not meet?
5. Using just the closing costs specifically stated in Figure 22-1, what range of costs should the buyer expect to pay (minimum and maximum)? What range of costs should the seller expect to pay? Assume that the house sold for $180,000.
6. Use your Loan Planner Tool to solve this problem. To buy the home you want, you will have to borrow $100,000 at 7 percent interest for 30 years (or 360 monthly payments). What will your monthly payment be?

PLANNING TOOLS

For related activities and links, point your browser to **www.mypf.swep.com**

As you work through the problems, watch for the Internet symbol, which will direct you to the World Wide Web. The Planning Tools icon indicates problems that can be solved using the Planning Tools software.

TO THE STUDENT

Welcome to the exciting world of personal finance! This textbook focuses on your role as a citizen, student, family member, consumer, and active participant in the business world. The intent of *Managing Your Personal Finances* is to inform you of your various financial responsibilities and to provide you with opportunities for self-awareness, expression, and satisfaction in a highly technical and competitive society.

★ Would you like to learn ways to maximize your earnings potential?
★ Do you need to develop strategies for managing your financial resources?
★ Are you interested in exploring skills for the wise use of credit?
★ Do you want to gain insight into the different ways of investing your money?

This book will help you investigate many important areas of interest that will enhance your financial security. You will also better understand your own wants, needs, and values, and how these affect personal financial decisions. Understanding the concepts presented in this text will enable you to make wise decisions that will help your financial future and make you a more effective consumer.

To help you learn about personal finance, this text has a number of special highlights.

Terms to Know are vocabulary words that are printed in bold and defined within the chapter.

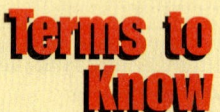

Up Front presents a story that's tailored to the chapter's contents. By reading the story, you'll have an overview of the chapter's main topics.

Goals are clearly stated learning objectives that begin each lesson and offer an overview of the information you'll study.

Personal Perspective is a full-page feature that will extend your knowledge by acquainting you with real-world issues. Critical thinking questions help you go deeper into the topics.

Throughout the book, certain features will help you relate chapter concepts as they apply to the real world of personal finance. These include **Did You Know?**, **Communication Connection**, **Career Links**, **Pros and Cons**, **Net Notes**, **Around the Globe**, and **Math Minute.**

At the end of each lesson, **Check Your Understanding** contains activities to help you review terms and concepts you've learned.

Chapter Review gives you the opportunity to tie your learning together. *Summary* is a bulleted list of chapter concepts for quick review. *Review Terms* helps you acquire a vocabulary of personal finance terms. *Review Facts and Ideas* tests your recall of the chapter's main points. *Apply Your Knowledge* and *Solve Problems* challenge you to dig deeper into issues. As you work through the problems, watch for the *Internet* symbol, which will direct you to the World Wide Web. The *Planning Tools* icon indicates problems that can be solved using the Planning Tools software.

A **Project** ends each unit. It's an opportunity for you to apply and extend your knowledge about personal finance with exercises relevant to your own life.

Contents

UNIT Six Risk Management   708

UNIT Seven Consumer Rights And Responsibilities   794

Unit one

Career Decisions

Chapters

Unit 1 prepares you to analyze choices and develop the tools to get and keep temporary, part-time, or full-time employment, now or in the future. This unit is based on the idea that making wise career decisions is crucial to managing your personal finances and all future financial planning.

The chapters describe career options and how to cope with changes that will affect your choices. You will learn why people work, how to begin career planning, and where to find up-to-date information. You also will find out how to compete with other applicants in getting a job. Then you will explore how to adapt to and keep the job—important skills that lead to good work relations and work history.

Chapter 1

Choosing Your Career

Up Front

"To be truly happy in what you do for a living, you need three things: You must be good at it, it must come easily for you, and you must enjoy it." —Unknown

A junior in high school, Mark worked every afternoon sorting and moving boxes. He was unhappy with his job, and he was trying to find out why. His friends told him it was because he wasn't paid enough money. But Mark knew that there was more to it. He didn't look forward to going to work, and he was bored with the work itself. Once he reminded himself that this job wasn't permanent and that it was just a part-time, after-school job to earn spending money, he was much happier.

"When I choose my career, I'll be sure to pick something that I like doing so I can enjoy going to work," he told himself. Now Mark has to decide what that right career choice is.

Lesson 1.1 — Considering Careers

Goals

★ Discuss career and job trends, and describe sources of job information.

★ Complete a job analysis, listing the positive and negative features of potential career choices.

Careers of the Future

Your grandparents or even your parents may have worked for one employer for many years before retiring, but your career path will likely look much different. New products and services, together with global competition and the computerized work environment, have changed the expectations and needs of employers. The job you accept will likely change quite a bit within a few years. In fact, you will probably retrain, upgrade, or change jobs several times during your working life.

Technology creates newer, better, and faster ways of getting things done. **Technology** is a general term for improvements in work methods and equipment that increase productivity. **Productivity** is the amount a worker produces in an hour. Businesses must constantly increase their output and lower their costs to stay competitive. Companies today must become very efficient in order to be profitable and stay in business.

Why is it likely that you will retrain, upgrade, or change jobs several times during your working life?

Major Occupational Groups

In the early 1900s, farmers made up more than one third of the total workforce of the United States. Now, they make up less than 3 percent, and that number is decreasing. Today, in most occupations the collection, use, and distribution of information is the job. Computers and the Internet are key tools for gathering, transmitting, and storing information.

One of the largest career groups is the *professions*, where knowledge is the key job skill. For example, the professions include doctors, lawyers, and accountants. Professional employees also work in the information field, with the creation, processing, storage, and retrieval of information as important parts of the job. As computers and the Internet continue to evolve, many new professional careers will emerge. For example, people who work as Web designers and database administrators are in rapidly growing professional fields.

Service jobs are a large—and increasing—sector of the market. They also are dominated by technology and information needs that determine what will be produced and how it will be made available to customers. Service employees are using highly sophisticated information storage and retrieval devices, from point-of-sale computers to optical scanners for inventory counting.

This extraordinary transformation of occupations has been variously labeled the "space age," "electronic era," "global village," "technological revolution," and "information age." All of these terms refer to technology and the rapid increase of knowledge that affect virtually all career choices today.

Job Titles and Descriptions

Some of today's careers may seem the same as they were 20 years ago. However, you will find that most are considerably different when you compare present-day job descriptions, job qualifications, and employment opportunities with earlier counterparts.

Careful research into job titles and descriptions of potential careers will help you prepare to make career choices. Several U.S. government publications provide detailed descriptions of many job titles. Three of them are available in most public libraries and also online: the *Dictionary of Occupational Titles (DOT)*, the *Occupational Outlook Handbook (OOH)*, and the *Monthly Labor Review*. You can find the *DOT* online at http://www.oalj.dol.gov/libdot.htm or by entering the keywords "Dictionary of Occupational Titles" in your browser. Eventually a new online publication called *O*NET* is expected to replace the *DOT*. You can find *O*NET* at http://online.onetcenter.org. To find the *OOH* online, go to http://stats.bls.gov/ocohome.htm or enter the keywords "Occupational Outlook Handbook." For the *Monthly Labor Review* online, go to http://stats.bls.gov/opub/mlr/mlrhome.htm, or use the keyword "Bureau of Labor Statistics." Then search the publications section for the *Monthly Labor Review*.

The *Dictionary of Occupational Titles*, published by the U.S. Department of Labor, classifies jobs by nine-digit categories according to functions and duties. Listed within the major categories are numerous jobs available in the United States. Figure 1-1

0/1 Professional, Technical, and Managerial Occupations

(D.O.T. 024.381-010 to 079.131.010)

This category includes occupations concerned with the theoretical or practical aspects of such fields of human endeavor as art, science, engineering, education, medicine, law, business relations, and administrative, managerial, and technical work. Most of these occupations require substantial educational preparation (usually at the university, junior college, or technical institute level).

024.381-010 LABORATORY ASSISTANT (petrol & gas) alternate titles: analyst, geochemical prospecting; core analyst; laboratory tester

Tests sand, shale, and other earth materials to determine petroleum and mineral content and physical characteristics: Performs routine chemical or physical tests of earth samples in field or laboratory to determine content of hydrocarbon or other minerals indicating presence of petroleum and mineral deposits. Tests core samples brought up during well drilling to determine permeability and porosity of sample, fluid content of sand and shale, salinity of drilling mud, and other conditions affecting oil well drilling operations.
GOE: 02.04.01 STRENGTH: L GED: R4 M4 L3 SVP: 5 DLU: 77

025 OCCUPATIONS IN METEOROLOGY

This group includes occupations concerned with the investigation of atmospheric phenomena with specializations, such as synoptic meteorology, climatology, dynamic meteorology, physical meteorology, radar and radio meteorology, and hydrometeorology.

025.062-010 METEOROLOGIST (profess. & kin.) alternate titles: weather forecaster

Analyzes and interprets meteorological data gathered by surface and upper-air stations, satellites, and radar to prepare reports and forecasts for public and other users: Studies and interprets synoptic reports, maps, photographs, and prognostic charts to predict long and short range weather conditions. Operates computer graphic equipment to produce weather reports and maps for analysis, distribution to users, or for use in televised weather broadcast. Issues hurricane and other severe weather warnings. May broadcast weather forecast over television or radio. May prepare special forecasts and briefings for particular audiences, such as those involved in air and sea transportation, agriculture, fire prevention, air-pollution control, and school groups. May direct forecasting services at weather station, or at radio or television broadcasting facility. May conduct basic or applied research in meteorology. May establish and staff weather observation stations.
GOE: 02.01.01 STRENGTH: L GED: R5 M5 L5 SVP: 7 DLU: 89

025.264-010 HYDROGRAPHER (waterworks)

Analyzes hydrographic data to determine trends in movement and utilization of water: Reads meters and gauges to measure waterflow and pressure in streams, conduits, and pipelines, and records data. Measures water level in lakes, reservoirs, and tanks. Calculates seepage and evaporation rates for dams and reservoirs. Measures depth of water in wells and test holes to determine ground water level. Measures snow characteristics to evaluate water yield from snow runoff. Prepares graphs and charts to illustrate water patterns. Positions sluice gates to direct water onto spreading grounds. Installs, calibrates, and maintains metering instruments. Recommends locations for metering stations and instrument placement.
GOE: 02.04.01 STRENGTH: M GED: R4 M4 L4 SVP: 6 DLU: 77

Source: Excerpted from the U.S. Department of Labor, *Dictionary of Occupational Titles*, 4th Ed., Rev. 1991, <http://www.oalj.dol.gov/public/dot/refrnc/dot01b.htm> (7 December 2000).

is an excerpt from the *DOT* that lists some specific jobs under "Professional, Technical, and Managerial Occupations." To use the *DOT*, first consult the index to locate the reference number for "0/1 Professional, Technical, and Managerial Occupations." Jobs may be further divided into functions and duties, with a brief description of these.

The *Occupational Outlook Handbook* is a yearly publication of the U.S. Department of Labor. It provides in-depth job descriptions and includes additional information about job opportunities nationwide. As you can see in the Figure 1-2 excerpt, the *Handbook* refers to the *O*NET* numbers for the jobs it describes. The *Handbook* descriptions include topics such as nature of the work, working conditions, employment, training and qualifications, job outlook, earnings, related occupations, and sources of additional information.

Additional statistics and graphic information are available in the *Monthly Labor Review,* published by the U.S. Department of Labor. Articles in this publication provide current information about specific *occupation clusters* (groups of similar occupations) across the nation.

Job Analysis

While considering the type of work for which you would be best suited, you may find it useful to do a job analysis, such as the one shown in Figure 1-3 on page 8. A **job analysis** is an evaluation of the positive and negative attributes of a given career choice. After careful analysis, you may find that a certain job will not meet most of your career objectives. When this happens, continue with your analyses of other careers that interest you. Because you will probably spend a number of years in your first career choice, selecting the right one is very important.

What are some of the positive features that your chosen career will provide you?

Positive Features of Employment

Your chosen career will provide you with many positive features. The most important is usually the **salary,** which is the amount of monthly or annual pay that you will earn for your labor. You should also consider whether there are scheduled salary increases after a month, six months, or a year. Some companies offer frequent evaluations, merit raises, and liberal pay schedules. **Benefits** are also important. They are company-provided supplements to salaries.

Writers and Editors, Including Technical Writers

Significant Points
- Most jobs require a college degree in the liberal arts—communications, journalism, and English are preferred—or a technical subject for technical writing positions.
- Competition is expected to be less for lower paying, entry-level jobs at small daily and weekly newspapers, trade publications, and radio and television broadcasting stations in small markets.
- Persons who fail to gain better paying jobs or earn enough as independent writers usually are able to transfer readily to communications-related jobs in other occupations.

Nature of the Work
Writers and editors communicate through the written word. *Writers* develop original fiction and nonfiction for books, magazines and trade journals, newspapers, technical reports, online distribution, company newsletters, radio and television broadcasts, movies, and advertisements. Editors select and prepare material for publication or broadcast and review and edit a writer's work.

Writers either select a topic or are assigned one by an editor. Then they gather information through personal observation, library and Internet research, and interviews. Writers select the material they want to use, organize it into a meaningful format, and use the written word to express ideas and convey information to readers. Often, writers revise or rewrite sections, searching for the best organization or the right phrasing.

Working Conditions
Some writers and editors work in comfortable, private offices; others work in noisy rooms filled with the sound of keyboards and computer printers as well as the voices of other writers tracking down information over the telephone. The search for information sometimes requires travel and visits to diverse workplaces, such as factories, offices, laboratories, the ballpark, or the theater, but many have to be content with telephone interviews and the library.

Employment
Writers and editors held about 341,000 jobs in 1998. Nearly one-third of salaried writers and editors works for news-papers, magazines, and book publishers. Substantial numbers, mostly technical writers, work for computer software firms.

Job Outlook
Employment of writers and editors is expected to increase faster than the average for all occupations through the year 2008. Employment of salaried writers and editors for newspapers, periodicals, book publishers, and nonprofit organizations is expected to increase as demand grows for their publications. Magazines and other periodicals increasingly are developing market niches, appealing to readers with special interests. Also, online publications and services are growing in number and sophistication, spurring the demand for writers and editors. Businesses and organizations are developing Internet websites and more companies are experimenting with publishing materials directly for the Internet. Advertising and public relations agencies, which also are growing, should be another source of new jobs.

Earnings
Median annual earnings for writers and editors, including technical writers, were $36,480 in 1998. The middle 50 percent earned between $27,030 and $49,380 a year. The lowest 10 percent earned less than $20,920 and the highest 10 percent earned over $76,660. Median annual earnings in the industries employing the largest numbers of writers and editors of nontechnical material in 1997 were as follows:

Advertising	$38,100
Periodicals	35,900
Books	35,200
Newspapers	28,500
Radio and telelvision broadcasting	26,300

Median annual earnings of technical writers and editors in computer data and processing services were $39,200 in 1997.

Related Occupations
Writers and editors communicate ideas and information. Other communications occupations include news analysts, reporters, and correspondents; radio and television announcers; advertising and public relations workers; and teachers.

O*NET Codes: 34002B, 34002C, 34002D, 34002E, 34002F, 34002G, 34002J, 34002L, 34002M, and 34005

Source: Excerpted from the U.S. Department of Labor, *Occupational Outlook Handbook*, 2000–01, <http://stats.bls.gov/oco/ocos089.htm>

Figure 1-3 *Job Analysis Form*

JOB ANALYSIS

Job Title: _____

Positive features:

Beginning salary: _____

Benefits: _____

_____

_____

_____

Promotion opportunities:

_____

_____

_____

Other considerations:

_____

_____

_____

Negative features:

Employee expenses: _____

_____

_____

_____

Work characteristics:

_____

_____

_____

Other considerations:

_____

_____

_____

These extras may include sick pay, vacation time, profit-sharing plans, and health insurance, as discussed in Chapter 6.

Another important feature is the opportunity for **promotion**— the ability to advance, to accept more responsibilities, and eventually to work your way up to higher positions. Promotions give you recognition for your achievements, higher pay, and more challenging work. For example, a junior accountant will want to work for a company in which advancement to senior accountant and partner is possible.

You may also want to consider commuting distance and parking, company stability in the community, work hours and flexibility, and personnel policies. It's important to examine all features of a field of work and specific jobs, so you will have some idea where the career path may lead you. You should evaluate both rewards and additional investments you may need to make. These investments can include retraining and upgrading, moving to a new location, and advanced education or specialized skill development such as learning new computer programs, new electronic equipment, or new industry-specific technology.

Negative Features of Employment

Every job or occupation also has its negative features. You should try to see these negatives as challenges that go along with the positive aspects of employment.

Employee expenses include any costs paid by the employee that are not reimbursed by the employer (for example, uniforms or other special clothing and its cleaning). Although such expenses may be tax deductible, they can be very costly and can make the job less attractive. It is important to carefully balance employee expenses against benefits in a prospective job.

Work characteristics are the daily activities at work. They might include indoor versus outdoor work, working alone or with people, job pressures, time between breaks, supervisory relationships, number of employees with whom you will work, time spent at a computer terminal, and company rules and policies. Because you will do this work for eight or more hours a day, it is important to match work characteristics to your own needs and preferences.

To gain insight into how employees in actual careers feel about their jobs, read *Vocational Biographies* or *Working* by Studs Terkel. Both publications are a series of short descriptions of workers in many different occupations. In addition to discussing their job likes and dislikes, these workers give more details about their jobs than you may find elsewhere.

You can continue your in-depth career research by searching the subject headings in your library's card or online catalog and magazine indexes, such as the *Business Periodicals Index* and the *Readers' Guide to Periodical Literature*. Most career information sources can be found in the reference section of the library, which typically provides Internet links and online research assistance. Online career sites, such as Monster.com, often provide information about different jobs as well as openings.

Entrepreneurship

Many people would like to own their own business and be their own boss. An **entrepreneur** is someone who organizes, manages, and assumes the risks of a business or enterprise. There are many opportunities for people to start their own business or purchase an existing business or franchise. While long hours of work and dedication usually accompany such a move, rewards are also great because you can better control your own life and future.

With careful planning, training, advice, financing, and support, many young people today will eventually own and run their own businesses. Small business management and entrepreneurship courses, information, and assistance are often available in high schools, community colleges, and through local business organizations such as Junior Achievement. *Incubator projects* (in which cities or counties provide reduced-cost sites with incentives and subsidies to get a small business on its feet) and Small Business Assistance Centers also provide ongoing training, education, and assistance as needed. The Small Business Administration Web site is a valuable resource for people thinking about going into business for themselves. Visit the site at http:www.sba.gov/.

An entrepreneur assumes the risks of a business. Why might someone want to become an entrepreneur?

✓ Check Your Understanding

Review Terms

1. technology
2. productivity
3. job analysis
4. salary
5. benefits
6. promotion
7. employee expenses
8. work characteristics
9. entrepreneur

Review Concepts

1. Why are terms such as "information age" and "electronic era" used to describe today's occupations and career environment?
2. What are some U.S. government publications you could use to research careers?
3. What are some positive features of employment? What are some negative features?
4. Why might a person want to be an entrepreneur?

The Challenge of Change

Goals

★ Describe the techniques for coping with change.
★ Explain changing career patterns in a world economy and the need for job networking.

Coping with Change

With rapidly advancing technologies, change is certain. There are three things you can do about change: accept it, reject it, or ignore it. If you accept change, you can be part of it and help it happen. If you reject change, you will be run over by it; progress cannot be stopped. If you ignore change, you will be left behind, wondering what happened. By rejecting or ignoring change, you will be very frustrated, unemployed, or both. By reading, becoming a lifetime learner, taking classes, and completing a self-assessment, you can be aware of changes and make an action plan that will enable you to cope with changes and reduce the stress of uncertainty.

+PROS and CONS-

Change is a fact of life in business. Here are some issues that play a role in whether or not employees accept organizational changes: the amount of input employees have; whether communication lines between management and employees are open; whether employees perceive a need for the changes; and whether employees trust the initiators of the change.

Think Critically: Why do many attempts to overcome resistance to change fail? Can you think of reasons why employees might resist change?

Read Widely

A variety of resources follow national and international trends, from general technology to specific industries. Computer magazines or online technology news sources, such as CNET and *Wired* magazine, will keep you informed of technological advances entering the marketplace. In addition, you need to read newspapers and magazines to keep up with what is going on in the United States and in the world.

Be a Lifetime Learner

Both at work and in your personal life, be interested in what is going on. Ask questions. Talk to people. Follow news and special events. Participate in community activities. Care about what is going on in your area and in the world. Joining professional and service organizations will also keep you informed of what's new in specific job areas. You can find out about workshops and seminars that will keep you aware of trends. This will make you a more interesting person to talk to, to work with, and to be around. And it is essential to your successful career development.

Take Classes

Sometimes technological advances are too complex to learn by yourself, so you should actively seek new knowledge by taking classes to gain new skills. **Upgrading** is advancing to a higher level of skill to increase your usefulness to an employer. Many jobs, especially those affected by technological improvements, will require regular upgrading by employees. **Retraining** is learning new and different skills so that an employee can retain the same level of employability. Community college and vocational training is being geared as much to retraining displaced employees as to preparing employees for entry-level positions.

Technical courses are often available through corporations for retraining their own employees. Those who volunteer and are eager to learn will position themselves for advancement. Other training is available through technical schools, vocational centers, job placement services, business colleges, and community colleges. Training over the Internet is becoming increasingly common. For many careers, applicants will need a college degree before they will be considered for employment.

Young people are staying in college longer before entering the workforce than ever before. **Advanced degrees** are specialized, intensive programs (taken after the first college degree) that pre-pare students for higher-level work responsibilities with more challenges and higher pay. An advanced degree may be a master's, a doctorate in a specialized field, or a professional degree in medicine, law, engineering, and so on. A master's degree often requires one year beyond the first college degree. A Ph.D. may require an additional three years after a master's degree. It is also possible to earn a Ph.D. without first obtaining a master's degree. This path usually takes longer (up to five years).

Complete a Self-Assessment

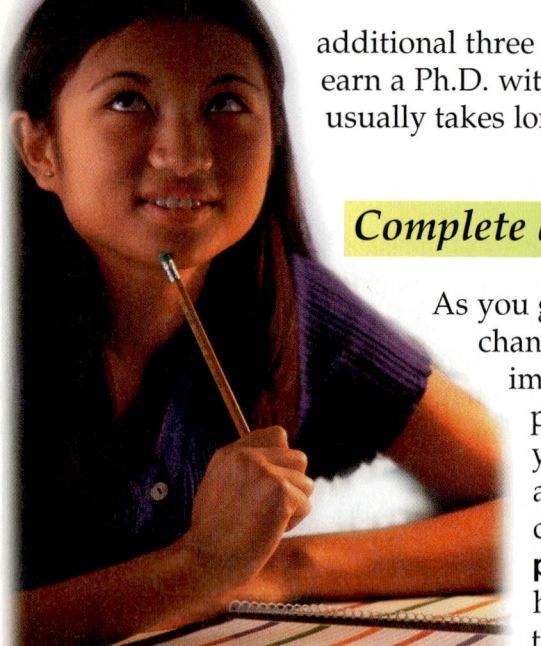

How could a self-assessment inventory help you prepare for a career?

As you go through life, your needs and values will change. It is important to look inward to define what is important to you and then use this knowledge to plan your future. You should think about what you like doing, what you do well, and what skills and knowledge you want to enhance. Located at a college or technical training institute, a **college placement center** offers advice and counseling to help you determine a career direction. Vocational testing is also available through these college placement centers. You can compare your interests with those of successful people in various professions. A values clarification test will help you determine what is important to you both personally and professionally. You can find many self-assessment questionnaires at online career sites or by searching with the keyword "self-assessment."

Private career counselors are listed in the Yellow Pages and may be consulted for a fee ranging from $25 to $75 an hour. A less expensive and more productive approach is to do your own research, using the sources listed in this chapter as well as *The American Almanac of Jobs and Salaries*. This book evaluates job opportunities in many career fields and gives a full range of salaries for positions and levels. You can do industry research and look into major job categories (service, professional, and so on, as listed in Chapter 2).

Specific company research will help you determine which companies can offer you the best career opportunities. You might want to check your library to find sources such as *Standard & Poor's Register of Corporations, Directors and Executives, United States and Canada,* or *The 100 Best Companies to Work for in America* to read about major American companies and why they are successful. You might also want to visit company Web sites and read their descriptions of themselves. Finally, you can do field research and talk to people working in careers that interest you. These interviews will show you strengths and weaknesses in some careers that you might not have anticipated. All this information is crucial in determining your needs and matching them to an appropriate career.

A **self-assessment inventory** lists your strong and weak points and gives you an idea of how to prepare yourself for a career. As you improve your weak points, they become strengths in your inventory. Figure 1-4 is a self-assessment inventory that lists a typical young person's assets, liabilities, and plans for action. Completing a similar inventory based on your personal qualifications will help you determine areas that need work. You might ask another person to objectively assess your strengths and weaknesses. A different point of view can sometimes help clarify your self-assessment.

Checklist **Figure 1-4**

Strengths	Weaknesses	Plan of Action
Education: High school diploma including business courses	Education: Weak in office skills	Take extra computer classes to learn new word processing and spreadsheet programs.
Experience: Cooperative job in office—part-time summer job as clerk; volunteer work at church	Experience: Need experience using computer programs	Look for work experience which includes computer applications in database management.
Aptitudes and Abilities: Good hand-eye coordination; work well with people	Aptitudes and Abilities: Poor speaker	Practice speaking in small groups; lead a class at church; attend more social functions.
Appearance: Neat and clean	Appearance: Wardrobe needs more professional work clothes	Start buying clothes that are appropriate for work.

Changing Career Opportunities

Career planning is changing as never before. A career choice is not a permanent decision but is subject to rapid, unpredictable change. To understand how the job market will be affected, let's examine some of the major changes sweeping the country and the world.

Long-Term Planning

Businesses must be concerned with what will happen in the long run. Otherwise, they will be totally unprepared when new technologies that require massive changes emerge. Individuals also must look to long-term planning to protect themselves from the effects of a rapidly changing technology. They must be in the midst of the change and help it happen. Career plans must span several decades and must be as broad, diversified, and open to future opportunities and challenges.

A World Economy

The idea that we can isolate ourselves from the rest of the world and live in total peace and security is a myth. We are now part of a worldwide, interdependent economy. The Internet has helped to open the world market to companies of all sizes. As a nation, we must seek ways to survive and grow internationally. As individuals, we must be aware of the changes occurring worldwide, particularly in *Third World countries*. Third World countries are nations with developing economies.

Our nation is part of a worldwide, interdependent economy. How does this affect our job market?

The twenty fastest growing economies of the 1990s were all in Third World nations, including the oil-exporting countries, South Korea, Singapore, the Dominican Republic, Taiwan, Mexico, and Brazil. The economic powers of the Third World are taking over the industrial production tasks formerly controlled by more developed countries, and they have the potential workforce to do it.

Should we try to go back and recapture our role as leader of a modern Industrial Revolution? Most experts agree that the answer is no. Instead, we should adapt and move forward in the area in which we are the leader—information.

Networking

Businesses and individuals are moving away from formal, individual-oriented structures and toward networks. **Networks** are communication lines established for people to talk to each other and share information. Networking includes making phone calls, sharing lunch, and creating opportunities to give ideas, share resources, and receive needed information from someone who has it. To find a career, you will need to establish a network of contacts—people you know who have information you need. Through networking, you can get inside information without being an "insider."

You can begin now to create your network by making a master list of people you know through your parents, school and business acquaintances, and personal friends and associates. By communicating within your network, you will learn how to prepare yourself for a job, where the openings are, and how to pursue them.

Check Your Understanding

Review Terms

1. upgrading
2. retraining
3. advanced degrees
4. college placement center
5. self-assessment inventory
6. networks

Review Concepts

1. What steps can you take to deal with change and reduce uncertainty?
2. Why must individuals consider long-term planning, a world economy, and networking when making career plans?

PERSONAL PERSPECTIVE

A Career in Computers . . . or Not?

Computer-related careers are among the most rapidly growing. Perhaps you are interested in the "hard sciences." If so, your future may lie in computer programming, computer systems design, or computer maintenance. Or maybe your interests lie with the "soft sciences." If so, you might look into information management, data entry and retrieval, or computer-aided decision-making, which includes marketing and management. No matter what your interests, computer-related fields offer numerous opportunities for employment, training, and advancement.

According to the U.S. Census Bureau, the electronic economy has three primary components—the supporting infrastructure, electronic business processes (how business is conducted), and electronic commerce transactions (buying and selling).

★ E-business infrastructure is the hardware, software, and telecommunication networks. It is also the human support services needed in electronic business.

★ E-business processes are the methods used to conduct business over a computer network. These processes include production, customer service, and internal and external management.

★ E-commerce is any transaction completed over a computer network that involves the transfer of ownership or rights to use goods and services. For example, when you buy a product over the Internet, you have participated in e-commerce. Businesses must consider how and when to include the Internet in their sales and marketing strategy.

In the fall of 1999, the Census Bureau began measuring e-commerce activities and use. The electronic economy is here, and the Census Bureau is preparing to collect the data and identify the future for potential careers in e-commerce.

Think Critically

1. What computer skills do you have?
2. Are you interested in one of the three fields of e-commerce? If so, which one and why?
3. What are some resources you might use to help you gain knowledge and experience in e-commerce?

1.1 Considering Careers

- Careers of the future will be based on technology to increase productivity.
- Careers will change rapidly in requirements and skills.
- Service jobs will continue to grow.
- People will depend more on the gathering and use of information.
- Evaluate positive features of a job, such as salary, benefits, promotions, and fulfillment.
- Evaluate negative features of a job, such as employee expenses, job pressures, and stress.
- Consider owning your own business.

1.2 The Challenge of Change

- Read widely and be a lifetime learner.
- Take classes for upgrading and retraining.
- Earn advanced degrees.
- Complete a self-assessment inventory to learn your strengths and weaknesses.
- Make career planning a long-term strategy.
- Recognize that a world economy means that you may work internationally or with foreign companies.
- Maintain your network of contacts.

Review Terms

Directions: Can you find the definition for each of the following terms used in Chapter 1?

advanced degrees
benefits
college placement center
employee expenses
entrepreneur
job analysis
networks
productivity
promotion
retraining

salary
self-assessment
    inventory
technology
upgrading
work characteristics

1. An evaluation of the positive and negative attributes of a given career choice.
2. One who organizes, manages, and assumes the risks of a business or enterprise.
3. A source of career counseling available at colleges or technical training institutes.
4. Improvements in work methods and equipment that increase productivity.
5. Communication lines established for people to talk to each other and share information.
6. The amount of monthly or annual pay.
7. The daily activities at work, such as indoor or outdoor work, or working alone or with people.
8. Expenses paid by employees and not reimbursed by employers.
9. The chance to advance, accept more responsibility, and work your way up the corporate ladder.
10. Company-provided supplements to salaries, such as sick pay and vacation time.
11. Specialized, intensive post-baccalaureate programs.
12. Advancing to a higher level of skill.
13. Learning new and different skills in order to remain employable at the same level.
14. A listing of strong points, weak points, and plans for action.
15. The amount a worker produces in an hour.

1. What do most occupations center on today?
2. What is one of the largest career groups today?
3. List three publications of the U.S. government that will assist you with career choices.
4. Describe the types of information that would be listed on a job analysis.
5. List some employee expenses that you might expect to pay in your first occupation choice.
6. What are the three things you can do about change?
7. List four ways you can keep up with new technologies and stay prepared for tomorrow's career choices.
8. How much education do you need in order to earn an advanced degree?
9. List some major changes that are sweeping the country and the world.
10. What is meant by a world economy?
11. List some Third World countries that have made great economic gains.

APPLY YOUR KNOWLEDGE

1. Describe some new technology that has been introduced in the past few months.
2. Describe some technological advance made just a year or two ago that is now obsolete.
3. What is the role of information in many of today's careers?
4. How has world interdependence changed our lives as Americans?
5. What are some positive features of employment that you have observed in the work of your parents or others?

6. What are some negative features of employment that you have observed in the work of your parents or others?
7. Describe ways you can keep in touch with what is going on in the world technologically.
8. What types of independent research can you do to determine the type of work you want and the company you want to work for?
9. Why is long-term planning necessary for individuals as well as for businesses?

Solve Problems

1. Look up three career choices in the *Dictionary of Occupational Titles*. Summarize your findings in one paragraph about each choice. Look up the same three occupations in the *Occupational Outlook Handbook* and add a second paragraph about each. If you have Internet access, use the online versions of these publications.

2. From a current issue of *Monthly Labor Review* or from the online version of this publication, summarize an article about an industry or employment trend.

3. From the September 2000 issue of the *Monthly Labor Review* in print or online, write a paragraph reviewing the article entitled "Looking for a 'Better' Job: Job-Search Activity of the Employed."

4. Using the *Occupational Outlook Handbook* (at the library or online) and the format shown in Figure 1-3, prepare a career report for one occupation in which you are interested. (Note that the form shown in Figure 1-3 is provided as a worksheet in Activity 1.1 of the *Student Activity Guide*.)

5. Complete a job analysis, using the form in Figure 1-3 as a guide, for three different occupations. To get this information, consult one of the sources listed in this chapter, or interview someone working in each occupation field. List your source(s) of information on the job analysis form.

6. Explain to a friend why it is necessary to be aware of what is new and what is happening technologically in the world. Give suggestions as to what she or he can do to keep up with changes.

7. Pick a large company you think you would like to work for in the future. Do some research to learn more about the company. (Suggestion: Check Standard & Poor's *The 100 Best Companies to Work for in America.* Also, look up the company's Web site and read the company's description of itself.) Summarize your findings in one or two paragraphs.

8. Develop a networking plan—a list of all your possible communication sources—and add to it each time you make a contact. List contacts you plan to set up, people you would like to meet, and places you would like to visit.

For related activities and links, point your browser to
www.mypf.swep.com

Chapter 2

Planning Your Career

Up Front

"To be happy in your work life, you must be able to work as if you don't have to." —Dr. Alfred Mukakis

Jamal was energetic and outgoing. He enjoyed being around other people and helping them. He often volunteered in a retirement center, and it made him happy to support others in doing things they couldn't do by themselves. Jamal was strong and physically fit but not especially interested in athletics. He hoped to find a career that would allow him to use his natural talents and help others at the same time.

"I think I'd like to be a physical therapist," he told his high school counselor. "What steps should I take now, while I'm still in high school, to help me decide if this career is really right for me? If the career is a good fit for me, then what I can do to get there as quickly as possible?"

Goals

★ List reasons why people work and factors that affect career choices.
★ Identify and describe good career planning techniques.

Why People Work

The majority of people work most of their lives. After completing high school and additional training or education, you will probably work for 25 to 40 years! Perhaps you're a teenager with a part-time job. Maybe you're from a two-income household. You or a member of your family may even have more than one job. Many people work even after retirement to supplement fixed incomes and find fulfillment.

People work to meet their needs, wants, and goals. They work to provide food, clothing, shelter, vacations, education, and luxuries. If working does not help them achieve personal goals, people are likely to become frustrated or unhappy in the job.

People also work to gain a sense of **identity**—of who they are. Because work is typically the central activity of a person's life, it often becomes a *way* of life, strongly linked to that person's identity. For example, since you are a student, your main activities center on school. Your identity is that of student. When you are asked what you do, you describe activities, favorite classes in school, sports you play, and events related to your education. When you are finished with school, your identity will probably be based on your career.

What are some reasons why people work?

Factors Affecting Career Choice

Because your career will affect nearly every part of your life, your choice of career is very important. Many factors will affect your decision. Among them are your values and lifestyle, aptitudes and interests, and personal qualities and traits.

What is the difference between values and lifestyle?

Values and Lifestyle

Values are the ideals in life that are important to you. While you are living at home, your values may reflect those of your parents. During high school, you begin to form values of your own—keeping some of your parents' values and rejecting others. For example, you may retain your parents' value that it is appropriate to wear a tie while attending a formal dinner, while rejecting a value that modern music is worthless.

AROUND THE GLOBE

In Japan, the percentage of unmarried, 25- to 29-year-old women has doubled, from 24 percent in 1980 to 48 percent in 1998. Many of these women live with their parents. With the country's workforce rapidly aging, experts are concerned that more Japanese women aren't choosing marriage and child rearing. However, many young women believe that in order to develop full-time careers, they must delay marriage. In Japan, child-care facilities are scarce and expensive.

Think Critically: Should the Japanese government do anything in order to help Japanese women raise children and develop meaningful careers? Do you think that women in other countries have similar problems with their careers?

Lifestyle is the way people choose to live their lives, based on the values they have chosen. Your lifestyle is evident to others from the clothes you wear and the things you buy, use, do, say, and enjoy. A career is an important value in most people's lives because it influences lifestyle. With careful planning, you can find a career that will be rewarding and also provide the money you need to support the lifestyle you want.

Aptitudes and Interests

An **aptitude** is a natural physical or mental ability that allows you to do certain tasks well. Examples of aptitudes include finger dexterity (the ability to use your fingers to move small objects quickly and accurately) and manual dexterity (the ability to move your hands skillfully). Certain types of work require specific types of aptitudes. Aptitude tests can help you realize your strengths and weaknesses. Counseling or career guidance departments of most high schools offer aptitude tests. You may want to test your physical and mental abilities before you begin making career plans.

In addition to your aptitudes, you should think about your **interests**—the things you like to do and the reasons you enjoy doing them. By examining the types of things you enjoy, you can choose a career that has activities you will find interesting and satisfying. For example, a person who enjoys being with people will likely prefer a job working with others, such as sales or a helping profession, to one working alone. Use Figure 2-1 to help identify the activities you most enjoy.

The Internet offers a number of questionnaires to help job seekers identify their interests. Use keywords such as "interest test" to search for these questionnaires. They are fun to fill out. Plus, they may reveal something about you that will help you find a good career fit.

Types of Work Activities **Figure 2-1**

Which of these work activities appeal to you?

analyzing and recording	physically inactive work
creating and designing	presenting or speaking
following directions	repetitive tasks
helping others	self-motivated work
indoor work	thinking work
managing people and resources	various tasks
manual work	working alone
outdoor work	working on a computer
physically active work	working with machines

Personal Qualities

Your **personality** is made up of the many individual qualities that make you unique. Personal qualities include such things as your appearance, intelligence, creativity, sense of humor, and general attitude. Most jobs require an individual with a particular set of personal qualities. For example, a person who represents a company to the public or to potential customers needs a different set of personal qualities than does a machine operator. Examining your personal qualities can help you choose a career that's right for you. How many of the qualities listed in Figure 2-2 apply to you?

Career Planning

Planning for your future career is an important task. Consider the total time spent working: 8 hours a day, 5 days a week, 50 weeks a year totals 2,000 hours each year. If you work the average career span of 43 years (from age 22 to age 65), you will have spent 86,000 hours on the job! Because your work will likely take so much of your time, you will need to plan your career carefully.

Steps in Career Planning

What are the steps involved in career planning?

Effective career planning involves careful investigation and analysis —a process that you should start now and revisit throughout your work life. Career planning involves self-analysis, research, a plan of action, and re-evaluation.

1. *Self-Analysis.* Using resources available from schools, employment offices, testing services, and online, you can explore personal factors that relate to your career choice. You should:
   a. Determine your wants and needs.
   b. Determine your values and desired lifestyle.
   c. Assess your aptitudes and interests and determine how they match job descriptions and activities.
   d. Analyze your personal qualities— those that are satisfactory and those you need to improve.

Check each of these that apply:

1. Has a good attitude toward own work and that of others.
2. Shows courtesy and respect toward others.
3. Is dependable and will do what is promised.
4. Has a desire to succeed and to do a good job.
5. Has enthusiasm for the job and for life.
6. Is clean and has a healthy appearance.
7. Is friendly and helpful.
8. Has a good sense of humor and cares about others.
9. Desires and respects giving a day's work for a day's pay.
10. Is willing and able to learn new skills.
11. Is able to adapt to change quickly and easily.
12. Is capable of working in a stressful and rapidly changing environment.

2. *Research.* Based on a good self-analysis, you can determine which careers interest you most and which suit you best. You should:
   a. Seek information in books, magazines, Web sites, and other resources available from libraries, counseling centers, online resources, and employment offices.
   b. Compare some of your interests, abilities, and personal qualities to job descriptions and requirements. Most careers can fit into one of the classifications shown in Figure 2-3 on page 30. Can you choose one or more of these areas whose requirements you can meet? Can you decide which cluster the job of your choice would fit into?
   c. Interview people in the fields of work you find interesting.
   d. Observe occupations, spend time learning about jobs and companies, and seek part-time work to get direct exposure and experience. Sometimes job shadowing (following someone through his or her workday) will give you real insight into the daily activities and requirements of a career.

Job Classification	Description of Activities	Training Needed	Working Hours	Beginning Salary	Examples
Clerical/Secretarial	Work in office setting. Involves contact with people and machines. Must operate computer, have telephone skills, etc.	High school diploma plus special training in keyboarding, accounting, etc.	40 hours/week during normal business hours.	Urban. $10-12/hr.; $1,600-1,920/mo.	Secretary, office assistant, word processor operator
Professional	Involves use of highly specialized knowledge. Often stressful. High-level responsibility implied.	4+ years of college. May require special training and/or apprenticeship.	40 hours/week during normal business hours plus overtime.	Urban. $37,500-62,500/yr.	Physician, lawyer, teacher, accountant
Skilled Labor	Emphasis on use of highly specialized skill. Special clothing required. Involves use of tools, machines, etc.	High school diploma plus special training, apprenticeship, licensing, or bonding.	40 hours/week plus overtime.	Minimum wage to set salary. Urban. $12-15/hr.; $2,000-2,400/mo.	Builder, mechanic, construction worker
Sales and Marketing	Emphasis on persuading others to buy products and services. Salesperson represents company, self.	High school diploma plus special training. License usually required.	Varied. Often seasonal.	Commission, sometimes with base salary of $1,000-3,000/mo.	Real estate agent, insurance agent, retail salesperson
Service	Involves labor that does not produce a material good. May or may not involve personal contact.	None to specialized 2-year degree program.	Varied. Split shift, as needed.	Min wage, plus tips, avg. $1,500/mo.; $2,000-2,500/mo. for supervisor/trainee. $2,500-4,000/mo.; exp., $4,000-5,000/mo.	Custodian, barber, chef, police officer
Management	Emphasis on supervision of operations, decision making, and direction giving.	College degree plus in-service training.	40 hours or more/week.	Urban. $2,500-4,000/mo.; exp., $4,000-5,000/mo.	Store manager, bank officer, supervisor
Semiskilled and Unskilled Labor	Involves assembly line and other manual work. Physical fitness and good health needed.	In-service training or vocational diploma.	40 hours/week plus overtime.	$15-25/hr., $2,400-4,000/mo.; unskilled, $8.50-12/hr. (after training).	Assembly worker, farm laborer
Entertainment and Recreation	Emphasis on entertaining people. Special quality or talent needed.	None required. Dancing, singing, and music lessons helpful.	Varied. Often under contract.	$0 to unlimited.	Singer, dancer, athlete, talk show host
Military Service	Emphasis on defense of the country. Discipline and training stressed. Ability to follow orders needed. Must fulfill minimum service requirement.	High school diploma usually required.	Daily during set number of years' commitment.	$24,000 + all expenses, rises by rank.	Armed Forces service people

3. *Plan of Action.* After you have done some job research, you will need to develop a plan of action that will eventually bring you to your career goals.

  a. Use good job search techniques. Get organized, make a plan, follow through, and don't give up.

  b. Develop necessary skills by taking courses (traditional and online) and gaining exposure to the field in which you want to pursue a career.

  c. Seek a part-time or volunteer job to gain experience.

  d. Evaluate what you have done. If at any point you think you are following the wrong career path, change your mind before you stay on it too long.

4. *Re-evaluation.* Because the world around us changes rapidly, we all need to prepare ourselves to meet the changes and challenges ahead. You may wish to re-evaluate your choices and prepare for career changes in order to take advantage of new opportunities. About every five years you need to think about what you will be doing and where you would like to be in the next five years.

The hiring wave that swept millions of employees into Internet-related businesses took a sharp downturn in the year 2000. More than 30,000 Internet-related jobs were eliminated.

The Importance of Goals

A **goal** is a desired end toward which efforts are directed. We all need goals in order to have a sense of direction and purpose in life. There are three types of goals: short-term, intermediate, and long-term.

A *short-term goal* is one you expect to reach in a few days or weeks. You must work consistently and with certainty to achieve it because you will have to account for the results in a very short time. A short-term goal could be preparing to pass a math test next week. You know you must plan your studying to be ready for the test, or else suffer the consequences.

Intermediate goals are those you wish to accomplish in the next few months or years. Some examples are graduation from high school, a vacation trip, or plans for summer employment.

Long-term goals are those you wish to achieve in five to ten years or longer. They might include college, career, marriage, and family.

If goals are to be meaningful, they should be defined and written down, to become a part of your life. Many people find a checklist a handy way to help them reach their goals. Figure 2-4 shows a typical goal checklist. Use it as a guide to create your own checklist.

Making the Right Choices

How do you know what kind of job is best for you? How can you possibly decide now, in high school, what you will want to do for the rest of your life? You may not be able to decide. Yet, unfair as it may seem, what you do now can greatly affect what you will do in the future.

You learn about a career through experience. **Experience** is the knowledge and skills acquired from direct participation in a career field. Furthermore, the more experience you gain, the more you learn, the more qualified you become, and the more desirable you become as an employee in that field. Thus, you can set yourself up for a career in a certain field, make yourself worth more to an employer, and increase your earnings by continuing in that field. Your lifestyle will be based on that work and the salary you receive.

Figure 2-4 *Checklist*

CHECKLIST
Week of ___Sept. 1___

Accomplished

Short-term goals (today/this week)
1. Buy birthday gift for mom.
2. Get haircut (Saturday).   _____
3. See counselor about chemistry class.   _____

Intermediate goals (next month/year)
1. Get a C or better on chemistry test (test in 2 weeks).   _____
2. Prepare for SAT test (test in October).   _____
3. Finish term report (due November 9).   _____
4. Complete college admission forms (by January 15).   _____

Long-term goals (future)   *Things to do now*
1. Graduate from college.   — Extra work in science
2. Begin full-time job.   — Bring up GPA to 3.5
3. Buy a car.   — Update placement folder
                                    — Get part-time job (save
                                       $50 a month)

PERSONAL PERSPECTIVE

Help Wanted

The following is a typical ad from a newspaper's Help Wanted section. It poses a dilemma for many young people today. How can you have education *and* experience? If no one will hire you, how can you ever get that "experience"?

> WANTED: Web designer. Must have course work in HTML programming and platform management. Degree preferred. Two years sales experience required. Starting salary $36,000 plus benefits.

There are a number of ways you can meet this employer's requirements of both education and experience. As you complete your formal education in the classroom, you can also prepare for your future career in the following ways:

1. *Cooperative Work Experience.* A job after class, part-time, evenings, and weekends—while you are in school—will add valuable experience. It will give you insight into the work environment you will experience, along with the type of work, skills, and activities that are performed day to day.
2. *Summer Work.* During the summers, you could work at a job that sounds exciting or interesting to you. To do this, try:
   a. *Temporary Work.* A company that places temporary help may be able to find you a job filling in for a regular employee. While the position is only temporary, it gives you valuable insight and work experience.
   b. *Volunteer Work.* As a volunteer, you may be giving up pay, but you will gain important skills and be able to observe working conditions.
3. *Internship.* An internship is an on-the-job training experience that usually pays only your expenses. The employer pays you only your cost of getting to work and any extra expenses you incur. You receive training and exposure to the job requirements.

These suggestions will help you find ways to avoid the "education but no experience" dilemma. Plan ahead and be ready for that opening!

Think Critically

1. Does the career you want require that you have experience in order to be hired for an entry-level position?
2. What are some specific ways you can gather experience for this career at the same time you are completing your formal education?

Unfortunately, the longer you work at one type of job, the greater the chance of becoming **locked in**—a feeling that you cannot change to another type of work. Often, you cannot afford to take the pay cut that may accompany starting over. Taking a temporary position to earn a living while you are preparing for your chosen career is a common practice. However, to achieve your career goals, you must continue to pursue jobs in your field.

Check Your Understanding

Review Terms
1. identity
2. values
3. lifestyle
4. aptitude
5. interests
6. personality
7. goal
8. experience
9. locked in

Review Concepts
1. If your job does not help you achieve your personal goals, what will likely happen?
2. How can taking an aptitude test help your career planning?
3. How can job shadowing help you evaluate a career option?
4. Why is it important to re-evaluate your choices occasionally?

Lesson 2.2 — Finding Career Opportunities

Goals

★ List sources of job opportunity information.
★ Itemize and explain good job search techniques, and formulate a personal plan of action to get the job you want.

Sources of Job Opportunity Information

You can find out about job opportunities in a number of ways: word of mouth and personal contacts; school counseling and placement services; periodicals, books, and other publications; public and private employment agencies; newspaper, telephone book, and private job listings; and online.

Contacts

Many job openings are never advertised. They are filled from within the company, or by people outside who have been privately informed of the opening by a contact within the company. A **contact** is a person you know who can help you get an interview for a job. People such as relatives, friends, and former employers are contacts. They can provide you with inside information on job openings. Therefore, the more people you know, the better your chances of hearing about a job opening.

If you are seeking a job in a field in which you have no contacts, you'll want to get to know people who can tell you about openings. If, for example, you want to work in a bank, you should meet people who work in banks and make yourself known to the human resource manager and other key employees. You can do this through acquaintances and friends in business, professional organizations, and community activities, and through school-sponsored visits, job shadowing, job fairs, or other activities.

How could you find out about job openings that aren't advertised?

School Counseling and Placement Services

Many schools have programs to assist students in preparing for careers, in making career choices, and in securing part- or full-time work. One such program is the cooperative work experience, or supervised field experience. In this type of program, students receive high school credits for on-the-job experience that directly relates to classroom studies in a chosen career field. Students placed in work situations are given grades on their work and are paid minimum wage for their efforts. Employers receive tax credits for the wages they pay the students during training.

School counselors and teachers are also good sources of job opportunity information. They often know about specific job openings and are asked by employers to recommend students for them. If you are interested in an office job, you should talk to counselors and business teachers as you complete business courses.

Colleges and universities (and some high schools) offer placement centers. These offices help students find employment. The services are usually offered free of charge. Job openings are posted at the school, and qualified students are given information so they can apply. These services also include keeping a placement folder on each student that contains school records, including attendance, academic, and disciplinary records. When employers ask for information about a student, they are given copies of information from the student's placement folder. If your school has a placement center, examine your folder and have teachers and other adults write recommendations to put in it. You should also see that all school records are in the folder. Be sure to check at your school to see what other types of assistance are available.

Periodicals, Books, and Other Publications

Your local public and school libraries are good resource centers for information about jobs. You can find facts about which jobs will be available in the future and which may not be around very long. You can read job descriptions and find other information about opportunities for employment, benefits, and requirements.

One good job sourcebook is the *Occupational Outlook Handbook*, described in detail in Chapter 1. At the library you will also find many government and industry publications that present information about job trends, kinds of jobs, employment possibilities, skills needed, and education requirements.

In addition, many current periodicals contain timely information about selected occupations. You might want to look at magazines such as *Time, Newsweek, U.S. News & World Report, Fortune,* and *BusinessWeek.* The *Readers' Guide to Periodical Literature,* and computerized library databases that permit interlibrary loans and other services, will assist you in locating information by topic, article, title, or author.

Public and Private Employment Agencies

All major cities have public and private employment agencies. Their business is to help you find jobs for which you are prepared and help employers locate the best applicants for job openings. Private employment agencies may or may not charge a fee for their services. Such fees vary from agency to agency, so you should compare prices before you sign with one. Some of these agencies charge a fee to the employer. Others charge the prospective employee when a job is found, and still others divide the fee between the employer and the hired employee.

The state employment office does not charge a fee because it is a government agency. There you can also obtain information about government jobs training assistance programs, YES (Youth Employment Services), Youth Corps, Civil Service (state and federal), and apprenticeship boards, as well as other government employment programs that exist from time to time. You may qualify for one or more of these types of work programs.

Newspaper, Yellow Pages, and Private Job Listings

The Help Wanted ads in the classified section of your local newspaper list job openings in your area. Brief descriptions of the positions are given, often with salary ranges specified. By watching these ads closely, you can respond quickly when a new job enters the market. Both employers and employment agencies advertise job openings to attract qualified applicants. You may be asked to send a letter of application and a resume to an employer before you will be granted an interview. In Chapter 3 you will learn how to prepare these materials.

The Yellow Pages of the telephone book is an alphabetically arranged subject listing of businesses advertising their services. If you are looking for a job in a certain field, determine the subject heading under which that type of work might be classified. You will find under that heading a list of companies that may be offering jobs in your field. You may want to send letters of application and resumes to all those listed, asking to be considered for the next opening.

Many companies, government offices, and schools place job opening announcements on bulletin boards, circulate them within the company, and post them in other special locations. Checking in these places may give you the inside information you need to apply for a position at the right time. Often the first applicants for a job opening have an advantage over those who apply at the last minute.

Online Job Information

Searching the Internet using keywords related to your field will provide many new sources of job information. A number of sites currently exist, such as www.resumeblaster.com; www.guru.com; www.techies.com; www.cooljobs.com; www.hotjobs.com; www.monster.com; and www.headhunter.net. These and other sites offer job information and assistance with finding and applying for job openings. Many of these sites allow you to post your resume for employers to see and even apply for a job online.

Companies often list their job openings on their own Web site. Find the sites of companies you would like to work for. Read the information the companies supply about themselves. Then follow the links to their list of openings. The site will tell you how to apply.

COMMUNICATION CONNECTION

Interview a friend or relative who recently conducted a job search. Ask what techniques that person used in order to locate a position. Was there anything he or she would do differently next time? Prepare a one-page report, describing the person's job-search experience.

Job Search Techniques

Finding and getting the right job takes hard work, careful planning, and often a great deal of time. Nevertheless, it is important that you put in sufficient time to ensure that you get a job you enjoy and can stay with. Dissatisfaction leads to frequent job changing, which may damage your employment chances in the future. Your **work history** is a record of the jobs you have held and how long you stayed with each employer. It will provide important information to future employers. If, for example, your record shows that you changed jobs six times in six months, you will appear immature and unstable to future employers. Thus, your work history could hurt your chances of getting a job you might want very much.

Job search techniques that will help you find and get the right job are discussed in the following paragraphs. The key elements in a successful job search involve getting organized, making a plan, following up, and not giving up.

Get Organized

After you have decided what kind of job you want, the first step is to get organized. You may want to prepare a checklist of things to do and check them off as you complete them.

1. Assemble all the information you will need about the type of work you want to do.
2. List prospective companies for which you would like to work.
3. Gather your sources of information and research job descriptions, skills and aptitudes needed, and other job requirements.
4. Make lists of personal contacts, places to go, and people to see.
5. Prepare a current resume and a letter of application.
6. Ask previous employers, teachers, or others to write letters of recommendation for you. Also, ask them if you may use their names as references for employment purposes.
7. Update your placement folder at school.

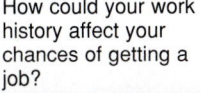

How could your work history affect your chances of getting a job?

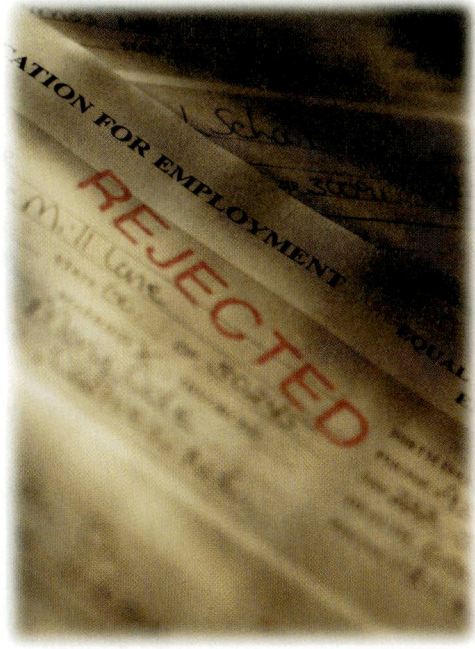

Make a Plan

A plan is important to the success of your job search because it keeps you organized, shows what you have done, and indicates what you need to do in the immediate future. A good plan lists all your goals and shows a time frame for getting them done. As you accomplish each step or goal, check it off. A plan you might want to follow is shown in Figure 2-5 on page 40.

Figure 2-5 *Plan to Get a Job*

Job Leads:
State employment office
Help Wanted ads (newspaper)
School placement office
Marketing teacher
Search online

Contacts:
Uncle Henry (knows manager
of local Penney's)

Time Line — Week 1

Day 1:
Prepare resume and letter
of application.
Check Help Wanted ads in
newspaper and online.
Make list of local stores from
Yellow Pages.

Day 2:
Send two application letters.
Get two personal references.
Call Uncle Henry to set at date
for lunch.

Conducting a job search involves "selling"
yourself to a potential employer. Focus on
communicating why your qualifications
make you an ideal match for the job.

Follow Up

After you have contacted a potential employer by letter or by filling out an application for a job opening, or after you have met a human resource manager or had an interview, it is important that you follow up. This means checking back from time to time to say you are still interested in the job. Call back in a day or two to check on the job, and always try to be courteous and upbeat.

Don't Give Up

Before you get a good job, you will probably not get several other jobs for which you applied. Remain calm and courteous, and keep checking back for openings. Try all your job leads. Be prepared at all times, so that if you are called for an interview on short notice—even on the same day—you can go. Continually check the want ads for new openings. Call back when you have established a contact, and check with your contacts frequently. Although a good job search may take several weeks or months, it will pay off. With careful planning and research, you can find the job that will meet your needs, wants, and goals.

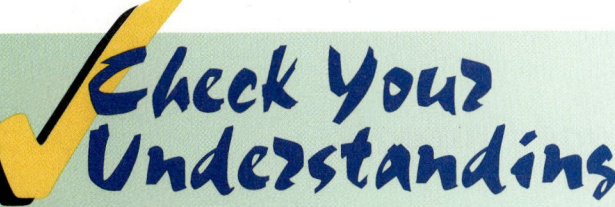

Check Your Understanding

Review Terms
1. contact
2. work history

Review Concepts
1. How do companies fill jobs without advertising?
2. What can your contacts do for you?
3. How can the Internet help your job search?

2.1 Finding a Good Career Fit

- Do a self-analysis to identify your values, lifestyle, aptitudes, interests, and personal qualities.
- Research careers that best fit the characteristics revealed in your self-analysis.
- Make a plan to reach your career goals and re-evaluate your choices from time to time.
- Create a checklist of your short-term, intermediate, and long-term goals, and check them off as you accomplish them.
- Look for ways to gain experience in your chosen field.

2.2 Finding Career Opportunities

- Search for job opportunity information through your contacts, placement services, magazines and books, newspaper ads and private job listings, the Yellow Pages, employment agencies, and online company and job sites.
- For a successful job search, get organized, make a plan, follow up, and don't give up.

Review Terms

Directions: Can you find the definition for each of the following terms used in Chapter 2?

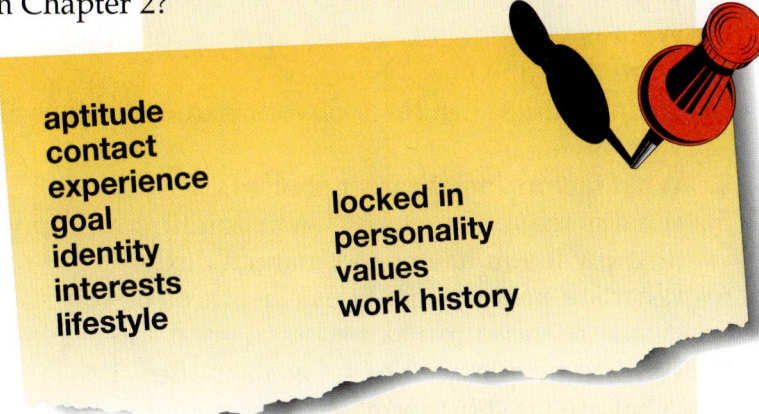

aptitude
contact
experience
goal
identity
interests
lifestyle

locked in
personality
values
work history

1. The things in your life that are important to you.
2. A natural physical or mental ability.
3. Individual qualities that make you unique.
4. Person you know in a business who can give you inside information about a job.
5. The record of jobs you have held.
6. A sense of who you are.
7. The way you choose to live your life, based on your values.
8. An end toward which efforts are directed.
9. Knowledge, skills, and practice gained from direct participation in a career field.
10. Describes the condition of feeling that you cannot change to another type of work because you cannot afford to start over in pay.
11. The things you like to do.

Review Facts and Ideas

1. Why do people work?
2. What is your identity at this time in your life? (You may have more than one.)
3. Define values. List three of your parents' values and three of your own.
4. What factors affect career choices?
5. What is manual dexterity? Why might it be important to you to know if you have good manual dexterity?
6. What are personal qualities? List three of yours.
7. What are the four major steps in good career planning?
8. Why do people need to set goals in life?
9. What are (a) short-term, (b) intermediate, and (c) long-term goals?
10. How can you establish personal contacts within a business where you don't know anyone?
11. What are placement services? What types of placement services are available at your school?
12. List five sources of job opportunity information.
13. Where can you find job opportunity information online?
14. Why should you check with different private employment agencies before signing up with one of them?
15. Why is a plan important to the success of your job search?

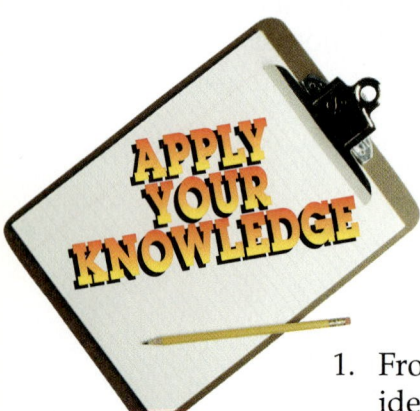

1. From Figure 2-1, list the activities that appeal to you. Then identify several occupations that offer these types of activities.
2. Describe your desired lifestyle in 10 years. Develop a plan of action to get a job that will support your desired lifestyle.
3. Using Figure 2-4 as an example, prepare a checklist of your short-term, intermediate, and long-term goals. At the end of one week, check to see what you have accomplished.

4. Cut these types of want ads from the classified section of your local newspaper: three ads by private employers; three ads by private employment agencies; one ad for someone to make a cash investment; one ad for someone in a sales position (to work on commission rather than for a salary); and one ad that gives the beginning salary in a dollar amount.

5. Using your telephone book, list five private employment agencies, their addresses, and their phone numbers. Also list the address and phone number of the state employment office. With your instructor's permission, call one of the private agencies and ask a counselor the fee for a job that will pay approximately $2,000 a month, and ask who would pay the fee.

6. Find the Web site of a major national company that has job openings listed. Briefly describe the available jobs. Then find the company's description of its business. Make a list of key information about the company you found there.

7. Write a paragraph describing your work history. It can be current or what you would like it to be in 10 years.

8. Using Figure 2-5 as an example, prepare a plan to get yourself a job using a one-week timetable. List your job leads, your contacts (or potential contacts), and a daily plan to accomplish several things each day.

9. Using a search engine on your computer, type in key words such as "job" and "career." Write a one-page paper on your findings of current Internet resources to help you plan your career.

Solve Problems

1. Jory McLean has decided that her long-term goal in life is to become an astronaut. She is now a sophomore in high school and hasn't done any planning. Jory's grades are average. She is active, outgoing, and bright. What can Jory do now, in the next few years, and beyond to prepare herself for a career as an astronaut?

2. Using Figure 2-3 as a guide, classify each of the following job titles into one of the job classifications. You may have to do some research to determine types of activities performed, skills and education required, working hours, and beginning pay. Next to each occupation, indicate whether or not you would be interested in the job. Next to job classification, indicate whether or not you would be interested in this type of career.

   a. Webmaster
   b. court reporter
   c. sheet-metal worker
   d. technical writer
   e. building custodian
   f. underwriter
   g. mechanical engineer
   h. sonar operator
   i. cosmetologist
   j. physical therapist
   k. computer programmer
   l. radio announcer
   m. singer
   n. infantry officer
   o. administrative assistant
   p. FBI special agent
   q. tailor
   r. graphic designer

3. Mei-ling Park wants to be an accountant when she completes high school. She is taking accounting courses and is working part-time at an ice cream store. What should Mei-ling be doing to prevent herself from becoming locked into her job at the ice cream store?

4. Fernando Suarez would like to work as a merchandising manager for a large department store. He has all the qualifications, education, and skills necessary, but he doesn't know anyone in any large stores, and most openings are filled before he even knows they existed. What can Fernando do to find out about job openings in the large department store?

5. Jermaine Reese is a sophomore in high school. He plans to use the placement service of his high school to help get a part-time job in his senior year. What should Jermaine do between now and his senior year to be sure his placement folder is ready when he is ready to find a job?

6. Mike Kriz has worked part-time after school for the past two years. He worked for two weeks as a cook, but rarely got to work on time and was fired. He worked for two months as a busboy but quit because he didn't get enough tips. Mike also worked for three weeks as a janitor but was laid off. Finally, he worked for four months as a plumber's assistant but quit because the work hurt his back. What is Mike's record of job changes called? What does it say to potential employers? Would you hire Mike?

For related activities and links, point your browser to
www.mypf.swep.com

Chapter 3

Getting the Job

Terms to Know

letter of application
return address
letter address
salutation
body

complimentary close
resume
references
scannable resume
letter of reference

employment
   application
job interview
thank-you letter

Up Front

A'yanna planned to get the right part-time job while she finished high school and prepared to go to college. Rather than waiting until spring when there would be far more competition, she decided to get the job in March and be all set when summer arrived. She had three interviews coming up, and she needed to mail or e-mail her resume before her appointments. She also wanted to draft a letter of application to which she would attach her resume.

"Getting a job can be a job in itself," A'yanna told her mother. "I have to be organized and have all my materials in order. I'm really glad I have two letters of reference ready to go. The good part is I'll get valuable experience for my resume. But for now, this isn't easy. In fact, it's pretty challenging."

Goals

★ Explain the purpose of, describe the parts of, and prepare a letter of application.
★ List the guidelines for and prepare a resume and scannable resume.
★ Describe the letter of reference and explain why it is useful to job applicants.

The Letter of Application

To apply for a job opening, or to inform a prospective employer of your interest in a future job opening, you need to mail or e-mail a letter of application, together with a resume. The **letter of application**, or cover letter, introduces you to the potential employer and gives you a chance to "sell" your qualifications. The letter of application that you write is really a sales letter. It is often your first contact with a new employer, and it is important to make a good impression.

Why is a letter of application really a "sales" letter?

Contents of an Application Letter

The letter of application should be specific, interesting, and direct. The first paragraph should identify the purpose of the letter—why you are writing. Be *specific*; tell the employer what job you are seeking. If you know of an opening, tell the employer how you learned about it.

The middle paragraph or paragraphs should give reasons why you are a good choice for the job. Use full sentences that explain your key qualifications—those that best fit this employer's job. Also express interest in the company as well as the job. Briefly describe any of your experiences, classes, or skills that relate to the job requirements. Your tone should be enthusiastic. Make your writing style conversational; you should be able to "hear yourself talking" throughout the letter.

The closing paragraph should wrap up the letter in a friendly yet assertive manner. Be *direct*; ask for an interview. For example, give the employer your telephone number and a good time to call.

In a friendly manner, make it clear that you would like to hear from the employer soon and that you are available for an interview.

Some experts believe that an application letter has only eight seconds to make an impression on the reader, before the employer decides positively or negatively about the applicant.

Preparing the Letter of Application

Generally, when you are sending the letter of application by mail, print it on white, standard-size (8-½ × 11-inch) paper of good quality. Choose a mailing envelope of the same color and quality. Personal letterhead stationery, with matching envelope, is also appropriate.

Figure 3-1 shows a letter of application prepared in a word processing software. Word processing programs allow you to choose different fonts (or type styles) and sizes when preparing documents. Choose a common, easy-to-read font for the body of your letter. You may use a different font and size in your heading if you want, but don't get too fancy. Your letter should look professional.

Along with your letter of application, enclose a resume. You may also want to include a copy of your transcripts (school records) and a letter of reference. Be sure to refer to all enclosed items in the body of your letter. Enclosures should also be listed at the end of the letter in a separate notation.

Parts of the Letter of Application

A letter of application should contain five basic parts. As you can see from Figure 3-2 (page 52), they are the return address, the letter address, the salutation, the body, and the complimentary close.

Return Address

The **return address** is the writer's address and the date at the top of the letter. The employer will need your address to write back to you. The standard return address contains your complete street address, a blank line space, and the date. If you have an e-mail address, add it below your city, state, and zip code.

234 Maple Street
Eugene, OR 97401-4321
tadams@stargaze.net

June 15, 20--

Ms. Marcia Hosteger, Owner
The Music Emporium
P.O. Box 8264
Eugene, OR 97405-8264

Dear Ms. Hosteger:

I would like to apply for your company's next opening in an office staff position.

I have prepared for this type of work and would appreciate the opportunity to visit with you about what I have to offer your company. As you can see from my resume, I have counter experience as well as accounting, clerical, and telephone skills. My course work in high school was in business and management, and I plan to continue my education as I work part-time for the next several years.

I am available for full-time work for the summer and part-time for the school year. I plan to continue my studies in business management, and my long-term goals include a permanent position in management that leads to increasing challenge and responsibility.

You can reach me at (503) 555-2000 after 3 p.m. daily. I am available to interview at your convenience. I look forward to discussing possible present or future employment with your company.

Sincerely,

Terrell B. Adams

Terrell B. Adams

Enclosure

Figure 3-2 *Parts of a Letter of Application*

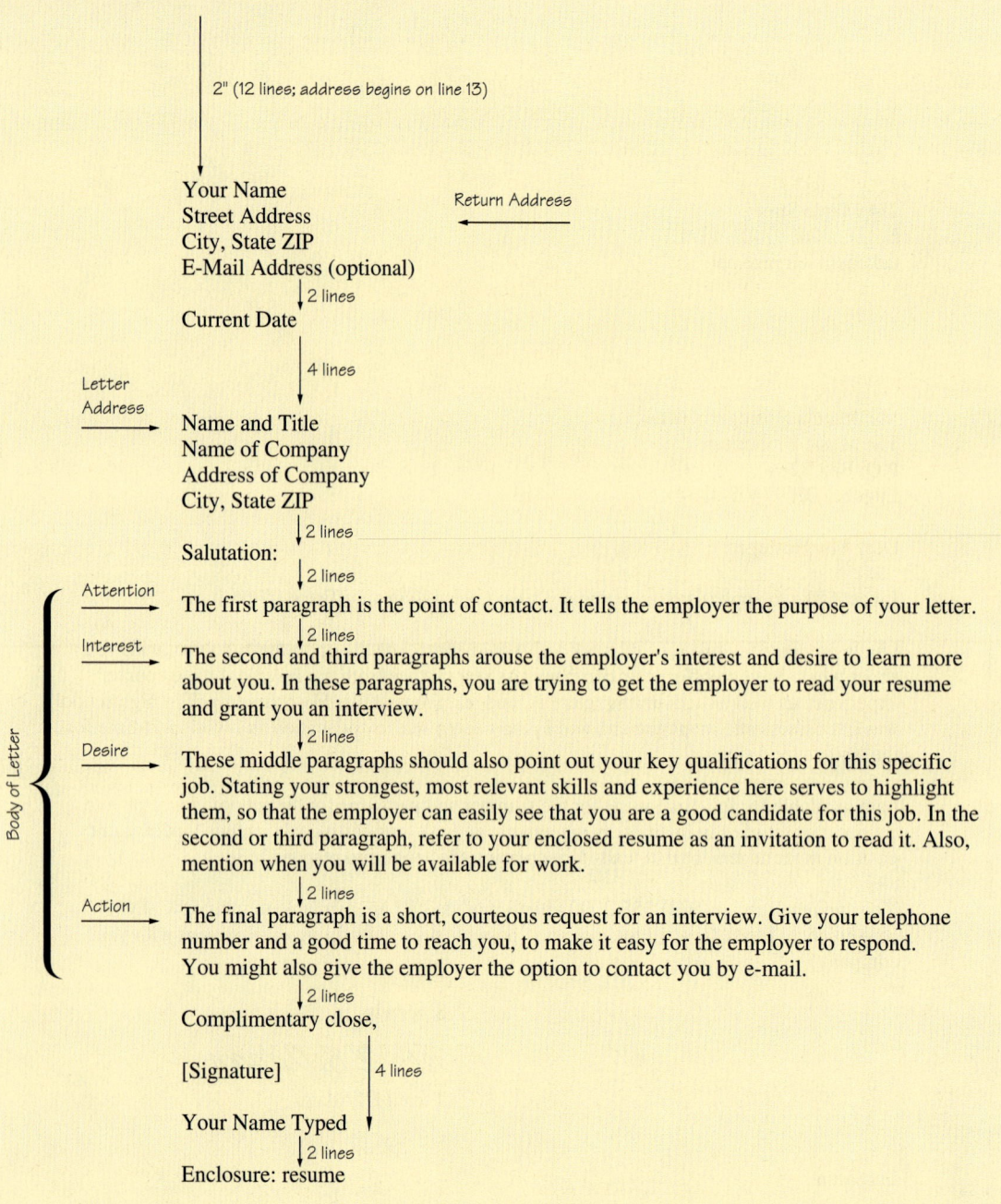

2" (12 lines; address begins on line 13)

Your Name
Street Address   ⟵ Return Address
City, State ZIP
E-Mail Address (optional)
↓ 2 lines
Current Date
↓ 4 lines

Letter Address ⟶

Name and Title
Name of Company
Address of Company
City, State ZIP
↓ 2 lines
Salutation:
↓ 2 lines

Attention ⟶ The first paragraph is the point of contact. It tells the employer the purpose of your letter.
↓ 2 lines
Interest ⟶ The second and third paragraphs arouse the employer's interest and desire to learn more about you. In these paragraphs, you are trying to get the employer to read your resume and grant you an interview.
↓ 2 lines
Desire ⟶ These middle paragraphs should also point out your key qualifications for this specific job. Stating your strongest, most relevant skills and experience here serves to highlight them, so that the employer can easily see that you are a good candidate for this job. In the second or third paragraph, refer to your enclosed resume as an invitation to read it. Also, mention when you will be available for work.
↓ 2 lines
Action ⟶ The final paragraph is a short, courteous request for an interview. Give your telephone number and a good time to reach you, to make it easy for the employer to respond. You might also give the employer the option to contact you by e-mail.
↓ 2 lines

Body of Letter

Complimentary close,

[Signature]   4 lines

Your Name Typed
↓ 2 lines
Enclosure: resume

Letter Address

The **letter address**, also called the inside address, contains the name and address of the person or company to whom you are writing. Try to find out the person's name and title, so you can address the letter directly to him or her. If you can't find out the person's name or you don't know whether the person is male or female, use the simplified version of a business letter shown in Figure 3-3 on page 54.

Salutation

The **salutation** is the greeting that begins your letter. The person's name or other form of address may be followed by a colon or by nothing at all. Do not use a comma. "Dear Mr. Sanchez:" and "Dear Sir or Madam:" are examples of salutations. Avoid addressing application letters "To Whom It May Concern." There is no salutation in the simplified format. Instead, there is a subject line. This makes the letter less personal, but also avoids choosing a title for the person, such as Mr., Ms., Mrs., Miss, or Dr.

Body

The **body** is the message section of the letter. As you can see in Figure 3-2, the body contains four basic parts and should be three or four paragraphs long. These paragraphs should attract the employer's attention, inspire the employer's interest in learning more about you, arouse the employer's desire to read your resume, and request that the employer take action in the form of an interview. These parts of the body are often referred to as AIDA—attention, interest, desire, and action.

Complimentary Close

The **complimentary close** is a courteous phrase used to end a letter. Phrases commonly used in business are "Sincerely," "Sincerely yours," and "Cordially." Your typed name should appear several lines below the complimentary close to allow space for your signature. The simplified format does not include the complimentary close but goes directly to your name, again eliminating the personal touch. Below your typed name are the notations for enclosures that will accompany the letter.

Preparing an E-Mail Letter of Application

To send your information by e-mail, prepare your letter of application in your e-mail message window. Your message will be dated

Figure 3-3 *Simplified Letter of Application*

2" (12 lines; address begins on line 13)

234 Maple Street
Eugene, OR 97401-4321
tadams@stargaze.net

↓ 2 lines

June 15, 20--

↓ 4 lines

Human Resource Manager
Excel Wholesale Company
818 Magnet
Eugene, OR 97401-0011

↓ 2 lines   (All caps)

POSITION POSTING OF JUNE 11, 20--, NO. 41826, ACCOUNTING CLERK

↓ 2 lines

Please consider me an applicant for the position posting referred to above.

↓ 2 lines

As you can see from my resume, I have completed the course work required to qualify
for an entry-level accounting clerk position. Also, I have worked for six months in a clerk
position where I learned about serving customers, keeping cash records, recording
purchases, and answering a multi-line telephone during busy hours.

↓ 2 lines

My long-term goal is to be a manager. I would like to work in a challenging job with
increasing responsibilities that use my business and accounting skills. I am available for
part-time employment now. In the fall, I plan to attend the community college part-time
to continue my studies in business and accounting.

↓ 2 lines

I am available for an interview at your convenience. Please call me at (503) 555-2000 to
discuss current or future employment opportunities with your company. If you prefer, you
can contact me by e-mail at tadams@stargaze.net. I look forward to hearing from you.

↓ 4 lines

Terrell B. Adams

TERRELL B. ADAMS   (All caps)

↓ 2 lines

Enclosure: resume

automatically, so you need not type the date. Start your message with the salutation. Omit the inside address and move your return address to the bottom of the message, below your name.

The body of your message should contain the same content as any other letter of application. End the message with a complimentary close and your typed name. Below your name, type your street address, e-mail address, and phone number. Send your resume as an e-mail attachment. You need not include an enclosure notation since the attachment will show automatically.

With e-mail, what you see on your screen is not necessarily how your message will appear on your receiver's screen. The receiver's software may not be able to accept special formatting. Therefore, place everything flush left and use no special formatting or tabs.

The Resume

The **resume** is often called a personal data sheet, a biographical summary, a professional profile, or a vita. It is a brief summary of personal information of interest to a prospective employer. The resume describes your work experience, education, abilities, interests, and other information such as awards, offices, and activities. The resume is a valuable tool when applying for a job because it tells the employer neatly and concisely who you are, what you can do, and your background and special interests. Always have an up-to-date resume ready for potential employers. Figure 3-4 on page 56 shows a commonly used resume style.

General Guidelines for a Resume

There are no set rules for preparing a resume. You should choose the style that best presents you to an employer. However, here are some guidelines that have proven successful:

1. Keep your resume to one page, if possible, by carefully arranging the information you choose to include. If your resume extends onto a second page, but doesn't fill it, place your references on a separate page to keep the resume to one page.
2. Include all information pertinent to the job for which you are applying. An employer wants to know that you are interested in the specific job opening. Rather than prepare a "generic" resume to fit all possible openings, use key words

Figure 3-4 *Resume*

TERRELL B. ADAMS
234 Maple Street
Eugene, OR 97401-4321
(503) 555-2000
tadams@stargaze.net

CAREER OBJECTIVE

Office or accounting clerk position with challenge, responsibility, and opportunity for advancement to administrative assistant.

EDUCATION

1998-2001   Madison High School, Eugene, Oregon (GPA 3.00)
Major Course of Study: Business and Accounting

Relevant Course Work:

		Relevant Skills:
Word Processing	Accounting I and II	Typing (70 wpm)
Computer Applications	Marketing I and II	Word processing and
Business Math	Business Law	spreadsheet software

Extracurricular Activities:

Member: National Honor Society, 1999-2001
Member: Future Business Leaders of America, 2000-2001
Competitor at regional skills event in area of accounting

WORK EXPERIENCE

Accounting Clerk, Video Image Plus, Springfield, Oregon (six months)
Cooperative work experience position through Madison High School.
Duties included answering telephone, preparing statements, serving customers, keeping cash records, recording purchases, and filing.

Office Assistant, Madison High School, Eugene, Oregon (one year)
Work in the front office included helping new students get to classes, answering the telephone, running errands, typing forms, and calling parents.

Newspaper Carrier, Register-Guard, Eugene, Oregon (two years)
Delivered morning newspapers in one route for one year, and on two routes for one year. Duties included keeping good records, collecting from customers, sorting and doing inserts, making special deliveries, and substituting for others.

REFERENCES

Provided on request.

from a job posting or ad in the paper to show that you match that particular job.

3. Choose fonts and arrange your information in a way that is attractive yet professional-looking and easy to read. Place the most important items in the upper third of the page.

4. Proofread carefully. Remember, your computer's spell check catches only misspelled words. It will not catch errors such as "then" instead of "than." Your resume must have no errors.

5. Use a high-resolution printer to print out the resume on good quality, $8\frac{1}{2} \times 11$-inch paper. Avoid bright colors, odd sizes, and paper with stains or discolorations.

Parts of the Resume

A simple resume should include limited personal information, a career objective, education, work experience, additional qualifications and skills or special items of interest, and references. You may arrange your resume according to personal preference. However, generally you should show your most favorable section first, just below your career objective. For example, if your work experience relates to the open job more closely than your education does, list work experience ahead of education. Following is a discussion of the basic parts of a resume.

Personal Information

This section usually appears first on the resume and includes your name, address, telephone number, and e-mail address, if you have one. You may also wish to include a cell phone or pager number where the employer can leave messages. Include your area code. However, omit information such as age, gender, marital status, number of dependents, or ethnic background. These do not give information about your skills or qualifications.

Career Objective

The career objective is a short, assertive statement indicating your career goal. For example, your goal might be to rise to a particular position. Make the statement forward-looking, interesting, and specific. This statement helps the employer identify with your plans and reveals your interest and enthusiasm for the job and for your future. Avoid weak and unimpressive statements such as "any type of work in the office." The career objective statement can be omitted in cases where it might be too limiting or too specific.

As your resume gets more detailed, this is the first part you should drop to make room for more important information.

Education

List all high school and post-high school institutions you have attended, starting with the most recent and working backwards. You may wish to include major areas of study, grade point average, extracurricular activities, scholastic honors, specific courses that apply to the job opening, or any other pertinent facts that you think will create a favorable impression on the employer. For example, extracurricular activities tell an employer that you are a well-rounded person and that you possess different abilities and interests. Offices held in school organizations will show the employer that you have leadership capability.

Work Experience

List all jobs, paid and unpaid, that you have held, including assisting at school functions, working as a teacher's aide, and any part- or full-time summer or vacation jobs (such as camp counselor). You may write this section of your resume in paragraph or outline form. Include information such as name and address of employer, job title, work duties, employment dates or length of time employed, and specific achievements while with this employer. Point out tasks you performed that relate directly to the open position.

Why is work experience an important part of the resume?

Additional Qualifications

Educational and employment records present an overview of your personal and professional qualifications. However, you may have additional skills that you wish to bring to a potential employer's attention. For example, you may want to list special equipment you have learned to operate, software you have learned to use, foreign languages you know, or special talents you have (such as playing the piano). You can also list honors you have received or contests you have won. All of these things give an employer a better picture of you.

References

References are people who have known you for at least one year and can provide information about your skills, character, and achievements. References should be over age 18 and not related to you. The best types of references include teachers, school counselors, former employers, and adults in business. Be sure to ask permission from the people you wish to list as references before including them on your resume. If you choose not to list references on your resume, state "references available upon request." Then have names, addresses, telephone numbers, and e-mail addresses ready for employers who ask for them.

Scannable Resumes

Some employers use scanners and special software to search for key words and phrases that match the skills required in their job descriptions. They can scan hard copy as well as electronic resumes. The scan determines which resumes will be considered further and which will not.

A **scannable resume** is a resume that has been designed for easy reading by a scanner and contains key words from the applicant's career field. To make the scanner's cut, describe your qualifications using key words from your field. For example, a publisher looking for an editor might scan for key words such as English or journalism degree, writing, editing, and copyediting. To make your resume easy for the scanner, use the following formatting:

- A simple, standard font, such as Times Roman or Arial
- Type size of 11 or 12 point for the body of the resume
- Headings no larger than 14 point bold or caps

Avoid the following:

- Fancy fonts, italic, underlines, condensed type, shading, shadows, and white type on a black background
- Multiple columns
- Horizontal or vertical lines, boxes, and graphics

Letters of Reference

A **letter of reference** is a statement, in letter form, attesting to your character, abilities, and experience, written by someone who can be relied upon to give a sincere report. When you ask people to write a letter of reference for you, be sure to give them enough time to prepare it. It is also helpful to give them a copy of your current resume or a short summary of your accomplishments and background. Be sure to ask business references to print out the letter on letterhead stationery. A sample letter of reference is shown in Figure 3-5.

When you receive the letter of reference, make photocopies to give to employers along with your resume and letter of application. Keep the original for your files, because you may need to make additional copies for other job applications.

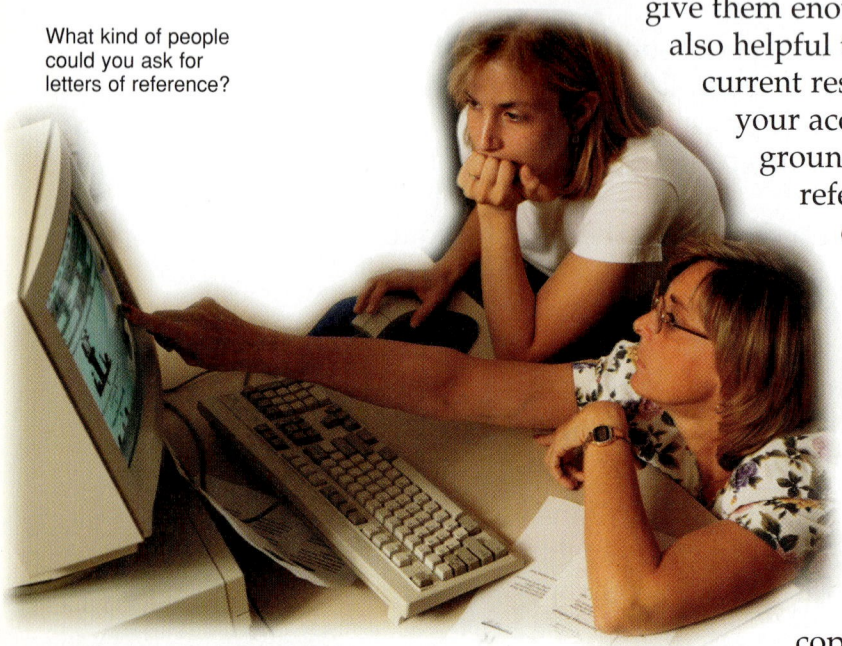

What kind of people could you ask for letters of reference?

FARWEST TRUCK CENTER

402 First Street, NW
Eugene, OR 97402-2143

June 4, 20--

To Whom It May Concern:

RE: Terrell B. Adams

I have known Terrell Adams as an employee for one and a half years. Terrell began working for Farwest as a work-study student in the cooperative education program at his high school. He proved to be such a good employee that, at the end of the school year, we kept Terrell as a full-time summer worker. He now works for us part-time after school and on weekends.

Terrell is a fine young man. I have found him to be honest and sincere. He is always on time and is genuinely eager to do a good job. Terrell gets along well with other employees and customers. He has filled in for vacationing office employees and has been able to assume additional responsibilities very quickly.

Without hesitation I can recommend Terrell to you as a fine person and an outstanding employee. He will, I am sure, be an asset to any company for which he works.

If you have any further questions, please do not hesitate to call me.

Sincerely,

Harriet Chen

Harriet Chen
Manager

PERSONAL PERSPECTIVE

Your Networking Notebook

Most people use networking as a way to find out about jobs and advancement opportunities. Networking is an important skill throughout life. A networking notebook is one way to prepare an organized job search. It's also valuable when you decide to change careers in the future.

To prepare a networking notebook, you'll need the following supplies:

1. A notebook, at least 2" thick
2. Plastic protective sheets
3. Section dividers (5)

To start with, your notebook might contain five sections:

1. A master resume (one that contains every job you ever had, every reference, every skill, etc.)
2. A list of references and original letters of reference
3. Transcripts, certificates of achievement, and other evidence of accomplishments
4. A contact list for people you know, meet, and would like to meet
5. An action section where you keep track of job interviews, follow-up, research about companies, etc.

A networking notebook will be useful in a number of ways. First, when you are considering applying for a new job, you will have all of your information in one place. With a master resume, you can pick and choose the information that best matches the job opening. Likewise, you can include references on your resume, or have a separate sheet that includes those references that would be most beneficial for the current opening.

Transcripts can take several weeks to receive, so having them on hand can save you time and effort. Other evidence of your achievements will help to sell you to prospective employers. Consider placing material in your notebook that showcases work you have performed in the past and that could be used as a portfolio to present your qualifications. People you know will serve as valuable channels of information; keeping track of their addresses and keeping in touch of them will be important over time.

Think Critically

1. What types of informal networking do you do already?
2. How could you use the networking notebook to help you prepare better for interviews?
3. As you move through your career, what types of information might you insert into the notebook over time?

✓ Check Your Understanding

Review Terms

1. letter of application
2. return address
3. letter address
4. salutation
5. body
6. complimentary close
7. resume
8. references
9. scannable resume
10. letter of reference

Review Concepts

1. List the parts of a letter of application.
2. Why should you avoid special formatting when preparing an e-mail letter of application?
3. What information is contained in a resume? List the parts of a resume.
4. Name three people who would be good references to list on your resume or who would write a letter of reference for you.

Lesson 3.2

Applying, Interviewing, and Following Up

Goals

★ Prepare a job application form, prepare for a job interview, and list methods of making a good first impression.

★ Explain the purpose of, describe the content of, and prepare a thank-you letter.

The Application Form

When you visit a company to interview or to inquire about a job opening, you will probably be asked to complete an **employment application**, like the one shown in Figure 3-6. When possible, ask to take the application form home. Then complete it carefully and return it. If you must do it on the spot, fill it out completely, using a good pen. Some companies supply their application form online. You may be able to download the form, fill it out on your computer, and submit it electronically. When completing an employment application, follow these steps:

1. Print neatly using a black or dark blue pen that does not skip or blot. Keep your responses within the space provided. Handwriting must be easy to read and clear.

How is an employment application different from a letter of application?

EMPLOYMENT APPLICATION

Date: _7/15/20--_ Job you are applying for: _Clerk/Office Assistant_ ☐ Full Time ☒ Part Time

Social Security Number: _Provided at employment_

First Name: _Terrell_ Middle Initial: _B._ Last Name: _Adams_

Mailing Address: _234 Maple Street_ City: _Eugene_ State: _OR_ Zip: _97401_

Home Phone: _(503) 555-2000_ Work Phone: (   )

Have you worked for this company before? ☐ Yes ☒ No **From:** ____ **To:** ____ **What location?**

Your name at that time: _—_ Position when you left: _—_

If you are under 18, give your birthdate: _—_ / _—_ / _—_ and work permit number (if applicable): _____

Date available for work: _7/15/01_

Please indicate the hours that you are available to work on each of these days.

(Hours)	SUNDAY	MONDAY	TUESDAY	WEDNESDAY	THURSDAY	FRIDAY	SATURDAY
From	8	1	1	1	1	1	8
To	8	8	8	8	8	8	8

START WITH CURRENT OR LAST EMPLOYER—INCLUDE MONTH AND YEAR IN DATES

FROM	COMPANY		POSITION HELD	
Mo. 9 Yr. 00	*Video Image Plus*		*Accounting Clerk*	BEGINNING PAY *Min. Wage*
TO	STREET and NUMBER	CITY and STATE		ENDING PAY *Min. Wage*
Mo. 2 Yr. 01	*1121 West 18th Springfield, OR 97477*			
SUPERVISOR'S NAME	TITLE	REASON FOR LEAVING		
Jewel Clark	*CWE Coordinator*	*end of program*		
FROM	COMPANY		POSITION HELD	
Mo. 9 Yr. 99	*Madison High School*		*Office Assistant*	BEGINNING PAY *Volunteer*
TO	STREET and NUMBER	CITY and STATE		ENDING PAY *Volunteer*
Mo. 6 Yr. 00	*Eugene, OR 97401*			
SUPERVISOR'S NAME	TITLE	REASON FOR LEAVING		
Andy Williamson	*Office Manager*	*end of year*		
FROM	COMPANY		POSITION HELD	
Mo. 6 Yr. 99	*Register-Guard*		*Newspaper Carrier*	BEGINNING PAY *Commission*
TO	STREET and NUMBER	CITY and STATE		ENDING PAY *Commission*
Mo. 9 Yr. 99	*Eugene, OR 97401*			
SUPERVISOR'S NAME	TITLE	REASON FOR LEAVING		
Mary Adamson	*Supervisor*	*to go to school*		

MAY WE CONTACT YOUR PRESENT EMPLOYER? ☒ Yes ☐ No

SCHOOL NAME	ADDRESS	FROM	TO	DEGREE/DIPLOMA
HIGH SCHOOL				DIPLOMA ☒ Yes ☐ No
Madison High School	*Eugene, OR 97401*	*1998*	*2001*	TYPE:
BUSINESS/VOCATION SCHOOL				DIPLOMA ☐ Yes ☐ No
				TYPE:
COMMUNITY COLLEGE/UNIVERSITY				DIPLOMA ☐ Yes ☐ No
				TYPE:
UNDERGRADUATE COURSEWORK EMPHASIS				CUM GPA
GRADUATE COURSEWORK EMPHASIS				CUM GPA

I understand that any offer of employment is conditioned upon the satisfactory completion of this verification process and that the complany will hire only those individuals who are legally authorized to work in the United States and who present acceptable proof of their lawful employment status and identity.

Terrell B. Adams _7 / 15 / 20--_
SIGN HERE **DATE**

2. Fill in all the blanks. When you cannot answer a question, write "N/A" (for "not available" or "not applicable") or use a line (——) to indicate to the employer that you have not skipped or ignored the question.

3. Be truthful. Give complete answers. Do not abbreviate unless the meaning of the abbreviation is clear.

4. Have with you all information that might be requested on the application form, such as telephone numbers, dates of employment, addresses of references, or work permit number. Calling later with the rest of the needed information inconveniences the employer and makes you look unprepared. You should avoid giving confidential data, such as your social security number, until you have secured employment.

5. Whether you are completing the form by hand or by computer, proofread it carefully!

The Job Interview

A **job interview** is a face-to-face meeting with a potential employer to discuss your job qualifications. During the job interview, the employer will have your completed job application, together with your resume, letter of application, letter(s) of reference, and any other information you provided. The interviewer may question you about statements you made on any of these documents or about any other job-related matters. Therefore, you should spend at least as much time preparing for the interview as you did in getting the interview.

Preparing for the Interview

Review your resume so that all your personal information and qualifications will be fresh in your mind. Be prepared to answer open-ended questions such as "Tell me about yourself," "Why do you want to work for us?" or "What would you like to be doing in five years?" These types of questions are designed to learn more about you than just the information contained in your answers. Your responses show how well you organize your thoughts, speak, and think under pressure. Avoid rambling on, talking about personal information, or talking negatively about others. Emphasize your skills, achievements, and career plans. Rehearse what you will say if you are asked this type of question.

It is also important to learn something about your potential employer. Find out what the company makes or sells, where its branches are, how rapidly it has grown, and what its prospects are for the future. Think of questions you might ask the interviewer about the company and about the position for which you are applying. The prospective employer will be more interested in you as an employee if you show that you are interested in the company. This kind of information can be obtained from such sources as these:

Why should you spend time preparing for an interview?

1. The Yellow Pages may have an advertisement that lists the company's products or services.
2. Find out from the company itself. Simply call and request the information or visit the company's Web site and read about its products, history, financial performance, and other data.
3. Ask for information from a friend or acquaintance who works for the company.
4. Review the company's annual reports, available at public and university libraries and often online at the company Web site. Annual reports describe the company and its financial resources.
5. Find articles in current periodicals and newspapers, including online publications, which discuss the company's economic health or plans for expansion.

Making a Good First Impression

Since it may affect your whole future, the interview is an important moment in your life. Prepare for it carefully. Discussed below are some ways to make a favorable impression.

1. *Arrive on Time.* Better yet, arrive five to ten minutes early so you have time to check your appearance and compose yourself. Never be late to an interview. The interviewer will consider your tardiness an indication of your expected job performance. Time your travel route before the day of the interview. Then allow extra time for traffic and parking.

2. *Dress Appropriately.* If you are seeking work in a bank, dress like those already employed at the bank. Whatever you wear, be neat and clean. Don't overuse jewelry, perfume, or after-shave. Be conservative in dress, hairstyle, and appearance. In other words, look like you already have the job and are preparing for the job beyond.

3. *Go Alone.* Don't bring along a friend or relative. Only you will perform the job if hired; therefore, the interviewer wants to talk with you alone.

4. *Be Prepared.* Have copies of your resume, reference letters, and school transcripts with you. All should be neat, up-to-date, and accurate. Take a pad of paper and one or two good pens, articles you have found about the company, and other information you may need. Bring your papers in a briefcase or some type of carrying folder to keep them neat and organized.

5. *Appear Poised and Self-Confident.* It's normal to be nervous, but don't let your emotions control you. It's important to appear relaxed and comfortable. Maintain good eye contact with the interviewer. Don't chew gum, smoke, or display nervous habits. An occasional smile shows you are relaxed and feel good about yourself. Avoid chattering to fill quiet times. Allow the interviewer to lead the discussion.

6. *Be Courteous.* Even if you are asked to wait, respond with courtesy and understanding. Convey an attitude of composure and congeniality. Use "please" and "thank you."

7. *Think Before You Answer Each Question.* Take a moment to organize your thoughts before answering. Be polite, accurate, and honest. Use correct grammar; be especially careful of verb tenses. Say "yes" rather than "yeah." Avoid slang and informal speech. Speak slowly and clearly.

8. *Emphasize Your Strong Points.* Talk about your most relevant school subjects, grades, attendance, skills, work experience, activities, and goals in a positive manner. Negative comments reflect badly on your personality.

9. *Be Enthusiastic and Interested in the Company and the Job.* Show that you are energetic and able to do what is asked with a willing attitude. Let the interviewer know that you are interested in the company, in the job, in your future, and in what's going on in the world. Above all, let common sense guide you throughout the interview. Look for nonverbal and other cues from the interviewer. Listen carefully and try to understand the needs and wants of the company.

When the interview is over, thank the interviewer for his or her time. Say you will check back later. Then do so. Leave a copy of your resume, letters of reference, and other information with the interviewer, if he or she does not already have these documents. Exit with a smile and a comment along the lines of "I look forward to hearing from you."

Career Links

Human resources managers recruit and interview employees, and advise on hiring decisions that have been established in conjunction with top management. Human resources manager positions usually require a bachelor's degree in human resources, personnel administration, or industrial and labor relations. The field demands a range of personal qualities and skills. Dealing with people is an essential part of the job. Knowledge of computers and information systems is also useful.

For more information, refer to the *Occupational Outlook Handbook* at www.bls.gov or search the Internet using such key words as "careers," "jobs," and "human resources."

The Thank-You Letter

After the interview, the employer is left to choose from various candidates. Follow-up is essential on your part. Positive contact with the employer after the interview will remind the person of who you are and could improve your chance of getting the job. A **thank-you letter**, such as the one in Figure 3-7 on page 70, is an excellent follow-up tool to remind the interviewer of your qualifications and desire to work for the company.

Figure 3-7 *Thank-You Letter*

234 Maple Street
Eugene, OR 97401-4321
tadams@stargaze.net

June 25, 20--

Mr. R.B. Rivera, Manager
Magna Music Company
2345 Main Street
Eugene, OR 97401-0013

Dear Mr. Rivera:

Thank you for the time you spent with me during our interview yesterday afternoon. I enjoyed meeting you and having the opportunity to see how your company operates.

Your description of the data entry position sounded very interesting and challenging to me. As you know, I worked as an accounting clerk as part of my cooperative work experience. In that position, I gained skills in entering data into accounting spreadsheets. You can be assured that I will do my best on the job and will continue to improve my skills to be more valuable to your company in the future.

If there is any further information I can supply to you, please feel free to contact me. You can reach me in the evenings at (503) 555-2000, or anytime by e-mail at tadams@stargaze.net. I look forward to hearing from you.

Sincerely,

Terrell B. Adams

Terrell B. Adams

Basic Rules for the Thank-You Letter

Follow the same format and guidelines that you used in preparing your letter of application. You may want to enclose an additional letter of reference or other information that may help convince the interviewer to hire you. Remember to address the interviewer by name. If more than one person interviewed you during your visit, write a brief letter to each person.

Body of the Letter

The first paragraph should remind the interviewer of your interview by making reference to it. A good way to begin is as follows: "Thank you for giving me the opportunity to speak with you on (date and time of interview) concerning . . ."

The second paragraph reminds the interviewer of your interest in and desire to work for the company. Take this opportunity to remind the interviewer of one or two of your key qualifications that best fit the open position.

The final paragraph should courteously express your eagerness to hear from the interviewer when he or she has reached a decision. Include your telephone number and good times to reach you. This paragraph should end on a positive note.

Keep your letter short and to the point, and make sure it is error-free. Your final opportunity to represent yourself to the potential employer through a thank-you letter may make the difference that will get you the job.

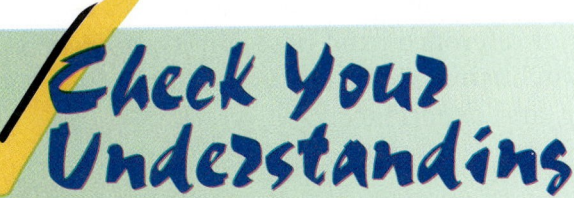

Check Your Understanding

Review Terms
1. employment application
2. job interview
3. thank-you letter

Review Concepts
1. What are some important steps to remember when filling out an employment application?
2. List several things you should do to prepare for a job interview.
3. What are some good ways to make a good first impression at a job interview?
4. What is the purpose of the thank-you letter?

Summary

3.1 Getting an Interview

- A letter of application sent by mail should include a return address, inside address, salutation, body, and complimentary close.
- When you prepare a letter of application in the body of an e-mail, avoid special formatting, place everything flush left, and send the message in plain text format.
- The purpose of the letter of application is to interest the employer in reading your resume and granting you an interview.
- A resume is a concise summary of your work experience, education, abilities, interests, and other information of interest to a prospective employer.
- To make your resume easy for a scanner to read, avoid fancy fonts and formatting.
- Ask for a letter of reference from past employers, teachers, and adults in business who can vouch for your skills, character, and experience.

3.2 Applying, Interviewing, and Following Up

- Fill out employment application forms completely, accurately, and honestly.
- Prepare for an interview by reviewing your materials, researching the company, and rehearsing answers to questions you might be asked.
- Arrive at the interview on time, dress appropriately, go alone, and be courteous, and enthusiastic.
- After an interview, follow up with a short thank-you letter that reminds the interviewer of your key qualifications and your interest in the job.

Review Terms

Directions: Can you find the definition for each of the following terms used in Chapter 3?

body
complimentary close
employment application
job interview
letter address
letter of application
letter of reference
references
resume

return address
salutation
scannable resume
thank-you letter

1. The part of a letter that shows the writer's name, street address, city, state, ZIP Code, e-mail address (optional), and current date.
2. The greeting that begins a letter.
3. The part of a letter that shows the name and address of the person or company to whom you are writing.
4. A summary of personal information, education, experience, additional qualifications, and references of the job-seeker.
5. The message section of a letter.
6. People over 18, not related to you, who have known you for at least one year and can report on your skills, character, and achievements.
7. A statement, in letter form, attesting to your character, abilities, and experience, written by someone who can be relied upon to give a sincere report.
8. A form you fill out when you apply for a job.
9. A face-to-face meeting with a potential employer to discuss your job qualifications.
10. A letter that introduces you to the potential employer and gives you a chance to "sell" your qualifications.
11. The phrase that courteously ends a letter.
12. A tool to remind the employer of your qualifications and interest in the job, written after the interview.
13. A resume that has been designed for easy reading by a scanner and contains key words from the applicant's career field.

Review Facts and Ideas

1. What is the purpose of a letter of application? What action does the writer desire? What do the letters AIDA stand for?
2. What size of paper should you use for a letter of application or a thank-you letter?
3. List and describe briefly the five basic parts of a letter of application.
4. When would you use the simplified letter format for a letter of application?
5. What is a resume? Describe the parts you will include in your own resume.
6. What should you do to make your resume scannable? What should you avoid?
7. Why should you list extracurricular activities on your resume?
8. Which kinds of people should be used as references on a resume?
9. List four rules for filling out an application for employment.
10. What information should you include in the second paragraph of a thank-you letter?

APPLY YOUR KNOWLEDGE

1. Follow the instructions in the chapter to prepare a letter of application to a business or company that you would like to work for.
2. Prepare your resume, using your own design. Include all information that applies to you, emphasizing your strong points. Format it to be scannable.
3. Visit Career Consulting Corner online at www.careercc.com/ or another Web site that offers resume advice. Write a paragraph about the resume tips you find there. Which tips do you plan to follow when you prepare your own resume?
4. Call, write, or speak directly to each person listed on your resume as a reference (or anyone you would use when asked for references). Ask permission to use their names on your resume or for job interview purposes. Ask one person to write a letter of reference for you.

5. Obtain and complete an application for employment from a local business. Or, search company sites on the Internet for an application you can download.

6. Write a thank-you letter for a job interview. Assume you were interviewed by the person to whom you sent your letter of application (see Question 1). You should know the interviewer's name now. Address the person by name and title.

Solve Problems

1. Hitesh Nizami wants to work as a forest ranger when he graduates from college. At present, he knows of no openings, but he does know the address of the local Bureau of Land Management, which occasionally hires students during summers to help in the forest. Hitesh takes science courses and does well. He is available to work all summer, and could even work without pay if his living expenses were covered. Because you are Hitesh's friend, you have offered to help him write a letter of application. Make up a return address, letter address, salutation, body, and complimentary close. Use the sample letters of application in the chapter as guides.

2. Naomi Rodriguez must provide a resume in order to answer an advertisement in the local newspaper. Write in outline form a summary of the basic rules of writing a resume. On another piece of paper, sketch a resume and label its parts. You do not need to insert fictional information—just describe what kinds of information Naomi should use.

3. Pam Olefson tells you that she has a job interview tomorrow. She has never been on a job interview before, and she is very nervous. Pam asks you to point out to her what she should and should not do during her interview. On a piece of paper, make a list for Pam of at least five things she should be sure to do and five things she should avoid during her job interview.

4. Lee O'Leary has just completed a job interview. Lee knows that his competition is tough, but believes he stands a good chance of getting the job because he is available to work right away, his grades are high, and he has taken three marketing courses. Would you advise him to write a follow-up (thank-you) letter? What might he say?

For related activities and links, point your browser to
www.mypf.swep.com

Terms to Know

hearing
listening
sympathetic listening
critical listening
creative listening
horizontal
　　communication

downward
　　communication
upward
　　communication
e-mail
human relations
empathy

productivity
self-esteem
self-actualization
hygiene factors
motivators

Up Front

Stage fright is a common fear experienced by people who perform for audiences. It refers to the anxiety that is felt by a person who is confronted with doing something he or she is not comfortable doing.

Joel had to give a presentation to his marketing class. He remembered the important things he learned in a previous speech class—to relax, to look directly at the audience, to speak slowly, to take deep breaths—but still he didn't feel comfortable. According to Joel, "My dad says I have to get used to this sort of thing. He says I'll have to communicate at work every day. Sometimes it will be one-on-one, but at times I'll have to speak in front of a group. He says this class presentation will be good for me. Fine, but I'm still nervous. The good thing is that I get a little less nervous every time I do this."

Goals

★ List and describe effective communication strategies, including listening, informal and formal speaking, communication among employees, and communication among employees and employers.

★ Discuss techniques of effective human relations.

Effective Communication at Work

Today's jobs and those in the future will depend on good communication skills. Of all the job activities you perform in a day, 80 percent involve communication in one form or another. You may think that writing is the most frequent form of communication. Actually, 60 percent of job communication involves listening and speaking. Figure 4-1 on page 78 illustrates the amount of time spent in the four forms of communication (listening, speaking, writing, and reading) during the average workday in America.

What is the difference between hearing and listening?

Listening

Hearing is not the same as listening. **Hearing** is the process of perceiving sound. It requires little or no thinking and very little effort. **Listening** is an active hearing process that requires mental concentration and effort. There are several rules to follow to become a good listener:

1. Look at the speaker and maintain eye contact to show interest in what the speaker is saying.
2. Ask questions and get actively involved in the conversation.
3. Avoid interrupting or changing the subject.
4. Control your emotions. Listen to what the speaker says, and then evaluate it with an open mind.

Figure 4-1   *Communication on the Job*

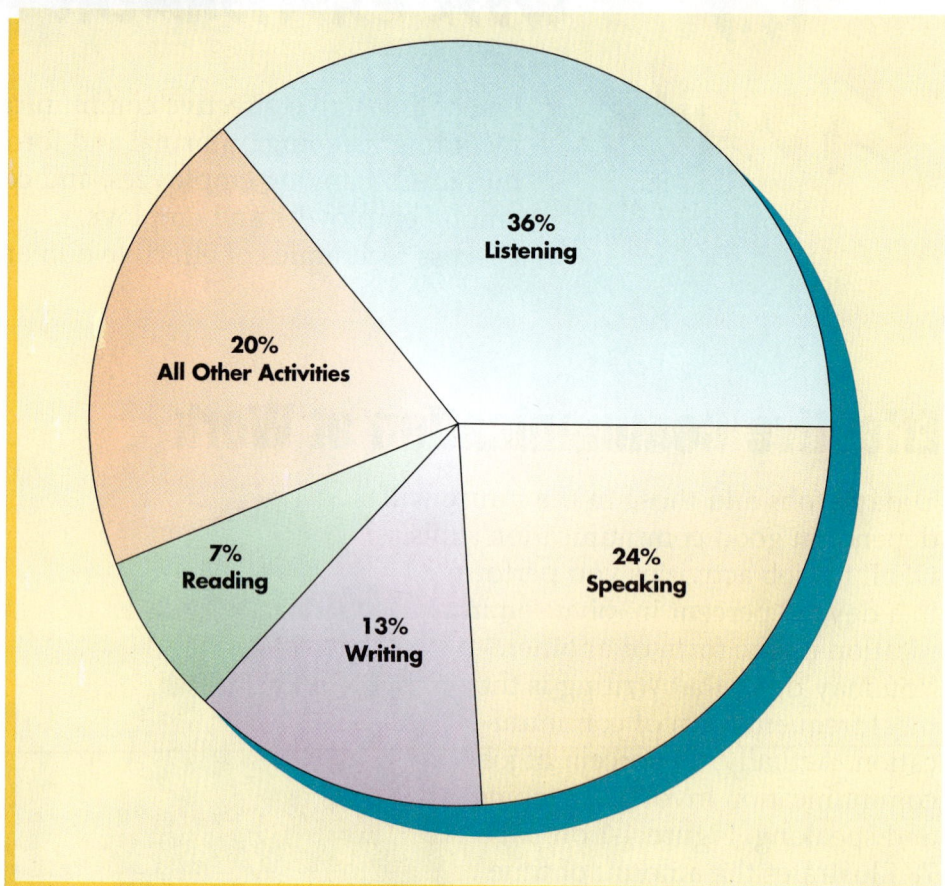

36%
Listening

20%
All Other Activities

7%
Reading

13%
Writing

24%
Speaking

You will need different types of listening at different times. The three types of effective listening are sympathetic, critical, and creative.

Sympathetic Listening

Sympathetic listening, sometimes called empathetic listening, is the ability to perceive from another person's point of view and to sense mentally and emotionally what the person is feeling. To listen with empathy, keep your eyes and attention on the speaker. Do not interrupt with your opinions. Ask questions that lead the speaker to make further explanations and analysis. Do not make body gestures or expressions indicating approval, disapproval, or opinion. With sympathetic listening, you should not give your own opinions unless asked for.

Critical Listening

Critical listening is the ability to differentiate facts from fiction or useless trivia. When analyzing information about a product or service you are considering purchasing, you will need to use critical listening. For example, claims that a product is "the best buy," "top quality," or "one of a kind" do not tell you anything about the product. But when you hear descriptors that provide important information describing a product, such as "100 percent cotton," "one-year guarantee," or "wrinkle-resistant," you are receiving useful information.

Creative Listening

Creative listening is the ability to hear new ideas that can help you develop a plan of action. Creative listening is often used in problem solving. Brainstorming is a common component of creative listening. In this process, all ideas are written down, regardless of quality. Then, after every possible piece of information is gathered, the best parts are put together to make a workable plan. Creative listening is difficult because it is a group process.

Listening is considered both a sign of politeness and a valuable skill in business negotiations in Japan. The Japanese often think North Americans need to listen more attentively, not talk as much, and certainly not interrupt when someone else is speaking.

Informal Speaking

At most workplaces, about 24 percent of the average employee's time is spent in oral communication. Most of the speaking you will do will be informal speech. Informal speech is used in four major ways: to make contact with others, to exchange information, to influence others, and to solve problems.

1. *To make contact with others,* you greet people, exchange social conversation, report on people and events, establish personal relationships, and find common ground for discussion. All relationships, formal or informal, begin with this initial contact, which often leads to more conversations where you discover and develop common interests. This type of informal speech is a daily event for most people at work. It's

important to be able to initiate conversations and begin relationships this way.

2. *To exchange information,* you explain an idea, clarify a difficult point, and illustrate with examples. This is often accomplished by relating to others through some common experience, which you discover by asking and answering questions. Workers must share information in order for the company to produce its goods and services.

3. *To influence others,* you stimulate feelings, present new viewpoints, and convince through basic appeals to emotion, logic, and evidence. To get people to accept your viewpoint and make it their own, you might describe personal experiences, encourage open communication, give advice, or share a strong belief. You will need to convince others of the validity of a new idea, or when you feel strongly about changing something.

4. *To solve problems,* you identify or define the problem and specify its causes. Then you consider all possible alternatives and propose solutions. Finally, after rational elimination of the least desirable choices, you select the best option. To effectively solve problems, you must have the cooperation of others with whom you are communicating. Unfortunately, you can't solve problems if you haven't mastered the first three informal speech methods.

Formal Speaking

There are three basic purposes for formal speaking: to inform, to entertain, or to persuade. Information is presented in different ways, depending on which kind of speech you are making.

1. *To Inform.* In this type of presentation, you attempt to convey information to your audience. The information should be given in a manner that is easily understood. You can give facts and then reach your conclusions (inductive reasoning), or you can give the conclusions first, followed by the reasons (deductive reasoning).

2. *To Entertain.* This type of speech is humorous or stimulating from beginning to end. The purpose is to get the members of your audience to relax and enjoy themselves. Entertainment speaking may seem fun and easy, but it is probably the most difficult form of formal speech, because you depend on the audience's reaction. For example, if the audience doesn't respond favorably, you may find it difficult to keep going.

3. *To Persuade.* This is a speech designed to convince your audience to take some action or to believe something. To be convincing, you must use solid information based on facts and statistics. You must appear to be honest and to believe in what you are saying. Persuasive speech takes a great deal of practice and motivation. If you are not sincere, your audience will sense it.

To give your formal speaking added dimension and style, use visual aids. For example, consider using overhead projectors, video, computerized slide shows with presentation software, Internet screen captures, audio recordings, slides, display boards, flip charts, chalkboards, maps and graphs, real objects, models, or handouts. The setting, which includes lighting, room layout, seating, speaker's stand, and microphone, can also contribute to the positive acceptance of a speech.

Stage fright (nervousness) is a natural and common reaction. Many experienced speakers are tense before speaking. Here are several things you can do to control stage fright:

1. *Build Your Confidence.* Prepare in relatively non-threatening speaking situations. Talk before small groups, including friends and family. Take speech classes and observe other speakers carefully.
2. *Be Well Prepared.* First, outline what you want to say. Then time yourself giving the speech on several occasions. Prepare an additional "comfort zone" of several minutes' worth of

What are some things you can do to control stage fright while speaking formally?

material in case time goes faster than you thought it would. Most people talk faster when they are nervous, so make allowances for this.

3. *Practice Public Speaking.* Begin with short speeches and build to longer ones. Practice speaking slowly and carefully when expressing your thoughts. Volunteer to speak before classes, clubs, and groups. Record your voice and evaluate its effectiveness. This will help you keep your voice low and clear, avoiding high pitches, slang, talking too fast, and so on.

Communication Among Employees

While upward and downward exchanges of information tend to be more formal, **horizontal communication** (communication among employees of equal rank) is usually informal. Within all groups there are invisible ranks and communication barriers. These can be minimized through effective communication and interpersonal skills. The most common types of horizontal communications are face-to-face conversations (described earlier in the "Informal Speaking" section), e-mail messages, and small group meetings.

Small group meetings may be organized (with specific purposes in mind), or they may be spontaneous and informal. Common functions of small group meetings include problem solving, decision making, and information sharing.

Usually employees who are in small groups tend to be of equal rank. Ideas and suggestions promoted by a group tend to be put into practice more often than when the same information comes from one person. Some companies encourage small group meetings to get good advice, desired feedback, and varied approaches to problem solving. These companies find that involving employees is a good way to solve problems and to increase employees' commitment to the solutions.

Communication Between Employees and Employers

There are two types of communication between employers and employees: downward and upward. **Downward communication** is communication that flows from higher to lower levels in an organization. Managers use it to keep employees informed and to give them job-related instructions and feedback about their performances. Downward communication needs to be consistent, fair, and easily understood by employees. Some communications will be public and verbal, some written, and others will occur in private or group meetings. Information needs to be clearly presented so employees can respond appropriately.

Upward communication is communication that flows from lower to higher levels in an organization. Employees transmit information to managers. Upward communication includes information about work-related problems, organizational policies and procedures, and suggestions for improving company practices. The effectiveness of this flow of information depends on relationships between employers and employees; the quality of the employee's presentation of the message; the extent to which the message is positive or negative; the timeliness of the message; and its apparent usefulness to the employer. When upward communication is free-flowing and encouraged, employees tend to be more productive and efficient because they believe they have a significant role within the company. Good upward communication also supplies job satisfaction, which motivates the employees.

+PROS and CONS

Business and labor have often been at odds in America. Many employees feel that their employers do not care about them and that they are "only a number" and easily replaceable. But employers and managers have to be competitive to stay in business. Since wages are the largest expense of most businesses, that's the logical place to make cuts.

Think Critically: Do you agree with the logic of each side? Are there more points that could be made? Do you think the state of the economy plays a role in this issue?

E-Mail Communication

E-mail is the transmission of messages using computers. It is the fastest growing form of communication in business today. E-mail flows in all directions in an organization—up, down, and horizontally. Messages between employees and managers are generally worded more formally than messages between employees of the same rank. However, the rules of good writing still apply. When you write an e-mail message, use good grammar and proofread before sending. Keep your messages concise. People in business don't want to plow through a mountain of words before coming to your point.

E-mail has several advantages as a communication tool. It is fast. Messages go from one computer to another almost instantly. It is inexpensive. Messages can be sent all over the world without having to pay postage or long-distance charges. Messages can also be sent to many people at the same time. Finally, e-mail is easy to learn and use.

One disadvantage of e-mail arises from an advantage. E-mail is so easy that people tend to use it too much. Businesspeople often complain of information overload caused by e-mailboxes full of unnecessary messages. To be a good e-mail communicator at work, don't overuse it. Resist the temptation to send messages to many people unless they all really need the information.

Another disadvantage is lack of privacy. Employers can monitor employees' e-mail. Even if you delete messages from your computer at work, the messages remain on the company's large server computers. You may be fired for using e-mail or the Internet at work for non-business purposes.

Human Relations at Work

Human relations means getting along with others. As technological advances become more complex and sophisticated, our need for genuine and caring human relationships increases. To be truly competent in human relations, you need to have a good understanding of yourself and of others and a genuine concern for their needs and feelings. Here are some ways you can improve your relationships:

1. *Accept Differences.* Everyone is different. Accept others as they are, tolerate differences of opinion, and recognize that other ways of doing things may also be effective. It is important to be able to disagree without being disagreeable.
2. *Treat Others as Individuals.* Take time to discover the individuality in others. Learn people's names and use them. Take an interest in what others are doing. Every person needs and deserves to be respected as a human being.
3. *Empathize with Others.* **Empathy** is the ability to see others' points of view and understand their feelings. It does not mean you agree with them or with what they are feeling, but rather that you understand what they are saying, feeling, or experiencing.
4. *Praise Others.* Be consistent in praising the achievements of others. Seek good things that are true and complimentary,

Why are human relations at work important?

and praise them freely. But avoid untrue or exaggerated claims that will appear to be forced and fake.

5. *Describe Problems.* When problems with someone else occur, you will get the person's cooperation by describing the problem rather than the person or personality differences. To do this, avoid accusations. For example, say, "That report was not what the auditors needed," rather than "You did not prepare the report properly for the auditors."

6. *Accept Responsibility.* Take responsibility for your actions. Everybody makes mistakes. Take responsibility for yours. Your willingness to accept responsibility and say, "I messed up" will be respected by co-workers and employers.

7. *Avoid Dogmatic Statements.* A dogmatic statement asserts an opinion as if it were a fact. A user of dogmatic statements soon becomes known as a "know-it-all." To avoid appearing dogmatic, restrict your judgments to possibilities rather than absolutes.

8. *Treat Others as Equals.* Treat each person you associate with as though he or she is making worthwhile contributions. Don't talk down to people by telling them what they should know or should do. Allow others to make their own decisions without criticism.

9. *Trust Others.* People will live up to, or down to, your expectations. Therefore, think the best of others and expect the best. When they know you trust them, most people prove to be trustworthy.

10. *Control Your Emotions.* Withhold judgments, comments, or decisions until you gather all information. Reacting emotionally may affect your decisions, and you may later regret the display of emotions as well as the decision you made. Be slow to show emotions, and hold off as long as you can to be sure you have reached the right conclusion.

Check Your Understanding

Review Terms
1. hearing
2. listening
3. sympathetic listening
4. critical listening
5. creative listening
6. horizontal communication
7. downward communication
8. upward communication
9. e-mail
10. human relations
11. empathy

Review Concepts
1. Have you made presentations that have been uncomfortable for you? If so, what could you have done differently?
2. List situations in which you do sympathetic, critical, and creative listening.
3. What was your favorite presentation? What parts do you remember—in other words, what techniques were used effectively?

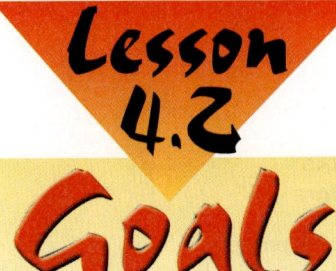

Goals

★ Describe employer expectations and policies such as written and unwritten work rules, attitudes, and absenteeism.

★ Explain motivation and levels of need as described by Maslow and Herzberg, and discuss the results of job satisfaction.

Employer Expectations and Policies

Employers have expectations and policies to inform and guide employees in meeting the goals of the business. These expectations are often expressed as work rules and policies concerning absenteeism and attitudes on the job. Employees who thrive in the workplace exceed these expectations.

Work Rules

Most businesses have written and unwritten *work rules* that all employees generally understand. *Unwritten work rules* often are commonly understood without being documented or verbally communicated. A dress code is one example. Observe how other employees dress. Then dress in a similar manner. An employer expects employees to know from common sense some of the work rules that apply to their jobs. Courtesy and teamwork are expected. Loyalty, a positive attitude, safety, punctuality, and good grooming are rules that are often unwritten and unspoken.

Written work rules are usually posted in employee work areas or included in an employee manual to remind employees of strict policies that they must follow. These rules are generally written for the benefit and protection of all employees. When everyone adheres to the rules, the work flows smoothly and everyone shares in the responsibilities. Breaking a rule can cause hard feelings among employees. Figure 4-2 on page 88 is an example of work rules that might be posted in an employee break room.

Because the rules shown in Figure 4-2 are basic disciplinary rules, employees who break them are subject to immediate discipline. When one employee is permitted to break the rules, others will see this and feel justified in doing the same thing. It is important

Figure 4-2   *Work Rules*

COMPANY WORK RULES
Sanders Department Store

1. Work begins promptly at 8 a.m. or 2 p.m. and ends promptly at 5 p.m. or 10 p.m. These are our hours of operation, and the store must be covered.

2. No food, drink, or smoking is allowed in the store.

3. No smoking is permitted in the building. Outside smoking areas are provided at the south and north entrances. Please do not smoke within 15 feet of the doorway.

4. All employees will be clean and properly groomed at all times. Facial hair is permitted if it is well groomed. Use good judgment in what you wear.

5. When a worker is sick, he or she must call in by 7 a.m. for the day shift, or by 4 p.m. for the evening shift.

6. Vacations are taken according to seniority; no more than three employees may take vacations during the same week. All vacations must be arranged two weeks in advance.

for new employees to follow all the rules to the letter to show the employer that they can fit in and be a part of the team. New employees should arrive early, leave on time, and never stay over-time on a break or sneak food into the work area. While these infractions are not acceptable in regular employees, they are tolerated even less in new employees.

Recent studies have shown that rates of illicit drug and heavy alcohol use were higher among workers age 18–25 than among older workers, and higher among males than females. In addition, rates were higher among those with less than a high school education than among those with a high school diploma or more education.

Work Attitudes and Absenteeism

Employees' work attitudes are important to employers because they affect morale, output (production), and public relations. Every employee in a company represents that company to the public.

A good attitude makes a favorable impression. Good public relations are important to a company's future growth and profitability. Employees in today's best-run organizations follow these simple rules to create a favorable impression:

1. Remember customers' names.
2. Make an unusual effort to help.
3. Demonstrate knowledge, enthusiasm, and interest in customers.
4. Display genuine concern for the quality of products and services.
5. Care about people and meeting their needs.
6. Listen sympathetically to customer complaints.
7. Take pride in yourself and your work.

Why are employees' work attitudes important to a business?

Employers appreciate employees who "go the extra mile." This means doing more than required and doing it with a positive attitude.

Absenteeism is a special kind of problem. How to deal with it depends on the reasons for the absence. One expert observed that of all absences:

- 60 percent are due to serious or chronic illnesses, injuries, or family emergencies;
- 20 percent are due to acute, short-term illnesses (such as the flu), work-related accidents, or personal problems;
- 10 percent are due to a minor illness such as a cold, and to employees whose decision to report to work or not depends on their attitudes about their jobs; and
- 10 percent are due to a pretend illness so that the employee can enjoy a day off.

The absentees making up the last 20 percent are of greatest concern to businesses. Industrial psychologists call this "voluntary absence syndrome" and warn that these patterns can lead to serious emotional imbalance and disturbance in the absentees' lives.

Types of Absentees

Absentees usually fall into groups with similar characteristics. Most fit into these six categories:

1. *Chronic.* These are the people who seem to have little tolerance for pressure on the job or off. They need to be aware that their absence is a problem and is causing other difficulties.
2. *Vacationing.* These are people who work only long enough to pay their bills and put a few dollars in their pocket before they head down the road. Vacationers make a conscious choice to be absent from work as much as work rules will allow.
3. *Directionless.* This group of employees is generally made up of young people. Until they decide what they want to do with their lives, they are likely to be poor employees and may take advantage of opportunities to be absent from work.
4. *Aggressive.* These are people who willfully stay away from work, intending their absences to cause problems. This kind of behavior requires professional counseling to correct.
5. *Moonlighters.* People who hold more than one job are often either too tired to come to work or trapped by conflicting work schedules. Very often the moonlighter is forced to make a choice between jobs.
6. *Occasional.* These employees' absences are legitimate, and their illnesses are real. But while their absences can cause temporary problems in the workplace, these absentees need a mixture of sympathy, understanding, and good advice.

Effects of Absenteeism

The absentee is not the only one affected by absenteeism but is usually the most seriously affected. Typically, the results range from penalties, fines (such as pay deductions), and warnings, to temporary layoffs, poor recommendations, lack of respect (from employers and fellow employees), and eventually to termination of employment.

When employers do not take action, they are in effect giving their approval to the absences, thereby encouraging other employees to feel free to be absent often. The working employees resent having to do another employee's work when the employer takes no corrective action.

PERSONAL PERSPECTIVE

Do You Have an Absentee Problem?

Chronic absenteeism is a leading reason for firing younger employees. If you have a job and can answer yes to any of the following questions, you may have an absentee problem. But you can change your behavior before it endangers the rest of your career.

1. Is getting to work a problem (real or imagined)?
2. Are off-the-job pressures (such as family troubles) so overwhelming that they weaken your decision to go to work?
3. Do you feel the work is boring, disagreeable, unattractive, or somehow not measuring up to your expectations?
4. Are your working relationships unpleasant?
5. Are there serious problems in your life that need immediate attention (emergencies, serious illness, court appearances, and so on)?
6. Has lateness or absenteeism become a habit that you find hard to break?

Do you recognize yourself? If you do, now is the time to take action—before you get fired. Losing your job would have many negative effects. Before you put your job in jeopardy due to absenteeism, consider the following consequences of getting fired:

1. You won't be able to use this employer as a reference for your next job application.
2. If you list this job on your resume, you will likely have to explain why you were fired. Employers don't like to hire people with a record of chronic absenteeism.
3. If you don't list this job on your resume, there will be a period of time during which you will appear to have been unemployed. How will you explain that?
4. If you are fired for just cause (such as chronic absenteeism), you will not be able to collect unemployment benefits.

If you've ever been fired, laid off, or asked to resign, then you know how it feels. It's an unpleasant, often humiliating experience, and something most people want to avoid.

Think Critically

1. Why is it important to report for work consistently?
2. What types of penalties have you experienced at work or at school for absenteeism?
3. How would you feel if your employer fired you?

Costs of Absenteeism

High rates of absenteeism cost companies thousands of dollars annually. The U.S. Department of Labor uses the formulas shown in the Math Minute feature to compute the rate of absenteeism and the costs of absenteeism to a business. Most labor experts agree that an absentee rate of 2.0 is low, while a rate of 5.0 is high. In the Math Minute example, Chandler's Bakery has an absentee rate of 2.08 percent. The company can conclude that its absenteeism is reasonable. However, Rosario's has a rate of 4.69 percent. From this number, Rosario's can see that it has a problem with absent employees and should search for causes and solutions.

Cost of Absenteeism

Chandler's Bakery operates 24 hours a day, 365 days a year. Employees work three 8-hour shifts. In an average month, 12 employees work 30 days. On average, a total of 180 hours are missed from work per month (the equivalent of 7.5 days). The *rate of absenteeism* is determined as follows:

$$\text{Rate of Absenteeism} = \frac{\text{Absent Days per Month}}{\text{Work Days per Month} \times \text{Number of Employees}}$$

Using this formula, Chandler's absenteeism rate is 2.08%, or 7.5 ÷ (30 × 12).

The formula to determine *cost of absenteeism* is described as follows:

Cost of Absenteeism = Annual lost time × Average wage rate × 2

The formula multiplies the cost of wages by 2 to include the costs of benefits paid to absent employees and the costs of paying temporary workers to replace the absent workers.

Chandler's average wage rate is $7.50 per hour. Using the formula, the cost of absenteeism is determined as follows:

Annual lost time = 180 hours per month × 12 months in a year = 2,160 hours
Cost = 2,160 hours × $7.50 = $16,200 wages paid to absent employees
    $16,200 × 2 = $32,400 annual cost of absenteeism

Based on the preceding example, compute the absenteeism rate and annual cost in the following situation:

Rosario's operates two 8-hour shifts a day. The company is open for business 24 days a month, with employees working two 8-hour shifts. Eight employees work 24 days per month. On average, a total of 144 hours are missed from work per month (the equivalent of 9 full days). The average wage rate is $12 per hour.

Solution: 9 ÷ (24 × 8) = 4.69% absenteeism rate
    144 × 12 = 1,728 hours lost annually
    1,728 × $12 = $20,736 wages paid to absent employees
    $20,736 × 2 = $41,472 annual cost of absenteeism

Motivation and Needs

All human beings have some needs that are basic to survival and other needs that go beyond mere physical existence. Unfulfilled needs motivate people to work toward satisfying those needs. For example, hunger motivates a person to look for food. Abraham Maslow, a psychologist, developed a human behavior model called the *hierarchy of needs*. Maslow's hierarchy divides human needs into five categories, as shown in Figure 4-3.

Maslow's Hierarchy of Needs

Employment can help satisfy all five levels of needs. Levels 1 and 2 are things that are essential to physical survival: employees need pay that is adequate to provide food, clothing, and housing and sufficient job security to feel safe and comfortable. Until the job meets these basic needs, the employee will not be motivated to greater achievement. According to Maslow, in general, lower-level needs must be satisfied before higher-level needs motivate a person's behavior. Once a need is met, another emerges to take its place. People are constantly striving to satisfy some higher need.

Maslow's Hierarchy of Needs   **Figure 4-3**

Level 5
Self-
Actualization

Level 4
Self-Esteem

Level 3
Love and Belonging

Level 2
Safety and Security

Level 1
Food, Clothing, and Shelter

However, the relationship among needs is complex. Several needs may affect a person's behavior at the same time.

Once physical needs are met, the needs in levels 3, 4, and 5 motivate workers to greater productivity. **Productivity** is the amount a worker can produce per unit of time, such as an hour. It is a measure of efficiency. A quality standard is often incorporated into the measure of productivity.

Every person needs fulfillment beyond physical requirements. Most businesses consider it the responsibility of management to provide opportunities for employees to meet their needs. The resulting increase in productivity will benefit the business.

Maslow's Level 3 is the need for love and the need to belong to a group: to be accepted, to have friends, and to be valued as a member of the team. In the workplace, employees can meet this need through caring work relationships and through working and socializing with groups of co-workers.

Level 4 is the need for **self-esteem**, or self-respect and recognition from others. When work is challenging and rewarding, employees feel good about their jobs and about themselves, and they want to do more. Workers trying to meet their need for self-esteem will be motivated by managers' and co-workers' praise and recognition.

Level 5 is the need for **self-actualization**. This is the need to reach one's full potential, to grow, and to be creative. Workers can fulfill this need if they are able to do the work they choose, as they choose, and receive appropriate rewards for a job well done. To aid employees in achieving to their full potential, many managers challenge employees by providing greater decision-making responsibility and more complex work gradually as the employees become capable of handling it.

AROUND THE GLOBE

Many large French corporations are using online employee training ("e-learning"). Companies consider it to be an important factor in developing employee expertise, thereby reinforcing their competitiveness and efficiency. About 70 percent of large French companies are already offering this type of training. Their goal: to create more flexibility, since employees can learn directly from their desktops, and to train employees better and more quickly, at a lower cost.

Think Critically: How might employee training lead to greater productivity and work satisfaction? Can you relate this to Maslow's Hierarchy of Needs?

Herzberg's Two-Factor Theory

Frederick Herzberg studied employees to find out what satisfied and dissatisfied them about their jobs. From his research, he formulated his *two-factor theory*. Herzberg found that elements of a job that lead to job satisfaction or dissatisfaction fall into two groups: hygiene factors and motivators.

Hygiene factors are job elements that dissatisfy when absent but do not add to satisfaction when present. For example, pay, fringe benefits, and the workplace environment are hygiene factors. A clean, roomy workspace will help maintain a level of satisfaction but will not increase motivation to work hard or increase satisfaction. However, a dirty, cramped workspace would increase job dissatisfaction.

Motivators are job elements that increase job satisfaction. For example, challenging work, responsibility, recognition, achievement, and personal growth motivate workers to greater productivity and add to satisfaction in the job. Therefore, to motivate employees to achieve and to promote greater job satisfaction, employers must offer hygiene factors to avoid dissatisfaction plus provide motivators. For example, jobs need to be designed to meet employees' need for challenging, rewarding work.

Results of Job Satisfaction

When employees can meet their needs in their jobs, several positive outcomes benefit both the employees and the employer.

Increased Productivity

When employees are motivated, they are more productive. They use time wisely and produce more and higher quality work in less time. Increased productivity leads to higher profits for the employer and subsequent rewards for the employees—both tangible (raises, bonuses, or promotions) and intangible (praise and self-esteem).

Self-Esteem and Self-Actualization

To put forth your best effort; to win the praise of your employer and co-workers; to strive for new challenges—all are valid bases for career development and satisfaction. As you achieve these goals, you will gain personal pride and enjoyment that are satisfying beyond the paycheck. Because you will probably work most of your adult life, why not strive to achieve to the best of your ability?

How can job satisfaction benefit employees?

Rewards and Opportunities

Employers often seek to motivate employees by using praise and pay as reinforcements for desirable results. Your rewards will vary: oral or written commendations from employers; admiration and respect of other employees; pay raises (often called merit pay); increased opportunities for challenging work (new job assignments with increased responsibilities); opportunities for advancement to higher-paying positions; and respect from others inside and outside your organization. You could become known as "one of the best in the field" and gain recognition in your community and beyond. This not only makes you valuable to your own employer, but it also makes you more employable in the future should you desire to move to another job. Increased opportunities within your field are created by excellence in work accomplishments and should be a part of your long-term career plans.

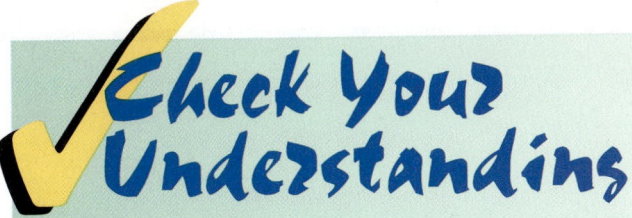

Check Your Understanding

Review Terms
1. productivity
2. self-esteem
3. self-actualization
4. hygiene factors
5. motivators

Review Concepts
1. Why are work rules, both written and unwritten, important to employers?
2. What are some things you can do to create a favorable impression with an employer?
3. How are motivators different from hygiene factors, according to Herzberg?

Summary

4.1 Communicating in the Work Environment

- Effective communication requires good listening, including sympathetic, critical, and creative listening.
- People communicate informally at work to make contact, exchange information, influence others, and solve problems. The goal of a formal speech may be to inform, to entertain, or to persuade.
- To reduce stage fright, build your confidence by speaking to small groups of friends and family first, prepare your speech well, and record your speaking practices so that you can evaluate your voice quality.
- Communication in the workplace occurs horizontally among employees of the same rank as well as upward to managers and downward from managers to employees.
- E-mail is fast, inexpensive, easy to learn and use, and can send messages to multiple people at a time. However, e-mail communication lacks privacy and can lead to information overload.
- To improve your human relations, accept differences; treat others as individuals; empathize with others; praise them; describe problems; accept responsibility; avoid dogmatic statements; treat others as equals; trust them; and control your emotions.

4.2 Thriving in the Work Environment

- Some expectations on the job are unwritten, such as loyalty, punctuality, and a good attitude. Others are written work rules posted in the workplace or included in the employee manual.

- Employees' work attitudes are important to employers because they affect morale, output, and public relations. Employees can make a good impression by showing genuine concern for producing high-quality products and meeting customers' needs.
- Unnecessary absenteeism costs the company money and can cost the employee in loss of respect from co-workers, docking of pay, and eventually termination.
- Maslow's hierarchy of needs theory holds that people are motivated to behave in ways that will meet their needs. As lower needs are satisfied, higher needs motivate behavior. Jobs can help satisfy all five levels of needs.
- Herzberg's two-factor theory differentiates between hygiene factors (which dissatisfy when absent but do not add to satisfaction when present) and motivators (which increase satisfaction).
- Both employees and employers benefit when jobs satisfy employee needs. Employees are rewarded by greater pay, advancement opportunities, and praise. Employers benefit from increased productivity, which leads to greater profits and company growth.

Review Terms

Directions: Can you find the definitions for each of the following terms used in Chapter 4?

creative listening
critical listening
downward communi-
      cation
e-mail
empathy
hearing
horizontal communication
human relations
hygiene factors

listening
motivators
productivity
self-actualization
self-esteem
sympathetic listening
upward communication

1. Communication among employees of equal rank.
2. Active hearing that requires mental concentration and effort.
3. Communication that flows from higher to lower levels in an organization.
4. Job elements that dissatisfy when absent but do not add to satisfaction when present.
5. Job elements that increase job satisfaction.
6. A type of listening in which you differentiate fact from fiction.
7. Communication that flows from lower to higher levels in an organization.
8. Self-respect and recognition from others.
9. Getting along with others.
10. The amount a worker can produce per unit of time, such as an hour.
11. The type of listening in which you listen but offer no advice.
12. A type of listening in which all ideas are considered and the most workable parts are saved.
13. Reaching one's full potential, growing, and being creative.
14. The process of perceiving sound.
15. The ability to see others' points of view or understand their feelings.
16. Transmission of messages using computers.

Review Facts and Ideas

1. List four ways informal speaking is used on the job.
2. In percentages, how much time on the job is spent on these activities?
   a. listening
   b. speaking
   c. writing
   d. reading
   e. other activities (traveling, filing and retrieving, data entry, running errands, cleaning up, organizing, thinking, planning, and so on)
3. What are the differences among the following types of listening?
   a. sympathetic listening
   b. critical listening
   c. creative listening
4. List three purposes of formal speeches.
5. List three things you can do about stage fright.
6. Distinguish among these types of communication:
   a. horizontal communication
   b. downward communication
   c. upward communication
7. Describe some advantages of e-mail as a business communication tool. Describe two disadvantages.
8. What is meant by good human relations?
9. List five techniques for maintaining effective human relations.
10. What percentage of all absences is due to serious or chronic llness, injuries, or family emergencies?
11. What is voluntary absence syndrome?
12. List six categories of absentees.
13. What are some effects of absenteeism on the absentee? On other employees?
14. List in order from bottom to top Maslow's five levels of needs.
15. List several hygiene factors and several motivators in a job.
16. What are three major results of job satisfaction?

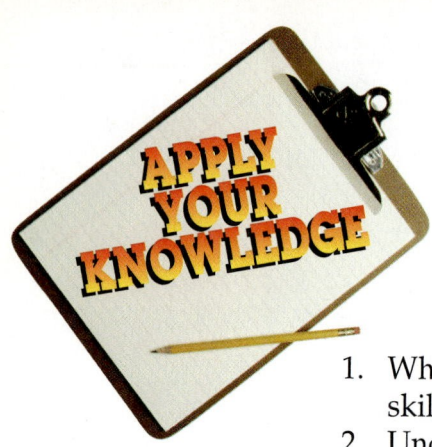

1. What are some things you can do to improve your listening skills?
2. Under what circumstances would you use sympathetic listening? critical listening? creative listening?
3. What type of speech or presentation did you hear recently (informational, entertaining, or persuasive)? Describe it.
4. Have you ever experienced stage fright? What did you do to reduce it?
5. What are three types of horizontal communication? Describe each.
6. Why are human relations important in any career or workplace?
7. Why is it important for a new employee to observe all unwritten and written work rules?
8. How might you benefit from excellent work performance?
9. Think about a job you have held or work you have done as part of a school or community group. What kinds of things motivated you to do your tasks well? Did these same things make the job more satisfying for you? What kinds of things made you less satisfied with the work?

Solve Problems

1. Search the Internet using the keyword "emoticon." Write a brief explanation of what an emoticon is. Then print out or copy several emoticons to share with the class. Together with your classmates, discuss how emoticons can aid e-mail communication.
2. Use the questions below to interview employees about the need to get along with others at work. Then ask an employer the same questions.
   a. Do you feel that human relations is an important part of each job where you work?
   b. Does the employer (supervisor) feel that human relations is important?

c. What types of company policies or unwritten rules are in place to ensure good human relations?

3. Salvador works for a small delivery service and believes that he is underpaid. He brags to friends, "When I'm making deliveries, sometimes I stop for a pizza. Sometimes I even visit my girlfriend. Why should I knock myself out on what I earn?" What advice would you give Salvador?

4. Make a list of unwritten rules that you observe in your home or in your classroom. Compare your list to a friend's list to see the similarities and differences.

5. Use the formula given in the Math Minute to compute the rate of absenteeism and annual cost of absenteeism based on these facts:
   - Number of employees: 45
   - Number of workdays in an average month: 22
   - Work days lost during an average month: 26
   - Work hours lost during an average month: 624
   - Average hourly wage: $8

6. Interview a person working full time and ask how the job helps to meet the following needs: Level 1 (food, clothing, and shelter); Level 2 (safety and security); Level 3 (love and belonging); Level 4 (self-esteem); and Level 5 (self-actualization).

For related activities and links, point your browser to
www.mypf.swep.com

Chapter 5

Keeping Your Job

Up Front

Midori worked part-time after school during high school, and full-time during the summers. She decided to stay with her job while attending college because the manager was willing to give her flexible hours that would permit her to study and earn money to pay for college at the same time.

"I like my job because my employer deals with me fairly," Midori told a friend. "I'm paid adequately, working conditions are good, and I like my supervisor. As a part-timer, I don't get a lot of benefits, but I'm able to attend classes for my degree. That flexibility makes me feel good about my job, and I'm motivated to give my best. It's a win-win situation. My employer wins because I'm loyal and serve the customers well. I win because I'm able to pursue my career goals and have a job that helps me pay for college expenses, too."

Goals

★ Understand and complete appropriate work forms, such as W-4, W-2, social security number application and benefits statement, and work permit application forms.

★ List and define provisions of basic employment laws enacted for the protection and security of workers.

Required Work Forms

The government requires employees to complete a number of forms. If you are under the age of 16, some forms are required to obtain the documents you need to hold a job, such as a social security card and work permit. Other forms, such as the W-4, you will complete when you begin work. Still others, such as the W-2, your employer must fill out for you. You should be familiar with these forms because you may need to make corrections or changes from time to time, and because you will use the information on some of these forms for filing income taxes.

Form W-4, Employee's Withholding Allowance Certificate

When you report to work, you will be asked to fill out a **Form W-4**, like the one shown in Figure 5-1 (page 106). The information you put on this form determines the amount your employer will withhold from your paycheck for income taxes. The employer sends this money to the government as partial payment of your income taxes.

The form supplies a simple worksheet to help you calculate your allowances. **Allowances** are a number that reduces the amount of tax withheld from your paycheck. The more allowances you claim, the less tax you will have withheld. However, claiming more allowances does not decrease the tax you will eventually owe. It only decreases the tax payments your employer makes for you from your paycheck during the year. If you have too little withheld, you will have a huge tax bill to pay at the end of the year.

If you qualify, you may claim **exempt status**. This status applies only to people who will not earn enough that year to owe

Figure 5-1 *Form W-4*

Form **W-4**	**Employee's Withholding Allowance Certificate**	OMB No. 1545-0010
Department of the Treasury Internal Revenue Service	▶ For Privacy Act and Paperwork Reduction Act Notice, see reverse.	

1 Type or print your first name and middle initial	Last name	2 Your social security number
Marisa M.	Clark	682-40-5896

Home address (number and street or rural route)
685 West Circle Avenue

3 ☒ Single ☐ Married ☐ Married, but withhold at higher Single rate.
Note: *If married, but legally separated, or spouse is a nonresident alien, check the Single box.*

City or town, state, and ZIP code
Cincinnati, OH 45227-6287

4 If your last name differs from that on your Social Security card, check here and call 1-800-772-1213 for more information . . . ▶ ☐

5 Total number of allowances you are claiming (from line G above or from the worksheets on page 2 if they apply) . | 5

6 Additional amount, if any, you want withheld from each paycheck . . . . | 6 $

7 I claim exemption from withholding and I certify that I meet **ALL** of the following conditions for exemption:
● Last year I had a right to a refund of **ALL** Federal income tax withheld because I had **NO** tax liability; **AND**
● This year I expect a refund of **ALL** Federal income tax withheld because I expect to have **NO** tax liability; **AND**
● This year if my income exceeds $600 and includes nonwage income, another person cannot claim me as a dependent.
If you meet all of the above conditions, enter "EXEMPT" here . . . . ▶ | 7 | EXEMPT

Under penalties of perjury, I certify that I am entitled to the number of withholding allowances claimed on this certificate or entitled to claim exempt status.

Employee's signature ▶ *Marisa M. Clark*　　　Date ▶ January 3 ,20 - -

8 Employer's name and address (Employer: Complete 8 and 10 only if sending to the IRS)	9 Office code (optional):	10 Employer identification number

any federal income tax. Line 7 of the form in Figure 5-1 shows the requirements to qualify. If you qualify, simply write the word *exempt* on Form W-4, as Marisa Clark has done in the figure. Then no money will be withheld from your paycheck for federal income taxes. The maximum amount of earnings necessary to qualify varies annually.

Social Security Forms

Because all workers in the United States must pay a social security tax from wages earned, all must have a social security number. Your **social security number** is your permanent work identification number. While you are working, your employers withhold social security taxes from your pay and contribute matching amounts. The amounts you earn and the amounts contributed for social security throughout your work life are credited by the Social Security Administration to your account under your assigned number. When you become eligible, usually at retirement, benefits are paid to you monthly, based upon how much you have paid into your account.

SOCIAL SECURITY ADMINISTRATION

Form Approved
OMB No. 0960-0466

☐ **SP**

Request for Earnings and Benefit Estimate Statement

To receive a free statement of your earnings covered by Social Security and your estimated future benefits, all you need to do is fill out this form. Please print or type your answers. When you have completed the form, fold it and mail it to us.

1. Name shown on your Social Security card:

   Marisa   M.

   First Name   Middle Initial

   Clark

   Last Name Only

2. Your Social Security number as shown on your card:

   6 8 2 - 4 0 - 5 8 9 6

3. Your date of birth   08   21   85
      Month   Day   Year

4. Other Social Security numbers you have used:

   ☐☐☐ - ☐☐ - ☐☐☐☐
   ☐☐☐ - ☐☐ - ☐☐☐☐

5. Your sex: ☐ Male   ☒ Female

6. Other names you have used
   (including a maiden name):

   None

7. Show your actual earnings for last year and your estimated earnings for this year. Include only wages and/or net self-employment income covered by Social Security.

   A. Last year's actual earnings: *(Dollars Only)*

   $ ☐ ☐ 2 , 0 8 4 . 0 0

   B. This year's estimated earnings: *(Dollars Only)*

   $ ☐ ☐ 4 , 0 0 0 . 0 0

8. Show the age at which you plan to retire:

   6 5   *(Show only one age)*

9. Below, show the average yearly amount you think you will earn between now and when you plan to retire. We will add your estimate of future earnings to those earnings already on our records to give you the best possible estimate.

   Enter a yearly average, not your total future lifetime earnings. Only show earnings covered by Social Security. Do not add cost-of-living, performance or scheduled pay increases or bonuses. The reason for this is that we estimate retirement benefits in today's dollars, but adjust them to account for average wage growth in the national economy.

   However, if you expect to earn significantly more or less in the future due to promotions, job changes, part-time work, or an absence from the work force, enter the amount in today's dollars that most closely reflects your future average yearly earnings.

   Most people should enter the same amount they are earning now (the amount in 7B).

   Future average yearly earnings: *(Dollars Only)*

   $ ☐ ☐ 4 , 0 0 0 . 0 0

10. Address where you want us to send the statement.

    Marisa M. Clark

    Name

    685 West Circle Avenue

    Street Address (Include Apt. No., P.O. Box, or Rural Route)

    Cincinnati   OH   45227-6287

    City   State   Zip Code

11. ☐ Please check this box if you want to get your statement in Spanish instead of English.

I am asking for information about my own Social Security record or the record of a person I am authorized to represent. I understand that if I deliberately request information under false pretenses I may be guilty of a federal crime and could be fined and/or imprisoned. I authorize you to use a contractor to send the statement of earnings and benefit estimates to the person named in item 10.

Please sign your name (Do not print)

Marisa M. Clark

Signature

1/9/--   (513) 555-8684

Date   (Area Code) Daytime Telephone No.

Form SSA-7004-SM (2-93) Destroy Prior Editions

Work Permit Application

Federal and some state laws require **minors**—people under the age of legal adulthood—to obtain a work permit before they are allowed to work. The work permit is signed by the parents or legal guardian of people under age 16. You can obtain an application for a work permit from the Department of Labor, a school counseling center, or work experience coordinator. There is usually no charge for obtaining the form, but you will have to provide your social security number and proof of age, and have your parent or legal guardian sign. Additional information may be required in some states. Figure 5-4 is an example of a work permit application. Processing of the work permit application takes three to six weeks, so early application is advisable.

Form W-2, Wage and Tax Statement

Each company for which you worked during the year will give you a **Form W-2**, like the one shown in Figure 5-5 on page 112. This form is a summary of the income you earned that year and all amounts the employer withheld for taxes. These amounts include federal, state, and local income taxes, and social security tax. Compare your W-2 to your paycheck stubs to be sure that the reported amounts are accurate. Your employer will also send a copy of your Form W-2 to the government.

The employer must provide you with a Form W-2 no later than January 31 of the year following the one in which you were employed. This is true even if you worked only part of the year and were not working as of December 31. If you do not receive a W-2 from each employer you worked for during the year, contact the employer to get the W-2. You must file your W-2 forms with your tax return.

Career Links

Records processing workers maintain, update, and process a variety of records, such as payrolls or bank statements. Their duties usually vary with the size of the firm. The growing use of computers and financial software has enabled records clerks to become more productive, while still interacting with co-workers and customers. Employers typically require applicants to have at least a high school diploma. On-the-job training is necessary to learn company procedures.

For more information, refer to the *Occupational Outlook Handbook* at www.bls.gov or search the Internet using such key words as "careers," "jobs," and "records management."

STATE OF OREGON
BUREAU OF LABOR AND INDUSTRIES

APPLICATION FOR A WORK PERMIT

INSTRUCTIONS: You must be at least 14 years old.

The permit will not be issued unless all blanks are filled in and clearly readable.

Proof of Age must be attached. The following documents are acceptable to prove your age:

    Birth Certificate, Baptismal Certificate, Hospital Certificate, Resident Alien Card, Driver's License or Learner's Permit issued by DMV.

Print your full name (Do not use nickname).

Print your Social Security Number clearly.

You and a parent or guardian must sign this application.

Send complete application, proof of age and self-addressed stamped envelope for postage and handling to: Bureau of Labor and Industries, Work Permit Unit, # 1160, 800 NE Oregon St. # 35, Portland, OR 97232. Telephone No. 731-4074

YOUR PROOF OF AGE WILL BE RETURNED TO YOU.

Duplicate Work Permits: Call the nearest BOLI office.

WORK PERMIT APPLICATION

Work Permit No. _____
(For office use only)

Eduardo		B.	Valdez	
Name	(First)	(Middle)	(Birth last name)	(Current)
3/28/87		Male	252-43-4557	
Birthdate		Sex	Social Security Number	

1350 Harrison Street   503-555-3485

Mailing Address   Telephone No.

Portland	Multnomah	Oregon	97232
City	County	State	Zip Code

Portland   OR

Birthplace (City)   State

Eduardo B. Valdez   *Carmen A. Valdez*
Minor's Signature   Parent or Guardian Signature

Figure 5-5 *Form W-2*

1 Control number				
	22222	OMB No. 1545-0008		

2 Employer's name, address, and ZIP code
Hanson Motors 85 Briar Street Cincinnati, OH 45230-5162

6 Statutory employee ☒	Deceased ☐	Pension plan ☐	Legal rep. ☐	942 emp. ☐	Subtotal ☐	Deferred compensation ☐	Void ☐

7 Allocated tips	8 Advance EIC payment

9 Federal income tax withheld	10 Wages, tips, other compensation
	$2,084.00

3 Employer's identification number	4 Employer's state I.D. number
93-81256791	OH4422

11 Social security tax withheld	12 Social security wages
$129.21	$2,084.00

5 Employee's social security number
682-40-5896

13 Social security tips	14 Medicare wages and tips
	$2,084.00

19 Employee's name, address, and ZIP code
Marisa M. Clark 685 West Circle Avenue Cincinnati, OH 45227-6287

15 Medicare tax withheld	16 Nonqualified plans
$ 30.22	

17	18 Other

20	21	22 Dependent care benefits	23 Benefits included in Box 10

24 State income tax	25 State wages, tips, etc.	26 Name of state	27 Local income tax	28 Local wages, tips, etc.	29 Name of locality
$14.04	$2,084.00	Ohio	$41.60	$2,084.00	Cincinnati

Copy 2 To Be Filed With Employee's State, City, or Local Income Tax Return

Department of the Treasury—Internal Revenue Service

Form **W-2 Wage and Tax Statement   20--**

Employee's and employer's copy compared ☐

Employment Laws

In the last 50 years, many laws have been enacted to protect American workers. Federal immigration law requires that you show a prospective employer an original social security card, together with other evidence of your citizenship and right to be employed, such as a driver's license, birth certificate, passport, or other identification.

The Department of Labor is responsible for overseeing several important labor laws. The main provisions of employment laws covering all workers do the following:

1. Establish a minimum wage.
2. Provide regular working hours.

3. Provide unemployment, disability, and retirement insurance benefits.
4. Provide equal employment opportunities and prohibit discrimination.
5. Establish safe working conditions.

Other laws have provisions for specific workers that do not apply to all workers. Laws covering minors require the following:

1. Specific safety precautions and working conditions that are more extensive than for adults.
2. Maximum number of hours and times minors can work during the school year.
3. A work permit for those under age 16.

Employees who believe they have not received benefits as required by law may turn to the government for *recourse*, or remedy. If you think you have a legitimate complaint, you should contact the state Department of Labor, which will assist you without charge. Employers found in violation of labor laws are subject to fines, payment of damages to employees, and other penalties determined by a court.

Social Security Act

The **Social Security Act**, passed in 1935, established a national social insurance program that provides federal aid for the elderly and for disabled workers. In 1965, the Medicare provision was added. It provides hospital and medical insurance protection for elderly retired workers and other qualified people. Originally known as OASDHI, social security provides these benefits: **o**ld **a**ge retirement income, **s**urvivorship income, **d**isability income, and **h**ealth **i**nsurance. Benefits received depend on the amount of contributions made. Self-employed workers pay their social security contributions when they pay their income tax. For employees in occupations covered by social security, contributions are mandatory. Social security (FICA) tax is deducted from your pay and sent to the U.S. Treasury for proper crediting to your social security account.

Unemployment Compensation

The Social Security Act requires every state to have an **unemployment insurance** program. This insurance provides benefits to workers who lose their jobs through no fault of their own. After a waiting period, laid-off or terminated workers may collect a portion of their regular pay for a certain length of time. Premiums for unemployment insurance are usually paid by employers.

Each state has its own regulations for waiting periods, maximum benefits, and deadlines for filing claims. Usually, benefits are paid for a maximum of 26 weeks through the local state employment office. In most states, an unemployed worker must wait for at least one week before receiving benefits. To receive benefits, a worker must have been employed for a minimum period of time (6 months to one year, depending on the state) and for a minimum amount of earnings ($400 or more per month in most states). Workers fired for a good reason, such as poor performance, will not receive benefits.

Fair Labor Standards Act

Popularly known as the *Wage and Hour Act*, the **Fair Labor Standards Act** establishes a minimum wage and requires hourly workers to be paid 1½ times their hourly rate for hours worked beyond 40 per week. A **minimum wage** is the legally established lower limit on wages employers may pay. Tips are not considered wages, so they are not included in calculating the minimum wage. In 1997, the minimum wage reached $5.15 an hour. Many states require higher minimum wages than the federal minimum wage. For example, in the state of Washington, minimum wage as of January 1, 2001 was $6.72 an hour, which was considerably higher than the national minimum wage.

Each state enforces wage and hour laws, which include federal provisions and additional state regulations. These laws require every employer to establish regular paydays. For example, in the state of Oregon, payment of wages to new employees must begin no later than 35 days after the date the employees begin work. Also, state laws vary in the maximum number of hours they allow minors to work.

Workers' Compensation

Workers' compensation is an insurance program that pays benefits to workers and their families for injury, illness, or death that occurs as a result of the job. The employer is responsible for employee injuries and illnesses that are the result of employment, even though the employer may have done nothing to cause the injury or illness. Today all 50 states have workers' compensation laws. Employers pay the insurance premiums in most states. However, in some states, employees are required to pay all or part of the premium. Benefits include payments to doctors and hospitals, to the employee for temporary or permanent disability, and to survivors in the event of death.

Family and Medical Leave Act

The **Family and Medical Leave Act** of 1993 allows employees to take up to 12 weeks of unpaid, job-protected leave in a 12-month period for family and medical reasons. During the leave period, all insurance and health benefits are maintained for the employee. To be eligible for FMLA, the employee must have worked for the employer for at least 12 months. Any of the following reasons are considered adequate for this unpaid leave:

1. Birth and care of a newborn child, including adoption of a child.
2. Care of an immediate family member (spouse, child, or parent) with a serious health condition.
3. Medical leave when the employee is unable to work because of a serious health condition (such as injury, illness, impairment, or physical or mental condition).

To find out more about FMLA, go to the Employment Standards Administration Web site at http://www.dol.gov/dol/esa, and follow the links to FMLA.

Laws Against Discrimination in Employment

A number of laws protect workers from unfair treatment in the workplace. Here is a brief description of the most important of these laws:

What is the Americans with Disabilities Act?

1. **Equal Pay Act:** Prohibits unequal pay for men and women doing substantially similar work.
2. **Civil Rights Act of 1964:** Prohibits discrimination in hiring, training, and promotion on the basis of race, color, gender, religion, or national origin.
3. **Age Discrimination in Employment Act:** Prohibits discrimination in employment decisions against people age 40 and over.
4. **Americans with Disabilities Act:** Prohibits discrimination on the basis of physical or mental disabilities.

These laws are enforced by the Equal Employment Opportunity Commission (EEOC). Discrimination complaints can be filed with the EEOC.

Check Your Understanding

Review Terms

1. Form W-4
2. allowances
3. exempt status
4. social security number
5. minors
6. Form W-2
7. Social Security Act
8. unemployment insurance
9. Fair Labor Standards Act (Wage and Hour Act)
10. minimum wage
11. workers' compensation
12. Family and Medical Leave Act
13. Equal Pay Act
14. Civil Rights Act of 1964
15. Age Discrimination inEmployment Act
16. Americans with Disabilities Act

Review Concepts

1. If you do not properly fill out the Form W-4 and thus claim too many allowances, what is likely to happen?
2. What should you do if you lose your social security card?
3. What law allows you to take unpaid leave when you have a new baby?

Goals

★ Explain employee responsibilities at work, including responsibilities to employers and to other employees.
★ Describe employer responsibilities to employees.

Employee Responsibilities

To be successful as a new employee, you will have to meet a number of responsibilities. These include personal responsibilities to your employer, to other employees, and to customers.

Responsibilities to Employers

Your employer hires you and pays you at predetermined intervals. In return for this pay and other benefits, the employer expects certain things from you, as discussed below.

Competent Work

You should do your best to produce the highest quality finished product for your employer. The work needs to be **marketable**—that is, of such quality that the employer can sell it or use it to favorably represent the company. If, for example, you type an e-mail message to a client that has so many mistakes that it would make the company look incompetent or uncaring to the client, the message is not a marketable product.

Thrift

When using an employer's property, you should be as thrifty as possible, conserving supplies and caring for equipment with as much diligence as you would your own.

Punctuality

Arrive at work on time, take no more than the allotted time for breaks, and don't leave before quitting time. Being punctual means being ready to start working at the appointed time. For example, rather than arriving at 8 A.M. (starting time), you should be at your workstation at 8 A.M.

Pleasant Attitude

On any job, it is important to be pleasant and easy to get along with. You should be willing to follow orders and take directions. Your employer also has the right to expect you to be courteous to customers, because you represent the company to others.

Loyalty and Respect

While working for a company, you should never spread rumors or gossip about your employer or job. As long as you are on the company "team," you are expected to be loyal. Loyalty includes showing respect to the employer and the company on and off the job.

Dependability

Why do you, as an employee, have a responsibility to be pleasant and easy to get along with?

When you say you will do something, follow through. The employer should be able to depend on you to do what you were hired to do. A person who is dependable has a good reputation and will be considered for increased responsibilities and promotions.

Initiative

You should not have to be told everything to do. Employees who stand idle after completing a task are of very little value to employers. **Initiative** means that you do things on your own without being told to; you're a self-starter.

Interest

It is important for you to show an interest in your job and your company. You should project an attitude of wanting to learn all you can and of giving all tasks your best effort. Being enthusiastic about your job shows an employer your sincere interest in being a cooperative and productive worker.

Self-Evaluation

The ability to take criticism and to assess your own progress is important to you and your employer. You cannot improve your weak points unless you are willing to admit they exist and to work on them. Employers must evaluate employees' work to determine raises and promotions. Employees should be able to recognize their own strong points and limitations and do a realistic self-evaluation of their job performance.

Responsibilities to Other Employees

In addition to your responsibilities to your employer, you also have duties to your co-workers. These include the following obligations:

Teamwork

You are part of a team when you work with others in a company, and you need to do your share of the work. Employees must work cooperatively in order to produce a high-quality final product. When friction and personality conflicts occur, the productivity of the whole company decreases.

Thoughtfulness

Be considerate of co-workers to promote a good work atmosphere for everyone, including customers. Having a pleasant attitude will result in a more enjoyable time for yourself and others. Personal problems and conflicts have no place at work.

Loyalty

In addition to being loyal to your employer, you should be loyal to co-workers. This includes not spreading rumors about them. Gossiping leads to a breakdown of teamwork.

Responsibilities to Customers

As an employee, you represent the company. To the customer who walks in the front door, *you* are the company. Thus, your attitude toward a customer often will be the deciding factor in whether he or she continues to do business with your company. Therefore, remember that on behalf of your employer you have the responsibility to greet the customer with an attitude of helpfulness and courtesy.

Helpfulness

It is your responsibility to help customers find what they want or to do what is needed to make a sale. When customers contact you with a problem, you are responsible for solving the problem or finding another employee who can. An attitude of helpfulness reflects well on the company and is an important part of any job.

Courtesy

Whether or not you like the customer, that customer actually pays your wages by keeping your employer in business. Without the customer, the business could not exist. Therefore, your attitude toward the customer should always be respectful and courteous, never hostile or unfriendly. Customer loyalty to a business is often built by friendly, helpful employees.

Employer Responsibilities

Employers also have responsibilities to employees. Some responsibilities are required by law; others are simply sensible practices for keeping employees happy and on the job. Failure to meet these responsibilities can result in a high employee turnover rate (with resulting high costs for finding and training new workers), increased premiums for unemployment insurance, and employer fines for unfair labor practices.

What are some of the responsibilities that employers have to their employees?

Adequate Supervision

Employees need proper supervision to do a good job. Supervision includes providing appropriate instruction in the use of equipment and safety standards; training new employees in their job tasks; helping employees solve problems on the job; and distributing information downward from management and upward to management.

Fair Human Resource Policies

Policies on hiring, firing, raises, advancement, and dispute resolution need to be fair and well defined. Employees should know clearly what is considered acceptable and unacceptable performance, what the standards are for advancements and raises, and what constitutes grounds for suspension or discharge.

Safe Working Conditions

All employees must be provided with safe equipment, a safe working environment, and adequate training for working under dangerous conditions. Special protective equipment and clothing and warning signs must be provided to employees working in hazardous situations. Laws governing working conditions for minors are stricter than those for adults in most industries.

Open Channels of Communication

Employers need to communicate with employees so that all employees have the opportunity to express concerns, ask questions, and make suggestions. Lack of open channels of communication can result in poor morale for workers and low work output. Employees need to know they are an important part of the company and that their opinions are valuable.

Take a sheet of paper and draw a vertical rule down the center. On one side, list employees' responsibilities to an employer. On the other side, list an employer's responsibilities to its employees. What happens if either group doesn't meet these responsibilities?

Recognition of Achievement

Employers need to provide some form of reward for above-average performance. Merit pay raises, bonuses, and advancement opportunities encourage workers to do their best work. Employees also respond well to non-monetary rewards, such as providing extra time off or simply complimenting exceptional work in front of other employees. When achievement is not recognized, employees lose the desire to be as productive as possible.

Compliance with Employment Laws

Employers must obey state and federal laws designed to protect workers from discrimination in employment on the basis of race, color, sex, national origin, religion, age, or disability. The employer is responsible for observing workers' rights. Failure to do so can result in severe penalties for the employer.

PERSONAL PERSPECTIVE

Sexual Harassment

A safe working environment also means one that is comfortable and free of unwanted conduct that interferes with work performance. Sexual harassment is any unwelcome advance, request for sexual favors, and other verbal or physical conduct that is offensive.

Workers are protected by the Equal Employment Opportunity Commission (EEOC) from these types of behaviors. Harassment on the basis of sex violates the Civil Rights Act of 1964, and employers have the responsibility to prevent and eliminate sexual harassment in the workplace. EEOC guidelines state that an employer is responsible for the actions of employees as well as non-employees on work premises.

Unfortunately, sexual harassment is widespread. Studies show that at least 50 percent of working women and 15 percent of working men have experienced sexual harassment on the job. Fortunately, steps are being taken to reduce and eliminate this problem.

Until a decade ago, the only recourse to sexual harassment was through a lawsuit against the offending person. Today, complaints are investigated by the EEOC. When sexual harassment is found, the victim may receive a remedy such as back pay, a promotion, or reinstatement if he or she had been fired. When the victim's rights are not protected, the EEOC will sue the employer.

Many companies have policies to prevent sexual harassment. All employees are entitled to respect, courtesy, and tactful behavior. Abusing the dignity of anyone through ethnic, sexist, or racial slurs or any derogatory or objectionable conduct is cause for disciplinary action. Objectionable conduct includes suggestive remarks, physical contact, and intimidation.

All employees should be aware of what sexual harassment is and how to avoid it. For example, employees who tell inappropriate jokes or engage in suggestive behavior, such as flirting, may find themselves in embarrassing situations. It is important to dress and act professionally at all times, so that you can truly say you did nothing to contribute to the situation.

Think Critically

1. What would you do if you received unwanted physical or verbal contact on the job?
2. What are some things you can do to reduce your risk of sexual harassment?

Check Your Understanding

Review Terms
1. marketable
2. initiative

Review Concepts
1. In a part-time or volunteer job you have had, what did your employer expect from you in terms of responsibilities?
2. What things are most important to you about an employer or place of employment?

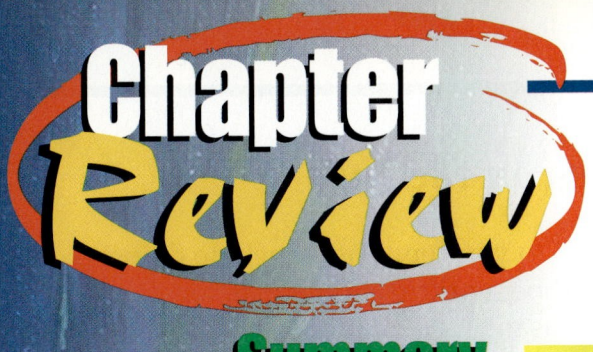

5.1 Work-Related Forms and Laws

- The information you supply on Form W-4 determines the amount your employer will withhold from your paycheck for taxes. The more allowances you claim, the less will be withheld.
- Your social security number is your permanent work identification number. The amounts you and your employer contribute to your social security account throughout your work life determine the payments you will receive from the government when you retire.
- If you are under age 16, you will probably have to obtain a work permit to hold a job.
- Every employer you worked for during the year must give you a Form W-2. This form summarizes wages and amounts withheld. You must submit all Forms W-2 with your tax return.
- The Social Security Act is a national social insurance program that provides aid for the elderly and for disabled workers. This law also requires states to provide unemployment insurance to pay benefits to workers who lose their jobs through no fault of their own.
- The Fair Labor Standards Act establishes a minimum wage and overtime pay.
- Workers' compensation pays benefits for injury, illness, or death that occurs as a result of the job.
- The Family and Medical Leave Act allows employees to take unpaid leave for family and medical reasons.
- Major laws that protect employees against discrimination include the Equal Pay Act, Civil Rights Act of 1964, Age Discrimination in Employment Act, and Americans with Disabilities Act.

5.2 Responsibilities on the Job

- Your responsibilities to your employer include doing competent work and being thrifty, punctual, loyal, dependable, and pleasant. You should take initiative and be willing to work to improve your weaknesses.
- Your responsibilities to your co-workers include working well with others as a member of the team, being considerate of co-workers, and avoiding rumors or gossip.
- Your responsibilities to customers include helping them with their purchase decisions and company-related problems and treating them with courtesy and respect.
- Your employer is responsible for providing you with good supervision, safe working conditions, fair human resource policies, open communications, rewards, and compliance with employment laws.

Review Terms

Directions: Can you find the definitions for each of the following terms used in Chapter 5?

Age Discrimination in
   Employment Act
allowances
Americans with Disabili-
   ties Act
Civil Rights Act of 1964
Equal Pay Act
exempt status
Fair Labor Standards Act
   (Wage and Hour Act)
Family and Medical Leave
   Act
Form W-2
Form W-4
initiative
marketable
minimum wage
minors
Social Security Act
social security number
unemployment insurance
workers' compensation

1. The number that you calculate on Form W-4 that reduces the amount of tax withheld from your paycheck.
2. Your permanent work identification number.
3. A summary of the income you earned that year and all amounts the employer withheld for taxes.
4. Work of such quality that an employer can sell it or use it to favorably represent the company.
5. People under the age of legal adulthood.
6. Law that established a national insurance program that provides financial help for the elderly and for disabled workers.
7. A part of the Social Security Act that requires benefits to be paid to workers who lose their jobs through no fault of their own.
8. A form you fill out when you begin working that determines the amount your employer will withhold from your paycheck for income taxes.
9. Status that applies only to people who will not earn enough that year to owe any federal income tax.
10. The ability to do things without being told.
11. Insurance program that pays benefits to workers and their families for injury, illness, or death that occurs as a result of the job.
12. Law that establishes a minimum wage and requires hourly workers to be paid 1½ times their hourly rate for hours worked beyond 40 per week.
13. The lower limit on wages that employers can pay workers per hour.

14. Law that allows employees to take up to 12 weeks of unpaid, job-protected leave in a 12-month period for the birth or adoption of a child and for personal illness or the illness of an immediate family member.
15. Law that prohibits unequal pay for men and women doing substantially similar work.
16. Law that prohibits discrimination in hiring, training, and promotion on the basis of race, color, gender, religion, or national origin.
17. Law that prohibits discrimination in employment decisions against people age 40 and over.
18. Law that prohibits discrimination on the basis of physical or mental disabilities.

Review Facts and Ideas

1. What is the purpose of Form W-4?
2. Why do you need to have a social security number before you begin work?
3. Besides retirement income, what other benefits are provided by social security?
4. Where can you obtain a work permit application?
5. What information is listed on Form W-2?
6. What should you do if your employer during the past year does not send you a Form W-2?
7. Why should you request a social security statement?
8. What benefits does the Social Security Act provide?
9. Who may receive unemployment insurance benefits?
10. How does the Fair Labor Standards Act protect employees?
11. Explain the provisions of the FMLA.
12. What laws protect people from employment-related discrimination?
13. List at least five responsibilities that you, as an employee, owe your employer.
14. List at least three responsibilities that you, as an employee, owe to your co-workers.
15. What responsibilities do you, as an employee, have to your employer's customers?
16. List and describe three responsibilities that your employer owes you as an employee.

APPLY YOUR KNOWLEDGE

1. Obtain a Form W-4 from the nearest office of the Internal Revenue Service or download one by going to the IRS Web site at www.irs.ustreas.gov and following the links to forms and publications. Complete the W-4 form properly, claiming exempt status if you are entitled to do so.

2. Locate the Web site of your state Department of Labor. Check labor laws in your state. What is your state's minimum wage? Does your state require a work permit? If so, ask for a request form or download one and fill it out. (Your counseling center or work experience coordinator will probably have work permit forms also.)

3 Download and complete an application for a Social Security card (SS-5) at www.ssa.gov/online/ss-5.html.

4. Complete a Request for Social Security Statement online by going to the Social Security Administration site at www.ssa .gov and following the links to a statement request form.

5. Visit the Social Security Administration online at www.ssa.gov or look up the Social Security Act in an encyclopedia or historical reference book in your library. Obtain this information: (a) Why did the president at the time consider social security necessary? (b) Who was the president at the time? (c) Describe the history of benefits, deductions from paychecks, and purpose of social security.

6. Obtain from your state Department of Labor the provisions of state laws regarding employment of minors. Find out: (a) the maximum hours per week that can be worked, (b) latest hour in the evening that a minor can work, (c) whether a work permit is required for workers under 16, and (d) any other provisions to protect a minor working part- or full-time.

7. Research the history leading up to the Civil Rights Act of 1964. Write a two-page paper describing the controversy surrounding this law and how it eventually won passage.

8. On a piece of paper, list in the order you think most important the responsibilities that employees have to their employers. Then ask a working parent or other working person to list employee responsibilities in order of importance. Compare the two lists. Then, if possible, ask an employer to list in order what she or he considers important responsibilities that employees have to their employers.

9. A popular expression used in business today is "total customer satisfaction." What do you think this expression means?

10. What responsibilities do you think employers should have to employees besides the regular payment of wages earned? Ask a person who is working full-time the same question. Compare answers.

Solve Problems

1. Your friend Ai-Ling discovered that the amount of wages paid to her during the year appears to be different from the amount listed on the W-2 she received from her employer. She asks you what to do. How would you reply?

2. Leah O'Shane worked for three employers last year. Now it's February 1 of the following year, and she has received Form W-2 from only two of those employers. She asks you what she should do about it. What would you tell her?

3. Because last year Manuel did not earn enough money at his part-time job to have to pay any federal taxes, his employer asked him if this year he would like to claim exempt status on his W-4. Explain to Manuel how he can claim to be exempt and what this means to him.

4. Marita, age 14, has decided that she wants to work part-time this summer doing whatever kind of work she can find to earn money to buy school clothes. Tell her what things she should do to prepare for work. Also tell her what forms she may have to complete when she begins work.

5. Millie Angelino just received her W-2 form from her employer and noticed that her social security number is wrong on the form. What should she do? What can happen if she does nothing?

6. Antwan Simpson worked for over a year for the same employer but then was laid off because business was slow. He is looking for another job, but he needs income now to make his rent payment. You told Antwan that he may be eligible for unemployment insurance payments. Explain how he could qualify and whom he should see to find out about unemployment benefits.

7. Chi Wang, who has a visual disability, applied for a position as an assistant credit manager at a local retail store. David Burrow, the store's human resource manager, tested Chi's eyesight by having him read a chart written in small print. Chi failed the test and, on that basis alone, was rejected for the position. Investigate the Americans with Disabilities Act and determine if Chi's employment rights have been violated.

For related activities and links, point your browser to
www.mypf.swep.com

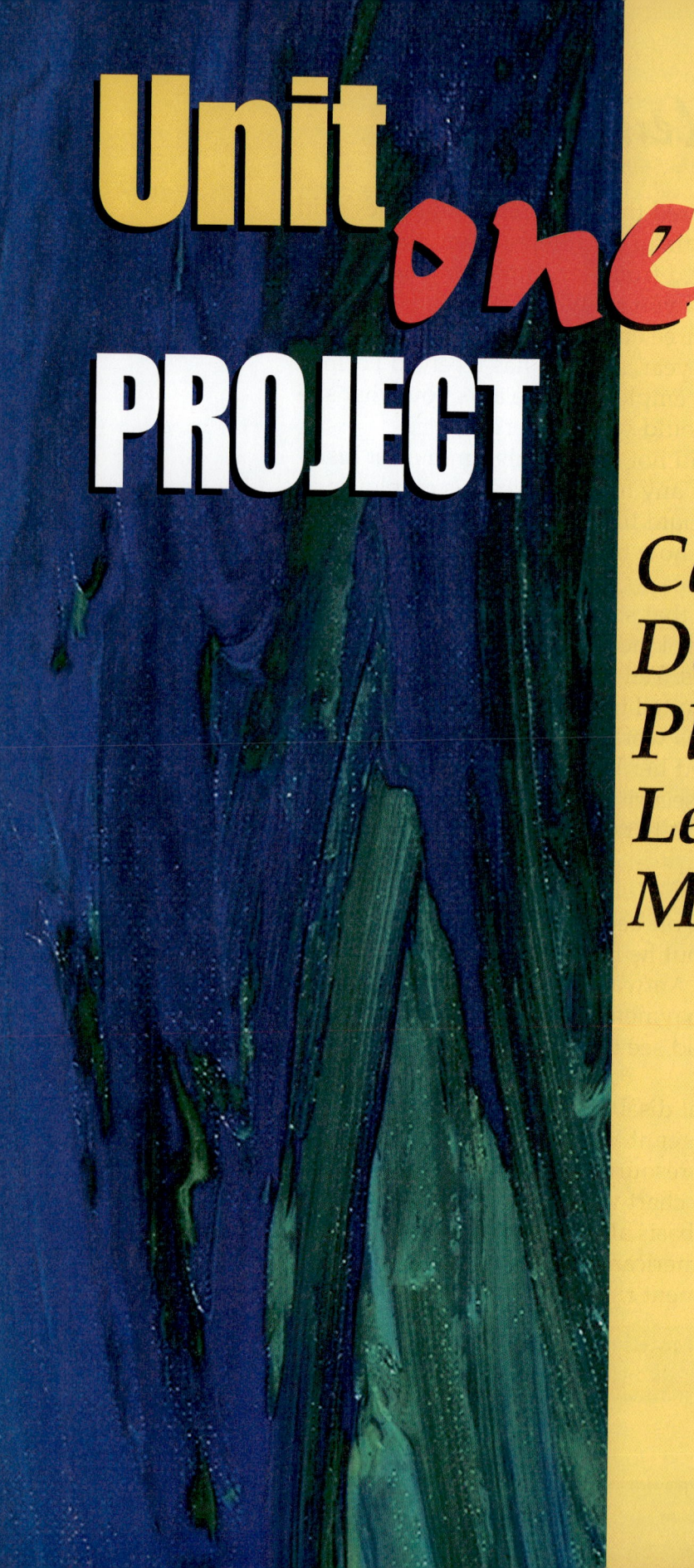

Unit *one*
PROJECT

Career Development: Planning and Leading a Meeting

Project 1

This project is designed to help you acquire leadership skill as part of career development. If you've ever attended a meeting that failed—people were bored, there was no clear direction, or nothing was decided—you know why it is important to run effective meetings.

Planning a Successful Meeting

If you are merely announcing information, you don't need a meeting—just a memo or an e-mail will do. The time to have a meeting is when you need input or opinions, when you want the group to make a decision that is binding, when you need to stimulate creative thinking, or when you want everyone to hear important information at the same time. Here are some guidelines for planning a successful meeting:

1. Whenever possible, plan meetings to last no more than an hour. If the meeting must exceed an hour, provide drinks and a break. If it must last more than two hours, you also should provide food.
2. Make sure the meeting space is sufficient for participants to be comfortable. It must be large enough, have enough chairs, provide the right atmosphere, and include needed accessories, such as a flipchart, white board, or audio-visual equipment.
3. Give at least a week's notice, or preferably, two, so people can plan their schedules and make necessary arrangements. Figure U1-1 (page 134) shows a typical meeting notice.
4. Never call a meeting late in the afternoon, unless you also have arranged a time of relaxation and entertainment. Friday afternoons are rarely a good time to schedule meetings. People are tired from the week's activities.
5. Provide, in advance, an agenda of topics to be discussed, so that people can prepare their contributions and bring related information with them. Figure U1-2 (page 134) shows a typical agenda.
6. Plan no more topics than can be completed in the scheduled time. Attention wanes when a meeting runs longer than participants expect.

MEETING NOTICE

The Teen Consumers Group will have its monthly meeting and will hear a presentation by Ms. Eva Diaz of the Better Business Bureau. Ms. Diaz will discuss Internet shopping.

Date: Thursday, February 15, 20--

Time: 3:00 p.m. to 4:30 p.m.

Place: Western High School Library

If you can't attend, please call LaMont Russell at 555-7825 or e-mail him at 1russell@omega.net.

AGENDA

Teen Consumers Group
February 15, 20--
3:00 p.m.

Facilitator—LaMont Russell
Note-Taker—Sun-Yi Wong

1. Opening comments—LaMont Russell
2. Report on next month's fund-raising car wash—Midori Tanaka
3. Report on consumer Web sites of interest—Barry Coogan
4. Presentation on Internet shopping—Ms. Eva Diaz, Better Business Bureau
5. Closing comments—LaMont Russell

Setting Up the Meeting

A round table or circle is often a good way to encourage participation. Prepare and copy handouts ahead of time and have them waiting for people to arrive. Have extra paper and pencils available for participants who want them.

Set up and test your audio-visual tools ahead of time, such as computer presentation or video equipment, flipcharts, white boards, and markers. Make sure everything is ready to go when the meeting starts. Each participant should be able to see without obstruction. If you expect participants to write, make sure the table offers ample space for each person.

Room ambiance can be especially important. If the room is too cold or too dark, group members will be unable to concentrate. If the room is too hot or too bright, group members will be in a hurry to leave rather than to participate.

Make pre-arrangements to avoid meeting interruptions. For example, if refreshments will be served, arrange to have them delivered at a set time. You should stay with the meeting at all times rather than attend to details that you could have taken care of in advance.

Conducting a Successful Meeting

As the meeting leader, you are responsible for keeping the meeting moving and accomplishing its purpose. Here are some suggestions for keeping the meeting productive:

- Give a preview. Before you start the meeting, tell the participants what will happen, what will be expected from them, and what outcomes are desired.
- Make introductions. Unless everyone in the room already knows each other, have group members introduce themselves, or give a short introduction of each person yourself, briefly describing each person's role in the group.
- Assign someone to take notes and prepare the meeting summary. Figure U1-3 (page 136) shows a typical meeting summary.
- Keep the group focused on the purpose of the meeting. Some rambling is normal, but avoid getting too sidetracked. To be productive, the meeting must accomplish its main purpose.

MEETING SUMMARY

**Teen Consumers Group
February 15, 20--
3:00 p.m.**

Attendees: Barry Coogan; Joel D'Aurizio; Cate Ewing; Deondra Holcomb; Danny Martinez; LaMont Russell; Midori Tanaka; Nancy Williams; Sun-Yi Wong; Mishelle Zambito

1. LaMont reminded the group that our picture for the school yearbook will be taken on Friday, February 23, in the lobby. Everyone should meet there at noon.
2. Midori handed out instructions for March's fund-raising car wash in the school parking lot. If you have questions, see her.
3. Barry provided a list of new Web sites that we should look at before our next meeting. Each group member will review one site and prepare a one-paragraph description. E-mail your information by March 10, to Barry at bcoogan@omega.net
4. Ms. Eva Diaz presented a helpful and informative discussion on the pros and cons of Internet shopping. She distributed some brochures from the Better Business Bureau and suggested that we contact the BBB if we experience problems.
5. LaMont closed the meeting with a reminder that the next meeting will take place on Thursday, March 15, at 3:00 p.m. in the Library. Last-minute details about the car wash will be discussed, and the reports on the consumer Web sites will be reviewed.

- If the purpose of the meeting is to generate ideas or come up with a creative solution to a problem, try *brainstorming*. With this technique, you present the topic or problem and ask participants to say their ideas out loud as they come to mind, no matter how wild the ideas. Do not judge the responses at this point. Just record them where participants can see them. The purpose of brainstorming is to allow a free flow of ideas. One person's wild idea may trigger a more workable idea from someone else. To encourage everyone to make suggestions, you could try going around the table, asking each person, in turn, for an idea, but allowing people to pass if they don't have one. Then keep going around the table until the group seems to have run out of ideas. Once all ideas are recorded, lead the group in discussing the ideas and selecting the best one to implement.

- No matter what your meeting format, keep everyone involved. Some people tend to be more reluctant to speak than others. To encourage their participation, use written feedback or ask directly for every person's opinion, allowing each person the same time to express his or her view. Everyone should feel safe and free to make contributions that will help accomplish the purpose of the meeting.

- To disarm disrupters, place time limits on comments. Acknowledge what they say with a comment such as "We hear you," and then move on to the next item or ask someone else to speak. Ask the group as a whole if they want to stop and address the issue at hand or deal with it at another time. When negativity creeps in, use humor to change the mood back to a positive tone. If you have known disrupters who will come prepared to sabotage the meeting, meet them head on by acknowledging their concern and setting a meeting time to deal with that issue specifically.

- Use consensus decision-making, when appropriate. When building a consensus decision, every person in the group must agree to and "buy into" the final outcome. This means negotiating, with give and take, until all participants feel they have been heard and each person is willing to accept the final decision of the group. You will need to ask questions such as "What will it take to make you comfortable with our decision?" until everyone is satisfied that the best possible agreement has been reached.

- Wrap up the meeting with a summary of what the group decided and the next steps to be taken. People who have agreed to certain actions should be reminded of their commitments. Congratulate everyone for their hard work and contributions.

Unit One Project

After the Meeting

Soon after the meeting, distribute a copy of the meeting summary or *minutes* to each participant and to group members who could not attend. Include handouts for absent group members and reminders of subsequent actions to be taken and their time-frames. File the meeting summary for future reference. Include the names of all people who attended and the date of the meeting.

Follow-Up Assignment

1. Ask someone you know who works in an office to arrange for you to observe a meeting. Take notes on the following issues and write a report for your class:
   a. Was an agenda distributed ahead of the meeting?
   b. Was the meeting room adequate? Was the audio-visual equipment set up and in working order at the start of the meeting? What elements of the physical environment could have been improved?
   c. What was the purpose of the meeting? Did the purpose seem clear to everyone?
   d. How well did the discussion stay focused on the pur-pose? What sidetracking occurred? How did the leader bring the discussion back to the purpose?
   e. How did the group go about accomplishing the meeting purpose? How did the leader help this process? How could the group process have been improved?
   f. Did everyone participate? How did the leader encourage participation? Were there disrupters? How did the leader handle disruptions? What could have been done to improve participation?
   g. What were the outcomes of the meeting? Did the meeting accomplish its purpose? Did everyone seem to agree with the decisions made and know their responsibilities for further action?
   h. Overall, how productive do you think the meeting was? Explain.
2. Using the issues listed in question 1, critique a meeting that you attend as a participating member. Summarize your find-ings in a report.

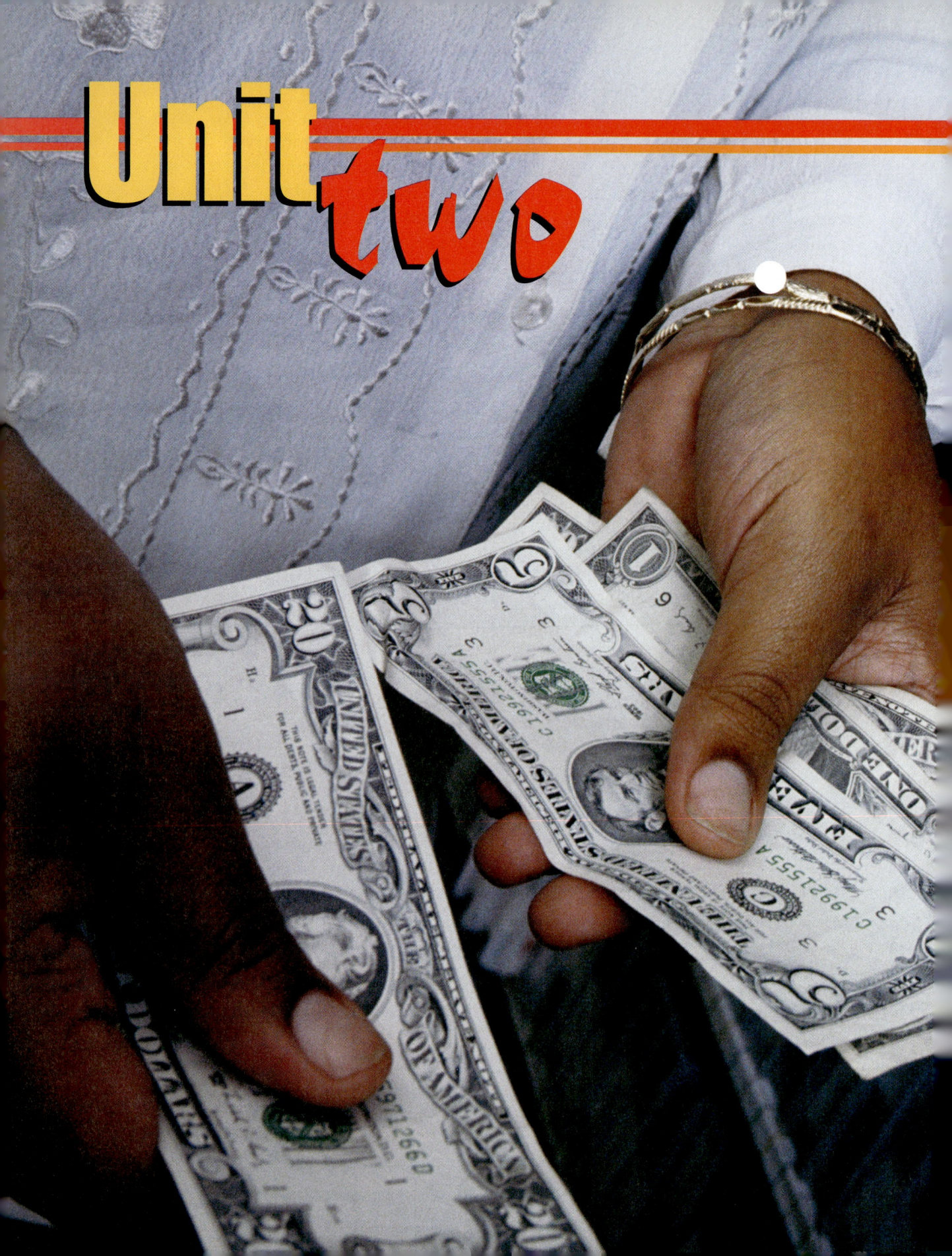

Unit *two*

Money Management

Unit 2 begins with an examination of your paycheck and benefits. You will also look at trends in the workplace that affect your career and opportunities for advancement. Then you will learn about preparing your income tax.

Next you will study financial management, beginning with preparing budgets and other financial records. You will also find out about informal and formal contracts that you enter into daily.

Finally, you will learn how to use a checking account, including writing checks, keeping a checkbook register, and reconciling your account. You will discover how to choose the right bank and services that meet your needs.

Chapter 6

Pay, Benefits, and Working Conditions

Terms to Know

gross pay
overtime
deductions
net pay
benefits
incentive pay
employee services

vested
flextime
compressed
    workweek
job rotation
job sharing
labor union

collective
    bargaining
seniority
strike
professional
    organization
lobbying

Up Front

Lisa just got a job at XYZ Corporation. When she was hired, her employer provided a packet containing all kinds of information, from union membership to sick pay. She will receive two weeks of paid vacation every year, after her first year of employment. The company allows 10 paid sick days per year. The company will grant a leave of absence in the case of pregnancy or death of a family member, and she is fully vested in the pension plan once she has been employed for five years. Also provided for employees is a full package of group health, dental, vision, and life insurance coverage. In addition, the company has a child care facility, altered workweeks, and job sharing.

"Wow, I'm sure glad I read that packet," Lisa said to herself. "There are a lot of things I need to understand."

Lesson 6.1

Understanding Pay, Benefits, and Incentives

★ Compute payroll deductions and net pay from information and tables provided.
★ Identify optional and required employee benefits and recognize their value as additions to net pay.

Gross Pay, Deductions, and Net Pay

When you take a job, you agree to perform certain tasks in exchange for regular pay. **Gross pay** is total pay before any deductions are subtracted. If you work for an hourly wage, any overtime pay you earned during the pay period must be added to your regular pay to determine your gross pay.

Hourly Wages

Figure 6-1 (page 144) shows a paycheck for M. J. Smith. As you can see, Ms. Smith works for $6.50 per hour. Her employer keeps a record of the hours she works. For this pay period, Ms. Smith worked 40 regular hours. To determine Ms. Smith's regular gross pay, multiply the pay rate by the number of hours:

$$\$6.50 \times 40 \text{ hours} = \$260.00$$

Overtime

Ms. Smith also worked some overtime during this pay period. **Overtime** is time worked beyond the regular hours. A standard workday is 8 continuous hours with scheduled breaks plus an unpaid lunch period. A standard workweek is 40 hours in a 5-day period of 8 hours each day. According to the Fair Labor Standards Act, employers must pay hourly workers for overtime at the rate of $1\frac{1}{2}$ times the regular rate of pay. As you can see on Ms. Smith's paycheck stub, her regular rate of pay is $6.50 an hour. Her overtime

Figure 6-1 *Paycheck with Stub*

Marshall Manufacturing Co.

14 Ault Street   El Paso, TX 79925-6457

88-0581 / 1120

PAYROLL CHECK

Co. Code	Department	File No.	Clock No. ID	Social Security No.	TO THE ORDER OF	Pay Date	Check No.
R&T	000108	43329	501 A	555 12 3344	M.J. SMITH	02 10 —	BELOW

PAY THIS AMOUNT / NET PAY

Two hundred thirty-four and 83/100 dollars — $234.83

M.J. SMITH
1133 ELM STREET
EL PASO, TX 79930-3264

DISBURSING AGENT FOR ABOVE EMPLOYER

EL PASO BANK
EL PASO, TEXAS

Jermaine Davis

AUTHORIZED SIGNATURE

⑆1120058⑆ 010450 001995⑈

Marshall Manufacturing Co.

14 Ault Street   El Paso, TX 79925-6457

Co. Code	Department	File No.	Fed. Status	Name	Pay Period Ending	Pay Date
R&T	000108	43329	501 A	SMITH, M.J.	02 10 —	02 10 —

Hours Units	Rate	Earnings	Type	Deduction	Type	Deduction	Type
40 00	6 50	260 00	REG	20 00	CR UN		
5 00	9 75	48 75	OT	11 00	H INS		
				2 50	UN DUES		
				3 80	ACC INS		

	Gross	Fed. With. Tax	OASD	Medicare	Other Deductions		Net Pay
This Pay	308 75	13 00	19 14	4 48	37 30		
YTD	1,852 50	78 00	114 84	26 88	223 80		234 83

---

rate, then, is $9.75 an hour ($6.50 × 1.5). You can compute Ms. Smith's gross pay as follows:

40 hours × $6.50 an hour (regular pay)	=	$260.00
5 hours × $9.75 an hour (overtime pay)	=	48.75
Gross pay	=	$308.75

Ms. Smith's gross pay appears under "Gross" at the bottom left of her paycheck stub. The letters "YTD" mean "year-to-date." The amounts on this line are Ms. Smith's cumulative totals up to this point in the year.

Salary

Perhaps you will work for a salary rather than an hourly wage. In most cases you will work regular hours, but you will not receive additional pay for overtime work. In this case, your gross pay will be the same as your salary.

Your salary may be stated as an annual, or yearly, amount. If so, your employer will divide the yearly salary into equal amounts to be paid each month or pay period. For example, suppose you agree to work for $24,000 a year. Your monthly gross pay will be $2,000 ($24,000 divided by 12 months in a year). If you are paid every two weeks, your paycheck will be $923.08 every two weeks:

52 weeks in a year/2 weeks per pay period = 26 pay periods

$24,000/26 pay periods = $923.08 per paycheck

Notice that you will receive 26 paychecks using this method. If you were paid twice a month rather than every two weeks, you would receive only 24 paychecks (12 months in a year × 2 paychecks per month). In a later chapter, you will learn about budgeting when you receive paychecks weekly, biweekly (every two weeks), or monthly.

Deductions

Amounts subtracted from your gross pay are called **deductions**. Some deductions, such as social security, federal income tax, and state income tax (if your state has an income tax), are required by law. Other deductions are optional and you may elect one or more of them. For example, you can have your employer automatically deduct an amount to deposit into your company-sponsored savings plan. As you can see in Figure 6-1, Ms. Smith has deductions for a credit union payment, health insurance, union dues, and accident insurance.

Employers are required to keep detailed records of wages earned and hours worked for inspection by the Department of

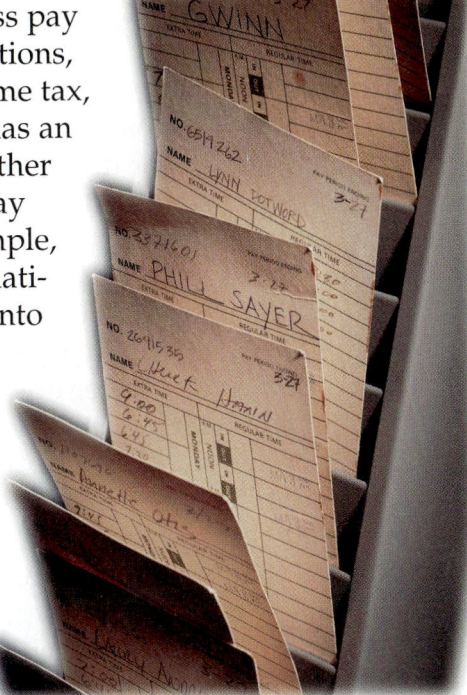

Why would an employer track the number of hours an employee works?

Labor. With each paycheck, you will receive a detailed list of all deductions taken from your gross pay. Optional deductions may not be withheld without your written consent except by court order. This does not apply to taxes, social security, and other deductions required by law to be withheld from all paychecks.

Net Pay

When all deductions are taken out of your gross pay, the amount left is your **net pay**. This is the amount of your paycheck, or the money you can actually spend. Net pay is often called "take-home pay" because it is the amount you can actually use as you wish. Stated mathematically:

Regular Wages or Salary + Overtime = Gross Pay

Gross Pay − Deductions = Net Pay

Figure 6-2 shows an employee withholding sheet. It lists weekly gross pay, deductions, and net pay. Save your withholding sheets or paycheck stubs that list the amounts withheld from your gross pay. You can use these to check the accuracy of the Form W-2 your employer gives for your income tax return.

Required deductions include federal, state, and local taxes, and social security and Medicare taxes. In Figure 6-1, the deductions for M. J. Smith appear at the bottom of the paycheck stub. "OASD" means "old age, survivors, and disability." This is the social security deduction.

The amounts to be withheld are determined from tax tables. Figures 6-3 and 6-4 (pages 148–149) show weekly and monthly withholding tables for the state of Oregon. Figures 6-5 and 6-6 (pages 150–151) show federal withholding tax tables.

To determine the proper amount to withhold, first determine whether the pay is weekly or monthly and use the appropriate table. For example, Shari Gregson in Figure 6-2 is being paid weekly, so use the weekly table in Figure 6-3 to find the state withholding. Move your finger down the left side of the table to the range that includes the employee's gross pay. Shari's gross pay of $276 falls in the table's range of $260–$280. Then run your finger to the right until you get to the proper number of allowances and marital status. Shari's form shows that she is single and claims 1 allowance. In Figure 6-3, the number that falls in the column for a single person with 1 allowance, making between $260 and $280, is $16. Notice that $16 shows in the state income tax line on Shari's withholding sheet.

EMPLOYEE WITHHOLDING SHEET

Employee Name   Shari Gregson   Social Security Number   898-40-7426

Pay Period: ☒ weekly   ☐ bimonthly   ☐ monthly

Number of allowances: 1   ☐ married   ☒ single

GROSS PAY

   1. Regular Wages: _40_ hours at $ _6.00_ /hr.   = $ 240.00

or

   2. Regular Salary: =   _____

   3. Overtime: _4_ hours at $ _9.00_ /hr.   =   36.00

   GROSS PAY . . . .$ 276.00

REQUIRED DEDUCTIONS

   4. Federal Income Tax (use tax tables) . . . .$ 26.00

   5. State Income Tax (use tax tables) 16.00

   6. Social Security Tax (use 6.2% × gross pay, up to $80,000) 17.11

   7. Medicare Tax (use 1.45% × gross pay) 4.00

OTHER DEDUCTIONS

   8. Insurance . . . .   _____

   9. Union Dues. 3.00

   10. Credit Union 20.00

   11. Savings . . . .   _____

   12. Retirement . . . .   _____

   13. Charity . . . .   _____

   14. Other: _____   . . . .   _____

              _____   . . . .   _____

   TOTAL DEDUCTIONS (total lines 4 through 14) . . . .$ 86.11

   NET PAY (subtract total deductions from gross pay) . . . .$ 189.89

Following the same process, you can find Shari's federal with-holding from Figure 6-5. Try it. Did you find the number $26 in the table, as shown on Shari's withholding sheet for federal income tax?

The social security deduction is currently withheld at the standard rate of 6.2 percent of the first $80,000. The Medicare tax

Figure 6-3 *State Tax Withholding Table—Weekly Payroll*

Weekly payroll period (Oregon)
Amount of tax to be withheld

NUMBER OF WITHHOLDING ALLOWANCES

WAGE AT LEAST	BUT LESS THAN	TWO OR LESS SINGLE 0	1	2	MARRIED 0	1	2	THREE OR MORE SINGLE OR MARRIED 3	4	5	6	7	8	9	10	11	12	13	14
0–	20	0	0	0	0	0	0	0	0	0	0	0	0	0	0	0	0	0	0
20–	40	1	0	0	0	0	0	0	0	0	0	0	0	0	0	0	0	0	0
40–	60	2	0	0	0	0	0	0	0	0	0	0	0	0	0	0	0	0	0
60–	80	3	2	0	1	0	0	0	0	0	0	0	0	0	0	0	0	0	0
80–	100	4	3	1	2	1	0	0	0	0	0	0	0	0	0	0	0	0	0
100–	120	5	4	3	3	2	0	0	0	0	0	0	0	0	0	0	0	0	0
120–	140	6	5	4	5	3	2	0	0	0	0	0	0	0	0	0	0	0	0
140–	160	8	6	5	6	4	3	1	0	0	0	0	0	0	0	0	0	0	0
160–	180	9	8	7	7	6	4	3	1	0	0	0	0	0	0	0	0	0	0
180–	200	11	10	8	8	7	5	4	3	1	0	0	0	0	0	0	0	0	0
200–	220	12	11	10	9	8	7	5	4	2	0	0	0	0	0	0	0	0	0
220–	240	14	13	11	10	9	8	6	5	4	2	0	0	0	0	0	0	0	0
240–	260	15	14	13	12	10	9	8	6	5	3	2	0	0	0	0	0	0	0
260–	280	17	16	14	13	11	10	9	8	6	5	3	2	0	0	0	0	0	0
280–	300	18	17	16	14	13	12	10	9	8	7	5	3	2	0	0	0	0	0
300–	320	20	19	17	16	14	13	12	11	10	8	7	5	3	2	0	0	0	0
320–	340	21	20	19	17	16	15	14	12	11	10	9	7	5	4	2	0	0	0
340–	360	23	22	21	19	17	16	15	14	13	11	10	9	7	5	4	2	0	0
360–	380	24	23	22	20	19	18	17	15	14	13	12	10	9	7	5	4	2	0
380–	400	26	25	24	22	21	19	18	17	16	14	13	12	11	9	7	5	4	2
400–	420	28	26	25	23	22	21	20	18	17	16	15	14	12	11	9	7	6	4
420–	440	29	28	27	25	24	22	21	20	19	17	16	15	14	13	11	9	7	6
440–	460	31	30	28	26	25	24	23	21	20	19	18	17	15	14	13	11	9	7
460–	480	33	31	30	28	27	25	24	23	22	21	19	18	17	16	14	13	11	9
480–	500	35	33	31	30	28	27	26	25	23	22	21	20	18	17	16	14	13	11
500–	520	37	35	33	32	30	29	27	26	25	24	22	21	20	19	17	16	15	13
520–	540	38	37	35	34	32	30	29	28	26	25	24	23	21	20	19	18	16	15
540–	560	40	39	37	35	34	32	30	29	28	27	25	24	23	22	21	19	18	16
560–	580	42	40	39	37	36	34	32	31	29	28	27	26	25	23	22	21	20	18
580–	600	44	42	40	39	37	36	34	32	31	30	29	27	26	25	24	22	21	20
600–	620	46	44	42	41	39	37	36	34	32	31	30	29	28	26	25	24	23	21
620–	640	47	46	44	43	41	39	37	36	34	33	32	30	29	28	27	25	24	23
640–	660	49	48	46	44	43	41	39	38	36	34	33	32	31	29	28	27	26	25
660–	680	51	49	48	46	45	43	41	39	38	36	35	33	32	31	30	29	27	26
680–	700	53	51	49	48	46	45	43	41	39	38	36	35	34	32	31	30	29	28
700–	720	55	53	51	50	48	46	45	43	41	39	38	36	35	34	33	32	30	29
720–	740	56	55	53	52	50	48	46	45	43	41	40	38	37	36	34	33	32	31
740–	760	58	57	55	53	52	50	48	47	45	43	41	40	38	37	36	35	33	32
760–	780	60	58	57	55	54	52	50	48	47	45	43	41	40	39	37	36	35	34
780–	800	62	60	58	57	55	54	52	50	48	47	45	43	41	40	39	38	36	35
800–	820	64	62	60	59	57	55	54	52	50	48	47	45	43	42	40	39	38	37
820–	840	65	64	62	61	59	57	55	54	52	50	49	47	45	43	42	41	40	38
840–	860	67	66	64	62	61	59	57	56	54	52	50	49	47	45	44	42	41	40

FOR WAGE OF 860 AND OVER—
9.00 PERCENT OF AMOUNT OVER 860 PLUS—

860—OVER		68	66	65	63	62	60	58	56	55	53	51	50	48	46	44	43	42	41

deduction is withheld at the rate of 1.45 percent of all pay earned. Congress periodically increases the withholding rate and maximum amount as needed to keep enough tax money coming in to pay social security benefits.

In addition to required deductions, the optional deductions an employee has authorized will be subtracted from gross pay to arrive at net pay. The most common of these deductions are insurance payments, union dues, credit union payments, savings deposits, retirement contributions, and charitable deductions.

Monthly payroll period (Oregon)
Amount of tax to be withheld

| WAGE | | TWO OR LESS | | | | | | THREE OR MORE SINGLE OR MARRIED | | | | | | | | | | | |
| AT LEAST | BUT LESS THAN | SINGLE | | | MARRIED | | | | | | | | | | | | | | |
		0	1	2	0	1	2	3	4	5	6	7	8	9	10	11	12	13	14
0—	40	0	0	0	0	0	0	0	0	0	0	0	0	0	0	0	0	0	0
40—	80	0	0	0	0	0	0	0	0	0	0	0	0	0	0	0	0	0	0
80—	120	1	0	0	0	0	0	0	0	0	0	0	0	0	0	0	0	0	0
120—	160	3	0	0	0	0	0	0	0	0	0	0	0	0	0	0	0	0	0
160—	200	5	0	0	0	0	0	0	0	0	0	0	0	0	0	0	0	0	0
200—	240	8	2	0	0	0	0	0	0	0	0	0	0	0	0	0	0	0	0
240—	280	10	4	0	1	0	0	0	0	0	0	0	0	0	0	0	0	0	0
280—	320	12	7	0	4	0	0	0	0	0	0	0	0	0	0	0	0	0	0
320—	360	15	9	2	6	0	0	0	0	0	0	0	0	0	0	0	0	0	0
360—	400	17	11	5	9	2	0	0	0	0	0	0	0	0	0	0	0	0	0
400—	440	20	14	8	11	5	0	0	0	0	0	0	0	0	0	0	0	0	0
440—	480	22	16	10	13	8	1	0	0	0	0	0	0	0	0	0	0	0	0
480—	520	24	19	13	16	10	3	0	0	0	0	0	0	0	0	0	0	0	0
520—	560	27	21	15	18	12	6	0	0	0	0	0	0	0	0	0	0	0	0
560—	600	29	23	18	21	15	9	1	0	0	0	0	0	0	0	0	0	0	0
600—	640	31	26	20	23	17	11	4	0	0	0	0	0	0	0	0	0	0	0
640—	680	34	29	23	25	19	14	7	0	0	0	0	0	0	0	0	0	0	0
680—	720	37	32	26	28	22	16	10	2	0	0	0	0	0	0	0	0	0	0
720—	760	40	35	30	30	24	18	13	5	0	0	0	0	0	0	0	0	0	0
760—	800	43	38	33	32	27	21	15	8	0	0	0	0	0	0	0	0	0	0
800—	840	46	41	36	35	29	23	17	11	3	0	0	0	0	0	0	0	0	0
840—	880	49	44	39	37	31	26	20	14	6	0	0	0	0	0	0	0	0	0
880—	920	52	47	42	40	34	28	22	16	9	1	0	0	0	0	0	0	0	0
920—	960	55	50	45	42	36	30	25	19	12	4	0	0	0	0	0	0	0	0
960—	1000	58	53	48	44	39	33	27	21	14	7	0	0	0	0	0	0	0	0
1000—	1040	62	56	51	47	41	35	29	24	17	10	2	0	0	0	0	0	0	0
1040—	1080	65	59	54	49	43	37	32	26	20	13	5	0	0	0	0	0	0	0
1080—	1120	68	62	57	51	46	40	34	28	23	16	8	1	0	0	0	0	0	0
1120—	1160	71	65	60	54	48	42	36	31	26	19	12	4	0	0	0	0	0	0
1160—	1200	74	68	63	56	50	45	39	34	29	23	15	8	0	0	0	0	0	0
1200—	1240	77	72	66	59	53	48	43	37	32	26	19	11	4	0	0	0	0	0
1240—	1280	80	75	69	61	56	51	46	40	35	30	23	15	8	0	0	0	0	0
1280—	1320	83	78	72	65	59	54	49	43	38	33	26	19	11	4	0	0	0	0
1320—	1360	86	81	75	68	62	57	52	46	41	36	30	22	15	7	0	0	0	0
1360—	1400	89	84	78	71	65	60	55	49	44	39	33	26	18	11	3	0	0	0
1400—	1440	92	87	82	74	68	63	58	53	47	42	37	29	22	14	7	0	0	0
1440—	1480	95	90	85	77	71	66	61	56	50	45	40	33	26	18	11	3	0	0
1480—	1520	98	93	88	80	75	69	64	59	53	48	43	37	29	22	14	7	0	0
1520—	1560	101	96	91	83	78	72	67	62	56	51	46	40	33	25	18	10	3	0
1560—	1600	104	99	94	86	81	75	70	65	59	54	49	44	36	29	21	14	6	0
1600—	1640	107	102	97	89	84	78	73	68	62	57	52	47	40	32	25	17	10	2
1640—	1680	110	105	100	92	87	81	76	71	66	60	55	50	44	36	29	21	14	6
1680—	1720	113	108	103	95	90	85	79	74	69	63	58	53	47	40	32	25	17	10
1720—	1760	116	111	106	98	93	88	82	77	72	66	61	56	50	43	36	28	21	13
1760—	1800	120	114	109	101	96	91	85	80	75	69	64	59	54	47	39	32	24	17

AROUND THE GLOBE

In Western Europe, workers traditionally have had far more rights and protections than U.S. workers. However, in recent years thousands of poor immigrants have flooded Europe from China, India, Southeast Asia, and the old Soviet Union, only to end up working as forced laborers in illegal factories, sweatshops, and service industries. Organized gangs exploit this immigrant labor and have created an underground economy that ironically has helped European business growth and competitiveness.

Think Critically: One expert says that Europeans have actually benefited economically from this illegal immigration. Do you think this statement is true? What have been the economic benefits and drawbacks of this situation?

Figure 6-5

Federal Tax Withholding Tables—
Weekly Payroll

SINGLE Persons—WEEKLY Payroll Period
(For Wages Paid in 20--)

If the wages are—		And the number of withholding allowances claimed is—										
At least	But less than	0	1	2	3	4	5	6	7	8	9	10
		The amount of income tax to be withheld is—										
$0	$55	$0	$0	$0	$0	$0	$0	$0	$0	$0	$0	$0
55	60	1	0	0	0	0	0	0	0	0	0	0
60	65	2	0	0	0	0	0	0	0	0	0	0
65	70	3	0	0	0	0	0	0	0	0	0	0
70	75	3	0	0	0	0	0	0	0	0	0	0
75	80	4	0	0	0	0	0	0	0	0	0	0
80	85	5	0	0	0	0	0	0	0	0	0	0
85	90	6	0	0	0	0	0	0	0	0	0	0
90	95	6	0	0	0	0	0	0	0	0	0	0
95	100	7	0	0	0	0	0	0	0	0	0	0
100	105	8	1	0	0	0	0	0	0	0	0	0
105	110	9	2	0	0	0	0	0	0	0	0	0
110	115	9	2	0	0	0	0	0	0	0	0	0
115	120	10	3	0	0	0	0	0	0	0	0	0
120	125	11	4	0	0	0	0	0	0	0	0	0
125	130	12	5	0	0	0	0	0	0	0	0	0
130	135	12	5	0	0	0	0	0	0	0	0	0
135	140	13	6	0	0	0	0	0	0	0	0	0
140	145	14	7	0	0	0	0	0	0	0	0	0
145	150	15	8	1	0	0	0	0	0	0	0	0
150	155	15	8	1	0	0	0	0	0	0	0	0
155	160	16	9	2	0	0	0	0	0	0	0	0
160	165	17	10	3	0	0	0	0	0	0	0	0
165	170	18	11	4	0	0	0	0	0	0	0	0
170	175	18	11	4	0	0	0	0	0	0	0	0
175	180	19	12	5	0	0	0	0	0	0	0	0
180	185	20	13	6	0	0	0	0	0	0	0	0
185	190	21	14	7	0	0	0	0	0	0	0	0
190	195	21	14	7	0	0	0	0	0	0	0	0
195	200	22	15	8	1	0	0	0	0	0	0	0
200	210	23	16	9	2	0	0	0	0	0	0	0
210	220	25	18	11	4	0	0	0	0	0	0	0
220	230	26	19	12	5	0	0	0	0	0	0	0
230	240	28	21	14	7	0	0	0	0	0	0	0
240	250	29	22	15	8	1	0	0	0	0	0	0
250	260	31	24	17	10	3	0	0	0	0	0	0
260	270	32	25	18	11	4	0	0	0	0	0	0
270	280	34	27	20	13	6	0	0	0	0	0	0
280	290	35	28	21	14	7	0	0	0	0	0	0
290	300	37	30	23	16	9	1	0	0	0	0	0
300	310	38	31	24	17	10	3	0	0	0	0	0
310	320	40	33	26	19	12	4	0	0	0	0	0
320	330	41	34	27	20	13	6	0	0	0	0	0
330	340	43	36	29	22	15	7	0	0	0	0	0
340	350	44	37	30	23	16	9	2	0	0	0	0
350	360	46	39	32	25	18	10	3	0	0	0	0
360	370	47	40	33	26	19	12	5	0	0	0	0
370	380	49	42	35	28	21	13	6	0	0	0	0
380	390	50	43	36	29	22	15	8	1	0	0	0
390	400	52	45	38	31	24	16	9	2	0	0	0
400	410	53	46	39	32	25	18	11	4	0	0	0
410	420	55	48	41	34	27	19	12	5	0	0	0
420	430	56	49	42	35	28	21	14	7	0	0	0
430	440	58	51	44	37	30	22	15	8	1	0	0
440	450	59	52	45	38	31	24	17	10	3	0	0
450	460	61	54	47	40	33	25	18	11	4	0	0
460	470	63	55	48	41	34	27	20	13	6	0	0
470	480	65	57	50	43	36	28	21	14	7	0	0
480	490	68	58	51	44	37	30	23	16	9	2	0
490	500	71	60	53	46	39	31	24	17	10	3	0
500	510	74	61	54	47	40	33	26	19	12	5	0
510	520	77	63	56	49	42	34	27	20	13	6	0
520	530	79	66	57	50	43	36	29	22	15	8	1
530	540	82	69	59	52	45	37	30	23	16	9	2
540	550	85	72	60	53	46	39	32	25	18	11	4
550	560	88	75	62	55	48	40	33	26	19	12	5
560	570	91	77	64	56	49	42	35	28	21	14	7
570	580	93	80	67	58	51	43	36	29	22	15	8
580	590	96	83	70	59	52	45	38	31	24	17	10
590	600	99	86	73	61	54	46	39	32	25	18	11

MARRIED Persons—MONTHLY Payroll Period
(For Wages Paid in 20--)

| If the wages are— | | And the number of withholding allowances claimed is— | | | | | | | | | | |
At least	But less than	0	1	2	3	4	5	6	7	8	9	10
		The amount of income tax to be withheld is—										
$0	$540	$0	$0	$0	$0	$0	$0	$0	$0	$0	$0	$0
540	560	3	0	0	0	0	0	0	0	0	0	0
560	580	6	0	0	0	0	0	0	0	0	0	0
580	600	9	0	0	0	0	0	0	0	0	0	0
600	640	14	0	0	0	0	0	0	0	0	0	0
640	680	20	0	0	0	0	0	0	0	0	0	0
680	720	26	0	0	0	0	0	0	0	0	0	0
720	760	32	1	0	0	0	0	0	0	0	0	0
760	800	38	7	0	0	0	0	0	0	0	0	0
800	840	44	13	0	0	0	0	0	0	0	0	0
840	880	50	19	0	0	0	0	0	0	0	0	0
880	920	56	25	0	0	0	0	0	0	0	0	0
920	960	62	31	0	0	0	0	0	0	0	0	0
960	1,000	68	37	6	0	0	0	0	0	0	0	0
1,000	1,040	74	43	12	0	0	0	0	0	0	0	0
1,040	1,080	80	49	18	0	0	0	0	0	0	0	0
1,080	1,120	86	55	24	0	0	0	0	0	0	0	0
1,120	1,160	92	61	30	0	0	0	0	0	0	0	0
1,160	1,200	98	67	36	6	0	0	0	0	0	0	0
1,200	1,240	104	73	42	12	0	0	0	0	0	0	0
1,240	1,280	110	79	48	18	0	0	0	0	0	0	0
1,280	1,320	116	85	54	24	0	0	0	0	0	0	0
1,320	1,360	122	91	60	30	0	0	0	0	0	0	0
1,360	1,400	128	97	66	36	5	0	0	0	0	0	0
1,400	1,440	134	103	72	42	11	0	0	0	0	0	0
1,440	1,480	140	109	78	48	17	0	0	0	0	0	0
1,480	1,520	146	115	84	54	23	0	0	0	0	0	0
1,520	1,560	152	121	90	60	29	0	0	0	0	0	0
1,560	1,600	158	127	96	66	35	5	0	0	0	0	0
1,600	1,640	164	133	102	72	41	11	0	0	0	0	0
1,640	1,680	170	139	108	78	47	17	0	0	0	0	0
1,680	1,720	176	145	114	84	53	23	0	0	0	0	0
1,720	1,760	182	151	120	90	59	29	0	0	0	0	0
1,760	1,800	188	157	126	96	65	35	4	0	0	0	0
1,800	1,840	194	163	132	102	71	41	10	0	0	0	0
1,840	1,880	200	169	138	108	77	47	16	0	0	0	0
1,880	1,920	206	175	144	114	83	53	22	0	0	0	0
1,920	1,960	212	181	150	120	89	59	28	0	0	0	0
1,960	2,000	218	187	156	126	95	65	34	3	0	0	0
2,000	2,040	224	193	162	132	101	71	40	9	0	0	0
2,040	2,080	230	199	168	138	107	77	46	15	0	0	0
2,080	2,120	236	205	174	144	113	83	52	21	0	0	0
2,120	2,160	242	211	180	150	119	89	58	27	0	0	0
2,160	2,200	248	217	186	156	125	95	64	33	3	0	0
2,200	2,240	254	223	192	162	131	101	70	39	9	0	0
2,240	2,280	260	229	198	168	137	107	76	45	15	0	0
2,280	2,320	266	235	204	174	143	113	82	51	21	0	0
2,320	2,360	272	241	210	180	149	119	88	57	27	0	0
2,360	2,400	278	247	216	186	155	125	94	63	33	2	0
2,400	2,440	284	253	222	192	161	131	100	69	39	8	0
2,440	2,480	290	259	228	198	167	137	106	75	45	14	0
2,480	2,520	296	265	234	204	173	143	112	81	51	20	0
2,520	2,560	302	271	240	210	179	149	118	87	57	26	0
2,560	2,600	308	277	246	216	185	155	124	93	63	32	1
2,600	2,640	314	283	252	222	191	161	130	99	69	38	7
2,640	2,680	320	289	258	228	197	167	136	105	75	44	13
2,680	2,720	326	295	264	234	203	173	142	111	81	50	19
2,720	2,760	332	301	270	240	209	179	148	117	87	56	25
2,760	2,800	338	307	276	246	215	185	154	123	93	62	31
2,800	2,840	344	313	282	252	221	191	160	129	99	68	37
2,840	2,880	350	319	288	258	227	197	166	135	105	74	43
2,880	2,920	356	325	294	264	233	203	172	141	111	80	49
2,920	2,960	362	331	300	270	239	209	178	147	117	86	55
2,960	3,000	368	337	306	276	245	215	184	153	123	92	61
3,000	3,040	374	343	312	282	251	221	190	159	129	98	67
3,040	3,080	380	349	318	288	257	227	196	165	135	104	73
3,080	3,120	386	355	324	294	263	233	202	171	141	110	79
3,120	3,160	392	361	330	300	269	239	208	177	147	116	85
3,160	3,200	398	367	336	306	275	245	214	183	153	122	91
3,200	3,240	404	373	342	312	281	251	220	189	159	128	97

Benefits and Incentives

Many employers offer **benefits**, which are forms of employee compensation in addition to pay. Common benefits include insurance, retirement savings plans, pension plans, paid sick leave and vacations, and profit sharing. Some of these benefits are required by law. Among them are unemployment compensation, workers' compensation, and matching social security and Medicare payments. These federal programs were discussed in Chapter 5. Many employers also provide some of the optional (not required by law) benefits discussed below.

Profit Sharing

Profit sharing is a plan that allows employees to receive a portion of the company's profits at the end of the corporate year. The more money (profits) the company makes, the more the company has to share with employees. Most companies that provide profit sharing consider it **incentive pay**—money offered to encourage employees to strive for higher levels of performance. Employers offer profit sharing because it links part of employee compensation with company profit goals, making employees more likely to reduce waste and increase productivity.

Paid Vacations and Holidays

Most businesses provide full-time employees with a set amount of paid vacation time. This means that while you are on vacation, you are paid as usual. It is not uncommon to receive a week's paid vacation after a year of full-time employment, two weeks after two years, three weeks after five years' employment, and so on.

A benefit that you are likely to receive for any full-time job is paid time off for holidays. Generally, full-time employees who are receiving a salary are entitled to have off, with pay, those holidays designated as "paid holidays." These include Christmas, Thanksgiving, Fourth of July, Labor Day, and Memorial Day. Other holidays that many companies consider paid holidays are New Year's Day, Veterans' Day, Martin Luther King Day, and Presidents' Day. An employee required to work on a holiday is usually paid double or more than double the regular hourly rate of pay.

Employee Services

Employee services are the extras that companies offer in order to improve employee morale and working conditions. Many companies offer employee discounts on merchandise sold or made by the company. For example, if you work at a clothing store that allows employee discounts, you can purchase your clothing for a reduced price. Other services include social and recreational programs, free parking, tuition reimbursement for college courses, company newsletters, day-care centers, and counseling for employee problems.

Child Care

Child care is a major issue for working parents. Many companies provide on-site child-care facilities as well as coverage of child-care expenses as a part of employee benefit packages. Federal legislation is likely to change child care significantly in years to come. Legislation will focus on high-quality, affordable programs for children of working parents.

Sick Pay

Many businesses also provide an allowance of days each year for illness, with pay as usual. This benefit is usually available to full-time employees only. It is customary to receive three to ten days a year as "sick days" without deductions from pay.

Leaves of Absence

Some employers allow employees to leave their jobs (without pay) for certain reasons, such as having children or completing education, and return to their jobs at a later time. While a leave of absence may be unpaid, it has an important advantage: it gives job security and permits you to take time off for important events in your life.

The Family and Medical Leave Act (known as FMLA) was discussed in Chapter 5. Employers with 50 or more employees must give up to 12 weeks unpaid leave per year for the birth or adoption of a child, or care for a spouse, child, or parent with a serious illness, or for the employee's own serious illness. Employers are required to maintain health coverage during the leave, and job reinstatement rights are guaranteed.

Insurance

Most large companies provide group health insurance plans for all employees. A few plans are paid for almost entirely by the employer, as a part of employee compensation. Other plans require paycheck deductions if employees elect to participate in the plan or if employees wish to cover dependents (spouse and children). Insurance plans typically include health, dental, vision, and life insurance.

Health Insurance

A typical health insurance plan has an employee-paid amount, or *deductible.* After the deductible has been reached, the plan pays 80 percent of most doctor bills and prescriptions and 100 percent of hospitalization charges and emergency bills. Traditional insurance plans generally will not cover routine physical examinations. As an alternative to a traditional plan, your employer may offer you a health maintenance organization (HMO) plan or another variation of this health care program. Health insurance will be discussed in Chapter 27.

What types of services are usually covered in insurance plans?

Life Insurance

Many companies offer life insurance. Life insurance pays a cash benefit to a designated person, called a *beneficiary,* when the insured dies. The purpose of life insurance is to partially offset the income lost when a wage earner dies. When you leave your current employment, the group policy does not go with you. The employer generally pays an amount each month for standard coverage for each employee. Employees who want additional coverage can pay for it through payroll deductions. Life insurance is discussed in detail in Chapter 27.

Dental Insurance

Most dental plans provide a maximum benefit per year per family member. Orthodontia (braces) may not be covered. Routine exams and cleanings are usually covered 100 percent, while most other services are covered at 80 percent of a predetermined fee range. If, for example, a dentist charges $110 for a filling, and the insurance plan pays a high of $80 for this service, the plan will pay 80 percent times $80, or $64. The patient must pay the remainder. In addition, most non-routine work, such as crowns, bridges, or root canals, is covered at a lesser rate, such as 50 percent. Dental insurance may have a small deductible, such as $50 per person per year.

Vision Insurance

Vision insurance covers the cost of prescription lenses and eye examinations once every few years. As the employee gets older, more frequent exams may be allowed. Generally, frames are not covered, but sometimes coverage is available for contact lenses. Vision and dental insurance are explained further in Chapter 27.

Bonuses and Stock Options

Bonuses are incentive pay based on quality of work done, years of service, or company sales or profits. A factory manager may offer all workers a $100 year-end bonus as a reward for having no serious on-the-job accidents during the year. Holiday bonuses are often based on years of service. If a division of a company reaches a particular sales goal in a year, all top-level managers might receive a bonus equal to a percentage of their current salaries.

Today, employers must keep their costs and prices down to compete worldwide. Therefore, some companies rely on lower fixed salaries and the incentive of bonuses for high-performance employees. As a result, the days of a salary that increases year after year are going away. Instead, employees are more likely to receive a base salary that is enhanced by programs such as merit bonuses.

Stock-purchase options give employees (usually executives) the right to buy a set number of shares of the company's stock at a fixed price by a certain time. The employees gain as long as the stock price goes up. Many types of stock option plans exist.

Pension and Savings Plans

Some employers provide pension plans for retirement. Pension plans are completely funded by the employer. When an employee retires, he or she receives a monthly check. In some cases, an employee may withdraw funds early in part or in full, or retire early and begin collecting reduced benefits. Employees are fully **vested** (entitled to the full retirement account) after a specified period of time, such as five years. We will discuss retirement planning in a later chapter. This benefit will have special value for you as you grow older.

Employer-sponsored savings plans, such as a 401(k) for private employers or a 403(b) for government employers, are also retirement plans. Employers do not bear the full cost of these plans. As a result, many companies are switching from pensions to savings plans. In an employer-sponsored savings plan, the employee makes contributions to his or her own account. The employer then contributes money to the employee's account. The employer's contribution may equal the employee's or may be a percentage of it. Generally, withdrawing funds from savings plans before retirement will result in severe financial penalties.

Travel Expenses

Companies that require employees to travel in the course of their work often provide a company car or a mileage allowance if employees use their own car. Generally, car insurance, gasoline, and repair and maintenance expenses for the company automobile are also provided. While out of town, employees receive a daily allowance, or have their motel, meals, and other travel expenses paid. In some cases, employees are expected to pay the costs of their travel, keep receipts as evidence of purchases, and submit a report in order to be reimbursed.

Evaluating Employee Benefits

Many of these optional benefits are of great value to employees. Benefits generally are not currently taxable to employees (except bonuses and other benefits paid in cash), yet they provide valuable coverage and advantages. Generally, large companies provide more extensive optional benefits than do small companies.

In recent years, employee benefits have been expanded to meet the needs of different life situations. *Cafeteria-style* employee benefits are programs that allow workers to base their job benefits on personal needs. Flexibility in the selection of benefits has become quite common. For example, a married employee with children might opt for increased life and health insurance, while a single parent may choose child-care services.

✓ Check Your Understanding

Review Terms

1. gross pay
2. overtime
3. deductions
4. net pay
5. benefits
6. incentive pay
7. employee services
8. vested

Review Concepts

1. What is included in gross pay?
2. If you are paid every two weeks, how many paychecks do you receive in a year?
3. How are employer-sponsored savings plans different from pension plans?

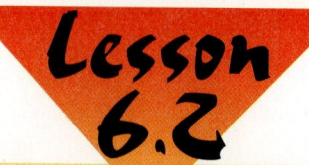

Lesson 6.2

Work Arrangements and Organizations

★ Explain flexible job arrangements, such as flexible schedules, job rotation, job sharing, and permanent part-time employment.
★ Describe the role of unions and professional organizations in the workplace.

Flexible Work Arrangements

Many employers are responding to changing lifestyles and needs of their employees. By designing more flexible jobs, employers can reduce absenteeism, burnout, and turnover.

Altered Workweeks

Many firms have experimented with altered workweeks to get away from the standard eight-hours-a-day, five-days-a-week work schedule. Flextime is one work schedule alternative. Another is the compressed workweek.

Flexible schedules, or **flextime**, allow employees to choose their working hours within defined limits. All employees must be present during a specified core time period. Employees can then choose the rest of their work hours around this core period. Employees negotiate their starting times, usually within a three- to four-hour period. This allows them to begin working as early as 6 A.M. or as late as 9 or 10 A.M. Even though starting times are flexible, most employers require employees to work a set number of hours per day. For example, a person arriving at 6 A.M. would be finished by 3 P.M. (having a one-hour unpaid lunch break), while a person arriving at 10 A.M. would be finished at 7 P.M. The *core time period* is a crucial time during the day when all employees must be working. This core period may be between 10 A.M. and 3 P.M., the peak hours for business activity.

Flextime decreases absenteeism and tardiness. Production increases because employees are responsible for working a full day regardless of when they arrive on the job. Employees experience greater job satisfaction because flextime helps them fulfill their personal goals. For example, employees who need to pick up children from school would find it convenient to be off at 3 P.M. Flextime also allows for the scheduling of medical or other appointments, and it reduces stress caused by the pressure of meeting strict work schedules.

A **compressed workweek** is a work schedule that fits the normal 40-hour workweek into less than five days. The typical compressed workweek is 10 hours a day for 4 days, followed by 3 days off. Some types of work are better suited to a compressed schedule than are others. For example, some kinds of taxing physical or mental work are probably not suitable for a compressed workweek.

Job Rotation

Job rotation is a job design in which employees are trained to do more than one specialized task. Employees "rotate" from one task to another. Job rotation gives employees more variety in their work and allows them to use different skills. It reduces boredom and burnout, leading to greater job satisfaction for employees and greater productivity for the employer. A major advantage of job rotation for both employer and employee is that information and ideas are freely exchanged among employees, so that everyone knows how to do each task. If one worker is absent, another can take over and keep production rolling.

Job Sharing

Job sharing is a job design in which two people share one full-time position. The employees split the salary and benefits according to the amount of each employee's contributions. Job sharing is especially attractive to people who want part-time work. By satisfying employees' needs for more personal time, job sharing reduces absenteeism and tardiness, lowers fatigue, and improves productivity.

Permanent Part-Time and Telecommuting

Many employees are choosing to work only part-time (16 to 25 hours a week). Companies can save on salary and benefits by hiring permanent part-time employees. Part-time work usually provides some benefits to the employee, including job security, while also allowing freedom to spend more time away from work. Parents with small children, older employees, and others may find that permanent part-time work is best suited to meeting their financial and psychological needs.

For what kinds of jobs might telecommuting work well?

Advances in technology make another flexible work arrangement feasible: *telecommuting*. Telecommuters can work at home or on the road, and stay in contact with their manager and co-workers through e-mail, fax, and mobile phone. Employees who telecommute often do computer-related work, such as data entry, Web design, information processing, or software development. Working at home is convenient and gives the worker flexibility. Telecommuting does not work well in jobs that require frequent face-to-face inter-action among employees or that require employees to work together in one place to create a product.

DID YOU KNOW

The world leader in the number of regular teleworkers, as a fraction of the workforce, is Finland (10.8%), followed by the Nether-lands (8.3%), Sweden (8.0%), and the U.S. (6.8%).

Labor Unions and Professional Organizations

Many jobs involve union membership or participation in a profes-sional organization as a requirement of employment. Unions are groups of people joined together for a common purpose. A **labor union** is a group of people who work in the same or similar occu-pations, organized for the benefit of all employees in these occu-pations.

History of Unions

Unions developed in the United States in the late 1800s. The first unions were local groups organized by skilled craftspeople to pro-tect themselves from competition by untrained and unskilled employees. In 1886, the American Federation of Labor (AFL) was organized by Samuel Gompers.

Unions had very little power until 1935, when the National Labor Relations Act (the Wagner Act) gave unions the right to organize and bargain with employers. In 1938, John L. Lewis became the first president of a new union, the Congress of Industrial Organizations (CIO). Unions continued to grow in number, power, and size until 1947, when Congress passed the Labor-Management Relations Act, commonly called the Taft-Hartley Act. This act limited the powers of unions and curbed strikes. In 1955, the AFL and CIO merged and became the largest and most powerful union in the United States.

In the middle 1980s, with the pressures of competition and international trade, companies began looking for ways to cut costs. Membership in unions began declining as jobs were lost. In the 1990s, labor unions struggled to survive in many industries.

Functions of Unions

The importance of labor unions in American life cannot be measured by the number of employees in unions alone. Many nonunion employers are influenced by the standards set by union agreements with other employers, and many employees reap the benefits of unionization even though they do not belong to a union. Labor unions have four major functions: (1) to recruit new members, (2) to engage in collective bargaining, (3) to support political candidates who are favorable to the union, and (4) to provide support services for members.

Unions get their power from having a large membership. Therefore, new employees in unionized occupations are strongly urged or required to join the union. Political candidates who express opinions favorable to a particular union may receive campaign funds and/or endorsements from union leaders. These endorsements usually mean that large numbers of the union members will vote for the candidate. Unions provide support for their members by helping to keep them employed, negotiating job transfers, providing credentials for job-seeking employees, and providing the education members need to obtain and keep jobs.

The main function of unions is **collective bargaining**, which is the process of negotiating the terms of employment for union members. Terms of the agreement are written into an employment contract. The contract is usually quite detailed and is divided into these major sections: wages and supplements; employees' rights on the job; union rights in relation to the employer; management rights in relation to the union; and the grievance procedure. A *grievance* is a formal complaint, by an employee or by the union, that management has violated some aspect of the contract.

The labor contract stipulates wages to be paid for certain jobs and types of work. Paid holidays, vacations, overtime rates, and hours of work are also specified in the contract. Most labor contracts also list benefits. Union contracts usually provide for **seniority** rights, a policy in which the last workers hired will be the first fired when jobs must be cut. So, when the company needs to reduce its workforce, it will lay off newer workers ahead of more experienced workers. Under this policy, the longer you work for the employer, the more job security you are entitled to. Seniority may be used to determine transfers, promotions, and vacation time according to most union contracts.

When the union and employer cannot reach a contract agreement, the dispute can be mediated. Congress created the Federal Mediation and Conciliation Service as part of the Taft-Hartley Act. Through *mediation,* the union and the employer receive the help of a neutral third party (the mediator or specialist). The mediator helps to bring about concession and compromise. Mediators cannot issue binding decisions. When employers and union officials cannot agree on the terms of a new contract, the union may decide to **strike,** a job action in which union members refuse to work until an agreement is reached.

Types of Unions

Unions are self-governing organizations that can be classified into three types: craft unions, industrial unions, and public-employee unions. Major decisions are made by elected leaders. Many unions have developed a high degree of professionalism and power. Union leaders often work full time in their positions. Unions often employ their own lawyers, doctors, economists, educators, and public relations officials. Dues collected from members pay for the services of these professionals.

Career Links

Labor relations managers coordinate industrial labor relations programs. They interpret and administer labor relations contracts with respect to grievances, wages and salaries, employee welfare, health care, pensions, union and management practices, and negotiations. Employers usually seek college graduates, often with backgrounds in business, human resources, personnel administration, or labor relations. Some labor relations managers specialize in preventing or resolving labor disputes.

For more information, refer to the *Occupational Outlook Handbook* at www.bls.gov or search the Internet using such key words as "careers," "jobs," and "labor relations."

Craft Unions

Membership in a craft union is limited to those who practice that craft or trade (for example, bricklayers, carpenters, or plasterers). Major craft unions exist in the building, printing, and maritime trades, and for railroad employees.

Industrial Unions

Membership in industrial unions is composed of skilled, semiskilled, or unskilled employees in a particular place, industry, or group of industries. Examples include the AFL-CIO, Teamsters, and United Auto Workers. Most of this country's basic industries (steel, automobiles, rubber, glass, machinery, mining) are heavily unionized.

What kinds of employees are members of industrial unions?

Public-Employee Unions

Municipal, county, state, or federal employees such as firefighters, teachers, and police officers may organize public-employee unions. These unions are organized much like craft and industrial unions except that they generally do not hire outside officers. In other words, municipal or county workers would also serve as union representatives and officers, sometimes with released time and pay from union dues.

Professional Organizations

A **professional organization** is an organization of people in a particular occupation that requires considerable training and specialized skills. For example, medicine and law are considered professions. Professional organizations also collect dues from members and provide support services. In some cases, membership in a professional organization may be required. Notable professional organizations include the American Bar Association (required) for lawyers and the American Medical Association (optional) for doctors. To be licensed or "admitted to the bar," lawyers must pass rigorous tests administered by their state's bar association. Lawyers who commit serious misconduct may be "disbarred," which means they can no longer practice law.

What role does a bar association play for lawyers?

Professional organizations have six major purposes: (1) to establish and maintain professional standards, including procedures for self-improvement; (2) to support legislation and political action that is beneficial to the profession, called **lobbying**; (3) to encourage individual growth and achievement; (4) to publish a professional journal or magazine; (5) to provide pension, retirement, and insurance benefits for members; and (6) to keep members up-to-date on current information and procedures. Because most doctors and lawyers are self-employed, their professional behavior is not regulated except through membership in these organizations and through lawsuits. Exams, accreditations, admission procedures, and other standards are administered through these organizations.

Another professional organization, sometimes called a union (the largest one nationwide), is the NEA (National Education Association). An educator who joins a local association must also join the state and national associations. Each branch of the NEA charges dues, just as do the national, state, and county bar associations.

PERSONAL PERSPECTIVE

The American Bar Association

The American Bar Association (ABA) was founded in 1878. The legal profession as we know it today barely existed then. Lawyers were trained under a system of apprenticeship. There was no national code of ethics. Today, the stated mission of the ABA is to "be the national representative of the legal profession, serving the public and the profession by promoting justice, professional excellence, and respect for the law."

ABA membership is open to lawyers admitted to practice and in good standing before the bar of any state or territory of the United States. One organizational goal is to maintain high ethical standards for the legal profession. The current version of the ABA's ethical standards, the Model Rules of Professional Conduct, was adopted in 1983. The association also accredits law schools under the authority of state high courts and the United States Department of Education.

Other association activities include efforts to increase access to legal services for all people, through support of lawyer-donated services and legal assistance programs, and by providing consultation to emerging countries in Central and Eastern Europe. Policies of the association are determined by a house of delegates representing the legal profession and administered by the board of governors. Headquarters of the ABA are in Chicago and in Washington, D.C.

The ABA maintains a Web site at www.abanet.org, where you can get dependable information about law, including a glossary of legal terms. You can also find a lawyer through their directory of local legal services programs. The site offers insight into Supreme Court cases and public policy issues. The site also provides information for students about careers in the law and nationwide online youth summits.

Think Critically

1. Visit the ABA Web site and write a report on your findings in an area of interest to you.
2. If you were interested in a legal career, what steps would you take in getting the appropriate education and experience for that career?

Check Your Understanding

Review Terms

1. flextime
2. compressed workweek
3. job rotation
4. job sharing
5. labor union
6. collective bargaining
7. seniority
8. strike
9. professional organization
10. lobbying

Review Concepts

1. Which form of flexible work arrangement is most attractive to you? Why?
2. How do unions benefit their members?
3. What are the purposes of professional organizations such as the AMA?

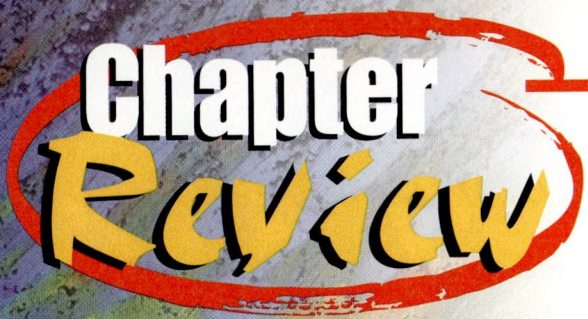
6.1 Understanding Pay, Benefits, and Incentives

- Your gross pay includes your regular pay plus any overtime wages you earned that pay period.
- Deductions (both required and voluntary) are subtracted from gross pay to determine your net pay—the money you actually take home.
- Many companies offer benefits and incentives in addition to pay. These may include profit sharing, paid time off, employee services, insurance plans, bonuses, stock options, and retirement plans.
- Benefits add significantly to an employee's overall compensation. Some companies offer cafeteria-style plans, allowing employees to choose the benefits that best meet their needs.

6.2 Work Arrangements and Organizations

- Many companies now offer flexible work schedules and job designs to meet the needs of employees and reduce absenteeism, burnout, and turnover.
- Permanent part-time work, telecommuting, and on-site child-care facilities offer options to meet the needs of working parents and other employees who value flexibility.
- Labor unions—including craft unions, industrial unions, and public-employee unions—negotiate the terms of work contracts with employers on behalf of their members.
- Professional organizations serve people in highly skilled occupations. These organizations maintain standards and keep members current in their fields.

Review Terms

Directions: Can you find the definition for each of the following terms used in Chapter 6?

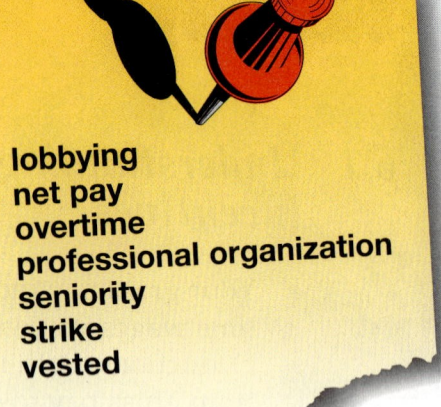

benefits
collective bargaining
compressed workweek
deductions
employee services
flextime
gross pay
incentive pay
job rotation
job sharing
labor union

lobbying
net pay
overtime
professional organization
seniority
strike
vested

1. Organization of people in a particular occupation that requires considerable training and specialized skills.
2. A job action in which employees refuse to work until an agreement with management is reached.
3. An effort to support legislation that would benefit a certain group.
4. Total pay before deductions are subtracted.
5. Pay remaining after deductions are subtracted.
6. Entitled to the full amount accumulated in a retirement plan.
7. A group of people in the same or similar occupations, organized for the benefit of all.
8. Amounts subtracted from gross pay.
9. A negotiation between unions and employers about terms of employment.
10. Workplace policy in which the last workers hired will be the first fired when jobs must be cut.
11. Money offered to encourage employees to strive for higher levels of performance.
12. Work schedule that allows employees to choose their working hours within defined limits.
13. Job design in which employees are trained to do more than one specialized task and move from one task to another.
14. Job design in which two people share one full-time position.
15. Work schedule that fits the normal 40-hour workweek into less than 5 days.
16. Extras that a company offers in order to improve employee morale and working conditions.

17. Forms of employee compensation in addition to pay.
18. Time worked beyond the regular 40-hour workweek.

Review Facts and Ideas

1. How is gross pay different from net pay?
2. How much must an employer pay an hourly employee for hours worked beyond a regular workweek?
3. What is an important difference between employees who work for a salary and those who work for an hourly wage?
4. List five optional deductions you may elect to have withheld from your gross pay.
5. What is a leave of absence?
6. What is a core time period?
7. What is a major advantage of job rotation to employers?
8. What was the significance of the Wagner Act to American labor?
9. What are the major functions of labor unions?
10. Describe the collective bargaining process.
11. Explain the principle of seniority.
12. How is mediation used in labor negotiations?
13. What are the three types of labor unions?
14. How are labor unions funded? That is, who pays for the services they provide?
15. Name a professional organization.

APPLY YOUR KNOWLEDGE

1. Compute gross pay for these situations:
   a. Regular hours worked: 40
      Overtime hours worked: 5
      Regular rate of pay: $5.85 an hour

b. Total hours worked: 43 (in 5 days)
   Regular rate of pay: $6.10 an hour
   c. Annual salary: $18,000
   Compute monthly gross pay.
2. Using the payroll tax withholding tables in Figures 6-3 through 6-6, find the state and federal withholding amounts for each of the following cases:
   a. For a single person, one allowance, who made $110 last week.
   b. For a single person, no allowances, who made $222 last week.
   c. For a married person, two allowances, who made $1,120 last month.
   d. For a married person, six allowances, who made $1,479 last month.
3. Visit the Social Security Administration online at www.ssa.gov and look up the current-year Social Security changes. List the maximum taxable earnings for Social Security and for Medicare, and the current tax rate on earnings.
4. Visit the American Bar Association online at www.abanet.org and list or print out the 11 goals of the association.

Solve Problems

1. Teresa Valencio works for a weekly paycheck. She is single and claims no allowances. Last week she worked 5 days for a total of 44 hours. Her regular rate of pay is $7.60 an hour. In addition to federal income tax, state income tax (use tables shown in Figures 6-3 through 6-6), and social security tax, Teresa also has insurance of $16 a week withheld and puts 6 percent of her gross pay into a retirement account. Compute her gross pay, deductions, and net pay.

2. Dontae Jones works for a weekly paycheck. He is single and claims one allowance. Last week he worked 5 days, for a total of 48 hours. His regular rate of pay is $6.80 an hour. In addition to required deductions, he also has $10 a week sent to his credit union account and gives $5 a week to United Fund (a charity). Compute his gross pay, deductions, and net pay.

3. Hector Fuentes works for a monthly salary. He is married and claims four allowances. Last month Hector worked 22 days. He does not get paid for overtime. His monthly salary is

$1,780. In addition to required deductions, Hector also pays insurance premiums of $23 a month and sets aside for retirement 6 percent of his gross monthly pay. Compute his gross pay, deductions, and net pay.

4. Jazmine Peak works for a monthly paycheck. She is married and claims two allowances. Her yearly salary is $20,700. Last month she worked 21 days. In addition to required deductions, she also contributes $14 a week (assume a four-week month) to the Heart Fund and sets aside $50 a month, paid directly to her savings account. Compute her gross pay, deductions, and net pay.

5. Assume that Jazmine in question 4 continues to save $50 a month. She had $200 in her account when she started her monthly contributions, and the account earns 7 percent. Use your Savings Planner Tool to determine how much she will have in her account at the end of two years.

PLANNING TOOLS

6. Ying Ho makes an annual salary of $32,000. However, he gets paid every two weeks. How much is his gross pay on each paycheck?

For related activities and links, point your browser to
www.mypf.swep.com

Chapter 7

Federal Income Tax

Up Front

When Andrae started his after-school part-time job last year, he filled out a Form W-4 declaring zero exemptions. At the end of the year, his employer sent him a Form W-2 listing the amounts that were withheld for taxes. Because Andrae must now prepare his first tax return, he needs to pick up a tax form at the local IRS office, or download a copy online.

"This is great," says Andrae, as he reads through the direction page that comes with Form 1040EZ. "I'm looking at a refund. I had a lot more withheld than I'll owe in taxes. Next year, I think I'll plan a little better. It's nice to have a refund, but it would be better to have the right amount withheld so I have full use of my money during the year. I could have earned interest on that money if I had put it away."

Goals

★ Discuss the purpose of taxes, different types of taxes, and the history of taxes in the United States.
★ Describe components of the tax system, including the IRS, the power to tax, and paying your fair share.

Types of Taxes

In a free enterprise system, such as that of the United States, the government collects money from citizens and businesses in the form of taxes. The government then spends this money, called **revenue**, according to priorities determined by Congress. The largest source of government revenue is income taxes. Other taxes providing government revenue include social security taxes, unemployment insurance taxes, inheritance and estate taxes, excise taxes, import duties, and personal property taxes.

A commonly accepted principle of tax fairness is that individuals with high incomes should pay more taxes than people with low incomes. This theory is called the *ability-to-pay principle.*

Progressive taxes are taxes that take a larger share of income as the amount of income grows. Federal income taxes are progressive. For example, someone with a low income may pay 15 percent of income as taxes. Someone with a high income may pay 28 percent for income taxes. Everyone who receives income from employment or any other source must pay income taxes.

Regressive taxes are taxes that take a smaller share of income as the amount of income grows. Sales taxes are regressive, because people with lower incomes pay a larger percentage of their income for sales taxes than do people with higher incomes. For example, your state may charge a 5 percent sales tax. If you buy an item worth $10, your tax would be 50 cents ($10 × 0.05 = $0.50), and you would pay $10.50 for the item. For someone who earns $50 a week, this 50 cents represents 1 percent of income ($0.50/$50 = .01 = 1%). For someone who earns $100 a week, this 50 cents represents only half a percent of income ($0.50/$100 = .005 = .5%).

Almost all consumption taxes are regressive. Another type of tax on consumption is an *excise tax.* Excise taxes are sales taxes

What is the difference between progressive, regressive, and proportional taxes?

imposed on specific goods and services, such as gasoline, cigarettes, alcoholic beverages, air travel, and telephone service.

Proportional taxes or *flat taxes* are taxes for which the rate stays the same, regardless of the amount on which the tax is imposed. Property taxes are proportional. For example, all people owning property in the same community pay the same tax rate, whether their property is worth $50,000 or $500,000.

On a local level, taxes provide services such as education, parks and playgrounds, roads, and police, fire, and health departments. On a national level, they provide salaries for Congress and funds for national defense, highways, wildlife refuges, welfare, foreign aid, and other services. Most of the services (local, state, and national) are provided for the general welfare of all citizens, although as an individual, you may not benefit from all of them directly.

Some states don't have individual income taxes on wages. Other states don't have sales taxes.

History of Taxes

For many years the United States operated without an income tax. Many of the new residents came to America to evade taxation, and therefore society was careful to avoid it. While our country was a colony of England, the British government imposed certain taxes.

However, when the Revolutionary War brought independence, there was no direct income tax imposed on citizens. The Constitution, drawn in 1787, included the option to tax but not to tax individuals directly. Excise taxes and customs duties produced enough revenue to meet the nation's needs at that time.

The Revolutionary War was financed by contributions from sympathetic countries such as France. The War of 1812 brought a temporary income tax; but when the war debts were paid, the tax was dropped. While the government did not levy *income* taxes against the citizens, it also did not provide services for them.

When the Civil War became an economic burden, an income tax to finance the war became necessary. In 1862, President Abraham Lincoln signed a law that provided for progressive income taxes on wages earned. When the war debts were paid off, the tax expired.

In 1909, Congress introduced the first permanent income tax with the 16th Amendment to the Constitution, which was ratified by three-fourths of the states by 1913. However, only nominal taxes were levied as a result of this Amendment.

World War I (1917) was paid for by income taxes. After that war, the country prospered until the Great Depression of 1929. At that time the government provided few services, and many people suffered badly as a result. But President Franklin D. Roosevelt's "New Deal" sought prosperity through taxation and redistribution of income. In 1935, the Social Security Act was signed into law, creating the Internal Revenue Service (IRS). The IRS was designed to collect taxes and turn them over for the payment of government debt, commitments, and benefits. Money withheld from wages for social security was deposited with the U.S. Department of the Treasury.

During World War II, taxes were increased to finance the war. This increase set a precedent for the changing tax rates we know today. The government increases income tax rates to pay for the growing demand for services and needs of the government.

Components of the Tax System

Our tax system is complex. Both businesses and individuals pay income taxes and must file income tax returns each year. The basic components that allow the tax system to operate are the IRS, the country's power to tax income, and each taxpayer's willingness to pay his or her fair share.

The IRS

The Internal Revenue Service is an agency of the Department of the Treasury. It has headquarters in Washington, D.C., and seven regional offices throughout the country. Each regional office is a major data processing center that oversees at least 10 district and local offices. The main functions of the IRS are to collect income taxes and to enforce tax laws.

The IRS also provides services to taxpayers. In local offices, IRS employees assist taxpayers in finding information and forms. The IRS prints pamphlets to aid taxpayers in preparing their returns. It also furnishes tax information and instruction booklets free to schools and colleges. The IRS maintains a Web site at www.irs.gov, where citizens can get tax information, download tax forms, and even file their taxes electronically.

The Power to Tax

The power to levy taxes rests with Congress. The Constitution provides that "all bills for raising revenue shall originate in the House of Representatives." Proposals to increase or decrease taxes may come from the president, the Department of the Treasury, or a member of Congress representing the interests of a geographic area. The House Ways and Means Committee studies the proposals and makes recommendations to the full House. Revenue bills must pass a vote in both the House and the Senate and then be signed by the president before they become law.

Paying Your Fair Share

Our income tax system is graduated. This means that tax rates increase as taxable income increases. Tax rates apply to income ranges, or **tax brackets**. Currently, there are five tax brackets: These brackets are being reduced to 10 percent at the low end and 35 percent at the high end, phased in through 2006. For example, suppose that you earned $29,000 in a year. If the 28 percent tax bracket that year included incomes between $27,000 and $65,000, then your income would be taxed at the 28 percent rate. Congress increases the tax rates when needed to bring in more money to balance its budget. When the government spends more than it receives in revenue, it has a *deficit,* or shortage. It must then borrow money to pay its expenses.

Our income tax system is based on *voluntary compliance.* What does this mean?

Our income tax system is based on *voluntary compliance,* which means that all citizens are expected to prepare (or have prepared) and file income tax returns. Taxes are due by April 15 of each year. Responsibility for filing a tax return and paying taxes due rests with the individual. Failure to do so can result in a penalty: interest charges on the taxes owed plus a fine and/or imprisonment. Willful failure to pay taxes is called **tax evasion**, which is a serious crime punishable by a fine or imprisonment or both.

+PROS and CONS

Taxes collected from individuals and businesses provide our government with the money necessary to provide services. However, many people do not pay their fair share of taxes. Some people believe the government is corrupt or doesn't spend their money wisely. Others feel that taxes are simply too high. When everyone doesn't pay their fair share, the burden is passed along to others who can't avoid taxation— usually wage earners who have taxes withheld from their paychecks.

Think Critically: How do you feel about taxes in this country? What benefits do you receive even though you may not be paying taxes? Do you feel that penalties for tax evaders are too tough? Not tough enough?

An IRS Audit

Every year, the IRS calls thousands of taxpayers for an **audit**, or examination of their tax returns. Taxpayers being audited have three choices. First, they can represent themselves all the way to an appeal in Tax Court, if necessary. Second, they can give someone the power to take their place, as long as the designated person is a lawyer, certified public accountant, a member of the immediate family, or an enrolled agent (someone who is licensed to prepare tax returns). Third, they can bring anyone at all (tax preparer, attorney, or other representative) for support during the session. Most audit sessions involve nothing more than confirming supporting documentation. Therefore, most taxpayers can go alone unless the matter is unusually complicated.

A correspondence audit is much more common than an office audit, where the taxpayer sits down with the auditor to answer questions and produce records. In a correspondence audit, the IRS asks the taxpayer to respond to specific questions or produce evidence of deductions or other entries on the tax return. A field audit is similar, except that an IRS agent or local representative visits the taxpayer to verify information or ask specific questions.

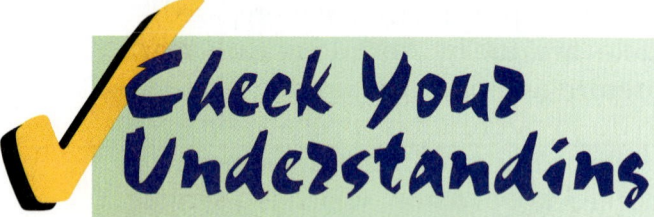

Check Your Understanding

Review Terms
1. revenue
2. progressive taxes
3. regressive taxes
4. proportional taxes
5. tax brackets
6. tax evasion
7. audit

Review Concepts
1. What is the purpose of the Internal Revenue Service (IRS) within our income tax system?
2. Who has the power to levy taxes in the United States?
3. Explain why voluntary compliance is a vital component of our democracy.

PERSONAL PERSPECTIVE

Taxpayer Advocate Service

The Taxpayer Advocate Service is an IRS program that provides an independent service to taxpayers. The National Taxpayer Advocate heads the program; each state has at least one taxpayer advocate. The taxpayer advocate is independent of the IRS and its goals are to protect individual taxpayer rights, to improve customer service, and to reduce taxpayer burden.

The taxpayer advocate represents your interests and concerns by ensuring that taxpayer problems are resolved promptly and handled fairly. The advocate will listen to your point of view and work to address your concerns. The service is available to taxpayers suffering from hardships, including excessive professional fees (accounting and/or legal). It specializes in informing you, the taxpayer, about your rights when dealing with the IRS and helping to resolve claims. In some instances, enforcement (collection) action may be suspended while your case is being reviewed. Most cases are resolved without the need for court appearances. The National Taxpayer Advocate reports to Congress twice a year, summarizing problems and making recommendations.

You can locate the Taxpayer Advocate Service by phoning 1-877-777-4778 toll free or by calling the general IRS toll-free number (1-800-829-1040) and asking for the Taxpayer Advocate Service. For more information, go online at www.irs.ustreas.gov/prod/ind_info/advocate.html.

Think Critically

1. How might you use the services provided by the Taxpayer Advocate Service?
2. What benefit is there to having such a service, even if the average taxpayer never uses it?

Lesson 7.2

Filing Tax Returns

Goals

★ Define and discuss the significance of exemptions, dependents, and taxable and nontaxable income on tax returns.

★ Prepare tax Forms 1040EZ and 1040A.

Definitions of Terms

You should prepare your tax forms with the idea of paying your fair share while taking advantage of the tax breaks legally available to you. Before you can understand how to prepare tax forms, you need a working knowledge of the tax vocabulary. The terms described in the following paragraphs appear on income tax returns, in IRS instruction booklets, and on forms and schedules you will use.

Filing Status

You must select the filing status that best fits you from among these five choices:

1. Single person (not married)
2. Married person filing a joint return (even though only one spouse may have earned income)
3. Married person filing a separate return
4. "Head of household" (you may qualify as a head of household whether you are married or single if you meet certain conditions in providing a home for people dependent on you)
5. Qualifying widow(er) with a dependent child

You mark your filing status on the front of the tax form. The tax instruction booklet contains a more complete description of these classifications. After you file your first tax return, each year thereafter you will automatically receive a tax booklet containing the necessary forms in the mail for use in preparing your tax returns.

Exemptions

When figuring taxes, an **exemption** is an amount you may subtract from your income for each person who depends on your income to live. You would then not have to pay tax on this amount. As a taxpayer you are automatically allowed one exemption for yourself unless someone else (such as a parent) claims you on his or her return. If you are filing a joint return, you can take an exemption for your spouse.

A dependent is a person who lives with you and who receives more than half his or her living expenses from you. Each exemption you claim on your income tax form excludes a certain amount of your income from being taxed. In a recent year, each exemption excluded $2,800 from taxation, with this amount increasing according to the cost of living each year. Dependents are usually children, a spouse, elderly parents, or disabled relatives living with and depending on the taxpayer. However, dependents can be anyone who meets the requirements spelled out in the information that accompanies the tax form.

What are the five choices of filing status?

Gross Income

Gross income is all the taxable income you receive, including wages, tips, salaries, interest, dividends, unemployment compensation, alimony, workers' compensation benefits, and so forth. Scholarships and grants may be taxable for amounts used for expenses other than tuition and books. If you just take classes without pursuing a degree, more of the scholarship or grant money you receive will likely be taxable. Also, employer-reimbursed tuition is in most cases taxable. Certain types of income are not taxable and are not reported as income. These include child support, gifts, inheritances, life insurance benefits, and veterans' benefits.

You are also taxed on other forms of income, including winnings from gambling, bartering income, pensions and annuities, rental income, royalties, estate and trust income, and income on sale of property.

Wages, Salaries, and Tips

This category on your Form W-2 includes all income you receive through employment. If you receive tips on your job, you must report your tips to your employer. Your employer then includes these earnings with your wages on your Form W-2.

Interest Income

Your interest income includes all taxable interest from banks, savings and loan associations, credit unions, series HH savings bonds, and so on. You should receive Form 1099-INT from the payers of such interest.

Dividend Income

Dividends are money, stock, or other property that corporations pay to stockholders in return for their investment. You will receive a Form 1099-DIV for each investment, listing the dividend income.

Unemployment Compensation

If you receive any unemployment compensation during the year, you will receive a Form 1099-G, which shows the total you received. You must enter this amount as income on the tax return.

Social Security Benefits

If you receive social security payments during the year, 85 percent of this money is taxable if your total income exceeds $25,000 for single taxpayers and $32,000 for married taxpayers filing jointly. You would receive a Form SSA-1099, listing the total paid for the year.

Child Support

Money paid to a former spouse for support of dependent children is called **child support**. This income is not taxable for the person receiving it, nor is it deductible for the person paying it.

Alimony

Money paid to support a former spouse is called **alimony**. It is taxable for the person receiving it and deductible for the person paying it. (You would have to fill out the long Form 1040.)

Adjusted Gross Income

The law allows you to subtract some types of spending from gross income. You can "adjust" your income by subtracting such things as contributions to IRAs (retirement accounts you will learn about in Chapter 11). After these adjustments are subtracted from gross income, the result is **adjusted gross income**. You will use your adjusted gross income as a basis for computing other deductions on your tax return.

Taxable Income

In Chapter 6, you learned that *deductions* are amounts subtracted from your gross pay to arrive at your take-home pay. On tax returns, **deductions** are expenses the law allows you to subtract from your adjusted gross income to determine your taxable income. To get the tax benefit from your deductions, you must list or **itemize** these allowable expenses on your tax return. To itemize deductions, you must use Schedule A and Form 1040. Common expenses you may deduct are medical and dental expenses beyond a specified amount, state and local income taxes and property taxes, home mortgage interest, gifts to charity, losses from theft or property damage, and moving expenses.

If you do not have many deductions, your tax may be less if you take the **standard deduction**. This is a stated amount that you may subtract from adjusted gross income instead of itemizing your deductions. Figure 7-1 on page 184 shows the standard deduction in a recent year for most people based on their filing status. If your individual deductions do not add up to the standard deduction, then you can reduce your total tax by taking the standard deduction rather than itemizing.

Once you have subtracted your standard deduction (or itemized deductions), you need to compute exemptions. You may deduct a stated amount for each exemption to arrive at your **taxable income**, which is the income on which you will pay tax. You can then determine your tax by looking up your taxable income on a tax table. The Math Minute feature shows the formula for determining your taxable income.

Taxable Income Formula

$$
\begin{array}{l}
\text{Gross Income} \\
-\ \text{Adjustments} \\
\hline
\text{Adjusted Gross Income} \\
-\ \text{Standard Deduction } or \text{ Itemized Deductions} \\
-\ \text{Exemptions} \\
\hline
\text{Taxable Income}
\end{array}
$$

Figure 7-1 *The Standard Deduction*

STANDARD DEDUCTION FOR MOST PEOPLE	
If your filing status is:	**Your standard deduction is:**
Single	$4,400
Married filing jointly	7,350
Married filing separately	3,675
Head of household	6,450

Preparing to File

Once you have gathered your income and expense records, you can make a rough draft of your tax return. You should also study the tax booklet that accompanies the printed forms. This contains the latest tax information you will need in order to prepare your return. Read the instructions carefully to be sure you are taking advantage of every possible deduction and are reporting all taxable income. A simple 1040EZ tax return may require only 15 minutes to prepare. The long Form 1040 may require most of a day after you have gathered all information. In addition to a federal tax return, you may have to file a state income tax return.

Who Must File?

You must file a tax return if your filing status, age, and gross income are as shown in Figure 7-2. In addition to the requirements given in Figure 7-2, people claimed as dependents on another person's tax return may also have to file a tax return (see tax booklets). You may also have to file if (1) you owe any special taxes, such as social security tax on tips; (2) you earned $400 or more from self-employment; or (3) you earned $100 or more from a church or church-controlled organization that is exempt from employer social security taxes. If you did not earn enough to owe taxes but you had taxes withheld from your paychecks, you must file a return to reclaim the taxes withheld. If you do not file, you will not get a refund.

United States citizens living abroad are required to file annual U.S. income tax returns and report their worldwide income if they meet the minimum filing requirements for their filing status and age.

You must file if your gross income was at least the amount shown in the last column. *Gross income* means all income you received in the form of money, goods, property, and services that is not exempt from tax, including income from sources outside the United States (even if you may exclude all or part of it).

Marital Status	Filing Status	Age	Gross Income
Single	Single	Under 65	$7,200
		65 or older	$8,300
	Head of household	Under 65	$9,250
		65 or older	$10,350
Married, with child, Living apart	Head of household	Under 65	$9,250
		65 or older	$10,350
Married, living with spouse	Married, joint return	Under 65 (both spouses)	$12,950
		65 or older (one spouse)	$13,800
		65 or older (both spouses)	$14,650
	Married, separate return	Any age	$2,800
Married, living apart	Joint or separate return	Any age	$2,800
Widowed, not remarried	Single	Under 65	$7,200
		65 or older	$8,300
	Head of household	Under 65	$9,250
		65 or older	$10,350
	Widow(er) with dependent child	Under 65	$10,150
		65 or older	$11,000

When to File?

You must file no later than April 15 of the year after you earned income. If April 15 falls on a weekend or holiday, your tax return is due on the next regular weekday. If you file late, you will have to pay penalties and interest charges.

Short Form or Long Form?

Although there are nearly 400 federal tax forms and schedules, all taxpayers must use one of three basic forms when filing their return. You must decide whether to fill out a short form (1040A or 1040EZ) or to itemize your deductions using the long form (1040). Figure 7-3 lists the requirements for using each form. Which form you choose will depend on the type and amount of your income, the number of your deductions, and the complexity of your tax situation. In general, if your deductions add up to more than the standard deduction, your total tax will be lower if you use Form 1040 and itemize your deductions.

Where to Begin?

During the year, save all receipts and proofs of payment for your itemized deductions. You will need these receipts to prove the accuracy of your tax return if you are audited. Save all employee withholding records, such as your paycheck stubs. By January 31 you should receive your Form W-2 from each of your employers. Compare it with your records to check for accuracy. Any discrepancy between the Form W-2 and your records should be reported immediately to the employer and corrected. Social security tax withholding rates increase periodically, and a current IRS tax preparation booklet will give you the current rates.

It is wise to prepare your tax return early—as soon as you receive your Form W-2 and any Forms 1099, which reflect other income you received. Gather all other necessary information, including tax preparation booklets and last year's tax return as a model for preparing this year's return. If you owe additional taxes, mail your return and the amount due in sufficient time to have the envelope postmarked by April 15. If you have a refund coming, the sooner you file, the sooner you will receive it. If you wait until April 1, your refund may be delayed for months. You will not receive interest on refunds.

Once you have gathered all your information, prepare both the short and the long form to determine whether you can save money by itemizing deductions. Read all directions carefully and fill out all schedules completely.

If you did not have enough taxes withheld during the year to cover the tax, you may have to pay a penalty and will have to increase withholdings for the next year. If you receive a large refund, you should increase the number of allowances you claim

All individual taxpayers use one of three basic tax forms: Form 1040EZ, Form 1040A, or Form 1040. Forms 1040EZ and 1040A are shorter and take less time to fill out than Form 1040. However, if you have many deductions, you should use Form 1040 so that you can list and benefit from all of them.

Form	Filing Status	Number of Exemptions	Taxable Income	Source of Income
Form 1040EZ	• Single • Married, filing jointly	One for self; one for spouse (no dependents)	Less than $50,000 on Line 6	• Wages, salaries, tips • Taxable scholarships • Interest of $400 or less • Unemployment compensation
Form 1040A	• Single • Married, filing jointly • Married, filing separately • Head of household • Qualifying widow(er) with dependent child	All exemptions you are entitled to claim	Less than $50,000 on Line 25	• Wages, salaries, tips • Taxable scholarships • Interest • Dividends • Unemployment compensation
Form 1040	• Single • Married, filing jointly • Married, filing separately • Head of household • Qualifying widow(er) with dependent child	All exemptions you are entitled to claim	Any amount of taxable income on line 39	• Wages, salaries, tips • Taxable scholarships • Interest • Dividends • Unemployment compensation • Taxable social security and railroad retirement benefits • Self-employment • Rents and royalties • Pensions, annuities, IRAs • Taxable state and local tax refunds • Capital gains • Alimony received

for next year to reduce the amount withheld during the year. Ideally, you want the amount withheld to end up very close to the amount of your tax. That way, you can have as much of your money as possible in the bank earning interest for you, rather than allowing the government free use of it during the year.

Even if you hire a professional tax preparer, you are responsible for supplying accurate and complete information. Hiring a tax preparer will *not* guarantee that you are paying the correct amount. If you discover an error in a tax return after it has been filed, you may file an amended return (Form 1040X) to claim a refund or credit, or to pay additional tax due.

Save copies of the tax returns you file, together with all supporting evidence (receipts) for six years. Tax returns should be kept in a safe deposit box or in another safe place, together with copies of Forms W-2 and other supporting information.

Filing Electronically

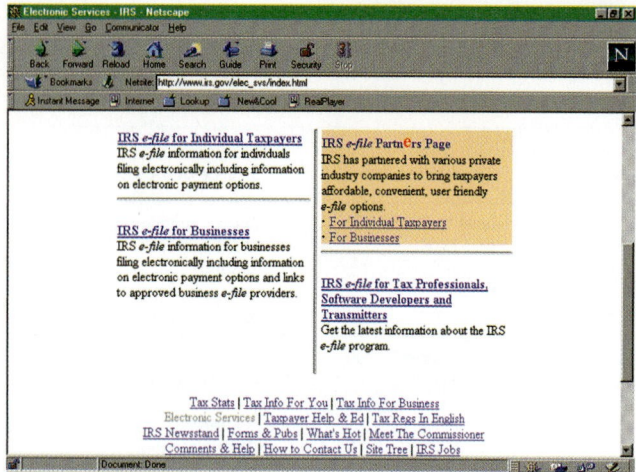

The IRS Web site gives valuable information on filing electronically. Who is eligible to do so?

For people who use Form 1040EZ or 1040A, the IRS allows electronic filing of tax returns and electronic payment of taxes due. You can file paperlessly by visiting www.irs.gov. This Web site also allows you to pay electronically using a debit card or a credit card. If the government owes you a refund, the Web site promises quicker processing. If you file electronically, be sure to print a copy of the tax return for your records.

Preparing Your Income Tax Return

You must complete the tax return in ink or typed with no errors or omissions. The booklets provided by the IRS have line-by-line instructions that explain each section and type of income or deduction.

NET NOTES

Having trouble making sense of taxes? Check out the Tax Interactive Web site at www.irs.gov/taxi. It presents an online 'zine for understanding taxes, including a glossary of tax terms, a history of taxes in the U.S., information on how to file your taxes electronically, and an explanation of tax deductions. There are even facts about how teen entrepreneurs can set up their own businesses.

Tax Preparation Software

Most professional tax preparers use a tax preparation computer program. You can use tax preparation software to do your own taxes if you like. Good software provides all the necessary forms and leads you through the process of filling out the forms. Most tax software also provides tips and additional information to help you identify all the deductions you are allowed. Tax preparation software is available for all types of computers and costs from about $20 to $50.

You may use Form 1040EZ if you are single or married and claim no dependents. Your taxable income must be less than $50,000. Line-by-line instructions for filling out Form 1040EZ are given on the back of the form. Highlights of the instructions are described in the following paragraphs.

Figure 7-4 (page 190) shows Form W-2 for Roberto Flores. Figure 7-5 (page 191) shows his completed Form 1040EZ tax return. Roberto is single and claims one exemption. His wages are found on the W-2, which he previously checked for accuracy. Roberto earned $134 in interest on his savings account. No one else can claim him as a dependent. Follow along on Roberto's Form 1040EZ as you read the instructions below.

Step 1: Name, Address, and Social Security Number

Fill in your name, address, and social security number. If you have filed a tax return in previous years, the IRS will supply a printed name and address label for you for this year's return. Stick this self-adhesive label in this place on the form rather than write your information.

Check the "Yes" box if you want $3 to go to the Presidential Election Campaign Fund. This is a fund established by Congress so that taxpayers can share in the costs of election campaigns. The $3 comes from taxes already withheld, so you will not have to pay more income taxes if you check this box.

Step 2: Report Income

First, enter your total wages, salaries, and tips, as shown on your W-2 form(s). On Roberto's Form W-2, you can see that he earned $14,720. He entered this amount on his Form 1040EZ.

Second, enter interest earned on savings accounts (this amount cannot be more than $400) and any unemployment compensation you may have received. Add these figures together. This is your adjusted gross income.

Next, you must indicate if you are claimed as a dependent on another person's tax return. If so, you will lose most or all of the standard deduction. If not, you can enter the total standard deduction and personal exemption allowed on the 1040EZ ($7,200 at this writing). Subtract this amount from adjusted gross income to obtain your taxable income.

Figure 7-4 *Sample W-2*

a Control number	22222	Void ☐	For Official Use Only OMB No. 1545-0008		

b Employer identification number 93-899348488		1 Wages, tips, other compensation $14,720.00	2 Federal income tax withheld $1,501.00

c Employer's name, address, and ZIP code Blanton School District T-31 23855 SW 85th Portland, OR 97215-4562	3 Social security wages $14,720.00	4 Social security tax withheld $912.64

5 Medicare wages and tips $14,720.00	6 Medicare tax withheld $213.44

7 Social security tips	8 Allocated tips

d Employee's social security number 465-84-3894	9 Advance EIC payment	10 Dependent care benefits

e Employee's name (first, middle initial, last)	11 Nonqualified plans	12 Benefits included in box 1

13 See instrs. for box 13	14 Other

Roberto J. Flores
285 SW 28th Street, #8
Portland, OR 97214-4562

15 Statutory employee ☐	Deceased ☐	Pension plan ☐	Legal rep. ☐	Deferred compensation ☐

f Employee's address and ZIP code

16 State OR	Employer's state I.D. no. 2384762	17 State wages, tips, etc. $14,720.00	18 State income tax $946.00	19 Locality name	20 Local wages, tips, etc.	21 Local income tax

Form **W-2** Wage and Tax Statement **20--**

Department of the Treasury—Internal Revenue Service

Copy A For Social Security Administration—Send this entire page with Form W-3 to the Social Security Administration; photocopies are **not** acceptable.

For Privacy Act and Paperwork Reduction Act Notice, see separate instructions.

Cat. No. 10134D

Do NOT Cut, Fold, or Staple Forms on This Page — Do NOT Cut, Fold, or Staple Forms on This Page

Step 3: Compute Tax

Now enter the total federal tax withheld, as shown on your W-2 form(s). This is the amount of tax you have already paid. To find out the total tax you are required to pay, look up your taxable income in the tax table that comes with your return. It will look similar to the one in Appendix A. In the tax table in Appendix A, Roberto Flores found that his taxable income of $7,654 fell within the range of $7,650–$7,700. In that row, he located his tax liability (the total tax he is obligated to pay) of $1,151 in the "single" column.

Form 1040EZ

Department of the Treasury—Internal Revenue Service

Income Tax Return for Single and Joint Filers With No Dependents (U) **20--**

OMB No. 1545-0675

Use the IRS label here

Your first name and initial: *Roberto J.* Last name: *Flores*

If a joint return, spouse's first name and initial: Last name:

Home address (number and street). If you have a P.O. box, see page 12. *285 SW 28th Street* Apt. no. *#8*

City, town or post office, state, and ZIP code. If you have a foreign address, see page 12. *Portland, OR 97214-4562*

Your social security number 465 84 3894

Spouse's social security number

Presidential Campaign (p. 12)

Note. Checking "Yes" will not change your tax or reduce your refund. ▶
Do you, or spouse if a joint return, want $3 to go to this fund?

You: ☒ Yes ☐ No   Spouse: ☐ Yes ☐ No

		Dollars	Cents

Income

Attach Form(s) W-2 here. Enclose, but do not attach, any payment.

1. Total wages, salaries, and tips. This should be shown in box 1 of your W-2 form(s). Attach your W-2 form(s). — **1** — 14,720.

2. Taxable interest. If the total is over $400, you cannot use Form 1040EZ. — **2** — 134.

3. Unemployment compensation, qualified state tuition program earnings, and Alaska Permanent Fund dividends (see page 14). — **3**

4. Add lines 1, 2, and 3. This is your **adjusted gross income.** — **4** — 14,854.

Note. You must check Yes or No.

5. Can your parents (or someone else) claim you on their return?
   ☐ **Yes.** Enter amount from worksheet on back.
   ☒ **No.** If **single,** enter 7,200.00. If **married,** enter 12,950.00. See back for explanation. — **5** — 7,200.

6. Subtract line 5 from line 4. If line 5 is larger than line 4, enter 0. This is your **taxable income.** ▶ **6** — 7,654.

Payments and tax

7. Enter your Federal income tax withheld from box 2 of your W-2 form(s). — **7** — 1,501.

8a. **Earned income credit (EIC).** See page 15.
  b. Nontaxable earned income: enter type and amount below.
   Type _____ $ _____ — **8a**

9. Add lines 7 and 8a. These are your **total payments.** — **9** — 1,501.

10. **Tax.** Use the amount on **line 6 above** to find your tax in the tax table on pages 24–28 of the booklet. Then, enter the tax from the table on this line. — **10** — 1,151.

Refund

Have it directly deposited! See page 20 and fill in 11b, 11c, and 11d.

11a. If line 9 is larger than line 10, subtract line 10 from line 9. This is your **refund.** — **11a** — 350.

  b. Routing number
  c. Type: ☐ Checking ☐ Savings   d. Account number

Amount you owe

12. If line 10 is larger than line 9, subtract line 9 from line 10. This is the **amount you owe.** See page 21 for details on how to pay. — **12**

For Official Use Only   1 2 3 4 5   6 7 8 9 10

I have read this return. Under penalties of perjury, I declare that to the best of my knowledge and belief, the return is true, correct, and accurately lists all amounts and sources of income I received during the tax year.

Sign here ▶

Keep copy for your records.

Your signature: *Roberto J. Flores*

Date: *3/15/20--*   Your occupation: *Mechanic*

Spouse's signature if joint return. See page 11.

Date: Spouse's occupation:

May the IRS discuss this return with the preparer shown on back (see page 21)? ☐ Yes ☐ No

For Disclosure, Privacy Act, and Paperwork Reduction Act Notice, see page 23.   Cat. No. 11329W   20-- **Form 1040EZ**

Step 4: Refund or Amount Owed

If the amount of federal taxes withheld (the amount you already paid) is larger than your total tax obligation (from the tax table), you will receive a refund. If you owe more tax than was withheld, you must pay the difference. Write your check to the United States Treasury and attach it to your return.

When Roberto Flores subtracted his tax liability of $1,151 from his taxes withheld of $1,501, the difference was $350. The amount of tax withheld was greater by $350 than the tax Roberto was required to pay, so he will receive a refund for that amount.

Step 5: Sign the Return

Sign your tax return. Make sure your W-2 form(s) and check (if applicable) are attached to the completed return, and mail the return to the regional IRS office designated for your area.

Form 1040A

Individuals who have less than $50,000 in taxable income can use Form 1040A. With Form 1040A, you also can take deductions for individual retirement account (IRA) contributions and a tax credit for child-care expenses. Married people filing jointly with dependents may choose to file Form 1040A or Form 1040. Figures 7-6A and 7-6B on pages 193–194 show the Forms W-2 for Michael J. and Melissa B. Anderson. Figures 7-7A and 7-7B on pages 195–196 show their joint return using Form 1040A. Follow along on their Form 1040A as you read the instructions below.

Step 1: Name and Address

Write the name, address, and social security number for each person filing the return. Michael and Melissa are filing a joint return, so they entered this information for both of them. If you receive a printed label from the IRS, use the label rather than write the information. Each person filing can elect to give or not give to the Presidential Election Campaign Fund.

Step 2: Filing Status

In this section, you select your tax filing status. You must fill in your spouse's name and social security number if filing separately, names of dependents if head of household, and year spouse died, if filing as a widow(er).

a Control number	22222	Void ☐	For Official Use Only OMB No. 1545-0008		

b Employer identification number 92-186848		1 Wages, tips, other compensation $12,811.40	2 Federal income tax withheld $611.00

c Employer's name, address, and ZIP code

A&W Welding Supply
85 West Bensington Blvd.
Chicago, IL 60615-2358

3 Social security wages $12,811.40	4 Social security tax withheld $794.31
5 Medicare wages and tips $12,811.40	6 Medicare tax withheld $185.77
7 Social security tips	8 Allocated tips

d Employee's social security number 411-86-3214	9 Advance EIC payment	10 Dependent care benefits

e Employee's name (first, middle initial, last)

11 Nonqualified plans	12 Benefits included in box 1
13 See instrs. for box 13	14 Other

Melissa B. Anderson
312 East 34th Street
Chicago, IL 60604-5214

15 Statutory employee ☐	Deceased ☐	Pension plan ☐	Legal rep. ☐	Deferred compensation ☐

f Employee's address and ZIP code

16 State IL	Employer's state I.D. no. 33-261	17 State wages, tips, etc. $12,811.40	18 State income tax $820.00	19 Locality name	20 Local wages, tips, etc.	21 Local income tax

Form **W-2** Wage and Tax Statement **20--**

Department of the Treasury—Internal Revenue Service
For Privacy Act and Paperwork Reduction Act Notice, see separate instructions.

Copy A For Social Security Administration—Send this entire page with Form W-3 to the Social Security Administration; photocopies are **not** acceptable.

Cat. No. 10134D

Do NOT Cut, Fold, or Staple Forms on This Page — Do NOT Cut, Fold, or Staple Forms on This Page

Step 3: Exemptions

In the exemptions section, claim yourself and your spouse if you are filing jointly, and enter the names and social security numbers of your dependents. Total your exemptions.

Step 4: Total Income

Enter wages, salaries, tips, and other income as shown on your Form W-2. The Andersons, filing jointly, entered the total earnings from their two Forms W-2.

You must also report taxable interest and dividend income. If you received over $400 in interest, you must list the name of each payer and the amount in Part I of Schedule 1. (See Figure 7-8, page

Figure 7-6B *Sample W-2 Statements—Joint Return*

a Control number	22222	Void ☐	For Official Use Only OMB No. 1545-0008		

b Employer identification number 91-4813141		1 Wages, tips, other compensation $11,028.60	2 Federal income tax withheld $591.00

c Employer's name, address, and ZIP code A Art Studios 48 East 11th Avenue Des Plaines, IL 60601-3132	3 Social security wages $11,028.60	4 Social security tax withheld $683.77
	5 Medicare wages and tips $11,028.60	6 Medicare tax withheld $159.91
	7 Social security tips	8 Allocated tips

d Employee's social security number 323-40-6128	9 Advance EIC payment	10 Dependent care benefits

e Employee's name (first, middle initial, last)	11 Nonqualified plans	12 Benefits included in box 1
Michael J. Anderson 312 East 34th Street Chicago, Il 60604-5214	13 See instrs. for box 13	14 Other

15 Statutory employee ☐	Deceased ☐	Pension plan ☐	Legal rep. ☐	Deferred compensation ☐

f Employee's address and ZIP code

16 State IL	Employer's state I.D. no. 226421	17 State wages, tips, etc. $11,028.60	18 State income tax $706.00	19 Locality name	20 Local wages, tips, etc.	21 Local income tax

Form **W-2** Wage and Tax Statement **20- -**

Department of the Treasury—Internal Revenue Service

For Privacy Act and Paperwork Reduction Act Notice, see separate instructions.

Copy A For Social Security Administration—Send this entire page with Form W-3 to the Social Security Administration; photocopies are **not** acceptable.

Cat. No. 10134D

Do NOT Cut, Fold, or Staple Forms on This Page — Do NOT Cut, Fold, or Staple Forms on This Page

197.) If you received more than $400 in dividends on your investments, you must list each payer and amount in Part II of Schedule 1. Then transfer the total interest and dividend amounts from Schedule 1 to lines 8a and 9 on Form 1040A. The Andersons did not earn more than $400 in interest or in dividends, so they did not use Schedule 1. However, they still had to report their amounts on Form 1040A.

If you received any tax-exempt interest, you would list it on line 8b, even though you would not have to pay tax on it. The rest of the Income section of Form 1040A requires you to report the taxable amount of any money received from IRAs, pensions, and social security benefits, as well as any unemployment compensation you received. If you received any unemployment compensation during the year, you must attach Form 1099G.

Form **1040A**	Department of the Treasury—Internal Revenue Service		
	U.S. Individual Income Tax Return (99) **20--**	IRS Use Only—Do not write or staple in this space.	

OMB No. 1545-0085

Label
(See page 20.)

Use the IRS label.
Otherwise, please print or type.

L A B E L H E R E	Your first name and initial *Melissa B.*	Last name *Anderson*	Your social security number *411 86 3214*
	If a joint return, spouse's first name and initial *Michael J.*	Last name *Anderson*	Spouse's social security number *323 40 6128*
	Home address (number and street). If you have a P.O. box, see page 21. *312 East 34th Street*	Apt. no.	▲ **Important!** ▲
	City, town or post office, state, and ZIP code. If you have a foreign address, see page 21. *Chicago, IL 60604-5214*		You **must** enter your SSN(s) above.

Presidential Election Campaign (See page 21.) ▶

Note. Checking "Yes" will not change your tax or reduce your refund.
Do you, or your spouse if filing a joint return, want $3 to go to this fund? . . ▶

You ☒ Yes ☐ No   **Spouse** ☒ Yes ☐ No

Filing status

Check only one box.

1 ☐ Single
2 ☒ Married filing joint return (even if only one had income)
3 ☐ Married filing separate return. Enter spouse's social security number above and full name here. ▶ _____
4 ☐ Head of household (with qualifying person). (See page 22.) If the qualifying person is a child but not your dependent, enter this child's name here. ▶ _____
5 ☐ Qualifying widow(er) with dependent child (year spouse died ▶ _____). (See page 23.)

Exemptions

If more than seven dependents, see page 23.

6a ☒ **Yourself.** If your parent (or someone else) can claim you as a dependent on his or her tax return, **do not** check box 6a.

b ☒ **Spouse**

No. of boxes checked on 6a and 6b	2

c **Dependents:**

(1) First name Last name	(2) Dependent's social security number	(3) Dependent's relationship to you	(4) ✓ if qualifying child for child tax credit (see page 24)
Billy Anderson	*316 84 2915*	*Son*	☐
Diane Anderson	*382 38 4814*	*Daughter*	☐
			☐
			☐
			☐
			☐

No. of your children on 6c who:
• lived with you — **2**
• did not live with you due to divorce or separation (see page 25)

Dependents on 6c not entered above

Add numbers entered on lines above	4

d Total number of exemptions claimed.

Income

Attach Form(s) W-2 here. Also attach Form(s) 1099-R if tax was withheld.

If you did not get a W-2, see page 26.

Enclose, but do not attach, any payment.

7	Wages, salaries, tips, etc. Attach Form(s) W-2.	7	*23,840*
8a	**Taxable** interest. Attach Schedule 1 if required.	8a	*284*
b	**Tax-exempt** interest. **Do not** include on line 8a.	8b	*168*
9	Ordinary dividends. Attach Schedule 1 if required.	9	
10	Capital gain distributions (see page 26).	10	
11a	Total IRA distributions. 11a	11b Taxable amount (see page 26). 11b	
12a	Total pensions and annuities. 12a	12b Taxable amount (see page 27). 12b	
13	Unemployment compensation, qualified state tuition program earnings, and Alaska Permanent Fund dividends.	13	
14a	Social security benefits. 14a	14b Taxable amount (see page 29). 14b	
15	Add lines 7 through 14b (far right column). This is your **total income.** ▶	15	*24,292*

Adjusted gross income

16	IRA deduction (see page 31).	16	*2000*
17	Student loan interest deduction (see page 31).	17	*2000*
18	Add lines 16 and 17. These are your **total adjustments.**	18	*4000*
19	Subtract line 18 from line 15. This is your **adjusted gross income.** ▶	19	*20,292*

For Disclosure, Privacy Act, and Paperwork Reduction Act Notice, see page 55.   Cat. No. 11327A   Form **1040A** (20--)

Figure 7-7B *Joint Income Tax Return (continued)*

Form 1040A (20--)   Page **2**

Taxable income	**20**	Enter the amount from line 19.	20	*20292*
	21a	Check if: ☐ **You** were 65 or older ☐ Blind ☐ **Spouse** was 65 or older ☐ Blind **Enter number of boxes checked ▶** 21a ☐		
	b	If you are married filing separately and your spouse itemizes deductions, see page 33 and check here . . . . . . ▶ 21b ☐		
	22	Enter the **standard deduction** for your filing status. **But** see page 33 if you checked any box on line 21a or 21b **or** if someone can claim you as a dependent. • Single—$4,400 • Married filing jointly or Qualifying widow(er)—$7,350 • Head of household—$6,450 • Married filing separately—$3,675	22	*7350*
	23	Subtract line 22 from line 20. If line 22 is more than line 20, enter -0-.	23	*12942*
	24	Multiply $2,800 by the total number of exemptions claimed on line 6d.	24	*11200*
	25	Subtract line 24 from line 23. If line 24 is more than line 23, enter -0-. This is your **taxable income.** ▶	25	*1742*
Tax, credits, and payments	**26**	**Tax** (see page 34).	26	*261*
	27	Credit for child and dependent care expenses. Attach Schedule 2. 27		
	28	Credit for the elderly or the disabled. Attach Schedule 3. 28		
	29	Education credits. Attach Form 8863. 29		
	30	Child tax credit (see page 37). 30		
	31	Adoption credit. Attach Form 8839. 31		
	32	Add lines 27 through 31. These are your **total credits.**	32	
	33	Subtract line 32 from line 26. If line 32 is more than line 26, enter -0-.	33	
	34	Advance earned income credit payments from Form(s) W-2.	34	
	35	Add lines 33 and 34. This is your **total tax.** ▶	35	*261*
	36	Federal income tax withheld from Forms W-2 and 1099. 36 *1202*		
	37	2000 estimated tax payments and amount applied from 1999 return. 37		
If you have a qualifying child, attach Schedule EIC.	**38a**	**Earned income credit (EIC).** 38a		
	b	Nontaxable earned income: amount ▶ and type ▶		
	39	Additional child tax credit. Attach Form 8812. 39		
	40	Add lines 36, 37, 38a, and 39. These are your **total payments.** ▶	40	*1202*
Refund Have it directly deposited! See page 48 and fill in 42b, 42c, and 42d.	**41**	If line 40 is more than line 35, subtract line 35 from line 40. This is the amount you **overpaid.**	41	
	42a	Amount of line 41 you want **refunded to you.**	42a	*941*
	▶ b	Routing number ☐☐☐☐☐☐☐☐☐ **▶ c** Type: ☐ Checking ☐ Savings		
	▶ d	Account number ☐☐☐☐☐☐☐☐☐☐☐☐☐☐☐☐☐		
	43	Amount of line 41 you want **applied to your 2001 estimated tax.** 43		
Amount you owe	**44**	If line 35 is more than line 40, subtract line 40 from line 35. This is the **amount you owe.** For details on how to pay, see page 49.	44	
	45	Estimated tax penalty (see page 49). 45		

Sign here
Joint return? See page 21. Keep a copy for your records.

Under penalties of perjury, I declare that I have examined this return and accompanying schedules and statements, and to the best of my knowledge and belief, they are true, correct, and accurately list all amounts and sources of income I received during the tax year. Declaration of preparer (other than the taxpayer) is based on all information of which the preparer has any knowledge.

Your signature	Date	Your occupation	Daytime phone number
Melissa B. Anderson	*4/15/0X*	*Student/Cashier*	
Spouse's signature. If a joint return, **both** must sign.	Date	Spouse's occupation	May the IRS discuss this return with the preparer shown below (see page 50)? ☐ **Yes** ☐ **No**
Michael J. Anderson	*4/15/0X*	*Student/Clerk*	

Paid preparer's use only

Preparer's signature ▶	Date	Check if self-employed ☐	Preparer's SSN or PTIN
Firm's name (or yours if self-employed), address, and ZIP code ▶		EIN	
		Phone no. ( )	

Form **1040A** (20--)

Schedule 1
(Form 1040A)

Department of the Treasury—Internal Revenue Service

Interest and Ordinary Dividends
for Form 1040A Filers   (99)   **20--**

OMB No. 1545-0085

Name(s) shown on Form 1040A

Your social security number

Part I

Interest

(See page 62 and the instructions for Form 1040A, line 8a.)

Note. If you received a Form 1099-INT, Form 1099-OID, or substitute statement from a brokerage firm, enter the firm's name and the total interest shown on that form.

1 List name of payer. If any interest is from a seller-financed mortgage and the buyer used the property as a personal residence, see page 62 and list this interest first. Also, show that buyer's social security number and address.

Amount

	1	

2 Add the amounts on line 1.   2

3 Excludable interest on series EE and I U.S. savings bonds issued after 1989 from Form 8815, line 14. You **must** attach Form 8815.   3

4 Subtract line 3 from line 2. Enter the result here and on Form 1040A, line 8a.   4

Part II

Ordinary dividends

(See page 62 and the instructions for Form 1040A, line 9.)

Note. If you received a Form 1099-DIV or substitute statement from a brokerage firm, enter the firm's name and the ordinary dividends shown on that form.

5 List name of payer. Include only ordinary dividends. If you received any capital gain distributions, see the instructions for Form 1040A, line 10.

Amount

	5	

6 Add the amounts on line 5. Enter the total here and on Form 1040A, line 9.   6

For Paperwork Reduction Act Notice, see Form 1040A instructions.   Cat. No. 12075R   Schedule 1 (Form 1040A) 20--

After listing income received from all sources, you would add them up to determine total income for line 15 of Form 1040A.

Step 5: Adjusted Gross Income

You can deduct contributions to an Individual Retirement Account (IRA). All employed workers who earn at least $2,000 can contribute up to $2,000 to an IRA, if they qualify. Rules for eligibility are explained in the guide for preparing taxes. If both taxpayers are eligible, IRA deductions are entered and totaled, as the Andersons have done in Figure 7-7A. You would then subtract the total from gross income to determine your adjusted gross income (line 19).

Step 6: Taxable Income

Next you would compute your taxable income, as shown in Figure 7-7B. First, copy your adjusted gross income from the bottom of the first page of the form to the top of the second page. Then check if you or your spouse is 65 or older or blind, if you are claimed as a dependent by another taxpayer, or if you are married filing separately. Then enter the standard deduction stated on your form for your filing status. In Figure 7-7B, the Andersons entered $7,350 because they are married filing jointly.

Subtract the standard deduction from adjusted gross income. Then multiply the number of exemptions claimed by the amount allowed for each exemption (at this writing, the exemption amount is $2,800). On the first page of their form, the Andersons had claimed 4 exemptions, so they multiplied $2,800 by 4 to arrive at their $11,200 deduction. Subtract the result from adjusted gross income to determine taxable income.

Step 7: Tax, Credits, and Payments

For this section of Form 1040A, find your tax by looking up your taxable income in the tax table in your instruction booklet. Appendix B shows a recent tax table for use with Form 1040A. The Andersons had a taxable income of $1,742. In Appendix B, this income falls in the range $1,725–$1,750. Reading across the row to the column marked "Married filing jointly," they found that their tax was $261. They entered this number in line 26 of their form.

In this section of the form, you may claim any credit due for child-care expenses. You would complete Schedule 2, Part 1, to determine the amount of the credit, and subtract it from the tax liability. (Note that a tax credit directly reduces taxes.) Then subtract your credits to determine your total tax liability for line 35.

Finally, enter the amount of federal income tax withheld, as shown on your W-2 form, which you will attach to the tax return. For the Andersons, the amount withheld was the total of the federal withholdings listed on their two Forms W-2. Their total was $1,202. If you qualify for the earned income credit (EIC), you would enter it as if it were taxes withheld.

Step 8: Refund or Amount Owed

If the amount withheld plus credits exceeds the tax liability, the difference is your refund. But if you have more tax liability than the amount withheld or computed as a credit, you owe taxes. You must attach a check for the amount owed.

Step 9: Signature

In this section, taxpayer and spouse must both sign and date a joint return even though only one may have earned or received income. Anyone who was paid to prepare your tax return for you also must sign and date the return.

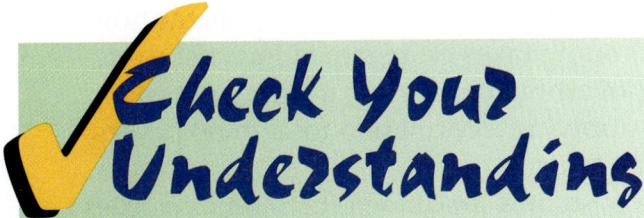

Check Your Understanding

Review Terms
1. exemption
2. gross income
3. child support
4. alimony
5. adjusted gross income
6. deductions
7. itemize
8. standard deduction
9. taxable income

Review Concepts
1. Who is eligible to use Form 1040EZ to file their income taxes?
2. Who is eligible to use Form 1040A to file their income taxes?
3. Who is required to use Form 1040 (the long form) to file their income taxes?

Chapter Review

Summary

7.1 Our Tax System

- The government collects money, or revenue, from citizens and businesses to spend as specified by Congress.
- Progressive taxes take a larger share as income grows; regressive taxes take a smaller share as income grows; and proportional or flat taxes take the same percentage regardless of the amount on which the tax is imposed.
- Income taxes were levied starting in the mid-1800s to finance war. The 16th Amendment to the Constitution authorizes continuing taxes on personal income.
- The IRS is the governmental agency in charge of collecting taxes and supplying information to help taxpayers prepare their tax returns.
- The income tax system is graduated. Different tax rates apply to different income ranges or tax brackets.

7.2 Filing Tax Returns

- Gross income consists of all taxable income received, including wages, salaries, tips, interest, dividends, unemployment compensation, social security benefits, and alimony.
- To determine taxable income, subtract adjustments, deductions, and exemptions from gross income.
- File the short form, 1040EZ, if your income is less than $50,000, and you have no dependents.
- File Form 1040A if you do not have enough deductions to itemize and have less than $50,000 income.
- If the amount withheld from your paychecks exceeds your total tax, you will receive a refund. If the amount withheld is less than your total tax, you must pay the difference when you file your tax return.

Review Terms

Directions: Can you find the definition for each of the following terms used in Chapter 7?

adjusted gross income
alimony
audit
child support
deductions
exemption
gross income
itemize
progressive taxes
proportional taxes
regressive taxes

revenue
standard deduction
tax brackets
tax evasion
taxable income

1. Money collected by the government through taxes.
2. Taxes that take a larger share of income as the amount of income grows.
3. Taxes for which the rate stays the same regardless of the amount on which the tax is imposed; also called flat taxes.
4. Taxes that take a smaller share of income as the amount of income grows.
5. Stated amount taxpayers may subtract from adjusted gross income instead of itemizing their deductions.
6. Income ranges to which different tax rates apply.
7. Willful failure to pay taxes.
8. The process of listing allowable deductions on a tax return.
9. An amount taxpayers may subtract from their income for each person who depends on their income to live.
10. All the taxable income received during the year, including wages, tips, salaries, interest, dividends, alimony, and unemployment compensation.
11. Gross income minus allowed adjustments.
12. Money paid to a former spouse to support dependent children.
13. Money paid to support a former spouse.
14. Expenses the law allows taxpayers to subtract from their adjusted gross income to determine their taxable income.
15. Income on which you will pay tax.
16. An examination of a tax return by the IRS.

1. What is the United States government's largest source of revenue?
2. Describe the three basic types of taxes.
3. List five other taxes providing government revenue besides income taxes.
4. What is the purpose of the IRS?
5. List at least five services the government provides for all citizens from taxes collected.
6. When was the first permanent income tax ratified?
7. List three services provided by the IRS.
8. Who has the ability to levy taxes on the citizens of the United States?
9. What is meant by a tax system based on voluntary compliance?
10. What can happen to you if you deliberately do not file your tax return and pay taxes due?
11. List five types of income that are taxable.
12. How is child support different from alimony in terms of taxation?
13. Explain the standard deduction and when you should itemize.
14. When must you file your federal income tax return? Why?
15. What should you do if you discover an error after you have filed your tax return?
16. If you file electronically, how do you pay the tax you owe?
17. Under what circumstances would you file the long Form 1040 tax return?
18. Why should you file your tax return early when you expect a refund?
19. If you check the "Yes" box on your return to contribute to the Presidential Election Campaign Fund, does it increase your taxes by $3?

1. Explain the need for taxes in this country. How does everyone benefit from taxes?
2. Summarize how taxing income came about in this country. Do you think that the time will ever come when taxation will no longer be needed? Explain.
3. Explain how new federal taxes are imposed.
4. How does your filing status affect the amount of taxes you will pay?
5. How does the number of exemptions claimed affect the amount of taxes you will pay?
6. What are deductible expenses?
7. Use your browser to search the Internet for a tax calculator. Some calculators figure the income taxes you would pay if our country had a flat tax. Others calculate taxes based on today's system and rates. If you have a job, enter numbers based on your earnings. Estimate any numbers you don't have. Then enter different income levels to see how the tax changes as income rises.
8. When should you use Form 1040EZ? 1040A?
9. What must you do if you are married and wish to deduct charitable contributions on your tax return?
10. Visit www.irs.gov, follow the link to forms and publications, and download this year's Form 1040EZ. Fill out the form using estimates if you don't know the real numbers for yourself. Use the tax tables in Appendix A to find your tax obligation based on your estimates.
11. Many people believe that someday we will all file our income taxes electronically. Go to the IRS Tax Interactive site at www.irs.gov/taxi/ and find out how to file taxes electronically. Write a one-page paper describing the process.

1. Acquire a copy of Form 1040EZ. Prepare a tax return for Tomeka Hunt. Use Appendix A tax tables and the following information:

>Tomeka M. Hunt (social security number 541-33-9892)
>54 Center Street
>San Francisco, CA 96214-3627

Tomeka is a part-time engineer. She wants $3 to go to the Presidential Election Campaign Fund. She is single and claims only herself as an exemption. Tomeka's salary is $28,200, plus interest of $155. No one else claims her as a dependent, and she had $3,660 in federal taxes withheld.

2. Using Figure 7-8, Form 1040A, and the tax tables in Appendix B, calculate the tax liability of Mack R. Rueoff, an auto mechanic. Mack's gross income is $24,000. He has a $2,000 IRA deduction, claims the standard deduction, and had $2,280 in federal taxes withheld. He is single and is entitled to one exemption. Based on this information and Appendix B tax tables, how much does Mack owe, or how much is his refund?

3. Using Figure 7-8, Form 1040A, and the tax tables (Appendix B), calculate the tax liability of Yi Chang, a part-time teacher. Yi's wages totaled $16,201; interest income, $190; tax-exempt interest, $200. He has an IRA contribution of $500, claims the standard deduction, and had $1,656 in federal taxes withheld from his wages. He is single and is entitled to one exemption. How much does Yi owe in taxes, or how much is his refund?

4. Acquire a copy of Form 1040A and Schedule 1 to prepare a joint tax return for Mell and Janis Saperstein.

>Mell K. and Janis B. Saperstein
>(SS#s 895-10-9008, 485-01-9089)
>2450 West 18th Avenue
>Dallas, TX 75201-7242

Mell is a construction worker, and Janis is a preschool teacher. They both want to contribute $3 to the Presidential Election Campaign Fund. Married, filing jointly, Mell and Janis have one dependent child, Mark J. Saperstein, who is age 17 and lives with them. Mark's social security number is 354-58-6102. They each contributed $2,000 to IRAs. Mell's and Janis's combined incomes totaled $38,400 (Janis's is $18,400). They had a total federal tax of $3,672 withheld. Mell and Janis had interest income of $1,400: First National Bank, $300; interest on a private loan to J. Smith, $600; certificate of deposit at State Savings & Loan, $500. Tax-exempt interest income was $400. Dividend income amounted to $1,100: $411 from CDK stock, $621 from Investors' Mutual Fund, Inc., and $68 from I.P.Q. Manufacturing Co. Use Appendix B tax tables.

For related activities and links, point your browser to
www.mypf.swep.com

Chapter 8

Budgets and Financial Records

Up Front

Ahmad has a part-time job, attends school six hours a day, and participates in two after-school sports. He no longer receives a monthly allowance from his parents. He pays for all of his own clothes, gas, insurance, and entertainment. Last year, he was able to save over $600.

"How do you do it?" asked Carrie. "I work more hours than you do, my parents pay for my clothes and most of my expenses, and I still don't have any money left over for entertainment. I didn't save a dime last year!"

"I have a budget," said Ahmad. "Every time I get paid, I put aside money for savings. I know how much I spend on everything I buy. Keeping a good record of income and expenses helps me plan better, so I don't run out of money. That doesn't mean I buy anything I want, but it does mean that I know how much I can spend, so I can stretch my money to cover as many things as possible."

Budgeting and Record Keeping

Goals

★ Describe the budgeting process and prepare personal budgets.

★ Explain the purpose of record keeping and be able to prepare a personal net worth statement and a personal property inventory.

Importance of Financial Planning

Do you have unlimited resources to buy all the things you want? Some people do, but if you are like most Americans, to achieve financial success you will have to plan and work for it. Budgeting and maintaining financial records are a significant part of financial planning, and they provide the road map to financial security. Budgeting is the first step.

Your **disposable income** is the money you have left to spend or save after taxes have been paid. In order to use this income to your best advantage, you need to create a financial plan.

All the money you receive is spent, saved, or invested. You may spend it for things you need or want, save it for future needs, or invest it to earn more money. A **financial plan** is an orderly program for spending, saving, and investing the money you earn. Financial planning helps you do the following:

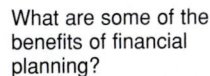

What are some of the benefits of financial planning?

1. Determine and evaluate your options for using your money.
2. Make sure you use your limited funds for the things you want most.
3. Prevent careless and wasteful spending.
4. Organize your *financial resources* (sources of income) so that you can maintain a plan of personal financial fitness.
5. Avoid money worries by planning your saving, spending, and borrowing to stay within your financial means.

Preparing a Budget

The first step in attaining financial fitness is to plan. A **budget** is a spending and saving plan based on your expected income and expenses. In a budget, money coming in (earnings plus borrowing) must equal money going out (spending plus saving). The budget must balance. A budget helps you plan your spending and saving so that you won't have to borrow money to meet your daily needs.

Figure 8-1 shows a high school student's budget for one month. This student expects to receive a total of $380, and plans to use the money for certain needs and wants and to save part of it as well. Notice that the total income equals the total of expenses plus savings. The budget balances.

Steps in Preparing a Budget

Preparing a budget can be done in a series of steps:

1. Estimate total expected income for a certain time period. Include all money you expect to receive. You may wish to

Figure 8-1   *Simple Budget*

BUDGET FOR SEPTEMBER

Income

Work (part-time)	$320.00
Allowances for household chores	20.00
Lunch money	40.00
Total income	**$380.00**

Expenses

Daily lunches	$ 80.00
Supplies	20.00
Snacks	40.00
Entertainment (movies and golfing)	140.00
Total expenses	**$280.00**

Savings

To Columbia County Credit Union	$100.00
Total expenses plus savings	**$380.00**

use a weekly, biweekly, or monthly budget, whichever best matches how often you expect to receive money.

2. Decide how much of your income you want to save—to set aside for future needs. Most financial experts advise saving at least 10 percent of your disposable income each pay period. By saving at least this amount, you will have money to pay for future needs, both expected and unexpected.

3. Estimate your expenses, or money you will need for day-to-day purchases—for example, lunches, fees, personal care items, and clothing.

4. Balance your budget. If your expenses plus savings exceed your income, you must adjust your plan to make them match. You can't spend or save money you don't have. You may have to delay buying some items you want but don't need. Or, you may decide to save a little less this month. If you don't want to do either of these options, you'll have to find a way to bring in more money.

A Typical Monthly Budget

Figure 8-2 (page 210) shows the monthly budget of Mike and Jennifer Harris. Mike and Jennifer have no children, and both are working. The Harrises estimated their expected income by adding together their two take-home incomes (paychecks), along with anticipated interest on savings and earnings on investments. They would like to save at least 10 percent every month, setting aside money for emergency savings, short-term savings, and long-term investments as shown.

Would vacation costs be considered fixed or variable expenses? Explain your answer.

Fixed expenses are costs you are obligated to pay at specific times, regardless of other events. You cannot change them without making a major revision in your lifestyle. For example, you must pay your rent or

Figure 8-2 — Monthly and Yearly Budget for a Married Couple

BUDGET — Mike and Jennifer Harris

	Monthly	Yearly
Income		
Salary (Mike) after taxes	$ 1,600	$19,200
Salary (Jennifer) after taxes	1,800	21,600
Interest on savings	50	600
Earnings on investments	50	600
Total income	$ 3,500	$42,000
Expenses		
Fixed expenses:		
Rent	$ 1,000	$12,000
Utilities	150	1,800
Car payment	300	3,600
Insurance:		
Car	100	1,200
Life and Health	75	900
Total fixed expenses	$ 1,625	$19,500
Variable expenses:		
Telephone	$ 45	$ 540
Gasoline	150	1,800
Car repairs and maintenance	60	720
Cable television	40	480
Groceries	400	4,800
Clothing	200	2,400
Personal care:		
Dry cleaning, household	50	600
Drugs, cosmetics	50	600
Insurance deductibles and co-pays	50	600
Recreation and entertainment	100	1,200
Gifts, donations, miscellaneous	300	3,600
Total variable expenses	$ 1,445	$17,340
Total fixed and variable expenses	$ 3,070	$36,840
Cash surplus (total income minus total expenses)	$ 430	$ 5,160
Allocation of cash surplus:		
Emergency savings fund	$ 100	$ 1,200
Short-term savings	100	1,200
Long-term investments	230	2,760
Total savings and investments	$ 430	$ 5,160
Total expenses plus savings	$ 3,500	$42,000

mortgage, utility bills, car loan, and insurance premiums when they are due, no matter what else is going on in your life. Most financial experts recommend that a family have no more than 50 to 60 percent of take-home pay set aside for fixed expenses. However, this standard is difficult to achieve for young people just starting life on their own. But with time, pay raises, and careful budgeting, a family can achieve that goal.

Variable expenses are costs that vary in amount and type, depending on events and the choices you make. For example, your grocery bill can be larger or smaller, depending on what you choose to buy. Other examples of variable expenses are costs for eating out, going to movies, and buying clothes.

NET NOTES

The Budget Resource Center is a place to find free tips and valuable information on how to budget for yourself and your household. The Web site provides downloadable budgeting kits plus a Budgeting Guide, which has facts and answers to help you secure your financial future. A free e-mail-based budgeting course is also offered. Once a day for four days you'll receive an e-mail with helpful money-saving budgeting techniques. Check out this Web site at www.budgetresource.com.

What are the different kinds of financial records you should keep?

Personal Records

Good personal record keeping makes budgeting and long-range planning easier. Your records also form the basis for completing income tax returns, credit applications, and other financial forms. You should keep four types of personal records: income and expense records, a statement of net worth, a personal property inventory, and tax records. Many people keep financial records on their computer, usually password-protected. As with any important files you keep electronically, always keep a current backup of your financial records.

Records of Income and Expenses

Your W-2 forms show the money earned and deductions taken from your paycheck during the year. The W-2 forms also state the amount of taxes and social security tax withheld. You may need the W-2 forms later when you want to collect benefits. Other records of income include statements from banks showing interest earned on savings and statements from investment companies listing dividends earned from stock or other investments. Expense items include receipts listing charitable contributions, medical bills, or work-related expenses. When you prepare your budgets and tax returns, these receipts and statements serve as documentation (proof) of income and expenses. Store these documents in a safe place for future reference.

Statement of Net Worth

A *net worth statement,* such as that shown in Figure 8-3, is a list of items of value that a person owns, called **assets**; amounts of money owed to others, called **liabilities** or debts; and the difference between the two, known as **net worth**. If your assets are greater than your liabilities, you are said to be *solvent,* or in a favorable financial position. But if your liabilities are greater than your assets (you owe more than you own), you are said to be *insolvent,* or in a poor financial position.

You will need your net worth information (lists of assets and liabilities) when you ask for a loan or apply for credit. The bank or other financial institution will want you to be solvent and a good risk who will likely pay back the loan. It also helps you keep track of how you spend your money and what you have to show for it at the end of the year.

NET WORTH STATEMENT
Nygen Phomn
January 1, 20--

ASSETS		LIABILITIES	
Checking account	$ 500	Loan on car	$1,800
Savings account	800	Loan from mother	100
Car value	3,000		
Personal property:		Total liabilities	$1,900
(inventory attached)	5,000		
		NET WORTH	
Total assets	$9,300		
		Assets minus liabilities	$7,400
		Total	$9,300

Personal Property Inventory

A personal property inventory, such as the one shown in Figure 8-4 on page 214, is a list of all valuable items you own, along with their purchase prices and approximate current values. Personal property includes anything of value inside your home—clothing, furniture, appliances, and so forth. A personal property inventory is especially useful in the event of fire, theft, or property damage. The inventory will help you list your lost items and their value when you make an insurance claim. As a further safeguard, photograph items of value, attach the photographs to the inventory, and keep this information in a safe deposit box or other secure place to use as evidence in the event the property is damaged, lost, or stolen. A personal property inventory also helps you see what you have to show for the money you have spent. Reviewing it will help you assess your spending patterns. As you buy new items and dispose of others, revise the inventory.

Tax Records

All taxpayers should keep copies of their tax returns, W-2 forms, and other receipts verifying income and expenses listed on tax returns for three years after the tax return is filed. For good planning purposes, tax returns should be kept much longer, along with W-2 forms and other important documentation. Information used

Figure 8-4   *Personal Property Inventory*

PERSONAL PROPERTY INVENTORY
Nygen Phomn
January 2, 20--

Item	Year Purchased	Purchase Price	Approximate Current Value
Sphinx XTL DVD Player with big-screen TV	2001	$3,200	$1,300
Bedroom furniture (bed, dresser, lamp, clock)	1999	2,000	1,200
Clothing, jewelry	-----	3,000	500
MBD motor bike	1998	1,800	1,000
CD collection, digital camera, scanner, CD burner	1999	2,000	1,000
		$12,000	$5,000

in preparing tax returns should be kept in a safe place in the event of an audit. The IRS has the legal right to audit your tax returns and supporting records for three years from the date of filing the return (longer if fraud or intentional wrongdoing on your part can be proved).

Check Your Understanding

Review Terms
1. disposable income
2. financial plan
3. budget
4. fixed expenses
5. variable expenses
6. assets
7. liabilities
8. net worth

Review Concepts
1. What is the first step in budgeting?
2. How are fixed expenses different from variable expenses?
3. Why would you prepare a personal statement of net worth?

Legal Documents and Filing Systems

Goals

★ Explain the elements of legal contracts and negotiable instruments and describe your rights and responsibilities.

★ Discuss ways to set up a filing system for personal records.

Contracts and Agreements

A **contract** is a legally enforceable agreement between two or more parties to do or not to do something. We all have many transactions in our daily lives that can be properly classified as contracts or lawful agreements. Contracts are part of personal business situations even though they may not be consciously acknowledged. If you buy a suit and you want it altered, the clerk fills out a ticket. The ticket lists the changes requested and the promised date of completion. This ticket is a contract between you and the store. The store agrees to make the alterations by the stated date and for the stated price, and you agree to pay the price.

Other common legal agreements are credit plans, mortgages, and rental agreements. When you sign up for a retail credit plan, the store agrees to give you products now in exchange for your regular payments over time. When you rent an apartment, the landlord agrees to let you live in the apartment, and you agree to pay the rent by a certain day each month. Each of these cases constitutes an express agreement between two or more people. *Express agreements* can be oral or written; what makes them *express* is that the terms have been agreed upon between the parties in words.

Figure 8-5 (page 216) shows a credit application from a retail store. A credit application asks you to agree to certain conditions before opening an account. Attached to the application will be an explanation of finance charges and how they are computed. You will sign the application to show that you understand the finance charges and agree to pay them if your balance is not paid in full each month. Be sure you have read everything contained in the agreement before you sign it. If something is not clear, ask for an explanation so you can understand your rights and responsibilities before you enter into the contract.

Figure 8-5 *Credit Application*

CREDIT CARD APPLICATION
(Please print. Not valid unless signed below.)

Title (optional): Mr. ☒ Mrs. ☐ Ms. ☐ Other _____

First Name __Richard__ MI __J__ Last Name __Washington__

Street Address __45 Cleveland Avenue__ Apt. # _____

City __Portland__ State __OR__ Zip + 4 __97201-1072__

Home Phone __(513)555-0181__ Business Phone __(513)555-9213__ E-Mail _____

Soc. Sec. # __482-51-9384__ Est. Monthly Charges __$100.00__ # Cards Desired __1__

Former Address __-----__
(if less than 1 year at current address)

City _____ State _____ Zip + 4 _____

Mother's Maiden Name __Hawkins__ Years Employed __3__ Position __Payroll specialist__

Present Housing: Own ☐ Rent ☒ Live with Parents ☐

# of Dependents (exc. self) __1__ Student? Full ☒ Part ☐

Note: An applicant, though married, may apply for a separate Account in his or her own name. If your spouse will use this Account, please indicate his or her name, and social security number for credit reporting purposes.

First Name of Spouse __----__ MI ____ Last _____ Soc. Sec. # _____

I HAVE READ AND AGREE TO BE BOUND BY THE TERMS OF THIS APPLICATION (INCLUDING THE ADDITIONAL APPLICATION PROVISIONS AND ACCOMPANYING FEDERAL AND STATE NOTICES AND SUMMARY OF CREDIT TERMS PRINTED TO THE RIGHT AND BACK).

I understand and agree that if I am approved for an Account, (i) the Central Credit Bank, N.A., Retail Installment Credit Agreement (the "Agreement") that I will receive with my credit card, will govern my Account, (ii) the Agreement is incorporated by reference into and made a part of the Application, and (iii) THE AGREEMENT INCLUDES AN ARBITRATION PROVISION THAT MAY SUBSTANTIALLY LIMIT MY RIGHTS IN THE EVENT OF A DISPUTE, INCLUDING MY RIGHT TO LITIGATE IN COURT OR HAVE A JURY TRIAL, DISCOVERY AND APPEAL RIGHTS, AND THE RIGHT TO PARTICIPATE AS A REPRESENTATIVE OR MEMBER OF A CLASS IN A CLASS ACTION. I MAY REQUEST THE COMMERCIAL ARBITRATION RULES OF THE AMERICAN ARBITRATION ASSOCIATION, WHICH SERVES AS ARBITRATION ADMINISTRATOR, BY CALLING 1-800-555-0155. I understand and agree that the Bank will first consider this application with respect to the credit card program described in this application. If for any reason, at the Bank's sole discretion, I do not qualify for this program, I request the Bank consider this application with respect to alternative credit card programs. My signature on this Application represents my signature on the Agreement.

NOTICE TO THE APPLICANT: (1) DO NOT SIGN THIS APPLICATION/AGREEMENT BEFORE YOU READ IT OR IF IT CONTAINS ANY BLANK SPACES. (2) YOU ARE ENTITLED TO A COMPLETELY FILLED IN COPY OF THE RETAIL INSTALLMENT CREDIT AGREEMENT

X *Richard J. Washington* 3/11/- -
Signature of Card Applicant Date

In addition to written agreements, you take part in many unwritten agreements. When you ride a bicycle or rent a video, you have made an *implied agreement*. Whether you realize it or not, you have agreed to certain things by riding on public streets or renting the video. For example, when you ride your bicycle, you agree to obey traffic laws, ride in a safe and responsible manner, and observe the rights of other riders, pedestrians, and cars around you. A violation of one of these unwritten agreements can result in a traffic ticket and fine.

Elements of an Enforceable Contract

To accomplish its purpose, a contract must be binding on all who enter into it. Some contracts must be in writing and signed by everyone involved in order to be legally binding. Examples of contracts that must be written are contracts for the sale of real property (homes and land), contracts that cannot be fully performed in less than a year, contracts involving $500 and over, and contracts in which one person agrees to pay the debts of another.

To be legally binding, enforceable agreements, contracts must have all of the following elements:

1. Agreement
2. Consideration
3. Contractual capacity
4. Legality
5. Genuine assent
6. Legal form

Agreement

A contract has **mutual assent** when an offer is made and accepted. In order to prove mutual assent, two conditions are required by law: a valid offer and an acceptance of that exact offer. One person makes the offer; another person accepts it. When one person makes an offer and another person changes any part of it, the second person is making what is known as a *counteroffer*. The counteroffer is a new offer and has to be accepted or rejected by the first person.

Consideration

The **consideration** is anything of value exchanged as part of a contract. Consideration may be in the form of an object of value, money, a promise, or a performed service. If one person is to receive something but gives nothing in return, the contract may

How does the element of consideration come into play when a person buys a house?

not be enforceable. The idea behind consideration is that each party to the agreement receives something of value. When you buy a pair of shoes, you get the shoes and the store gets your money. The shoes and the money are items of consideration.

Contractual Capacity

Contractual capacity refers to the competence (legal ability) of the parties to enter a contract. *Competent parties* are people who are legally capable of giving binding assent. Those who are unable to protect themselves because of mental deficiency or illness, or who are otherwise incapable of understanding the consequences of their actions, cannot be held to contracts. Minors have limited contractual capacity, which means that they may legally set aside contractual obligations. This privilege is allowed in order to protect minors from those who would take advantage of them. Married people under age 18 are considered competent to enter into agreements. All people 18 or older are considered legally competent to enter into a contract unless they are declared incompetent by a court.

Legality

To be legally enforceable, a contract must be lawful. A court will not require a person to perform an agreed-upon act if it is illegal. Without a lawful objective, the agreement has no binding effect on a person.

PERSONAL PERSPECTIVE

Minors and the Law

A minor is a person under the age of legal adulthood. In most states, a person is legally an adult at age 18. When you turn 18, you take on all the rights and responsibilities of an adult (except some privileges that are reserved for age 21).

One way you can obtain full capacity to enter into binding agreements before you reach age 18 is to become emancipated. Being *emancipated* means that you are legally responsible for yourself. In most states, you can apply to be legally emancipated if you are employed and have the maturity and the means to support yourself. In other states, you cannot be emancipated prior to age 18 without permission from your parents. Emancipation is a serious undertaking. Once you are independent, you are not entitled to receive financial support or other benefits, such as health insurance coverage, from your parents.

When you are emancipated, you have the right to make your own decisions, and you also must accept full responsibility for the consequences of your actions. For example, if you commit a crime as an emancipated youth, you will face penalties that are appropriate for an adult. When you commit a crime as a minor, the juvenile justice system is designed to reform rather than to punish. In many states, you can have your juvenile record cleared or sealed after you become an adult.

Finally, once you are emancipated, you cannot reclaim your minority status. You will remain responsible for all future actions, contracts, and obligations.

Think Critically

1. What are some advantages of becoming emancipated?
2. What are some disadvantages of emancipation?
3. What is the age of adulthood in your state? What rights are you given when you reach that age? Are some privileges deferred until later?

Genuine Assent

It is possible for a contract to be unenforceable, even though two parties with full legal capacity have entered into the agreement for a legal purpose and even though it is supported by consideration. This occurs when there is no genuine assent because there is misrepresentation, a mistake, duress, or undue influence.

Misrepresentation is also called *fraud* and contains four elements: (1) misrepresentation of a material fact with (2) the intention to deceive; (3) the innocent party has justifiably relied on this misrepresented fact and (4) has been injured (damaged) as a result. *Duress* is the use of force or fear to make a person enter into a contract. *Undue influence* arises from special relationships (such as guardianship) in which one party's free will is overcome by the other.

Legal Form

State laws provide that contracts must contain the necessary information to be enforceable. The contract may be a printed form, drawn up by attorneys, or it may be in some other readable and understandable form. It must state the date, duration of contract, people involved, consideration, terms of agreement, and other necessary information to explain the purpose of the contract and the intentions of the people entering into it. In some cases the contract must be recorded. When a contract is recorded, it is made a public record, and a photocopy is stored by the county recorder. Before a document can be recorded, it must meet specific requirements that are set out by state law.

Valid, Void, and Voidable Contracts

Contracts must be enforced for an economic system to operate efficiently. Both consumers and businesses benefit from contract enforcement. Without it, dishonest consumers or business owners could refuse to honor their agreements, and our daily business activities would be disrupted. Contracts can generally be classified as valid, void, and voidable.

Valid Contracts

Valid contracts are those that contain all of the essential elements: mutual assent, consideration, competent parties, lawful objective, genuine assent, and legal form. They are legally enforceable. A valid contract sometimes becomes an unenforceable contract because the time limit for filing suit to enforce it has passed.

Void Contracts

Void contracts are those that are missing one or more of the essential elements. These contracts are null and void, and are not enforceable in court. An example of a void contract is one that will require doing something illegal. If you enter into an agreement and later learn that you will be doing something against the law, you cannot be forced to fulfill your part of the contract.

Voidable Contracts

A voidable contract is a contract that can legally be avoided by one of the parties. If that party chooses avoidance, or disaffirms the agreement, it will not be enforced. An example of a voidable contract is the purchase of an automobile on credit by a minor. The minor may disaffirm the contract because contracts with minors do not meet the competent-party test of a legally binding contract. However, if the minor continues to make payments on the contract after reaching age 18, he or she has ratified the agreement (has made that contract valid) and is legally responsible for fulfilling the terms of the contract.

Consumer Responsibilities in Agreements

As a consumer, you have the following responsibilities regarding the contracts and agreements you enter into:

1. Understand all clauses and terms contained in the agreement. Do not sign it until you have read it. Your signature acknowledges that you have read and understood the contract.
2. Keep a copy of the agreement. Put it in a safe place for future use.
3. Be sure the agreement is dated correctly.
4. Be sure all blank spaces are filled in or marked out and that no changes have been made after you have signed it. Your initials at the bottom of each page will prevent substitution of pages.
5. Be sure all terms agreed upon are written clearly. Because interpretation may vary, vague phrases are often not enforceable.
6. Be sure all dates, amounts, and other numbers are correct and written clearly.
7. Be sure proper disclosure is made by the seller. The buyer is entitled to proper and complete information about the

rate of interest, total finance charges, cash payment price, and so on.

8. Be sure all cancellations and adjustments are made in accordance with the contract.

Although consumers are protected by numerous consumer protection laws, occasionally you may need legal services. But your best protection is to guard yourself in advance by understanding the agreements you enter into.

Negotiable Instruments

The word "negotiable" means legally collectible. A **negotiable instrument** is an unconditional written promise to pay a specified sum of money upon demand of the holder. The negotiable instruments most people are likely to use are checks (discussed in Chapter 9) and, to a lesser extent, promissory notes. A negotiable instrument is legally collectible if the following conditions are met:

1. It must be in writing (not oral) and signed by the maker.
2. It must contain an unconditional promise to pay a definite amount of money.
3. It must be payable on demand or on a fixed or determinable future date.
4. It must be payable to the order of a particular person or to the holder of the note.
5. It must be delivered to the payee.

If any one of the above conditions is missing, the document is not a negotiable instrument. It is no longer legally collectible.

A promissory note, such as the one shown in Figure 8-6, is a written promise to pay a certain sum of money to another person or to the holder of the note on a specified date. A promissory note is a legal document, and payment can be enforced by law.

The person who creates and signs the promissory note and agrees to pay it on a certain date is called the *maker*. The person to whom the note is made payable is known as the *payee*. A promissory note is normally used when borrowing a large sum of money from a financial institution.

In some cases creditors (those extending credit) will require a co-signer with a good credit rating as additional security for repayment of a note. A **co-signer** is a person who promises to pay the note if the maker fails to pay. The co-signer's signature is also on a note. Young people and people who have not established a credit

PROMISSORY NOTE

$ __400.00__   January 15_____ , 20 _-_-

I (we) __Marilyn Huykamp_____ , jointly and severally,
do agree and promise to pay to __Emerald Furniture Co.___
the sum of ___Four hundred and 00/100_____ dollars
with interest at the rate of __9%__ from __January 15, 20--__ , payable in
monthly installments of $ 69.67 beginning __February 1_____ , 20 _-_-
and on a like day each month until paid in full, the last payment
due ___July 1_____ , 20 _-_-_ . Said payment shall include interest.
In the event of default, the maker hereof agrees to pay attorneys' fees and
court costs in collection of this note.

Marilyn Huykamp
Maker

rating are often asked to provide a co-signer for their first loan. If
someone asks you to co-sign a loan, do so only if you are sure the
person is financially responsible. If that person fails to repay the
debt, you would be legally responsible to repay it.

Warranties

A **warranty**, also called a guarantee, is a statement about a product's qualities or performance that the seller assures the buyer are
true. If the product fails to live up to the standards specified, the
warranty usually states what the seller will do as a remedy, such
as return the purchase price or repair the product at no extra
charge. The warranty may be in writing or assumed to exist by the
nature of the product. However, a warranty is not a safeguard
against a consumer's poor buying decision.

All products contain implied warranties, and some also have
written guarantees stating responsibilities that the manufacturer
agrees to. For example, all products carry the warranty of mer-
chantability. This means that a product is supposed to do what it is
made to do, whether or not standards are stated in writing. For
example, a tennis ball must bounce. If it does not bounce, you can
return the defective ball, even if there is no written warranty.

Specific written warranties often guarantee that a product will
perform to your satisfaction for a certain period of time. Many

Figure 8-7   *Limited Warranty*

Limited Warranty   12 Y 845

This product is guaranteed for one year from the date of purchase to be free of mechanical and electrical defects in material and workmanship. The manufacturer's obligations hereunder are limited to repair of such defects during the warranty period, provided such product is returned to the address below within the warranty period.

This guarantee does not cover normal wear of parts or damages resulting from negligent use or misuse of the product. In addition, this guarantee is void if the purchaser breaks the seal and disassembles, repairs, or alters the product in any way.

The warranty period begins on the date of purchase. The card below must be received by the manufacturer within 30 days of purchase or receipt of said merchandise. Fill out the card completely and return it to the address shown.

Owner's Name: _____

Address: _____

City, State, Zip: _____

E-Mail Address: _____

Date of Purchase: _____

Store Where Purchased: _____

Return to: ALCOVE ELECTRICAL, INC.
42 West Cabana
Arlington, VA 23445-2909

To register your warranty online, visit our Web site at www.alcoveelectrical.com.

Serial No.   12 Y 845

written warranties state that you may return a product for repair or replacement if it ceases to work because of a defect. However, warranties will not protect against normal wear and tear of the product.

Figure 8-7 illustrates a limited warranty that might accompany a home product. Read it carefully to determine what the manufacturer does and does not guarantee.

DID YOU KNOW

A service contract, like a warranty, provides repair and/or maintenance for a specific time period. Warranties, however, are included in the price of the product, while service contracts cost extra and are sold separately. Before considering a service contract, make sure you know what your warranty coverage is.

Filing Systems for Personal Records

Keeping a good filing system for your personal records will help you organize, store, and retrieve needed information. An electronic filing system can be a convenient way to organize some records.

Paper Filing System

A typical home filing system would include folders and labels and a file cabinet. Most households need folders for each category shown in Figure 8-8 (page 226). You may have additional categories. Name your folders with a descriptive word or short phrase that tells you immediately what records it contains. File your folders alphabetically.

COMMUNICATION CONNECTION

Gather a stack of paper slips or index cards. Set up a paper filing system appropriate for your or your family's personal records. On each slip or card, write the name of a folder along with the various records that folder would contain. Then file your "folders" alphabetically.

Keep records and receipts in the appropriate folder. For example, in the "automobile" folder, you might want to keep track of oil changes, tune-ups, repairs, and other car expenses. Original copies of important documents such as insurance policies and wills should be kept in a safe deposit box. After you submit your tax return, file your receipts and tax records in your filing system.

What are some of the advantages of using a computerized system for personal financial planning?

Electronic Record Keeping

Many people invest in home computers and software for personal financial planning. The advantages of computerized systems include (1) ease of updating information, (2) ease of record storage, and (3) speed of making new computations and comparisons.

Many software programs are available to consumers at reasonable prices. A **spreadsheet** is a computer program

Figure 8-8 *Home Filing System*

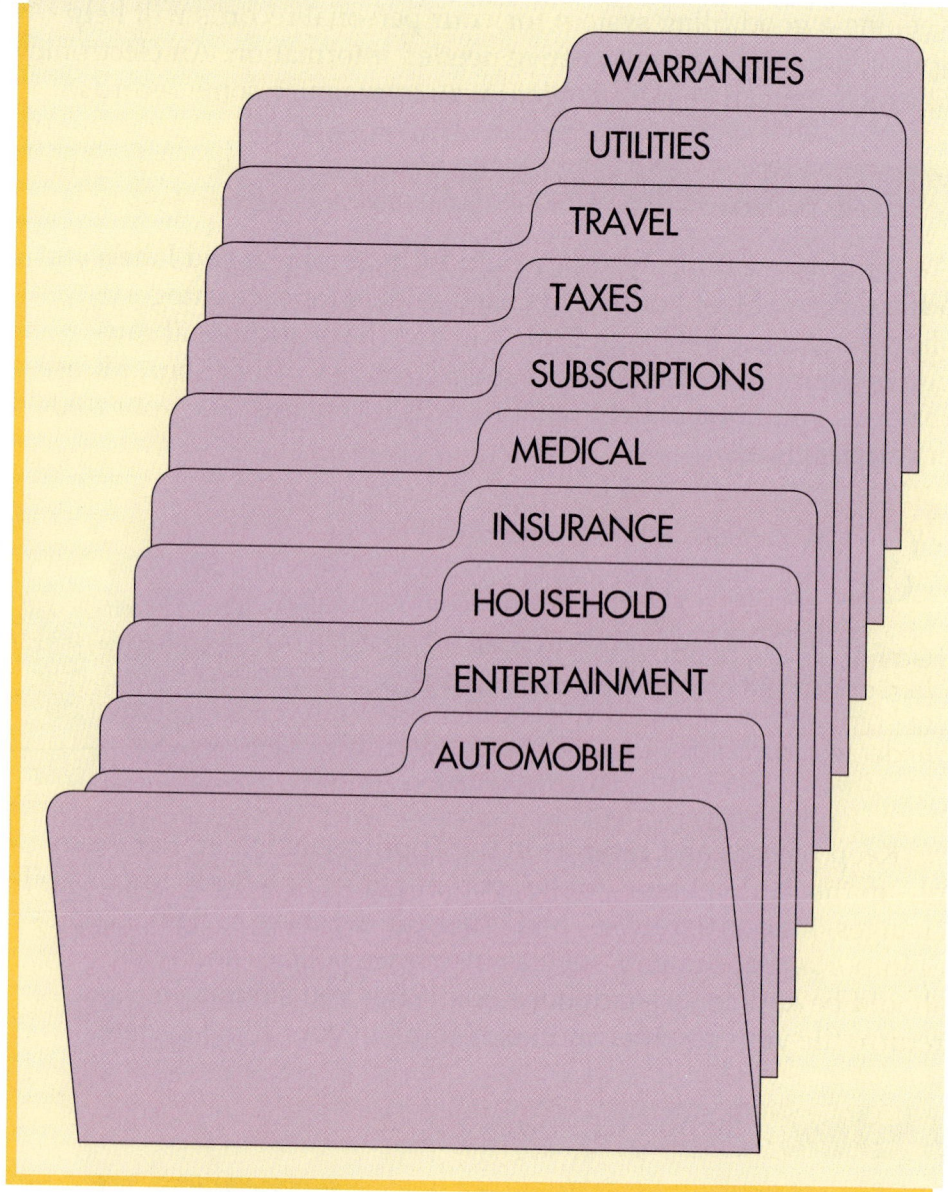

WARRANTIES

UTILITIES

TRAVEL

TAXES

SUBSCRIPTIONS

MEDICAL

INSURANCE

HOUSEHOLD

ENTERTAINMENT

AUTOMOBILE

that organizes data in columns and rows and can perform calculations using the data. You can use a general-purpose spreadsheet program to maintain a list of your income and expenses. You can enter a formula that will add them up. When you enter a new expense, the formula will recalculate the new sum automatically. You can even design your own budget worksheet in a spreadsheet program.

A **database** is a computer program that organizes data for easy search and retrieval. The program can sort the data in many ways. For example, if you entered all your expenses into a database program, you could ask it to give you a report of all expenses associated with travel.

A general-purpose database program can be rather sophisticated. However, several good software packages are available that are specially designed for financial planning and record keeping. These programs provide spreadsheet and database forms already set up for personal financial management. For example, Microsoft Money and Quicken both offer easy ways to keep track of your income and expenses, keep an electronic checkbook, and create budgets.

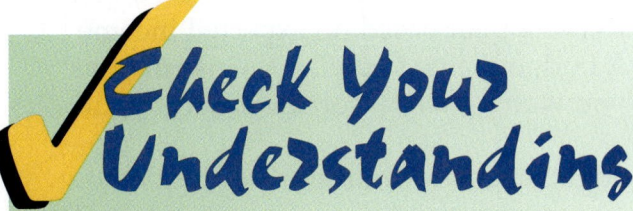

✓ Check Your Understanding

Review Terms
1. contract
2. mutual assent
3. consideration
4. negotiable instrument
5. co-signer
6. warranty
7. spreadsheet
8. database

Review Concepts
1. How is an express contract different from an implied contract?
2. What contracts have you agreed to?
3. Why should you read a contract before signing it?

Summary

8.1 Budgeting and Record Keeping

- The first step in financial planning is to create a budget, a spending and saving plan based on expected income and expenses. A budget helps you plan the use of your money so that you won't have to borrow to meet your daily needs.
- To prepare a budget, estimate your income, decide how much you want to save, and estimate your expenses. If your expenses plus savings exceed income, you'll have to adjust your spending or saving to balance your budget, or find a way to bring in more money.
- You should keep four types of personal records: income and expense records, a statement of net worth, a personal property inventory, and tax records.
- The statement of net worth lists items of value (assets) and money owed to others (liabilities). The difference between assets and liabilities is your net worth.
- A personal property inventory is used to keep track of items of value, and it serves as proof of value in the event items are damaged or stolen.

8.2 Legal Documents and Filing Systems

- Contracts are legally binding agreements. They can be express (in words) or implied (based on your actions).
- An enforceable agreement has six elements: offer and acceptance, consideration, contractual capacity, legality, genuine assent, and legal form.
- Contracts are valid (have all six elements), voidable (one of the elements is defective), or void (one or more of the elements is missing).

- It is your responsibility to read and understand an agreement before you sign it.
- Negotiable instruments are unconditional written promises to pay a specified sum of money upon demand of the holder. Two common types of negotiable instruments are checks and promissory notes.
- Good filing systems can involve paper or electronic files. Spreadsheet and database programs, especially those designed for financial planning, can facilitate budgeting and record keeping.

Review Terms

Directions: Can you find the definition for each of the following terms used in Chapter 8?

assets
budget
consideration
contract
co-signer
database
disposable income
financial plan
fixed expenses
liabilities
mutual assent

negotiable instrument
net worth
spreadsheet
variable expenses
warranty

1. An offer made and accepted.
2. Costs you are obligated to pay at specific times, regardless of other events.
3. Costs that vary in amount and type, depending on events and the choices you make.
4. A legally enforceable agreement between two or more parties.
5. Anything of value exchanged as part of a contract.
6. Things of value that a person owns.
7. A person who promises to pay a note if the maker fails to pay.
8. A statement about a product's qualities or performance that the seller assures the buyer are true.
9. An orderly program for spending, saving, and investing your income.
10. A spending and saving plan based on your expected income and expenses.
11. Money that you owe to others, also known as debts.
12. An unconditional written promise to pay a specified sum of money upon demand of the holder.
13. A computer program that organizes data in columns and rows and can perform calculations using the data.
14. A computer program that organizes data for easy search and retrieval.
15. Money you have left to spend or save after taxes have been paid.
16. Difference between assets and liabilities.

Review Facts and Ideas

1. Why should you prepare a budget?
2. What are the four steps in preparing a budget?
3. What choices do you have if your initial budget doesn't balance?
4. If you had to reduce your spending to balance your budget, which would you try to reduce first: fixed or variable expenses? Why?
5. What four types of personal records should you prepare and keep in a safe place?
6. Besides for obtaining credit, what is another good reason for preparing a personal property inventory?
7. How is an implied contract different from an express contract?
8. In order to be legally enforceable, contracts must contain what six elements?
9. Give three examples of contracts that must be in writing in order to be enforceable.
10. What is the difference between a void contract and a voidable contract?
11. What is the most commonly used form of negotiable instrument?
12. List the five conditions of negotiable instruments that make them legally collectible.
13. List five consumer responsibilities when entering into a contract.
14. Explain the concept of a filing system for personal records and list several file labels you would choose.

1. Using Figure 8-1 as a model, prepare a simple budget for yourself, listing expected income, savings, and expenses for a month. Make sure your budget balances. How much will you set aside for savings? Now assume that you can set aside this same amount each month. Use your Savings Planner Tool to calculate your total savings after 12 months, at 6 percent interest, starting with $0 savings.

2. How will your budget change in the next few years? What are your short-term and intermediate goals?

3. Using Figure 8-3 as a model, prepare a net worth statement. List your assets and liabilities. Compute your net worth. How can you use this information?

4. Using Figure 8-4 as a model, prepare a personal property inventory, listing items of personal property in your room at home. Why should you and your family keep a record such as this?

5. After examining the credit application in Figure 8-5, list the kinds of information requested by a retail store. Why do you think a store needs or wants this type of information?

6. Following the example of Figure 8-6, handwrite a promissory note from you to John Doe, payable in one year of monthly payments, in the amount of $50 with interest at 11 percent and monthly payments of $4.63. Are you the maker or the payee? Using your Notes & Interest Planner Tool, calculate the amount of interest you would earn on this note.

7. Bring to class an express warranty from a product you or your family recently purchased. What does the warranty specifically promise to do? List any restrictions (exceptions) that the manufacturer has placed in the warranty.

8. Go online to search for articles or reviews about financial planning software. Write a one-page description of what you could do with the software and what features make one software better than another.

Solve Problems

1. Based on the information given, prepare a monthly and yearly budget for TayVon and Keyondra Harbour. Use Figure 8-2 as a model.

   Average Income
   Net paychecks total $1,800 monthly
   Interest on savings = $50 monthly

   Average Monthly Expenses
Rent payment	$400
Utilities	120
Gasoline	100
Insurance	150
Groceries	200
Clothing	100
Car payment	210
Car maintenance	50
Telephone	40
Entertainment and Recreation	200

   Cash Surplus
Savings	To be Determined
Investment fund	60
Miscellaneous	120

2. Based on the information given, prepare a monthly and yearly budget for Elena Espinoza. Follow the style shown in Figure 8-2.

   Average Income
   Net monthly pay is $1,400

   Average Monthly Expenses
Rent	$410
Insurance	60
Utilities	50
Gasoline	60
Clothing	60
Entertainment	100
Savings	120
Telephone	15
Car payment	150
Car repairs	20
Groceries	150
Personal care	50
Miscellaneous	155

3. Revise Elena's budget when she agrees to share her apartment with a friend. Some expenses can be shared equally. Assume the telephone expense increases to $30, utilities to $60, and insurance to $70. These expenses along with rent are shared equally. What will you have her do with the added funds?

4. Based on the information given, prepare a net worth statement for Sako Masuta. Follow Figure 8-3. Sako owns a car worth about $3,000, but owes $1,500 on it to the bank. He has $500 in savings and $100 in checking. His personal property totals $3,000, and he also owes $90 to his credit union.

PLANNING TOOLS

5. Sako has five payments left to pay off the remaining $1,500 of his car loan. He is paying 8 percent interest. Use your Loan Planner Tool to determine his monthly payments.

6. Based on the information given, prepare a personal property inventory for Sako Masuta. Follow Figure 8-4.

Sako has these furnishings in his apartment:
- JWA CD stereo system, Model 252, SN 975923, bought last year for $600, presently worth $500
- sofa, presently worth about $800
- Bright alarm clock, SN 630AM and Blare radio, Model 2602, SN 413T, bought four years ago, total worth about $100.

Sako also has the following personal items:
- miscellaneous clothing and jewelry, presently worth about $800
- Quantex wristwatch, presently worth about $100
- coin collection, valued last year at $600.

Sako has photographs of these items. (List a hypothetical purchase price for all items except the CD system in preparing your property inventory.)

For related activities and links, point your browser to
www.mypf.swep.com

Chapter 9

Checking Accounts and Other Banking Services

Terms to Know

check
demand deposit
canceled check
overdraft
floating a check
checkbook register

reconciliation
blank endorsement
special endorsement
restrictive
   endorsement
certified check

cashier's check
stop payment
  order

Up Front

Angela works part-time after school and one weekend a month. She receives a paycheck once a week from her employer.

"I can't cash my paychecks," Angela told her boyfriend, "unless my mom goes with me to her bank. They told me that I need my own account. They recommended a checking account that has a savings account attached to it. That way I can transfer the money I don't need each month into savings, where I can earn higher interest."

The bank told Angela that her mother has to be a joint account holder with her until she reaches age 18. Then she can have her own private account. But for now, a joint account with her mother will allow Angela to deposit her checks into her checking account and manage her own money.

Goals

★ Describe the purpose of a checking account.
★ Discuss how to prepare a signature authorization form, checks, check endorsements, deposit slips, a checkbook register, and a bank reconciliation.
★ Be able to distinguish between different types of checking accounts.

Purpose of a Checking Account

Financial institutions such as banks and credit unions offer a number of services. The first service you will likely want is a checking account. A *checking account* is an account that allows depositors to write checks to make payments. A **check** is a written order to a bank to pay the stated amount to the person or business (payee) named on it. A checking account is also called a **demand deposit**, because the money can be withdrawn at any time—that is, "on demand." Only you, the depositor, can write checks on the account. Financial institutions often charge a fee for checking services, or require depositors to keep a minimum balance in the account. In shopping for a checking account, you will find a wide variety of account types and fees.

DID YOU KNOW

The banking industry has been consolidating sharply. In the mid-1970s, there were around 14,000 banks. By the year 2000, this number had decreased to 10,000.

Checks follow a process through the banking system. Your payee cashes your check. The bank that cashed the check returns it to your bank. To reimburse the payment, your bank withdraws the money from your account and sends it to the other bank. Your bank then stamps the back of your check, indicating that it has "cleared," or successfully completed its trip through the system. A **canceled check** is a check that bears the bank's stamp, indicating that it has cleared. Because of this stamp, you can use your canceled checks as proof of purchase or of payment if a dispute arises.

Your canceled checks should become part of your record keeping system.

A checking account offers several advantages:

1. It provides a convenient way to pay your bills.
2. Writing a check is often safer than using cash, especially when making major purchases in person, paying bills, or ordering merchandise through the mail.
3. A checking account has a built-in record keeping system that you can use to track expenses and create budgets.
4. As a checking account customer, you have access to other bank services, such as instant loans and 24-hour access to your money through ATMs.

In exchange for the convenience of using a checking account, you must accept certain responsibilities. First, you must write checks carefully and keep an accurate record of checks written and deposits made. Second, you must verify the accuracy of the bank statement you receive each month. Third, you must keep canceled checks among your permanent records.

In addition, you must maintain sufficient funds in your account to cover all the checks you write. A check written for more money than your account contains is called an **overdraft**. A financial institution receiving an overdraft usually stamps the check with the words "insufficient funds" and returns the check to the payee or the payee's institution. When an overdraft occurs and a check is returned, the check has "bounced." In addition, your bank will charge you a fee of $20 or more for each NSF ("non-sufficient funds") check processed. When checks are returned, the institution notifies the account holder of its action.

You are **floating a check** when you realize your account contains insufficient funds, but you write a check anyway, hoping that a deposit will clear before the check is cashed. Floating a check is riskier in the computer age, because computers process checks very quickly. Purposely overdrawing your account by floating a check is illegal in most states. Writing a "bad check" can result in a fine, imprisonment, or both.

What are some advantages of having a checking account?

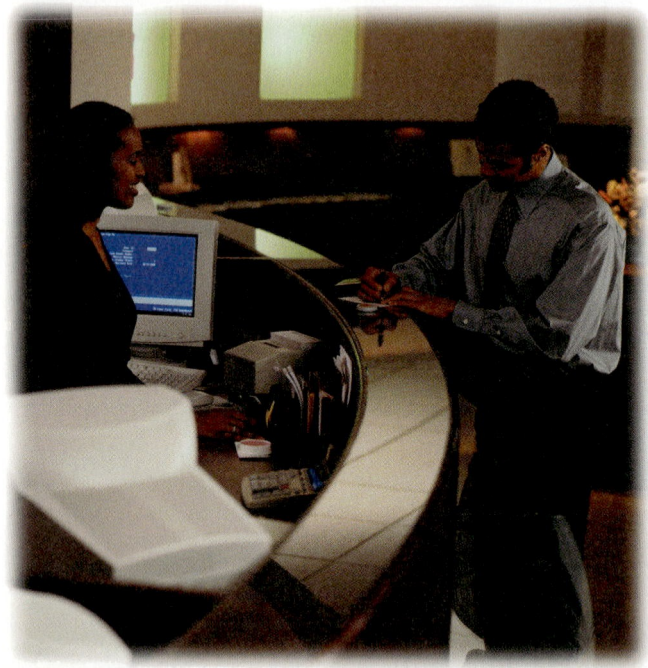

Opening a Checking Account

To open a checking account, you must fill out and sign a signature authorization form, such as the one shown in Figure 9-1. The signature form provides an official signature that the bank can compare to the signature you write on your checks. This is done to

Signature Authorization Form **Figure 9-1**

FIRST INDEPENDENT MUTUAL SAVINGS BANK
CHECKING SIGNATURE VERIFICATION

Customer Name *Ardys Johnson*   Date *4/28/--*
Account No. *08 40 856*   Individual *X* Joint
Address *4250 West 18th Avenue*   Daytime Phone *555-8925*
City/State/ZIP *Chicago, IL 60601-2180*   Evening Phone *555-0100*
Social Security No. *482-81-8096*   DOB *11/20/78*
Occupation *Accountant*   How long? *2 years*
Employer *Cho and Jackson, Inc.*   Phone *555-8925*
Contact in cast of emergency:
        Harold Johnson   Phone *555-2322*
Relationship *father*
Mother's Maiden Name or other code word *Williams*

JOINT ACCOUNT HOLDER (if any):

Customer Name   Date
Account No.   Individual   Joint
Address   Daytime Phone
City/State/ZIP   Evening Phone
Social Security No.   DOB
Occupation   How long?
Employer   Phone
Contact in cast of emergency:

                                            Phone

Relationship
Mother's Maiden Name or other code word

SIGNATURES: ___*Ardys Johnson*___   #1 Date ___*4/28/--*___
_____   #2 Date _____

(Use second page if more signatures are needed.)

verify that the checks were not forged. Most banks also require that you have an initial deposit of $50 or more.

In Figure 9-1, Ardys Johnson completed and signed the form. Additional space is allotted for a joint account holder. (Signature forms look different at various banks, but they contain the same basic information.) Ardys also listed her mother's maiden name for use in identification. Anyone forging Ardys's signature is not likely to know her mother's maiden name when questioned by a teller.

Parts of a Check

A check consists of 10 parts. Look at the lettered elements of the check in Figure 9-2 as you read their explanations below.

A *Check Number.* Checks are numbered for easy identification. In Figure 9-2, Check 581 has been pre-numbered by the bank.

B *ABA Number.* The American Bankers Association (ABA) number appears in fraction form in the upper right corner of each check. The top half of the fraction identifies the location and district of the bank from which the check is drawn. The bottom half helps in routing the check to the specific area and bank on which it is drawn.

C *Maker's Pre-Printed Name and Address.* Most checking account owners prefer to have their name, address, and sometimes telephone number preprinted on the top left of each check. Most busi-

Figure 9-2 *Check*

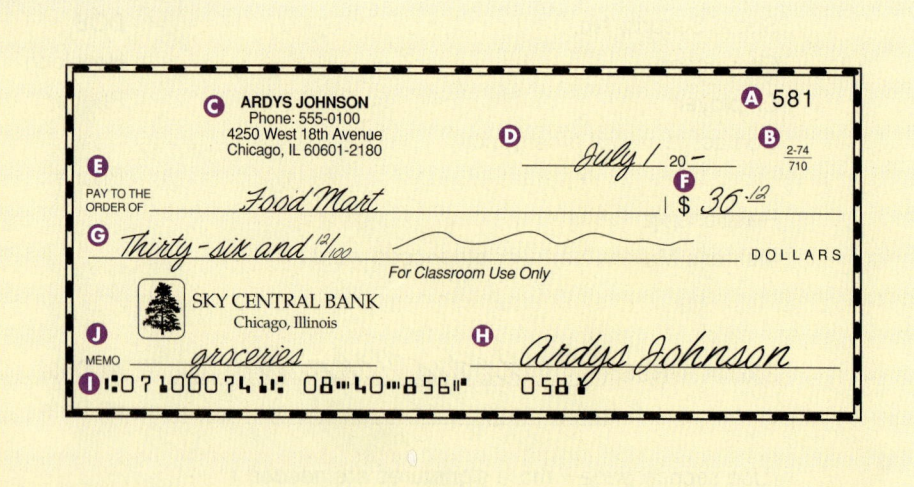

240

Money Management

nesses are reluctant to accept a check unless it is preprinted with at least the name and address.

D *Date.* In this blank, fill in the date you write the check. Do not postdate checks; that is, do not write a future date in this blank. Banks will not cash a check before the date written on it, or they may charge a fee for holding the check until the date arrives. Also, banks may not honor checks over six months old.

E *Payee.* The payee is the person or company to whom a check is made payable. Food Mart is the payee in Figure 9-2.

F *Numeric Amount.* The numeric amount is the amount of dollars and cents being paid, written in figures. Write the amount neatly and clearly as close as possible to the dollar sign, with the dollars and cents clearly distinguished. Many people raise the cents above the line of writing, as shown in Figure 9-2, and insert a decimal point between the dollar and cent amounts.

G *Written Amount.* The written amount shows the amount of dollars and cents being paid, written in words. The word "dollars" is preprinted at the end of the line. Write the word "and" to separate dollar amounts from cents; the word replaces the decimal point. When checks are written by computers, the "and" is usually omitted. Always begin writing at the far left of the line, leaving no space between words, and draw a wavy line from the cents to the word "dollars," as shown. In Figure 9-2, the fraction $^{12}/_{100}$ means 12 cents, which is 12 hundredths of a dollar.

H *Drawer or Maker.* The drawer, or maker, is the person authorized to write checks on the account. Ardys Johnson is the maker of the check in Figure 9-2 because she is the person who opened the checking account and deposits money into it. The bank has a copy of Ardys's signature on file so they can stop someone attempting to forge her name on a check.

I *Account Number.* The account number appears in bank coding at the bottom of each check. In Figure 9-2, 08 40 856 is Ardys's checking account number; 0581 is the preprinted check number that also appears at the top of the check; and 071000741 is the bank's identification code for the electronic sorting and routing of checks.

J *Memo.* A memo line is provided at the bottom left of each check so that the maker can write the purpose of the check. This line does not have to be filled in. It is provided for the account holder's convenience.

Some banks provide inexpensive "stock" checks to customers, but many customers prefer to order checks with special designs or colors rather than use plain stock checks. You will pay more for checks with special designs.

Using Your Checking Account

Checking accounts can help you manage your personal finances, but only if you use them correctly. Careless or improper use of a checking account can result in financial loss. Here are some tips on using a checking account.

Writing Checks

When writing checks, be sure to do the following:

1. Always use a pen, preferably one with dark ink that does not skip or blot.
2. Write legibly. Keep numbers and letters clear and distinct, without any extra space before, between, or after them.
3. Sign your name exactly as it appears preprinted on the check and on the signature card you signed when you opened the account. If you opened your account under your full name, don't use a nickname when writing a check.
4. Avoid mistakes. When you make a mistake, *void* (cancel) the check and write a new one. To cancel a check, write the word VOID in large letters across the face of the check. Save the voided check for your records.
5. Be certain you have deposited adequate funds in your account to cover each

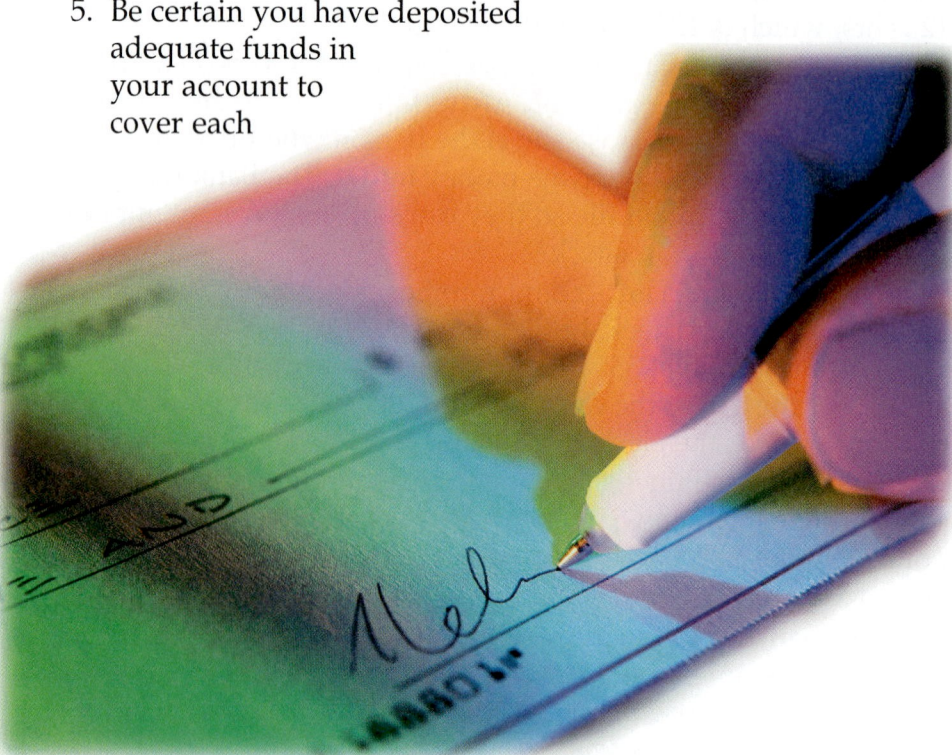

When writing a check, how should you sign your name?

check you write. A check is a negotiable instrument. It represents your written promise to pay the stated amount to the payee when it is cashed.

Making Deposits

You must complete a form each time you want to deposit or withdraw money from your account. Figure 9-3 illustrates a deposit slip. To prepare a deposit slip, follow these guidelines:

1. Insert the date of the transaction.
2. In the "cash" section, write in the amount of currency (paper money) and coin you are depositing.
3. If you are depositing any checks, write the amount of each check, together with the ABA check number (top part of fraction), in the "checks" section of the slip.
4. Total the currency, coin, and check amounts. Write this figure on the subtotal line.
5. If you wish to receive some cash at the time of your deposit, fill in the desired amount on the "Less Cash Received" line.
6. Subtract the cash received from the subtotal, and write the final amount of the deposit on the "Net Deposit" line.
7. If you will receive cash, write your signature on the line above the words "Sign here for less cash in teller's presence" (this wording will vary). If you do not want cash back, leave this signature line blank.
8. Keep one copy of this deposit slip as proof of the amount of your deposit. Financial institutions can make errors in crediting an account.

Deposit Slip **Figure 9-3**

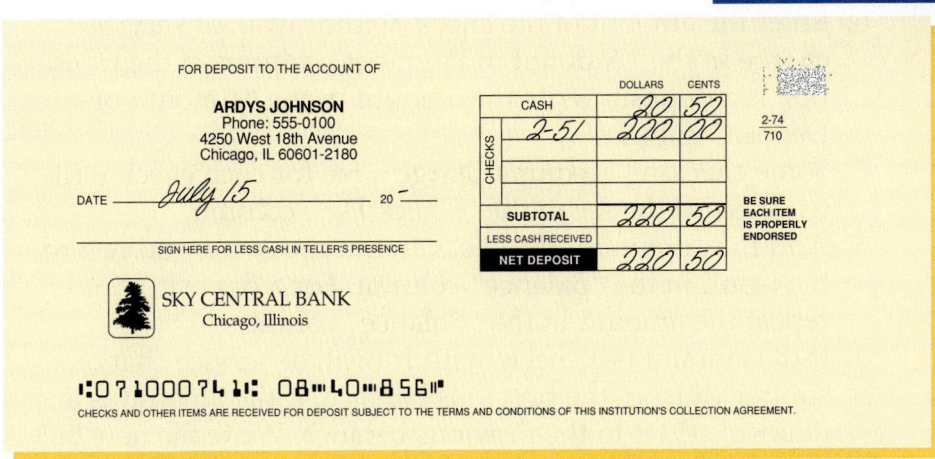

Checking Accounts and Other Banking Services

When writing deposit slips, carefully count the currency and coins you are depositing and recheck all addition and subtraction. Make sure all checks being deposited are properly endorsed (see pages 247–250). Hand the deposit slip to the teller with the currency, coins, and checks you are depositing. You can also make deposits at automated teller machines (see page 255).

Using a Checkbook Register

A **checkbook register** is a booklet used to record checking account transactions. Figure 9-4 shows a page from the checkbook register of Ardys Johnson. Through the use of her checkbook register, Ardys can keep track of all checks written, service fees paid, interest earned, and deposits made to the account. To fill out a checkbook register, follow these guidelines:

1. Record the current amount in your account at the top of the "Balance" column. When you fill a page in the checkbook register and turn to the next page, copy your account balance from the bottom of the previous page to the top of the new page.
2. As soon as you write a check or make a deposit, record the transaction in your checkbook register.
3. Write the preprinted check number in the first column. If the transaction is not a check, draw a diagonal slash in this column, or use another distinctive notation.
4. Write the month, day, and year of the transaction in the "Date" column.
5. Enter the name of the payee on the first line of the "Description" section. On the second line, if one is provided, write the purpose of the check.
6. Enter the amount of the check, withdrawal, or service charge in the "Amount of Payment" column. If the transaction is a deposit, write the amount in the "Amount of Deposit" column.
7. Some checking accounts charge a fee for each check written. Record the fee in the "Check Fee" column.
8. Add the amount of the check to the check fee, and record the result in the "Balance" column. For a deposit, simply repeat the amount in the "Balance" column.
9. If the amount is a check, withdrawal, or service charge, subtract it from the previous balance. If the amount is a deposit, add it to the previous balance. Write the new balance on the next line of the column.

Money Management

Checkbook Register   **Figure 9-4**

ITEM NO. OR TRANSACTION CODE	DATE	DESCRIPTION OF TRANSACTION		AMOUNT OF PAYMENT OR WITHDRAWAL (-)		✓	TAX OR OTHER	AMOUNT OF DEPOSIT OR INTEREST (+)		BALANCE FORWARD	
										800	—
581	7/1	TO	Food Mart							36	32
		FOR	Groceries	36	12		.20			763	68
—	7/15	TO	Deposit							220	50
		FOR	Paycheck					220	50	984	18
—	7/16	TO	W/D							20	—
		FOR	ATM	20	—					964	18
582	7/20	TO	Bellvue Apts							600	20
		FOR	Rent	600	—		.20			363	98
—	7/31	TO	Service Charge							5	—
		FOR	July	5	—					358	98
		TO									
		FOR									

10. The column headed by a check mark is provided so that you can check off each transaction when it appears on your monthly bank statement. The check mark shows that the transaction has been cleared by the bank and is no longer outstanding.

Always keep your checkbook register handy so you can write down the necessary information each time you make a transaction. Prompt recording will help you keep track of your personal finances.

Reconciling Your Checking Account

Financial institutions that offer checking accounts provide each customer with a regular (usually monthly) statement. This lists checks received and processed by the bank, plus all other withdrawals and deposits made, service charges, and interest earned.

Most financial institutions return your canceled checks with your bank statement. Some, however, make copies of the processed checks and destroy the originals. If necessary, you can get copies of your canceled checks for a small fee.

The process of matching your checkbook register with the bank statement is known as **reconciliation**. The back of the bank statement is usually printed with a form to aid you in reconciling your account. Figure 9-5 represents both sides of a typical bank statement.

On the left in Figure 9-5 is a simple statement of the bank's record of activity in the checking account. Canceled checks and

Figure 9-5   *Bank Reconciliation*

Bank Statement
SKY CENTRAL BANK

Ardys Johnson
4250 West 18th Avenue
Chicago, IL 60601-2180

For month ended   July 31, 20--:

Checks		Deposits	Balance
	7/1		800.00
32.00	7/1		768.00
36.12	7/5		731.88
22.00	7/8		709.88
	7/15	220.50	930.38
40.00	7/20		890.38
10.00	7/25	400.00	1280.38
1.00 SC*			1279.38

| Ending balance | | | 1279.38 |

* Service charge of 20 cents per check processed

Other charges and deductions: none

Bank Reconciliation

1. Write ending balance as shown on bank statement: *1,279.38*

2. Add credits or deposits made that do not appear on statement: *100.00*

3. Total lines 1 and 2:   *1,379.38*

4. Write total checks outstanding (not processed):   *139.90*

Check No.	Amount	
586	14	-
591	30	-
602	85	90
604	10	-

5. Subtract line 4 from line 3 and write balance (should agree with checkbook balance)   *1,239.48*

If Donald's name had been written incorrectly on the face of the check, he would correct the mistake by endorsing the check with the misspelled version first and then with the correct version of his name, as shown here.

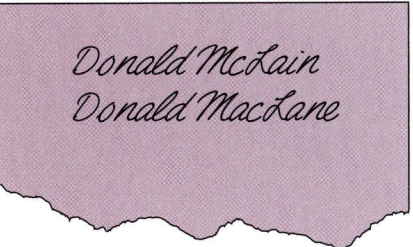

Special Endorsement

A **special endorsement**, or an endorsement in full, is an endorsement that transfers the right to cash the check to someone else. It consists of the words "Pay to the order of [new payee's name]" and the signature of the original payee. In the following illustration, for example, Donald MacLane uses a check written to him to pay a debt owed to Diane Jones. By using a special endorsement, Donald avoids having to cash the check before repaying Diane.

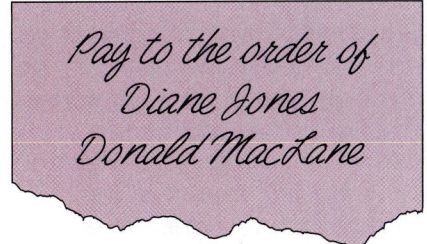

Restrictive Endorsement

A **restrictive endorsement** restricts or limits the use of a check. For example, a check endorsed with the words "For Deposit Only" above the payee's signature can be deposited only to the account specified. The restrictive endorsement is safer than the blank endorsement for use in mailing deposits, in night deposit systems, or in other circumstances that may result in loss of a check. If a check with a restrictive endorsement is lost, it cannot be cashed by the finder.

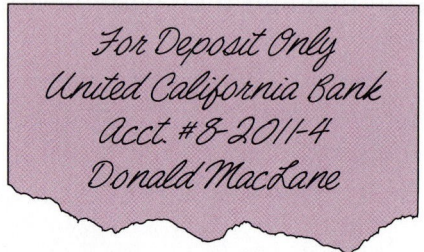

For Deposit Only
United California Bank
Acct. #8-2011-4
Donald MacLane

Types of Checking Accounts

Financial institutions offer many types of checking accounts. You should carefully study your options, because a wise choice can save you money. Most banks still offer free checking (no service fees) if you maintain a certain balance or agree to certain conditions (such as using ATMs rather than using teller services). Free checking is also available to senior citizens, nonprofit groups, and to others during special bank promotions, such as the opening of a new bank or branch.

Career Links

Bank tellers conduct most of a bank's routine transactions, such as cashing checks, accepting deposit and loan payments, and processing withdrawals. Being a teller requires a great deal of attention to detail, along with the ability to use computers. In many banks, tellers are also trained to perform functions of customer service representatives. Most tellers have at least a high school education and usually receive training from the bank. Experienced tellers may advance to higher-level positions, including those as managers.

For more information, refer to the *Occupational Outlook Handbook* at www.bls.gov or search the Internet using such key words as "careers," "jobs," and "banking."

Joint Accounts

Accounts can be either joint or individual. A *joint account* is opened by two or more people. Such an account is also called a *survivorship account* because any person who signs on the account has the right to the entire amount deposited. If one person using the account dies, the other (the survivor) then becomes the sole owner of the funds in the account. All of the checking accounts discussed in this chapter can be joint accounts.

When opening a joint account, you must decide if it will be an "or" account in contrast to an "and" account. If it is specified as an "or" account, any authorized account holder can write checks on the account. An "and" account with two owners, on the other hand, would require the signatures of both owners on checks.

Special Accounts

Most banks offer a special checking account to customers who write only a small number of checks each month. Service fees are charged at a flat rate per month with an additional fee for each check written (for example, $3 per month plus 15 cents for each check cashed). Banks may charge service fees only when the number of checks written in a month exceeds the set limit (such as more than 10 checks in a given month). If you write only a few checks each month, this type of account might be right for you.

Another type of special account is one where you are assessed a small or no fee, but if you use banking services, such as making a deposit or withdrawal at a teller station, you agree to pay a fee for each service used. This type of account is good for people who have their paychecks deposited automatically by their employers and who use ATMs for withdrawals and other transactions.

Standard Accounts

A standard account usually has a set monthly service fee of between $5 and $12 but no per-check fee. Often, if you are able to maintain the average minimum balance the bank requires, you can avoid service fees entirely. Many banks give a package of services for this type of account, such as free traveler's checks, an ATM card, or a free safe deposit box. Some banks offer reduced interest rates on credit card balances to customers who also have checking, savings, and other accounts at their bank.

Interest-Bearing Accounts

Most financial institutions offer checking accounts that earn interest. With these accounts, your account balance must not fall below a minimum average set by the bank during any month. The minimum may be $500 or more.

How financial institutions determine the balance you must maintain to waive fees can make a big difference in the cost of an account. With the passage of the Truth-in-Savings Law in 1993, depositors must receive interest on their full balance every day. The *average-daily-balance method* triggers a fee or service charge only if the monthly average of each day's balance drops below a certain dollar amount.

Interest rates rise and fall with economic conditions. When overall interest rates drop, you may receive as low as 1 percent; when overall interest rates rise, you might expect 5 percent or more. Keeping money in a low-interest account can cost you money in interest lost because you could have invested elsewhere. Yet, it also is useful in avoiding bank service charges.

Share Accounts

Most credit unions offer *share accounts*. These are checking accounts with low (or no) average daily balance requirements and no service fees. If you are eligible for credit union membership, this type of account may be the least expensive and most convenient checking method for you. Credit unions and the types of services they offer will be discussed in Chapter 10.

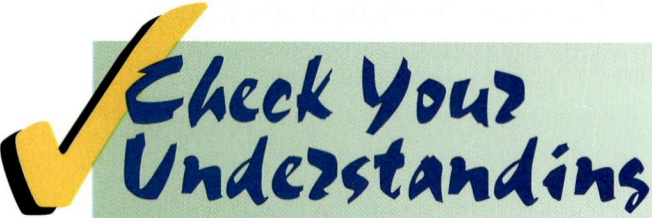

Check Your Understanding

Review Terms
1. check
2. demand deposit
3. canceled check
4. overdraft
5. floating a check
6. checkbook register
7. reconciliation
8. blank endorsement
9. special endorsement
10. restrictive endorsement

Review Concepts
1. What is an overdraft? Why is it important to avoid overdrafts?
2. Why should you keep a checkbook register?
3. Why might you use a special endorsement?

Lesson 9.2

Other Banking Services and Fees

Goals

★ Describe various banking services other than checking accounts available to consumers.
★ Identify services for which banks commonly charge a fee.

Other Banking Services

A full-service bank is one that offers every possible kind of service, from checking accounts to credit cards, safe deposit boxes, loans, and automated tellers (ATMs). Other services commonly offered are certified checks, cashier's checks, money orders, and debit cards. Most banks offer FDIC (Federal Deposit Insurance Corporation) insurance, which protects the deposits of customers against loss up to $100,000 per account.

AROUND THE GLOBE

Most Cambodians don't use banks, either because they are too poor or they don't trust them. But many are learning that banks have their uses. Acleda Bank has become the most active lender in Cambodia's struggling economy. The bank began as a "micro-loan" agency, making loans for as little as $25 in an attempt to make entrepreneurs of Cambodia's poor. It is now a full-fledged commercial bank, with fixed-rate savings accounts, bank transfers, and payroll services.

Think Critically: Why would a bank make a loan for as little as $25? Does this make good business sense?

Guaranteed-Payment Checks

A **certified check** is a personal check that the bank guarantees or certifies to be good. Sometimes a payee might want you to get your personal check certified to reduce the risk of accepting your check in payment. For example, if you buy a used car from someone, the owner might want a certified check before allowing you to take the car.

To get a check certified, write your check in the normal manner. Then take it to your bank. A bank officer will immediately deduct the amount from your checking account, stamp the word "certified" on the check, and initial it. In effect, the bank puts a hold on that amount in your account so that the money will be there when the certified check is presented for payment. Most financial institutions charge the account holder for this service; typically, the fee ranges from $2.50 to $5 per check.

A **cashier's check**, also called a *bank draft*, is a check written by a bank on its own funds. You can pay for a cashier's check through a withdrawal from your savings or checking account, or in cash. After receiving your payment, the teller makes out the cashier's check to your payee, and an officer of the bank signs it.

Cashier's checks are generally used when the payee requires a guaranteed payment but cash is not desirable. A cashier's check also might be requested instead of a personal check when the payee questions your credit standing or you do not have a credit history established. A cashier's check also can be used for transactions in which you wish to remain anonymous. The bank is listed as the maker of the check, and your identity need not be revealed. As with certified checks, many banks charge a fee for issuing cashier's checks.

Money Orders

Banks sell money orders to persons who do not wish to use cash or do not have a checking account. A money order is like a check, except that it can never bounce. There is a charge for purchasing a money order. It could cost from 50 cents to $5 or more, depending on the size of the money order. You also can purchase money orders through the post office and local merchants.

Debit Cards

Debit cards allow immediate deductions from a checking account to pay for purchases. The debit card is presented at the time of purchase. When the merchant presents the debit card receipt to the bank, the amount of the purchase is immediately deducted from the customer's checking account and paid to the merchant. The debit card transaction is similar to writing a check to pay for purchases. The issuing bank may charge an annual fee for the card or a fee for each transaction. (Note: There is no credit extended to you when you are using a debit card.) Debit cards can also be used for cash withdrawals at ATMs.

Bank Credit Cards

You can apply to a full-service bank for a bank credit card such as VISA or MasterCard. If you meet the requirements, you can use the card instead of cash at any business that will accept it. Banks offering national credit cards usually charge both an annual fee for use of the card and interest on the unpaid account balance. The topics of credit and credit cards will be discussed in detail in Unit 4.

Automated Teller Machines

Most banking transactions can now be made through electronic funds transfer (EFT). The main component of the EFT system is the automated teller machine (ATM). Using an ATM and an ATM (debit) card, you can make cash withdrawals from or check deposits to any of your accounts, make payments on loans, and pay bills. Using a VISA or MasterCard, you can receive a cash advance electronically. To use 24-hour ATMs, you must have a card that is electronically coded. You also must know your personal identification number (PIN), which usually is some combination of numbers and letters. For safety, memorize your personal identification number. Do not keep a written copy of it with your bank card.

What kinds of transactions can you make through ATMs?

Online and Telephone Banking

Most financial institutions offer online and telephone banking services to their customers. These services give you the ability to access your accounts from a computer or telephone, transfer money from one account to another, and pay bills by authorizing the bank to disburse money. You can find out your current balance, what checks and other deductions have cleared, and which deposits and other credits have been entered. You will need a secret code or password to gain entry into your account record. The advantage of online and telephone banking is that information is up-to-date and can be checked anytime, day or night.

Stop Payment Orders

A **stop payment order** is a request that the bank not cash a specific check. The usual reason for stopping payment is that the check has been lost or stolen. By issuing a stop payment order, the check writer can safely write a new check, knowing that the original check cannot be cashed if it is presented to the bank. Most banks charge a fee (usually $10 or more) for stopping payment on a check.

Safe Deposit Boxes

Safe deposit boxes are available at most financial institutions for a yearly fee that is based on the size of the box. Annual rental fees may range from $25–$100 or more. The customer is given two keys for the box and is allowed to store valuables and documents there. Documents commonly kept in a safe deposit box are birth certificates, marriage and death certificates, deeds and mortgages, and stocks and bonds. Jewelry, coin collections, and other small valuables also are commonly stored there. Keeping important documents and other items in a safe deposit box ensures that the items won't be stolen, lost, or destroyed. Documents that can be easily replaced with a duplicate need not be stored there.

What items are commonly kept in safe deposit boxes?

When you rent a safe deposit box, you will fill out a signature card. Then each time you enter your safe deposit box, you must sign a form so that your signature can be compared to the one on file. This procedure prevents unlawful entry to your box by an unauthorized person.

Loans and Trusts

Financial institutions also make loans to finance the purchase of cars, homes, vacations, home improvements, and other items. Banks also can provide advice for estate planning and trusts. (You'll learn more about estates and trusts in Chapter 15.) In addition, banks can act as trustees of estates for minors and others. A *trustee* is a person or an institution that manages property for the benefit of someone else under a special agreement.

Financial Services

Many larger banks offer financial services such as purchasing or selling savings bonds and discount brokerage services to their depositors. You may buy and sell stocks and bonds through the brokerage service at reduced rates. But you receive no advice or counseling. The purchases and sales are "cleared" through your checking or savings accounts with the bank. Brokerage services will be discussed in Chapter 12. Many banks also purchase a block of bonds (debt obligations) that they allow their members and depositors to purchase. Generally there is no additional fee to buy or sell these securities (the fee is included in the purchase price). To access this service, however, usually a minimum purchase such as $1,000 is required.

Bank Fees

Banks charge fees to their customers to help cover their operating costs. For example, when a bank grants you a loan, it charges you a loan fee. When the bank acts as a trustee, it charges a fee for this service. Banks also charge non-customers for services such as check cashing. If you want to cash a check at a bank where you do not have an account, the bank may charge you a fee or refuse to cash the check. Non-depositors pay for other services that may be free to depositors, such as traveler's checks, certified checks, and notary services.

Under the Truth-in-Savings Act (1993), checking advertised as "free" must carry no hidden charges or conditions. The bank or savings institution cannot charge regular maintenance or per-check fees or require balance minimums to avoid fees. However, it still may charge for a box of checks and for ATM transactions.

Check Your Understanding

Review Terms
1. certified check
2. cashier's check
3. stop payment order

Review Concepts
1. To withdraw money from your account using an ATM, what do you need besides an ATM card?
2. What would you put into a safe deposit box?
3. What fees does the Truth-in-Savings Act allow banks to charge on "free" checking accounts?

PERSONAL PERSPECTIVE

Shopping for the Right Bank

A checking account is a personal choice. Some people choose the bank closest to their home or work. Others choose the biggest bank or the one with the most ATMs. While all of these are good reasons, there are many other considerations in choosing your bank.

Finding the right bank to get started with can take a lot of time. All banks and services are not the same; they vary a great deal. A good way to start is to make a list of the features that are very important to you. Rank them 1 to 10. For example, #1 may be a low interest rate on a VISA card; #2 may be a low minimum deposit for a free or interest-bearing account; and #3 may be low or no service fees. Arrange your features into a table, either on paper or in a word processor or spreadsheet. At the top, list the banks that you are considering. Your table might look like this:

	Bank 1	Bank 2	Bank 3	Bank 4	Bank 5
1. Debit card provided					
2. Low/no minimum deposit					
3. Low/no service fee					
4 Online banking available					
5. Telephone banking available					
6. Low-cost bank credit card available					

Fill in your table by inserting information you find out about the five different banks. Then compare information to determine which bank overall provides the best services and costs for you.

Think Critically

1. Which is your favorite bank or financial institution? Why?
2. What features do you think are the most important when choosing a financial institution for your checking account?
3. What would cause you to switch from your bank to another one?

Chapter Review

Summary

9.1 Checking Accounts

- A checking account has many advantages, such as convenience, safety, value as a record keeping method, and access to other banking services.
- To open a checking account, you must fill out a signature authorization form and make an initial deposit.
- To write a check, fill in the current date, name of the payee, and the amount in figures and words. Then sign the form. For reference, you can note in the memo section the purpose of the check.
- As soon as you make any checking transaction, record the transaction in your checkbook register. When you receive your monthly bank statement, reconcile it with your register and correct any errors.
- Checks must be endorsed to be cashed. A blank endorsement is simply the payee's signature on the back of the check. A special endorsement signs the check over to someone else. A restrictive endorsement limits the use of the check to the specified purpose, such as depositing to an account.
- Financial institutions offer checking accounts with different fees and restrictions. Some checking accounts earn interest, but they require holders to keep a certain minimum balance.

9.2 Other Banking Services and Fees

- When your payee requires you to pay with a check guaranteed to be good, you can get a certified check or cashier's check from your bank for a small fee.

- If you don't have a checking account, you can buy a money order to use like a check. If you have a checking account, you can pay for purchases or make ATM transactions using a debit card.
- Bank customers can make transactions and access account information anytime, night or day, using online and telephone banking.
- Banks charge fees for services such as loans and other transactions to help cover their operating costs.

Review Terms

Directions: Can you find the definition for each of the following terms used in Chapter 9?

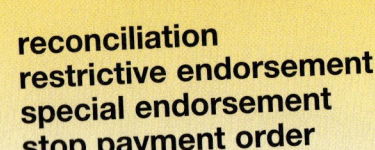

blank endorsement
canceled check
cashier's check
certified check
check
checkbook register
demand deposit
floating a check
overdraft

reconciliation
restrictive endorsement
special endorsement
stop payment order

1. A check written for more money than the writer's account contains.
2. A request that the bank not cash a specific check.
3. Comparing your checkbook register with the bank statement each month.
4. A check that bears the bank's stamp, indicating that it has cleared.
5. An endorsement that consists only of the payee's signature.
6. An endorsement, such as the words "For Deposit Only," that limits use of the check.
7. A booklet used for recording checking account transactions.
8. An endorsement that transfers the right to cash the check to someone else.
9. A personal check guaranteed by the bank to be good.
10. Money on deposit in a bank that can be withdrawn at any time.
11. A written order to a bank to pay a stated amount to the person or business named on it.
12. Intentionally writing a check on an account without sufficient funds in the hope of making a deposit before the check is cashed.
13. A check written by a bank on its own funds.

Money Management

Review Facts and Ideas

1. What are reasons for having a checking account?
2. What responsibilities do checking account owners have when using their account?
3. Why is a checking account called a demand deposit?
4. What is a canceled check, and why is it important to the checking account owner?
5. Why do you need to reconcile your checking account promptly when you receive the monthly bank statement?
6. Why would you be asked your mother's maiden name when opening a bank account?
7. List three types of endorsements and give a written example of each.
8. What is a joint checking account?
9. What types of checking accounts are offered by financial institutions? Briefly describe each type of account.
10. How is a bank debit card different from a bank credit card?
11. What is the purpose of a PIN (personal identification number)?
12. List at least four banking services provided by financial institutions.

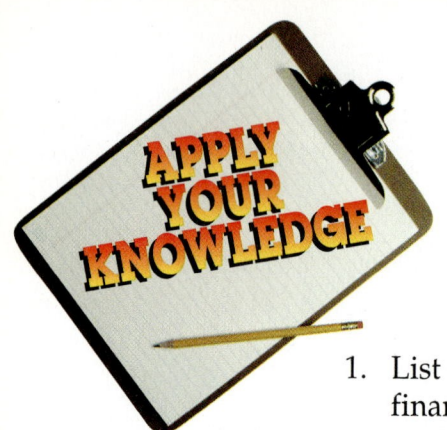

APPLY
YOUR
KNOWLEDGE

1. List the names, addresses, and telephone numbers of five financial institutions in your community, and list the services provided by each. What type of checking account might you choose? Why?

2. Visit three banks at their Web sites and compare the types of accounts and services they offer. Do all of them allow you to do your banking online?

3. Using Figure 9-2 as an example and following the guidelines on pages 242–243, write these checks:
    a. Check No. 12 to Melvin Quigly for $34.44, written today.
    b. Check No. 322 to Save-Now Stores for $15.01, written today. The purpose of your check is to buy school supplies.
    c. Check No. 484 to M.A. Rosario for $91.10, written today.

Note: Blank checks are available in the *Student Activity Guide.*

4. Using Figure 9-3 as an example and following the guidelines on page 243, prepare these deposit slips:
    a. Today's date; currency $40.00; coins $1.44; Check No. 18-81 for $51.00; no cash received back with the deposit transaction.
    b. Today's date; Check No. 40-22 for $300.00 and Check No. 24-12 for $32.00; $20.00 cash received back with the deposit transaction.

Note: Blank deposit slips are available in the *Student Activity Guide.*

5. Using Figure 9-5 as an example, determine your ending reconciled checkbook balance when all of the following six conditions exist:
    a. Your ending checkbook balance is $311.40 (before the service fee is deducted).
    b. You made an error, resulting in $30.00 less showing in your account than should be.
    c. The service fee is $6.00.
    d. The ending bank balance is $402.00.
    e. Outstanding deposits total $100.00.
    f. Outstanding checks total $166.60.

6. Determine your ending reconciled checkbook balance when all of the following six conditions exist:
   a. Your checkbook ending balance is $800.40 (before the service fee is deducted).
   b. The service fee is $3.00.
   c. The ending bank balance is $1,100.00.
   d. Outstanding deposits total $50.00.
   e. Outstanding checks total $352.60.
7. Write on plain paper the information needed for a signature authorization form, as shown in Figure 9-1.

Solve Problems

1. Find the errors in the following check.

RICHARD McGUIRE
Phone: 555-0109
2802 Saratoga Street
Ogden, UT 79393-4081

518

June 1 20 --

97-145
1243

PAY TO THE ORDER OF _*Best Buys*_ | $ *35.00*

Thirty five and 00/100 _____ DOLLARS

For Classroom Use Only

PEAK BANK AND TRUST
OGDEN, UTAH

MEMO _____

Rick McGuire

⑆124301452⑆ 0518 024⑆90759⑆

2. The deposit slip shown here was written to deposit the check in Question No. 1. Find the errors on the deposit slip.

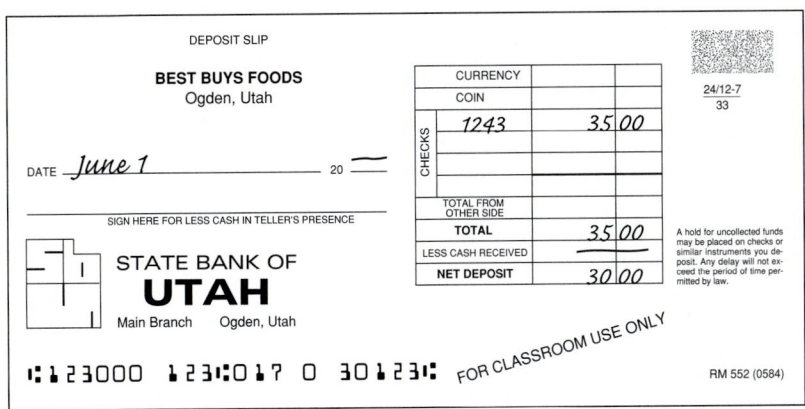

3. Complete the bank reconciliation form shown here by first finishing the checkbook register below, entering the service charge, and then computing balances. (Don't write in your textbook. Use another piece of paper.)

PLEASE BE SURE TO *DEDUCT* ANY PER ITEM CHARGES OR SERVICE CHARGES THAT MAY APPLY TO YOUR ACCOUNT

ITEM NO.	DATE		PAYMENT ISSUED TO OR DESCRIPTION OF DEPOSIT	AMOUNT OF PAYMENT		✓	(−) CHECK FEE (IF ANY)		AMOUNT OF DEPOSIT			BALANCE FORWARD	
												100	00
101	3/1	To	Grocery Mart	24	75						Payment or Deposit	24	75
		For	Groceries								Balance	75	25
102	3/3	To	Independent Phone Co.	13	00						Payment or Deposit	13	00
		For	Feb. charges								Balance		
/	3/5	To	Deposit						30	00	Payment or Deposit	30	00
		For									Balance		
103	3/8	To	Local High School	10	00						Payment or Deposit	10	00
		For	Band donation								Balance		
104	3/10	To	Alan's Bakery	3	80						Payment or Deposit	3	80
		For	Bread								Balance		
105	3/15	To	Grocery Mart	18	20						Payment or Deposit	18	20
		For	Groceries								Balance		
/	3/18	To	Deposit						42	00	Payment or Deposit	42	00
		For									Balance		
106	3/20	To	Acme Hardware	4	18						Payment or Deposit	4	18
		For	Hammer								Balance		

BANK STATEMENT
Hometown Bank

For month ended   March 31, 20--

Beginning balance · $100.00

Checks cashed		Deposits	Date	Balance
$24.75			3/7	$75.25
13.00		$30.00	3/8	92.25
10.00	$3.80		3/11	78.45
1.20 SC				77.25
Ending balance ·				$77.25

BANK RECONCILIATION

Ending balance as shown on bank statement $ _____

Add deposits not shown on bank statement $ _____

                                                                                    _____   _____

Subtract checks written but not shown
  on bank statement   _____

                                                                                    _____   _____

Adjusted balance (should be same as
  ending balance in checkbook) $ _____

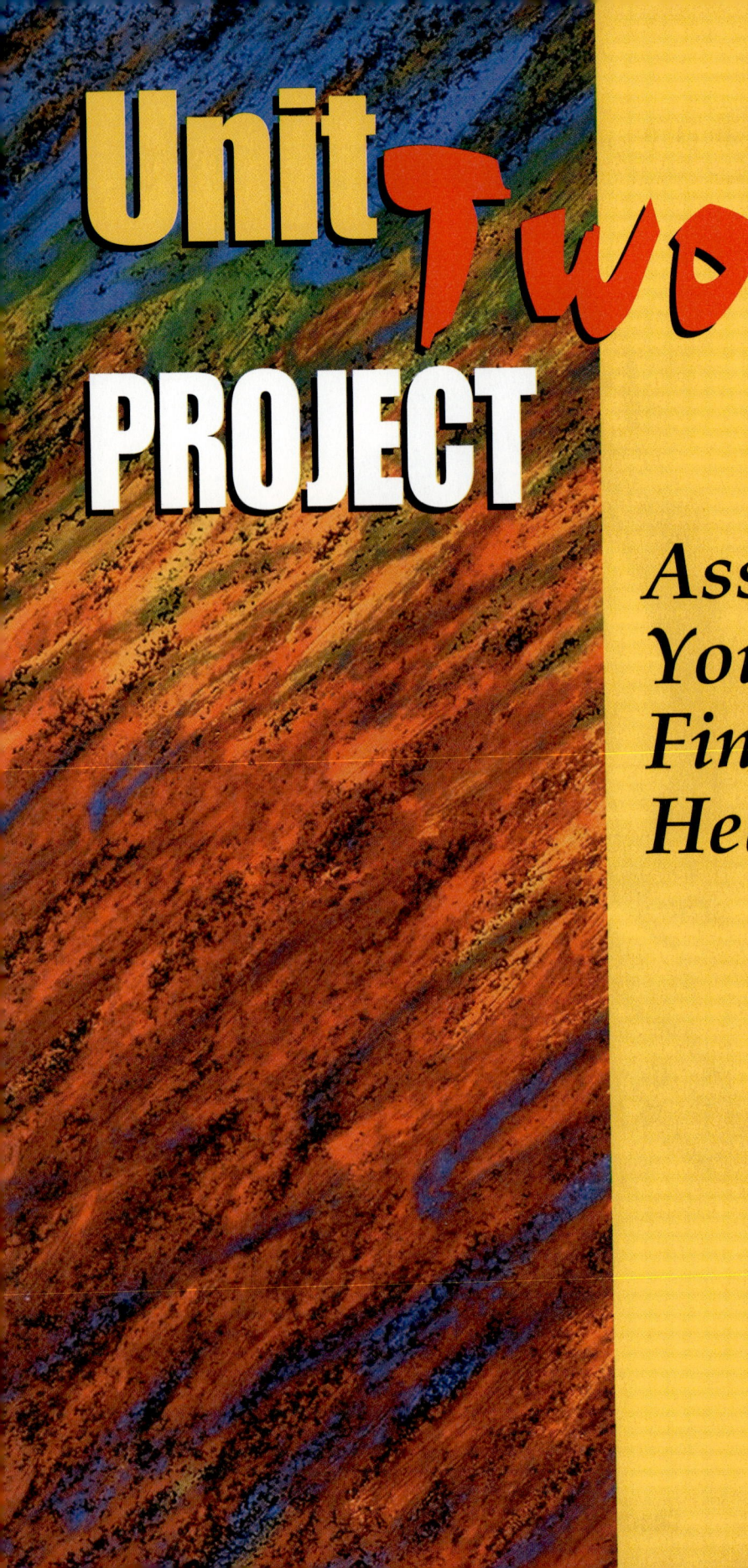

Unit Two PROJECT

Assessing Your Financial Health

Project 2

This project is designed to help you begin the financial planning process. Here you will assess your financial health by carefully examining your present financial condition. By taking inventory of where you are now, you can begin to build a plan for the future.

Your Job

We'll begin with your job. The money you earn affects what you are able to purchase and save now as well as your future prospects for financial stability. It's important to rate your job in terms of your opportunities for advancement, the company's chances for survival, and your job satisfaction. If you feel you are in a dead-end job, working for a weak or financially unstable company or in an obsolete industry, start looking for a more promising situation. On the other hand, if you like your work, and the future looks good for the company and the industry, then examine your opportunities for advancement. In addition, consider your own mental attitude, skills, and aptitudes for higher-level positions. If you aren't currently working, interview a person who has the type of job you'd like to have.

Remember that the pay you receive in any job is only part of what you get as an employee. You also should consider benefits, training received, and opportunities for making contacts that could be important in your career plans.

Worksheet 1 (Rate Your Job) is designed to help you assess your current job and any potential job you might consider. Complete Worksheet 1 provided in the *Student Activity Guide*. (For your reference, it also appears at the end of this project.) When you examine the scores, you will have a clearer picture of the direction you should pursue. The time to do career research is now, not when you've invested several years of your life in the wrong job, the wrong employer, or the wrong industry.

Worksheet 1 Scores: A score of 25 points is possible for each section. A score between 20 and 25 for any section indicates stability and good prospects for the future. A score between 15 and 20 indicates that you should examine the characteristics carefully before making long-term commitments. A score between 10 and 15 indicates that you should start looking for a new job, a new employer, or a new type of career soon. A score under 10 indicates that you are in a hopelessly dead-end job that has no future and should be viewed as only temporary.

Your Income and Outgo (Cash Flow)

Having completed the budgeting exercises in Chapter 8, you recognize the importance of keeping track of dollars that regularly flow through your hands. Worksheet 2 is a Cash Flow Statement that will help you identify where your money comes from and where it goes. In addition, it allows you to make projections for future income and outgo on a yearly basis. It's important to pinpoint your spending habits, analyze them, and take steps to improve your financial picture.

Examine your cash flow closely, looking for places where your income may be leaking away. Plugging the small leaks will help you build larger cash reserves and spend money more wisely. For example, think about three things you bought last year and later regretted. What is the total amount of money you could have saved? What other things could you have purchased?

Complete Worksheet 2, which is provided in the *Student Activity Guide.* (For your reference, it also appears at the end of this project.)

Your Net Worth

An assessment of where you stand begins with what you own and owe at the moment. Worksheet 3 is a Net Worth Analysis that is used for listing your assets and liabilities and making projections of where you would like to be at some future date (such as a month, a year, or five years).

The purpose of the net worth analysis is threefold: (1) to show you your strong and weak areas, (2) to help you plan for specific short-term changes, and (3) to allow you to project goals into the future based on those decisions.

Complete Worksheet 3 in the *Student Activity Guide.* (For your reference, it also appears at the end of this project.)

Your Tax Liability (for Extra Credit)

Based on the income tax returns you prepared in Chapter 7, use Worksheet 4 (Tax Liability) to analyze your tax liability and determine whether or not you can reduce your taxes through careful planning. Keep copies of your tax returns. Compare tax liability by preparing Forms 1040EZ, 1040A, and the long Form 1040. Use the form that gives the greatest tax advantage (that is, the lowest amount of taxes). Then study tax booklets and other information to see where you can benefit from taking more deductions.

Complete Worksheet 4 (Tax Liability) in the *Student Activity Guide.* (For your reference, it also appears at the end of this project.)

WORKSHEET 1
Rate Your Job

Directions: Rate each of the following characteristics on a 1 to 5 point scale. A score of 5 means *always;* a score of 4 means *usually;* a score of 3 means *as often as needed;* a score of 2 means *sometimes;* a score of 1 means *never;* and a score of 0 means *not applicable.* If you do not have a job, complete this worksheet after doing research about your desired future job.

Your Score

1. You enjoy the work you do, and you look forward to going to work each day. _____
2. You are willing to get extra training, education, or extra skills in order to be challenged. _____
3. You seek additional responsibility and can do the job well. _____
4. You like the work environment, and others recognize you as someone who will help and be a team player. _____
5. You receive regular pay raises large enough to keep you ahead of inflation and support your desired lifestyle. _____

Your total _____

Job Score

1. The product or service is in demand and prospects look good for the future. _____
2. The industry is growing as a whole, with opportunities for advancement in other companies similar to yours. _____
3. The product or service is inflation-resistant (rising prices don't greatly affect sales). _____
4. Turnover among employees is generally low. _____
5. Pay scale and fringe benefits compare well with other companies in the same field. _____

Job total _____

Employer's Score

1. Your boss calls on you to handle tough assignments and gives you credit for your accomplishments. _____
2. The boss regularly solicits your suggestions and follows them. _____
3. The company promotes from within. _____
4. The company has a large number of customers rather than just a few big ones. _____
5. The company is well established and still growing. _____

Employer's total _____

Total of all points _____

WORKSHEET 2
Cash Flow Statement

Directions: Keep a record of income and expenses for a month (you might want to do this for a year to build a budget base for the following year). In the first column, list each item you receive or spend in a month. In the second column, project your annual income or expense for each item. In the third column, check any items that need attention. In the fourth column, indicate how much (increase or decrease) each item should change monthly—what you'd like to accomplish. In the fifth column, indicate how much additional money you would save (or spend) annually by making the changes in the fourth column.

Example:	THIS MONTH	YEARLY TOTAL	NEED CHANGE	MONTHLY CHANGE	YEARLY EFFECT
Entertainment expense	$38.00	$456.00		$12.00	$144.00

| | 1 | 2 | 3 | 4 | 5 |
| | THIS | YEARLY | NEED | MONTHLY | YEARLY |
ITEM	MONTH	TOTAL	CHANGE	CHANGE	EFFECT
Income:					
Take-home pay					
Bonuses/gifts					
Interest income					
Other					
Totals					
Outgo:					
Savings					
Totals					

Analysis:
List ways you can cut expenses or increase income (such as by substituting activities, buying cheaper products, or working odd jobs in the summer).

WORKSHEET 3
Net Worth Analysis

Directions: Fill in the blanks below. In column 1, write in the market value of each item you possess or debt you owe. See Chapter 8 for definitions of terms (assets, liabilities, and net worth). In column 2, write in what each item will be worth in one year. In column 3, indicate the value of each item in five years. You can assume an item will increase it if gains in value over time (through interest or inflation) or if you add to or purchase an item from that category.

ITEM	1 TODAY'S BALANCE	2 ONE-YEAR PROJECTION	3 FIVE-YEAR PROJECTION
Assets:			
	$_____	$_____	$_____
Total assets			
Liabilities:			
Total liabilities			
Net worth			

Analysis: List major purchases that you wish to make and how you plan to pay for them.

WORKSHEET 4
Tax Liability

Directions: To complete this worksheet, first list your gross income, taxable income, and tax liability for the last three years you have filed tax returns and paid income taxes. If you have not yet filed a tax return, use the projected gross income that you would receive in the entry-level position of your choice (used for Worksheet 1). Compute taxes owed on that amount (see Chapter 7). Then compute how much you could save in income taxes if you made changes as shown. Finally, list some of the tax deductions available on the Form 1040 in the *Student Activity Guide* that you might use to decrease your tax liability.

	YEAR	GROSS INCOME	ADJUSTED GROSS INCOME	INCOME TAXABLE	TAX LIABILITY
1.	_____	_____	_____	_____	_____
2.	_____	_____	_____	_____	_____
3.	_____	_____	_____	_____	_____

How would each of the above years' tax liabilities have changed *if* you could have had the following changes:

YEAR	CHANGE	TAX DECREASE
1	IRA deduction of $2,000	$_____
2	Child care credit of $500	$_____
3	One more exemption	$_____

Analysis:
Examine Schedule A of Form 1040 (itemized deductions) in the *Student Activity Guide.* Identify some deductions you might wish to take advantage of to reduce your tax liability.

Examine Form 1040 in the *Student Activity Guide* and list additional types of income and deductions that are required and/or permitted when this form is used.

Unit *three*

Financial Security

Chapters

Unit 3 starts with a basic explanation of saving, investing, investment alternatives, investment risks, and how to invest wisely.

You will explore the types of stock. You will also look at bonds, mutual funds, real estate, precious metals, gems, and collectibles, as well as futures and options.

You'll end this unit learning about retirement and estate planning, wills, trusts, and the taxation of your estate.

Chapter 10

Saving for the Future

Terms to Know

discretionary income
principal
interest
compound interest
annual percentage
    yield (APY)

share account
securities
stockbroker
liquidity
certificate of deposit
    (CD)

maturity date
money market
    account

Up Front

Radwynn saves regularly from her allowance and the money she gets from relatives and friends for special occasions. She makes it a point to set aside some of what she receives, rather than spending all of it.

"For every dollar I save, Mom will contribute 10 cents to my savings," Radwynn told her best friend. "That gives me a 10 percent return, in addition to the interest I earn on my savings account. Mom wants me to save money for the future. I'm going to college some day, and I want to minimize the amount of student loans I'll need. It may not seem like a lot of money each month, but every year my savings grow. This year, I'll have enough to get a CD at the bank. That way, I get a higher interest rate on money deposited. Sure, it's tempting to spend some of my savings on fun stuff, but I have to pay back the 10 percent to my mom on everything I take out. It's kind of like a tax on spending, isn't it?"

Lesson 10.1 — Savings Goals and Institutions

Goals

★ Describe different purposes of saving.
★ Explain how money grows through compounding interest.
★ List and describe the financial institutions where you can save.

Why You Should Save

The best reason to save some of your income as you earn it is to provide for future needs, both expected and unexpected. If you set nothing aside for these inevitable needs, frustration, financial trouble, and even bankruptcy can result. Let's begin by examining some reasons why you should start saving regularly.

Short-Term Needs

Often you will have short-term needs that require money beyond what you can cover with your current paycheck. You will have to pay for these things out of savings. Some of these needs you can anticipate. For those, you can plan the savings into your budget. Others you can't foresee, but you must have enough in savings to cover them anyway. Some short-term needs you might encounter include the following:

What are some short-term needs that could require you to save?

1. Emergencies—such as unemployment, sickness, accident, or death in the family.
2. Vacations—short weekend trips or longer excursions.
3. Social events—weddings, family gatherings, or other potentially costly special occasions.
4. Major purchases—a car, major appliances, remodeling, or other expenses that become necessary as time goes by. Things do wear out and have to be replaced, repaired, or remodeled.

Long-Term Needs

Some needs won't occur until years into the future. Long-term needs can require a lot of money, so you must start saving for them now in order to have enough when you need it. These long-term needs include outlays for such things as home ownership, education, retirement, and investing.

Home Ownership

A down payment on a house amounts to thousands of dollars. The larger the down payment you can make, the smaller your monthly payments will be. Many people consider owning their own home a very important part of their future.

Education

Many high school graduates will borrow money, obtain grants and scholarships, or pay for their own post-secondary training. Education for one or both spouses may involve completing a bachelor's or master's degree, an advanced degree (such as law or medical), or mastering some special skill or trade through a vocational or apprenticeship program.

In addition, many couples begin a savings plan when children are born. Then when the time comes for college, they have money for their children's education.

NET NOTES

For many families, the greatest financial worry is whether they will be able to afford a college education for their children. The National Association of State Treasurers sponsors a Web site called the College Savings Plans Network, which provides links to state savings programs for college. The state-sponsored savings plans promote planning for education expenses and saving for such expenses instead of relying on debt or government aid programs. Check out the site at www.collegesavings.org.

Retirement

Social security was never designed to provide a comfortable retirement. It is meant to be a supplement to an individual's own savings. To have a financially secure retirement, you must begin to save regularly as early in life as you can.

Investing

To earn higher average returns over a long time period, people may invest in a business, real estate, insurance, stocks, collectibles, or a number of other alternatives. Because investments are often risky, you should make them in addition to—not instead of—regular savings. Types of investments will be described in later chapters.

Financial Security

Probably the best reason to save is the peace of mind that comes from knowing that when needs arise, you will have adequate money to pay for them now and into the future. The amount of money you save will vary according to several factors: (1) the amount of your **discretionary income**—what you have left over after you have paid your bills; (2) the importance you attach to savings; (3) your anticipated needs and wants; and (4) your will power, or ability to give up present spending in order to provide for your future.

How Your Money Grows

The amount of money deposited by a saver is called the **principal**. For use of the saver's money, the financial institution pays the saver money called **interest**. **Compound interest** is interest computed on the original principal plus accumulated interest. Figure 10-1 illustrates how interest is compounded annually. Notice how the interest earned increases each year because the saver is earning interest on the previous year's interest *as well as* on the initial deposit.

Compounding Interest Annually   **Figure 10-1**

Year	Beginning Balance	Interest Earned (5%)	Ending Balance
1	$100.00	$5.00	$105.00
2	105.00	5.25	110.25
3	110.25	5.51	115.76

Figure 10-2 | *Compounding Interest Quarterly*

Quarterly Compounding
Annual Interest Rate = 6%

Year	Beginning Balance	Rate	Quarterly Interest 1	2	3	4	Ending Balance
1	$100.00	.015	$1.50	$1.52	$1.55	$1.57	$106.14
2	$106.14	.015	$1.59	$1.62	$1.64	$1.66	$112.65
3	$112.65	.015	$1.69	$1.72	$1.74	$1.77	$119.57

The more often interest is compounded, the greater your earnings. (See the Math Minute feature.) Figure 10-2 illustrates what happens when 6 percent interest is compounded quarterly (every three months) and added to the principal before more interest is calculated. Notice that you will earn more interest with quarterly compounding than with annual compounding. Today, many financial institutions offer interest compounded each day savings are on deposit. They use computers to rapidly compute the compounding daily interest.

Earnings on savings can be measured by the *rate of return* or *yield*. *Yield* is the percentage of increase in the value of your savings due to earned interest. Because financial institutions compound interest in many ways, comparing yields can be difficult. To solve this problem, the law requires all financial institutions to tell consumers the **annual percentage yield (APY)** on their accounts. This is the actual interest rate the account pays per year, with compounding included. Because all financial institutions must calculate APY the same way, you can use APY to easily compare the yields on different accounts.

Where You Can Save

Most cities have commercial banks, savings banks, savings and loan associations, credit unions, and brokerage firms. Most of these institutions have greatly expanded their services in recent years, so the differences among them are becoming increasingly blurred. Interest rates vary among all savings institutions. No one type will always offer the best deal.

MATH MINUTE

Computing Interest Compounded Quarterly

Compound interest means earning interest on principal, and then allowing the interest to remain on deposit so you will then earn interest on both your principal and your previous interest. Let's look at how this happens when interest is compounded quarterly for three years. To compute interest compounded quarterly, divide the annual interest rate by 4 to get the quarterly rate. For monthly compounding, divide the annual interest rate by 12. For interest compounded every 6 months (a half year), divide the annual rate by 2. Round all interest computations up if the remainder is .5 or greater.

Suppose you deposit $100 in a share account that will pay you 6 percent per year, compounded quarterly. This means that for each quarter, you will receive 1/4 of the yearly interest. Six percent divided by 4 is 1.5 percent each quarter. At the end of the first quarter, you will have earned $1.50 in interest, using the following computation:

$$\$100 \times .015 = \$1.50$$

At the beginning of the second quarter, you now have $101.50 in your account ($100 + the $1.50 interest). At the end of the second quarter, you will earn interest as follows:

$$\$101.50 \times .015 = \$1.52$$

At the beginning of the third quarter, you have $103.02 ($101.50 + the $1.52 interest). At the end of the third quarter, you will earn interest as follows:

$$\$103.02 \times .015 = \$1.55$$

At the beginning of the fourth quarter, you have $104.57 ($103.02 + the $1.55 interest). At the end of the fourth quarter (the end of the first year), you will earn interest as follows:

$$\$104.57 \times .015 = \$1.57$$

Your balance at the end of the first year is $106.14. You earned a total of $6.14 in interest for the year. At the end of Year 3, your balance is $119.57. That's a total interest of $19.57 on your original deposit of $100, as shown in Figure 10-2.

Based on the previous example, compute your quarterly interest for three years if you deposit $500 at 8 percent, compounded quarterly.

Year	Beginning Balance	Rate	Quarterly Interest 1	2	3	4	Ending Balance
1	$500.00	___	$_____	$_____	$_____	$_____	$_____
2	$_____	___	$_____	$_____	$_____	$_____	$_____
3	$_____	___	$_____	$_____	$_____	$_____	$_____

Solution:

Year	Beginning Balance	Rate	Quarterly Interest 1	2	3	4	Ending Balance
1	$500.00	.02	$10.00	$10.20	$10.40	$10.61	$541.21
2	$541.21	.02	$10.82	$11.04	$11.26	$11.49	$585.82
3	$585.82	.02	$11.72	$11.95	$12.19	$12.43	$634.11

Commercial Banks

Commercial banks provide the widest variety of banking services of any financial institutions. Many people prefer to keep their checking and savings accounts in the same bank for ease in transferring funds and making deposits and withdrawals. Commercial banks offer many kinds of savings and checking accounts. They provide bank cards, ATMs, overdraft protection, a variety of loans, and other services. Almost all commercial banks are insured by the Federal Deposit Insurance Corporation (FDIC). This insurance protects depositors from loss due to bank failure, up to $100,000 per account. Most large commercial banks have many branches, making it easy to find one near your home or job. Commercial banks may be either nationally chartered or state chartered.

DID YOU KNOW

Despite signs of health, Russia's banking system is still in fragile condition. Few Russian citizens trust banks enough to deposit savings on a large scale, afraid of bank and currency collapses. Analysts estimate Russians keep between $30 billion and $40 billion in savings under mattresses and out of banks.

Savings Banks

Savings banks are usually referred to as mutual savings banks. These financial institutions are few in number—about 500 of them in roughly a dozen states, mostly throughout New England and the Northeast—but substantial in size. Savings banks are state chartered and are insured by the FDIC. Two primary services offered by these institutions are savings accounts and loans on

Why might people prefer to keep their checking and savings accounts in the same bank?

real property, including mortgages and home-improvement loans. Because of deregulation of the banking industry in the 1980s, savings banks also offer checking accounts and other types of consumer loans.

Savings and Loan Associations

Savings and loan associations (S&Ls) are organized primarily to lend money for home mortgages. S&Ls offer many of the services of commercial banks, including interest-bearing checking accounts, special savings plans, loans to businesses, major credit cards, and ATMs. In the 1980s, many S&Ls failed as a result of careless loan practices and poor investments. Since then, many have merged with banks. All S&Ls today are insured by the FDIC.

Credit Unions

Credit unions are not-for-profit organizations established by groups of employees in similar occupations who pool their money. To use a credit union, you must be a member of the employee group. Credit unions generally offer higher interest rates on savings and lower interest rates on loans. Their membership in the NCUA (National Credit Union Administration) provides insurance for depositors' accounts, up to $100,000.

Credit unions are owned by their members. A savings account at a credit union is usually called a **share account**. Credit union members save their money in the form of "shares," or part ownership in the credit union. From funds accumulated by these shares, the credit union makes loans to its members. Credit unions also offer IRAs (Individual Retirement Accounts), share draft accounts (checking accounts), consumer loans, certificates of deposit, and other services. Credit unions are growing rapidly in most parts of the country and consequently are offering more diversified services.

Brokerage Firms

Brokerage firms buy and sell different types of securities. **Securities** are stocks and bonds issued by corporations or by the government. Stocks represent equity, or ownership. Bonds represent debt, or a loan. In other words, when you buy stock, you become an owner of the company. When you buy a bond, you are loaning money to the company or to the government. Investors buy and sell securities through a **stockbroker**, who works for the brokerage firm.

✓ Check Your Understanding

Review Terms

1. discretionary income
2. principal
3. interest
4. compound interest
5. annual percentage yield (APY)
6. share account
7. securities
8. stockbroker

Review Concepts

1. Why do you need to start saving now to cover long-term needs?
2. Explain how compounding interest makes your savings grow.
3. How can you compare interest rates on accounts that compound differently?

Lesson 10.2 ▽

Savings Options, Features, and Plans

Goals

★ Explain the features and purposes of savings accounts, certificates of deposit, and money market accounts.
★ Discuss some of the factors that influence the selection of a savings plan.
★ Explain at least two ways to save regularly.

Savings Options

Once you have decided to establish a savings program, you need to know about the different types of savings options available. You may want to deposit money in several types of accounts, because each can contribute to your overall plan in different ways.

Career Links

Financial planners use their knowledge of tax and investment strategies, securities, insurance, pension plans, and real estate to develop and implement financial plans for persons and businesses. Financial planners can work for credit unions, counseling firms, or banks, or may be self-employed. Although a college education is not necessary to become a financial planner, most planners have a bachelor's or master's degree. Courses in accounting, business administration, economics, and finance are very helpful.

  For more information, refer to the *Occupational Outlook Handbook* at www.bls.gov or search the Internet using such key words as "careers," "jobs," and "financial planning."

Regular Savings Account

A regular savings account has a major advantage—high liquidity. **Liquidity** is the ability of an asset (a resource owned) to be converted into cash quickly without loss of value. A regular savings account is said to be very liquid because you can withdraw your money at any time without penalty. The tradeoff for high liquidity, however, is lower interest. A regular savings account generally pays the least amount of interest of the savings options.

Why is a regular savings account said to be very liquid?

Once you have opened the account, you are free to make withdrawals and deposits. Some financial institutions charge service fees when you make more than a maximum number of withdrawals in a certain period of time. Other institutions charge a monthly fee if your balance falls below a set minimum. In most cases, you will receive a debit or ATM card that goes with the account so that you can make withdrawals and deposits at ATMs. You can also check your balance online and by using a touch-tone telephone.

Certificate of Deposit

A **certificate of deposit (CD)**, or time deposit, is a deposit that earns a fixed interest rate for a specified length of time—for example, 5 percent for six months. A CD requires a minimum deposit. The interest rate on a CD is usually higher (although the difference may be small) than on regular savings accounts because CDs are less liquid. You must leave the money in the CD for the full time period. If you take out any part of your money early, you will pay an early withdrawal penalty. Generally, the penalty is in the form of substantially less interest earned on the CD.

A CD has a set **maturity date**—the date on which an investment becomes due for payment. Within so many days after the maturity date, your certificate will renew automatically. You may prefer to redeem it for cash or purchase a new certificate for a different time period. Financial institutions offer CDs that allow the interest to accumulate to maturity. Often you can choose to receive a check periodically for the interest earned or have the interest deposited in a separate regular account.

Money Market Account

A **money market account** is a combination savings-investment plan in which money deposited is used to purchase safe, liquid securities. Brokerage firms as well as banks offer money market accounts. Money may be deposited or withdrawn from a money market account at any time without a fee. As a result, this account is quite liquid.

Money market accounts with brokerage firms are not insured. At banks, some money market accounts are insured by the FDIC. Others are not. However, even without insurance, money market accounts are generally considered safe because the securities backing these funds are very stable. Managers of these accounts frequently use the money to purchase short-term (one year or less) securities issued by the U.S. Treasury. Therefore, the chance of losing your money is very low.

Unlike regular savings accounts, the interest rates on money market accounts go up and down with the stock market. Banks and brokerage firms may change their rates on these accounts as much as weekly, or even more often. However, interest rates on money market accounts are typically higher than on regular savings accounts, and the rate changes are small. Usually money market accounts require a minimum balance, such as $500 or more. These accounts also may have restrictions on the number of checks you can write over a period of time and the minimum amount for which you can write each check.

Selecting a Savings Plan

There are a number of important factors to consider in selecting a savings account and a savings institution. Among any savings or investment options, there is usually a tradeoff between liquidity or safety and yield. The safer or more liquid an investment, the less earning potential it is likely to have. Use the following criteria in judging which savings options best meet your needs.

What are some important factors to consider when selecting a savings account and a savings institution?

Liquidity

Liquidity (how quickly you can turn savings into cash when you want it) may be important to you. The need for liquidity will vary, based on your age, health, family situation, and overall wealth. For example, if you have little money left over after paying your bills, you may need to keep this money liquid so you can get it quickly, without penalty, if you face some emergency. In this case, a regular savings account or money market account would be best for you.

CDs impose a penalty if you withdraw early, so you should choose this option when you don't expect to need the money before the maturity date.

Safety

You want your money to be safe from loss. Most financial institutions are insured by a government agency, the FDIC. Accounts protected by this insurance are safe for up to $100,000 per depositor. You should be sure the financial institution of your choice has federal insurance to protect your deposit. Deposits in banks, no matter what type, are almost always safer than investments in the stock market.

Convenience

People often choose their financial institution because of convenience of location and the services offered. Interest rates on various savings accounts and certificates of deposit may vary only slightly. Fees charged are often very similar within a community.

Many banks have several branches within a limited geographic area, which makes your banking convenient. If a bank has only one branch located several miles from your home, the inconvenience of driving there might outweigh a slightly higher interest rate at this bank. A very large bank may have branches in other states, giving you banking privileges while out of town.

Many banks offer drive-up windows with expanded weekday and Saturday hours. Branches are often located in grocery stores or residential areas. You may want to look for a bank that offers ATMs near your home or job, or at other locations you frequent, such as the local shopping mall.

Interest-Earning Potential (Yield)

You want to earn as much interest as you can on your deposit, while maintaining the degree of liquidity, safety, and convenience you want. Shop around for the best rates in your area for the type of account you want. Usually, the more liquid your deposit, the less interest it will earn. A regular account usually earns a low rate because you can maintain a low minimum balance and withdraw money as needed. CDs tie up your money for some length of time. In exchange for your commitment to leave this money with the bank for this time period, you will usually earn higher interest.

INTEREST RATES FOR CONSUMERS

For the week ended December 10, 20--
(reported at the end of every business week):

REGULAR SAVINGS ACCOUNT:	Commercial banks	3.5%
	Credit unions	3.8%
MONEY MARKET ACCOUNTS:	Commercial banks	3.1%
	Credit unions	3.5%
	Brokerage firms	4.1%

Figure 10-3 gives examples of interest rates being paid in a local area. As you can see from the chart, yield depends on the type of account.

Fees and Restrictions

Different accounts and institutions have different rules. Before you open an account, be sure to understand the withdrawal restrictions, minimum balances, service charges, fees, and any other requirements. For example, some accounts charge a fee for using a live teller rather than making your transactions through an ATM. CDs exact a heavy cost in lost interest for withdrawing money before maturity. Fees for use of an ATM can vary as well. Some banks may charge nothing to use their ATMs but charge a hefty fee for using another bank's ATM.

Saving Regularly

Everyone should have saving as a goal. In simplest terms, you can grow your savings only by spending less than you take in. It is important not just to save, but to save regularly. Over time, and with compounding interest, your savings can grow into a substantial sum. Figure 10-4 on page 292 illustrates the effect of compounding when you make regular deposits and earn interest on interest.

DID YOU KNOW

Coffee, a doughnut, and a newspaper purchased every working day might cost a person $15 or more per week—or $750 per year!

Figure 10-4 *Compounding Interest and Making Additional Deposits*

Year	Beginning Balance	Deposits	Interest Earned (5%)	Ending Balance
1	$ 0.00	$100.00	$ 5.00	$105.00
2	105.00	100.00	10.25	215.25
3	215.25	100.00	15.76	331.01
4	331.01	100.00	21.55	452.56

Obviously, no savings plan is effective unless you have the will power to set aside money. The safe storage of funds for future use is a basic need of every individual. There are ways to make regular saving easier, including direct deposits and payroll deductions.

Direct Deposit

Both employers and financial institutions offer the direct deposit of paychecks into bank accounts. This service helps you because your money is available in your account faster. You can also have part or all of your direct deposit put into your savings account. Then you could transfer what you need to cover your bills into checking and save the rest. This way, you are truly paying yourself first. You can earmark the money you set aside for a vacation or some other special purpose.

Automatic Payroll Deductions

Having a certain amount withheld from your paycheck and deposited into a savings account is another method of "paying yourself." Contributions to savings are part of pre-authorized payment systems. In this case, money is automatically deducted from your paycheck and deposited in your savings account.

You may authorize your employer to make automatic deductions from your paycheck each month. Many people participate in *payroll savings plans,* in which money is taken out of each paycheck and deposited in a bank or credit union or used to buy government savings bonds.

PERSONAL PERSPECTIVE

Saving to Keep Life Simple

Saving is often defined as deferred spending. In other words, you set money aside today so you can spend it in the future. But saving money can be more than providing for some future need. Saving itself can be a virtue.

Abraham Lincoln said, "Most people are about as happy as they make up their minds to be." But what is happiness? According to many philosophers, it is enjoying what you have, not in wishing for more. Consider what some people learn well into their lives—that the accumulation of possessions does not bring happiness! By keeping your life simple, you don't get used to having more and more and keeping up with what everyone else is buying. This means not buying "things" that have to be protected and maintained. Instead, you can enjoy life without having to earn large sums of money to achieve some high standard of consumer spending.

Most people "buy things they don't need, with money they don't have, to impress people they don't like." Those you love and who care about you aren't impressed with how much money you spend or all the possessions you own. Wouldn't it be better to put money aside so that you can retire early, enjoy traveling, or live comfortably without the stress of keeping up with the rat race? Remember, even if you win the rat race, you're still a rat!

Think Critically

1. Do you buy things that you later wish you hadn't? If you had the money back, what would you do with it instead?
2. Do you know someone who is "happy" and at peace with his or her life? If so, describe the person's lifestyle.

Check Your Understanding

Review Terms
1. liquidity
2. certificate of deposit (CD)
3. maturity date
4. money market account

Review Concepts
1. Explain how a savings account is more liquid than a certificate of deposit.
2. To earn a higher interest rate, what tradeoff will you likely have to make?
3. In what way is the interest paid on a money market account different from interest paid on a regular savings account?

Chapter Review

Summary

10.1 Savings Goals and Institutions

- Savings provide money to meet short-term needs. Some of these needs, such as vacations and major purchases, you can anticipate and include in your budgeted savings. Others, such as emergencies and special social events, you may not foresee but need to save for anyway.
- You must start saving early to accumulate enough money to meet your long-term needs, such as home ownership, education, retirement, and investing, and to achieve financial security.
- Compounding, or interest earned on both principal and previous interest, makes savings grow faster. To compare accounts with different compounding methods, simply compare annual percentage yields.
- Commercial banks, savings banks, savings and loan associations, credit unions, and brokerage firms offer a variety of accounts and services.

10.2 Savings Options, Features, and Plans

- Savings options include savings accounts, certificates of deposit, and money market accounts. Regular savings accounts usually pay the lowest interest of these options because they offer the highest liquidity and safety.
- In selecting a savings plan, consider liquidity, safety, convenience, earning potential, and fees and restrictions.
- Saving regularly helps you meet your goals more quickly. Direct deposit and automatic payroll deductions are methods of forcing yourself to save.

Review Terms

Directions: Can you find the definition for each of the following terms used in Chapter 10?

annual percentage yield (APY)
certificate of deposit (CD)
compound interest
discretionary income
interest
liquidity
maturity date

money market account
principal
securities
share account
stockbroker

1. Ability of an asset to be converted into cash quickly without loss of value.
2. The date on which an investment becomes due for payment.
3. Money paid by a financial institution for the use of the saver's money.
4. A savings account at a credit union.
5. A sum of money in a savings account on which interest accrues.
6. Interest computed on the principal plus accumulated interest.
7. Amount of money left over after the bills are paid.
8. Person who buys and sells securities for investors.
9. A combination savings-investment plan in which the money deposited is used to purchase safe, liquid securities.
10. Deposit that earns a fixed interest rate for a specified length of time.
11. Stocks and bonds issued by corporations or by the government.
12. Actual interest rate an account pays per year, with compounding included.

Review Facts and Ideas

1. List several short-term needs that you expect to have in the next few months or years.
2. List your long-term plans that will require money in the next five years or more.
3. What are some personal factors that help determine the amount of money you will save?
4. Why might people choose to save their money in a commercial bank when another type of financial institution offers a higher interest rate?
5. How is a credit union different from a savings and loan association?
6. How much is an account insured for by the FDIC?
7. Why does a regular savings account pay less interest than a certificate of deposit?
8. What types of penalties might you face for early withdrawal of all or part of your savings from (a) regular savings, (b) certificates of deposit, or (c) money market funds?
9. What things should you consider when choosing a financial institution for your savings?
10. Describe ways you can force yourself to save.

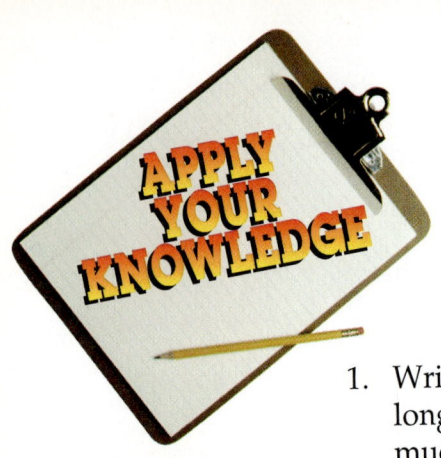

APPLY YOUR KNOWLEDGE

1. Write out your savings plans, listing your short-term and long-term goals and how you plan to achieve them. How much money will you save to meet them? Using the Savings Planner, calculate how much you would have to save each month to total the amount you need to meet your short-term goals. Assume that you will be saving for five years and will earn 7 percent on your savings.

2. What does discretionary income have to do with saving?

3. If two savings accounts offered 5 percent interest, but one was compounded quarterly and the other was compounded daily, which account would have the higher APY? Why?

4. Select a situation—amount saved and yield—and show the difference between simple and compounded interest. Figure the annual interest earned over a five-year period. Calculate the compound interest manually or use the Savings Planner Tool to help you.

5. Search the Internet for a savings calculator. Plug in different numbers and note the results. For example, try a certain regular savings amount compounded annually, then quarterly, then monthly. Note the differences that occur because of the different compounding method. Then try different savings amounts using the same compounding method. How does saving just a little more each month affect your total savings in, say, 10 years? Then try different interest rates with the same savings amounts and compounding method. Write a page about the conclusions you drew from your research.

6. Collect advertisements offering various financial services. What factors would you consider before using these services and the financial institutions that offer them?

7. Visit one or more financial institutions in your community and describe the following:
   a. types of savings accounts
   b. services available to depositors
   c. fees charged for services
   d. requirements, such as minimum deposits
   e. other enticements to get your business

8. Call a credit union in your area or find one online. Who can be a member of this credit union? What services does the credit union offer its members?

9. Miguel Correa is considering buying a certificate of deposit with the $500 he has in regular savings. Explain to him what factors he should consider when choosing a certificate of deposit.

10. Suppose you need to withdraw the money in a two-year CD before the certificate matures. Ask a local bank what the penalty is for withdrawing early from a two-year CD. What is the penalty for withdrawing all or part of your money from a regular savings account?

11. Visit www.money2000.org online and write a page about suggested ways to cut spending and save more.

Solve Problems

1. Compute the interest compounded for Kisha Burke, assuming that she deposits $1,000 in a CD with interest compounded every six months at the rate of 8½ percent. The certificate matures in three years. Use this format on a separate sheet of paper:

Year	Beginning Balance	First-Half Interest	Second-Half Interest	Total Interest	Ending Balance
1	$1,000	_____	_____	_____	_____
2	_____	_____	_____	_____	_____
3	_____	_____	_____	_____	_____

PLANNING TOOLS

2. Marita Reyes wishes to save $100 a month. Her bank computes compound interest monthly. The current rate for a regular savings account is 5½ percent. Compute the ending balance in her account after one year. Use this format on a separate sheet of paper:

Month	Beginning Balance	+ Deposit	= Total	+ Interest	= Ending Balance
1	_____	_____	_____	_____	_____
2	_____	_____	_____	_____	_____
3	_____	_____	_____	_____	_____
4	_____	_____	_____	_____	_____
5	_____	_____	_____	_____	_____
6	_____	_____	_____	_____	_____
7	_____	_____	_____	_____	_____
8	_____	_____	_____	_____	_____
9	_____	_____	_____	_____	_____
10	_____	_____	_____	_____	_____
11	_____	_____	_____	_____	_____
12	_____	_____	_____	_____	_____

3. Compute the interest compounded quarterly on a deposit of $500 for three years at 8 percent APY. Use the following format on a separate sheet of paper:

			Interest				
Year	Beginning Balance	First Quarter	Second Quarter	Third Quarter	Fourth Quarter	Total Interest	Ending Balance
1	$500	____	____	____	____	____	____
2	____	____	____	____	____	____	____
3	____	____	____	____	____	____	____

4. Compute your total savings if you keep $1,000 in a regular savings account at 5¼ percent, compounded quarterly, for two years. Use this format on a separate sheet of paper:

REGULAR SAVINGS ACCOUNT

			Interest				
Year	Beginning Balance	First Quarter	Second Quarter	Third Quarter	Fourth Quarter	Total Interest	Ending Balance
1	$1,000	____	____	____	____	____	____
2	____	____	____	____	____	____	____

For related activities and links, point your browser to
www.mypf.swep.com

Chapter 11
Investing for Your Future

Terms to Know

investing	annual report	stock
inflation	bonds	futures
risk	discount bond	option
diversification	mutual fund	penny stocks
financial advisers	annuity	

Up Front

Antonio has saved some money that he will use for college expenses in a few years. Right now, it's in his savings account, earning 3 percent a year.

"My dad says I can do better," Antonio told his best friend. "If I invest the money, I could get 8 to 12 percent, or maybe even better. So I've been checking my options. You know what I've found so far? That risk is a big part of investing. If I'm willing to take a lot of risk, then I may be able to earn more money. But I also stand a chance of losing part or all of my money. So I have to decide what my goals are, weigh the tradeoffs, and make the best choice to meet my goals. This is interesting stuff, but it isn't as easy as it sounds."

Goals

★ Describe the stages of investing and the relationship between risk and potential return.
★ Explain effective investment strategies, criteria for choosing an investment, and steps for investing wisely.

Stages of Investing

Your goals for saving and investing will be different, depending on your lifestyle, age, purposes for saving or investing, and income. Typically, as your excess income grows, you can progress through stages from temporary savings into different kinds of investing and greater amounts of risk.

Stage 1. Put-and-Take Account

When you first begin to earn a paycheck, your savings will be temporary. You will put your paycheck into an account and take money out as needed to pay your bills. This money is your *emergency fund,* or your "put-and-take" account. (See Figure 11-1 on page 304.) The purpose of this money is to pay for your short-term needs with enough left over to cover unexpected expenses. For example, you would use this money to pay your rent and utility bills, buy food and clothes, and pay for unexpected expenses, such as car repairs. Then your next paychecks would replenish the fund for later needs or expenses.

If your car needed repairs, where would you likely get the money?

Figure 11-1   *Stages of Investing*

BUDGET
- Income
- Expenses
- Savings

		Type of Investment	Strategy	Considerations
① Put-and-Take Account (Emergency Account) (excess)	Temporary	Short-term savings (3 to 6 months' pay)	Safety	• Security • Future expected and unexpected needs
② Beginning Investments (excess)		Conservative, low risk	Diversification	• Tax advantages
③ Systematic Investment (excess)	Permanent Investment	Retirement planning	Long-range	• Growth • Future financial security
④ Strategic Investment		Self-management of investment options	Maximization of return in the medium term (5–10 yrs.)	• Diversification • Planning • Hedging against risk
⑤ Speculation (excess)		Taking chances to realize quick profit potential	Risk	• Uncertain future income • Short-term profit potential

Spend and Enjoy

Many financial advisers recommend that you have three to six months' net pay set aside for this type of fund. Then, should a need arise, you won't dip into permanent, long-term investments to pay for temporary, short-term needs. Your main concern in saving these funds should be safety.

Stage 2. Beginning Investing

Investing is the use of savings to earn a financial return. The overall objective of investing is to earn money with money. As shown in Figure 11-1, investing really begins when your savings are "permanent" rather than "temporary put-and-take." Your initial investments should be conservative and low risk. At this stage, you don't have a lot of money to invest, so you don't want to risk losing it. Once you have established a safe cushion of investment, you can afford to make riskier (and potentially more profitable) investments. Typically, young workers in their 20s and early 30s begin investing when their budgets are stable and their excess cash is increasing.

Stage 3. Systematic Investing

Once you are comfortable with your beginning investments, you can then enter a stage called *systematic investment*—investing on a regular and planned basis. You would regularly set aside a certain amount for investing each month, increasing the amount as your excess income grows. At this stage, your goals are long-range. You are investing for a financially secure retirement. This ability to contribute regular sums of money usually happens in middle age, when earning potential is peaking.

Stage 4. Strategic Investing

Strategic investing is the careful management of investment alternatives to maximize growth of your *portfolio* (collection of investments) over the next 5–10 years. For example, when the growth prospects for one investment, or type of investment, seems to be declining, you would move your money into another type of investment where the prospects for growth seem greater. You would invest in different types of securities to try to maximize your returns.

Stage 5. Speculative Investing

When you are investing regularly in a broad collection of investments but you still have money available to take bigger risks, then you can choose to move into the final stage, called *speculation*. In this stage, you can make—or lose—a great deal of money in a short period of time. You must be aware of the risks and be prepared to lose the money you invest. Typically, odds are small that you will make a profit in a speculative investment, but when the speculation pays off, the profit can be great. Beginning investors should avoid speculation because they cannot take the loss that is likely to occur. Many investors never choose to speculate. Instead, they prefer to invest regularly over their lifetimes in solid securities with moderate risk.

Reasons for Investing

Investing is a proven and powerful way to strengthen your financial position over time. It is more than just an option. It is an essential part of providing for present and future needs. It provides a source of income in addition to a paycheck as you invest successfully and make money on money.

Investing Helps Beat Inflation

Inflation is a rise in the general level of prices. Investors should seek investments for the long term that will grow faster than the prices of goods and services, or the rate of inflation. For example, if the annual inflation rate is 6 percent, you will want your overall portfolio to yield a rate of return higher than 6 percent. During inflationary times, when prices are rising rapidly, you may not be able to earn a return that will keep pace with the inflation rate.

AROUND THE GLOBE

Unsettled by years of slow economic growth, runaway inflation, and high unemployment rates, some Latin American nations are turning to the U.S. dollar for economic stability. Panama, Ecuador, and El Salvador have "dollarized" their economies. This means that the national currencies are phased out and are replaced by U.S. dollars. Supporters of dollarization insist that it drives down inflation and interest rates, and softens the blow of international financial crises.

Think Critically: Opponents of dollarization say that it involves a nation's surrendering its financial independence. What do you think?

Investing Increases Wealth

Financial success grows from the assets that you build up over time. Investing helps you accumulate wealth faster than if you simply saved your excess cash in a savings account. Over the long run, investments earn higher profits than savings do. When you invest in stocks and bonds, you are participating in helping businesses make and sell new products and services, and you will be rewarded with dividends and interest that will add to your personal wealth.

Investing Is Fun and Challenging

Investors make choices and hope to pick winners. Once you get experience, you can have fun choosing the right investments, buying and selling when the time is right, and planning for your financial security based on your own knowledge and skill.

Risk and Return

Risk is the chance that an investment's value will decrease. All types of investing involve some degree of risk. The greater the risk you are willing to take, the greater the potential returns. A safe investment has a minimal risk of loss. Some people are willing to take more risks than others. Those who are willing to accept a reasonable amount of risk will likely make considerably more in the long run than investors who are *risk averse* (afraid to make investments in which they might lose some or all of their investment). However, *risk-takers* (investors who like to take on a great deal of risk) could make a lot or lose a lot. The best plan for most investors is to plot a moderate course, somewhere between no risk and extreme risk, wherever they feel comfortable.

Diversification

One way to minimize risk is through **diversification,** or the spreading of risk among many types of investments. Rather than buying only one kind of investment, you should choose several types of investments, such as stocks, bonds, and real estate. Also, you should diversify among types of stocks. For example, you might select some low-risk stocks to balance others with greater risk.

Is there any type of investing that does not involve some degree of risk?

Diversification reduces overall risk because not all of your choices will perform poorly at the same time. If one choice does not do well, the others will likely make up some or all of the loss.

Here's an easy way to think about the concept of diversification: "Don't put all your eggs in one basket." Diversification can't eliminate risk. But it can help you balance risk.

Types of Risk

Short-term investments are generally less risky than long-term investments. You can predict much more accurately what will happen in a week, a month, or a year than you can in 10 or 20 years.

During inflationary times, there is *interest-rate risk* that the return on an investment will not keep pace with the inflation rate. Inflation makes your fixed-rate investments worth less because they are "locked in" at lower rates of interest. The value of a fixed-rate investment decreases when overall interest rates increase. The value increases when overall interest rates decrease. For example, if you own a security paying a fixed interest rate (say, 5 percent) and interest rates are increasing (more than 5 percent), your investment will be worth less over time.

Government actions that affect business conditions are the basis of *political risk*. Increased taxes and certain regulations, such as costly environmental controls that businesses are required to apply, can make some investments less attractive.

Market risk, which affects many types of investments at once, is caused by business declines, sudden national or world events, or interest rate fluctuations. *Company* or *industry risk* is produced by events that affect only one company or industry. For example, if you invest in the candy industry, a nationwide trend toward dieting or the avoidance of sugar may adversely affect the value of your investment.

Investment Strategies

Many individuals never start an investment program because they think they don't have enough money. But even small sums of money grow over time. To achieve financial security, start investing as soon as you can and continue to invest over your lifetime. The suggestions that follow will help you make wise investment decisions.

Criteria for Choosing an Investment

Some investments increase in value at a rate higher than the rate of inflation. Some do not. Some investments provide for increases in value that do not show up as taxable income for many years. Others do not. Evaluate your investment options according to these factors:

1. Safety (minimal risk of loss)
2. High liquidity (getting your money quickly)
3. High dividends or interest
4. Growth in value that exceeds the inflation rate
5. Reasonable (low) purchase price (or initial cost)
6. Tax benefits (saving or postponing tax liability)

No investment offers all of these. Each investment choice represents a tradeoff. For example, in exchange for tax benefits, you would likely have to give up a high return and liquidity. However, you should choose investments that offer, for example, the highest degree of safety you can get for the expected return. A diversified portfolio of investments achieves a balance among these factors. It would include some safe but low-yield investments as well as some riskier, higher-growth choices plus some tax-deferred investments. Most of these factors will be examined in the discussion of specific types of investments in Chapters 12–15.

Wise Investment Practices

People commonly make mistakes in connection with their investment practices. Some mistakes are minor and can be corrected easily. Others cause serious financial damage. To avoid investment mistakes and maximize your investing returns, follow the investment practices described below.

Define Your Financial Goals

In Chapter 8 you were introduced to the importance of setting goals as you developed a budget. If you clearly define your financial goals, you will know which investments to purchase to best meet them. To be useful, investment goals must be specific and measurable.

Go Slowly

Before making investment decisions, gather the information you need in order to make a wise decision. Don't act on impulse or because something sounds good. Allow yourself adequate time to obtain and analyze the needed information and to make a good choice.

Follow Through

Putting off plans and never taking action will lead to failure in meeting financial goals. Act on your important goals now. Don't wait for a future day that may not come. A common mistake is keeping too much money in the "put-and-take" account and not taking advantage of the higher rates of return of permanent investments.

Keep Good Records

In order to keep a clear view of your future needs and goals, you need to keep good financial records. Your personal net worth statement, plus lists of insurance policies and investments, account balances and the location of bank accounts, and the contents and location of your safe deposit box, are essential information. Unless you know where you have been and where you are now, it is difficult to plan where you are going.

Seek Good Investment Advice

Don't be afraid to ask questions. Many people think they can make wise investments without seeking advice from an expert. In the long run, these investments may prove to be expensive, because poor investments can cost a great deal in lost income. In general, it is wise to seek competent advice from a trained professional before making any investment decision.

Keep Investment Knowledge Current

You should be aware of what is new in the financial market, what kinds of investments are currently good prospects, when to sell, and when to buy. The economy is a major consideration in making investment decisions. You need to understand how it works and what various economic indicators mean. Although you should seek advice before making a major investment move, it is your responsibility to know when to ask questions and to make the final decisions about your investments.

The Internet has greatly affected the financial world. In 1997 there were 17 firms that offered online trading; by 2001 there were more than 100. By 2002, it is predicted that there will be approximately 14.4 million online accounts, containing approximately $688 billion in assets—up from 3 million accounts and $120 billion in assets in 1998.

Know Your Limits

Understand your risk tolerance and the amount of money you can afford to risk, so you can maximize returns within your risk comfort zone. If you are uncomfortable taking large risks, then avoid them. The chance of making huge profits is not worth being stressed out by the risk.

Review Terms
1. investing
2. inflation
3. risk
4. diversification

Review Concepts
1. Why do you need an emergency fund before you start investing?
2. How does investing help you beat inflation?
3. What is diversification and what is its purpose?

Lesson 11.2 Exploring Investment Options

Goals

★ List and describe sources of financial information useful for making investment decisions.

★ List and define basic investment options, rated by risk.

Sources of Financial Information

Investment information can be found in print, online, and through other sources. When you want to evaluate investment options, you can find plenty of information to make an informed decision.

Newspapers

Most newspapers contain *financial pages.* Reading these pages daily will help you keep track of financial markets and obtain information needed to make wise investment decisions. *The Wall Street Journal* is a daily publication that provides detailed coverage of the business and financial world. *Barron's* is a weekly newspaper that also provides charts of trends, financial news items, and technical analysis of financial data. Both of these publications offer online subscriptions as well as free articles and data available at their Web sites: http://public.wsj.com/home.html (*The Wall Street Journal*) and www.barrons.com (*Barron's*).

What are some sources of investment information?

Investor Services and Newsletters

Companies called *investor services* provide extensive financial data to clients. Main resources are *Moody's Investors Service* (www.moodys.com), *Standard and Poor's Reports* (www.standard-andpoors.com), and *Value Line* (www.valueline.com). These publications are found in public libraries and brokerage firms, as well as online. They contain precise current and historical financial data. Many investors subscribe to weekly or monthly investment newsletters, which give them the latest financial data and information.

Financial Magazines

A number of weekly and monthly magazines specialize in business and financial information. Most of them interpret financial data and give opinions and recommendations. Weekly magazines include *Business Week* (www.businessweek.com) and *Forbes* (www.forbes.com). Monthly magazines include *Money* (www.money.com), *Fortune* (www.fortune.com), *Kiplinger's Personal Finance* (www.kiplinger.com), and *The Economist* (www.economist.com). Once you have made your choices, these magazines will keep you current, so you can determine when it is time to buy, hold, or sell. All of these publications offer financial news and stock market performance data at their Web sites.

Brokers

Full-service brokers provide clients with analysis and opinions based on their judgments and the opinions of experts at the company they represent. However, you cannot expect a broker to pick winners for you every time. Almost all full-service brokerage firms provide monthly market letters giving advice on the purchase and sale of certain securities. Some well-known brokers include Merrill Lynch (www.ml.com), Fidelity Investments (www.fid-inv.com), and American Express (www.americanexpress.com).

Some people are well informed and know what they want to buy and sell. For these investors, a discount broker is adequate. *Discount brokers* buy and sell securities for clients at a reduced commission. The commission can be half of that charged by a full-service broker, or even less. A discount broker usually provides little or no investment advice to a client. A pioneer in the discount trading business is Charles Schwab (www.charlesschwab.com). Two other well-known online discount brokers are Ameritrade (www.ameritrade.com) and E*Trade (www.etrade.com). Also, because of the increasing popularity of inexpensive trading, many full-service brokers also offer discount trading at their Web sites.

Many banks and some savings and loans have discount brokers available to customers who want to trade securities. In most cases, you will be required to have a checking or savings account at that institution. Money can be transferred from your account to pay for securities purchased, or deposited to your account to reflect securities sold. A bank or savings and loan will also maintain a brokerage account for you and send you account statements showing the current value of your securities.

With most types of brokerage accounts, you can manage your account online. You can give buy and sell orders, transfer money among investment accounts, and track the progress of your investments either with your own software or with a platform supplied by the broker or bank.

Financial Advisers

Professional investment planners are called **financial advisers**. They are trained to give informed overall investment advice based on your goals, age, net worth, occupation, investment experience, lifestyle, family responsibilities, and other factors. You will be asked to fill out confidential information showing assets, liabilities, net worth, income, and budget as well as your financial goals. The financial adviser usually receives a fee for services rendered, although some advisers receive fees when they sell you investment products (such as stocks, bonds, or life insurance policies). Generally, you will get better overall advice when the adviser does not stand to make a profit on the investment you choose to buy.

Annual Reports and Financial Statements

An **annual report** is a summary of a corporation's financial results for the year and prospects for the future. The Securities and Exchange Commission (SEC) requires all corporations to prepare this report at the end of each year and send it to their stockholders. Investors can use the information contained in the report to evaluate the corporation as an investment prospect.

The annual report gives the financial history of the company, current financial statements including the balance sheet and the income statement, comparisons of data for several years, and a

PERSONAL PERSPECTIVE

Choosing the Right Financial Adviser

Selecting the right financial adviser can be tricky. If you choose the wrong adviser, the financial results could be painful. The most important factor in selecting a financial adviser is *trust*. You must feel comfortable with your adviser, be willing to give him or her a full and complete picture of your finances and financial goals, and then follow his or her advice.

Many people begin their investing with a trusted family friend who is in the business of giving financial advice at a bank, brokerage firm, or other financial institution. Or, you may know someone who has worked with a particular adviser for several years and can recommend him or her. If so, your choice will be somewhat easier.

Some people consult with financial advisers at credit unions or through employee assistance plans. Others participate in group seminars offered by employers or professional organizations. In many cases, you can get good general advice about investment strategies that are effective for people with investment goals similar to yours.

The trick to finding and building a relationship of trust with a financial adviser involves taking the time to ask questions and to discuss thoroughly your income, assets, liabilities, risk comfort level, and financial goals. Be sure to ask potential financial advisers about their training, background, and experience. Ask their philosophy of investing, fees (how they earn money), and investment strategies. You also should know how clients have done in the past with their investment recommendations. Ask for copies of references. Take them home and read them carefully. Good advisers will tell you about their past successes. You can also check up on the past performance of stockbrokers through the National Association of Securities Dealers. The association monitors complaints and actions taken against its members. Remember: If you don't feel comfortable with a prospective financial adviser, keep looking until you find one who you feel can help you achieve your investment goals.

Think Critically

1. If you needed financial advice, whom would you ask? Why?
2. What are the characteristics you would look for in a successful financial adviser? What would it take to build your trust?
3. Locate the names and addresses of three or more financial advisers in your area.

description of its products and services. In addition, you will find an assessment of the company's future growth plans and prospects, plus information about competitors and the company's position in the industry. All major trends are discussed for the company and the industry, including current and future expansions or consolidations that could affect the value of the stock. Charts and graphs are used to display financial trends and comparisons to previous years or similar businesses.

You can find annual reports online at the SEC Web site (http://www.sec.gov/edgarhp.htm). Corporations often publish financial performance data about themselves in the investor section of their Web sites. If you are interested in learning about or investing in a corporation, you can receive a copy of the annual report by writing the company and asking for it, or requesting it at the company Web site. In addition, some large libraries keep copies of annual reports of major corporations.

Online Investor Education

In addition to the Web sites of print publications and brokers, the Internet offers many educational sites for new investors. Teenvestor (www.teenvestor.com) is dedicated to helping teens learn how to invest and manage their money. The Motley Fool (www.fool.com) offers money management tips in its personal finance section. Its "fool's school" presents investment basics in reader-friendly language. The National Association of Investors Corporation (www.better-investing.org) is a nonprofit site dedicated to investor education. This organization also helps investment clubs get started. These are just a few of the many educational sites available to investors online. A Web search using a search engine or a directory from a popular home page, such as Yahoo! (www.yahoo.com), will produce many more.

Investment Options

Once you have established your emergency fund and have some additional money in savings, it's time to consider other investment alternatives. The following discussion groups different types of investments according to their degree of risk and expected return. In Chapters 12 through 15, you will explore each type of investment more thoroughly.

For your first investments, you will likely want to consider fairly safe investments, even though their returns will be relatively low. Even as you grow as a sophisticated investor, however, you will probably continue to include some low-risk investments as part of your diversified portfolio.

Corporate and Municipal Bonds

Bonds are debt obligations of corporations (*corporate bonds*) or state or local governments (*municipal bonds*). When a corporation or government body sells a bond to an investor, it is borrowing from the investor. When you buy a corporate bond as an investment, the corporation pays you a fixed amount of money (called interest) at a fixed interval (usually every six months). The corporation also must repay the principal (amount borrowed) at maturity. The maturity date of a bond is the date on which the borrowed money must be repaid. When you loan money to a government authority, such as a city, county, community college district, or utility district, you are also paid interest on your investment. Your principal is repaid when the bond matures. Typically, interest earned on government bonds is tax-free, giving the investor a tax advantage. Bonds are explained in detail in Chapter 13.

U.S. Government Savings Bonds

When you buy a savings bond, you are lending money to the United States government. A *Series EE savings bond* is a **discount bond**, because you buy it for less than its maturity value. The purchase price of a Series EE bond is one half of its maturity value. For example, you would buy a $50 bond for $25 and a $100 bond for $50. At maturity, you receive the full value of the bond. The difference between the purchase price and the maturity value is the amount of interest earned. Generally, EE bonds mature in 10 years but can be extended for up to 30 years.

DID YOU KNOW

To commemorate the U.S. Bicentennial in July, 1976, many banks sold the $25 savings bond for $17.76 instead of the usual $18.75.

The interest accumulates every six months. You receive the interest at the time you cash in your bond. Interest earned on Series EE savings bonds is exempt from state and local taxes. It is not subject to federal taxation until the bonds are cashed in. These bonds earn a variable rate of interest and have a higher rate of return than regular savings accounts and some CDs.

A *Series HH savings bond* pays interest semiannually (every six months) and matures in 10 years. These bonds can be purchased only in exchange for maturing EE bonds. Series HH bonds may be redeemed at any time after being held for a minimum of six months.

You can buy savings bonds from commercial banks or through payroll deductions. Savings bond certificates should be stored in a safe deposit box.

If you are seeking safety, savings bonds are a good investment. They are also very liquid. You can hold them to maturity or cash them in anytime at a bank for their current value. Their interest is not subject to state or local taxes, only federal. Some savings bonds used to finance a college education are free of federal taxation as well. If savings bonds are lost, stolen, or destroyed, they can be replaced without cost.

Treasury Securities

U.S. Treasury bills (called *t-bills*) are available in denominations of $10,000 and then in increments of $5,000 more. A Treasury bill matures in one year or less. The bill is usually a three-month, six-month, or one-year government obligation.

Treasury notes are issued in units of $1,000 or $5,000. Maturities range from two years to ten years. Interest rates for Treasury notes are slightly higher than for Treasury bills.

Treasury bonds are issued in minimum units of $1,000 with maturities that range from 10 to 30 years. Interest rates for Treasury bonds are generally higher than interest rates for either t-bills or Treasury notes. Interest paid every six months is taxed by the federal government, but it is exempt from state and local income taxes.

Medium Risk/Medium Return

When you feel secure enough to take more risk and you have additional money to invest, you are ready to step up to the medium-risk range to increase your return. Some of these medium-risk options involve investing with companies that manage the investment.

Mutual Funds

Suppose you have $500 to invest but do not know which stocks or bonds to buy, when to buy them, or when to sell them. You can buy shares in a large, professionally managed group of investments called a **mutual fund**. A mutual fund pools the money of many investors and buys a large selection of securities that meet the fund's stated investment goals. Two major advantages of a mutual fund for an investor are professional management and diversification. Since the fund invests in a wide variety of securities, it provides diversification that small investors could not otherwise achieve with their limited resources.

Although some mutual funds fall in the speculative category and others fall in the low-risk category, such as those that specialize in money market securities, most mutual funds fall somewhere in the broad medium range in terms of risk and return. You can further diversify your portfolio by investing in mutual funds with different objectives. For example, some funds buy securities in riskier small companies, hoping to earn a higher return. Others stick to well-established, safe companies to earn a lower but stable return. By investing money in both funds, you are diversifying your investments. If your riskier fund does not do well, your stable fund will limit your losses.

Mutual funds are the fastest-growing segment of the United States' financial services industry. You will learn more about mutual funds in Chapter 14.

Annuities

An **annuity** is a contract sold by an insurance company that provides the investor with a series of regular payments, usually after retirement. Generally, you receive income monthly, with payments to continue as long as you live. You usually buy an annuity directly from a life insurance company. The interest on the principal, as well as the interest compounded on that interest, builds up free of current income tax. Taxes are deferred until you receive payments from your annuity. The payments from an annuity are normally used to supplement retirement income. The annuity is often described as the opposite of life insurance. It pays while you are alive; life insurance pays when you die.

Self-Managed Retirement Accounts

Profit-seeking companies may provide 401(k) retirement accounts for their employees. Not-for-profit and government employers provide 403(b) retirement accounts, which are the equivalent of the 401(k) type of account. Employers usually offer a variety of investments, often mutual funds, from which employees may choose for investing their retirement account money. Within these accounts, you can choose the type of investing strategy, such as fixed (low risk, low return), a balanced fund (medium risk, medium return), or aggressive stock funds.

An *IRA (individual retirement account)* is a retirement savings plan in which an individual sets aside a certain amount of money (up to a specified maximum) each year for retirement. The advantage of an IRA is that the money put into an IRA each year may be tax deductible. You will pay taxes on the IRA when you start withdrawing funds at age 59½ or older.

A *Keogh plan* is similar to the IRA but to qualify, the investor must be self-employed. Keogh plans allow for larger annual investments than IRAs do. Similarly, a *Simplified Employee Pension Plan (SEP)* is aimed at small employers. An employee may contribute to a SEP even if covered by another pension plan. The allowable contribution is higher than for an IRA. Annuities, IRAs, Keogh plans, and SEPs will be discussed in more detail in Chapter 15.

Real Estate

What are some advantages of investing in real estate?

Many people like to invest in real estate—houses and land. While this type of investment usually represents a large and often non-liquid investment of cash, it has proven to be protection against inflation in most parts of the United States. In some areas, prices of homes have increased faster than the inflation rate. Real estate investments also have tax benefits. Certain costs associated with home ownership are deductible from gross income, and therefore they lower taxable income. For people who don't want to own real estate but want to invest in it, REITs (Real Estate Investment Trusts) are available. While investing in your own home carries little risk, investment in other types of real estate can be very risky. Chapter 14 presents a more in-depth explanation of real estate investing.

High Risk/High Return

High-risk/high-return options involve considerable uncertainty. Returns can be high, but they can also be low, none at all, or a loss to principal (the amount of the original investment). If you are willing to take the risks involved with these choices, you stand to make high returns over time. But you also risk losses if your investments prove to be poor performers.

Stocks and Trading Instruments

Stock is a unit of ownership in a corporation. The owner of stock is called a *stockholder*. A stockholder receives a stock certificate, which is evidence of the ownership. When you are a stockholder, you will share in a corporation's profits, which are paid to you as dividends. If the company does well, you earn returns in two ways: in dividends and in the increased value of the stock you own. Stocks generally carry more risk than choices with fixed interest, such as savings bonds, because a stockholder's earnings can go up or down, depending on the company's fortunes. Stocks in well-established companies are reasonably safe, while stocks in less-stable companies can be quite risky. You will learn more about investing in stocks in Chapter 12.

Futures

Futures are contracts to buy and sell commodities or stocks for a specified price on a specified date in the future. The investor is betting that the price of the commodity or stock will be higher on that future date than it is at the time of the contract. Thus, trading in futures is very risky speculation. If prices fall, the investor loses. If prices rise, the investor stands to make a lot of money. This type of investment is not for beginners or for individuals who cannot afford to lose their investment.

Options

An **option** is the right, but not the obligation, to buy or sell a commodity or stock for a specified price within a specified time period. As with futures, the investor is betting that, during the option period, the price of the stock will rise. If it does, the investor can choose to buy it at the lower option price, resulting in an instant profit. Typically, options are short-term investment devices used by speculators to make a quick profit. They are risky and not for novice investors.

Penny Stocks

Penny stocks are low-priced stocks of small companies that have no track record. The stock usually sells for under a dollar per share. The small companies often have no revenues or earnings and no assets to assure future growth. Dot-com (Internet) companies typically begin this way. Many of them fail, and the stock is worthless. Occasionally, a penny stock will be successful, and the investor will make a large windfall. But generally they are highly risky.

Collectibles

Many people like to collect items such as coins, art, memorabilia, ceramics, or other items that are popular from time to time, such as Beanie Babies or baseball cards. If you collect an item that goes up in value rapidly, you can reap large rewards. If, however, you don't sell when your items are a hot commodity, they are likely to lose their value just as quickly, making them a risky investment. Collectors must be aware of the market and realize that their collections are subject to changing public tastes and can be difficult to sell.

COMMUNICATION CONNECTION

Interview a friend or relative who collects a certain item. Does the person collect for fun and/or profit? Write a one-page essay that describes the collection and the person's point of view. From your perspective, is the collection really an investment? Why or why not?

✓ Check Your Understanding

Review Terms
1. financial advisers
2. annual report
3. bonds
4. discount bond
5. mutual fund
6. annuity
7. stock
8. futures
9. option
10. penny stocks

Review Concepts
1. What are some sources of financial information useful for making investment decisions?
2. Why should beginning investors choose safe investments?
3. Why is investing in stock considered risky?

11.1 Investing Fundamentals

- As you begin to earn a regular income, your first goal will be to save enough to cover your current needs and unexpected emergencies. As your income grows beyond current needs, you will progress through stages into different kinds of investing and greater amounts of risk.
- Risk is the chance that an investment's value will decrease. All investments involve some degree of risk. Choose investments with a risk level within your comfort zone. You can minimize your overall risk by building a diversified portfolio of investments.
- Investing will help you increase wealth, stay ahead of inflation, and strengthen your financial position over time.
- There are several types of investment risk, including interest-rate (inflation) risk, political risk, market risk, and company or industry risk.
- Evaluate your investment options for their degree of safety, liquidity, dividends or interest, growth, cost, and tax benefits. All investments involve tradeoffs among these criteria.
- To make wise investment choices, define your goals, go slowly, keep good records, get good advice, keep your investment knowledge current, and know your limits.

11.2 Exploring Investment Options

- Sources of information about investment choices include newspaper financial pages, investor newsletters, financial magazines, brokers, financial advisors, and annual reports. Much of this information is also available online.

- Investment options can be low risk/low-to-medium return, medium risk/medium return, or high risk/high return. Generally, the more risk you are willing to take, the more you stand to gain or lose.
- Low risk/low-to-medium return investment options include corporate or government bonds and Treasury securities.
- Medium risk/medium return investment options include mutual funds, annuities, self-managed retirement accounts, and real estate.
- Stocks can be risky or not so risky, depending on the stability of the issuing company. However, with highly risky investments, such as futures, options, penny stocks, and collectibles, you can lose some or all of the money you invested or make a big profit.

Value	Change	%Change
3,006.62	38.97 ▲	1.31%
2,649.71	33.35 ▲	1.27%
807.90	2.93 ▲	0.36%
10,744.54	96.03 ▲	0.90%
1,367.40	13.28 ▲	0.98%
626.42	4.70 ▲	0.76%

Review Terms

Directions: Can you find the definition for each of the following terms used in Chapter 11?

annual report
annuity
bonds
discount bond
diversification
financial advisers
futures
inflation
investing

mutual fund
option
penny stocks
risk
stock

1. A bond purchased for less than its maturity value.
2. A contract sold by an insurance company that provides the investor a series of regular payments, usually after retirement.
3. An investment strategy for spreading risk among different types of investments.
4. The use of savings to earn a financial return.
5. A rise in the general level of prices.
6. The chance that an investment's value will decrease.
7. An SEC-required summary of a corporation's financial results for the year and prospects for the future.
8. Unit of ownership in a corporation.
9. Professional investment planners who are trained to give investment advice.
10. An investment that represents the debt of a company or a government.
11. A professionally managed group of investments bought using a pool of money from many investors.
12. Contracts to buy and sell commodities or stocks for a specified price on a specified date in the future.
13. The right, but not the obligation, to buy or sell a commodity or stock for a specified price within a specified time period.
14. Low-priced stocks of small companies that have no track record.

Review Facts and Ideas

1. Explain the difference between temporary and permanent investments.
2. List the stages investors usually go through as their excess income increases over time.
3. List three reasons for investing money.
4. How does risk relate to potential return?
5. Identify criteria you can use to evaluate an investment.
6. What are seven wise investment practices?
7. What questions might you ask in selecting a financial adviser?
8. Name at least six main sources of financial information.
9. Where can you find investment information online?
10. Explain the difference between stocks and bonds.
11. Distinguish among t-bills, Treasury notes, and Treasury bonds.
12. What are some advantages of investing in mutual funds?
13. Why are futures and options risky investments?

APPLY YOUR KNOWLEDGE

1. Explain the put-and-take concept. Why is it important that money set aside remain a permanent investment? How will you personally design an investment plan? Will it include a put-and-take or emergency account? Explain.
2. Why is risk such an important consideration when investing? Write a paragraph explaining your comfort level with risk and how it will affect your investment decisions.
3. Explain why it is not possible for one investment to satisfy all the criteria for choosing an investment. Which criteria are most important to you?

4. Read the financial section of your local newspaper. Write a few paragraphs summarizing the type of information covered and its usefulness to you as an investor.

5. Visit a library and get a copy of a current annual report for a major corporation that does business in your state. Or, visit a large corporation online and go to its investor page to find its financial data. Outline the contents of the report or the online financial data and give a brief oral review of your findings to the class. Give your opinion of whether or not this corporation would be a good investment choice, and present reasons why you feel this way.

6. Consult a financial newspaper or magazine or search the Internet to find the following information:
   a. the current rate being offered on Series EE savings bonds
   b. the current rate of one-year Treasury bills
   c. the current rate of two-year Treasury notes
   d. the current rate of thirty-year Treasury bonds

7. Using key words such as "investment," "stock," or some others you can think of, search the Internet for resources to help you make investing choices. List the names and URLs of three sites that you think would help you most. Briefly describe the types of investment information available at those sites.

8. Visit a discount brokerage firm online to find out how to open an account. Summarize their requirements in a paragraph.

Solve Problems

PLANNING TOOLS

1. Your friend Amanda, who is 19 and in college, has just inherited $1,000. She does not need the money for her put-and-take account. What would you tell her to do with it? If Amanda invested the money in a stock that earned, on average, 10 percent return, how much would her investment be worth in five years? Use your Savings Planner Tool for your calculations.

2. Rick Suarez is considering investing $500. Explain to him what factors he should consider when choosing investment alternatives.

3. Friends of your family, who were recently married, are now finding that they have money left over each month that they could invest. They would like to consult a financial adviser but don't know one. What tips would you give them about selecting a financial adviser?

4. Joanne Chen would like to invest in XYZ Corporation. She heard that the company was big and powerful. You've never heard of it. What kinds of information should she have before she invests in this company? Where can she get that information?

5. Lynda Goldberg would like to invest $10,000 that she inherited from her uncle. She would like to have the money for her daughter's college education starting in eight years. She does not like to take a lot of risk because she cannot afford to lose the $10,000. What course of action would you suggest for Lynda?

6. Assume that Lynda Goldberg in question 5 invested her $10,000 in a way that earned an average of 6 percent annual return. Use your College Planner Tool to find out how much more she would have to invest each year to cover her daughter's college costs. Assume that college will cost $5,000 a year for four years.

PLANNING TOOLS

7. Choose at least six of the investment alternatives presented in this chapter. Rank the choices from high to low on the factors of safety, risk, and liquidity. Assume that 3 is the highest score and 1 is the lowest score for each factor. Based on the results of your review of possible investments, which three alternatives would you select as permanent investments? Why?

For related activities and links, point your browser to
www.mypf.swep.com

Chapter 12
Investing in Stocks

Up Front

LeVar worked hard for the summer and managed to save $500 to invest. He decided he wanted to buy a stock and see what happened.

"I've been doing research about a medical research company, and I think it's on the verge of something big," he said to his discount broker in an e-mail. "I think the stock price is low now because the company isn't paying dividends. Instead, management is using company profits to develop new products. The president and management team are very strong. All the information I've gathered online suggests that the company is solid. I think this growth stock is worth the risk. Please buy me as many shares as my money will purchase."

Lesson 12.1 — Evaluating Stocks

Goals

★ Describe the features of common stock and compare it to preferred stock.
★ Discuss stock investing classifications and why you would choose one over another.
★ Explain how stock values are determined.
★ Discuss factors that affect a stock's price.

Characteristics of Stock

Nearly 50 million people in the United States own stocks. There are more than 34,000 public corporations from which to choose. A *public corporation* is a company whose stock is traded openly on stock markets.

Stockholders, also known as *shareholders*, are the owners of the corporation. If the corporation does well, stockholders will profit in two ways. One is through dividends. **Dividends** are the part of the corporation's profits paid to stockholders. The other way stock-holders profit when the corporation does well is through **capital gain**. This is an increase in the value of the stock above the price initially paid for it. For example, if you bought stock for $5 per share and the corporation thrived, its stock price might go up to $10 per share. If it did, you could sell it for a substantial profit. Part of the risk in owning stock, however, is that the price could also go down below the price initially paid for it, resulting in a *capital loss.*

Also, a capital gain becomes profit only when you sell the stock. Until then, it is a profit only on paper.

Stockholders can lose all of their investment should the company fail. However, one advantage to owning stock is that stockholders can lose no more than their investment in the stock. The owner of a small business, on the other hand, can also lose personal assets when the business fails.

Why is owning a stock risky?

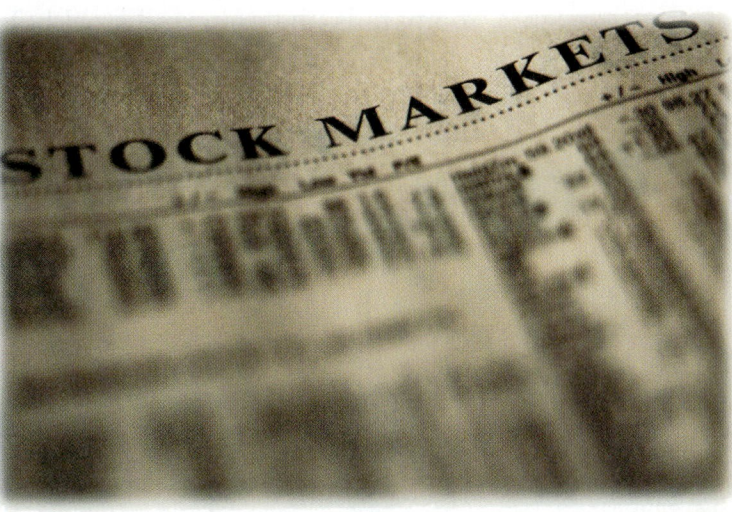

Stocks are traded in round lots or odd lots. A *round lot* is 100 shares or multiples of 100 shares of a particular stock. An *odd lot* is fewer than 100 shares of a particular stock. Brokerage firms usually charge slightly higher per-share fees for trading in odd lots. Odd lots must be combined into round lots before they can be traded.

Common Stock

Common stock is a type of stock that pays a variable dividend and gives the holder voting rights. The *board of directors*, elected by stockholders to guide the corporation, decides the amount of the dividend each year. Common stockholders do not directly manage the corporation, but they may vote on major policy decisions, such as whether to issue additional stock, sell the company, or change the board of directors. Each share has the same voting power, so the more shares a stockholder owns, the greater the power to influence corporate policy.

Common stockholders may vote in person at the stockholders' meeting or by proxy. A **proxy** is a stockholder's written authorization to transfer his or her voting rights to someone else, usually a company manager. Most stockholders sign the proxy rather than attend the meetings.

Preferred Stock

Preferred stock is a type of stock that pays a fixed dividend and carries no voting rights. Preferred stockholders earn the stated dividend, regardless of how the company is doing, making preferred stock less risky than common stock. In the event the company fails, the preferred stockholder would be paid ahead of common stockholders. As with most investments, however, the tradeoff for less risk is lower return. Dividends on preferred stock may be lower than common stockholders would earn on a thriving corporation over time.

An investment club is a group of people who pool their money to make investments. The group usually decides to buy or sell based on a majority vote of the members. Each member may actively participate in investment decisions.

Classifying Stock Investments

When evaluating common stock investments, investors often classify stocks into different categories. Common categories of stocks include income, growth, blue chip, defensive, and cyclical. Which category is best for you will depend on how much risk you are willing to assume for a chance to earn larger returns on your investments. Also, most investors buy stocks in several of these categories to diversify their risk.

Income versus Growth Stocks

Corporations can use their profits in two ways. They can distribute the profits to stockholders as dividends, or they can reinvest the profits in the business to help it grow. Stocks that have a consistent history of paying high dividends are known as **income stocks**. Investors choose income stocks in order to receive current income in the form of dividends. Preferred stocks pay the most certain and predictable dividend income and are often the choice of retired people and others investing for income from dividends.

Corporations that pay high dividends put less profit back into the business. As a result, income stocks usually do not grow in value as quickly as growth stocks. **Growth stocks** are stocks in corporations that reinvest their profits into the business so that it can grow. These corporations may pay little or no dividends. Instead of current income, investors buy growth stocks for future capital gains. If the reinvested profits do make the business grow, the stock will be worth substantially more in the future, when the investor is ready to sell it. As a result, growth stocks are long-term investments. If the value of the stock increases, stockholders must decide whether to sell it at the higher price now or to continue to hold it, hoping that it will go up even more. When stockholders decide to sell, the difference between their original purchase price and the selling price they receive is their capital gain.

Less-Established versus Blue Chip Stocks

Stocks in young, often small corporations have higher overall risk than stocks of companies that have been successful for many years. These young companies may be on their way to becoming highly profitable. Or, they may be among the many small companies that fail every year. Because the future of these companies is so uncertain, their stocks are often inexpensive but risky.

Why are blue chip stocks a conservative investment?

Blue chip stocks are stocks of large, well-established corporations with a solid record of profitability. Most people have heard of these companies because their products and services have been around for decades—they are companies like IBM and Coca-Cola. Blue chip stocks are a conservative investment. Investors choose them for relatively safe, stable, but moderate returns.

Defensive versus Cyclical Stocks

A *defensive stock* is one that remains stable and pays dividends during an economic decline. Generally, companies in this category have a history of stable earnings. A defensive stock is not subject to the ups and downs of business cycles. Examples include utilities, drugs, food, and health care. In other words, the demand for these products is consistent regardless of economic conditions. Therefore, stocks in these industries protect the investor from sharp losses during bad economic times.

Cyclical stocks do well when the economy is stable or growing but often do poorly during *recessions,* when the economy slows down. Examples of cyclical stocks are travel-related companies such as airlines and resorts, manufacturing companies, and agriculture. For example, during a recession, many people lose their jobs or earn less than they would during good economic times. As a result, people have less money for luxuries, such as leisure travel, causing reduced profits for travel-related companies such as airlines and resorts. In response to this poor profit performance, the value of the stocks in these companies will likely decline.

Determining a Stock's Worth

When you buy stock, you expect to hold it for a period of time and then sell it, hopefully for a profit. Whether or not you make a profit on the sale of your stock depends on how much someone else is willing to pay for it when you are ready to sell.

Stock Value

When you purchase stock, you may receive a stock certificate or have it held electronically. The certificate states the number of shares you own, the name of the company, the type of stock (common or preferred), and the par value. The **par value** is an assigned (and often arbitrary) dollar value.

An old stock certificate may still be valuable even if the stock no longer trades under the name on the certificate. The company may have merged with another business or simply changed its name. Even if you learn that a certificate has no value, it may be considered a collectible.

Par value is an artificial number. It has nothing to do with a stock's **market value**, which is the price for which the stock is bought and sold in the marketplace. Market value reflects the price investors are willing to pay for the stock. How a company currently is doing, its track record, and how well it is expected to perform in the future determine market value.

Some stocks perform very well, yet their market value seems too low—or a "real bargain." These "undervalued" stocks are worth more than the price for which they are selling. Stocks that are undervalued make good bargains for investors, while creating a dangerous situation for businesses. With this condition, the corporation is vulnerable to a takeover by a large investor or company. The result is often loss of jobs for workers and a company that is broken into parts for sell-off. Takeovers may be unfavorable for employees but can be very favorable for stockholders, because the market value of the stock is likely to rise.

On the other hand, stocks can be "overvalued," which means they are selling at a price that is not justified by their earnings potential. This situation is very risky for the investor, because it is likely that the price of the stock will drop.

Stock prices go up and down constantly. The wider the price swings, the riskier the stock. That is, a stock that has a history of very high highs and very low lows is a riskier investment than a stock that goes up and down only moderately over time.

Stock Price

Several things affect the price you will pay for a share of stock: the financial situation of a company, current interest rates, the market for a company's products or services, and earnings per share.

1. *The Company.* When a company is performing well (meeting its current obligations and making a profit), the company's stock is attractive. Investors consider the company's earning power (its ability to continue to make a strong profit), as well as its debt obligations (how much the company owes). If the company seems to be in a good financial position, the stock price will continue rising.

2. *Interest Rates.* When interest rates are low, people who would normally put money in savings accounts and certificates of deposit look for more profitable places to invest their money. As interest rates rise, however, people tend to move their money to the safer investments. Generally, when interest rates fall below the current rate of inflation, people buy more stock, and stock prices rise.

3. *The Market.* The marketplace determines a company's ability to sell its product or service now and in the future. If the company is in a popular industry and its products or services are selling well, its stock price will rise. For example, when people are buying computers, software, and related items, companies in the high-tech industry are considered wise investments. If the demand for a particular product or service declines, the price of the stock will decrease.

4. *Earnings per Share.* **Earnings per share** are a corporation's after-tax earnings divided by the number of common stock shares outstanding, that is, shares in the hands of investors. For example, assume that in a given year, XYZ Corporation had after-tax earnings (net profit) of $1,000,000. It had 100,000 shares of common stock outstanding. Therefore, its earnings per share at that time were $10 ($1,000,000/100,000 = $10). Stockholders use earnings per share as a measure of a company's profitability.

Return on Investment

Because you can make money on stocks from dividends and from an increase in the price of the stock (capital gain), you should consider both when computing the return on your investment. Figure 12-1 shows the formula for computing a stock's *return on investment (ROI)*. Your ROI is the profit you earned on the stock as a percentage of the total cost of buying the stock. Your profit is the difference between what you paid for the stock and what you sold it for, plus any dividends you earned. To compute the total costs, add any commission you paid to the stockbroker to the purchase price of the stock. Then find the ROI percentage by dividing profit by cost.

Computing a Stock's Return on Investment (ROI) **Figure 12-1**

Computing a Stock's One-Year ROI

$$\frac{\text{Current Profit on Stock}}{\text{Purchase Price} + \text{Commission}} = \text{Return on Investment (ROI)}$$

Example: Current stock price: $40/share
Dividends received during the year: $1/share
Purchase price: $38/share
Discount brokerage fee: $19
Number of shares owned: 100

Computations:
Current profit: $40/share − $38/share = $2/share x 100 = $200 + dividends ($100) = total profits of $300.

$$\frac{\$300}{(100 \times \$38) + \$19} = \frac{\$300}{\$3,819} = 7.86\%$$

Check Your Understanding

Review Terms

1. stockholders
2. dividends
3. capital gain
4. common stock
5. proxy
6. preferred stock
7. income stocks
8. growth stocks
9. blue chip stocks
10. par value
11. market value
12. earnings per share

Review Concepts

1. In what two ways can you make money from owning stock?
2. How is an income stock different from a growth stock?
3. Why do stockholders want to know a corporation's earnings per share?

Goals

★ Describe market channels and the process for buying and selling securities.
★ Describe short- and long-term investment strategies when buying and selling stocks.
★ Explain how to read the stock listings in financial publications and how to use stock indexes.

The Securities Market

The securities market consists of the channels through which you buy and sell securities—stocks and bonds. To purchase common or preferred stock, you need a trading agent. Your agent will buy or sell for you in a securities marketplace, which is either a securities exchange or the over-the-counter market.

Securities Exchanges

A *securities exchange* is a marketplace where brokers who are representing investors meet to buy and sell securities. The largest organized exchange in the United States is the New York Stock Exchange (NYSE). The smaller American Stock Exchange is also in New York City. Regional exchanges are located throughout the country. To have a stock listed with the NYSE or AMEX, a company must meet a minimum number of public shares and dollar market-value requirements.

In the New York Stock Exchange building, the trading floor (where stocks are bought and sold) is about two-thirds the size of a football field. Around the edge of the trading floor are booths with computer terminals that are open at both ends, with room inside for a dozen or more floor brokers. *Floor brokers* buy and sell stocks on the exchange. Only brokers who are members of the exchange may do business there.

Spaced at regular intervals around the trading floor are trading posts, which are horseshoe-shaped counters, each occupying about 100 square feet on the floor. Behind each counter are specialists— the brokers to the floor brokers. All buying and selling is done around trading posts. About 90 different stocks are assigned to each post. Post display units above each counter show which stocks are sold in each section, the last price of that stock, and whether that price represents an increase or a decrease from the previous price.

Orders received at a brokerage firm or discount brokerage are phoned or sent by computer to that firm's booth at the exchange. A message is printed out and is given to the floor broker to carry out. When the transaction is completed, the clerks for the brokers who bought and sold the stock report back to their respective brokerage firms. The buyer and seller can then be advised that the transaction has been concluded.

The exchange is a form of *auction market* where buyers and sellers are brought together to trade securities. Stock trading happens auction-style because in every transaction, stock is sold to the highest bidder (buyer) and bought from the lowest offeror (seller). Securities listed with the NYSE are traded only during official trading hours—9:30 A.M. to 4 P.M. New York time, Monday through Friday (except holidays).

Why is a securities exchange considered an auction market?

Career Links

Stockbrokers are used when investors buy or sell stocks, bonds, shares in mutual funds, insurance annuities, or other financial products. They also give advice on investments and other financial matters. A college degree and good sales ability are among the most important qualifications for this profession. Brokers should be knowledgeable about economic conditions and trends.

For more information, refer to the *Occupational Outlook Handbook* at www.bls.gov or search the Internet using such key words as "careers," "jobs," and "brokers."

Over-the-Counter Market

When securities are bought and sold through brokers but not through a stock exchange, the transaction is over-the-counter (OTC). The *over-the-counter (OTC) market* is a network of brokers who buy and sell the securities of corporations that are not listed on a securities exchange. Brokers in the OTC market do not deal face-to-face. Their marketplace is as large as the number of desks with brokers at work that day. Trades with other brokers are completed by telephone, and a computerized system displays current price quotations on a terminal in a broker's office. Brokers operating in the OTC market use an electronic quotation system called NASDAQ. (The letters were originally an acronym for the National Association of Securities Dealers Automated Quotation System.) To be listed with NASDAQ, companies must have issued at least 100,000 shares of stock worth $1 million.

NET NOTES

The CNBC Student Stock Tournament is a free, Internet-based stock game that gives high school students an opportunity to compete in a test of stock-picking skills. It familiarizes students with the workings of Wall Street and helps them improve their financial literacy. Using play money, student investment clubs invest in stocks from the New York Stock Exchange, American Stock Exchange, and/or NASDAQ. The group whose tournament portfolio has the greatest total return wins a grand prize. Interested? Check out the Web site at www.sss.cnbc.com.

Bull and Bear Markets

The stock market goes through cycles. For a period of time, stocks go up in value. Then the market corrects itself as people sell (to make a profit), and stock prices decrease. A **bull market** is a prolonged period of rising stock prices and a general feeling of investor optimism. Confidence about how the country is doing also serves to drive up stock prices.

A **bear market** is a prolonged period of falling stock prices and a general feeling of investor pessimism. It develops when investors become negative about the overall economy and start to sell stocks. In bear markets, stock prices may fall 20 percent or more. Bear markets are usually short and savage. The average bull market often lasts three to four times as long as a bear market.

Whether the stock market in general is bullish (on an upward trend in prices) or bearish (on a downward trend in prices) influences your decisions about when to buy stocks and which stocks to buy. To make a profit, you need to buy stock when the price is low and sell when the price is higher. However, nobody knows, including brokers, when a stock is at its lowest price or whether or not the price will rise. For this reason, you need to research individual stocks to judge which are most likely to earn a profit.

Investing Strategies

You can approach investing with either a short- or long-term strategy. Generally, if you buy and sell stock within a short period of time, you are a *speculator*, or *day trader*. If you hold your investment for a long period of time (a year or more), you are an investor.

Short-Term Techniques

When you buy and sell stocks for quick profits, you are "playing the stock market." The goal is to buy a stock that will soon increase in value. Then, when the price rises, you sell the stock. Many investors realize short-term gains through processes called buying on margin and selling short.

Buy on Margin

You can borrow money from your broker to buy stock if you open a margin account and sign a contract called a margin agreement. To establish a margin account, you must deposit a minimum of $2,000 in cash or eligible securities (securities your broker considers valuable collateral) with a broker. Let's assume you have $2,000 in your margin account. You want to buy 100 shares of XYZ Corporation at $20 per share ($2,000). You could use $1,000 from your margin account and borrow $1,000, with interest, from your broker. This strategy is called **leverage**—the use of borrowed money to buy securities. You use less of your own money and therefore can buy more stocks with less cash. You would still have $1,000 in your margin account to use toward another purchase on margin.

With a margin purchase, you are betting that the stock will increase in value. If it does, you sell the stock, repay the loan with interest and commission, and take your short-term profit. Figure 12-2 shows how margin buying works.

Unfortunately, if the value of the stock does not increase, you will have to make up the difference. When the market value of a margined stock decreases to approximately one-half of the original purchase price, the investor will receive a margin call from the broker. After the margin call, the investor must pledge additional cash or securities to serve as collateral for the loan. If you don't have the cash, the stock is sold and the proceeds are used to pay the loan.

Sell Short

Short selling is selling stock borrowed from a broker that must be replaced at a later time. To sell short, you borrow a certain number

Buying on Margin

Example: You buy $2,000 worth of stock with $1,000 of your own money and $1,000 borrowed from your broker at 6% annual interest. The stock increases in value and you sell it after 60 days for $2,800. Your broker's commission to buy and sell is $200.

Computing Profit:

Interest cost: $1,000 borrowed x .06 annual interest x $\left(\dfrac{60\ days}{360\ days\ in\ a\ year}\right)$
= $10 interest on the 60-day loan

Costs: $1,000 purchase price + $1,000 amount borrowed
+ $10 interest + $200 commission = $2,210 total cost

Profit: $2,800 selling price − $2,210 cost = $590 total profit

Computing Return on Investment:

$$\dfrac{\$590\ profit}{\$2,210\ cost} = 26.7\%\ ROI$$

of shares from the broker. You then sell the borrowed stock, knowing that you must buy it back later and return it to the broker. You are betting that the price will drop, so that you can buy it back at a lower price than you sold it for. However, if the stock price increases, you will lose money because you must replace the borrowed stock with stock purchased at a higher price. Figure 12-3 on page 344 shows how selling short works. There is usually no broker fee for selling short. The broker receives a commission when the stock is bought and sold.

Long-Term Techniques

As you may already suspect, investing in the stock market for short-term gains can be extremely risky. You cannot beat the market all of the time, but you can make some healthy profits if you study and follow the market carefully. However, most financial consultants advise you to invest for the long term. Records have shown that, over a long time, stock investments have consistently beaten rates for savings accounts, CDs, and other conservative options.

Buy and Hold

Most investors consider stock purchases as long-term investments. All stocks go up and down, but over a number of years, the overall

Figure 12-3 *Selling Short*

Selling Short

Example: You borrow 100 shares of stock of XYZ Corporation from your broker. You then sell 100 shares of XYZ at $28 per share and pay a $100 commission.

Income from sale = 100 shares x $28 per share − $100 commission
  = $2,700 initial income

Two weeks later, the stock price drops to $22 per share. You buy 100 shares to return to the stockbroker and pay a $100 commission.

Cost of buying back the shares: 100 shares x $22 per share + $100 commission
  = $2,300 cost

Profit from selling short: $2,700 income − $2,300 cost = $400 profit

Return on Investment: $\dfrac{\$400}{\$2,300}$ = 17.4% ROI

trend of non-speculative stocks is moderately up. Remember, a profit or loss occurs only when you sell the stock. If you "buy and hold" stocks for many years, you can ride out the down times. When you are ready to sell years later, most likely your stock will have gained value. In addition, many stocks pay dividends, so you are earning income while you hold the stock.

A stock split also can add to the value of the stock over time. A **stock split** is an increase in the number of outstanding shares of a company's stock. When a company increases its shares outstanding, it lowers the selling price in direct proportion. For example, if there were 1,000 shares outstanding with a market value of $60, then a 2:1 (two for one) stock split would result in 2,000 shares outstanding selling for $30. You will notice that the stock is still worth a total of $60,000. A stock split lowers the selling price of the stock, making the shares more affordable and encouraging investors to buy more. As investors buy more stock at the lower price, the share price often rises. If you held the stock before the split, then this price increase makes your stock worth more.

Dollar-Cost Averaging

The *dollar-cost averaging* technique involves the systematic purchase of an equal dollar amount of the same stock at regular intervals. The result is usually a lower average cost per share. To calculate the average cost per share, divide the total amount invested by the total number of shares purchased, as shown in Figure 12-4. In the figure, the investor purchased $100 worth of stock every quarter for one year. Over that time, the average price of the stock was $8. However, by investing at regular intervals over the time period, the investor's average cost per share was lower: $7.41.

Investors use this technique so they don't have to worry about timing their investment purchases. A regular purchase over a year's time will usually average out to a reasonable price per share. With dollar-cost averaging, the investor makes a profit when the selling price per share is higher than the average cost per share.

Direct Investment

You can save money using **direct investment**, or buying stock directly from a corporation. By buying directly, you avoid brokerage and other purchasing fees. You may also be able to obtain shares at prices lower than on open exchanges. Direct investment is often available to existing stockholders who may have the privilege of buying additional shares at fixed prices that are at or below market value.

Dollar-Cost Averaging **Figure 12-4**

Dollar-Cost Averaging

Monthly investment amount		Share price ($)		Number of shares
$100	÷	10	=	10
$100	÷	7	=	14.29
$100	÷	5	=	20
$100	÷	10	=	10
$400		$32		54
Total $ invested				Total number of shares

Average share price = $8
$32 ÷ 4

Your average cost per share = $7.41
total $ invested ($400) ÷ total number of shares (54)

Ending value = $540
last share price ($10) × number of shares (54)

Reinvesting Dividends

You can also save money by reinvesting your dividends. **Dividend reinvestment** means using dividends previously earned on the stock to buy more shares. Buying stock this way avoids a broker fee and other costs of receiving cash dividends on the stock.

Reading the Stock Listings

To make wise investments in the stock market, you will need to track the progress of your chosen investments to see how they are performing. Whether you are reading *The Wall Street Journal* or following your stocks online, you should see a listing similar to Figure 12-5 of the stocks that are bought and sold on stock exchanges or over-the-counter. Follow along in Figure 12-5 as you read the following explanation of each column.

1. *Columns 1 and 2.* These columns show the highest and lowest price this stock sold for during the year. For the ExeB stock in Figure 12-5, the high for the last 52 weeks was 57.00 and the low was 32.00. This means the stock sold for $57 a share at one point (high) and $32 a share at another (low), though it may have sold for many prices in between during the year.
2. *Column 3.* This column lists stocks alphabetically by name. You will notice that stocks are abbreviated. You may see additional abbreviations, such as "pf" (which means "preferred stock"), beside the name of the stock. There will be a legend at the bottom of the page that explains what these abbreviations mean. For example, a small "s" means that the stock has recently split. When a stock splits, each share owned is traded for additional shares. A 2:1 split would double your shares. If you owned 10 shares worth $50 each, you would now own 20 shares worth $25 each.
3. *Column 4.* This column shows the cash dividend per share for the year listed in dollars and cents. For the ExeB stock, 2.50 means that if you owned 100 shares of this company, you would have received a dividend of $250 for the year.
4. *Column 5.* Yld % stands for *percent yield,* or the percentage of the current price the dividends represent. In other words, divide the amount of annual dividends (Column 4) by the closing price (Column 10).

Reading Stock Listings

Excerpt from stock exchange listings:

52 wks High	52 wks Low	Stock	Div	Yld %	P/E Ratio	Sales 100s	High	Low	Close	Net Chg.
1	2	3	4	5	6	7	8	9	10	11
58.75	44.00	Enger	2.20	4.8	12	109	46.38	45.50	46.00	– .50
45.00	23.00	Eng pf	2.25	8.9	10	25	26.25	24.00	25.38	+ .38
10.50	9.00	Entld	.10	1.0	3	8	10.13	9.50	10.00	----
24.00	16.00	Epsco	1.00	5.0	7	12	21.00	19.00	20.00	+ .88
6.38	4.00	Exlab	--	--	15	300z	5.75	5.12	5.50	----
57.00	32.00	ExeB	2.50	5.7	11	48	46.00	43.00	44.00	+1.00

5. *Column 6.* The *P/E ratio* (price/earnings ratio) is the price of a share of stock divided by the corporation's earnings per share over the last 12 months. For example, if XYZ Corporation's stock is selling for $50 per share and XYZ's earnings per share are $10, the P/E ratio is 5 ($50/$10 = $5). The price/earnings ratio is a key factor that serious investors use to evaluate stock investments. A low P/E may indicate a solid investment, and a high P/E may indicate higher risk.

6. *Column 7.* This column shows sales in hundreds of shares from the previous day—how many round lots of stock were bought and sold. Multiply the number by 100 to get the number of shares.

7. *Columns 8, 9, and 10.* These columns show the highest, lowest, and closing price for this stock on the previous day. The closing price is the final price at the end of trading for the day.

8. *Column 11.* This column, called "net change," compares the closing price today with the closing price of the day before. A minus means the price has gone down. A plus means the price has risen. Stocks that have a price change of more than 5 percent are in boldface.

Keeping track of your *stock portfolio* (or stock holdings) can be as simple as checking the closing prices periodically. Some people check their investments only once a year to see if they should make changes to their portfolio. Investors might buy additional shares, sell, or choose a different type of stock after checking their portfolios.

The stocks shown in Figure 12-6 have been tracked for 10 days straight. As you can see, some stocks have done better than others in terms of market value as of a certain date. But remember, this chart does not take into account dividends received or the appreciation in value since a stock was purchased. The stock progress chart is merely a device for monitoring changes in the closing prices of stocks.

Many financial Internet sites allow you to follow stock prices. Using a stock's ticker symbol, you can find the stock's price up to the minute. If you want stock quotes sent to your computer automatically, you can sign up for the service with your Internet service provider. Most will allow you to specify the stocks you want to follow. You can even buy and sell stocks online. Most major stockbrokers maintain Web sites that allow online transactions.

What kinds of stock-related activities are available online?

AROUND THE GLOBE

Great Britain has one third of all European stockholders, but it accounts for only 7 percent of the European online brokerage market. The number of online investors is growing much more slowly there than elsewhere. Britain has been hesitant to move to cheaper, more efficient electronic systems. In addition, Britain has a very low savings rate—just 4 percent compared to 12 percent in the rest of Europe. Because British housing is so expensive, many residents have most of their wealth tied up in home mortgages.

Think Critically: Are you comfortable with the idea of online investing? How could an online broker make it easier or more attractive for people to invest?

Stock Indexes

A *stock index* is a benchmark that investors use to judge the performance of their investments. The most widely followed stock index is the *Dow Jones Industrial Average.* Often called simply *the Dow,* it is an average of the price movements of 30 major stocks listed on the New York Stock Exchange. This average provides a general overview of what stock prices are doing in the stock market as a whole. Investors compare the price fluctuations of their

Stock Progress Chart

Stock Names	Closing Prices for 10 days										Total Change (+ or −)
	1	2	3	4	5	6	7	8	9	10	
1. Enger	28	28.12	29	28	27	28	28.50	29	29.50	30	+2
2. Glastn	38	40	41	41.50	--	40	39	38	38	38	0
3. Karbr pf	61	61.25	61.13	61	61.38	61	62	62.38	61	61.13	+.13
4. Maxln	50.13	49	50	50.25	51	51	51.13	52	52	53.50	+3.37
5. Totlmb	10	11	11.13	11.50	11	10.88	10	9	8	8.50	−1.50

stocks against this average to judge how well their stocks are performing compared to the overall stock market. Indexes for judging the performance of all kinds of stocks are available online and in print publications. Other commonly used indexes are the Standard & Poor's 500 and the NASDAQ Composite Index.

Check Your Understanding

Review Terms
1. bull market
2. bear market
3. leverage
4. short selling
5. stock split
6. direct investment
7. dividend reinvestment

Review Concepts
1. What are two kinds of markets where securities are bought and sold?
2. Why is buying on margin a risky action?
3. How do you save money by reinvesting dividends?

PERSONAL PERSPECTIVE

Are You Risk Averse?

Answer the following questions to see if you are a risk taker, a moderate investor, a cautious investor, or risk averse.

1. When I vacation, I like to (a) travel without reservations and see what happens, (b) make plans but stay flexible, (c) plan the trip in great detail, (d) stay at home to save money.
2. When I choose friends, I prefer to (a) date people I meet over the Internet, (b) go on blind dates arranged by friends or dating services, (c) meet people at social events, (d) meet people through friends or relatives.
3. When I order a meat dish at a restaurant, I prefer to (a) eat it rare, (b) eat it medium, (c) have vegetarian choices, (d) bring my own food.
4. When I am unprepared for an exam, I will (a) attend class and see what happens, (b) ask the teacher for an extension, (c) miss school that day, (d) study day and night until I feel prepared.
5. When I am flying, my preferred mode of travel is to (a) fly stand-by, (b) use electronic tickets and show up at the last minute, (c) use electronic tickets and show up early, (d) have confirmed reservations and a printed ticket, and show up an hour early.
6. When driving, I almost always (a) drive at or above the speed limit, (b) drive carefully at or below the speed limit, (c) drive only during off-peak hours, (d) prefer that someone else drive.
7. When traveling for long periods of time, I prefer to (a) stay in hostels or to camp, (b) take my chances and show up unannounced, (c) make reservations as I travel, (d) have confirmed hotel reservations at every stop.

Scoring: Compute your score as follows: Answer (a) 4 points, (b) 3 points, (c) 2 points, (d) 1 point. **Interpretation:** Add up your points. Here's what the totals mean: 24–28 Points: Risk Taker—Go ahead and buy high-risk investments! 16–23 Points: Moderate Investor—Invest only what you can afford to lose. 11–15 Points: Cautious Investor—Avoid risk unless you have carefully decided to take this one-time risk. 7–10 Points: Risk Averse—Do not take risks; invest in conservative investments only.

Think Critically

1. Do you think your score on this risk test accurately predicts how you would feel about investments that offer big potential profits but with a high probability of losing your money?
2. Would you be more willing to make risky investments if you had a lot of extra money than if you were living paycheck to paycheck? Why or why not?

12.1 Evaluating Stocks

- Stockholders are owners of the corporation. They can profit from stock ownership through dividends and through capital gains.

- Owners of common stock receive a variable dividend and have the right to vote in stockholders' meetings. Owners of preferred stock receive a fixed dividend but have no voting rights. A corporation's preferred stock is less risky than its common stock, but the return is likely to be lower.

- Corporations can distribute their profits to stockholders as dividends (income stocks) or reinvest it in the business (growth stocks).

- Blue chip stocks provide a relatively safe but moderate return, while stocks in less well-established businesses have a higher potential profit but also a higher risk of loss.

- Defensive stocks remain relatively stable during good and bad economic times. Cyclical stocks do well when the economy is growing but do poorly during recessions.

- Par value is the value printed on the stock certificate. It is artificial and has nothing to do with the market value, which is the price at which investors are actually buying and selling the stock.

- The price of a stock depends on factors such as company performance, general level of interest rates, the market for the company's products, and the company's earnings per share.

- Both dividends earned and profit on the sale of the stock go into determining the return on your investment.

12.2 Buying and Selling Stock

- You can buy and sell securities through two channels: a securities exchange or over-the-counter. A securities exchange, such as the New York Stock Exchange, is a physical place where brokers buy and sell securities for their clients. The over-the-counter market is not a physical place. Buying and selling occurs by phone and computer.
- The stock market goes through cycles. A prolonged period of rising stock prices is a bull market. A prolonged period of falling stock prices is a bear market.
- Short-term investors are speculators who try to make a quick profit by buying on margin or selling short. These are risky techniques that can gain or lose a lot.
- Most investors invest for the long term. They buy and hold stocks for many years. Over time, the trends for most non-speculative stocks are generally up.
- Other long-term strategies are dollar-cost averaging (systematic purchase of stocks at regular intervals), direct investment (buying stock directly from the corporation), and reinvesting dividends (using earned dividends to buy more shares).
- You can track the progress of your stock by reading the stock listings in financial publications in print and online.

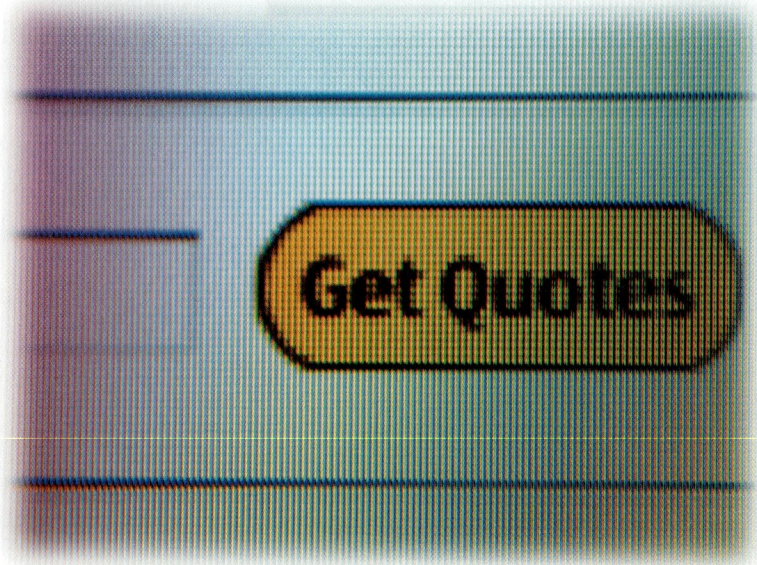

Review Terms

Directions: Can you find the definition for each of the following terms used in Chapter 12?

bear market
blue chip stocks
bull market
capital gain
common stock
direct investment
dividend reinvestment
dividends
earnings per share
growth stocks
income stocks

leverage
market value
par value
preferred stock
proxy
short selling
stock split
stockholders

1. A type of stock that pays a variable dividend and gives the holder voting rights.
2. Stockholder's written authorization to transfer his or her voting rights to someone else, usually a company manager.
3. Stocks with a consistent history of paying high dividends.
4. An increase in the number of outstanding shares of a company's stock.
5. The price for which a stock is bought and sold in the marketplace.
6. The use of borrowed money to buy securities.
7. A prolonged period of rising stock prices and a general feeling of investor optimism.
8. The part of the corporation's profits paid to stockholders.
9. A type of stock that pays a fixed dividend and carries no voting rights.
10. Stocks in corporations that reinvest their profits into the business so the company can grow.
11. Stock of large, well-established corporations with a solid record of profitability.
12. An assigned (often arbitrary) dollar value printed on a stock certificate.
13. A prolonged period of falling stock prices and a general feeling of investor pessimism.
14. A corporation's after-tax earnings divided by the number of shares of common stock outstanding.
15. Buying stock directly from a corporation.
16. Selling stock borrowed from a broker that must be replaced at a later time.
17. Using dividends previously earned on the stock to buy more shares.
18. Owners of a corporation.
19. An increase in the value of the stock above the price initially paid for it.

Review Facts and Ideas

1. How would you earn a capital gain on your stock?
2. How is common stock different from preferred stock?
3. What type of investor should purchase income stocks? growth stocks?
4. Which involves the greatest risk—stocks of young businesses or blue chip stocks? Explain the differences between the two types of stocks.
5. Why are defensive stocks not subject to the usual ups and downs of business cycles?
6. Explain the relationship between par value and market value.
7. What causes stock prices to rise and fall? List four factors that affect stock prices.
8. Which is the largest stock exchange in the United States? How does a company get listed on this exchange?
9. Why would a stock be listed on the NASDAQ rather than the NYSE or American Stock Exchange?
10. What characterizes a bull market? a bear market?
11. Explain two short-term strategies for investing in stocks.
12. Explain four techniques for long-term investing.
13. In stock listings, what do these symbols stand for: P/E, "s," pf?
14. How do investors use stock indexes?

APPLY YOUR KNOWLEDGE

1. If you own 100 shares of common stock, which you purchased for $28 a share, and the company declares a cash dividend of $.88 for the quarter, how much will you receive in dividends?
2. Common stockholders take more risk but have a higher rate of return than preferred stockholders. Explain why.
3. Assume a company has issued the following stock:
   2,000 shares of 5 percent preferred stock at $50 per share
   18,000 shares of common stock at $22 per share
   A cash dividend of $1.30 per share is declared for common stock, after preferred stockholders have received their 5 percent dividend.

Compute your total cash dividends for the year if you own:
a. 100 shares of preferred stock.
b. 100 shares of common stock.
c. 50 shares of preferred stock and 50 shares of common stock.

4. If you had an extra $1,000 that you just inherited, which type of common stock investment would you choose? Explain why.

5. Investing in blue chip stocks is said to be a conservative choice. Can you list several well-known stocks that are considered blue chip, besides the two mentioned in the text? (Hint: Read through the listing of stocks in the financial pages and mark the stocks you recognize. Or, look for listings online.)

6. Suppose you purchased 100 shares of stock in January for $48 a share. You received dividends of $1.25 per share on April 1 and July 1 and $.95 per share on September 1. You sold the stock in December for $50 a share. What would be the stock's return on investment for the year? Assume a broker commission of 3 percent on the purchase and sale of the stock.

7. Use the Internet or library resources to research the history of bull and bear markets. List the years and months when each type of market occurred during the 1980s and 1990s. Why is it important to understand bull and bear market trends?

8. You have $2,500 in cash in a margin account. You decide to buy stock on margin. You buy 50 shares of stock selling at $100 per share. Assume that the stock rises in value, and 30 days later you sell the stock for $110 a share. Interest on the amount borrowed is 7 percent. The commission on the purchase and sale is $150. What is the total return on investment?

9. You wish to sell short. You arrange to borrow from your broker 100 shares of stock in XYZ Corporation on January 2, 2001. You immediately sell 100 shares of XYZ at $60 per share. On April 1, 2001, you instruct your broker to purchase 100 shares of XYZ at $53 per share. You return 100 shares of XYZ stock to your broker. Assume the commission was $200. What is your return on investment for this transaction?

10. Search the Web for investment advice. In no more than one page, summarize what the experts are saying about which stocks are hot right now and which are not. Do the experts seem to agree or disagree with each other? Some sites you might try are listed below:

www.adviceamerica.com
www.morningstar.com
www.fremontfunds.com
www.vanguard.com
www.mystockoptions.com/

www.imoneynet.com
www.riskmetrics.com/

11. The Dow Jones Industrial Average has a rich history. Go to the Dow Jones site at http://averages.dowjones.com/home.html to learn more about it. In your own words, summarize what the Dow Jones Industrial Average is, how it originated, and why there was a need for it. List 10 companies that are among the 30 used to create the average.

Solve Problems

1. Your friend Ashley is considering investing in stocks. She has an extra $5,000 that she wants to invest. She won't need the money for five years, when she hopes to start medical school. Would you recommend common or preferred stock? Explain why.

2. Mr. and Mrs. Reynolds are in their late fifties and plan to retire within the next three to five years. They would like to put some of their money into the stock market because interest rates on savings accounts are low. Which of these options would you recommend to them? Give a brief reason for each choice.
   a. income or growth stocks?
   b. stocks of new small businesses or blue chip stocks?
   c. defensive or cyclical stocks?

3. Bill Candido has just been given a gift from his grandmother—10 shares of stock in a leading manufacturing company. In the upper right corner, the certificate states PAR VALUE, $10 per share. Bill is confused. His grandmother told him that the closing price for the stock was $50 per share on the day he received the gift. Explain this difference.

4. Moesha Rogers bought a stock one year ago. Since then, she has received quarterly dividends of $.50 per share. Her 50 shares are now worth $35 each. She paid $29 per share, plus a commission of $180. What is her return? Would you advise her to keep or to sell the stock?

5. Rosa and Ernesto have been married for less than a year. They are considering buying some stock to have a "nest egg" for their future children. Ernesto prefers to buy stock in a local company that is small and just getting started. Rosa prefers to buy the stock of a well-known company that is listed on a

major exchange. Discuss with them the pros and cons of each course of action.

6. Choose three stocks to follow for a week: one listed on the NYSE, one on the AMEX, and one on the NASDAQ. Pretend that you invested $1,000 in each stock. On the Internet, find the closing price for these stocks on the day you "purchased" them and at the end of every day for one week. Keep a table of the dates and closing prices. At the end of the week, make a graph of the closing prices for each day for all three stocks. Analyze your findings. Which stock price varied the most? Which had the highest high? The lowest low? Which had the most consistent upward trend? If you sold the stocks at the end of the last day, how much would you have gained or lost on each one?

For related activities and links, point your browser to
www.mypf.swep.com

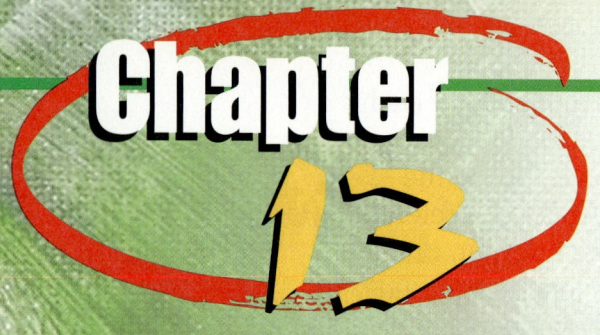

Chapter 13
Investing in Bonds

Up Front

Nguyen is a conservative investor. He wants to be certain his principal is safe and that it will be available to him in two years when he needs it to start his business.

"I want to get better return than I can get for a certificate of deposit," he told his investment advisor. "I'm thinking about investing my money in bonds. I read in the financial section of today's paper that there are some tax-free municipal bonds that are paying 7.5 percent. I'm also considering a high-grade corporate bond that pays 9 percent. While the rate is higher on the corporate bond, interest earnings are taxable. What would you advise?"

Characteristics of Bonds

Goals

★ Discuss the features and types of corporate bonds.
★ Explain how to calculate earnings and percentage yield on a corporate bond.
★ Describe federal and municipal government securities, and zero-coupon bonds.

Corporate Bonds

While a corporation may use both bonds and stocks to finance business activities, there are important distinctions between the two. First, bonds are loans that must be repaid at maturity. Stocks are shares of ownership in the corporation, not loans, so stocks do not need to be repaid. Second, interest payments on bonds are mandatory. Corporations may or may not pay dividends on stocks, as decided by the board of directors.

What are some differences between stocks and bonds?

As you learned in Chapter 10, some investments, such as bonds, become due for payment on their *maturity date.* Bond maturities vary widely. The loans can last a year or less or continue for 30 or more years. The most common bond maturity is 10 years. **Face value** is the amount the bondholder will be repaid at maturity. Face value is commonly $1,000. Face value is also referred to as *par value* because, like the par value on stock discussed in Chapter 12, the face value is the dollar amount printed on the certificate.

Features of Corporate Bonds

Corporate bonds are sold on the open market through brokers, just like stocks. Prices asked for bonds appear daily in *The Wall Street Journal* and the financial pages of major newspapers. However, only a tiny fraction of the bonds issued are listed in the newspaper.

Bonds are "fixed-income investments." They pay a specified amount of interest on a regular basis. A bond's *interest rate* is the percentage of face value that will be paid in interest to the bond-holder each year. Usually, payments of half the annual interest are made twice a year. For example, a $1,000 bond might pay 5 percent, or $50 a year. The bondholder would receive two $25 payments during the year. Interest you receive on corporate bonds is taxable. You must report the interest as ordinary income on your tax return.

The process for collecting the interest on your bond depends on whether it is a registered or a coupon bond. A *registered bond* is recorded in the owner's name by the issuing company. Interest checks for registered bonds are mailed semiannually, directly to the bondholder of record. A *coupon bond* (also called a *bearer bond*) is not registered by the issuing company. To collect interest on a coupon bond, bondholders must clip a coupon and then cash it in at a bank, following the procedures outlined by the issuer. Today, most bonds are registered in the holder's name and have no coupons. Bonds with coupons are assumed to belong to whoever possesses ("bears") them. Therefore, if a coupon bond is lost or stolen, whoever has it may collect the interest on it and redeem it. For this reason, only "older" bonds are on the market as bearer bonds. Newly issued bonds are generally registered.

A major disadvantage for individual investors is the cost of bonds. Very few corporate bonds are sold in denominations or units of less than $1,000. Bonds are commonly sold in units of $5,000. Bond purchases by an individual investor require a large sum of cash.

A bond may be issued with a call provision. A **callable bond** is a bond that the issuer has the right to pay off before its maturity date. The date when a bond can be called is identified at the time it is offered for sale. For example, a 10-year bond issued in 2000 with a maturity date of 2010 may be callable in the year 2005. If interest rates fall, corporations may choose to call the bonds because they can re-issue them at a lower interest rate. Generally, it is cost-effective for corporations to pay the costs of calling and re-issuing when interest rates drop by 2 percent or more. Corporations usually agree *not* to call bonds for the first five years after issuance. When the corporation does exercise its right to call the bond, it generally pays the bondholders a slight premium—an amount above the face value of the bond. A $1,000 bond may be called for $1,020.

Types of Corporate Bonds

For corporations, bonds are a primary way of raising capital. The money raised pays for expansion, new technology, and operating expenses. You can choose from three types of corporate bonds: debentures, mortgage bonds, and convertible bonds.

Debentures

A **debenture** is a corporate bond that is not backed by collateral but only by the general credit standing of the corporation. The issuer does not pledge any specific assets to assure repayment of the loan. An investor relies on the full faith and credit of the issuer for repayment of the interest and principal. When issued by reliable corporations, debentures are usually relatively safe investments.

Mortgage Bonds

A **mortgage bond**, or *secured bond*, is a corporate bond backed by specific assets as collateral to assure repayment of the debt. If the corporation fails to repay the loan as agreed, the bondholder may claim the property used as security for the debt. The asset or collateral used for security is typically real estate.

Convertible Bonds

A **convertible bond** is a corporate bond that can be exchanged, at the owner's option, for a specified number of shares of the corporation's common stock. If the bondholder converts to common stock, the corporation no longer must redeem the bond at maturity. Each bond is convertible into a certain number of common shares at a specific price per share. For example, say you purchase a $1,000 corporate bond convertible to 50 shares of the company's common stock. You can convert the bond to stock whenever the price of the company's common stock is $20 ($1,000/50 shares = $20) or higher. Assume the company's stock is selling for $22. In this situation, you would have an investment worth $1,100 on conversion ($22 × 50 shares = $1,100).

Earnings on Corporate Bonds

All bonds are issued with a stated face value and interest rate. Figure 13-1 shows interest payments on a $10,000, 10-year, 6 percent corporate bond. Let's assume that the bond was issued January 1, 2000, and interest payments are due June 30 and December 31 of each year. The maturity date of the bond is the date when the principal (face value) must be repaid in full. This 10-year bond would have a maturity date of January 1, 2010, or 10 years from the date of issue.

The return on the bond in Figure 13-1 is 6 percent per year. The yield is also 6 percent; in other words, there is no compounding effect. Half the annual amount of simple interest is paid every six months.

However, once a bond has been issued, its market value may rise above or fall below its face value. For example, a $10,000 bond may sell for more than that amount if interest rates are falling. People would be willing to pay more for the bond because it pays an interest rate higher than the current market rate. When bonds sell for more than their face value, they are selling at a *premium*. A $10,000 bond selling for $10,000 is at 100 percent of its face value, or "1." But if the bond sold for "104," it would have a premium of 4 percent. At 104, the market price would be $10,400:

$$\$10,000 \times .04 = \$400 \text{ premium}$$
$$\$10,000 + \$400 = \$10,400 \text{ market price}$$

Figure 13-1	Interest Payments on a Ten-Year, 6% Corporate Bond

Year	June 30 Interest	December 31 Interest
1	$300.00	$300.00
2	300.00	300.00
3	300.00	300.00
4	300.00	300.00
5	300.00	300.00
6	300.00	300.00
7	300.00	300.00
8	300.00	300.00
9	300.00	300.00
10	300.00	300.00

January 1, 2010: $10,000 principal is repaid

Yield on a 6% Corporate Bond Purchased at a Premium and at a Discount   **Figure 13-2**

$$Current\ yield = \frac{Annual\ interest\ dollar\ amount}{Market\ price}$$

	Interest	**Yield**
If you buy the $10,000 bond at face value	$600	6%
If you buy the bond at 104	$600	5.8%*
If you buy the bond at 96	$600	6.3%*

*A bond's current yield is computed by dividing its annual dollar amount by its current market price ($600/$10,400 and $600/$9,600).

In this case, the yield would be lower than 6 percent because the buyer had to pay more than face value to buy the bond.

Bonds also can sell below face value. For example, say that investors are not willing to pay face value for a bond yielding 6 percent when interest rates are rising. Therefore, the bond may have to be sold at a *discount,* or for an amount lower than face value, to entice buyers. If a bond sold for 96, it was sold at a 4 percent discount. The purchaser of the bond would pay only $9,600 for a $10,000 bond:

$$\$10,000 \times .04 = \$400\ discount$$
$$\$10,000 - \$400 = \$9,600\ market\ price$$

In this case, the buyer's yield would be higher than 6 percent because the buyer paid less than the face value for the bond.

Figure 13-2 shows how to compute the yield on bonds when they are issued at a premium or at a discount. Yield is not the same thing as the interest rate. In fact, yield may be higher or lower than the bond's stated interest rate, as you can see in Figure 13-2.

Government Bonds

In addition to loaning money to corporations, you also can loan money to the government. Government bonds can be issued by the federal as well as state or local government. There are five major types of government bonds: municipal, general obligation, Treasury, savings, and federal agency bonds.

Municipal Bonds

A bond issued by state and local governments is called a **municipal bond**. The minimum investment in a municipal bond is $5,000, although brokers often ask for a multiple of this amount as a minimum investment. Municipal bonds, often called "munis," can be backed by specific projects, or by the general taxing authority of a governmental unit. A **revenue bond** is a municipal bond issued to raise money for a public-works project. The revenues (income) generated by the project are used to pay the interest and repay the bonds at maturity. Major projects financed by revenue bonds include airports, hospitals, toll roads, and public housing facilities.

A **general obligation bond** (or GO) is a municipal bond backed by the power of the issuing state or local government to levy taxes and borrow. For example, school districts issue bonds to finance construction of new buildings. A city may issue bonds to pay for a new police or administrative center. States may issue bonds to pay for a new college campus or a new road system. A GO bond is repaid with general revenue and borrowings, in contrast to a revenue bond, which is repaid from the revenue of the specific facility built with the borrowed funds. Cities pay off the bonds from city income and sales taxes collected, fees, fines, and other sources. Schools and colleges pay off the bonds from property taxes collected, tuition, fees, and other sources.

Municipal bonds generally pay a lower interest rate than corporate bonds. However, the interest is exempt from federal taxes, so the effective rate is higher than the stated rate. Municipal bonds are also generally exempt from state and local taxes in the state where they are issued. As Figure 13-3 shows, the tax advantage of municipal bonds sometimes makes them a better deal than a corporate bond paying a higher interest rate. Figure 13-3 calculates net interest on both kinds of bonds for an investor in the 28 percent tax bracket.

Why might a state or local government issue a revenue bond?

Savings Bonds and Treasuries

You can buy U.S. savings bonds from commercial banks, through payroll deduction, or directly from a Federal Reserve bank. You can

	Corporate Bond	**Municipal Bond**
Face Value (Principal)	$10,000	$10,000
Rate of Interest	6%	5%
Amount of Annual Interest	$ 600	$ 500
Tax on Interest Earned (28%)	168	0
Net Interest	$ 432	$ 500

buy up to $15,000 worth of these bonds a year. Investors who buy Series EE bonds often hold them to maturity. These bonds are issued with maturity values that range from $50 to $10,000. You can postpone paying federal tax on the interest you earned on matured Series EE bonds by converting them to Series HH bonds.

+PROS and CONS

Traditionally, savings bonds have been purchased for babies and children. However, one expert advises that stock be bought instead, with the dividends and capital gains reinvested. This expert believes that over time, no financial asset performs as well as stock.

Think Critically: Would you agree with this philosophy? What advantages and disadvantages do you see?

Treasury securities are no longer issued as engraved certificates as are many stocks and corporate bonds. Instead, Treasuries exist as bookkeeping entries in the records of the U.S. Treasury Department itself or in the records of commercial banks. Unlike corporate bonds, Treasury obligations are not rated, since the backing of the U.S. government makes them virtually risk-free. Treasuries are exempt from state and local taxes and are usually *not* callable.

Agency Bonds

In addition to the U.S. Treasury, other federal agencies issue debt securities. Federal agencies that issue bonds include the Federal Home Loan Mortgage Corporation, Federal National Mortgage Association, Federal Land Bank, Federal Housing Administration, and the Tennessee Valley Authority. When you purchase an **agency bond,** you are loaning money to one of these agencies. Although agency issues are basically risk-free, they offer a slightly higher yield than securities issued by the Treasury. Both can be bought directly through banks or from brokers.

Zero-Coupon Bonds

A **zero-coupon bond** is a bond that is sold at a deep discount, makes no interest payments, and is redeemable for its face value at maturity. These bonds, whether issued by the U.S. government, corporations, or municipalities, are sold at as much as 50 to 75 percent below the face value of the bond. As the bond progresses toward maturity, it may appreciate, or increase in value. The bondholders make money by selling the bonds before maturity at a price higher than they paid for them. Or, they can hold the bonds to maturity and receive the face value.

With a zero-coupon bond, you must pay taxes on any interest earned each year (even though you don't actually receive it) until the bond is paid at maturity. Interest on zero-coupon municipal bonds, however, is not subject to taxation. Prices on zero-coupon bonds can fluctuate widely. Should you need to sell the bond before maturity, you may face a loss.

Check Your Understanding

Review Terms
1. face value
2. callable bond
3. debenture
4. mortgage bond
5. convertible bond
6. municipal bond
7. revenue bond
8. general obligation bond
9. agency bond
10. zero-coupon bond

Review Concepts
1. What is a callable bond? Does this feature make the bond more attractive to the investor?
2. Under what conditions would bonds sell at a premium?
3. What is a major advantage to government and municipal bonds?

Goals

★ Explain how to buy and sell bonds.
★ Describe how to evaluate different grades of bonds.
★ Explain how to read bond listings in financial publications.

How to Buy and Sell Bonds

Full-service brokers, who also sell securities, can assist you in purchasing all kinds of bonds. The broker will charge you a commission or a flat fee for this service. You also can use a discount broker to buy bonds. A *discount broker* charges a smaller fee or commission, usually half or less of what a full-service brokerage charges. You will receive no advice in your decisions to buy or sell. Full-service and discount brokerage firms are listed in the telephone book, and most can easily be found online. Also, many banks provide brokerage services.

The corporate bond market is large and liquid, with daily trading volume estimated at $10 billion.

You can buy a Treasury security through the Federal Reserve System. There are 12 Federal Reserve Banks and 25 regional branches spread across the nation. Check with your local financial institution to find the bank or branch closest to you. The Federal Reserve Bank will mail you an application form. You can send your check or money order with the application directly to the Federal Reserve. The Federal Reserve uses a system called *Treasury Direct* to record and store data about Treasury securities and their owners. You can even buy securities through Treasury Direct online at www.treasurydirect.gov. Interest (and principal when the bonds mature) is deposited directly into your bank account. Also, by using Treasury Direct, you can reinvest in Treasury securities automatically when existing securities mature. U.S. government securities also may be purchased through banks or brokers, but you will pay a commission.

You may wish to purchase savings bonds through payroll deductions. Your employer will withhold money as authorized. When your withholdings are sufficient, the bond will be purchased and sent to you. This process takes longer because your employer processes the money through a bank, which in turn purchases the bonds and returns them through your employer. It is often quicker to deal directly with a bank in your area.

You can buy municipal bonds through banks or brokers. In most states, you can set up a bank account to buy and sell municipal bonds. Generally, you are purchasing a bond from the inventory your bank has on hand. Banks buy large blocks of municipal bonds and make them available to their customers. There is a fee for this service, although it may be incorporated into the price of the bonds.

Most bond options require a minimum investment of $1,000. Only savings bonds can be purchased with small, regular payments. When you have a large sum of money to set aside, you can consider larger purchases of $5,000 or $10,000.

What are some ways in which you can buy Treasury securities?

Evaluating Bonds

Investors can earn a return on bonds in three ways. First, bondholders earn interest for each day they own the bond. Second, they can redeem the bond for its face value at maturity. Third, bonds often appreciate in value, and bondholders may be able to sell the bond before maturity for a price higher than they paid for it.

To help investors evaluate the risk level of different bonds, bonds are graded, or rated as to their safety. Independent rating services, such as Moody's (www.moodys.com) and Standard & Poor's (www.standardandpoors.com), base their ratings on the financial condition of the issuing corporation or municipality. The highest rating is AAA, or triple A. The lowest rating is a D. A D rating indicates that the bond is in *default*. This means that the issuer cannot meet the interest and/or principal payments. Because bonds are not insured, investors can lose their money if the corporation or municipality defaults.

Any bond with a rating of Baa or higher in Moody's, or BBB or higher in Standard & Poor's, is considered an **investment-grade bond**. These bonds are considered safe because the issuers are stable and dependable. For example, U.S. Treasury bonds provide maximum safety because these securities are backed by the federal government itself. Lowercase letters in a bond rating indicate more risk than capital letters. The letters stand for company stability, bond security, and general industry risk. Unfortunately, the higher the bond's rating, the lower the interest rate you will earn.

AROUND THE GLOBE

In 2001, the South-American country of Colombia planned to launch a new bond issue for $1.3 billion, with a partial guarantee from the World Bank. (The World Bank is an international institution that helps less-developed countries develop their basic industries and facilities.)

Think Critically: Why do you think the World Bank's involvement was necessary?

A **junk bond** is a bond that has a low rating, or no rating at all. Any bond with a rating of Ba/BB or lower is called a junk bond. Because of its low or no rating, this type of bond is highly speculative. Junk bonds have higher yields and at times appear to have reasonable levels of risk. However, in most cases, interest rates on junk bonds are high because they are high risk, since the companies issuing them are not financially sound. Carefully explore junk bonds before buying, and don't buy junk bonds at all if you can't afford to lose your investment.

Reading Bond Listings

Only one factor has a real effect on bond prices—interest rates. When interest rates rise, the value of bonds decreases. The bonds are paying less in comparison to other fixed-rate investments. Conversely, when interest rates drop, fixed-rate bonds will become attractive because they are "locked in" at higher rates.

To track bond prices, you need to understand the bond price listings in the financial section of your newspaper. Not all local newspapers contain bond quotations, but *The Wall Street Journal* publishes complete information on bond transactions. Most portal sites such as www.yahoo.com or the user home page offered by Internet service providers enable users to track securities prices. Users can key in the names of the securities they wish to track, and the home page will display the updated prices each day.

Figure 13-4 Reading Corporate Bond Listings

Name 1	Type/ Rating 2	Coup. 3	Mat. 4	3 P.M. Bid 5	Net Chg. 6	Yld 7
AK Steel	a/BB	9.125	12/06	98½	unch	9.46
Allied Waste	b/B+	10.00	8/09	102	unch	9.57
Am Std	a/BB+	7.375	2/08	98½	– 1¼	7.56
Chanclr	b/BB+	8.125	12/07	103	unch	7.36
Echostar	a/B	9.375	2/09	101¼	unch	9.52

Purchases and sales of corporate bonds are reported in tables similar to the one shown in Figure 13-4. In bond quotations, prices are given as a percentage of face value, which is usually $1,000.

1. *Column 1.* The first column lists the name of the bond, abbreviated.
2. *Column 2.* This column indicates the type of bond it is as its rating. The small letter "a" stands for a senior bond, a "b" stands for split coupon, a "c" stands for zero coupon bond, a "d" is an unsecured bond, and an "e" is a secured bond. The bond rating can range from AAA (highest) to C (junk bonds).
3. *Column 3.* This column shows the coupon rate of the bond (the guaranteed, fixed interest rate that will be paid annually on the bond). There may also be a volume column that lists the number of shares traded that day, in hundreds.
4. *Column 4.* This column shows the maturity date. A date of 12/06 means December, 2006.
5. *Column 5.* This column tells you what the final closing bid for the day was for this bond. It is similar to the closing price for stocks. For AK Steel, for example, the 3 p.m. price was 98½.
6. *Column 6.* The net change column compares the last price paid for the bond today with that paid on the previous day. "Unch" means "unchanged"; the price has not changed from the previous day.
7. *Column 7.* The yield column states the current yield for the bond. The current yield is computed by dividing the bond's coupon rate by its average current market value (not its closing value). This yield figure varies as market interest conditions change, and thus the yield may be above or below the actual coupon rate.

Check Your Understanding

Review Terms
1. investment-grade bond
2. junk bond

Review Concepts
1. How can you purchase savings bonds?
2. How are bonds graded?
3. What factor affects bond prices?

PERSONAL PERSPECTIVE

Tax Strategies

When choosing investment options, investors must keep one important consideration in mind—taxability. Some investments are fully taxable while others are tax-free. There are numerous options in between. The choice of an investment might hinge on its tax status.

An investment is *tax-exempt* when there is no tax due, either now or in the future. Tax-exempt investments include municipal bonds sold by state and local governments. However, to be free from both federal and state taxes, you must live in the state where the bond is issued. For example, if you live in California, tax-free bonds in Oregon will be subject to state income taxes in California.

An investment is *tax-deferred* when income will be taxed at a later time. Tax-deferred investments include annuities, which will be discussed in Chapter 15. While earnings are credited to your account now, you do not pay taxes on the earnings until you withdraw them. At that time, your tax rate may be lower, so you will owe less tax.

Taxes also are deferred on assets that appreciate in value. *Capital gains*, the profits from the sale of assets such as stocks, bonds, or real estate, are not taxed until the asset is sold. For example, if shares of stock you own are currently worth more than you paid for them, you will owe no taxes on the gain until you sell the stock.

Income and deductions can be *shifted* by postponing them to the following tax year, or accelerating them forward into a current year, when they will do you more good. If your income is higher this year than usual, you can shift some deductions to help offset this increased income.

Taxes can be *avoided* by selling securities on which you lost money to offset gains on the sale of other securities. You can deduct losses to reduce capital gains on securities you sold at a profit. This strategy is not the same as *tax evasion*, which is the use of illegal actions to reduce your taxes.

Think Critically

1. Why is it important to consider tax consequences when choosing investment alternatives?
2. What type of investor would likely choose a tax-exempt investment? What type of investor would choose tax-deferred?
3. Why should you seek professional advice when shifting income and avoiding taxes?

13.1 Characteristics of Bonds

- Bonds are loans that the corporation or government body must repay at face value, with interest. In contrast, stocks are shares of ownership in a corporation that need not be repaid and that may or may not pay a dividend.
- Corporate bonds are sold in the open market and are a fixed-income investment, in that they pay a specified interest at regular intervals. A registered bond pays interest directly to the owner of record, whereas a coupon bond pays interest to whoever presents the coupon to a bank.
- A callable bond may be "called" (paid off) by the issuer before maturity.
- Debentures are unsecured bonds. Mortgage bonds are secured by a specific asset. Owners of convertible bonds can exchange their bonds for common stock if they wish.
- Bonds whose interest rates are higher than the current market rate of interest will sell at a premium. Bonds whose interest rates are lower than the current market rate will sell at a discount.
- Government or municipal bonds generally are tax-free. General obligation municipal bonds are backed by the power of the issuing government unit to levy taxes.
- Both corporations and government bodies issue zero-coupon bonds. These bonds sell at a deep discount and make no interest payments. Holders of zero-coupon bonds make money by selling the bonds at a profit before maturity or redeeming them at face value at maturity.

13.2 Buying and Selling Bonds

- You can buy bonds through a broker, discount broker, financial institution, or the Federal Reserve System.
- Investors can earn a return on bonds from interest paid on them, by redeeming the bond for its face value at maturity, or by selling the bond before maturity for a price higher than they paid for it.
- To help investors evaluate bond risk, rating services grade bonds based on the financial condition of the issuing corporation or municipality. Bonds with a rating of Baa or higher in Moody's, or BBB or higher in Standard & Poor's, are safe investment-grade bonds. Bonds with a low rating or no rating are very risky junk bonds.
- Interest rates are the main factor that affects bond prices. When interest rates rise, the values of bonds fall, because bonds are paying less in comparison to other fixed-rate investments. Conversely, when interest rates drop, fixed-rate bonds will become attractive because they are "locked in" at higher rates.
- Bond listings in the financial section of the newspaper provide information about price fluctuations, yield, and maturity dates.

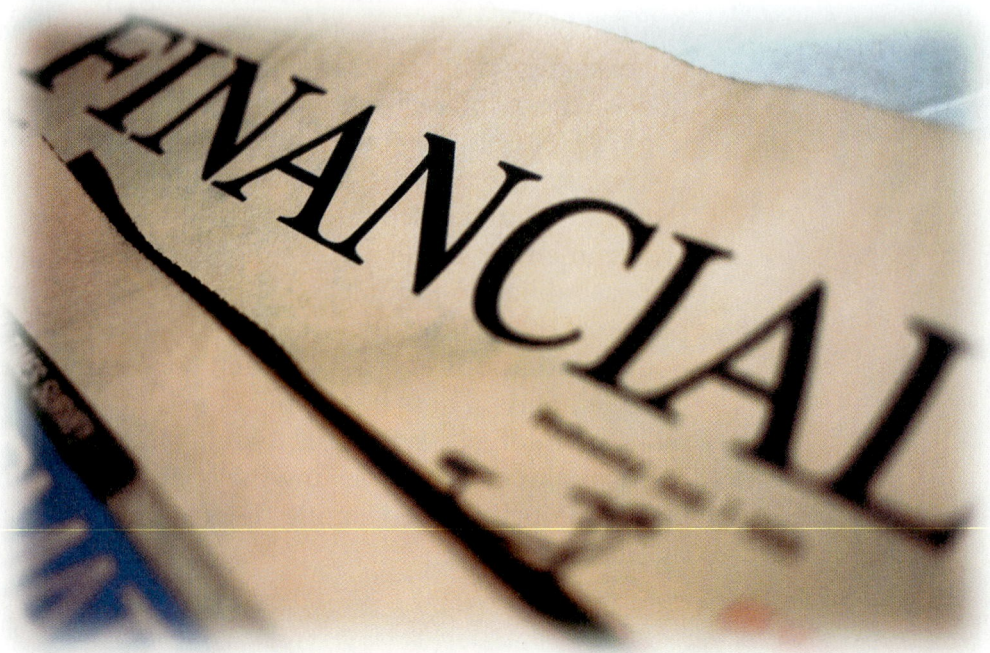

Review Terms

Directions: Can you find the definition for each of the following terms used in Chapter 13?

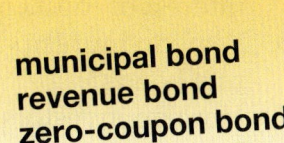

agency bond
callable bond
convertible bond
debenture
face value
general obligation bond
investment-grade bond
junk bond
mortgage bond

municipal bond
revenue bond
zero-coupon bond

1. A bond with a very low rating, or no rating at all.
2. A corporate bond that can be exchanged, at the owner's option, for a specified number of shares of the corporation's common stock.
3. A bond that the issuer has the right to pay off before its maturity date.
4. Debt security issued by federal agencies.
5. A bond that is sold at a deep discount, makes no interest payments, and is redeemable for its face value at maturity.
6. A corporate bond not backed by collateral but only by the general credit standing of the corporation.
7. A corporate bond backed by specific assets as collateral to assure repayment of the debt.
8. A municipal bond backed by the power of the issuing state or local government to levy taxes and borrow.
9. A high-quality bond considered to be a safe investment.
10. A bond issued by a state or local government.
11. The amount the bondholder will receive when the bond is repaid at maturity.
12. A municipal bond issued to raise money for a public-works project and repaid by the income from the project.

Review Facts and Ideas

1. In what two main ways are bonds different from stocks?
2. How does a bondholder make money from investing in bonds?
3. Why would a corporation issue callable bonds?
4. How are debentures different from mortgage bonds?
5. How do state or local governments pay off the principal and interest of municipal bonds issued?
6. Why do municipal bonds pay lower interest rates than corporate bonds?
7. How do investors make money on zero-coupon bonds?
8. What is "Treasury Direct"?
9. Why should you be concerned about a bond's rating before you buy it?
10. Why would anyone buy junk bonds?
11. How do interest rates affect the price (value) of bonds?

APPLY YOUR KNOWLEDGE

1. Why might an investor choose to buy bonds rather than stocks?
2. As a bondholder, would your investment in a corporate bond be more secure than a stockholder's investment? Why or why not?
3. Why might you choose a secured bond rather than an unsecured bond?
4. You bought a $10,000, 6 percent corporate bond at face value that matures in five years. What would be your total earnings during that five-year period?
5. Explain why you might choose a municipal bond paying 5 percent over a corporate bond paying 7 percent.
6. When buying Treasury bonds, which would you choose: full-service broker, discount broker, or Treasury Direct? Why?
7. Visit Treasury Direct online at www.treasurydirect.gov and find the answers to these questions:

    a. What are STRIPS?

b. What is the current national debt figure?

c. How can you replace a lost, stolen, or destroyed savings bond?

8. You have the choice of buying a municipal bond with a rating of Aaa paying 4 percent or a corporate bond with a rating of Ba paying 8 percent. Which bond would be your choice, and why?

9. You can buy a $1,000 face value zero-coupon bond for $600. The bond matures in 10 years. Describe the circumstances under which you would consider buying the bond.

10. A new bond issue you are considering has a face value of $1,000, an interest rate of 5 percent, and a maturity date eight years away. The bond is currently selling at 104. What is the current yield? What amount of interest would you earn in that time period?

11. Three $1,000 bonds have the following closing prices: $95\frac{3}{8}$, $103\frac{1}{4}$, and 99. What are the prices of the bonds in dollar amounts?

12. Visit the Federal Reserve System online at www.federalreserve.gov, and go to the consumer information section. Read one of the consumer information articles that interests you. In no more than a page, summarize, in your own words, what you learned from the article.

Solve Problems

1. Your friend Maria has just inherited $10,000. She considers the stock market too risky. She wants to preserve the safety of the principal she invests. Explain to her why buying a bond would be a safer investment than buying a stock.

2. Maria now asks you if she should consider a corporate bond. Explain to her how debt financing works, and the difference between the types of corporate bonds. What type of corporate bond would you recommend? Why?

3. Mike Ortega has just purchased a $10,000, 7.5 percent corporate bond that will pay interest semiannually for the next eight years. Prepare a chart showing how much in interest he will receive for the next eight years (total interest payments are 16).

4. Katrina McDonnel has chosen to buy a 5.5 percent, $1,000 corporate bond. The bond currently sells for 104. Compute her

current yield on the bond, and explain to her why it is not the same as the stated interest rate.

5. Tatsu Osaka is considering purchasing a $10,000 corporate bond yielding 9 percent. She also found that she could buy a municipal bond for 7 percent. Her federal income tax rate is 28 percent. Determine her net interest. Show your work.

6. Lionel has a regular job and is considering using payroll deductions to pay for savings bonds. If he could set aside $10 per month, how long would it take to buy a $500 EE bond? Explain to him how savings bonds work.

7. Using information from *The Wall Street Journal*, a local newspaper, or an online source, record the following data for three corporate bond issues you select. (Use a separate piece of paper.) Then briefly explain what each category of data means.

Source _____   Date _____

Stock Name	Current Yield	Volume	Close Price (or 3 p.m. Bid)
_____	_____	_____	_____
_____	_____	_____	_____
_____	_____	_____	_____

8. Mel is considering buying some junk bonds. He has some money set aside to use for speculation. He is willing to take the risk. Investigate how these bonds work. Then explain to him what junk bonds are.

9. Elena has narrowed her choice of bond purchases to two issues: MelMac, a 7 percent corporate issue selling for 102, or BrgPort, a 5 percent municipal issue selling for 96. Compute the current yield of each bond and advise her about which bond to choose.

10. Brian has $10,000 to invest. He is considering buying high-quality corporate bonds because interest rates on bonds are somewhat higher than on CDs. He has rejected stocks because of the risk involved. Brian feels that interest rates are going to continue to rise but, in the meantime, he needs a relatively safe place for his money. Explain to Brian how bond prices are affected by interest rates. Is he making the right decision? Explain.

11. Choose a corporate bond listed on the New York Bond Exchange. Use Moody's Industrial Manuals (available at many

public libraries) or Moody's online at www.moodys.com to answer the following questions about this bond issue.

a. What is Moody's rating for the issue?
b. What is the purpose of the issue?
c. Does the issue have a call provision?
d. What collateral, if any, has been pledged as security for the issue?
e. Based on the information studied, would the bond be a good investment for you? Why or why not?

For related activities and links, point your browser to
www.mypf.swep.com

Chapter 14

Investing in Mutual Funds, Real Estate, and Other Alternatives

Terms to Know

family of funds
growth fund
income fund
growth and income fund
balanced fund
bond fund
global fund

index fund
money market fund
prospectus
front-end load
back-end load
no-load fund
real estate
duplex

condominium
real estate investment trust (REIT)
participation certificate
mortgage
depreciation

Up Front

Karenna works 20 hours a week, lives at home, and can save $100 a month. She doesn't have a large lump sum to invest, but she's sure that she can set aside this amount permanently.

Karenna told her adviser, "I've thought about several different kinds of investments. I researched several mutual funds online, and I think I'm ready to buy shares in a fund that specializes in growth stocks. The one I'm most interested in has averaged 14 percent annual return over the last 15 years. That's good considering the ups and downs of the stock market. An important benefit I'll have is the ability to check my account daily if I want, by logging onto the fund's Web site. I can transfer my money from one fund to another electronically if I see that this would be a wise thing to do. And, once I buy in, I'm guaranteed to be able to keep buying shares of the fund, even if the fund is closed to new investors later on."

Goals

★ Explain why people invest in mutual funds and the types of mutual funds available for investing.
★ Describe how to evaluate mutual funds before buying.

What Are Mutual Funds?

As you will recall from Chapter 11, a *mutual fund* is a professionally managed group of investments bought using a pool of money from many investors. Individuals buy shares in the mutual fund. The fund managers use this money to buy stocks, bonds, and other securities. The kinds of securities they buy depends on the fund's stated investment objectives. For example, some mutual funds specialize in aggressive growth stocks. Others specialize in more conservative investments, such as bonds or money-market securities.

Most mutual fund companies offer a **family of funds**, which is a variety of funds covering a whole range of investment objectives. You can choose the funds that best match your own objectives. You are allowed to move back and forth among the company's funds. You can purchase one type of fund (such as a stock fund) and switch to another (such as a bond fund) at a later time.

Professional managers buy and sell according to their interpretation of market conditions, economic conditions, trends, and other factors. Fund managers research individual stocks and bonds and try to select good investments for their fund's investors. All fund investors share in any profits made by the mutual fund. They receive profits as dividends and as capital gains, both of which may be reinvested in the fund or distributed to investors as cash payments. The capital gains come from the profits made when the managers sell some of the fund's securities for more than they paid for them.

For most funds, you will have to make an initial purchase of $500 to $3,000 or more. Once you buy into a fund, you can make additional purchases as often as you like. Many people make regular purchases of $50 to $100 a month. To take money out of your fund, you may be able to simply call the company and place an order to sell your shares, or make your request online at the company Web site. The sale takes place at the end of the day (in some funds, sooner), and money is available to you the next morning.

Advantages of Mutual Funds

Investors often choose mutual funds for the convenience of professional management. You don't have to worry about following stock and bond markets or looking for hot new investments. Professionals are doing the work for you.

Also, your investment is liquid. You can get your money quickly if you need it, though there is some risk of loss if the fund's price is low when you choose to sell.

When you invest in mutual funds, you are diversifying, because mutual funds purchase a variety of stocks and bonds. When you have enough money to invest in more than one fund, you can further diversify by buying shares in funds with different investment objectives. In the same way that you would diversify individual stock purchases, you can buy some shares in riskier aggressive mutual funds and limit the risk by also purchasing shares in more conservative funds.

Another advantage of mutual funds is that you need not have a lot of money to invest. Many funds require only a small minimum investment. Also, through pooling your money with other investors in the fund, you can own, say, part of a $10,000 government bond without having $10,000 to buy the whole bond yourself.

Why is professional management an advantage of investing in mutual funds?

Types of Mutual Funds

Individual funds within a family have different investment goals and risk levels. In their publications and on their Web sites, investment companies describe the investment goal and level of risk for each fund in their family of funds. You should choose funds that match your investment goals and risk tolerance. As with any investment, the greater the potential return, the higher the risk.

Growth Funds

A **growth fund** is a mutual fund whose investment goal is to buy stocks that will increase in value over time. To do this, the fund's managers select stocks in companies that reinvest their profit in the company rather than distribute it to investors as dividends. Investors in growth funds earn their return through capital gains rather than through dividends. An aggressive growth fund invests in stock of new or out-of-favor companies and industries that the fund managers think will achieve above-average increases in value. The philosophy behind aggressive growth funds is to accept high risk of loss in exchange for a chance to earn high returns. Other growth funds follow a less risky philosophy. They invest in more stable companies that the fund managers expect to increase in value but at a slower, steadier rate than the stocks of aggressive growth funds.

Income Funds

An **income fund** is a mutual fund whose investment goal is to buy securities that consistently pay good dividends. Managers of income funds select stocks in companies that usually pay dividends rather than reinvest profit in the company for future growth. They also invest in bonds that pay regular interest. Investors in income funds are looking for income from their investments now rather than capital gains later. Income funds are considered to be of moderate risk and less risky than growth funds.

A **growth and income fund** is a mutual fund whose investment goal is to earn returns from both dividends and capital gains. Managers of these funds try to select securities that pay dividends as well as achieve some increase in market value over time. The risk level of this type of fund is moderate.

Balanced Funds

A **balanced fund** is a mutual fund that attempts to minimize risk by investing in a mixture of stocks (preferred and common) and bonds (corporate and municipal) that provide both current income and growth. Balanced funds are generally considered low-risk investments. The goal of a balanced fund is current income and long-term growth with safety.

Bond Funds

A **bond fund** is a mutual fund that invests in bonds to try to achieve stable income with minimal risk. Bond funds invest in government, corporate, or tax-exempt bonds with different maturity dates. A bond fund can be very risky if its stated objective is to invest in junk bonds to try to achieve exceptionally high yield. However, most bond funds are low to moderate risk. A bond fund might invest solely in tax-exempt bonds with a goal of providing tax-free income for investors. Tax-exempt bond funds appeal to investors in high income tax brackets.

Global Funds

A **global fund** is a mutual fund that purchases international stocks and bonds as well as U.S. securities. These funds appreciate when stock markets abroad are strong and world conditions favor certain overseas markets. Fluctuations in currency exchange rates also influence international stock values. Global funds run the whole range of risk, depending on the investment objective of the individual fund. For example, a global fund can be an income fund, growth fund, aggressive growth fund, or any other type, depending on the securities it buys.

Index Funds

As you learned in Chapter 12, an *index* is an average of the price movements of certain selected securities. Investors use indexes as benchmarks for comparison to judge how well their investments are doing. An **index fund** is a mutual fund that tries to match the performance of a particular index by investing in the companies included in that index. For example, an index fund might invest in companies included the Standard & Poor's 500 or the Dow Jones Industrial Average. The risk level of an index fund depends on the index it is tied to. Since the Dow includes only blue chip stocks, funds tied to this index would be relatively low risk. The NAS-DAQ Composite Index, on the other hand, averages stocks of some volatile high-tech companies. Funds tied to this index would be relatively risky.

Money Market Funds

Like a money market account in a bank, a **money market fund** invests in safe, liquid securities, such as Treasury Bills and bonds that mature in three weeks to six months. These short maturities provide current income and maximum safety. The goal of any money market fund is the preservation of principal and very high liquidity.

Evaluating Mutual Funds

There are thousands of mutual funds covering the whole range of investment objectives and risk levels. To choose the mutual fund that is right for you, you must know your own investment objectives and risk tolerance. Do you want income from your investments now, or can you wait for capital gains in the future? Do you need a tax-free or tax-deferred investment to reduce your current income taxes? Are you comfortable with risking your investment for a chance at big returns, or do you prefer a safe but lower return? Once you know your own requirements, you can read about the objectives and risk profiles of different funds and find one that matches your requirements.

Net Asset Value

Unlike stocks, mutual fund prices are not determined by what people are willing to pay for them. They are determined by *net asset value (NAV)*. The NAV is the total value of a fund's investment portfolio minus its liabilities, divided by the number of outstanding shares of the fund:

$$\text{NAV} = \frac{\text{Value of Portfolio} - \text{Liabilities}}{\text{Number of Shares}}$$

For example, suppose the value of all stocks in a fund's portfolio is currently $100,000. The fund has $90,000 in liabilities and has sold 500 shares of its fund to investors. The price for one of its shares, or its net asset value, would be $20 at this time:

$$\frac{\$100,000 - \$90,000}{500} = \$20$$

Because the value of the portfolio changes as the stocks and other securities are traded throughout the day, the NAV is calculated at the end of each business day.

Although a mutual fund provides professional management, you should continually monitor your fund's performance. Some funds consistently outperform the average among those with the same objective and risk. For example, if you own an income fund, you should compare its performance to that of other income funds. When considering the purchase of a fund, always examine its prospectus, its costs and fees, and the published comparisons among funds of the same type.

Over the long term, the success or failure of your investment in a mutual fund will depend on factors such as the fund's sales charges, fees, and expenses; the taxes you may have to pay on a distribution; the age and size of the fund; the fund's risks and volatility; and recent changes in the fund's operations.

The Prospectus

By law, investment companies must provide detailed information about their funds. A mutual fund company must provide a prospectus for each fund offered. The **prospectus** is a legal document that offers securities or mutual fund shares for sale. It must contain the terms, a summary of the fund's portfolio of investments, its objectives, and financial statements showing past performance. You can usually find this information on the investment company's Web site as well. Before choosing a mutual fund, read the prospectus carefully. Compare the fund's objectives with your own and compare its past performance with that of other funds you are considering.

Costs and Fees

If you buy a mutual fund through a broker, you will likely have to pay a sales fee, called a *load*. The broker's commission comes from this fee. A **front-end load** is a sales charge paid when you buy an investment. Sometimes you pay this fee on reinvested dividends as well. A **back-end load** is a sales charge paid when you sell an investment. Either way, loads can range from 2 to 8 percent of the value of the shares purchased.

In some cases, you can buy mutual funds directly from the investment companies. This kind of fund, called a **no-load fund,** does not charge a sales fee when you buy or sell because no salespeople are involved. You buy directly from the company by telephone, mail, or e-mail, or through the company's Web site.

Some mutual funds have a load—a sales fee that you pay when you invest in the fund. The fee goes to the salespeople who market the fund. Stock brokerages maintain load funds for their customers. On the other hand, no-load funds do not charge a sales fee because they have no salespeople.

Think Critically: What would be the advantages and disadvantages of loads versus no loads?

Other fees you should consider include annual management/administrative fees, which should average about 1 to 1½ percent of a fund's total assets. This charge is for the services of professional fund managers and for maintaining your account. The investment may also levy a *12b-1 fee* to defray the costs of marketing and distributing a mutual fund. These fees are a part of the fund's *expense ratio* and are expressed as a percentage of assets deducted each year for fund expenses.

Print and Online Sources of Mutual Fund Information

Financial publications, such as *Forbes*, *Fortune*, and *Money*, regularly review and rank mutual funds. They compare one-year, five-year, and ten-year performance of various funds with similar objectives. They also show the fees charged by each one, so that you can compare. Occasionally, entire sections of business magazines are devoted to listing, describing, and ranking mutual funds.

You can also find a great deal of information online. For example, www.morningstar.com issues reports that compare

If you were interested in a mutual fund, how might you get information about it?

mutual funds. Investorama is found at www.investorama.com. When you click on "mutual funds," you are given list of mutual fund families, such as Vanguard, Fidelity, and Dreyfus. Clicking on any of these names takes you to that fund's Web site, where you can download a prospectus or ask for specific information. At www.quicken.com, you can search for information on the better-performing funds by investment objective. You can also check a list of the top 25 performing funds and view NAVs for funds by their *ticker symbols* (abbreviated names). Another good site for educational information on mutual funds is at the Mutual Fund Investors Center at www.mfea.com. *Mutual Funds* magazine offers current articles on its Web site at www.mfmag.com.

Check Your Understanding

Review Terms
1. family of funds
2. growth fund
3. income fund
4. growth and income fund
5. balanced fund
6. bond fund
7. global fund
8. index fund
9. money market fund
10. prospectus
11. front-end load
12. back-end load
13. no-load fund

Review Concepts
1. Why might you choose a mutual fund over investing directly in stocks?
2. What is net asset value and how is it computed?

reluctant to make a loan. As a condition for a loan, you may have to make a larger down payment or pay a higher interest rate. When a renter takes possession of your house, you still have responsibilities. For example, as the owner, you must maintain the premises in a livable condition. You must provide running water, electrical circuits, sewer or septic hook-ups, and normal repairs and maintenance. If the roof leaks or a pipe breaks, it is your responsibility to fix it.

Duplexes, Apartments, and Condominiums

A **duplex** is a building with two separate living quarters. A duplex may be side-by-side living quarters with separate entrances, or it may be upper and lower floors of the building. The owner of a duplex has the same responsibilities to renters as the owner of a single-family home.

You might also choose to buy and rent a triplex (three units), quad (four units), or building with five to 100 or more apartments. When investing in large tracts of real estate, most people join investment groups. By pooling your cash with that of other investors, you can afford to buy larger and more expensive pieces of property. For example, if you and three others formed a partnership to buy an eight-unit apartment building, each of you would have to pay only one fourth of the total costs of buying and maintaining the property.

A **condominium**, or *condo*, is an individually owned unit in an apartment-style complex with shared ownership of common areas. The owner of a condo owns the individual apartment as well as a proportional share of common areas, such as the lobby, yard, and hallways. Condo

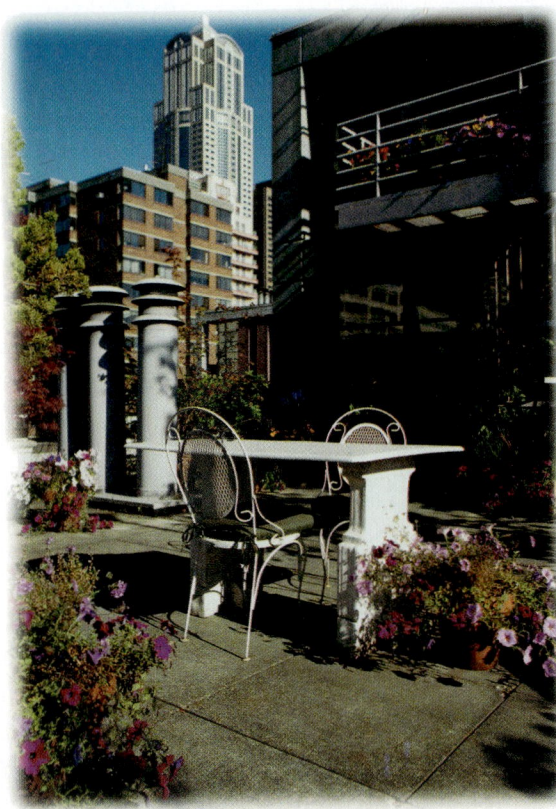

Why might you want to join an investment group when purchasing large tracts of real estate?

owners pay a monthly fee for the upkeep of the common areas, such as for mowing the lawn and maintaining a shared swimming pool. Condos are generally cheaper than detached houses because they use less land per unit and share roofs, walls, plumbing, and so on. Condos are particularly appealing to single people, young people, childless couples, and senior citizens.

Recreation and Retirement Property

Many people buy second homes for vacations or for their retirement years. Often the owners rent these properties to others during the times when they are not there, generating income for the owners. Of course, rented property will not be in brand-new condition when the owner retires to live there full time.

Recreation property includes beach and mountain cabins and even vacant land near vacation sites such as rivers, lakes, or an ocean. The owner can use and enjoy the property on weekends and during vacations, and at other times rent the property. However, absent owners must arrange for someone to take care of the property and manage the rental process. Real estate companies in popular vacation areas often provide these services for absent owners for a fee.

Indirect Real Estate Investments

In indirect investments, investors appoint a trustee to hold legal title on behalf of all the investors in a group. A *trustee* is an individual or institution that manages assets for someone else. Real estate syndicates, real estate investment trusts, and mortgage pools (in the form of participation certificates) are examples of indirect investments.

Real Estate Syndicates

A *real estate syndicate* (or *limited partnership*) is a group of investors who pool their money to buy high-priced real estate. This is a temporary association of individuals organized for the purpose of raising a large amount of capital. The organizer of the syndicate is called the general partner or syndicator. The people who contribute the capital are called limited partners.

Real estate syndicates work as follows: The general partner forms the partnership and assumes unlimited liability for all the obligations of the partnership. The general partner then sells participation units to limited partners whose liability is restricted to the amount of their initial investment (perhaps $5,000 or $10,000). Limited liability is especially important in real estate partnerships because the mortgage acquired to purchase real estate often exceeds the net worth of the partners.

A real estate syndicate often owns several properties for diversification. The commercial properties acquired are usually professionally managed.

Real Estate Investment Trusts (REITs)

A **real estate investment trust (REIT)** is similar to a mutual fund. It is a corporation that pools the money of many individuals to invest in real estate. Like a mutual fund, the REIT makes all buy and sell decisions. You can buy and sell REIT shares at will. REITs trade on stock exchanges or over-the-counter. Like stocks, REIT shares fluctuate with market conditions, and dividends are paid when the real estate investments do well. There are many types of REITs, investing in everything from rental properties for monthly income to mortgages for long-term income. REITs are found in the financial section of the newspaper along with stock, bond, and mutual fund price quotations.

There are about 300 REITs operating in the United States today. Their assets total over $250 billion. About two thirds of these trade on the national stock exchanges.

Participation Certificates

A **participation certificate** is an investment in a pool of mortgages that have been purchased by a government agency. Participation certificates are sold by federal agencies such as the Government National Mortgages Association ("Ginnie Mae"), the Federal Home Loan Mortgage Corporation ("Freddie Mac"), and the Federal National Mortgage Association ("Fannie Mae"). "Maes" and "Macs" are about as secure as Treasury securities.

At one time, you needed a minimum of $25,000 to invest in these certificates. However, many mutual funds invest entirely in them, making it possible to buy shares for as little as $1,000.

Owning and Managing Rental Property

A **mortgage** is a loan to purchase real estate. When buying real estate, most people make a down payment and get a mortgage to pay the balance. In Chapter 12, you learned that borrowing money to buy an investment is called *leverage*. A mortgage is a type of leverage. Only a small amount of the purchase price is your own money. For example, if you buy a duplex for $100,000 and make a down payment of $20,000 (a 20 percent down payment is usually required for rental property), you are borrowing $80,000 from the bank. As the property gains in value, the mortgage remains fixed. When you eventually sell the property, you keep the difference between the sales price and the mortgage. This difference is called *equity*, or ownership interest.

As your tenant makes rent payments, you make the mortgage payments to the bank. You would use the difference between the amount of rent and the mortgage payment to pay property taxes and the cost of upkeep on the property. If you have money left over after paying these expenses, you have a *positive cash flow*. If, however, you cannot collect enough rent to pay the mortgage, property taxes, repairs, and maintenance, then you have a *negative cash flow* and must make up the shortfall from your own pocket.

To manage your property, you can be a resident landlord or hire a resident landlord or property manager. A resident landlord lives at the rental site, takes care of all repairs and maintenance, collects the rent, and assures suitable living conditions. A property manager collects rent, hires and pays people to make repairs and maintain the property, charges a fee for his or her services, and remits the difference to the owner of the property.

Net Notes

Acting as a landlord can be a very complicated and time-consuming business. The mrlandlord.com Web site provides many free features and information for persons who own, manage, or control rental property. The site offers rental forms, management software, information on landlord/tenant law, and tips from Web site visitors, including real estate attorneys, authors, professional property managers, and hundreds of rental owners.

Depreciation is a decline in the value of property due to normal wear and tear. As the owner of rental property, you can deduct a depreciation expense on your taxes each year, reducing your taxable income. In addition, property taxes and other expenses of maintaining rental property are deductible. Thus, the expenses of ownership help to reduce the taxes you will have to pay on your rental income.

When you sell your property, you will have to pay taxes on the capital gain. But real estate can be difficult to sell. During slow economic times when people are not able to buy property, you may have to lower the price of your property substantially in order to sell.

You should also consider the risks of renting. Renters can damage or destroy your property to a degree far exceeding what a security deposit can pay for. When your units have vacancies, your rental income will decline, yet you still have to pay the mortgage and other expenses, thus cutting into your profits.

Real estate is also subject to zoning laws and other local use restrictions. Cities have laws that regulate what type of structure (single-family residence, apartment complex, office building, for example) that can be built in each area of the city. Before buying property, you should check the applicable zoning laws to make sure you will be allowed to use the property as you intend.

Check Your Understanding

Review Terms
1. real estate
2. duplex
3. condominium
4. real estate investment trust (REIT)
5. participation certificate
6. mortgage
7. depreciation

Review Concepts
1. What are some advantages of owning real estate as an investment?
2. Explain the concept of leverage as it applies to real estate.

Other Investment Choices

Goals

★ Identify potential investment choices in precious metals, gems, and collectibles.
★ Discuss the nature of futures and options markets.

Metals, Gems, and Collectibles

Investments in this category are speculative. They can return large profits or losses when sold. In some cases, the enjoyment of having and using the investment will far exceed any resale value. Although not inexpensive, precious metals, gems, and collectibles are easy to purchase. However, they can be very difficult to sell in a hurry and do not provide any current income in the form of interest or dividends.

Precious Metals

Gold, silver, and platinum are examples of *precious metals*. They are natural substances that people value. Inflation causes prices of precious metals to go up when the quantity and quality of the metal remains the same. However, prices of precious metals can be very volatile. Figure 14-1 on page 397 shows how gold and silver prices have fluctuated since 1967. Notice the wide swings in the prices. These swings are what make investments in precious metals very risky. If you had bought silver in 1980 at $32 an ounce and wanted to sell it in 2001, you would lose a lot of money!

You can buy gold and silver as coins, medallions, jewelry, and bullion. Storing precious metals safely may be a problem because of bulk and weight. Instead of storing your investment yourself, you can buy gold and silver in the form of a certificate stating how much you own of the metal being stored for you. You also can own gold indirectly by investing in gold-mining stocks or in mutual funds specializing in these stocks.

Other metals in which you can invest include aluminum, tin, copper, lead, nickel, and zinc. Prices for metals can be found in the financial section of newspapers and online. Prices vary greatly with changes in world economic conditions.

Gemstones

Gems are natural precious stones, such as diamonds, rubies, sapphires, and emeralds. Diamond prices are high and subject to dras-

Gold and Silver Prices — Figure 14-1

Date	Gold (Troy oz.)	Silver (Troy oz.)
6/1/67	$ 35.00	$ 1.80
6/1/80	850.00	32.00
6/1/83	437.50	11.80
6/1/89	368.30	5.27
6/1/93	364.20	3.25
9/1/94	390.20	3.55
6/1/97	322.40	4.01
3/1/01	266.20	4.45

tic change. Prices have fluctuated enormously in the last 30 years. For example, a flawless, Grade D, one-carat diamond purchased for $1,900 in 1970 would have sold for $50,000 in 1980, dropped to $17,500 in 1983, and then risen to $20,000 in 2001. Rubies, sapphires, and emeralds often increase in value during inflationary periods.

Precious metals and gems have their greatest value as jewelry. Stones that are one carat or more are rare and are much more valuable than smaller stones. Keep in mind, however, that the markup in jewelry made from precious metals and gems is typically 50 to 500 percent or more! When you, as an investor, purchase jewelry at retail prices, you are paying large markups. You will not be able to resell the jewelry for close to what you paid. Prices must increase substantially in the world market before you come near to recovering what you paid for the gem.

The biggest disadvantage of investing in gems (as well as precious metals) is that the market to resell them is very small and unpredictable. If you are eager to sell, you will face a loss. When purchasing gems and metals for an investment, remember that while it is easy to buy them, it is very difficult to resell them. No ready market exists. You must try to find an interested buyer.

While it is easy to buy gems, it is difficult to resell them. Why is this?

Collectibles

Collections of valuable or rare items, from antiques to comic books, are called *collectibles.* They are valuable because they are old, no longer made, unusual, irreplaceable, or of historic importance.

Coins are the most commonly collected items. Silver coins (rather than today's alloy coins) often are worth more than 20 times their face value. For example, a 50-cent piece dated before 1964 contains almost pure silver and is worth about $10, depending on its year and condition.

Commemorative coins are authorized by Congress and typically celebrate and/or honor American people, places, events, and/or institutions. Commemorative coins are available only from the U.S. Mint for a limited time, although they may remain available from collectors and coin dealers thereafter.

People like to collect favorite items, from porcelain figures to hubcaps, and hope that some day their collection will be valuable. Collecting can be a satisfying hobby. One advantage of collectibles is that you can start small and buy in small quantities. Unfortunately, collectibles can be hard to sell and are considered illiquid (not easily convertible to cash). You may find it difficult to locate a buyer who is willing to pay you the value of your collection, even when the value is well known. The trick is to collect wisely. Purchase only the highest quality of what you like. Buy what you can enjoy through the years, knowing that the item may or may not result in a profit.

Visit an antiques store, auction, estate sale, or the like. Speak with an appraiser, seller, or buyer to find out what that person thinks of collectibles. Would that person recommend investing in a collectible? Report back to your class, or prepare a one-page summary on your experience.

Financial Instrument Investments

As you learned in Chapter 11, *futures* are contracts to buy and sell commodities or stocks for a specified price on a specified date in the future. Commodities include farm products such as wheat, corn, and soybeans; cattle; and metals such as gold and silver. Commodity prices are volatile because supply and demand for commodities are disrupted by all kinds of mostly unpredictable situations from political upheaval to the weather.

Commodities are traded in both cash and futures markets. In a *cash market*, the commodity physically changes hands. Most of us are familiar with one type of commodities trading—the local farmer's market. Cash is exchanged for a farm product such as tomatoes or strawberries. Unlike the cash market, a commodity is not physically needed for trading in the futures market. For example, a farmer could sell a futures contract to deliver 5,000 bushels of wheat (one contract of wheat) one year from today. The futures market was created for those who want to know in advance what they will be paid. Farmers routinely sell in the cash market. They enter the futures market only for protection against volatile prices. Futures contracts are like an insurance policy against changes in prices. In this case, the farmers know in advance what they will be paid for their wheat.

Why are commodity prices unpredictable?

In Chapter 11, you learned that an *option* is the right, but not the obligation, to buy or sell a commodity or stock for a specified price within a specified time period. A *call option* is the right to buy 100 shares of stock at a set price by a certain expiration date. You can exercise the right at any time before the option expires. A *put option* is the right to sell stock at a fixed price until the expiration date. An investor who thinks a stock's price will increase during a short period of time may decide to purchase a call option. On the other hand, an investor who feels a stock's price will decrease during a short period of time may purchase a put option to safeguard the investment. Needless to say, options are risky business and not for the inexperienced investor. Options also apply to the purchase and sale of futures contracts.

Check Your Understanding

Review Concepts
1. Why are collectibles risky investments?
2. Explain how futures contracts work.

Chapter Review

Summary

14.1 Investing in Mutual Funds

- Mutual fund managers use money pooled from many investors to buy securities that fit the fund's stated investment objectives. All fund investors share in the fund's profits in the form of dividends and capital gains.
- Investors choose mutual funds for the convenience of professional management, the liquidity, the diversification, and the relatively small minimum investment required.
- Funds have different investment goals and risk levels. You should choose one that best matches your goals and risk tolerance.
- Investors choose growth funds to profit from capital gains in the future. They choose income funds to earn dividends now rather than capital gains later.
- Balanced funds and bond funds try to minimize risk while achieving a stable return. Global funds invest in international as well as U.S. securities. Index funds try to match the performance of a particular index. Money market funds invest in safe, liquid securities.
- A mutual fund's price is determined by its net asset value, calculated as the total value of the fund's investments minus its liabilities, divided by the total number of shares.
- To evaluate a fund, examine the prospectus, fees, and published comparisons among funds of the same type. Funds traded through a broker will likely include a sales fee when purchased (front-end load) or when sold (back-end load). Funds bought directly from the investment company carry no load.

14.2 Investing in Real Estate

- Real estate tends to increase in value over time, though not always. If you invest directly, you own legal title to the property. If you invest indirectly, a trustee holds legal title on behalf of the investor group.
- People invest in commercial property, such as office buildings, apartments, and condominiums, to produce lease or rental income.
- Indirect real estate investments may involve participating in a real estate syndicate, buying shares in a real estate investment trust (REIT), or investing in a federal agency's participation certificate.
- If your rental income exceeds your mortgage payment, property taxes, and upkeep expenses, then you have a positive cash flow. However, if vacancies cause your rental income to fall below your expenses, you will have a negative cash flow and have to make up the difference.
- As the owner of rental property, you are responsible for maintaining it. However, you benefit from tax deductions for depreciation and other expenses related to the property.

14.3 Other Investment Choices

- Investments in precious metals, gems, futures contracts, and options are all very risky and not for the novice investor.
- You can buy precious metals as coins, medallions, jewelry, or bullion and store it yourself, or you can buy a certificate of ownership of metals stored for you.
- Gems, such as diamonds and rubies, have their greatest value in the form of jewelry, but the retail price has a huge markup. The market for reselling gems is small and unpredictable.
- Collectibles can be very profitable but can also be worthless. Their value depends on the changing tastes of consumers.
- Financial instruments such as commodity futures and options are very high risk.

Review Terms

Directions: Can you find the definition for each of the following terms used in Chapter 14?

back-end load
balanced fund
bond fund
condominium
depreciation
duplex
family of funds
front-end load
global fund
growth and income fund
growth fund
income fund
index fund

money market fund
mortgage
no-load fund
participation certificate
prospectus
real estate
real estate investment
   trust (REIT)

1. A legal document that offers securities or mutual fund shares for sale.
2. A decline in the value of property due to normal wear and tear.
3. A variety of mutual funds offered by one investment company to cover a whole range of investment objectives.
4. A mutual fund whose investment goal is to buy stocks that will increase in value over time.
5. A mutual fund that attempts to minimize risk by investing in a mixture of stocks and bonds that provide both current income and growth.
6. A sales charge paid when an individual buys an investment.
7. A mutual fund for which investors pay no sales fee.
8. A building with two separate living quarters.
9. A mutual fund whose investment goal is to buy stocks and bonds that pay consistently good dividends.
10. A mutual fund that invests in bonds to try to achieve stable income with minimal risk.
11. A mutual fund that purchases stocks and bonds from around the world as well as the United States.
12. A sales charge paid when an individual sells an investment.

13. An individually owned unit in an apartment-style complex with shared ownership of common areas.
14. Land and any buildings on it.
15. A mutual fund whose investment goal is to earn returns from both dividends and capital gains.
16. A loan to purchase real estate.
17. A mutual fund that tries to match the performance of a particular index by investing in the companies included in that index.
18. An investment in a pool of mortgages that have been purchased by a government agency.
19. A mutual fund that invests in safe, liquid securities.
20. A corporation that pools the money of many individuals to invest in real estate.

Review Facts and Ideas

1. What determines the kinds of securities a mutual fund manager will buy?
2. Give some advantages of buying mutual funds rather than individual stocks or bonds.
3. List eight types of mutual funds, and briefly describe each.
4. What is the meaning of a mutual fund's NAV?
5. Explain the difference between a front- or back-end load fund and a no-load fund.
6. What kinds of comparisons among mutual funds can you find in print and online publications?
7. As the owner of rental property, what responsibilities would you have toward your tenants?
8. Why do many people join investment groups rather than purchase real estate individually?
9. How can vacancies in an apartment building you own affect you?
10. List some disadvantages of owning rental real estate.
11. Why are investments in precious metals, gems, and collectibles risky?
12. What are some advantages and disadvantages of collections as investments?
13. Describe the difference between a cash market and a futures market for commodities.
14. Explain the difference between put and call options.

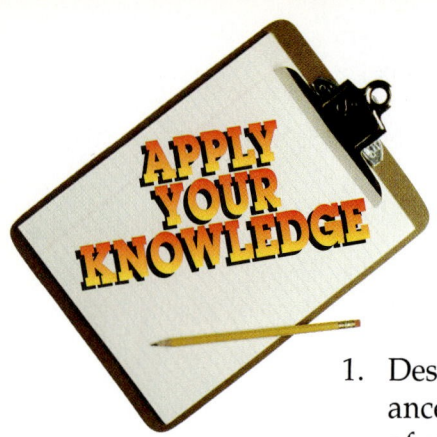

1. Describe the type of investor (in terms of goals and risk tolerance) who would be interested in each of the following types of mutual funds:
   a. growth funds
   b. income funds
   c. municipal bond funds
   d. money market funds
2. Why would a person choose a front- or back-end load fund over a no-load mutual fund?
3. Why should a new investor read the prospectus of a mutual fund carefully before purchasing the fund?
4. Visit the Web site of an investment company that offers a family of mutual funds. For example, you could go to Putnam Investments (www.putnaminvestments.com) or Fidelity (www.fidelity.com). Select five of the company's funds that are very different from each other. From the information given, describe the investment objective and risk level for each of the five funds. Draw a graphic that visually represents risk level, going from least to most risky. On the graphic, write the name of the most risky fund you selected at the high-risk end and the least risky fund at the low-risk end. Then place the other three funds at their appropriate risk level between the two extremes. In a paragraph, summarize what you learned about mutual funds and risk from this activity.
5. Describe what it would be like to be a landlord (your responsibilities and duties) if you owned:
   a. A single-family house that you rented to a family.
   b. A second home on the beach that you rented to vacationers in the summer.
   c. An eight-unit apartment building where you were the on-site manager.
6. Why would you wish to buy a piece of vacant land? Describe what your plans might be for the property in 10 or 20 years, including where you would buy such a lot and its potential uses.

7. Describe investors who might buy a second home, such as a cabin in the woods. Why should they purchase the property now rather than in the future, when they plan to use it full time for retirement?

8. Explain how leverage applies to buying real estate. Why is it desirable to have a positive cash flow from real estate you own?

9. What is the meaning of the statement "Real estate is an illiquid investment"?

10. Price changes for precious metals can be very unpredictable. Why would anyone want to invest in these items?

11. Collections are fun to have and can sometimes gain in value over the years. Name some collectible items you have seen, collected, or read about that have increased substantially in value over the years. What would you like to collect?

12. The Internet has provided a new way for buyers and sellers of collectibles to find each other. Search the Internet for sites dealing with a collectible that interests you. How is this item bought and sold online? Is there an association or club for your collectible? If so, how does the site help collectors?

Solve Problems

1. Hugh and Lacey have been married for three years and have managed to save some money to invest. They have decided on mutual funds but don't want to take too much risk. Still, they would like to have some additional income, and yet sell the shares for a good profit in five to ten years. Suggest to them some types of mutual funds that might fit their investment goals and risk tolerance. Which type(s) of fund would you choose for them?

2. Obtain a prospectus for a specific mutual fund. You can write to an address provided in an ad in the financial pages of your newspaper or *The Wall Street Journal,* get one from a brokerage firm or financial counselor, or locate the information at an investment company's Web site. Read the prospectus or online information and report on your findings: objectives (goals) of the fund; risk profile; tax status (are investments taxable or tax-free?); and performance of the fund for the last year and the last five years.

3. Your friend Matthew has saved almost $10,000 for a down payment and has decided to buy a small, single-family house that he will fix up and rent. He figures he can get at least $800 a month in rental income. He also has the money to cover the cost of $2,000 to fix up the house. Explain to Matthew the concept of leverage and the need for a positive cash flow once the house is fixed and rented.

4. Savita has decided to invest in real estate. She can't decide whether to buy a vacant lot for $25,000 or a one-fourth interest in a four-unit apartment building selling for $400,000. Explain to her the pros and cons of both of these alternatives.

5. Tomas and Calla Rodriguez will be retiring in less than 10 years. They are considering purchasing a house at the beach that they can use on weekends now and have as their home upon retirement. Explain to them the concept of buying recreation property and its potential as an investment.

6. Your grandmother has a wonderful collection of crystal, gold coins, diamond jewelry, and silver dating back to the early 19th century. When purchased, it cost very little, but today it could be worth a great deal of money. Explain to your grandmother, using a current issue of the newspaper or the Internet, what today's prices are for silver, gold, gems, and other valuables.

7. Your friend Tawana wants to buy a ruby ring at a local jewelry store. She believes it will make an excellent investment for the future, and that she can always sell the ring and make a profit. Explain to her the pros and cons of this type of investment.

8. Giorgio is a very nervous person. He is worried that his money is not earning enough interest to keep up with inflation. He was reading about commodities and thinks it would be a great way to make some quick money. Explain to him the risks involved in trading commodities.

For related activities and links, point your browser to
www.mypf.swep.com

Chapter 15

Retirement and Estate Planning

Terms to Know

reverse mortgage
heirs
estate
estate planning
will
codicil
power of attorney

trust
estate tax
inheritance tax
gift tax
individual retirement
    account (IRA)
Keogh plan

defined-benefit plan
defined-contribution
    plan

Up Front

"My grandparents say the time to think about retirement is when I get my first job," Frank told his co-workers. "But this isn't really my first job; it's just a part-time job while I go to school. When I get my first career-type job, then I'll start thinking about saving up for retirement."

"Your grandparents are right," replied Martina. "I have a great-uncle who is getting social security benefits. He barely has enough money to buy his groceries and pay the rent. Every time prices go up, he gets all stressed out because, in his words, he 'won't get a pay increase to make up for it.' I'm already thinking about the time when I won't be able to work. I think it's important to have enough money to live comfortably."

Goals

★ Describe how your needs will be different at retirement than they are now.
★ List the features of wills, powers of attorney, trusts, and joint ownership.
★ Discuss inheritance, estate, and gift taxes.

Defining Your Retirement Needs

When you get ready to retire, you will want to have enough financial resources to live comfortably. At that point, many people want to do the things they didn't have time for when they were working or raising families. To enjoy retirement, you must plan and save for it throughout your work life. Social security and a company pension may be insufficient to cover the cost of living. Inflation may decrease the purchasing power of your retirement savings.

How Much Income Do You Need?

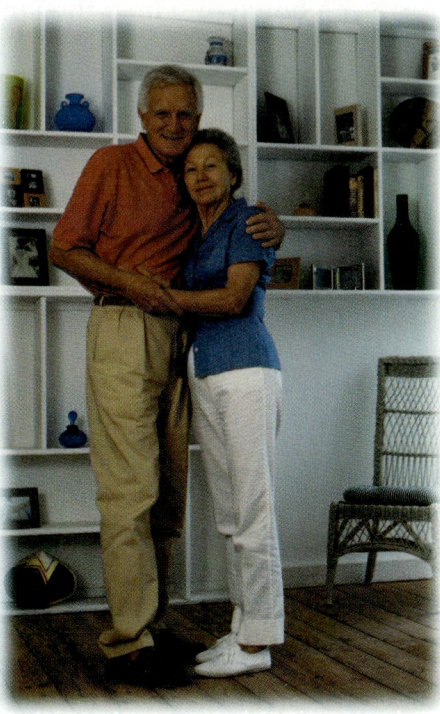

Many financial advisors tell clients that they will need between 60 and 80 percent of their before-retirement salary to live comfortably when they retire. This percentage may seem high. You may wonder how you can have that kind of income when you are no longer working. You can achieve a comfortable retirement only by limiting your current spending so that you can start saving now—at the beginning of your work life.

There will be times when you won't have much cash to set aside. You may be paying for a college education, children, cars, houses, furniture, and so on. But save regularly as much as you can without

Why must you save for retirement throughout your work life?

severely limiting your current lifestyle. Later in life, when you have fewer expenses, you can save even more. With regular saving and investing over many years, your nest egg can grow enough to meet your retirement needs.

Keep the House or Move?

Once their children are gone, many couples choose to sell their family home and find something smaller and easier to maintain. Current tax law allows married couples to sell the house they have lived in at least two years without paying taxes on the profits up to $500,000. For single people, the tax-free profit limit is $250,000. Thus, you will have the opportunity to sell the family home and keep the proceeds. Other people choose to keep their house because it is paid off. Before moving, consider the negative aspects. Moving is expensive. Also, if you move far away, you will be leaving friends and community behind.

Equity in a house is the property's value minus the amount of the mortgage not yet paid. As you make mortgage payments over the years, your equity in your home increases as the amount you owe decreases. However, equity is not income. It is money "tied up" in property. Some retirees need to turn their equity into current income. One way to do this is through a reverse mortgage.

A **reverse mortgage** is a loan against the equity in the borrower's home in which the lender makes tax-free monthly payments to the borrower. It works the opposite of a mortgage. Instead of making payments to the lender, the lender pays you. The loan amount must be repaid, with interest, when you sell your home, reach the end of the loan term, or die. For example, if you own a home worth $150,000 and your unpaid mortgage is $10,000, your equity is $140,000. With a reverse mortgage, the monthly payments to you would continue until they added up, together with interest, to the $140,000 equity. Once the loan is due, you may have to sell the home or get a regular mortgage to pay off the loan. If you die during the term of the loan, your heirs would have to pay it off. **Heirs** are people who receive property from someone who has died.

What Type of Investment Strategy?

Retired people view investments from a different perspective than when they were younger. Monthly income is often retirees' main goal for investments. For example, they may want to take dividends rather than reinvest them. Rather than saving for the future, investors at this stage are trying to preserve their financial position—that is, safeguard principal while earning a reasonable return. Fixed-income investments become a more practical choice. As people approach retirement, they often move some of their money out of growth stocks, which earn capital gains in the future, and into income stocks that produce dividends now. Many also move more of their investment into low-risk options, trading high-potential earnings for lower but more certain earnings.

What Type of Insurance?

When you retire, your insurance needs also change. While your need for life insurance has diminished, your need for other types of insurance has increased. You may have set up your life insurance to provide support and education for your children in case you died while they were still young. Now you may want to convert some of this asset into cash or income. You will learn more about insurance in Unit 6.

For retired people, the crucial need for insurance falls in the area of health—being sure that an illness or injury will not wipe out a lifetime of saving and investing. When you qualify for *Medicare*, government-sponsored health insurance for the elderly, you may need supplemental insurance to cover expenses not covered by Medicare. Also, there may be an interim period, between your retirement from work and when Medicare begins. This can be five or more years, during which time you must have your own health insurance. Also, retired people may want coverage for long-term care in a nursing facility.

How Do You Beat Inflation?

The probable loss of buying power due to inflation is one reason that planning for retirement is so important. As you will recall, *inflation* is a general increase in prices. Because of inflation, the cost of living goes up over time. Price increases diminish buying power. If prices are increasing at 8 percent while your retirement income is increasing at only 3 or 4 percent, you'll have to cut out something from your budget, or dip into your principal to maintain your living standard. Therefore, budgeting must continue through retirement. Part-time work is often the choice of seniors who need more income to offset inflation or who simply enjoy working.

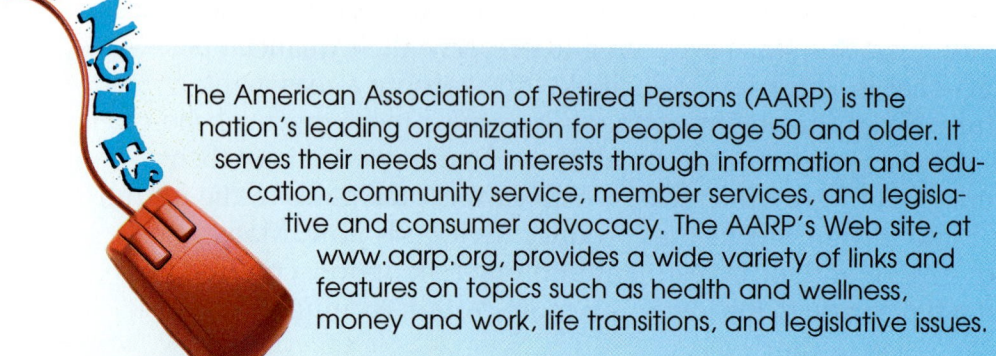

Estate Planning Tools

An **estate** is all that a person owns, less debts owed, at the time of the person's death. When people die, their possessions pass to other people, either as directed by the person who died (called the *decedent*), or by the laws of the state in which the person died. The estate may be taxed by the federal and/or state governments. **Estate planning** is preparing a plan for transferring property during one's lifetime and at one's death. Your goals in estate planning should be to minimize taxes on the estate, to make known how you want your possessions distributed, and to provide for a smooth transfer of your possessions to your loved ones upon your death. Some tools of estate planning include wills, powers of attorney, trusts, and joint ownership of assets.

Wills

A **will** is a legal document that tells how you want your estate to be distributed after your death. In your will, you name an *executor*, a person to carry out the transfer of your estate when you die. You also state your preferences for guardians of minor children and list the powers you want to give to the executor, guardians, or trustees. Any person who is 18 or older and of sound mind can make a legally valid will. Also, anyone who is legally emancipated—living independently from parents—can make a valid will. The person who makes the will is called the *testator*.

A *simple will* is a short document that lists the people you want to inherit and what you want each to receive. Simple wills take a short time to prepare, and they are fairly standard documents in each state. If your estate is relatively uncomplicated, you can prepare a will yourself, using an inexpensive kit or software purchased online or at an office products store. Whether you use a lawyer or not, you will need witnesses to your signature. Usually the witnesses must be two people not mentioned in the will. They must be 18 or older, not related to you, and able to attest to your mental competency at the time you signed the will. An example of a simple will is shown in Figure 15-1 on page 414.

A *holographic will* is a will written in a person's own handwriting. A handwritten will is legally valid in 19 states and should be witnessed, like other wills. Because a handwritten will is often easier to contest (question), a typed will is recommended.

When people die without a will, they are said to be *intestate*. In that event, the person's property is distributed according to the laws of the state where the decedent died. A typical intestate distribution might be as follows:

If the person is:	*Then distribution is:*
Married	All to spouse
Never married	All to parents
Married, one child	Half to spouse; half to child
Married, two children	Half to spouse; one-fourth to each child

By having a valid will, you can control who gets what, rather than allowing the state to make those decisions. Property reverts to the state when a person dies without heirs.

A person can make a will and later make small changes with a document called a **codicil**. The codicil lists the modifications and then reaffirms the rest of the original will document. A will cannot be legally amended by crossing out or adding words, or by removing or adding pages, or by making erasures. A codicil is drawn by an attorney and is executed and witnessed the same as a will.

Why is it important to prepare a will?

Figure 15-1 *Simple Will*

LAST WILL AND TESTAMENT OF ANTHONY JOHN HINTON

I, Anthony John Hinton, of the city of Dayton and state of Ohio, do make, publish, and declare this to be my Last Will and Testament in manner following:

FIRST: I direct that all of my just debts, funeral expenses, and the cost of administering my estate be paid by my personal representative hereinafter named.

SECOND: I give, devise, and bequeath to my beloved daughter, Carol Hinton Campbell, now residing in Englewood, New Jersey, that certain piece of real estate, with all improvements thereon, situated in the same city and at the corner of Hudson Avenue and Tenafly Road.

THIRD: All the remainder and residue of my property, real, personal, and mixed, I give to my beloved wife, Kimberly Sue Hinton, personal representative of this, my Last Will and Testament, and I direct that she not be required to give bond or security for the performance of her duties as such.

LASTLY: I hereby revoke any and all former wills by me made.

IN WITNESS WHEREOF, I have hereunto set my hand this tenth day of October, in the year two thousand --.

Anthony John Hinton
_____
Anthony John Hinton

We, the undersigned, certify that the foregoing instrument was, on the date thereof, signed and declared by Anthony John Hinton as his Last Will and Testament, in the presence of us who, in his presence and in the presence of each other, have, at his request, hereunto signed our names as witnesses of the execution thereof, this tenth day of October 20--; and we hereby certify that we believe the said Anthony John Hinton to be of sound mind and memory.

Vilbin Schaenbar	residing at	251 Wonderly Avenue Dayton, Ohio 45419-2521
Samuel Vance	residing at	3024 James Hill Road Kettering, Ohio 45429-2454
Irene Vasilhous	residing at	423 Goldengate Drive Centerville, Ohio 45459-2459

PERSONAL PERSPECTIVE

Challenging a Will

When you need a will, there are several ways you can do it and save money. You can go to a local stationery or office products store and buy a fill-in-the-blanks will that is supposed to be good in all states. Or you can simply sit down and write out your wishes in your own handwriting—a holographic will—which is legal in many states. But while the above choices may be legal, can these wills stand up in court if they are contested?

A person can contest the validity of another person's will if he or she feels excluded or forgotten, or believes the testator was mentally incompetent or *under undue influence.* A person who makes decisions under pressure from another person is said to be "influenced." The will may contain provisions that were not truly the "will" of the decedent. The court may agree with the person contesting the validity of a will in any of these circumstances. In addition, if you wait to draw your will until you are seriously ill, it could be contested based on your mental condition at the time.

If you want to *disinherit* a person who would ordinarily be entitled to an inheritance, you'll need a well-drawn will that will stand up to a court challenge. The most common challenge is from a possible heir who was omitted because of an outdated will. A child not mentioned in the will nor specifically disinherited will automatically share in the distribution of the decedent's estate. Adopted children inherit the same as do birth children.

How do you know for sure you have a will that can withstand a court challenge? The best way is to have an attorney prepare your will according to the laws of your state or have an attorney check a will you create from a kit or will-making software. You must mention all individuals who would normally inherit from you, and specifically disinherit any of them. To overcome a claim of insanity, undue stress, or physical illness impairing your ability to make decisions, many attorneys videotape the signing of your will. On the tape, you clearly state your intentions and your understanding of their consequences.

Think Critically

1. Have you considered to whom you would like to leave your property should something happen to you?
2. Under what conditions would you attempt to challenge the will of another person?
3. Why might you choose to have a will drawn by an attorney?

Power of Attorney

At some time in your life, you may become incapacitated and unable to make your own decisions. A **power of attorney** is a legal document authorizing someone to act on your behalf. For example, if you become incapable of caring for yourself, the power of attorney gives your appointed person the power to use money from your savings to pay your bills and hire people to care for you. The power of attorney may be limited or general in time or in scope. A limited power of attorney may be good for 30 days or a year, or it may pertain to a particular transaction. A general power of attorney gives another person the right to act completely for you. When you give a power of attorney to another person, you give that person the power to do anything you could have done. Of course, you must fully trust the person to whom you give this legal right.

Figure 15-2 shows a power of attorney form. You can hire a lawyer to write your power of attorney, or you can do your own, using a kit or software designed for creating legal documents. Many inexpensive programs are available online and in stores. Often software packages for writing wills, such as Nolo's Will-Maker and Quicken's WillWriter and Quicken Family Lawyer, also contain templates for creating powers of attorney and other common legal documents.

Trusts

A **trust** is a legal document in which an individual (the *trustor*) gives someone else (the *trustee*) control of property, for ultimate distribution to another person (the *beneficiary*). The trustee may be a financial institution or a person. A trust can exist during the lifetime of the trustor. This type of trust is called *inter vivos*, or a living trust. You simply transfer some property to a trustee, giving him or her instructions regarding its management and disposition while you are alive and after your death. The other type of trust is called a testamentary trust, or *trust will*. It takes effect upon the death of a trustor. Such a trust can be valuable if your beneficiaries are minor children or if you wish to avoid high taxes on your estate.

In order for money and property to be left to a minor child, the child must have a legal guardian who makes accountings of the child's property and money. Parents of small children typically create trust wills to provide for their children's education and

GENERAL POWER OF ATTORNEY

I, [YOUR FULL LEGAL NAME], residing at [YOUR FULL ADDRESS], hereby appoint _____ of _____, as my Attorney-in-Fact ("Agent").

I hereby revoke any and all general powers of attorney that previously have been signed by me. However, the preceding sentence shall not have the effect of revoking any powers of attorney that are directly related to my health care that previously have been signed by me.

My Agent shall have full power and authority to act on my behalf. This power and authority shall authorize my Agent to manage and conduct all of my affairs and to exercise all of my legal rights and powers, including all rights and powers that I may acquire in the future. My Agent's powers shall include, but not be limited to, the power to:

1. Open, maintain or close bank accounts (including, but not limited to, checking accounts, savings accounts, and certificates of deposit), brokerage accounts, and other similar accounts with financial institutions.

2. Sell, exchange, buy, invest, or reinvest any assets or property owned by me. Such assets or property may include income producing or non-income producing assets and property.

3. Purchase and/or maintain insurance, including life insurance upon my life or the life of any other appropriate person.

4. Take any and all legal steps necessary to collect any amount or debt owed to me, or to settle any claim, whether made against me or asserted on my behalf against any other person or entity.

5. Enter into binding contracts on my behalf.

6. Exercise all stock rights on my behalf as my proxy, including all rights with respect to stocks, bonds, debentures, or other investments.

7. Maintain and/or operate any business that I may own.

My Agent shall be entitled to reasonable compensation for any services provided as my Agent. My Agent shall be entitled to reimbursement of all reasonable expenses incurred in connection with this Power of Attorney.

My Agent shall provide an accounting for all funds handled and all acts performed as my Agent, if I so request or if such a request is made by any authorized personal representative or fiduciary acting on my behalf.

This Power of Attorney shall become effective immediately, and shall not be affected by my disability or lack of mental competence, except as may be provided otherwise by an applicable state statute. This is a Durable Power of Attorney. This Power of Attorney shall continue effective until my death. This Power of Attorney may be revoked by me at any time by providing written notice to my Agent.

Dated _____, 20-- at _____, _____.

[YOUR SIGNATURE]

_____
[YOUR FULL LEGAL NAME]

[WITNESS' SIGNATURE]   [WITNESS' SIGNATURE]

_____   _____
[WITNESS' FULL LEGAL NAME]   [WITNESS' FULL LEGAL NAME]

STATE OF _____, COUNTY OF _____, ss:

The foregoing instrument was acknowledged before me this _____ day of _____, 20-- by [YOUR FULL LEGAL NAME], who is personally known to me or who has produced _____ as identification.

_____
Signature of person taking acknowledgment

_____
Name typed, printed, or stamped

_____
Title or rank

_____
Serial number (if applicable)

living expenses. Then the balance of the estate is given to the children at some later age, such as 25 or 30, when all of them have reached adulthood.

The purpose of a trust is twofold. First, trusts provide for beneficiaries who might not be able to effectively manage assets for themselves. The trustee is held accountable for how money is spent and how the trust is administered. The trustee must file papers yearly with the court, reporting on how the trust is progressing. Also, the trustee typically receives a fee for these services. Second, a trust can minimize inheritance or estate taxes and avoid probate. *Probate* is a court-supervised process of paying your debts and distributing your property to your heirs upon your death. An attorney is required to complete the probate process. The estate pays the costs of probate before heirs receive any property. Property held in trust is not subject to probate. Therefore, the property can pass to beneficiaries quickly without a prolonged court proceeding and without the costs of probate.

Once probated, a will is a public record, and so is the final settlement and inventory of estate property. As such, these papers may be viewed by anyone. This fact may be a critical issue to some people, while others may not be concerned.

Joint Ownership

There are several ways to hold title to property. By putting property in *joint ownership,* two or more people own an undivided interest in the property. Joint ownership of property between spouses is very common. Joint ownership also may exist between parents and children, other relatives, or any two or more people. If you and your spouse own property as *joint tenants with right of survivorship* (JTWROS), the ownership is split 50-50 for estate tax purposes. If one spouse dies, the surviving spouse automatically becomes the sole owner of the property. No legal action is necessary to transfer title. This form of ownership is commonly used for land, automobiles, residences, bank accounts, and securities. Joint tenancy is a convenient and automatic way to pass property. It is perhaps the most widely used property ownership arrangement.

Two or more people can own property without survivorship. As joint tenants without right of survivorship, when one person dies, his or her interest in the property passes to his or her heirs, not to the remaining owners.

When a person holds ownership singly, with no joint owner or named beneficiary, that asset becomes part of the person's estate upon death and will be distributed according to the terms of the will. Joint ownership is an effective way to avoid probate and inheritance taxes in some states.

Taxation of Estates

Federal and state governments levy various types of taxes that must be considered in planning your estate. Three major taxes are estate, inheritance, and gift taxes.

Federal Estate Taxes

The federal government levies an **estate tax**, a tax on property transferred from deceased people to their heirs. An estate must be worth more than a certain amount to be subject to this tax. However, there is pressure to eliminate estate taxes altogether, and legislation has passed to that effect. The estate tax is paid from the assets of the estate, before anything can be distributed to heirs. An estate may have to sell property or investments in order to pay this tax.

Under present law, with intelligent estate planning and properly drawn wills, you may leave all of your property free of federal estate taxes to your surviving spouse. In addition to property transferred to a spouse, all property passed to qualified charitable organizations remains free of estate tax.

What are some different taxes that will affect your estate planning?

State Inheritance Taxes

Some states also levy an **inheritance tax**, a tax on an heir who receives property from a deceased person's estate. The difference between an estate tax and an inheritance tax lies in who pays the tax. The estate tax is deducted from the value of the estate, but the heirs pay inheritance taxes on property received. The amount of tax is based on the value of the property in the estate. In states where inheritance taxes are imposed, laws vary widely as to the rate of taxation and the treatment of property to be taxed.

Federal Gift Taxes

Gifts are a popular way of distributing some property to loved ones before death to avoid estate and inheritance taxes. However, you would not want to give away property you need in order to live comfortably. One way to retain possession is to create a life estate. A *life estate* allows you to pass title to real property to a loved one but retain your right to live on the premises for as long as you live. This means that your children cannot evict you even after the property is in their names.

A **gift tax** is a tax on a gift of money or property, to be paid by the giver, not the receiver, of the gift. You can give up to $10,000 per person per year without having to pay a gift tax. For gifts that exceed this amount, the gift tax rate is the same as the estate tax rate. Gifts to your spouse or to a charity are exempt from the gift tax. Also, gifts from a husband or a wife to a third party are considered as having been made in equal amounts by each spouse. Therefore, a husband and wife together may give as much as $20,000 per year to anyone, tax-free.

The timing of the gift also matters. Any gift given within three years of death is usually considered a "gift in contemplation of death." In this event, the estate still must pay taxes on the value of the gift, and the one receiving the cash or property would have to pay inheritance taxes.

Federal/State Income Taxes

When someone dies, income taxes must be paid on the income the decedent earned that year and on any income earned by the estate while its assets remain undistributed (such as interest or dividends). The executor or attorney representing the estate must file this tax return and pay the taxes from the estate before the estate can be distributed to heirs.

✓Check Your Understanding

Review Terms

1. reverse mortgage
2. heirs
3. estate
4. estate planning
5. will
6. codicil
7. power of attorney
8. trust
9. estate tax
10. inheritance tax
11. gift tax

Review Concepts

1. Why should you think about retirement when you are just beginning your work career?
2. Why is it important to have a will?
3. How does owning property jointly avoid probate?

Saving for Retirement

Goals

★ Describe the features of personal retirement accounts, including IRAs, Keoghs, SEPs, annuities, and pre-taxed savings.
★ Explain basic benefits available through employer- and government-sponsored pension plans.

Personal Retirement Accounts

Personal retirement accounts are ways to set money aside for your later life. You can select from tax-sheltered plans, such as individual retirement accounts (IRAs), Keoghs, and simplified employee pensions (SEPs) for which you qualify, as well as annuities. You should also include some savings on which you have already paid taxes.

Individual Retirement Accounts (IRAs)

An **individual retirement account (IRA)** is a retirement savings plan that allows individuals to set aside up to $2,000 per year (increasing to $5,000 per year) and delay paying tax on the earnings until they begin withdrawing it at age 59½ or later. People not covered by a pension plan at work may contribute the full amount per year, if they wish. Those who do participate in a pension plan at work can contribute to an IRA, but they may not be able to contribute the maximum, depending on their income.

With a *traditional IRA,* you can deduct your contribution each year from your taxable income. This allows you to delay paying the tax on that income and the earnings it accumulates in the account until you withdraw the money at retirement. At that time, your income

What is the value in contributing to a traditional IRA?

will likely be lower than it was while you were working. As a result, you would be in a lower tax bracket and would pay less tax.

A *Roth IRA* is a type of IRA that taxes the contributions but not the money withdrawn at retirement. With a Roth IRA, you pay tax on your income before you put it into the account, but you never have to pay tax on the earnings the account accumulates over the years. In a traditional IRA, you would pay tax on the earnings as well as the contributions when you withdraw the money at retirement.

You cannot withdraw your money from an IRA before age 59½ without a penalty. For early withdrawals, a 10 percent penalty is imposed on the amount withdrawn. This penalty can amount to a lot of money, so you should avoid withdrawing money early. In addition, the money you withdraw is subject to federal and state income taxes that year.

You can set up an *education IRA* if you have children under age 18. Contributions to an education IRA are not deductible. It is a trust created for the purpose of paying higher education expenses. Withdrawals for qualified expenses, such as tuition, books, fees, and supplies, are not taxable when withdrawn.

Keogh Plans

A **Keogh plan** is a tax-deferred retirement savings plan available to self-employed individuals and their employees. Keogh contributions are restricted to $30,000 or 25 percent of earned income in any one year, whichever is less. Earned income is your net income after business expenses, including contributions to the plan for employees. Employees must be covered in the plan in a nondiscriminatory manner. Thus, if you contribute 15 percent of your earnings to the plan as an employer, you must contribute 15 percent of any employee's salary as well.

The amounts an employer contributes are fully tax deductible. Earnings on Keogh plans are also tax-deferred. Withdrawals cannot be made before age 59½ without penalty, and withdrawals must begin by age 70½. Keogh plans must be administered by a trustee, such as a financial institution.

Simplified Employee Pension (SEP) Plans

Simplified employee pension (SEP) plans were authorized by Congress to encourage smaller employers to establish employee pension plans with IRAs as a funding method. Each employee sets up an

IRA at a financial institution. Then the employer makes an annual tax-deductible contribution of up to 15 percent of the employee's salary or $30,000, whichever is less. Employees also can make contributions up to a $2,000 limit. Employee contributions to these plans are also tax-deductible.

For example, assume you earn $15,000 a year. Your employer contributes $1,500 to your plan, or 10 percent of your salary. You can then contribute up to $500 to your plan, reaching the maximum of $2,000. On the other hand, assume your employer contributes $2,250 to your plan. In this case, you could make no personal tax-deductible contribution. The total going into the plan exceeds $2,000. As long as your annual salary remains at $15,000, the most your employer can contribute to the SEP is $2,250 (15% × $15,000).

Annuities

As you learned in Chapter 11, an *annuity* is an insurance company investment that provides a series of regular payments, usually after retirement. You can buy an annuity as your individual retirement account or as supplemental retirement income. An annuity can be bought with a single payment or with periodic payments. In recent years, *deferred annuities* have become popular because of the tax-free buildup of interest or dividends during the time the annuity contract remains in effect. Such annuities are often used by younger people to save money toward retirement.

Pre-Taxed Savings

Not all of your retirement savings should be in tax-deferred plans. Some should be savings and investments made with pre-taxed income (income on which you have already paid tax). When you retire and start taking money from your tax-deferred accounts, you will owe income taxes on the amount withdrawn. These taxes can add up to a significant sum. However, when you begin to use your pre-taxed savings, you will owe no further tax on the money.

Most financial advisors recommend that at least half of your retirement savings be pre-taxed. You will be able to withdraw these funds at any time, without tax consequences. Since there is no penalty for withdrawing these funds before retirement, you will have to restrain yourself from spending this part of your nest egg, so that it will be there for you when you retire.

Employer-Sponsored Retirement Plans

Another source of retirement income may be the pension plan offered by your company. With employer-sponsored plans, you and often your employer contribute to your tax-sheltered retirement savings. Contributions and earnings on employer-sponsored plans accumulate tax-free until you receive them.

Defined-Benefit Plans

Many larger companies provide defined-benefit plans for their employees. A **defined-benefit plan**, such as a pension, is a company-sponsored retirement plan in which employees receive, at normal retirement age, a specified monthly amount based on wages earned and number of years of service. The employer makes the entire contribution to the plan. To become *vested*, or entitled to the full amount in the plan, you must work for the company for a specified number of years. Employees who are vested but leave the company before retirement may withdraw the account balance in cash or "roll it over" (transfer it) to an IRA. In this situation, most people choose to roll the money into an IRA to delay paying taxes on it until retirement. If they take it as cash when they leave the company, they will have to pay tax on the full amount that year plus a 10 percent penalty if they are under age 59½.

Each pension plan has different rules and options. You should read the plan document to understand your choices.

If a company goes bankrupt or experiences serious financial difficulties, your plan may be protected by law. The Employee Retirement Income Security Act of 1974 (ERISA) sets minimum standards for pension plans in private industry and protects millions of workers from inadequately funded pension plans.

Defined-Contribution Plans

A **defined-contribution plan** is a company-sponsored retirement plan in which employees may choose to contribute part of their salary as a tax-deferred investment. The employer may or may not contribute to the employee's account as well. Each company's plan specifies the percentage of salary that an employee may contribute to his or her own account each year. The plan also specifies the amount the employer will contribute, if anything, but does not promise any particular benefit. When a plan participant retires or otherwise becomes eligible for benefits, the benefit is the total amount of money accumulated in the employee's account, including investment earnings on amounts put into the accounts. Two defined-contribution plans are 401(k) and 403(b) plans.

401(k) Plans

Employees of companies that operate for a profit may participate in 401(k) plans, if the company offers one. Under a *401(k) plan*, employees choose the percentage of salary they want to contribute to their account. The employer deducts this amount from their paychecks and puts it into the employees' individual accounts. This amount never becomes part of the employees' taxable income for the year, so they do not have to pay taxes on it until they withdraw the money at retirement. An investment company manages the accounts and invests the money. Usually employees may select the types of investments they want from among several options offered by the plan.

Frequently, employers match salary contributions by some percentage. For example, for every $1 of salary employees contribute to their account, the employer may add 50 cents (a 50 percent match). Companies usually set limits on how much they will match of an employee's salary contributed to a 401(k). Withdrawal restrictions and penalties apply when money is withdrawn early, except in the event of death, disability, or financial hardship. A 401(k) is usually an excellent investment for employees, particularly if the employer contributes. The employer's contribution is pure profit. In the example above, the 50 percent match is the same as making an immediate 50 percent return on your investment!

403(b) Plans

Employees of government or not-for-profit businesses may participate in 403(b) plans. A *403(b) plan* is an account for employees of schools, tax-exempt organizations, and government units. While the rules may vary slightly, the 403(b) plan operates similarly to 401(k). These plans have been called tax-sheltered annuities (TSAs) because originally the law permitted only deferred annuities to be purchased by employees who were qualified under this section of the tax code. In 1974 the law was amended to permit investments in mutual funds.

Earnings are tax-deferred, and early withdrawal penalties apply. Should an employee leave this type of employer, the 403(b) funds can be rolled into an IRA.

Government-Sponsored Pension Plans

You may be entitled to government benefit checks—in the form of social security, military retirement, or veterans' benefits. The Railroad Retirement System is the only retirement plan administered by the federal government that covers a single private industry. Many state, county, and city governments operate retirement plans for their employees.

Social Security Benefits

When you retire, you will be eligible for social security benefits if you paid social security taxes during your lifetime. The amount of your benefit is based on your earnings and contributions to social security. Remember, these withholdings from your paychecks were matched by your employer(s). However, social security is designed as a safety net, or supplement to an individual's own retirement savings. It was never intended to fully support people in retirement. To retire comfortably, you must have accumulated your own nest egg apart from social security.

If you were married for 10 years or more, you may be entitled to receive social security benefits based on your spouse's income. This benefit is available even if you are divorced.

Maximum social security retirement benefits are available at age 65. The government is raising the

Can you rely on social security for full retirement support?

retirement age, so the age when you can receive the maximum benefits may be later than 65. You can retire early, at age 62, and receive reduced benefits. As you are working, you should check your potential social security retirement benefits. Some federal government employees and railroad employees are not covered by social security retirement benefits, although recent federal employees are now paying into social security.

Remember, too, most or all of social security retirement benefits are taxable if your total income from all sources exceeds amounts set from time to time. In addition, 13 states currently tax social security benefits as income.

Military Benefits

Retired military personnel receive pensions after 20 years of active duty in the U.S. armed forces. Pensions are payable in full regardless of other sources of income and are subject to income taxes. In addition, military retirees may have special privileges that accrue from this status, such as the ability to purchase goods through military posts. These benefits can be very attractive, especially for people who retire from the military in their early 40s and continue working in different jobs for another 15 or 20 years.

The Veterans Administration provides regular pensions for many survivors of men and women who died while in the armed forces, and disability pensions for eligible veterans. In addition, veterans may be entitled to benefits ranging from low-interest mortgage loans to financing of a college education to low-rate car, life, or home insurance. Veterans should check to see what benefits are available—both now and at retirement.

COMMUNICATION CONNECTION

Write a page-long report on what you would like to do when you retire. Think about whether you would want to stay where you are, move to another climate, travel, work part-time, volunteer, and so on. Based on these plans, what kinds of savings and investments should you consider in order to achieve your goals?

Check Your Understanding

Review Terms
1. individual retirement account (IRA)
2. Keogh plan
3. defined-benefit plan
4. defined-contribution plan

Review Concepts
1. How is a traditional IRA different from a Roth IRA or an education IRA?
2. How is a 401(k) different from a 403(b)?
3. Who is eligible to collect social security retirement benefits?

15.1 Planning for Retirement

- After retirement, you will likely need between 60 and 80 percent of your before-retirement income to live comfortably. Social security and a company pension will probably not be enough. You must start building your nest egg now with regular saving and investing.
- The equity you build in your home can be a source of retirement income. You can get the money out of your home by moving to a smaller home or taking out a reverse mortgage.
- Your investment goals may change as you near retirement. You may choose investments that earn current income over those seeking capital gains in the future. You may also want to reduce the overall risk level of your portfolio at that time.
- Your insurance needs will change at retirement. Instead of life insurance, you will need to channel more dollars toward health insurance.
- You should plan your estate to minimize taxes, to make known how you want your possessions distributed after your death, and to provide for a smooth transfer of your assets to your loved ones.
- A will specifies how to distribute your assets. A power of attorney empowers someone else to act on your behalf. With a trust, you appoint a trustee to control property for your beneficiary, who will receive it at a later time. Joint ownership with right of survivorship transfers property at death without the costs and time involved in probate.
- Estate tax is deducted from the value of the estate before it is distributed to the heirs. Inheritance tax is paid by the heirs on property received.

- A gift tax applies to a gift exceeding $10,000 per person per year, to be paid by the giver.

15.2 Saving for Retirement

- An IRA allows individuals to set aside as much as $2,000 per year. A traditional IRA allows you to delay paying income tax on the contributions until you withdraw the money at retirement age. On a Roth IRA, you pay taxes on the contributions but pay no taxes on withdrawals at retirement.
- A Keogh plan is a tax-deferred plan for self-employed people. SEP plans are tax-deferred plans for employees of small businesses. An annuity is a tax-sheltered investment sold by insurance companies that provides regular payments after retirement.
- Under a defined-benefit plan, such as a pension, retired employees receive a specified amount based on wages earned and years of service. The employer completely funds the plan, and employees must be vested to receive benefits.
- Defined-contribution plans allow employees to contribute part of their salary to tax-deferred investments managed by an investment company. Employers may or may not contribute matching funds to employees' accounts. For-profit companies can set up 401(k) plans for their employees. Not-for-profit and government organizations can set up 403(b) plans for employees.
- Social security is a government-sponsored pension plan. You will be eligible for social security benefits at retirement if you paid social security taxes during your lifetime. If you were a member of the military, you may be eligible for a military pension.

Review Terms

Directions: Can you find the definition for each of the following terms used in Chapter 15?

codicil
defined-benefit plan
defined-contribution plan
estate
estate planning
estate tax
gift tax
heirs
individual retirement account (IRA)

inheritance tax
Keogh plan
power of attorney
reverse mortgage
trust
will

1. All that a person owns, less debts owed, at the time of the person's death.
2. A company-sponsored retirement plan in which employees receive, at normal retirement age, a specified amount based on wages earned and number of years of service.
3. A loan against the equity in the borrower's home in which the lender makes tax-free monthly payments to the borrower.
4. A retirement savings plan that allows individuals to set aside up to $2,000 per year and delay paying tax on the earnings until they begin withdrawing it at age 59½ or later.
5. A legal document that tells how a decedent wishes his or her property to be distributed after death.
6. People who receive property from someone who has died.
7. A legal document that empowers a trustee to control property for ultimate distribution to a beneficiary.
8. A federal tax on property transferred from deceased people to their heirs.
9. A state tax on an heir who receives property from a deceased person's estate.
10. A tax-deferred retirement savings plan available to self-employed individuals.
11. A company-sponsored retirement plan in which employees may choose to contribute part of their salary as a tax-deferred investment.
12. Preparing a plan for transferring property during one's lifetime and at one's death.
13. A legal document that makes small changes to a will.
14. A legal document authorizing someone to act on your behalf.
15. A tax on a gift of money or property, to be paid by the giver, not the receiver, of the gift.

Review Facts and Ideas

1. About how much income will you need at retirement to live comfortably?
2. How might your housing needs change as you near retirement?
3. How can you turn the equity in your home into income?
4. How might your investment strategy change as you near retirement?
5. How might your insurance needs change at retirement?
6. What are the goals of estate planning?
7. Why do you need a will?
8. What is the difference between a simple will and a holographic will?
9. Why would you need a power of attorney?
10. What is the difference between an *inter vivos* trust and a testamentary trust?
11. What governmental unit levies inheritance taxes? Who pays them?
12. Why would a person give property to another person during his or her lifetime rather than wait to pass property by a will?
13. When do you pay income taxes on the amounts in a Roth IRA?
14. Who can establish a Keogh retirement plan?
15. Explain the tax-deductible features of IRAs, SEPs, and Keogh plans.
16. How is a 401(k) plan different from a 403(b) plan?
17. Why should retirees not rely entirely on social security benefits?

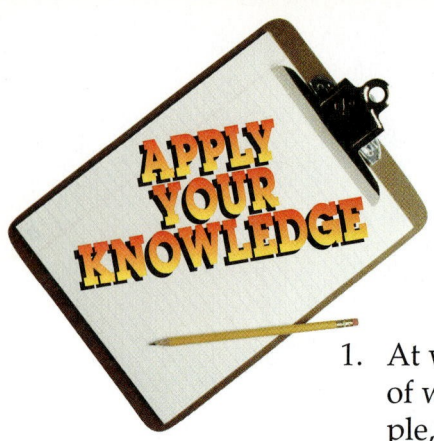

APPLY YOUR KNOWLEDGE

1. At what age would you like to retire? After how many years of work? Briefly describe your plans for retirement—for example, travel, leisure, and recreation.

2. Interview your colleagues and friends to get their views on retirement planning. Why are many young people who worry about the future often reluctant to plan for retirement?

3. Explain how you might invest your money to be sure your income keeps up with inflation. Assume that you will receive social security and pension benefits from an employer.

4. Visit the Vanguard investment company Web site at www.vanguard.com. Follow the link to the Personal Investors section and then click on "Plain Talk Library." Choose one investment topic, such as dollar cost averaging, and write a paragraph explaining what it is and how it works.

5. Visit the T. Rowe Price investment company Web site at www.troweprice.com to find out about social security benefits, taxes, inflation, and how to figure out how much you will need to save for retirement. Follow "Investment Insights" to "Retirement Planning." Choose the retirement planning worksheet, and write a one-page paper describing what you learned, based on your own projected retirement income needs.

6. To learn more about estate planning, visit www.netplanning .com/consumer. Here an alliance of estate planning attorneys offers advice about estate planning. Click on "Keys to Wealth" and select a topic that interests you. Then write a paragraph summarizing the key tips on that topic.

7. Visit the Roth IRA home page at www.rothira.com. From the information you find there, write a paragraph about Roth IRAs. Who would choose them and why?

8. Explain the advantages of using either a Keogh, IRA, SEP, 401(k), or 403(b) as part of retirement planning. Can you also list some disadvantages?

9. Prepare a simple will for yourself, following Figure 15-1. What would happen to your property if you did not have a will?

10. If you had minor children, you might create a trust to provide for them if you died while they were still young. Explain why a trust fund is important for managing the financial needs of minors.

11. What are some advantages of owning property jointly with another person? Why would people own property as joint tenants with the right of survivorship?

12. Suppose you gave a $20,000 gift to a friend. Would you pay a gift tax on $20,000 if you were single? If so, how much of the gift amount would be taxed?

Solve Problems

1. Mr. and Mrs. Gutierrez are getting older. Their children are grown and through college. Their home is nearly paid off. In five more years, they both plan to retire. Explain to them how their investment strategies today should probably be different from when they still had children to support.

2. Mrs. Chang is a widow. She has an employer-paid pension of $300 a month, together with social security benefits of $600 a month. She owns her home free and clear but has high medical bills. Explain to her how she can use her house equity to generate monthly income for her retirement years.

3. Georgina is self-employed. Every year, she has extra money she could save, but instead she spends it on trips and jewelry. She also pays high taxes because she earns considerable money from her business. Explain to her why she should strongly consider a Keogh plan for her retirement years.

4. Micah works and earns under $25,000 a year. He has never had an IRA because he thinks social security will be enough for retirement income. Explain to him how an IRA works, and why he should consider one.

5. Rondell has worked for over 45 years. He served in the military for 20 of those years. He is qualified to retire next year

when he reaches age 65. Explain to him what type of benefits he might expect to receive.

6. Your grandmother and grandfather have built a considerable estate. They are worried about how to avoid large estate and inheritance taxes. Their only heirs are your father and your uncle. Explain to them what type of will they could use. Do they need to create a trust, particularly for their grandchildren?

7. Sherry and Alan own a new car jointly with right of survivorship. Can Sherry leave her share of the car to another person when she draws up her will? Why or why not?

8. Your wealthy aunt has come to you for advice. How can she avoid estate taxes and inheritance taxes? She would be willing to give some of it away now and consider other options to avoid taxes, such as a trust. Should she establish a gift-giving program for her heirs? What type of trust arrangements might she consider?

9. Use the following information and your Retirement Planner Tool to plan for your retirement. You are 21 years old and have no savings yet, but you have a good job now and think you can start saving. You think you can retire comfortably at 65 on $30,000 a year, and plan to withdraw your savings until you are 85. On average, you think you can earn 8 percent on your savings. How much would you have to save each year to meet your savings goal? How much would you have to save each year if you didn't start until you were 35?

PLANNING TOOLS

For related activities and links, point your browser to
www.mypf.swep.com

Unit *three*

PROJECT

Assessing Your Financial Security

Project 3

At the end of Unit 2, you began your financial planning with a project that helped you carefully examine your financial position. Now you will plan how to build and protect your financial security through savings, investments, and retirement and estate planning.

Your Savings Plan

Saving is often defined as postponed spending. The money you set aside today will allow you to make purchases later. A good financial plan begins first with setting aside a portion of your current income to provide for future needs.

In Chapter 10, you learned how to calculate interest on savings deposits. When money is set aside, it gains interest until some point in the future when it is withdrawn and spent. Future value is the final compounded value of a deposit or series of deposits. Using future value tables (which are built into modern financial calculators), you can determine how much money you need to set aside today in order to reach a future goal.

Figure U3-1, on page 440, shows the future value (compound sum) of an amount deposited at several interest rates and allowed to compound for a number of compounding periods. Rather than compute interest for each period and add it to the previous balance, you can use this table. For example, if you deposit $5,000 at 8 percent and leave it for five years, compounded semiannually, you would use the table as follows: 8 percent a year is 4 percent per compounding period (8 divided by 2); five years, compounded semiannually, is 10 compounding periods (5 times 2). In the table, the factor for 4 percent and 10 periods is 1.48024. Multiply $5,000 times 1.48024, and the account total will be $7,401.20 after 5 years, at 8 percent interest, compounded semiannually.

When you make regular payments (rather than deposit a lump sum at irregular intervals) to your account, you can use another table to shortcut the calculations. Figure U3-2, on page 441, is the future value (compound sum) of an annuity. (You will recall that an annuity is a sum of money set aside regularly for the future.) Instead of calculating interest, adding a deposit, calculating interest, and so on, the table shown in Figure U3-2 simplifies the procedure. For example, say you deposit $1,000 per year for 12

Future Value (Compound Sum) of $1

Period					Percent				
	3%	4%	5%	6%	7%	8%	9%	10%	11%
1	1.03000	1.04000	1.05000	1.06000	1.07000	1.08000	1.09000	1.10000	1.11000
2	1.06090	1.08160	1.10250	1.12360	1.14990	1.16640	1.11810	1.21000	1.23210
3	1.09273	1.12486	1.15723	1.19102	1.22504	1.25971	1.29503	1.33100	1.36763
4	1.12551	1.16986	1.21551	1.26248	1.31080	1.36049	1.41158	1.46410	1.51807
5	1.15927	1.21665	1.27628	1.33823	1.40255	1.46933	1.53862	1.61051	1.68506
6	1.19405	1.26532	1.34010	1.41852	1.50073	1.58687	1.66710	1.77156	1.87042
7	1.22987	1.31593	1.40710	1.50363	1.60578	1.71382	1.82804	1.94872	2.07616
8	1.26677	1.36857	1.47746	1.59385	1.71819	1.85093	1.99256	2.14359	2.30454
9	1.30477	1.42331	1.55133	1.68948	1.83846	1.99901	2.17189	2.35795	2.55804
10	1.34392	1.48024	1.62890	1.79085	1.96715	2.15893	2.36736	2.59374	2.83942
11	1.38423	1.53945	1.71034	1.89830	2.10485	2.33164	2.58043	2.85312	3.15176
12	1.42576	1.60103	1.79586	2.01220	2.25219	2.51817	2.81266	3.13843	3.49845
13	1.46853	1.66507	1.88565	2.13203	2.40985	2.71962	3.06581	3.45227	3.88328
14	1.51259	1.73168	1.97993	2.26090	2.57853	2.93719	3.34173	3.79750	4.31044
15	1.55797	1.80094	2.07893	2.39656	2.75903	3.17217	3.64248	4.17725	4.78459
16	1.60471	1.87298	2.18288	2.54035	2.95216	3.42594	3.97031	4.59497	5.31089
17	1.65285	1.94790	2.29202	2.69377	3.15882	3.70002	4.32763	5.05447	5.89509
18	1.70243	2.02582	2.40662	2.54035	3.37993	3.99602	4.71712	5.55992	6.54355
19	1.75351	2.10685	2.52695	3.02560	3.61653	4.31570	5.14166	6.11591	7.26334
20	1.80611	2.19112	2.65330	3.20714	3.86968	4.66096	5.60441	6.72750	8.06231
25	2.09378	2.66584	3.38636	4.29187	5.42743	6.84848	8.62308	10.83471	13.58546
30	2.42726	3.24340	4.32194	5.74349	7.61226	10.06266	13.26768	17.44940	22.89230
35	2.81386	3.94609	5.51602	7.68608	10.67658	14.78534	20.41397	28.10244	38.57485
40	3.26204	4.80102	7.03999	10.28572	14.97446	21.72452	31.40942	45.25926	65.00087
45	3.78160	5.84118	8.98501	13.76461	21.00245	31.92045	48.32729	72.89048	109.53024
50	4.38391	7.10668	11.46740	18.42015	29.45703	46.90161	74.35752	117.39085	184.56483

years, earning 6 percent interest a year. In the table, the factor for 6 percent and 12 periods is 16.86994. Multiplying $1,000 times 16.86994, you get $16,869.94, which is the value of the deposits at the end of 12 years.

Using the two tables shown in Figures U3-1 and U3-2, complete Worksheet 1 (Future Values) in the *Student Activity Guide* (and illustrated on page 446).

For your own personal savings plan, you should set aside a predetermined amount each month. Complete Worksheet 2 (Your Savings Plan) in the *Student Activity Guide* (and illustrated on page 447). Then calculate the future values of money you can set aside.

Investments and Risk

After you have provided for savings, you can then begin investing. The purpose of investing is to earn a higher return than you

Future Value (Compound Sum) of an Annuity (Base Value $1)

Period	3%	4%	5%	6%	7%	8%	9%	10%	11%
1	1.00000	1.00000	1.00000	1.00000	1.00000	1.00000	1.00000	1.00000	1.00000
2	2.03000	2.04000	2.05000	2.06000	2.07000	2.08000	2.09000	2.10000	2.11000
3	3.09090	3.12160	3.15250	3.18360	3.21490	3.24640	3.27810	3.31000	3.34210
4	4.18363	4.24646	4.31013	4.37462	4.43994	4.50611	4.57313	4.64100	4.70973
5	5.30914	5.41632	5.52563	5.63709	5.75074	5.86660	5.98471	6.10510	6.22780
6	6.46841	6.63298	6.80191	6.97532	7.15329	7.33593	7.52334	7.71561	7.91286
7	7.66246	7.89829	8.14201	8.39384	8.65402	8.92280	9.20044	9.48717	9.78327
8	8.89234	9.21427	9.54911	9.89747	10.25980	10.63663	11.02847	11.43589	11.85943
9	10.15911	10.58280	11.02656	11.49132	11.97799	12.48756	13.02104	13.57948	14.16397
10	11.46388	12.00611	12.57789	13.18080	13.81645	14.48656	15.19293	15.93743	16.72201
11	12.80780	13.48635	14.20679	14.97164	15.79360	16.64549	17.56029	18.53117	19.56143
12	14.19203	15.02581	15.91713	16.86994	17.88845	18.97713	20.14072	21.38428	22.71319
13	15.61779	16.62684	17.71298	18.88214	20.14064	21.49530	22.95339	24.52271	26.21164
14	17.08632	18.29191	19.59863	21.10507	22.55049	24.21492	26.01919	27.97498	30.09492
15	18.59891	20.02359	21.57856	23.27597	25.12902	27.15211	29.36092	31.77248	34.40536
16	20.15688	21.82453	23.65749	25.67253	27.88805	30.32428	33.00340	35.94973	39.18995
17	21.76159	23.69751	25.84037	28.21288	30.84022	33.75023	36.97371	40.54470	44.50084
18	23.41444	25.64541	28.13239	30.90565	33.99903	37.45024	41.30134	45.59917	50.39594
19	25.11687	27.67123	30.53900	33.75999	37.37897	41.44626	46.01846	51.15909	56.93949
20	26.87037	29.77808	33.06595	36.78559	40.99549	45.76196	51.16012	57.27500	64.20283
25	36.45926	41.64591	47.72710	54.86451	63.24904	73.10594	84.70090	98.34706	114.41331
30	47.57542	56.08494	66.43885	79.05819	94.46077	113.28321	136.30754	164.49402	199.02088
35	60.46208	73.65223	90.32031	111.43478	138.23688	172.31680	215.71076	271.02437	341.58956
40	75.40126	95.02552	120.79977	154.76297	199.63511	259.05652	337.88245	442.59257	581.82607
45	92.71986	121.02939	159.70016	212.74351	285.74931	386.50562	525.85874	718.90484	986.63856
50	112.79687	152.66708	209.34800	290.33591	406.52893	573.77016	815.08356	1163.90853	1668.88115

can earn on savings. In order to do this, you must take more risk. When choosing investments, it is important first to decide how much risk you are comfortable taking. For example, investing in riskier stocks may be profitable, but it may not be appropriate for people who get very nervous when the stock market goes down.

Worksheet 3 shown on page 448 is a Risk Aptitude Test for Investors that lets you assess your tolerance for risk when you are planning your investment strategy. If you find you are risk-averse, you should choose lower-risk investments to avoid the stress that accompanies high-risk investments. If, however, you are a risk-taker, then you can take maximum risks and enjoy the uncertainty. Most people fall somewhere between the two extremes. They must try to balance their investments to earn maximum return for the risk involved.

Complete Worksheet 3 (Risk Aptitude Test) in the *Student Activity Guide.* Write a paragraph summarizing what you discovered about your own tolerance for risk.

Investment Strategy

An *investment strategy* is a plan that examines potential returns and rates investments according to desirability. To measure investment potential, two standards apply: the rate of inflation and the overall performance of the stock market. Inflation may be averaging 4 to 6 percent, and if your investment matches or exceeds that rate, you've done well. To estimate the return you're getting, follow the formula in Figure U3-3.

For example, let's say that four years ago you purchased 10 shares of stock at $35 each. The stock is now worth $38.50 a share. You have received dividends of $.50 per share for four years. Computation of the average rate of return is shown in Figure U3-4, on page 443.

If inflation was less than 3.9 percent on the average during those four years, your investment was worthwhile. However, if the inflation rate was higher than your average return of 3.9 percent, you should sell that investment and buy something else.

Calculate the average gain per year and average rate of return on investments shown, and rank the investments in order of desirability on Worksheet 4 (Investment Analysis) in the *Student Activity Guide* (and illustrated on page 449).

Your Investment Plan

A good investment plan is to begin slowly, choosing low-risk, predictable, and stable options. Then, as your comfort level increases

| Figure U3-3 | *Average Rate of Return Formula* |

Current market value of investment	$ _____ A
minus price you paid for it	_____ B
Gain (+) or Loss (–)	$ _____ C
plus dividends, interest, and other	
cash received	_____ D
Total Gain (+) or Loss (–)	$ _____ E
Average yearly gain:	
divide by number of years you've	
owned it (divide E by number of years)	$ _____ F
Average rate of return:	
divide average yearly gain (F) by	
original price (B)	_____ %G

Calculation of Average Rate of Return

Current value $38.50 × 10	$385.00 A
Original price 35.00 × 10	350.00 B
Gain (A − B)	$ 35.00 C
Dividends (.5 × 10 × 4)	20.00 D
Total gain	$ 55.00 E
Average yearly gain $55 ÷ 4	$ 13.75 F
Average rate of return $13.75 ÷ 350	3.9% G

and you have more money to risk, expand into moderate and high-risk ventures with greater potential profits (and losses). Complete Worksheet 5 (Investment Plan) in the *Student Activity Guide* (and illustrated on page 450). You may wish to refer to Chapters 12–14 to examine your options as you plan for future investments.

Your Retirement Plan

The time to begin planning for retirement is now—at the beginning of your work career. Otherwise, unforeseen events may prevent you from implementing plans needed to provide a secure retirement. Because people are living longer and healthier lives, it is important for all of us to consider those post-working years. With adequate financial resources, retirement can offer activities and opportunities that are satisfying and enjoyable.

The most difficult part of retirement planning is estimating your post-retirement income and needs. Generally, living expenses decrease following retirement. Bureau of Labor statistics show that retired couples are able to maintain a similar standard of living with about half the spendable income needed by the average family of four. Some financial advisers recommend that retiring individuals have 60 to 80 percent of their take-home pay to maintain their pre-retirement lifestyle. The types of expenses will also change. Health care and food become major budget items while house payments generally disappear because mortgages are paid off. Other expenses, such as utilities and property taxes, do not change significantly.

Between today and the day you retire, inflation will likely increase. However, your investments and savings should also increase. Therefore, when planning for retirement needs, prepare a budget based on today's dollars, knowing that in the future, prices will be higher, but your savings and investments will also be higher to offset inflation.

To prepare for retirement, you can cut your costs and increase your income. Worksheet 6 (Retirement Plan) will help you determine how much of each you need to do. Complete Worksheet 6 in the *Student Activity Guide* (and illustrated on page 451).

Social security payments probably will not be adequate to meet retirement expenses. Completing the retirement plan in Worksheet 6 should convince most people of the need to provide additional sources of income. Some of these will have a tax advantage; others will not. For example, IRA contributions that were deducted from gross income are now taxable when withdrawn. Therefore, when you withdraw money from an IRA or other tax-deferred accounts, such as a 401(k) or 403(b), you will pay income taxes on the full amount of principal and earnings. When computing the future monthly income to be derived from such sources, be sure to subtract the taxes (28 percent, for example).

Estate Planning

You learned about estate planning in Chapter 15. But there are several other matters to consider that were not covered in the text. For example, when a person dies, loved ones left behind have many decisions to make and expenses to pay. The costs involved when a person dies can range from a few hundred dollars to several thousand dollars. These expenses include final medical and hospital charges, the funeral and a casket (or other desired arrangements), and burial.

By preparing instructions and making provisions for these costs in advance, you spare your loved ones the emotional decision-making process. Survivors who are grieving the loss of a loved one often are unprepared to make the many decisions involved in planning a funeral and burial. At such an emotional time, a family may incur excessive expenses neither they nor the estate can afford.

Traditional funeral services may be performed in a church or in a funeral home. The cost can be $1,500 to $5,000 or more, which includes a casket, embalming, preparations, music, printed remembrances, and newspaper notices. All decisions about these matters must be made in a relatively short period of time.

Cremation is a process of reducing a body to ashes in a high-temperature oven. The ashes are placed in an urn that is presented to the family or placed in a vault. Cremation is less expensive than burial, but there are special requirements. When a body is not cremated within a certain time span, usually two days, it must be embalmed or otherwise prepared for burial. These costs must be paid, even though cremation is later chosen.

Many funeral homes have prearranged plans available at guaranteed costs. Money for the funeral is placed into an account that is insured by the FDIC or NCUA and earns interest. Although the money is for the funeral, it can be withdrawn in an emergency. Written instructions will save the family from overspending at the time of death, minimize emotional and financial distress, and assure the family that the type and cost of the funeral is as desired by the loved one.

A typical letter of final instruction is shown as Figure U3-5. It outlines a person's wishes and helps others to implement them.

Prepare Worksheet 7 (Letter of Instruction), which is in the *Student Activity Guide*, to outline your wishes.

Letter of Instruction　**Figure U3-5**

Date: _____

To my family,

This is a list of my last wishes and arrangements I have made which I hope will make decisions easier for you.

1. I wish to be cremated. I have prearranged services at the Bennet Funeral Home. These arrangements include the details of announcements, selection of urn, etc. I have prepaid these services, and the receipt is attached to this document.

2. I do not wish to be an organ donor. Please do not sign forms to indicate otherwise.

3. My Last Will and Testament is in my safe-deposit box at First Independent Bank, Main Branch, this city. A copy is also in my attorney's office (Anderson & Anderson, this city).

4. I have the following accounts and policies which should be included in my estate:

   Checking Account . . . . First Independent Bank
   Savings Account . . . . First Independent Bank
   Life Insurance Policy ($100,000) . . . New York Life
   Mortgage Insurance. . . . . Veterans Services

5. My safe-deposit box contains deeds to property I own, past tax returns, and lists of credit and charge accounts I hold.

_____
J. B. Adams

WORKSHEET 1
Future Values

Directions: For numbers 1–4, use Figure U3-1 to compute the value of each deposit at the rate given. For numbers 5–8, use Figure U3-2 to compute the value of each annuity at the given rate.

Future Value (Compound Sum) of $1

Deposit	Time	Annual Rate	Value
1. $5,000 Compounded quarterly	4 years	12%	$_____
2. $1,000 Compounded semiannually	10 years	6%	$_____
3. $7,500 Compounded annually	8 years	8%	$_____
4. $3,850 Compounded semiannually	2 years	8%	$_____

Future Value (Compound Sum) of an Annuity

Deposit	Time	Annual Rate	Value
5. $500/year	5 years	6%	$_____
6. $100/year	10 years	9%	$_____
7. $75/month ($900/yr)	2 years	8%	$_____
8. $250/year	10 years	5%	$_____

WORKSHEET 2
Your Savings Plan

Directions: In the spaces, project what you could save presently (either lump sum or monthly payment), and calculate the future value in 5, 10, and 20 years at the interest rate shown. Then project what you would like to be able to save (lump sum or monthly payment) in 5, 10, and 20 years.

Savings Amount	Interest Rates	Future Value
$_____ What you could set aside today	6% per year, compounded annually, in 5 years	$_____
	6% per year, compounded annually, in 10 years	$_____
	6% per year, compounded annually, in 20 years	$_____
$_____ What you want to be able to save 5 years from now	8% per year, compounded annually, in 10 years	$_____
	6% per year, compounded semi- annually, in 20 years	$_____
$_____ What you want to be able to save 10 years from now	5% per year, compounded annually, in 20 years	$_____
	6% per year, compounded semi- annually, in 5 years	$_____

Make a plan for the amount of money you will set aside now and in the future.

Directions: In the spaces below, write when you will set aside money, how much you will set aside and how often, your goal amount, and the future purpose of the amount saved.

Date	Amount Set Aside/How Often/Goal	Future Purpose of Saved Amount
_____	$_____/_____/_____	_____
_____	_____/_____/_____	_____
_____	_____/_____/_____	_____

WORKSHEET 3
Risk Aptitude Test

Directions: Answer the following questions, recording your answers in the spaces provided. Then compute your risk aptitude score as shown.

_____ 1. You have an extra $100 left over from your year-end bonus. Would you rather (a) put it all in savings, (b) spend some and save a little, (c) bet it on a lottery.

_____ 2. You are ready to buy a new car. Will it be a (a) small economy car, (b) conventional, standard car with a variety of options, (c) sports car emphasizing speed, style, or performance.

_____ 3. You have won a weekend trip of your choice. Will you (a) take cash instead, (b) go on a cruise or sightseeing trip, (c) fly to a mountain lodge for skiing.

_____ 4. You are considering a job offer. Which of these is most important to you? (a) job security (permanent employment), (b) higher salary with moderate security, (c) higher pay and less job security.

_____ 5. You are betting on a horse race. Which wager will you make? (a) bet on the favorite, even though winnings will be small, (b) select a horse with a good chance of winning and moderate payback if it does, (c) pick a long shot with high payback.

_____ 6. You have a mortgage on your home. Will you (a) make regular payments, paying off the loan on schedule, (b) repay the loan quicker than required so you can save interest, (c) refinance the loan and use the extra cash for other investments.

_____ 7. You are considering changing jobs. Which sounds best? (a) joining a well-established firm and doing similar work, (b) associating with a new company in a newly created position, (c) going into business for yourself.

_____ 8. You have a schedule conflict. The following three events are all scheduled for the same day and time. Which will you choose? (a) attending a seminar, (b) working on a committee, (c) giving a speech to a group of students.

_____ 9. Your dinner is "on the house." Which will you choose? (a) cold turkey sandwich and salad, (b) enchilada with hot peppers, (c) rare sirloin with fries.

_____10. You have a delayed flight and your plane will be four hours late. Will you (a) read a book and wait, (b) take in a short sightseeing trip, (c) book another flight.

Scoring: Give yourself 1 point for each question you marked (a); 3 points for each (b); and 5 points for each (c). Scores 40 and above indicate willingness to take risk (you are a risk taker); scores between 25 and 40 indicate a willingness to take moderate risk; and scores below 25 show high risk aversion. A score of 30 is average.

Analyzing Your Score:

Based on your score, what are some investments that have the amount of risk you are willing to take? (See Chapter 11.)

WORKSHEET 4
Investment Analysis

Directions: Calculate the average gain per year and average rate of return on investments shown, and rank the investments in order of desirability.

Asset Purchased	Original Price	Years Held	Current Value	Dividends or Interest Received	Avg. Gain/ Year	Avg. Rate Return	Rank
H&H Stock 25 shares	$14.00/sh	10	$16.00	$.30/share/ year	_____	_____	_____
Time CD	$5,000	5	$5,000	$1,055	_____	_____	_____
Mutual Funds 33 shares	$18.50/sh	7	$17.50	$.35/share/ year	_____	_____	_____
Gold 50 troy oz.	$325/oz.	3	$262/oz.	0	_____	_____	_____
ATZ Stock 50 shares	$29.50/sh	5	$35.50	$.50/share/ year	_____	_____	_____

WORKSHEET 5
Investment Plan

Directions: Complete the following worksheet by listing your investment and how much you expect to invest, how long you will keep the investment, and your potential return.

Investment Choice	Initial Cost	Time Kept	Expected Profit
Example: Time CD	$1,000	1 year	$80

Beginning Investments

1. _____
2. _____
3. _____

Systematic Investments

1. _____
2. _____
3. _____

Speculative Investments

1. _____
2. _____
3. _____

WORKSHEET 6
Retirement Plan

Directions: Fill in the amounts you project for each category in the spaces provided. In order to obtain realistic amounts, you may need to talk to a retired person or other person about projected benefits and costs.

1. Projected Income (monthly)

a. Anticipated benefits:
Social security $ _____
Pensions   _____
Annuities   _____
Part-time work   _____
Other   _____

b. Assets used for income:
Savings accounts $ _____
IRAs   _____
Investments   _____
Other   _____

Total projected
   monthly income $ _____

Projected   –   Projected   =   Surplus
Income   Costs   (Shortage)

_____ – _____ = $ _____

2. Projected Costs (monthly)

a. Fixed costs:
Property taxes $ _____
Insurance premiums   _____
Other   _____

b. Variable costs:
Food   _____
Utilities
   Gas or oil   _____
   Electricity   _____
   Telephone   _____
Household maintenance   _____
Transportation   _____
Clothing and cleaning   _____
Personal care   _____
Health care and medical   _____
Recreation/entertainment   _____
Miscellaneous   _____
Other   _____

Total projected expenses $ _____

Unit *four*

Credit Management

Chapters

Unit 4 begins with a chapter that serves as a general introduction to what credit is and why it is important to you as a consumer in the American economy.

In Chapter 17, you will learn about credit bureaus, ratings, and reports, and your rights and responsibilities as a credit user. You will also discover many credit laws that have been enacted to protect consumers.

In Chapter 18, you will study the responsibilities of consumer credit and its cost. You will also explore ways to minimize the cost of credit.

Finally, in Chapter 19, you will discover what happens when people become overextended and run into credit problems.

Terms to Know

credit
capital
collateral
finance charge
line of credit
deferred billing
open-ended credit

annual percentage rate (APR)
closed-end credit
service credit
loan sharks
usury laws
pawnbroker

Up Front

It was two days before the spring festival, and Marta still hadn't purchased the supplies she needed to make her costume. She had been saving her money for four months and was still $50 short of her goal.

"I'll just have to borrow the rest," she told her friends. "Otherwise, I won't be able to get the costume completed and that means I'll have let down the team. I really wanted to pay cash and not go into debt, but in this case, it can't be helped. Credit is serious because it's money I'll have to pay back in the future. I probably should have used credit a little sooner. Now I'll have to work all night in order to get this costume completed. I learned an important lesson. There's a time and a place for using credit."

What Is Credit?

Goals

★ Describe the history of credit in America.
★ Define basic credit vocabulary.
★ Discuss the advantages and disadvantages of using credit.

The History of Credit

When you borrow money or use a charge account to pay for purchases, you are taking advantage of the most commonly used method of purchase in the United States: credit. Over 80 percent of all purchases in the U.S. are made with credit rather than cash. **Credit** is money borrowed to buy something now, with the agreement to pay for it later.

The Early Years

The need for credit arose in the United States when the country grew from a bartering and trading society to a currency exchange economy. Most historians place this transition at the time of the Industrial Revolution. During that period, items were first manufactured for sale. People no longer produced everything exclusively for their own use.

Americans began to be dependent on one another. Instead of each family being wholly self-supporting, growing its own food and providing its own clothing and shelter, family members began working for others to earn wages. With their earnings, they bought the things they used to make themselves—beginning with food, clothing, and other essentials. Soon the need developed for sources of credit to help families meet their financial needs. Consumer credit had begun.

One of the earliest forms of credit was the account at the general store. Wage earners or farmers would pick up supplies and put the amount due "on account." Accounts would accumulate for a month, a season, or even a year. When the borrowers received a paycheck or harvested the crop, they would pay their account in full, and the charging process would begin again. The store rarely

How did the general store operate as a source of credit?

charged interest. Credit was a convenience that store owners provided for customers they knew well and trusted. The customers paid off their accounts as soon as they could.

Banks lent farmers lump sums of money as large as $500 to put in crops at the start of the planting season. The farmers repaid the loans after the harvest. This type of credit was very expensive, however. In the 1800s, bank interest rates were 25–50 percent, and loans generally were made only in emergencies. Most people, including bankers, knew very little about how credit worked. Consequently, banks charged high interest rates and were very reluctant to lend large sums of money. Also, most people did not easily accept credit, for it signified debt and dependence on others.

The 1900s

Since 1900, interest rates have dropped. This decrease is attributed to a new understanding of the advantages—especially the financial rewards—of lending money. At the turn of the century, the United States was changing from an agricultural economy, where the main occupation was farming, to an industrial economy of laborers and manufacturing. Lending institutions began to ask for security on loans (the pledging of property and income); consequently, they became more willing to make loans.

As the use of credit expanded, individual purchasing power also increased. Because credit increased people's ability to buy more goods and services, the American economy grew at a healthy pace. People bought luxuries as well as necessities with the help of credit, and the average American's standard of living rose. Businesses and consumers benefited from credit.

Between 1920 and 1990, buying on credit became the American way of life. No longer was credit saved for emergencies. Many different forms of credit developed to meet changing consumer needs and wants.

The 1970s brought the first powerful consumer credit protection legislation. No longer was "buyer beware" the rule in credit transactions. Laws were enacted to protect consumers from deceptive practices. Both government and private agencies were formed to assist consumers with their rights and responsibilities. The 1970s also ushered in a new occupation—credit counseling. People had begun to overuse credit. They needed credit counselors to advise them on how to use credit wisely, pay their bills, and get out of credit trouble.

In the 1990s, record numbers of people declared bankruptcy. They had overextended on credit. Overuse of credit cards was the main reason for this trend. With the economic prosperity of the decade, people were optimistic and willing to spend their income well into the future. But this overspending brought enormous credit debt.

DID YOU KNOW

Every day, companies nationwide appeal to consumers with poor credit histories. They promise, for a fee, to clean up your credit report so you can get a car loan, a home mortgage, insurance, or even a job. The truth is, they can't deliver. After you pay them hundreds or thousands of dollars in up-front fees, these companies do nothing to improve your credit report. Many simply vanish with your money.

The 1990s brought lower interest rates, which stimulated continued growth in the credit industry. Many non-banks began to issue general credit cards (Visa and MasterCard) to American consumers. These non-banks included General Motors, United Airlines, Eddie Bauer, Nordstrom, and even gasoline companies. These companies give credit users special bonuses for charging purchases on their accounts. For example, General Motors started to give points toward the purchase of a new car. Based on purchases, airlines began to give air miles toward free air travel.

Credit Today

Credit in the new millennium is abundant and easy to get. Merchants encourage consumers to use credit to buy all kinds of goods and services. The ease of buying over the Internet has opened new uses of credit cards that will likely increase credit debt into the future. Internet organizations as well as the government are looking for ways to improve the security of online credit purchases.

A smart card has an embedded computer chip that stores financial and other information. For many years, the smart-card industry was most profitable in Europe. But now, experts predict that tremendous growth will be seen in the U.S. market, due to the rise of e-commerce. While credit card numbers can be stolen from computer networks, smart cards can bypass the use of account numbers by using codes that authorize sales. Transactions can be carried out both quickly and securely.

Think Critically: Do you think that by making transactions so easy, smart cards might encourage people to shop excessively or recklessly? Explain your point of view.

The Vocabulary of Credit

Certain terms are commonly used to describe credit, its availability, and its cost. It's important to understand the vocabulary of credit before you sign a credit agreement.

When you borrow money or use credit, you are a *borrower* or *debtor*. The person or company who loans money or extends credit to you is called the *creditor*.

To qualify for credit, you must have the ability to repay the loan. Having a job or other income is important. Creditors may also expect you to have some capital. **Capital** is property you possess that is worth more than your debts. Having capital tells the creditor that you have accumulated assets and are on your way to being a responsible citizen.

You will probably want to pay for large purchases with credit. For large sums, creditors often want more than just your promise to repay. They want collateral. **Collateral** is property pledged to assure repayment of a loan. If you do not make your loan payments, the creditor can seize the pledged property. For example, when you buy a car on credit, the car serves as collateral. If you do not repay the loan, the car can be *repossessed*. Ownership of the car would revert back to the lending institution.

Once you have completed the credit purchase, you owe money to the creditor. The *principal* (amount borrowed) plus interest for the time you have the loan is called the *balance due*. You generally will make monthly payments until you repay the balance due in full. The payments include both principal and interest, and with each payment, the amount you owe is reduced. The interest you pay for the use of credit is called a **finance charge.** Finance charges may also be called *handling charges, service charges,* or *carrying charges.* Whatever term is used, it is the money you pay in order to use someone else's money to buy goods and services now.

Credit card statements usually specify a *minimum payment.* This is the least amount you may pay that month under your credit agreement, though you may pay more to further reduce your debt. All credit payments are due by a specific *due date.* Typically, you will be given 10 to 20 days from the date you receive a bill in which to pay. If you do not pay within the time allowed, you are likely to be charged a *late fee,* which is added to the balance due.

For particularly expensive purchases, you may have to sign an *installment agreement,* wherein you agree to make regular payments for a set period of time. At the end of that time, you will have repaid the entire debt. This is a type of *secured loan,* because the goods you purchased with the loan serve as collateral for the money loaned.

Advantages and Disadvantages of Consumer Credit

Some people use credit extensively while others pay cash for all purchases. Many people get into trouble each year by not using credit carefully. Credit can have several advantages for you, but you also need to be aware of its disadvantages.

Advantages of Credit

Used correctly, credit can greatly expand your purchasing potential and raise your standard of living. For example, credit allows you to purchase expensive items now that you do not currently have enough cash to buy, and then pay for them over time. As a result, you can enjoy items like furniture and a car earlier in your life than you otherwise could. Making your payments on time then helps you establish a good credit record that will help you get loans in the future.

Credit can also provide emergency funds. A sudden need for cash can be solved by a **line of credit,** which is a pre-established amount that can be borrowed on demand with no collateral. To establish a line of credit, you fill out the application at your bank. Bank officials look at your income and financial position and approve an amount that they believe you can repay. With a line of credit, money is always available should you need it.

Credit is convenient. Credit customers often get better service when they make a purchase because they can withhold payment until a problem is resolved. Regular charge customers receive advance notices of sales and special offers not available to the public, such as deferred billing. **Deferred billing** is a service available to charge customers whereby purchases are not billed to the customer until later. For example, merchandise purchased in October might not be billed to the customer until January, with no payment due until February.

The proof of purchase provided by a charge slip is usually more descriptive than a cash register receipt and helps in making adjustments when merchandise is returned. Finally, carrying a credit card is safer than carrying large sums of cash.

Disadvantages of Credit

What are some advantages and disadvantages of consumer credit?

Use of credit also carries some disadvantages. For instance, credit purchases may cost more than cash purchases. Merchants must pay the credit card company for using the card in transactions, and they often pass this fee on to customers in the form of higher prices. In addition, an item purchased on credit and paid for monthly costs more because of finance charges. A finance charge of 18 percent a year is $1\frac{1}{2}$ percent a month. On a $1,000 balance, the finance charge would be $15 a month. The larger your balance and the longer you take to pay it off, the greater the finance charges.

When you use credit, you tie up future income. You have committed to making payments, perhaps for several years. Over that time, those funds are not available to you for buying other products you may need. This situation can put a strain on your budget.

Buying on credit can lead to overspending. You can get into trouble with credit if you buy more than you can pay back comfortably. At the end of the month, when the bills come in, you may be surprised at how much you have really spent.

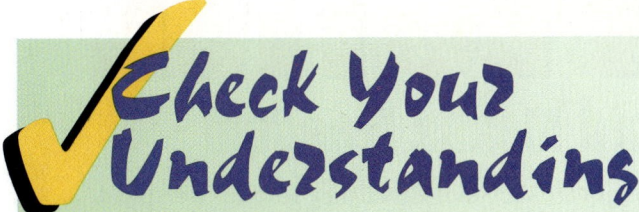

✓Check Your Understanding

Review Terms
1. credit
2. capital
3. collateral
4. finance charge
5. line of credit
6. deferred billing

Review Concepts
1. Compare the use of credit today to its use in this country's early years.
2. Why is it important to make credit payments by the due date?
3. For you, what is the greatest advantage and greatest disadvantage of credit?

Select Payment Method
Credit Card Type
Credit Card Number
Exp. Date
Name

PERSONAL PERSPECTIVE

Your Credit Card Means Freedom

Some people believe that credit cards are evil—that they lead to overspending, to debt problems, and to moral decline. But credit cards can also mean the difference between having a good vacation and staying at home. Consider the following:

1. In order to rent a car, you will need a credit card. The card must have a limit high enough to allow for charges of $150 or greater. Most rental companies will not accept cash or debit cards because they want assurance that there is a source of payment if you incur other charges, such as by keeping the car longer or by damaging it.
2. Motels and hotels usually also require a credit card. Once you have checked out and are ready to leave, they may allow you to use a debit card or cash, but in order to secure a reservation and in order to stay at the facility, you will need a valid credit card with space in your credit limit for charging.
3. While on the road, you may also need that credit card to buy gasoline. Many stations do not accept cash after dark. The only way to obtain self-service gasoline may be to use your credit card at the pump. If you have an emergency, such as needing a tow truck, the credit card provides a way to pay for it on the spot. When you're out of town, most merchants will not accept checks, so the credit card allows you the instant ability to buy necessities.
4. A credit card is a safer way to carry money when you travel. If the card is lost or stolen, you can get it replaced and can get cash advances from the card by calling the card issuer's toll-free number. If your cash is stolen, however, you cannot get it replaced.
5. If you are traveling in a foreign country, using your credit card will enable you to get the up-to-the-minute exchange rate, thus preventing merchants from giving you less than your fair dollar's worth. Both debit and credit cards can be used to get foreign currency from ATM machines abroad as well, also giving you the best exchange rate possible.

Credit cards are not evil. They're tools that can be used wisely to make your travel plans flow much more smoothly.

Think Critically

1. Have you been in a situation where a credit card would have been very useful? Describe what happened.
2. Explain why cash is not always the best thing to have to pay for your vacation expenses.

Goals

★ List and describe the kinds of credit available to the American consumer.
★ Describe and compare sources of credit.

Kinds of Credit

You will likely use several forms of credit throughout your life. Different types of credit are designed to meet different consumer needs.

Open-Ended Credit

Credit card accounts are open-ended forms of credit. **Open-ended credit** is an agreement to lend the borrower an amount up to a stated limit and to allow borrowing up to that limit again, whenever the balance falls below the limit. The borrower usually has a choice of repaying the entire balance within 30 days or repaying it over a number of months or years. Open-ended credit can be used again and again, as long as the balance owed does not exceed the limit.

Open 30-Day Accounts

In an open *30-day credit agreement*, a consumer promises to pay the full balance owed each month. Travel-and-entertainment cards, such as American Express and Diner's Club, are examples of 30-day open-ended credit agreements. On all charges, the balance must be paid in full when the bill is received. There is no credit extended beyond the 30-day billing cycle. In some cases, the billing cycle may be less than 30 days. A 25-day billing period is common. These cards are widely accepted nationwide and overseas, usually have high or no credit limits, and provide instant purchasing power.

Revolving Credit Accounts

In a *revolving credit agreement*, a consumer has the option each month of paying in full or making payments at least as high as the stated minimum. The minimum payment is based on the amount of the balance due. Department stores, gasoline companies, and banks typically issue credit cards based on revolving credit. Most merchants accept credit cards such as VISA, MasterCard, or Discover in order to increase their business by attracting customers who do not have accounts with their stores. Figure 16-1 shows a credit card statement for a revolving credit account.

Credit Card Terms

Credit card companies keep a record of transactions made on your account and bill you at the end of each month for all purchases. If you pay off the total each month, you probably can avoid a finance charge. But remember—a credit card is a form of borrowing. It usually involves a finance charge and sometimes other charges as well. Before selecting a credit card, learn which credit terms and conditions apply. Each affects the overall cost of the credit you will be using. Be sure to consider and compare the following terms.

1. *Annual Percentage Rate.* The **annual percentage rate (APR)** is the cost of credit, expressed as a yearly percentage. The Truth-in-Lending law requires all lenders to calculate APR the same way. As a result, you can compare the APR of different lenders to find the best deal. The APR must be disclosed to you when you open the account and must be noted on each monthly bill you receive. Usually the APR is a variable rate, and it is very high on credit cards.

2. *Free Period.* A free period—also called a *grace period*—allows you to avoid the finance charge by paying your current balance in full before the due date shown on your billing statement. Knowing whether a credit card plan gives you a free period is especially important if you plan to pay your account in full each month. If there is no free period of 10 to 25 days, the card issuer will impose a finance charge from the date you use your credit card or from the date each credit card transaction is posted to your account.

3. *Annual Fees.* Many credit card issuers charge an annual fee. The fee can range from $15 to $35 or more, and you must pay it whether or not you use the card.

4. *Transaction Fees and Late Fees.* A credit card also may involve other types of costs. For example, some card issuers charge a fee when you fail to make a payment on time or when you go over your credit limit.

5. *Method of Calculating the Finance Charge.* If your plan has no free period, or if you expect to pay for purchases over time,

McAdams

Account Number	Payment Due Date	New Balance	Minimum Payment Due	Indicate Amount Paid
779 19 9171	05/24/--	$244.61	$20.00	_____

0 7734 2704 20000 2446 10000 20004   70

ADDRESS CHANGE

ululululullululululullullulllululululululluullull

ELIZABETH SANCHEZ
3410 MAIN STREET
VANCOUVER WA 98684-0129

ADDRESS _____

CITY/STATE/ZIP _____

(AREA CODE) PHONE   5008440

Please return this portion
with your payment. Detach here ▼

- -

Account Number	779 19 9171	To avoid additional **FINANCE CHARGES** being applied to your current purchases on next month's statement, pay the new balance on this statement in full by the due date.	Page 1 of 1

Date	Store	Reference	Description	Charges	Payments Or Credits
3/28	021	108475936	SPECIAL CARE TREATMENT COSMETICS	60.00	
4/07	021	108476335	COSMETICS CLEANSERS, TONERS, MOISTURIZERS	80.00	
4/12	311	071070078	PAYMENT-THANK YOU		189.16
4/24	097		FINANCE CHARGE	4.61	

ANNIVERSARY TO DATE PURCHASES $1,853.39
ANNIVERSARY TO DATE DIVIDEND $5.96
YOU WILL EARN A 1% DIVIDEND ON MCADAMS PURCHASES
MADE PRIOR TO YOUR NEXT BILLING.
DIVIDEND WILL BE CREDITED ON YOUR JUNE 19-- STATEMENT.

Previous Balance	+ New Charges	– Payments Or Credits	Average Daily Balance (For Finance Charge Only)	+ FINANCE CHARGE (50¢ Minimum)	+ Late Payment Fee	= New Balance
289.16	140.00	189.16	307.19	4.61		244.61

Billing Date This Month	Payment Due Date	PERIODIC RATE	ANNUAL PERCENTAGE RATE	Credit Line	Amount Past Due	Minimum Payment Due
04/24/--	05/24/--	1.50	18.00	2,000		20.00

Payments or credits received after payment due date will appear on next month's statement. For customer service inquiries, please call 1-800-555-6200. **AMOUNTS DUE HEREUNDER MAY BE ASSIGNED. NOTICE: SEE REVERSE SIDE FOR IMPORTANT INFORMATION.**

McAdams

it is important to know how the card issuer will calculate your finance charge. This charge will vary, depending upon the method the card issuer used to figure your balance. The method used can make a difference, sometimes a big difference, in how much finance charge you will pay. Examples of how finance charges based on identical APRs can differ are explained in Chapter 18.

Closed-End Credit

To pay for very expensive items, such as cars, furniture, or major appliances, consumers often use closed-end credit. **Closed-end credit** is a loan for a specific amount that must be repaid, in full, including all finance charges, by a stated due date. Unlike open-end credit, closed-end agreements do not allow continuous borrowing or varying payment amounts. The borrower takes out a closed-end loan for a particular amount and then repays it with fixed payments, or *installments,* that include principal and interest. As a result, closed-end credit is sometimes called an *installment loan.*

The contract for closed-end credit tells, among other things, the amount loaned, the total finance charge, and the amount of each payment. Usually a down payment is required, and the product purchased with the loan becomes collateral to assure repayment.

Service Credit

Do telephone companies always expect payment in full by a certain time limit?

Almost everyone uses some type of **service credit,** which is an agreement to have a service performed now and pay for it later. Your telephone and utility services are provided for a month in advance; then you are billed. Many businesses—including doctors, lawyers, dentists, hospitals, dry cleaners, and repair shops—extend service credit. Terms are set by individual businesses. Some of these creditors do not impose finance charges on unpaid account balances, but they do expect regular payments to be made until the bill is paid in full. Others, such as utility and telephone companies, expect payment in full within a time limit. However, they usually offer a budget plan as well, which allows you to average bills to get lower monthly payments.

Sources of Credit

Credit is a service consumers buy. As with other things you buy, it pays to shop around to get the best deal.

Retail Stores

Retail stores are stores that sell directly to consumers, such as department stores, drugstores, clothing stores, hardware stores, restaurants, and most types of service businesses. Retailers purchase from wholesalers, who purchase from manufacturers and producers.

Retail stores take advantage of credit because customers like to shop where they can buy on credit. Many retail stores offer their own accounts and also accept bank credit cards and other well-known charge cards. Credit customers receive discounts, advance notice of sales, and other privileges not offered to cash customers.

+PROS and CONS

Where you purchase an item is not dependent only upon the credit extended by the retailer. For example, some consumers have loyalty to particular stores and may shop there even if credit or prices are higher than elsewhere. Other consumers shop around and may switch if they find better deals.

Think Critically: What advantages do you see to establishing a good relationship with a merchant? Are there disadvantages? What advantages are there to always shopping around? Are there disadvantages?

Banks and Credit Unions

Commercial banks and credit unions make loans to individuals and companies based on collateral, capital, income or ability to repay the loan, and credit records. Interest rates vary with location or financial institution and according to what the borrower is buying with the loan. Good reasons for a loan, such as the need to purchase a car or a home or the desire to take a vacation, are required. Regular bank customers who have established credit can get loans more easily than non-customers can.

Banks and credit unions also extend credit through credit cards available to account holders. In many cases, the rate of interest charged on these cards will be considerably higher than on closed-end loans for specific purchases. Credit card interest rates tend to fluctuate with national interest rates and therefore are often as high as the law will allow.

When you have a bank (or non-bank) credit card, you have an automatic line of credit up to the credit limit of the card. A *cash advance* is money borrowed against the credit card limit. In other words, you are taking out a cash loan from your line of credit rather than making a purchase with it. You can access this money at a teller machine, at a customer service desk in the bank, or by writing an *access check* against the credit card account. Access checks look just like regular checks. They are supplied by the credit card company and when written, are treated like a purchase. You must then pay back the cash advance in the same way that you pay for credit card purchases.

Credit unions make loans available to their members only. Interest rates are generally lower than those charged by banks because credit unions are nonprofit and are organized for the benefit of members. Credit unions are more willing to make loans because the members who are borrowing also have a stake in the success of the credit union.

Finance Companies

Often called small loan companies, *finance companies* usually charge high interest rates for the use of their money. The reason for the high rates is that finance companies are willing to take risks that banks and credit unions will not take. In many cases, people who are turned down by banks and credit unions can get loans at finance companies. Finance companies are second only to banks in the volume of credit extended.

There are two types of finance companies. A *consumer finance company* makes mostly consumer loans to customers buying consumer durables. Consumer durables are items expected to last several years, such as an automobile, refrigerator, or stereo. (Nondurable goods, such as food products, are consumed in a few days or months.) Durable goods can be financed because the purchase price is several hundred to several thousand dollars. Well-known consumer finance companies include Household Finance, AVCO, and Beneficial Finance.

The second type of company is the manufacturer-related *sales finance company* that makes loans through authorized representatives. For example, General Motors Acceptance Corporation (GMAC) finances General Motors automobile dealers and their customers. Both types of finance companies borrow money from banks and lend it to consumers at higher rates.

Finance companies take more risks than banks. Therefore, they must be more careful to protect their loans. If you do not make your payments when due, you can expect a call from someone at the finance company, who will ask for an explanation. The company will stay in constant contact with you until you make your payments as agreed. You can expect phone calls, letters, and even personal visits if you deviate even slightly from the agreed-upon payment schedule. High interest rates are another form of protection for the finance company.

Finance companies lend relatively small amounts of money repayable in monthly installments. These companies are regulated by states under the Uniform Small-Loan Law, which permits fairly high interest rates to cover the costs of making many small loans. Typically, the law permits loans of up to $5,000 and allows interest rates of up to 42 percent a year. The growth of finance companies is the result of efforts to eliminate **loan sharks**—unlicensed lenders who charge illegally high interest rates. Nevertheless, it is difficult to eliminate such practices, which take advantage of the poorest members of society who can least afford to pay.

Usury laws set maximum interest rates that may be charged for loans. In states where usury laws exist, finance companies charge the maximum. Where no usury laws exist, finance companies charge as much as the customer is willing to pay. When an emergency or other extreme need arises, consumers often feel forced to pay these higher rates to get the money they need.

Pawnbrokers

A **pawnbroker** is a legal business that makes high-interest loans based on the value of personal possessions pledged as collateral. Possessions that are readily salable (such as guns, cameras, jewelry, radios, TVs, and coins) are usually acceptable collateral. The customer brings in an item of value to be appraised. The pawnbroker then makes a loan for considerably less than the appraised value of the item. Some pawnshops give only 10 to 25 percent of

What do pawnbrokers usually accept as collateral? Why?

the value of the article. Most give no more than 50 or 60 percent.

For example, if you have a ring appraised at $500, you could probably borrow between $50 and $250 with the ring as collateral. You would turn the ring over to the pawnbroker and receive a receipt and a certain length of time—from two weeks to six months—to redeem the ring by paying back the loan plus interest. If you do not pay back the loan and claim the ring, the pawnbroker will sell it in the pawnshop and keep the proceeds. Property taken in by a pawnbroker is considered collateral for the loan because it is something of value that may be sold if you fail to pay off the loan.

Private Lenders

The most common source of cash loans is the private lender. Private lenders include your parents, other relatives, friends, and so on. Private lenders may or may not charge interest.

Other Sources of Consumer Credit

Life insurance policies can be used as an alternate source of consumer credit. As some life insurance policies build cash value, policyholders can borrow at low interest rates against the value of their policy. The loan does not have to be repaid, but interest will be charged; and the amount of the loan will reduce the value of the life insurance policy. (See the section on life insurance in Chapter 27.)

If you have a certificate of deposit with a financial institution, you can borrow money against the certificate. The certificate is used as collateral, and the interest rate charged is usually only 2 to 5 percent above the interest rate you are receiving on the certificate. If you cash in the certificate before maturity, you incur a penalty. If you borrow money using the certificate as collateral, you get a moderate rate of interest on the loan, and the certificate retains its full value.

"Affinity cards" are all-purpose credit cards sponsored by professional organizations, college alumni associations, and some members of the travel industry. An affinity card issuer often donates a portion of the annual fees or charges to the sponsoring organization, or qualifies you for free travel or other bonuses.

Check Your Understanding

Review Terms
1. open-ended credit
2. annual percentage rate (APR)
3. closed-end credit
4. service credit
5. loan sharks
6. usury laws
7. pawnbroker

Review Concepts
1. What is a revolving credit agreement?
2. Why should you get a bank loan rather than a loan from a finance company?

16.1 What Is Credit?

- Credit—money borrowed to buy now and pay later—began here when the U.S. grew from a bartering society to a currency exchange economy and manufactured products became available.
- Early forms of credit were accounts at the general store, offered by store owners to customers they knew and trusted. In the 1800s, bank loans were expensive and hard to get, and people viewed loans as unwanted dependence on others.
- In the 1900s, lenders began to ask for collateral, which made them more willing to make loans. Credit expanded people's purchasing power, and their purchases increased their standard of living and helped the economy grow.
- In the 1970s, the government passed laws to protect consumers from credit fraud. During this period, general overuse of credit got many people into debt trouble.
- Today, merchants encourage consumers to use credit, and Internet buying has opened new uses of credit as well as new avenues for fraud.
- To borrow, you must have sufficient capital to suggest that you will be able to repay. For large purchases, you will need collateral, or property to pledge as security for the loan. For the privilege of using credit, you will pay a finance charge.
- Advantages of credit are the ability to enjoy products now that you do not have the cash to buy, access to a source of emergency funds, the convenience of deferred billing, credit receipts as proof of purchase, and the safety of not having to carry large sums of cash.

- Disadvantages of credit are higher product prices, finance charges, decreased ability to spend in the future because of credit payments, and the tendency to overspend.

16.2 Types and Sources of Credit

- Open-ended credit allows you to borrow again and again, up to your established limit. Thirty-day agreements require you to pay the balance in full each month. Revolving agreements allow you to pay any amount between a stated minimum and payment in full each month.
- The annual percentage rate is the cost of credit, expressed as a percentage. A free period is the amount of time you have to make your payment before a finance charge will be assessed. Credit cards may also charge annual fees, transaction fees, and late fees.
- Closed-end credit is a loan for a specific amount that must be repaid, including finance charges, by a due date. It is most often used for expensive purchases, and the borrower repays in fixed monthly installments.
- Sources of credit include retail stores, banks, credit unions, finance companies, pawnbrokers, private lenders, and life insurance policies. Finance companies and pawnbrokers charge higher interest rates than do other financial institutions.
- Usury laws protect consumers from unfairly high interest rates. Loan sharks are unlicensed lenders who charge illegally high rates and prey on people who can least afford to pay.

Review Terms

Directions: Can you find the definition for each of the following terms used in Chapter 16?

annual percentage rate (APR)
capital
closed-end credit
collateral
credit
deferred billing
finance charge
line of credit
loan sharks
open-ended credit
pawnbroker
service credit
usury laws

1. Money borrowed to buy something now, with the agreement to pay for it later.
2. An agreement to have a service performed now and pay for it later.
3. Laws setting maximum interest rates that may be charged for loans.
4. A legal business that makes high-interest loans based on the value of personal possessions pledged as collateral.
5. A pre-established amount that can be borrowed on demand with no collateral.
6. A service to credit customers whereby purchases are not billed for several months.
7. Unlicensed lenders who charge illegally high interest rates.
8. An agreement to lend the borrower an amount up to a stated limit and to allow borrowing up to that limit again, whenever the balance falls below the limit.
9. A loan for a specific amount that must be repaid, in full, including all finance charges, by a stated due date.
10. Property owned that is worth more than the owner's debt.
11. Property pledged to assure repayment of a loan.
12. Interest paid for the use of credit.
13. The cost of credit, expressed as a yearly percentage.

1. When credit first began in this country, did loans have high interest rates?
2. When credit began, why were bankers and merchants reluctant to lend money and give credit?
3. How has credit affected the American economy?
4. How does collateral help assure repayment of a loan?
5. List several advantages of using credit.
6. List several disadvantages of using credit.
7. Why does the law require all lenders to calculate APR the same way?
8. What are two kinds of open-ended credit?
9. How is open-ended credit different from installment (closed-end) credit?
10. Give three examples of service credit.
11. How are consumer finance companies different from sales finance companies?
12. List the five major sources of credit for consumers.
13. Why do retail stores accept VISA, MasterCard, or Discover Card in addition to their own credit cards?
14. Why do credit unions offer lower interest rates on loans than do commercial banks?
15. Why do finance companies charge high interest rates on their loans?
16. Explain how pawnbrokers work.

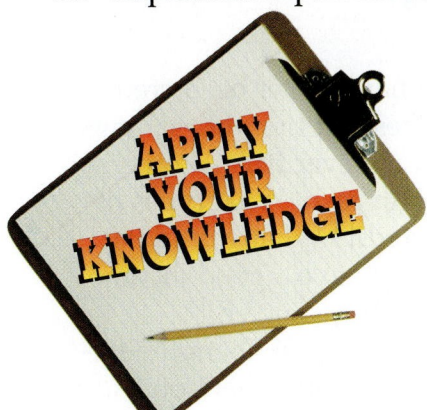

APPLY YOUR KNOWLEDGE

1. Give an example of a situation in which you would use collateral when making a purchase on credit.
2. How does your family make use of credit? Do you see credit

use in your family as a good or bad thing? Explain your answer.

3. Do you think consumers are being unfair when they accept a "free ride" based on a "grace period" for credit cards? Give reasons for your answer.

4. Banks compete for your credit card business by offering "low introductory rates." Search the Internet for any bank offering a special deal to new credit card customers. What is the "low introductory rate"? Now read the fine print. What would your rate be later, after the introductory period? At this regular rate, how much finance charge would you have to pay on a $1,000 balance each month? How much would the finance charge be if you maintained a $1,000 balance all year?

5. One major advantage of credit is that it helps consumers deal with emergencies. How does this advantage have special meaning where service credit is concerned?

6. If you were going into business for yourself, you would have to decide whether or not to accept credit cards from customers. Explain the points in favor of both positions.

7. Would it be possible to live without ever using coins, paper money, or checks? Explain how you might live on credit alone.

8. Does your state have usury laws? You can find out by consulting a current almanac or other references at your library or on the Internet. Identify some of the finance rates that states allow, including your state and neighboring states.

Solve Problems

1. Suppose that your elderly neighbors have never used credit. When they were children, their families lost their life savings in the Great Depression, and they have never trusted others enough to pay for anything except with cash. What types of problems can result from not using credit? What would be your advice to them, knowing that they have a good income from investments and have no need to buy on credit?

2. Interview three or four adults about credit. Ask them the following questions. Prepare a short report from what you learn.
   a. How do you feel about the use of credit?
   b. Do you use credit cards, such as store credit cards or bank credit cards?

c. Do you think the interest rates charged by stores and banks on unpaid balances are reasonable?

d. What are some typical interest rates that you have experienced?

e. How would you advise a young person just starting out about credit?

3. Do you feel that the advantages of using credit outweigh the disadvantages? Write a paper of no more than one page, either defending the use of credit or explaining why it should be avoided.

4. A friend of yours wishes to buy a new car. She has picked one out at a local dealer but has only enough money to make a down payment. She asks your advice about where she can finance the balance of her loan for $10,000. What will you tell her? Explain.

5. Your cousin Jason needs $100 immediately. He has a portable stereo worth at least $800 and wants to take it to a pawnbroker. Explain to him how much he can borrow against the stereo, and what will happen with pawnbroker credit.

For related activities and links, point your browser to
www.mypf.swep.com

Chapter 17

Credit Records and Laws

Terms to Know

credit history
credit bureau
credit report
subscribers
character

capacity
credit rating
discrimination
debt collector

Up Front

Janice is a full-time student and works part-time on weekends and during the summer. She has been able to save a little money, and now, at age 16, she is learning to drive.

"I'd like to buy my own car," she told her friend Chantel. "That way I can drive myself to work. If I had my own car, I could work after school too, and I'd have a way to get to more school activities. As it is, I depend on my mom to get me everywhere. She also works, so the car isn't always available to take me places. To get a car, I'll have to get a loan. My mom says I'll be establishing credit, but because I don't have any credit already, she'll probably have to co-sign for me to get my first car loan."

Goals

★ Discuss the importance of credit records and summarize how and why records are compiled.
★ Describe the five Cs of credit.
★ Explain how to get started using credit.

Credit Records

Before granting you credit, a *creditor* (a person or company that gives you credit) will ask about your past credit performance: Did you pay your bills on time? Did you pay your debts according to the loan agreement? How much total credit did you receive? How much do you owe now and how large are your payments? Your **credit history** is the complete record of your borrowing and repayment performance. This record will provide answers to these questions and thus help the creditor determine your ability to pay new debts.

Your Credit File

Every person who uses credit has a credit history on file at a credit bureau. A **credit bureau** is a company that gathers, stores, and sells credit information to business subscribers. Maintaining credit files is big business. Credit bureaus, numbering about 1,200 across the nation, assemble and distribute detailed credit information concerning an estimated 150 million consumers. When you open a new credit account with a business, a credit clerk at the business keys into a computer the relevant information from your application, along with details about the initial credit transaction. Then each time you use credit or make a payment, the business records the transaction. Once a month, the business electronically transmits the accumulated data about your borrowing and repayments to one or more of the three big national credit bureaus listed in Figure 17-1 on page 480. The credit bureau enters the information into your file and stores it under your social security number for identification. Local and regional credit bureaus hook into the Big Three's computer networks, making everybody's files widely accessible.

Figure 17-1   *Major U.S. Credit Bureaus*

Experian(TRW)
P.O. Box 2104
Allen, TX 75013-2104
(800) 682-7654
www.experian.com/
experian_us.html

Equifax
P.O. Box 105873
Atlanta, GA 30348
(800) 685-1111
www.equifax.com

Trans Union
P.O. Box 390
Springfield, PA 19064
(800) 916-8800
www.transunion.com

Career Links

Credit authorizers, checkers, and clerks review credit history and obtain the information needed to determine if a credit card applicant is worthy of credit. They also process and authorize applications for credit, including credit cards. A high school education is the minimum requirement for these entry-level positions. Good phone and organizational skills as well as the ability to pay close attention to details and meet deadlines are important. Computer skills are required so that the creditors can enter and retrieve data quickly.

For more information, refer to the *Occupational Outlook Handbook* at www.bls.gov or search the Internet using such key words as "careers," "jobs," and "creditors."

Credit bureaus issue credit reports about consumers. A **credit report** is a written statement of a consumer's credit history, issued by a credit bureau to its business subscribers. You can order a copy of your credit report online at the credit bureau's Web site or by writing to the bureau. You should check your local telephone book for the names and addresses of credit bureaus in your area that also can provide a credit report about you. Ordinarily, a credit bureau will charge $5 to $15 to give you your credit file information. If you are denied credit, you

Why might you want to order a copy of your credit report?

can get a free credit report if you ask within 30 days of being denied.

How Information Is Gathered and Used

Credit bureaus gather information from businesses, called **subscribers,** who pay a monthly fee to the credit bureau. Each subscriber supplies information about its accounts with customers—names, addresses, credit balances, on-time payment record, and so forth. Credit bureaus also gather information from many other sources. Articles about consumers found in local newspapers are clipped and added to files. Public records are searched for information to add to a file. When someone applies to a business for credit, the business asks the credit bureau for the applicant's credit report. Information in the credit report is then used as the basis for granting or denying credit. Usually credit grantors (banks and retail businesses) and employers, landlords, and insurance companies have an interest in credit reports. Before entering into a financial agreement with someone, they want evidence that the person is financially responsible.

Privacy is an important matter in credit issues. Your credit record may not be given to anyone who does not have a legitimate business need for it. Stores to which you are applying for credit may examine your record; curious neighbors may not.

Types of Information Stored

Any public information becomes part of your credit record. For example, if you fail to pay your property taxes, file for bankruptcy, file for a divorce, or apply for a marriage license, this information will appear in your credit record. Birth announcements published in newspapers, job promotions, lawsuits, and other visible activities are recorded. When you fill out a credit application, information requested such as occupation, length of employment, spouse's name and occupation, residence, length of occupancy, number of children and other dependents, and other related data is sent to the credit bureau by the subscriber.

Creditworthiness

Before potential creditors will grant credit to you, they must determine whether you are a good risk—that you are *creditworthy*. If you meet certain standards that creditors believe are important, you usually will qualify for the credit you desire.

A person who is considered a good credit risk usually meets five basic qualifications, called the five Cs of credit: character, capacity, capital, conditions, and collateral.

1. *Character: Will you repay the debt?* **Character** is a responsible attitude toward living up to agreements, often judged on evidence in the person's credit history. If you have character, you pay your bills on time, and your credit history will show it. Creditors often use *stability* as a measure of character as well. For example, a person who has moved six times during the past year might not be considered a good credit risk.

2. *Capacity: Can you repay the debt?* The financial ability to repay a loan with present income is known as **capacity.** Before lending you money, creditors want to make certain that your income is sufficient to cover your current expenses each month plus the payments on the new loan.

3. *Capital: Is the creditor fully protected if you fail to repay?* As you learned in Chapter 16, *capital* is property you possess that is worth more than your debts. In other words, when you add up all that you own (assets) and subtract all that you owe (liabilities), the difference (net worth or capital) should be sufficient to ensure payment of your debt.

4. *Conditions: What general economic conditions can affect your repayment of debt?* The state of the economy can affect your ability to repay. For example, if the economy is slowing and many people in your geographic area are losing their jobs, creditors may be less willing to loan to you. If you lose your job, you may not be able to meet your payments. Therefore, creditors want to know the following: How secure is your job? How secure is the firm you work for? How is the employment situation in your geographic location and in your occupation?

5. *Collateral: What assets back up your promise to pay?* You learned in Chapter 16 that *collateral* is property pledged to assure repayment of a loan. Collateral protects creditors, making them more willing to lend to you. If you do not repay your debt as agreed, they can sell the collateral to collect on the debt.

It is lawful and proper for creditors, in determining your credit-worthiness, to ask you for the following personal information:

- name
- age (provided it is not used as the basis for denying credit)
- source and amount of income
- number of dependents, their ages, and other obligations to them
- obligations to pay alimony, child support, or other such payments
- permanent residence and immigration status
- a list of assets
- place and length of employment
- history of employment
- outstanding debts and accounts
- telephone number (or whether you have a telephone)
- whether you rent or own your home
- length of residence at present address
- residence history
- savings and checking accounts in your name

A creditor may ask you about marital status only if you are making a joint application or if property that you legally share with your spouse will be used as collateral. In either case, a creditor may ask only whether you are married, unmarried, or separated.

Getting Started with Credit

Establishing a good credit record is a slow process. It can take several years of responsible money management to prove your credit-worthiness.

Begin with a Savings Account

Open a savings account with a financial institution, such as a bank or credit union. Try to start at a financial institution that will not charge you a monthly fee when your savings account balance is small. Many banks allow minors to establish accounts with small balances and waive normal fees charged to other depositors. Also, choose a financial institution that has full services available as you prove yourself: checking accounts, loans, and credit cards. Each month or pay period, make a deposit to your savings account. Keep your account growing through regular saving.

Open a Checking Account

What kind of savings account should you open if you want to establish a good credit record?

As soon as you have enough money in your savings account to allow you a little "cushion," open a checking account. This will provide a convenient method of paying your bills when you have credit accounts and will serve as a record-keeping system for your budget. Choose a checking plan that is the least expensive and most convenient for you. Then carefully manage your checking account. Do not write checks when your account contains insufficient funds to cover them. Bouncing checks will tarnish your credit-worthiness. Record all your transactions immediately in your check register and balance your checkbook as soon as you receive your statement. In this way, you will always know how much is in your account, so that you won't bounce a check accidentally.

Open a Store Credit Account

You may need your parents' assistance in opening your first credit account. They may need to act as co-signers. As you learned in Chapter 8, a *co-signer* is someone who promises to pay if the borrower fails to pay. Many department stores and other creditors will allow you to open a small account ($100 minimum, for example) with a parent's signature as co-signer. Make small purchases on your new account and pay the bills promptly, using your checking account. Be sure to make your monthly payments on or before the due date. Never pay late!

Get a Small Loan

Take out a small loan from the financial institution where you have your savings and checking accounts. Use the money to buy something you really need. Then pay back the loan as agreed. Make early payments if possible. A six-month loan is sufficient. Again, you may need to rely on your parents or another adult with a good credit record to co-sign your first loan.

Apply for a Credit Card

With credit established for a couple of years, a part-time job, and a few credit references, you might now be eligible for a credit card, such as a VISA or MasterCard account. Check the application carefully and ask about the income limit. If you do not make enough money to qualify for the card, do not apply until you do. In some cases you will have to be working full time and for the same employer for three years. Once you have a credit card and you make the payments without fail, you will find it easy to obtain additional credit for which you qualify.

Check Your Understanding

Review Terms
1. credit history
2. credit bureau
3. credit report
4. subscribers
5. character
6. capacity

Review Concepts
1. How do credit bureaus gather information for your credit file?
2. What does "creditworthiness" mean?
3. Why is it important to make payments on time?

PERSONAL PERSPECTIVE

Teenage Credit

Some businesses are finding it very financially rewarding to offer credit to teenagers. The logic is simple! Teenagers have a lot of money to spend, whether it is earned or supplied by parents. Because teenagers make many buying decisions, from clothing to automobiles, they are a market worth targeting.

Retail businesses that sell merchandise to teenagers are the first to admit that their teenage customers are important to them. By extending credit to teens, they are winning loyalty and at the same time helping teens get established with credit.

A typical teenage credit account might begin at age 16. The applicant (teenager) should have some steady source of income, whether it is from part-time, full-time, or summer jobs, or from parents. In most cases, the teenager needs permission from her or his parents. Permission is expressed in the form of a parent's signature as *co-signer* on the account. What this means to the parent is this: If the teenager fails to make the payments, the parent is responsible not only for the payments, but also for the entire balance owed.

Why would parents consider such a deal? Teenagers would be turned down if they asked for credit in their own name. A parent's signature on the credit application allows the credit grantor to rely on the parent's credit rating at first.

Typically, teen credit accounts also have a low credit limit, or maximum amount that they can spend on credit. However, even a $300 credit limit would allow a teenager to charge purchases, pay them off responsibly, and build a good credit record. By keeping the credit limit low, merchants and parents are assured that young people just beginning to use credit won't get carried away and get into debt trouble.

Think Critically

1. Do stores in your area extend credit to teenagers? If so, under what conditions?
2. Would you like to get established in credit early? How would you pay for purchases you make?
3. Pick several stores where you would like to have a credit account. Why did you choose these stores?

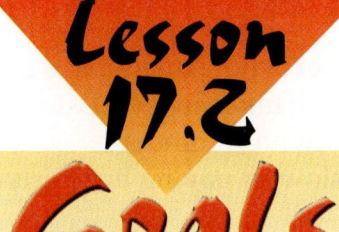

Lesson 17.2 — Credit Ratings and Legal Protection

Goals

★ Describe credit ratings and a point system for determining creditworthiness.
★ Outline the contents of a credit report.
★ Discuss the protections provided by the major credit laws.

Credit Ratings

Credit bureaus give each consumer a **credit rating,** which is a measure of creditworthiness based on an analysis of the consumer's financial history. Different bureaus use different rating systems, but a point system is common. In a *point system*, the bureau assigns points based on factors such as amount of current debt, number of late payments, number and types of open accounts, current employment, amount of income, and so on. Business subscribers then use these scores as part of their decision to grant or not grant credit. Your score is based on data provided to credit bureaus. If the data is wrong, so is your score.

Another rating system, which is accepted by many creditors, rates consumers according to how reliably they pay back money borrowed or charged. Credit bureaus merely supply credit files (names of customers, account balances, and payment records) to their subscribers, and the subscribers make their own rating decisions. Consumers may earn ratings such as excellent, good, fair, or poor.

To earn an *excellent credit rating*, sometimes called an *A Rating*, a customer must pay bills before the due date. If a payment is due on the fifth of the month, it must be received *before* the fifth. An excellent rating also means that the customer is well established (has used credit successfully for many years), has not missed any payments, and has made larger payments than the minimum amount required (paying off debts early).

To earn a *good credit rating*, which is designated a *B Rating*, a customer must pay bills on the due date or within a ten-day grace period. That is, if the payment is due on the first of the month, it must be received no later than the tenth of the month. (When a bill is paid within ten days of its due date, this is considered an automatic grace period.) A good customer pays around the due date, but never outside the grace period, and does not miss any payments.

A *fair credit rating* is earned by a customer who usually pays all bills within the grace period, but occasionally takes longer. Late charges are sometimes applied, but normally no reminder is needed. This person is often described as slow in paying but fairly dependable.

People with a *poor credit rating* are usually denied credit because their payments are not regular. They miss some monthly payments, and they must be reminded frequently. In many cases, they have failed entirely to pay back a debt, have filed for bankruptcy, or have otherwise shown that they are not a good credit risk.

Credit Reports

Credit files are updated continuously, and information stays in the file for seven years. In bankruptcy cases, information stays in the file for 10 years. Credit reports legally may be requested for investigations of credit applications, employment applications, and insurance matters. Reports from different credit bureaus may be arranged differently, but they will contain sections similar to those shown in Figure 17-2. These sections are described below.

Summary of Information

This first section is a summary of negative and positive items. It tells the subscribers what to look for as they go through the information that follows. Negative items are those that could harm your ability to get credit. Accounts in good standing are those that are favorable to your credit.

Public Record Information

This section lists information found in public records. You would expect to find any lawsuits, judgments, bankruptcy, marriage, divorce, adoption, and other public information available to anyone who searches public records.

Credit Information

This section lists the credit accounts, including department stores, credit cards, and other loans, that have been reported to credit bureaus. It reports details such as each account's high and payment status.

PERSONAL CREDIT REPORT

Prepared for	*Report Date*	*Report Number*
Jane Smith	June 1, 20--	108881

Summary of Information:
Potentially negative items:

Public records	2
Accounts with creditors	2

Accounts in good standing: 3

Public Record Information:

Source	Date Filed	Responsibility	Liability Amount	Comments
1. Jess County Courthouse	3/2000	Joint	$5,000	District Court complaint (defendant)
2. U.S. District Court	6/1997	Joint	$85,000	Bankruptcy discharged 11.97

Credit Information:

Source	Date Opened Last Report	Responsibility	Type/ Payment	High Amount	Status
3. Fidelity Bank (VISA)	6/1996	Individual	Revolv. $100 min.	$5,000	Late 2 pmts
4. CC & C Credit	10/2000	Individual	Install. $200/mo.	$8,500	Late charges-3
5. U.S. Finance Co.	3/2001	Joint	Install. $350/mo.	$18,000	Current

Account Detail:

Source	Date/Balance
6. U.S. Finance Co.	3/2001 $0 4/2001 $17,850 5/2001 $17,700 6/2001 $17,500 7/2001 $17,250 8/2001 $17,000
7. Merlo's Dept. Store	5/2000 $0 6/2000 $500 6/2000 $850 7/2000 $700 8/2000 $900 9/2000 $1,000 10/2000 $800 11/2000 $900 12/2000 $1,000 1/2001 $900 2/2001 $700 3/2001 $500 4/2001 $300 5/2001 $100 6/2001 $0

Between 5/2000 and 6/2001 your credit limit was $2,500.

Others Who Have Requested Your Credit History:
11/2000 Bill's Frame Shop (employment check)
2/2001   ABCD Mortgage Co. (related to real estate offer)
8/2001   Art's Motors (car loan application)

Requests Initiated by You:
5/2001   Credit report for denial of credit

Personal Information:

Names:	Jane L. Smith		*Social Security Number*: 541-00-9999
	Jane Louise Smith		
	J. L. Smith		

Residences:	123 Main Street Single-family house (owned)	4488 West Melody Lane Condominium (rental)
	Clio, CA 90001	Brighton, NJ 02411

Date of Birth: 9.23.1958
Telephone Numbers: 503.444.3331
                           253.622.4441

Driver's License Number: CA0948X23

Spouse's Name: John B. Smith
Employers: Cranston Bakery (Partner) $48,000 salary, reported 3/2/2001
               4480 West Palm Beach
               Clio, CA 90022

               McGraw School District $37,000 salary, reported 2/1/1996
               42 Maple Wood
               Clinton, NY 00442

What kind of credit information can be found in a credit report?

Account Detail

This section shows the monthly balances of accounts. It also lists the credit limits that have been reported.

Requests for Credit History

This section lists every business that has sought information from your credit file—requests by potential employers, creditors, insurance companies, and others, along with requests that you may have made to inspect your credit records.

Personal Information

This section lists the personal information that you have given when applying for credit or that is available through public records. It includes your name and previous names, your contact information, whether you own or rent, your date of birth and driver's license number, your spouse's name, your employers and salaries with each one, and your social security number.

AROUND THE GLOBE

Visa International, the payment-card company, sees Malaysia as a key market in terms of strategic value and size, as its population of 20 million presents good potential for payment card growth. Visa also plans to conduct pilot studies there, to develop new services and to bring consumers toward a cashless society. This would mean that a person is given the option to pay for daily goods and services with some form of card—credit, debit, or pre-paid.

Think Critically: What benefits do you see of a cashless society? What drawbacks?

Credit Laws

The government has passed a number of laws to protect consumers from unfair credit practices. Each law was intended to remove some of the problems and confusion surrounding the use of credit. Together, these laws set a standard for how individuals are to be treated in their daily credit dealings. Several of these laws are summarized on the following pages.

Consumer Credit Protection Act

The Consumer Credit Protection Act of 1968, known as the Truth-in-Lending Law, requires that consumers be fully informed about the cost of a credit purchase before an agreement is signed. Regulation Z of this act provides that the creditor must disclose all of these facts, in writing, to a borrower:

1. Cash price
2. Down payment and/or trade-in price
3. Amount financed
4. Insurance costs, filing costs, and other miscellaneous added costs of any kind
5. Finance charge
6. Annual percentage rate
7. Deferred payment price (deferred means "at a later time" or by the end of the credit agreement)
8. Amount(s) and date(s) of payment
9. Description of security interest (item being purchased)
10. Method of computing unearned finance charge (in case of early payoff)
11. Any other information that may be applicable or necessary

In addition, Regulation Z requires a grace period of three business days in which purchasers can change their mind about a credit agreement. The Truth-in-Lending Law also limits your liability to $50 after your credit card is reported lost or stolen. There is no liability at all if the card is reported lost prior to its fraudulent use.

Fair Credit Reporting Act

If you are denied credit based on a credit report, inaccurate information in your file may be the cause. Under the Fair Credit Reporting Act, you have a right to know what is in your file and who has seen your file. A listing of requests made for your file for credit purposes in the last six months, and for employment purposes in the last two years, must be available to you. You may see your credit file at no charge within 30 days of a credit denial. A small fee may be charged in the event you want to see your file at any other time for any reason. You have the right to have inaccurate information investigated, corrected, and deleted from your file and have a new report furnished to creditors. Or, if the information is essentially correct, you can write your own statement giving your side of the story. Your statement must be added to the file.

Fair Credit Billing Act

Under the Fair Credit Billing Act, creditors must resolve billing errors within a specified period of time. A *statement* is an itemized bill showing charges, credits, and payments posted to your account during the billing period. Suppose your monthly statement showed purchases you did not make. Perhaps the company billed you for merchandise you ordered but did not receive. Creditors are required to have a written policy for correcting such errors.

If you believe your bill contains an error, you should act immediately. Do not write on the bill sent to you. On a separate piece of paper, write a letter explaining what you believe the problem to be. Write clearly and give a complete explanation of why you believe there is an error. Be specific about the amount in dispute, when you noticed the error, and any details relevant to the disputed amount. Figure 17-3 shows an example of what you might say. Be sure to include your account number for identification and your contact information.

Your complaint must be in writing and mailed within 60 days after you receive the statement. The error or amount disputed must be dealt with by the company in a reasonable manner and within a reasonable period of time. The creditor must acknowledge your complaint within 30 days. Within 90 days after receipt of your letter, the creditor must either correct the error or show why the bill is correct. Customers are still liable for amounts not disputed while the error dispute is being settled. Figure 17-4 on page 494 shows an example of one company's written policy for handling billing errors.

The Fair Credit Billing Act allows you to withhold payment on damaged or poor-quality goods or services purchased with a credit card, as long as you have made a real attempt to solve the problem with the merchant.

Equal Credit Opportunity Act

The Equal Credit Opportunity Act of 1975 was designed to prevent discrimination in judgment of creditworthiness. **Discrimination** is treating people differently based on prejudice rather than individ-

P.O. Box 4848
Milwaukee, WI 40412-4848
April 10, 20--

Melon Visa Bank
Customer Service Center
24 Chambers Street
New York, NY 02040-3112

RE: ACCOUNT # 4902 3818 4783 1783
    Disputed Amount: $289.00 Melvin's, 3/21/--

As stated in my telephone conversation with Melanie at your 800 number on April 9, 20--, I am hereby disputing the above charge.

Enclosed are copies of the invoice and other documentation for the purchase I made on March 21. I am disputing the amount listed because the service provided was unsatisfactory. I was charged $589, but within a week, the same operational problem occurred. I asked Melvin's to correct the problem, but they said it was not their responsibility and that they would charge me an additional $200 in parts and labor. As you can see, I then went to Barlow's, and they fixed the defective part for $300. Therefore, I believe that of the $589, which is the fair market value of the product, I should not have to pay more than $289 to Melvin's.

You can reach me at (201) 555-2372 on weekdays. My e-mail address is listed below. Please let me know if you need any further information.

Thank you,

Jackie B. Chen

JACKIE B. CHEN
Jackiebc@starnet.com

Enclosure

ual merit. There are many legitimate reasons for denying an applicant credit. Some reasons, however, are considered discriminatory. The act provides that:

1. Credit may not be denied solely because you are a woman, single, married, divorced, separated, or widowed.
2. Credit may not be denied specifically because of religion, national origin, race, color, or age (except as age may affect your ability to perform, or your ability to enter into contracts; for example, minors cannot be held liable for their contracts because they are not considered competent parties).

Figure 17-4 *Error-Correction Policy*

IN CASE OF ERRORS OR INQUIRIES ABOUT YOUR BILL:

The Fair Credit Billing Act requires prompt resolution of errors. To preserve your rights, follow these steps:

1. Do not write on the bill. On a separate piece of paper, write a description as shown below. A telephone call will not preserve your rights.

   a. Your name and account number.
   b. Description of the error and your explanation of why you believe there is an error. Send copies of any receipts or supporting evidence you may have; do not send originals.
   c. The dollar amount of the suspected error.
   d. Other information that might be helpful in resolving the disputed amount.

2. Mail your letter as soon as possible. It must reach us within 60 days after you receive your bill.

3. We will acknowledge your letter within 30 days. Within 90 days of receiving your letter, we will correct the error or explain why we believe the bill is correct.

4. You will receive no collection letters or collection action regarding the amount in dispute; nor will it be reported to any credit bureau or collection agency.

5. You are still responsible for all other items on the bill and for the balance less the disputed amount.

6. You will not be charged a finance charge against the disputed amount, unless it is determined that there is not an error in the bill. In this event, you will be given the normal 25 days to pay your bill from the date the bill is determined to be correct.

3. Credit may not be denied because you receive public assistance (welfare), unemployment, social security, or retirement benefits.
4. Credit applications may be oral or written. However, a creditor is prohibited from asking certain questions, either orally or in writing, such as: Do you plan to have children? What is your ethnic origin? What church do you attend?
5. A creditor may not discourage you, in writing or orally, from applying for credit for any reason prohibited by the act (such as being divorced).

In addition to these pro-hibitions, the act states that creditors must notify you of any action taken on your credit application within 30 days of submission. If you are denied credit, the denial must be in writing and must list a specific reason for the denial. After a denial of credit, the creditor must keep for 25 months all information used to determine the denial and any written complaint from you regarding the denial. You have the right to appeal, and the creditor must give you the name and address of the federal agency that enforces compliance with the law.

What law was designed to prevent discrimination in the judgment of creditworthiness?

Also, the act requires new accounts to reflect the fact that both husband and wife are responsible for payment. In this way, both spouses establish their own credit histories. Existing accounts should be changed to assure that the wife, as well as the husband, receives credit for the payment record.

Fair Debt Collection Practices Act

The Fair Debt Collection Practices Act was designed to eliminate abusive collection practices by debt collectors. A **debt collector** is a person or company hired by a creditor to collect the overdue bal-ance on an account. The fee charged by the debt collector is often half of the amount collected. The law prohibits use of threats, obscenities, and false and misleading statements to intimidate the consumer into paying. It also restricts the time and frequency of collection practices, such as telephone calls and contacts at place of employment. Debt collectors are required to verify the accuracy of the bill and give the consumer the opportunity to clarify and dispute it.

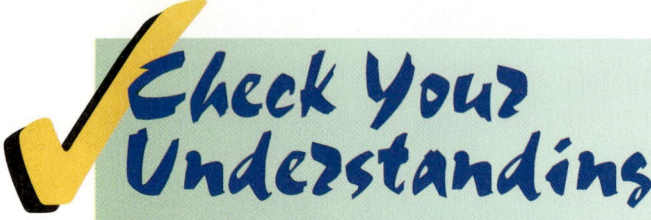

Check Your Understanding

Review Terms
1. credit rating
2. discrimination
3. debt collector

Review Concepts
1. What are some things you can do to maintain a good credit rating?
2. What is the purpose of a credit report?
3. What should you do if you believe there is an error on your credit card statement?

17.1 *Establishing Good Credit*

- Your credit history is a complete record of your experience with credit. This history is on file at a credit bureau.
- Credit bureaus collect information about consumers' credit transactions from businesses and prepare credit reports about individual consumers for their business subscribers. The businesses use this information to decide whether or not to grant credit to the consumer.
- Businesses judge your creditworthiness based on the five Cs of credit: character (evidence of financial responsibility); capacity (ability to repay the debt from income); capital (assets owned that exceed your total debt); conditions (general state of the economy); and collateral (property used as security for the loan).
- To start building a good credit history, open a savings account. Then open a checking account and use it responsibly. Open a store credit account and then get a small loan. Make all payments on time or early. Never miss a payment. Finally, apply for a credit card.

17.2 *Credit Ratings and Legal Protection*

- Credit bureaus rate consumers' creditworthiness using different systems. A point system assigns points based on debt, payment history, income, and other factors. Sometimes businesses determine their own ratings based on credit histories supplied by the credit bureau.
- Credit reports give personal and financial information about individual consumers, including a summary of potentially negative and positive items on the report, a list of information from public records, a list of credit

accounts and their status, details of monthly balances, and a list of all who have requested to see the consumer's credit history.

- Credit laws were designed to protect consumers from unfair credit practices.
- The Consumer Credit Protection Act (Truth-in-Lending Law) requires full disclosure of all facts related to credit, such as amount financed, total finance charge, and annual percentage rate.
- The Fair Credit Reporting Act gives you the right to inspect your credit file and to make changes or dispute information contained in the file.
- The Fair Credit Billing Act requires creditors to resolve billing errors within a reasonable time.
- The Equal Credit Opportunity Act prohibits discrimination in judgment of creditworthiness.
- The Fair Debt Collection Practices Act prohibits abusive collection practices by debt collectors.

Review Terms

Directions: Can you find the definition for each of the following terms used in Chapter 17?

capacity
character
credit bureau
credit history
credit rating
credit report

debt collector
discrimination
subscribers

1. Businesses that pay fees to a credit bureau in exchange for credit information collected and compiled into reports.
2. A person or company hired by a creditor to collect the overdue balance on an account.
3. A business that accumulates, stores, and sells credit information to business subscribers.
4. A responsible attitude toward living up to agreements, often judged on evidence in the person's credit history.
5. A written statement of a consumer's credit history, issued by a credit bureau to its business subscribers.
6. Financial ability to repay a loan with present income.
7. A complete record of a person's borrowing and repayment performance.
8. Treating people differently based on prejudice rather than individual merit.
9. A measure of creditworthiness based on an analysis of the consumer's financial history.

1. What does a credit bureau do to earn money? Who pays for its services?
2. What is the advantage for businesses of becoming subscribers of credit bureaus?
3. What types of public records become a part of your credit record?
4. Why is it important to pay your bills when they are due rather than a few days late?
5. Why do creditors care about how long you have worked at your present job and about how many jobs you have had?
6. List personal factors that creditors often consider.
7. What are the five Cs of credit?
8. What types of discrimination are unlawful in granting or denying credit?
9. What types of personal information can lawfully be asked of credit applicants?
10. What federal law protects consumers from unfair discrimination in credit?
11. Do you have a right to see your own credit file? Explain.
12. What is the purpose of the Truth-in-Lending Law?
13. What should you do if you are denied credit based on your credit file? What can you do if information in your credit file is basically correct but damaging to you as is?
14. What is the purpose of the Fair Credit Reporting Act?
15. What should you do if there is an error on your statement from a creditor?

APPLY YOUR KNOWLEDGE

1. Go to a local credit bureau and ask about the system the bureau uses for locating, storing, and using credit information. Write a one-page report describing the process. Be sure to include the credit rating system used and explain how customers are rated and by whom (the creditor or the credit bureau). Before visiting the credit bureau, prepare a list of questions to ask and call first to make an appointment.

2. You have filled out an application for credit at a local department store. The store has notified you that it cannot give you credit because you have a poor credit rating. What are your rights, and what are some things you should do? You have not paid late or missed any payments, and you have paid off previous debts as agreed. Suppose there is an error; what responsibilities to you does the credit bureau have?

3. As a teenager, you would like to get started in establishing a good credit history. Based on your personal situation and the stores and banks in your area, prepare a plan that you might follow in getting started using credit.

4. Visit the Federal Reserve Board's Web site entitled "Consumer Handbook to Credit Protection Laws" at www.hsh.com/pamphlets/cons_handbook_credit.html. Summarize in a one-page, double-spaced report three laws the Federal Reserve Board recommends that consumers be knowledgeable about.

5. Visit the Web site of one of the three major credit bureaus listed in Figure 17-1. In no more than one page, summarize what the bureau includes in its credit reports and outline the procedure you would have to follow to get a copy of your own report.

6. Describe what you must do if you believe a statement you receive from a creditor contains an error. Describe the process for error correction, including your responsibilities and time limits and the responsibilities and time limits of your creditor.

7. What kinds of credit do you think you will be using in five years? How will you establish a good credit rating to be eligible for increasing credit limits and privileges?

Solve Problems

1. Obtain a credit application from a local merchant or national credit card company. On a separate piece of paper, list each question on the form in a column on the left. To the right of the column of questions, make another column. Indicate beside each question whether it is (a) a personal question, (b) a payment record question, (c) an employment stability question, or (d) an income question.

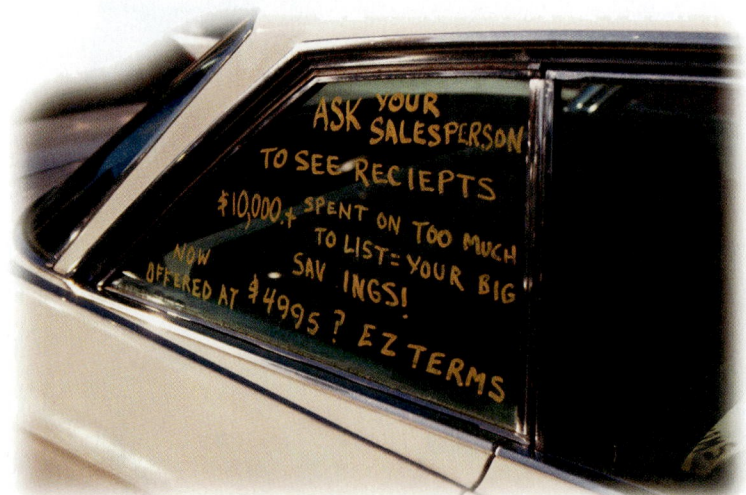

2. You have just received your monthly VISA bill. There is a charge on your bill of $42, but you have a receipt showing the amount should have been $24. You made the purchase at a local clothing store (you supply the name and address) one month ago. Write a letter to the bank that issued the VISA (choose a local bank) and explain the error.

3. Obtain a written error policy supplied by a local or national credit card company or other creditor. Companies that sell over the Internet should state their policy at their Web site. Compare the policy statement to Figure 17-4 and describe the similarities and differences.

4. Your friend Alice has just been turned down for credit. She works part-time and would like to buy clothing and jewelry on credit from a local department store. The department store stated lack of credit history as the reason for credit denial. Is there anything Alice can do?

5. Your friend Reggie was denied credit, so he asked for a copy of his credit report from one of the national credit bureaus. On examination of the report, he discovered several errors. For example, the report showed a previous employer and account that he never had. It also showed a previous address in another state that was not correct. What can Reggie do about this incorrect information?

6. Your neighbor recently purchased a refrigerator but was unable to continue making payments because he lost his job. In the last week he has had abusive telephone calls at home. A collector has come to your house looking for him and has made false and degrading comments about the neighbor's character. Your neighbor has volunteered to return the refrigerator, but the bill collector refuses and threatens him with public humiliation and all sorts of recriminations. What is your advice to your neighbor? What law protects him?

For related activities and links, point your browser to
www.mypf.swep.com.

Chapter 18

Responsibilities and Costs of Credit

Up Front

Jeremy was well on his way to managing credit and taking the next steps, such as buying a house and making a commitment to long-term payments.

"I learned the hard way that all credit isn't created equal," he thought. "Some credit cards have annual fees, and others charge very high interest rates. I switched from credit accounts that didn't meet my needs. Now I have a group of cards and accounts that have no annual fees, low interest rates, and the kinds of rebates that benefit me. I keep my accounts paid off and use credit cards mainly for emergencies and convenience. It wasn't always so easy, though. When I wasn't careful, I ended up spending a lot of money impulsively that I could have used later to buy something I wanted more."

Lesson 18.1 — Using Credit Responsibly

Goals

★ Describe the responsibilities of consumer credit.
★ Discuss how to protect your credit card from fraud.
★ Explain how you can reduce or avoid credit costs.

Responsibilities of Consumer Credit

Once you have established credit, you have the responsibility to manage it carefully. Failure to take this responsibility seriously can result in having your credit limited or, in some cases, withdrawn. Because using credit is important to your financial future, you should be aware of your responsibilities to yourself and to creditors. In return, creditors have responsibilities to you, their customer.

Responsibilities to Yourself

As a credit user, you have a responsibility to yourself to use credit wisely and not get into debt beyond an amount you can comfortably repay. Never having enough money and always scrambling to make your next payment is a stressful way to live.

You are also responsible for checking out businesses before making credit purchases. Better Business Bureaus and Chambers of Commerce have information about businesses and complaints that have been filed against them.

You owe it to yourself to comparison shop. Don't buy on impulse. Check prices in various stores. Take the time to evaluate the product and your other options before buying.

What responsibilities do you have to yourself as a credit user?

Comparison shop for credit as well. Compare features, costs, and availability of credit and make wise choices. Become familiar with billing cycles, annual percentage rates, and any special charges related to each credit account. Learn about state and local laws regarding the use of credit.

Finally, as a credit user, you should have the right attitude about using credit. Enter into each transaction in good faith and with full expectation of meeting your obligations and upholding your good credit reputation.

Responsibilities to Creditors

When you open an account, you are entering into a relationship with a store, bank, or other creditor. You are pledging your honesty and sincerity in the use of credit.

You have the responsibility to limit your spending to amounts that you can repay according to the terms of the credit agreement. By signing a credit application, you agree to make all payments promptly, on or before the due date. In addition, you are responsible for reading and understanding the terms of all agreements, including finance charges, what to do in case of error, how to return items, and any other provisions of the agreement.

It is your responsibility to contact the creditor immediately when you find a problem with the bill or discover that the merchandise is defective. If an emergency prevents you from making a payment, you must contact the creditor to make arrangements to pay at a later date.

Creditors' Responsibilities to You

Creditors also have responsibilities to consumers to whom they grant credit. These responsibilities include the following:

1. Assisting consumers in making wise purchases by honestly representing goods and services, with all their advantages and disadvantages.
2. Informing customers about all rules and regulations (such as minimum payments and due dates) and fees.
3. Cooperating with established credit reporting agencies, making credit records available to the consumer, and promptly discussing and clearing mistakes in records when they occur.

PERSONAL PERSPECTIVE

Maxing Out the Cards

Your credit cards are "maxed out" when there is no room left to charge. You cannot buy anything else on credit until you pay down the current balance. Maxing out is not a good idea. Here's why:

1. When you get really close to the top, it is very easy to "go over." Most credit card companies charge a fee for exceeding the card's credit limit. This fee may be $25 or more.
2. In some cases, the credit card company will not honor charges that exceed the credit limit. It can be very embarrassing to try to use your credit card, only to have it rejected by the verification machine.
3. When your cards are maxed out, you are paying maximum interest and maximum monthly payments. At the same time, you cannot use the card because the balance is going down very slowly and a single charge might take the card over the top once again.
4. Having maxed-out credit cards does not look good on your credit report. It tells potential creditors that you are already overextended and unable to pay down existing debts.
5. With a maxed-out credit card, having the credit card offers no advantages. In other words, you cannot use it for current purchases, to reserve a hotel room, or to rent a car. You must be very careful not to use it until you have created enough room for additional charges.
6. When you pay down your charges regularly, credit card companies will be more willing to raise your credit limit. But when the card is maxed out, the credit card company will not likely extend additional credit if you need it for a major purchase.

For all these reasons, avoid the practice of maxing out your cards.

Think Critically

1. How might maxing out your credit card affect your lifestyle?
2. If you were a creditor and someone with maxed-out cards asked you for a loan, would you grant it? Why or why not?

4. Establishing and carrying out sound lending and credit policies that do not overburden or deceive customers. This includes setting reasonable guidelines for credit use to avoid extending additional credit to customers who cannot afford it.
5. Establishing and maintaining fair and reasonable methods of contacting customers who fail to meet their obligations, assisting them whenever possible with payment schedules and other means for solving credit problems.

Protecting Yourself from Credit Card Fraud

Credit card fraud costs businesses and consumers millions of dollars each year. The most common type of fraud is the illegal use of a lost or stolen credit card or of credit card information intercepted online. While the credit card holder's liability is limited to $50, the merchant is not protected from loss. Consequently, merchants often raise their prices to cover such losses.

Safeguarding Your Cards

It is your responsibility to protect your cards from unauthorized use. Here are some commonsense tips for doing so:

1. Sign your cards as soon as you receive them.
2. Carry only the cards you need.
3. Keep a list of your credit card numbers, their expiration dates, and the phone number and address of each card company in a safe place.
4. Notify creditors immediately by phone when your card is lost or stolen and follow up with a letter so that you have written evidence of the notification.
5. Watch your card during transactions and get it back as soon as you can.
6. Tear up any carbon paper used for the transaction.
7. Do not lend your card to anyone or leave it lying around.
8. Destroy expired cards by cutting them up.
9. Don't give credit card numbers and expiration dates by phone to people or businesses you don't know.

10. Keep your sales receipts and verify all charges on your credit card statements promptly. Use the procedure printed on your statement to question charges that you think are in error.

Protecting Your Cards Online

Buying on the Internet has opened new avenues for criminals to steal credit card information for illegal use. Software makers and online organizations are fighting back by constantly developing new ways to offer secure electronic transmission of customer information. There are some steps you can take as well to help protect your credit card and personal information during online transactions.

What are some ways in which you can protect your credit online?

1. Deal only with companies online that you know and trust. If the retailer also has a physical "bricks-and-mortar" store, then it is likely to be safer than an unknown merchant that exists only online.

2. When making an online transaction, always look for your browser's symbol that indicates a secure site before entering your personal information. For example, the Internet Explorer and Netscape browsers display a small closed-lock symbol on the bottom of your screen when you have entered a secure Web page. The symbol should appear whenever a Web site asks you to enter credit card and other personal information, such as to make a purchase. Among other security measures, this symbol means that the information you enter will be *encrypted,* or put into code, before transmission. If you don't see the symbol, don't enter the information.

3. All legitimate online merchants should clearly state their privacy policy, explaining how they use the information you provide and how they protect your privacy. Review

the policy to make sure you are comfortable with it before dealing with that company. Many sites offer further assurance by displaying the seal of a nonprofit watchdog group, such as the Better Business Bureau or TRUSTe. Sites that follow the privacy principles set forth by these organizations are allowed to display their seal. This kind of oversight is not fully developed yet, so not all legitimate merchants display seals.

Many companies give you a choice on their Web site as to whether and how your personal information is used. These companies allow you to decline having personal information, such as your e-mail address, shared with other companies. Look for this as part of the company's privacy policy.

Avoiding Unnecessary Credit Costs

Credit can be very advantageous to if you use it wisely. Before deciding whether to borrow money, ask yourself these three critical questions: Do I need credit? Can I afford credit? Can I qualify for credit? If you can answer "yes" to these questions, then follow these guidelines to minimize the cost of credit:

1. *Accept only the amount of credit that you need.* Although having credit available when you need it may seem comforting, unused credit can count against you. **Unused credit** is the remaining credit available to you—that is, your credit limit minus the amount you have already spent. For example, if the limit on your credit card is $1,000 and you owe $200, your unused credit is $800. Other creditors may be reluctant to loan money to you because you could at any time charge the other $800, thereby reducing your ability to pay back another debt. Potential creditors, then, may view you as a bad risk because of your unused credit. Unused credit accounts are also temptations for you to use more credit than you need.
2. *Do not increase credit spending when your income increases.* Instead of spending that extra income, put it into savings or invest it. Avoid the trap of increasing spending with each

increase in your income. It is wiser to reduce existing debt or invest the additional income for future use.

3. *Keep the number of credit cards to a minimum.* Most credit counselors recommend carrying no more than one or two credit cards. The more credit cards you have, the more temptation you have to make purchases. A bank credit card is good at most places where you do business, which eliminates the need for having numerous individual charge accounts.

4. *Pay cash for purchases under $25.* If you make yourself pay cash for small purchases, you won't be surprised with a big bill at the end of the month. Paying cash will help you realize how much you are spending. Consequently, you may buy less and only when you really need the item.

Why is it a good idea to pay for small purchases with cash?

5. *Understand the cost of credit.* Think about how the finance charges, monthly payments, and length of time you will be committed to payments will affect your lifestyle. Study the costs carefully and consider how this commitment of future income to paying off debt might affect your budget in the months to come.

6. *Shop for loans.* The type and source of your loan will make a big difference in cost. Compare the cost of credit from three different sources. Plan your major purchases carefully. Never make such decisions on the spur of the moment. Don't sit and figure costs in the lender's office. Go home, figure all costs, and consider the purchase carefully without the lender being present.

7. *Use credit to beat inflation.* With the help of credit, you can often purchase needed items on sale that you would not buy if cash were your only payment option. In this way, you can avoid higher prices and save money.

8. *Time your credit card purchases carefully.* By purchasing immediately after the closing date of your billing cycle, you can delay your payment for approximately two months rather than one month. Your repayment time is usually 25 to 30

days. You can extend your time to repay to 60 days, interest free, if your timing is right.

9. *Take full advantage of rebate programs.* Many credit cards, from cards issued by retailers to car manufacturers to airlines, provide rebates. A **rebate** is a partial refund of an amount spent. For example, a credit card company might rebate a portion of the amount you charged during a period of time. The rebate may be computed monthly, quarterly, or annually. For example, XYZ card rebates to customers a percentage of all their purchases. If you charged $1,500 during the year, you could receive a check for $15 or more. Some credit cards allow you to accumulate points that can be used for free hotel accommodations, airline tickets, or car rentals. Still others pay cash or prizes for use of the card. However, do not use cards just to get rebates when it means paying higher finance charges than you might ordinarily pay.

+PROS and CONS

When you choose credit cards, there are trade-offs between the features you prefer and the cost of credit. These include the interest rate on purchases; the minimum monthly payment; the grace period; whether the card is acceptable in most places; and the annual fee.

Think Critically: Which credit card feature appeals to you the most? The least? When you use bank credit cards to pay for purchases, do you plan to pay the balance in full each month? Why or why not?

Check Your Understanding

Review Terms
1. unused credit
2. rebate

Review Concepts
1. List three responsibilities you have to your creditors.
2. List three responsibilities that creditors have to you.
3. List three things you can do to help avoid credit card fraud.

Credit Management

Lesson 18.2   Analyzing and Computing Credit Costs

Goals

★ Explain why credit costs vary.
★ Compute and explain simple interest and APR.
★ Compare methods of computing finance charges on revolving credit.

Why Credit Costs Vary

Several factors determine how much you will pay for the use of credit. One important factor is the method used to compute finance charges, explained later in the chapter. Other important factors include the following:

1. Source of credit
2. Total amount financed
3. Length of time you are making payments
4. Ability to repay debt
5. Type of credit selected
6. Collateral or security offered
7. Interest rates
8. Economic conditions
9. The business's costs of providing credit

As you learned in Chapter 16, the source of credit is important. Some creditors offer better credit plans than others. The more money you borrow and the longer you take to pay it back, the more you will pay in finance charges. The greater your ability to repay and, consequently, the higher your creditworthiness, the better your chances of being granted credit at reasonable rates. The type of credit plan selected will also determine the total amount of the finance charge.

When you buy an item that serves as collateral (security) for the loan, you are taking out a *secured loan*. Real estate is often considered the most solid collateral. Personal property pledged as collateral, such as an automobile, is often considered less secure. Secured loans, which often are for longer periods of time, generally have fixed interest rates that are lower than current variable rates charged on credit cards and open-ended credit. **Fixed-rate loans** are loans for which the interest rate does not change (up or down) over the life of the loan.

The current interest rate charged for the use of credit is often affected by the **prime rate,** which is the interest rate that banks offer to their best business customers, such as large corporations. Individuals pay more than prime-rate customers because the risk is greater to the lender. Generally, if the prime rate is 8 percent, consumers will pay 11 or 12 percent. The reasoning is that businesses borrow money for production, called *production loans,* while consumers borrow money to buy consumer goods, called *consumption loans.* With production loans, the businesses use the equipment, machinery, tools, and other assets they buy with the loans to generate income to repay the loans. With consumption loans, however, the item the consumer buys does not help generate income.

Inflation also has an effect on the cost of credit. Borrowers pay more for the use of credit during inflationary economic periods. When prices are rising (inflation), then money is more in demand in order to buy higher-priced goods and services. Because people need to borrow more money, lenders are able to charge higher interest rates.

In recent years, business costs for granting credit have risen. These business costs are related to delinquent accounts (overdue, but still collectible), bad debts (probably uncollectible), and bankruptcy. These debts add unpredictable and often uncontrollable costs to offering credit. Other costs of issuing credit include printing and mailing monthly statements, electronic authorization of credit charges, salaries for credit-support employees, computer support, and facilities for a credit department. Businesses pass along their costs for providing credit to consumers in the form of higher finance charges and higher product prices.

NET NOTES

RankIt by Visa is a Web site that provides financial information for students. Included are budget advice and resources (including a worksheet to track your budget); credit card facts and resources (including a credit card worksheet that helps you understand the real costs of using a credit card); financial tools (including a game on choices and decisions); and financial aid tips, links, and resources. Go to www.rankit.com and use the "finances" links.

Computing the Cost of Credit

Determining the cost of credit is easy using the formula for simple interest. The formula for calculating the total cost of installment credit is somewhat more complicated. The cost of a revolving charge account can be calculated using the previous balance method, the adjusted balance method, or the average daily balance method.

Simple Interest Formula

In Chapter 10, you learned that *interest* is money paid for the use of someone else's money. In the case of savings, interest is the amount the financial institution pays you for the use of your deposit. In the case of a loan, interest is the money you pay the business or financial institution for the use of its money. **Simple interest** is interest computed on the amount borrowed (or saved) only, without compounding. The simple interest method of calculating interest assumes one payment at the end of the loan period. The cost is based on three elements: the amount borrowed (or principal), the rate of interest, and the amount of time for which the principal is borrowed. The formula for computing simple interest is as follows:

$$\text{Interest (I)} = \text{Principal (P)} \times \text{Rate (R)} \times \text{Time (T)}$$

Principal

In Chapter 10, you learned that *principal* is an amount in a savings account on which interest accrues. The term has a similar meaning when referring to a loan. A loan's **principal** is the amount borrowed, or the unpaid portion of the amount borrowed, on which the borrower pays interest. For example, if you borrow $10,000 to buy a car, that $10,000 is the principal, or amount of the loan. Part of each payment you make goes toward paying down the principal. The rest of the payment is interest. After a number of payments, the principal on your car loan may drop to $8,000, which is the unpaid portion of the amount you borrowed.

Rate

The *interest rate* is expressed as a percentage. The higher the rate, the less desirable the loan for the consumer.

Time

The length of time the borrower will take to repay a loan is expressed as a fraction of a year: 12 months, 52 weeks, or 360 days. (In most business transactions, the standard practice is to use 360 as the number of days in a year for computing simple interest.) For example, if a loan is taken for six months, the time is expressed as ½. If money is borrowed for three months, the time is expressed as ¼. When a loan is for a certain number of days, such as 90, the time is expressed as ⁹⁰⁄₃₆₀, or ¼.

Figure 18-1 contains a simple interest problem showing the dollar cost of borrowing. In this problem, a person has borrowed $500 and will pay interest at the rate of 12 percent a year. The loan will be paid back in four months.

The simple interest formula also can be used to find principal, rate, or time when any one of these factors is unknown. For example, in Figure 18-2, the interest rate is 18 percent. The borrower paid a total of $26 in interest and repaid the loan in 18 months. What was the principal?

To find the missing rate, you can use the same formula. See Figure 18-3 for an illustration. In simple-interest problems, the rate stated—in this case, 9 percent—is also the *annual percentage rate*

Figure 18-1   *Simple Interest*

$$I = P \times R \times T$$

To multiply by a percent, first change it to a decimal: drop the percent sign, then move the decimal point two places to the left.

$I = ?$
$P = \$500$
$R = 12\%$
$T = 4 \text{ months}$

$$
\begin{aligned}
I &= 500 \times .12 \times \tfrac{4}{12} \\
&= 500 \times .12 \times \tfrac{1}{3} \qquad \text{(Four months is } \tfrac{4}{12} \text{ or } \tfrac{1}{3} \text{ of a year.)} \\
&= 60 \times .3333 \\
&= \$20
\end{aligned}
$$

Figure 18-2   *Simple Interest (Computing Principal)*

$$I = P \times R \times T$$

Or change the formula to read:

$I = \$26$
$P = ?$
$R = 18\%$
$T = 18 \text{ months}$

$$P = \frac{I}{R \times T}$$

$$
\begin{aligned}
26 &= P \times .18 \times \tfrac{18}{12} \\
&= P \times .18 \times \tfrac{3}{2} \ (1.50) \\
&= P \times .27
\end{aligned}
$$

$$= \frac{\$26}{.18 \times 1.50}$$

$$
\begin{aligned}
P &= 26 \div .27 \\
&= \$96.30
\end{aligned}
$$

$$= \frac{\$26}{.27}$$

$$= \$96.30$$

Credit Management

$$I = P \times R \times T$$

Or change the formula to read:

$$
\begin{aligned}
I &= \$18 \\
P &= \$300 \\
R &= ? \\
T &= 240 \text{ days}
\end{aligned}
$$

$$R = \frac{I}{P \times T}$$

$$
\begin{aligned}
18 &= 300 \times R \times {}^{240}/_{360} \\
&= 300 \times \tfrac{2}{3} \times R \\
&= 200 \times R
\end{aligned}
$$

$$= \frac{18}{300 \times \tfrac{2}{3}}$$

$$= \frac{18}{200}$$

$$
\begin{aligned}
R &= 18 \div 200 \\
&= .09 \text{ or } 9\%
\end{aligned}
$$

$$= .09 \text{ or } 9\%$$

(APR). As you learned in Chapter 16, the APR is the cost of credit stated as a yearly percentage.

As shown in Figures 18-2 and 18-3, you can either plug the numbers into the existing formula or rearrange the formula. Either way, you can find the unknown amount by simple mathematics.

Annual Percentage Rate Formula

Consumers often use an installment plan to pay for major items such as boats, cars, and furniture, making regular payments over time. To determine the APR for installment plans, in which the borrower repays the loan with more than one payment, use the formula in Figure 18-4 on page 518. Work through the problem in the Math Minute to see how to apply the formula.

An installment contract requires a **down payment**, or part of the purchase price paid in cash up front, reducing the amount of the loan. When you buy a car, you will probably have to pay at least 10 percent of the purchase price in cash. If you trade in your old car, the dealer will likely use the value of your trade-in as your down payment rather than give you cash for your old car.

In Figure 18-4, notice that the total price paid is more than the cash price. The total price includes all installment payments plus the down payment. Each payment includes principal and interest. The difference between the total price and the cash price is the finance charge.

By law, installment contracts must reveal the finance charge and the annual percentage rate. There are two ways to calculate APR: an APR formula and the APR tables. The APR tables are more precise; the formula only approximates the APR.

Figure 18-4

Formulas for Computing Finance Charge and APR

To calculate the finance charge, use the following formula:

Finance Charge = Total Price Paid − Cash Price

Where:
Total Price Paid = (number of payments x amount of each payment) + down payment
Cash Price = the total price you would have paid if you had paid in cash rather than with a loan

Then use the finance charge in the following formula to calculate the approximate annual percentage rate:

$$APR = \frac{2 \times n \times f}{P(N+1)}$$

Where:
n = number of payment periods in one year
f = finance charge
P = principal or amount borrowed
N = total number of payments to pay off amount borrowed

MATH MINUTE

Computing the Finance Charge and APR

The Espinosas are buying a new sofa. The cash price is $800. They decide to pay for it with an installment loan rather than pay cash. They put $100 down and borrow $700. They will pay off the loan principal in 12 monthly payments of $66 each. To determine their APR, you must first use the formula in Figure 18-4 to calculate their finance charge:

Total Price = (12 payments × $66) + $100 down payment = $892
Finance Charge = $892 total price − $800 cash price = $92

Then use the finance charge in the APR formula from Figure 18-4:

$$APR = \frac{2 \times 12 \text{ payments} \times \$92 \text{ finance charge}}{\$700 \text{ principal } (12 \text{ payments} + 1)} = \frac{2,208}{9,100} = .2426 = 24.26\%$$

Based on the above example, solve for finance charge and APR in the following case:

Mark and Dian bought a new refrigerator. The cash price was $1,200. They paid down $49, borrowing $1,151, which they will repay in payments of $49 per month for the next 27 months.

Solution:

Total price = (27 payments × $49) + $49 down payment = $1,372
Finance charge = $1,372 total price − $1,200 cash price = $172

$$APR = \frac{2 \times 2 \times 172}{1,151 (27 + 1)} = \frac{4,128}{32,228} = .1281 = 12.81\%$$

Credit Card Billing Statements

The cost of using an open-ended (revolving) credit account varies with the method the creditor uses to compute the finance charge. Creditors must tell you the method of calculating the finance charge. Finance charges are usually calculated based on the monthly billing cycle. Purchases made up to the closing date are included in the monthly bill. Finance charges are computed on the unpaid balance after the billing date. Creditors must tell you when finance charges begin on your account, so you will know how much time you have to pay your bills before the finance charge is added. Most creditors offering revolving credit give you a 25- to 30-day grace period to pay your balance in full before imposing a finance charge. Creditors may calculate finance charges on open-ended credit accounts using the adjusted balance method, the previous balance method, or the average daily balance method. The way the creditor determines the finance charge can make a big difference in the size of your credit card bills.

Adjusted Balance Method

When creditors use the adjusted balance method, they apply the finance charge only to the amount owed after you've paid your bill each month. For example, suppose your previous month's balance was $400. When the bill comes, you pay $300. If the creditor uses the adjusted balance method, you will pay a finance charge only on the unpaid balance ($400 − $300 = $100). As you can see in Figure 18-5, the adjusted balance method has the lowest finance charge.

Three Billing Systems — Figure 18-5

The adjusted balance method, the previous balance method, and the average daily balance method produce different results. This example is based on a billing period of 30 days:

	Adjusted Balance Method	**Previous Balance Method**	**Average Daily Balance**
Monthly Interest Rate	1.5%	1.5%	1.5%
Previous Balance	$400	$400	$400
Payments	$300	$300	$300 (on the 15th day)
Interest Charge	$1.50	$6.00	$3.75
	($100 × 1.5%)	($400 × 1.5%)	(average balance of $250 × 1.5%)*

*To figure average daily balance:

$$\frac{(\$400 \times 15\ days) + (\$100 \times 15\ days)}{30\ days} = \$250$$

To calculate the finance charge for this month, first determine the monthly rate by dividing the annual rate (18 percent) by 12 months. In this case, the monthly rate is 1.5 percent. Then multiply the balance due of $100 by 1.5 percent or .015 to derive the finance charge of $1.50. Then add the finance charge to the balance to determine the new account balance for the next billing cycle.

Previous Balance Method

When creditors use the previous balance method, they impose the finance charge on the entire amount owed from the previous month. This method allows no deductions for payments made. As shown in Figure 18-5, this method applies the monthly rate to the entire $400 (that month's balance). This is the most expensive way to figure the finance charge for the credit user.

Average Daily Balance Method

Most creditors use the average daily balance method for computing finance charges. Using this method, creditors calculate your balance on each day of the billing cycle. They then compute average daily balance by adding together all daily balances and dividing by the number of days in the cycle (usually 25 or 30). Payments made during the billing cycle are used in figuring the average daily balance. Because payments made during the period reduce the average daily balance, this method often results in a lower finance charge than does the previous balance method. The example in Figure 18-5 assumes a billing cycle of 30 days.

You can save as much as $1,000 or more each year in lower credit card interest charges by paying off your entire bill each month.

✓Check Your Understanding

Review Terms
1. fixed rate loans
2. prime rate
3. simple interest
4. principal (loan)
5. down payment

Review Concepts
1. Explain how economic conditions affect the cost of credit.
2. Why is a grace period important to you?

18.1 Using Credit Responsibly

- Your credit responsibilities to yourself include not going into debt beyond what you can comfortably repay, checking out businesses before you buy, comparison-shopping for products and for credit, and entering into credit transactions with the attitude that you will meet your obligations.

- Your responsibilities to creditors involve pledging your honesty and sincerity in the use of credit, limiting your spending to amounts you can repay, understanding the terms of the agreement, and contacting the creditor immediately if an emergency prevents you from making a payment.

- Creditors are responsible to consumers for assisting them in making purchases, applying fair credit policies and informing them of the rules, and dealing fairly with credit problems.

- To safeguard your credit cards, sign your cards immediately; carry only the cards you need; keep account information in a safe place; notify creditors immediately of a lost or stolen card; keep track of your card during transactions; destroy carbons and expired cards; do not lend your card; do not give card information to businesses you don't know; and verify your statements against your receipts each month.

- To protect your cards online, deal only with online companies that you trust; enter personal information only if you see the browser's symbol of a secure site; check the site's privacy policy; and look for the seal of an online oversight group.

- To reduce your credit costs, accept only the credit you need; do not increase spending when income increases; keep no more than one or two credit cards; pay cash for small purchases; understand how credit costs affect your lifestyle; shop for loans; buy items on sale; time your purchases with the billing cycle; and take advantage of rebates.

18.2 Analyzing and Computing Credit Costs

- Factors that determine the cost of credit include the source, length of time money is borrowed, type of credit, interest rates, collateral, economic conditions, and the business's costs of providing credit.
- Current interest rates charged for consumer loans are based on the prime rate (charged to business customers) plus a premium.
- The simple interest formula ($I = P \times R \times T$) does not involve compounding.
- The annual percentage rate (APR) formula calculates the costs of installment credit. It includes the down payment and all monthly payments in the total price. The difference between the total price and the cash price is the finance charge.
- Creditors calculate finance charges by the adjusted balance method, the previous balance method, or the average daily balance method. Costs vary depending on the method used.

Review Terms

Directions: Can you find the definition for each of the following terms used in Chapter 18?

down payment
fixed-rate loans
prime rate
principal (loan)
rebate

simple interest
unused credit

1. The total amount borrowed, or the unpaid portion of the amount borrowed, on which the borrower pays interest.
2. The remaining credit available to you—that is, your credit limit minus the amount you have already spent.
3. Interest computed on the amount borrowed (or saved) only, without compounding.
4. The interest rate that banks offer to their best business customers.
5. Partial refund of an amount spent.
6. Part of the purchase price paid in cash up front, reducing the amount of the loan.
7. Loans for which the interest rate does not change over the life of the loan.

Review Facts and Ideas

1. What responsibilities do creditors have toward consumers?
2. What is your liability and responsibility if your credit card is lost or stolen?
3. What can you do to protect your credit cards from unauthorized use?
4. What can you do to help protect your credit card and personal information when making online transactions?
5. List several things you can do to avoid unnecessary credit costs.
6. How can unused credit work against you when you apply for a new loan?
7. List several factors that affect the cost or interest rate you will have to pay to get a loan.
8. What is the formula for computing simple interest?
9. What is the formula for computing the APR on installment credit?
10. In calculating the finance charge in the APR formula, what makes up the total price?
11. Explain the three methods for determining the finance charge on revolving credit.

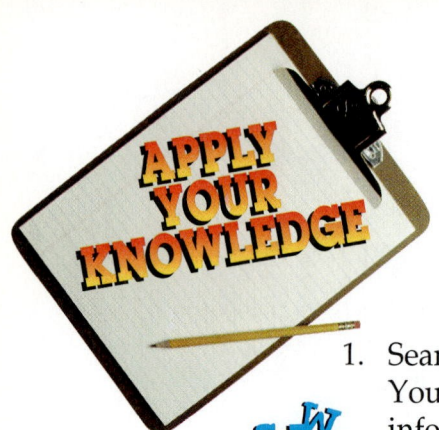

1. Search the Internet for current articles about online privacy. You might find an article about hackers who steal credit card information online, about current efforts to enhance online security, or about how to shop safely online. Read one of the articles you find. Then write a bulleted list of the key points in the article. Be prepared to share your findings with your class.

2. Visit the Federal Reserve System online at www.federalreserve.gov and click on "consumer information." Then go to "credit cards" for advice on how to compare and use them wisely. In one page or less, summarize in your own words the tips you found most useful.

3. Using the formula for simple interest, solve the following problems, rounding to the nearest penny.

   a. I = ?
      P = $500
      R = 18 percent
      T = 6 months

   b. I = ?
      P = $1,000
      R = 13.5 percent
      T = 8 months

   c. I = ?
      P = $108
      R = 15 percent
      T = 3 months

   d. I = ?
      P = $89.50
      R = 8 percent
      T = 9 months

4. The following simple interest problems have different elements missing. Solve for the missing elements, using the formula shown in this chapter. Round to the nearest penny.

   a. I = $8
      P = ?
      R = 12 percent
      T = 60 days ($^{60}/_{360}$)

b. I = $54
   P = ?
   R = 18 percent
   T = 18 months ($^{18}/_{12}$)
c. I = $510
   P = $2,100
   R = ?
   T = 2 years ($^{24}/_{12}$)
d. I = $36
   P = $108
   R = ?
   T = 18 months ($^{18}/_{12}$)

5. Using the process illustrated in Figure 18-4 and the Math Minute, determine the APR for the following problems:
   a. The purchase price of an item requires a down payment of $60, with the balance to be paid in 12 equal payments of $60 each. The cash price is $700.
   b. The purchase price of an item requires a down payment of $100 and 24 equal payments of $90. The cash price is $2,000.
   c. The cash price of an item is $200. The down payment is $20, and 10 equal payments of $22 each are to be made.
   d. The cash price of an item is $895. With $95 down, the balance is payable in 15 payments of $60 each.

6. The previous balance method of computing interest is determined by first calculating the finance charge and then subtracting the monthly payment to determine the new balance. On a separate sheet of paper, complete the following chart, using a calculator and rounding to the nearest penny. The APR is 12 percent. What is the total finance charge paid?

Balance	+	Finance Charge	=	Balance	−	Payment	=	New Balance
$100		_____		_____		$20.00		_____
_____		_____		_____		20.00		_____
_____		_____		_____		20.00		_____
Total Finance Charge		$_____						

7. With the adjusted balance method of computing interest, the monthly payment is subtracted before the finance charge is calculated. The amount of the finance charge is then added to obtain the new balance. On a separate sheet of paper, complete the following chart, using a calculator and rounding to the nearest penny. The APR is 18 percent. What is the total finance charge paid?

Balance	−	Payment	=	Balance	+	Finance Charge	=	New Balance
$500		$50.00		_____		_____		_____
_____		$50.00		_____		_____		_____
_____		$50.00		_____		_____		_____
Total Finance Charge						$_____		

Solve Problems

1. Your friend Jackie is proud of her ability to have and use credit. She buys lunch every day on credit, and at the end of the month she pays only the minimum balance due. When one credit card is at its limit, she switches to another credit card. She figures she can just go on charging forever because she can just make minimum payments. Do you see any problems with this behavior? Explain to Jackie how she is incurring finance charges.

2. Your cousin is considering whether to buy a new sound system. She can use installment credit at the store (18% APR), or she could put the purchase on her credit card. Her credit card has a variable rate, which is 9.9% right now, but is likely to increase in the next few months. What is your advice?

3. Your friend Abdul is unable to determine whether he is getting a good deal on a loan of $100 for 6 months when he pays back $114. What is the simple interest rate he is paying?

4. Tracy's aunt gave her a loan for $200 and asked her to repay the loan in nine months at 5 percent annual interest. Use your Notes and Interest Planner Tool to calculate how much Tracy will owe her aunt nine months from now?

PLANNING TOOLS

5. You are considering buying a used piano. The cash price of the piano is $600. The company selling the piano is willing to sell it to you for $50 down and 12 equal payments of $50. What is the total price? What is the finance charge?

6. If you were to purchase a major appliance and pay for it this year, borrowing $800 at 18 percent for 8 months, how much would you pay to finance this purchase?

7. You buy a new car that sells for $14,000 by trading in your car and using the trade-in allowance of $2,000 as a down payment. You pay the balance at $295 a month for 48 months. What is the APR?

8. Logan ran up a credit card debt of $1,000. He decided that he would not put any more purchases on the card until he had paid off the debt. He can pay $50 a month, and the interest rate is 18 percent. Use your Loan Planner Tool to find out how many monthly payments Logan will have to make to pay off his credit card debt. How many years will Logan be paying on the debt?

PLANNING TOOLS

For related activities and links, point your browser to
www.mypf.swep.com

Responsibilities and Costs of Credit

Chapter 19

Problems with Credit

Terms to Know

20/10 Rule
debtor
bankruptcy
unsecured debt
involuntary
    bankruptcy
voluntary bankruptcy

discharged debts
Chapter 11 bankruptcy
Chapter 7 bankruptcy
exempted property
Chapter 13 bankruptcy
reaffirmation

Up Front

Elbia has income of $1,500 per month, but when she totals her expenses, she has over $2,100 per month in bills to pay.

"I'm ready for some type of debt relief," Elbia told her credit counselor. "My income just doesn't cover my expenses. I didn't overspend, either. Last year I had to have extensive dental work. I had to get a different car because my old one was costing too much in repairs each month. And then my dog had to have surgery. The end result is that I'm buried. I have more expenses than income!"

GOALS

★ List and explain different methods for solving credit problems.
★ Outline bankruptcy laws, including exempted items, types of income excluded, and bankruptcy options.

Solving Credit Problems

One major disadvantage of credit is that it can lead to overextension (overspending). Many people get into trouble with credit every year, and they represent all levels of income and social standing.

Credit problems usually do not happen suddenly. Certainly, emergencies can and do occur, causing people to get buried in debt. Typically, however, credit problems arise after months and years of poor planning, impulse buying, and careless budgeting. If you recognize early enough that you are falling into an excessive debt problem, you can cure it before it becomes disastrous. However, it is less painful to plan your use of credit wisely and manage debt carefully from the beginning, so you don't have to face a serious financial problem.

The 20/10 Rule

Credit counselors often suggest use of the **20/10 Rule** to people beginning to use credit: Your total borrowing should not exceed 20 percent of your yearly take-home pay, and you should not take on monthly payments that total more than 10 percent of your monthly take-home pay. The 20/10 Rule does not apply to mortgage loans for housing. However,

What are some ways in which people can deal with credit problems?

it does apply to all other types of closed-ended as well as open-ended credit.

Suppose that your yearly take-home pay is $21,000 and your monthly take-home pay is $1,750. Your total borrowing should not exceed $4,200 (20 percent of your yearly take-home pay), and your monthly credit payments should not be more than $175 (10 percent of your monthly take-home pay). By following the 20/10 Rule, you avoid tying up future income with large credit payments. You can make reasonable fixed expenses and still have money left over for entertainment, clothing, and miscellaneous purchases.

Career Links

Bill and account collectors ensure that customers pay their overdue accounts. Some are employed by collection agencies, while others work for department stores or banks. Once collectors have found the debtors, they inform them of the overdue account and request payment. Collectors use computers and automated systems to track overdue accounts. A high school diploma is sometimes required for collector positions, and prior telemarketing experience is helpful. Collectors must be persistent and detail-oriented.

For more information, refer to the *Occupational Outlook Handbook* at www.bls.gov or search the Internet using such key words as "careers," "jobs," and "collection."

Credit Counseling

When you get into serious problems with credit, you can seek counseling from one of many private or government-sponsored counseling services. Sometimes the service charges a fee, usually according to your ability to pay. A counselor will help you set up a good budget and show you how to make your income do the most for you. The credit plan is voluntary; you are under no legal obligation to use it.

You cannot get loans from a credit counseling service, but you can get good advice for finding a workable plan for your situation. You can learn about credit counselors by looking under consumer credit counseling services in the Yellow Pages or online. A local nonprofit organization affiliated with the National Foundation for Consumer Credit (NFCC) is the Consumer Credit Counseling Service (CCCS). Anyone overwhelmed by credit obligations can phone, write, e-mail, or visit a CCCS office. The NFCC Web site at www.nfcc.org will help you find a CCCS office near you. You may even be able to work with a CCCS counselor over the Internet.

Some churches, private foundations, universities, military bases, credit unions, and state and federal housing authorities provide similar services. You can also find these nonprofit groups in the Yellow Pages and online.

Debt Adjustment

People who need stricter discipline than simply credit advice go to debt-adjustment companies. These companies charge a fee and require you to sign a contract. Then, they take over for you to help you get out of credit trouble. Often you will be asked to turn over your checkbook, paychecks, and bills to the debt-adjustment company. A credit advisor will contact your creditors to work out repayment plans and will use your accounts to make payments for you. Generally, the services include a five-step plan, similar to the one shown in Figure 19-1.

When you are desperate and cannot seem to control your purchases, you should consider getting help from a debt-adjustment company. You may not like the strict discipline involved, but the valuable training can help you avoid getting too deeply into debt again. Debt-adjustment companies, like credit counseling services, are listed in your Yellow Pages, in business directories, and online.

Debt-Adjustment Service Plan   Figure 19-1

1. Contact creditors and arrange for payments that can be made from your earnings.

2. Take your paycheck and checkbook and make debt payments for you. You are given an allowance until all bills have been paid off. This arrangement can take two years or more if you are in deep trouble.

3. Counsel you so that you understand how you got so far into debt and how to avoid doing so again in the future.

4. Work with you to create a reasonable budget that you can live with. Credit cards are taken away and given back slowly as the advisor becomes certain that you understand how to use them wisely.

5. Supervise your budget and help you make any needed changes or adjustments.

Credit Repair

After the damage is done and your credit rating is poor, you can take steps to repair it. You can obtain copies of your credit reports, challenge incorrect information, and respond to disputes. Or, for a fee, a credit-repair company will do these things for you.

According to experts, six out of ten Americans with bad credit ratings do not deserve them. The bad ratings are caused by credit bureaus and credit card companies that capture and spread incomplete and misleading information. You can take steps to assure that the information reported about you is correct. You can clear up debts in a responsible manner, making payment arrangements and requesting that corrected information be supplied to credit bureaus.

For people who become addicted to credit and are not able to control their credit use, the only wise course is to live debt-free. People who fall into this category should pay cash for all purchases and use credit only for emergencies, and then pay off the debt as quickly as possible.

Legal Recourse

A **debtor** is a person who owes money to others. When debtors are in severe debt trouble and cannot meet their bills, the final and most serious step is bankruptcy. **Bankruptcy** is a legal process that relieves debtors of the responsibility of paying their debts or protects them while they try to repay. Bankrupt debtors are said to be *insolvent*. They have insufficient income and assets to pay their debts (liabilities). Bankruptcy is a second chance, but it carries serious consequences.

Bankruptcy Laws and Their Purpose

Bankruptcy law in the United States has two goals. The first is to protect debtors by giving them a fresh start, free from creditors' claims. The second is to give fair treatment to creditors competing for debtors' assets. Many creditors complain that the bankruptcy code requires them to tighten credit because it is too easy for people to give up their debts rather than accept responsibility for them. On the other hand, bankruptcy casts a shadow over an individual's credit record.

Since the original federal Bankruptcy Act of 1898, various laws have been passed that have made it either easier or harder to file for bankruptcy. The Bankruptcy Reform Act of 1994 tightened the rules for bankruptcy but allowed insolvent debtors to keep more of their assets. Congress is considering ways to tighten bankruptcy laws and make it more difficult for people to use bankruptcy to avoid paying their credit card debts. The idea behind new legislation is to prevent people from abusing the protections provided by the laws.

Although bankruptcy provides debtors with a second chance, why is it such a serious issue to consider?

The U.S. population is about twice that of Japan. Yet, bankruptcies in the U.S. are more than 16 times the number in Japan. In the Japanese point of view, bankruptcy is shameful.

Bankruptcy laws treat two general classes of debt: secured and unsecured. As you learned in Chapter 18, *secured loans* are loans backed by specific assets that the debtor pledged as collateral to assure repayment. If the debtor does not pay, the creditor can take possession of the pledged asset. **Unsecured debt** is a loan that is not backed by pledged assets. In bankruptcy, all of the debtor's resources may be used to repay this kind of debt.

Types of Bankruptcy

Bankruptcy can be voluntary or involuntary. **Involuntary bankruptcy** occurs when creditors file a petition with the court, asking the court to declare you, the debtor, bankrupt. The court then decides whether or not you should be so declared. If the court agrees with your creditors, it takes over your property and other assets and pays off your debts as possible. Involuntary bankruptcy does not occur very often because most creditors prefer to be repaid in full over a period of time rather than settle only for a portion of your remaining assets.

Voluntary bankruptcy, the most common kind, occurs when you file a petition with a federal court asking to be declared bankrupt. The court notifies local newspapers and your creditors of your pending bankruptcy. Once notice is given, creditors may file claims. The court collects your assets and sells your property as needed.

Usually the value of all the bankrupt debtor's assets is not enough to pay off all the debts. The court sells the assets and gives each creditor a *proportional share,* in classes of creditors. For example, bankruptcy costs are paid first. Then secured loans are paid if assets remain. Credit card debts follow. Let's say that your total debt is $15,000 in one class, and your total assets are $5,000 for that class. You owe one creditor $1,500, which is 10 percent of the total debt. Therefore, this creditor will receive 10 percent of those assets, or $500. The remainder of that debt will be *discharged* after the bankruptcy is complete. **Discharged debts** are debts erased by the court during bankruptcy proceedings. Creditors can no longer seek payment for these debts. However, some debts, such as taxes, child support, and alimony, continue after bankruptcy. These debts cannot be discharged.

The bankruptcy process deals with debtors in one of two ways: liquidation or reorganization. Under *liquidation,* the court sells the debtors' assets and uses the proceeds to pay as much of the debts as possible. The remaining debt is then discharged. Under *reorganization,* debtors may keep their property but must submit a plan to the court for repaying a substantial portion of their debts.

The types of bankruptcy can be distinguished by which of these methods they use. **Chapter 11 bankruptcy** is a reorganization form of bankruptcy for businesses that allows them to continue operating under court supervision as they repay their restructured debts. The two kinds of bankruptcy available to individuals are Chapter 7 and Chapter 13.

Chapter 7 Bankruptcy

Commonly called *straight bankruptcy,* **Chapter 7 bankruptcy** is a liquidation form of bankruptcy for individuals that wipes out most debts in exchange for giving up most assets. To get debts dis-

Federally Exempted Items (as of January 1, 2001)   Figure 19-2

1. $15,000 equity in a home or burial plot ($30,000 on joint bankruptcy).

2. $2,400 interest in a motor vehicle.

3. Items worth up to $400 for a single item for household goods and furnishings, appliances, clothing, and personal items, for a total of not more than $8,000.

4. $1,000 in jewelry.

5. $1,500 in tools, books, and other items used in a trade or business.

6. Other property worth up to $800, plus up to $7,500 of the unused part of the $15,000 exemption for equity in a home or burial plot.

charged, debtors must give up all their property except for certain exempted items. **Exempted property** is the possessions that the bankrupt debtor is allowed to keep because they are considered necessary for survival. Federal laws exempt a number of items, as shown in Figure 19-2.

Some debts are not discharged and must still be paid, including child support, alimony, income taxes and penalties, student loans, and court-ordered damages due to malicious (intentional) acts. Once declared bankrupt, an individual cannot file for bankruptcy again for six years.

Chapter 13 Bankruptcy

Chapter 13 bankruptcy is a reorganization form of bankruptcy for individuals that allows debtors to keep their property and use their income to pay a portion of their debts over three to five years. Debtors work out a compulsory, court-enforced repayment plan. Under Chapter 13, often referred to as the *wage-earner's plan,* some debts are totally discharged, but family obligations still remain for child support and alimony.

Chapter 13 bankruptcy may seem more equitable and better for the debtor in terms of reestablishing credit. However, the blemish on the debtor's credit record caused by any form of bankruptcy is hard to overcome for many years.

Legal Advice

A person considering bankruptcy should seek good legal advice. In most states it is possible to file for bankruptcy without an attorney. But the law is complicated, and a good bankruptcy attorney can tell you which of your assets will be protected and which exempted items you can claim. The attorney can also assist you in deciding which bankruptcy plan will work best to help you solve your credit problems. Attorneys' fees for handling bankruptcies can range from $150 to $1,500, depending on the case, but good legal advice can save you that much and more.

Reaffirmation of Debts

Creditors may ask debtors to agree to pay their debts, even after bankruptcy has discharged them. The agreement to repay discharged debts is called **reaffirmation.** You may choose reaffirmation if a friend or family member co-signed the loan and you don't want to saddle this person with the debt. Also, you may choose to reaffirm rather than allow the collateral, such as a car, to be repossessed. Reaffirmation requires a court hearing, and debtors have 30 days to change their minds about promising to repay. A creditor is prohibited from harassing debtors to reaffirm after the court proceedings are over.

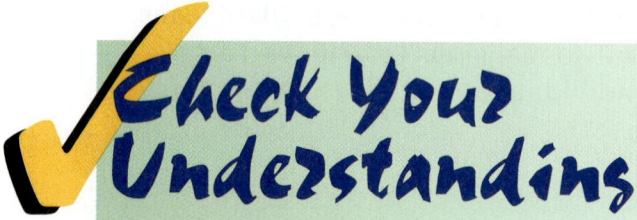

Check Your Understanding

Review Terms
1. 20/10 Rule
2. debtor
3. bankruptcy
4. unsecured debt
5. involuntary bankruptcy
6. voluntary bankruptcy
7. discharged debts
8. Chapter 11 bankruptcy
9. Chapter 7 bankruptcy
10. exempted property
11. Chapter 13 bankruptcy
12. reaffirmation

Review Concepts
1. Does the 20/10 Rule apply to open-ended credit or closed-ended credit?
2. When you are desperate and can't seem to control your purchases, what can you do?
3. What is credit repair?

illnesses
result in
bankruptcy,
they often
damage a
person's or
family's
finances for
many years.
For exam-
ple, a person
hospitalized
for a long time
with a critical ill[
could easily owe
a month for med[
room charges, ar
her savings can b
this type of debt
be years, even de
repaid, if ever.

Advantage[

For individuals v
offers a solution.
ruptcy does offer

1. *Debts are er*
   eliminates
   over. With
   avoid futur
   more diffic
   ruptcy. Del
   to repay th
   credit stanc
   no effort to
2. *Exempted as*
   to give up
   debts, they
   With these
   band and v
   start becom
   exempted i

Reconsidering Bankruptcy

Goals

★ Discuss the major causes of bankruptcy.
★ Describe the advantages and disadvantages of declaring bankruptcy.

Major Causes of Bankruptcy

Bankruptcy is a last-resort solution to credit problems. The most common reasons for claiming bankruptcy are business failure, emotional spending, failure to budget and develop a good finan-cial plan, and catastrophic injury or illness. Many creditors dislike the liberal bankruptcy code and want legislation that gives more rights to creditors while making bankruptcy less desirable for debtors.

Business Failure

Every year thousands of small businesses fail. For a number of rea-sons from bad economic conditions to poor financial planning, many small businesses do not make it beyond the first year. Other small business owners borrow more money and go further into debt in order to keep afloat until times get better. Owning and operating a small business can be very risky. Success depends on a great deal of luck in addition to good financial plans, knowledge of the product or service, favorable business location, and good eco-nomic conditions.

Emotional Spending

Consumers often get into trouble by buying based on emotion rather than reason. They may buy more than they can afford, often for instant gratification. They may spend to impress others rather than for items they really need. They may overuse credit, resulting in payments that are higher than they can comfortably repay with their current income. Usually, overuse of credit is gradual and, if recognized in time, can be overcome before it leads to bankruptcy. But a job loss, a business failure, or some other disaster can put

3. *Certain incomes are unaffected.* Bankruptcy will not affect certain types of income a debtor may have, such as social security; veterans' benefits; unemployment compensation; alimony; child support; disability payments; and payments from pension, profit-sharing, and annuity plans. These sources of income need not be considered even in a Chapter 13 bankruptcy, in which a compulsory payment plan is established.

4. *The cost is small.* Attorneys' fees and court costs in bankruptcy are relatively small in comparison to the amount of financial relief provided. When total debts reach such a level that income cannot stretch to pay them off, the relief is considerable in comparison to the cost involved. On the first visit to an attorney's office, a debtor will be given total cost estimates and information about the options available in bankruptcy proceedings.

Disadvantages of Bankruptcy

While bankruptcy offers debtors some relief, it carries serious consequences. Bankruptcy should be considered a last resort. Some of the disadvantages of bankruptcy are:

1. *Credit is damaged.* A bankruptcy judgment destroys your credit record for a long time. This judgment cannot be wiped off your credit records for 10 years. During that time, you could find it very difficult or impossible to obtain credit. You would have to pay cash for everything. If you did get credit, it would be at a very high interest rate because you would be considered a very high risk. Bankruptcy is a notice to creditors and others that, at one time, you were unable or unwilling to meet your financial responsibilities. Depending on the circumstances that caused the bankruptcy, people may continue to mistrust you in business affairs for well beyond the 10 years.

2. *Property is lost.* A person who declares bankruptcy does not necessarily get to keep exempt assets. Assume that you own a house worth $120,000 that has a mortgage of $90,000 against it. Your equity is $30,000. While the bankruptcy code allows you to keep the first $15,000 of equity in your home, you may be required to sell the home. You will be allowed $15,000 and the other $15,000 must be used to pay off creditors. Or, if you own a car valued at $5,000 and you owe

$2,800 on the car, your equity is $2,200. Since this amount is less than the allowance for a car, you will not have to sell the car. However, if you have a car valued at $8,000 with a loan of $5,000, your equity is $3,000. You are allowed only equity of $2,400, the legal limit. In this case, you will probably have to sell the car and use all proceeds over $2,400 to help pay off your creditors.

3. *Some obligations remain.* Regardless of the type of bankruptcy selected, all debt is not erased. Certain obligations, such as child support, must be paid in full. Other debts also remain: income taxes and penalties, student loans, and other debts at the discretion of the bankruptcy court. If a lender can prove that there was any type of false representation on the debtor's part in connection with a debt, the debt will not be discharged.

4. *Some debts can be reaffirmed.* You may feel the need to reaffirm some debts to protect your co-signers or avoid losing an important asset. However, by reaffirming, you will not get the fresh start that you probably need.

5. *Co-signers must pay.* After you have been declared bankrupt under Chapter 7, your co-signers must repay the loans they co-signed. Co-signers are likely to be your close friends or family members. Leaving them saddled with the debt can damage your personal relationships.

DID YOU KNOW

To conceal or illegally transfer assets, or to provide false information knowingly, is a crime under the bankruptcy laws.

Check Your Understanding

Review Concepts

1. What kinds of spending are most likely to get you into credit trouble? What can you do to avoid these dangers?
2. Do you believe that advantages of bankruptcy outweigh the disadvantages? Discuss.

PERSONAL PERSPECTIVE

An Abuse of Bankruptcy Protection

A dishonest person can use bankruptcy for personal advantage, as the following story will indicate.

John Smith (not his real name) was well established in credit when he lost his job. At that time, he held over ten charge cards from retailers and four bank credit cards.

He maintained his lifestyle during his unemployment (which lasted over two years), as though nothing had happened. He charged merchandise on his accounts to the maximum available and was careful to make all minimum monthly payments in a timely manner. As the months rolled by, he stretched every credit card to its absolute maximum credit limit, taking cash advances against the bank cards and buying all sorts of luxuries from watches to trips.

He sold his house, bought a smaller house with less than $15,000 equity, and hid away the profits from the sale in foreign bank accounts. He sold his expensive car and purchased one with a value of less than $2,400. He made sure all property in his name fell within the "exempt" category of bankruptcy law in his state. Meanwhile, he continued to use credit and make expensive purchases.

Finally, his credit ran out, and he could charge no more. He had amassed over $50,000 in debt. With no job and no assets remaining that could be used for collateral, he declared bankruptcy.

Think Critically

1. Do you see any ethical problems in this story? If so, what?
2. Were the bankruptcy laws designed to protect someone like John?
3. What lessons can be learned from this story?

19.1 Getting Unstuck

- The 20/10 Rule suggests that your total debt not exceed 20 percent of yearly take-home pay and your monthly payments not exceed 10 percent of your monthly take-home pay.
- Credit counseling services help you prepare a plan to manage your money and pay off creditors. Some are free while others charge a fee.
- Debt-adjustment companies often require you to turn over your checkbook, paychecks, and bills, and the advisor works out a repayment plan with your creditors and pays your bills from your income.
- Bankruptcy laws are designed to help people under severe debt get a new start. The debtor can file to be declared bankrupt, or creditors can file to have a debtor declared bankrupt.
- Bankruptcy deals with debt through liquidation or reorganization. Under liquidation, the court sells the debtors' assets to pay their debts. Under reorganization, debtors keep their property but must follow a plan to repay their debts.
- Chapter 11 bankruptcy is a reorganization form of bankruptcy for businesses that allows them to continue to operate as they repay their restructured debts.
- Chapter 7 bankruptcy is a liquidation form for individuals. Debtors must give up most of their assets in exchange for debt relief.
- Chapter 13 bankruptcy is a reorganization form for individuals. Debtors may keep their property but must follow a court-enforced repayment plan.

19.2 Reconsidering Bankruptcy

- Bankruptcy is most often caused by business failure, emotional spending, failure to budget, or catastrophic injury or illness.
- Bankruptcy offers the advantages of erasing some debts, allowing debtors to keep some possessions, allowing certain sources of income to remain unaffected, and providing considerable debt relief for the cost.
- Bankruptcy also carries serious consequences: Your credit is damaged for 10 years. You can lose much of your property. Some obligations are not discharged. Debt reaffirmation can hamper a fresh start. Leaving your co-signers saddled with your debt can damage your relationship with these people.

Review Terms

Directions: Can you find the definition for each of the following terms used in Chapter 19?

20/10 Rule
bankruptcy
Chapter 7 bankruptcy
Chapter 11 bankruptcy
Chapter 13 bankruptcy
debtor
discharged debts
exempted property
involuntary bankruptcy

reaffirmation
unsecured debt
voluntary bankruptcy

1. A legal process that relieves debtors of the responsibility of paying their debts or protects them while they try to repay.
2. Credit guideline stating that total borrowing should not exceed 20 percent of yearly take-home pay and monthly payments should not exceed 10 percent of monthly take-home pay.
3. A type of bankruptcy in which creditors file a petition with the court, asking the court to declare the debtor bankrupt.
4. A type of bankruptcy in which the debtor files a bankruptcy petition with the court, asking to be declared bankrupt.
5. Possessions that the bankrupt debtor is allowed to keep because they are considered necessary for survival.
6. A liquidation form of bankruptcy for individuals that wipes out most debts in exchange for giving up most assets.
7. A reorganization form of bankruptcy for individuals that allows the debtors to keep their property and use their income to pay a portion of their debts over three to five years.
8. Agreement to repay discharged debts.
9. A loan that is not backed by pledged assets.
10. A reorganization form of bankruptcy for businesses that allows the businesses to continue operating under court supervision as they repay their restructured debts.
11. A person who owes money to others.
12. Debt erased by the court as a result of bankruptcy proceedings.

Review Facts and Ideas

1. What sources of help in solving credit problems are available to you?
2. Where can you find out about the not-for-profit credit counseling services in your area?
3. What is the purpose of bankruptcy?
4. What are two ways that a debtor may be declared bankrupt?
5. What are two ways that the bankruptcy process deals with debtors?
6. Under Chapter 7 bankruptcy, what must a debtor give up in exchange for debt relief?
7. Which types of family obligations are not discharged by bankruptcy?
8. Why are some possessions exempted during bankruptcy?
9. Once you are declared bankrupt, how much time must pass before you can again file for bankruptcy?
10. How long does a bankruptcy judgment remain on your credit records?
11. How does Chapter 13 bankruptcy differ from Chapter 7?
12. Why is it a good idea to seek advice from an attorney before filing for bankruptcy?
13. Why might a debtor choose to reaffirm a debt after the bankruptcy process has discharged it?
14. List four common reasons for claiming bankruptcy.
15. List the advantages and disadvantages of filing bankruptcy.
16. Which types of income are not subject to the claims of creditors?

1. Read the classified section of your newspaper every day for one week, checking for bankruptcy notices. Most newspaper classified sections are available online. Collect the legal notices section and answer these questions:
   a. How many total bankruptcies were filed in the seven-day period?
   b. How many of the bankruptcies were joint bankruptcies (husband and wife)?
   c. What is the lowest amount of debt claimed?
   d. What is the highest amount of debt claimed?
   e. How many of those filers represented themselves? How many used an attorney?
   f. What was the lowest amount of property claimed as exempt?
   g. What was the highest amount of property claimed as exempt?
2. Search through the Yellow Pages, business directories, or online, and list several of the following:
   a. Not-for-profit credit counseling services
   b. Commercial debt-adjustment firms
   c. Attorneys specializing in bankruptcy
   d. Classes or other credit counseling services provided in the community, either for a fee or free
   Visit the Web site of one business of each type and write a brief summary of the kinds of information and services each provides.
3. Look up the original federal Bankruptcy Act of 1898 in a reference book or online, and write a report covering the following:
   a. Provisions of the law (in outline form)
   b. Exempted items allowed and types of income excluded
   c. Procedures or steps involved in filing bankruptcy

4. Search for articles online or in print magazines for information on the most recent Bankruptcy Reform Act and answer these questions:
   a. What key changes did this law make?
   b. How do these changes affect consumers and creditors?
   c. How will the law likely influence the availability of credit? Explain.
5. Search the Internet for advice on staying out of credit trouble. Make a list of at least five tips that you found most helpful. Note the URL where you found each tip.
6. Is it possible in your area to file bankruptcy without the aid of an attorney? What is the procedure for filing a bankruptcy, with or without an attorney? (You can find out by calling your local legal aid society or by asking at a courthouse.)

Solve Problems

1. Your friend Mariana has trouble paying her bills. She has taken a second job in order to make all her payments, but the long hours and hard work are causing her health problems. What suggestions do you have in helping her manage her credit problems?
2. Mark and Janice have decided to get help with their credit problems rather than declare bankruptcy. They want to extend the time for repaying loans, but they don't want to hand over their checkbook and credit cards to a debt-adjustment service. What other options do they have?
3. Savath owns a small store. The store has been losing money for some time. Savath is the sole owner of the store, and his personal assets are the store's assets as well. Explain to Savath the differences among Chapter 7, 11, and 13 bankruptcy.
4. Tarrence and Keyondra Churchwell are considering bankruptcy. They have the following assets. How much (total) will they be allowed in exempted items?
   a. $34,000 equity in home
   b. $5,000 interest in motor vehicle
   c. $500 in household goods and furnishings, $2,000 in appliances, $1,000 in personal items and clothing, and $2,000 in musical instruments
   d. $8,000 in jewelry

5. M. J. Majesky has filed for bankruptcy and has the following debts. After the bankruptcy, which debts will remain?
  a. $500 owed to a chiropractor
  b. $300 owed in child support
  c. $870 owed in student loans
  d. $1,200 owed in back taxes
  e. $530 owed to a department store
  f. $650 owed to an automobile repair shop
  g. $950 owed to a jewelry store

6. Aruna Patel has the following assets. What amounts would be considered exempted items?
  a. $3,500 equity in a home
  b. $3,000 interest in a motor vehicle
  c. $150 in household furnishings
  d. $300 in appliances
  e. $150 in personal items
  f. $300 in a pet parrot
  g. $1,500 in musical instruments
  h. $300 in jewelry
  i. $600 in tools
  j. $15,000 life insurance proceeds
  k. $300 a month in unemployment insurance benefits

For related activities and links, point your browser to
www.mypf.swep.com

Unit *four* PROJECT

Managing Credit and Debt

Project

4

Previous unit projects concentrated on examining your financial position, building and protecting your savings and investments, and planning your retirement and estate. In this project, you will learn more about credit and debt load and how to protect yourself from fraudulent use of your credit cards.

Your Use of Credit

Credit will enable you to enjoy a standard of living that otherwise would not be possible. Nearly everyone uses credit. Wise consumers analyze their use of credit annually, comparing sources, interest rates, minimum payments, and other features (such as rebates) of accounts. Figure U4-1, on page 554, illustrates a worksheet for analyzing your creditworthiness. Complete this analysis with Worksheet 1 in the *Student Activity Guide* to give you an idea of how you are handling credit in your life.

When examining your use of credit, you may want to keep control sheets for tracking your progress in paying off debts. A sample control sheet is shown in Figure U4-2, on page 555. You can make similar sheets for each credit card or account to track each monthly payment. At the end of the year, you can total the finance charges. Keeping the control sheets will also help you see the cost of your credit card purchases. The amount of the finance charge is shown on the monthly statement from the creditor, along with the previous balance, payments and returns (credits), new charges (debits), and the new monthly balance.

Your Debt Load

A *debt load* is the amount of outstanding debt at a particular time. Whether your debt load is acceptable to you will depend on your ability to meet the regular payments, your ability to pay off the debt quickly if a need or reason arises, and your level of comfort with the amount of debt you owe.

Figure U4-3, on page 556, shows a worksheet for determining whether you have a comfortable debt load. One rule says that

Credit Analysis

Directions: List each type of credit you have and its features. Then complete the analysis to determine what action can and should be taken.

	Monthly Payment	No. of Payments Left	Outstanding Balance	APR	Special Features	Ranking
Installment credit:						
Personal loans:						
Automobile	_____	_____	_____	____	_____	_____
Home improvement	_____	_____	_____	____	_____	_____
Other: _____	_____	_____	_____	____	_____	_____
_____	_____	_____	_____	____	_____	_____
Charge accounts:						
1._____	_____		_____	____	_____	_____
2._____	_____		_____	____	_____	_____
3._____	_____		_____	____	_____	_____

Total debt outstanding . . . .$ _____

Average APR . . . . _____

How long will it take to pay off the outstanding debt? (Total outstanding debt divided by total monthly payments) _____

Which debts do you feel comfortable with? _____

Which debts do you feel uncomfortable with? _____

Which debts will you pay off first (those with lowest ranking)? _____

_____

What are some anticipated future debt needs? _____

_____

Which credit sources will you use for future debt (those with highest ranking)?

_____

Control Sheet:
VISA Account

(1) Date	(2) Previous Balance	(3) Payments (Credits)	(4) New Charges (Debits)	(5) Finance Charge	(6) New Balance (2 3 4 5)
1/1	$280.63	$35.00	$20.00	$7.22	$272.85
2/3	272.85	35.00	0	7.01	244.86
3/2	244.86	35.00	15.00	6.88	231.74
3/4	231.74	35.00	0	6.55	203.29

installment debt should not exceed 20 percent of yearly take-home pay. Another holds that you should be able to pay off all installment debts in one year at your current monthly payments. Still another says that you should be able to pay off your debts within 30 days if absolutely necessary (with all the cash you can raise).

Complete your debt-load analysis, using Worksheet 2 in the *Student Activity Guide*. Compute your self-score. If you sense trouble with debt, the solution is to pay off old debts before taking on new ones. Assessment of your debt load will help you find ways to correct the potential problems with debt. Debts are future earnings already spent. Unfortunately, many people never assess how much future income they have already committed to debt and whether the types and sources of credit they use are most advantageous to them.

Protection from Credit Fraud

The cost of credit card fraud is in excess of $3 billion a year and growing. Maybe you will never be a victim, but everyone pays for credit card fraud through higher interest charges, membership fees, and other costs that are passed along to customers.

To protect yourself, you should do the following:

1. Shred receipts and carbons so that numbers cannot be read.
2. Do not allow store clerks to write your credit card numbers and expiration dates on checks.
3. Pay cash in cases where you suspect your credit information may not be secure.
4. Never give credit information over the telephone or on the Internet to a person or company you do not know.

Your Debt Load

Directions: Answer the following statements with a "Yes" or "No." Then read the information following the statements to make an assessment of your debt load.

1. You pay only the minimum amount due each month on charge and credit accounts.   YES   NO

2. You make so many credit purchases that your debt load (total debts outstanding) never shrinks.   YES   NO

3. You are usually not able to make it until the end of the month and must borrow from savings.   YES   NO

4. You have borrowed from parents or others and do not have plans to repay the debt.   YES   NO

5. You are behind on one or more of your payments.   YES   NO

6. You worry about money often and are discouraged.   YES   NO

7. Money is a source of arguments and disagreements in your family.   YES   NO

8. You often juggle payments, paying one creditor while giving excuses to another.   YES   NO

9. You really don't know how much money you owe.   YES   NO

10. Your savings are slowly disappearing, and you are unable to save regularly.   YES   NO

11. You've taken out loans to pay off debts, or have debt consolidation loans.   YES   NO

12. You are at or near the limit of your credit lines on credit and charge accounts.   YES   NO

13. You worry more about the amount of the payment than the amount of interest (interest rate) you are paying on loans.   YES   NO

ASSESSMENT: Total number of "Yes" answers _____

If you answered yes to 8 or more statements, you need immediate action to correct your debt load. If you answered yes to 4–7 statements, you should seek to remedy the defects in your debt load soon. If you answered yes to 1–3 statements, you are in pretty good shape and can solve your debt problems. If you answered no to all the statements, congratulations—keep up the good work!

5. When shopping online, check for your browser's security icon to make sure your transaction will be encrypted.
6. Never sign blank credit slips, and draw a line through blank spaces when you sign.
7. Verify your monthly statements to be sure you have been properly charged.
8. Notify creditors in advance of an address change.
9. Never lend your credit cards to anyone.
10. Never put your account number on the outside of an envelope or on a postcard.
11. Use a separate credit card with a low credit limit for purchases from merchants you don't know, for use on the Internet, and for times when you feel uncomfortable with the situation. This way you minimize the fraud that could occur.

You can probably think of many more ways to protect yourself from credit fraud. One bad experience will convince you that it's worth your time and trouble to take precautions. After reading the description of the following credit practices that mislead many consumers every year, ask yourself how you can avoid becoming a victim.

Credit Repair Fraud

Phony credit repair companies guarantee you that they can fix your credit history, get you out of debt, or get credit cards for you. They often use 900 numbers so you can contact them. These services cost you a large fee even though they are often provided at no charge by credit bureaus, not-for-profit credit counseling services, and legitimate organizations that counsel you and help you reestablish your credit responsibly.

In reality, credit repair companies do not magically "fix" your credit history. Once you have a poor credit history, bankruptcy, or other negative information in your record, it cannot be removed or changed. Instead, these companies find other sources of credit you can apply for. They sell you a list of companies that will issue credit cards to people with poor or no credit ratings. You could do this research yourself. For example, you can buy a book that contains a list of reputable card issuers that offer reasonable interest and no annual fees.

Advance-Fee Loans

These advertisements guarantee you a loan after you have paid a fee in advance, claiming bad credit or no credit is not a problem. You may hear on television or radio a claim that "no applicant is ever turned down." But what really happens is this: The applicant fills out an application and pays the advance fee. The fee is often substantial—from $25 to $200. Then credit is arranged and all payments are closely monitored. The borrower is not allowed to get even one day behind on payments, or aggressive debt-collection practices begin.

A legitimate lender usually does not charge a fee for applying for open-ended credit, nor will the lender guarantee that you will qualify for credit. Whenever it seems too easy, there is likely a good reason to be suspicious.

Ethical Decisions

Ethics are principles of morality or rules of conduct. Ethical behavior conforms to these rules; unethical behavior violates them. You may have many opportunities to take advantage of other people. When these opportunities come your way, stop and think how you might feel if you were victimized. Figure U4-4, on page 559, lists some circumstances involving credit. Think about how you might react to each circumstance. Complete the situational analysis in Worksheet 3 in the *Student Activity Guide* to develop skill in analyzing ethical issues.

Situational Analysis

For each situation described below, explain how you would respond and why. What are the ethical issues involved in each decision?

1. You walk by an ATM in a mall. You see a bank debit card that was left there by a previous user. You look around and there is no one nearby to claim the card. If you leave it there, someone else may find it. What would you do?

2. You make a payment on your credit account at a customer service center. The worker, who is new and in training, accidentally credits your account for more than you paid. For example, you gave her $25 and she credited your account for $50. What would you do?

3. Someone you know returns merchandise to a store and gets a credit on his charge account, knowing that he purchased the merchandise elsewhere. What would you do?

4. Your friend frequently buys clothing on credit, wears it to a special event, and returns it to the store before the account is due, claiming the garment is damaged or dirty. She then receives a credit or a refund for the merchandise. What would you do?

Unit *five*

Resource Management

Chapters

Unit 5 begins with personal decision making, where you will learn how to make good decisions based on your needs and wants.

When you leave home for the first time, you will have many housing options from which to choose. But there's also a lot to learn about renting and buying a residence.

Buying a car takes thought and preparation. You'll consider all the costs—from depreciation to accessories—and you'll learn ways to maintain your car's resale value.

The chapter on family decisions covers a wide range of topics. You will begin with marriage. From there you will examine family financial responsibility, divorce, and the financial aspects related to the death of a family member.

Chapter 20

Personal Decision Making

Chapter 20

Terms to Know

basic needs
values
collective values
innovations
custom
economy

product advertising
target market
company
  advertising
industry advertising
odd-number pricing

loss leader
cherry picker
micromarketing

Up Front

Rosa is preparing to go to college in the fall and isn't sure what she'll do with her summer. She can work full time and save more money, or she can go out with her friends and enjoy the break between high school and college.

"Making this decision is really tough," Rosa thought. "I'd like to have a fun summer with my friends. On the other hand, if I work, I can set aside more money. This would help reduce my student loans and make college less stressful in terms of financing. For me, it's a toss-up. Most of my friends are taking the summer off, and I could join them for one last time. Part of me says that's the right thing to do, but then part of me says it would be more responsible to set money aside for the future."

Making Better Decisions

Goals

★ Apply the decision-making process to solve consumer problems.

★ Explain economic needs and wants that influence consumer decision making.

The Decision-Making Process

Buying decisions play an important role in your efforts to manage your personal finances. Each buying decision requires a trade-off between current spending and saving for the future. Good decisions can save you money; bad ones can be expensive—in both time and money. For this reason, you should approach your purchase decisions with a rational, step-by-step process that will lead you through defining your needs and evaluating alternatives before making a final choice.

Step 1: Define the Problem

The first step in the decision-making process is to define the problem to be solved. Once you have pinpointed it, you can look for ways to solve the problem in a manner that fits your financial resources.

Defining the problem is not as easy as it sounds. For example, let's say you need a computer to do schoolwork. But what *specific* needs does this computer have to fulfill? Do you need to be able to use your computer at home and at school? Will

Why should you approach your purchase decisions with a step-by-step process?

your schoolwork require the use of a CD-RW drive, or would you just like to have this feature if you can afford it? To truly define the problem to be solved, you must identify all the specific functions you need this product to perform now and in the foreseeable future. You must also distinguish between "wants" and "needs." Since your resources are limited, you may have to give up some wants in order to fulfill your needs.

If you can't define the problem, then perhaps you should think more carefully about spending your money. Would you be buying on impulse? How badly do you really need this item?

Step 2: Obtain Accurate Information

Once you have determined the problem, you must then gather information on possible solutions. List all alternative solutions and the cost of each. In the computer problem example, you might list these possible solutions:

1. Use a computer at school (on campus) or at a public library.
2. Rent a computer at a copy center or technology store.
3. Buy a new computer and printer.
4. Buy a used computer and printer.

To make a wise decision, you need to know what products and services are available that will meet your needs and how much each will cost to use or purchase. For instance, you need to know where computer labs are located on the school campus. The cost of use will include a lab fee as well as mileage to and from campus and the time involved. Most libraries have computers available for students or the public to use, and these machines also provide Internet access for research purposes. Or, you could go to a full-service copy center or technology store that rents the use of computers. There is usually an hourly fee, plus a charge for printed pages. Most also offer Internet access.

For the possible purchase of a new or used computer, you need to list desired features and then visit various computer stores, department stores, and discount stores in person or online for comparative shopping. At each location, you should make a note of the brands available, features, costs, and warranties. The classified ads and the Internet are good sources for used computers and printers.

The Internet makes comparison shopping easy. With the click of the mouse, you can go quickly from store to store without the time and expense of traveling. Plus, many sites offer price comparisons among merchants selling the same product. For example, if you want to compare computer prices, you could go to a site such as My Simon at www.mysimon.com. Enter "computer" in the search engine and have immediate access to product and price comparisons for all kinds of computer equipment. Online product reviews can also help you compare features and prices. For example, some computer publications such as PC Magazine at www.zdnet.com/pcmag/ constantly review computers and related equipment. Consumer Reports Online at www.consumerreports.org offers reviews of all kinds of products for the price of a subscription. Since Consumer Reports accepts no advertising, its product reviews lack the bias that could creep into reviews offered by commercial publications.

Keep a written record of the information you collect on choices of products and services. By doing so, you can compare alternatives and costs more easily. Figure 20-1 on page 566 shows information collected for comparison in the computer problem.

Step 3: Compare Choices

When comparing total costs, you should consider time and convenience as well as dollar costs. In some cases, convenience may be more important than cost, as long as the cost is reasonable. Using the computer example, you may decide that the convenience of having your own computer is worth the extra dollar cost. You may also decide that even though the cost of owning a new computer will be greater, you prefer to avoid the uncertainty of possible repairs on used equipment. Purchasing used computers and printers is riskier because previous owners may not have maintained them properly.

Also, as your computer skills increase, you may find home as well as school uses for a computer. If so, buying may be a better decision for you than renting. You must weigh these kinds of factors along with dollar costs when comparing choices.

Modern technology services offer many advantages to consumers, but consumers should first make sure they can afford them. Check for hidden fees. Installation, monthly hardware rental fees, and cancellation fees can mount up. Often providers offer an incentive discount for signing up, but the real rate starts a few months later. Know what the total costs will be before you make a financial commitment.

Figure 20-1 *Information on Comparison Shopping*

	Per Month	**Per Year**
Option 1. Use a public/school computer lab		
Time: 5 hours each weekend	20 hours	240 hours
Gas: 6-mile round-trip each weekend	$3.00	$36.00
Lab Fee: $15 per year	1.25	15.00
Paper (1 ream per month)	3.00	36.00
	$7.25	$87.00
Option 2. Rent a machine at a copy center		
Time: 5 hours each weekend	20 hours	240 hours
Gas: 20-mile round-trip each weekend	$ 10.00	$ 120.00
Fee: $6 per hour	120.00	1,440.00
Cost of printing: $.10 per page	50.00	600.00
	$180.00	$2,160.00
Option 3. Buy a new computer and printer		
With student discount, laptop and printer	$800 cash or $900 financed	
Payments on one-year loan at 9%	$ 75.00	$ 900.00
Internet service provider charge	21.95	263.40
Paper (1 ream per month)	3.00	36.00
Toner for printer (2 per year at $30 each)	5.00	60.00
	$104.95	$1,259.40
Option 4. Buy a used computer and printer		
From private individual ($300 one-time cost)		$300.00
Internet service provider charge	$21.95	$263.40
Paper (1 ream per month)	3.00	36.00
Toner for printer (2 per year at $30 each)	5.00	60.00
	$29.95	$659.40

(plus cost of repairs or maintenance
if needed—no warranty)

Step 4: Make a Decision

If you follow the steps outlined in the preceding paragraphs, the decision you make will be based on a careful analysis of the problem, thorough information gathering, and analysis of that information. The wise decision in any situation is the one that best meets your needs, is within your budget, and gives you the most value for your dollar investment. Take the time you need to carefully evaluate the information you gathered about each choice before you make a decision, especially for expensive or complex products.

Step 5: Take Action

After you have selected the best choice, you must take action to implement your chosen solution. Because you have made a thorough analysis of choices for solving your problem, you can be sure that you have made the best decision you could with the available information.

Step 6: Re-evaluate

After several months have passed, revisit your decision. Are you happy with the choice you made? If not, what could you do differently next time to make a better decision? Should you do something different now? If your needs have changed or your initial decision isn't working out, go through the decision-making process again to decide whether to make a change.

Reflect on decisions you have made in the past. Do you now regret some of your decisions? If so, did you use the decision-making process or did you buy the first model you saw? While using a decision-making process won't make every decision perfect, it will help you make better decisions in the important aspects of your life.

Economic Wants and Needs

Basic needs are the ingredients necessary for maintaining physical life. They include food and water, shelter, and clothing. Some people would add safety and security to this list. Until people have met their basic needs, they have little need for anything else life has to offer.

Life-enhancing wants include, but are not limited to, the following:

1. Food, clothing, and shelter beyond what is necessary for biological survival.
2. Medical care to improve the quality and length of life.
3. Education to achieve personal goals, both social and economic.
4. Travel, vacations, and recreation to improve personal enjoyment of life.
5. Gadgetry or extra items to make life more fun and give it extra excitement or challenge.

You may have decided that many life-improving items are necessary for your happiness. But you must admit that they are really *wants,* not *needs.* You do not *need* them for your physical survival. You may simply have become used to them and therefore expect to have them.

Individual Wants

Beyond the basics, what you decide you want depends on a number of factors, including those discussed below. These factors are different among individuals and societies. All factors may change at different points in your life.

1. *Values.* Each person has his or her own set of values. **Values** are the principles by which a person lives. Different people value things differently. One person may highly value education. Someone else may highly value time with family. You make economic choices based on your values. For example, if you highly value education, you will probably decide to save a large portion of your income for college. The person who highly values time with family may choose to save toward a family vacation.

2. *Personal Preferences.* Personal preferences or *tastes* are your likes and dislikes. One person may enjoy a weekend alone in the mountains hiking, while another would choose a visit to Disneyland. Based on personal preferences, you make economic choices. You spend your money for things consistent with your personal tastes.

3. *Income.* The amount you earn will influence the type of consumer choices you can make. As you learned in Chapter 10, *discretionary income* is the money left over after you have paid your expenses. This is the money you can spend or save as you wish. The more discretionary income you have, the higher the quality and quantity of products you can consider. The ability to afford goods and services to fulfill the wants you consider important will affect your satisfaction with employment, your personal life, your goals, and other personal factors such as self-esteem. For example, if owning a lot of expensive "things" is important to you, then you may pursue educational goals that will likely land you a high-paying job.

4. *Leisure Time.* The amount of free time you have and the kinds of activities you enjoy also affect how you choose to spend your discretionary income. Retired people have a large amount of leisure time, so their wants are likely to include recreational spending for such things as travel and sportswear. If you enjoy skiing in your spare time, you will likely choose to spend your money on skis, lift passes, and ski apparel.

COMMUNICATION CONNECTION

Write a paragraph about each of the values that are important to you. Why is it important to consider your values when making decisions?

Collective Values

Collective values are those things important to society as a whole; all citizens share in their costs and in their benefits. The society in which you live influences your values, goals, and choices because it demands responsibility and accountability from citizens.

1. *Legal Protection.* One of the collective values a society shares is the desire for preserving legal and personal rights and being protected from others who would violate those rights. Law enforcement is the result of society's collective value for protection of citizens and property.
2. *Employment.* Most people who are able will work because it is expected and demanded in order to survive in this society. Most of us are aware of this subtle, yet very real, pressure to perform in the work arena. Therefore, we strive to do the best we can and to get a job that pays well for the effort we put forth. In this way, we can be personally satisfied with our productivity and at the same time satisfy society's demand for citizens who contribute.
3. *Progress.* The relative state of progress of the country in which you live (its technological advances and perceptions about the importance of those advances) will affect your purchase decisions. United States society is technologically advanced and places a high value on innovations. **Innovations** are new ideas, methods, or devices that bring about changes in the way we live. If you are like most Americans, you will likely buy products that offer the latest innovations.

What are collective values?

4. *Quality of Environment.* Natural resources are of great value and concern to society as a whole because they are very limited, and some cannot be replaced. Because of our collective priority of preserving a quality environment for ourselves and future generations, our society supports activities such as land-use planning, preserving natural beauty and wildlife, and establishing air pollution standards. We also expect producers to minimize the environmental damage caused by the production of their products and services. Environmental quality is important to society as a whole, and individuals respond to this concern by acting and purchasing accordingly.

5. *Public and Government Services.* Our country is organized to be "of the people, by the people, and for the people." We have a highly advanced and intricate system of government made up of the people, performing services for the people, with money contributed (through taxes) by the people. Our system of taxation takes money from those who have it and redistributes it to those who need it. Americans place high value on government-provided services for all citizens, from police protection to public parks.

✓ Check Your Understanding

Review Terms

1. basic needs
2. values
3. collective values
4. innovations

Review Concepts

1. How can the Internet help you gather information about different purchase options?
2. What should you consider in addition to dollar cost when comparing the total costs of alternative solutions?

Lesson 20.2 Spending Habits

Goals

★ List and describe factors that influence spending decisions.
★ Analyze marketing strategies that influence spending decisions.

Factors that Influence Spending

Consumer purchasing decisions are influenced by personal factors and by outside factors that work together and separately as incentives or deterrents to spending. When you plan a major purchase, you need to examine your motives to make sure you are buying for your own reasons and not because of outside influences that are not in your best interest.

Personal Factors

Many personal factors influence consumer spending decisions. Personal factors include such things as personal resources; position in life; customs, background, and religion; and values and goals.

1. *Personal Resources.* Your personal resources include your time, money, energy, skills and abilities, and available credit. The greater the quantity and the higher the quality of any one of these factors, the greater your purchasing power. For example, the amount of time you have available to compare prices and options before purchasing a product (time quantity) will affect your ability to make wise buying decisions. The job skills you possess will affect the amount of money you can earn and, consequently, your purchasing power.
2. *Position in Life.* Your position in life includes such factors as age, marital status, gender, employment status, and lifestyle. Spending patterns of single people are different from those of married couples and families. For example, a new parent will spend on baby products. Women will buy different kinds of clothes than do men.
3. *Customs, Background, and Religion.* A **custom** is a long-established practice that takes on the force of an unwritten law. Families may be faithful to traditions that their

571

Personal Decision Making

members have followed for generations. Cultures as well as religious and other groups share common customs. For example, people of a culture or religious group may observe special holidays that are not observed nationally. The customs of the groups to which you belong will influence your buying patterns.

4. *Values and Goals.* Values are deep-seated and slow to change, but they do change over time. Goals change often. You accomplish one goal and then move on to others. Your total value system may change as your goals in life are met or not met. Individual and family values and goals are expressed through choices of entertainment, literature, sports, luxuries, and so on. These choices are reflected in decisions to purchase goods and services, use of time and energy, and attitudes toward possessions and their accumulation.

Outside Factors

Factors outside yourself also affect your spending patterns. These include the economy, technological advances, the environment, and social pressures.

1. *The Economy.* The **economy** refers to all activities related to production and distribution of goods and services in a geographic area. Economists measure economic activity in different ways to describe the financial well-being of the nation. The general condition of the economy affects every one of us, and we react to it accordingly. For example, when interest rates on car loans are high, fewer people buy new cars. Consequently, older cars are kept longer. When the economy is strong and growing, people are more optimistic and willing to spend money more freely. When the economy is slowing down or in a recession, people hold back on buying items that can be postponed, such as luxury goods.

2. *Technological Advances.* You may be fascinated with new electronic games. Or you may be interested in the world's first mass-market electric-powered car. Perhaps you want to add a new solar heating device to your home to make it more energy efficient. Many Americans place a high value on new

technological advances. Many people want to have the newest, most convenient, modern, and interesting gadgets. As new goods and services are created to raise our standard of living, many people willingly purchase them.

3. *The Environment.* Concern for the environment can affect buying decisions. Citizens are concerned with home projects, community activities, and statewide programs to beautify and preserve, recycle, and protect existing resources and the environment. Thus, this interest in the environment affects consumers' actions and also their product preferences. People are buying more products that are ecologically safe, biodegradable, or recyclable.

4. *Social Pressures.* Social pressures often induce consumers to buy goods and services beyond their ability to pay. Your friends, relatives, and co-workers all influence your buying decisions. The media (radio, television, newspapers) also act as sources of social pressure for consumers. Through advertising, the media convince consumers to buy goods and services designed to keep them young, good-looking, and healthy.

Planning Major Purchases

Because major purchases generally tie up future income or take a big bite out of accumulated savings, carefully consider your needs and wants before committing to a large purchase. Ask yourself these questions, take time to reflect on your answers, and then make a final decision based on a rational—not emotional—perspective.

1. Why do I need or want this product?
2. How long will this product last?
3. What substitutes are available and at what cost?

4. By postponing this purchase, is it likely that I will choose not to buy it later?
5. What types of additional costs are involved, such as supplies, maintenance, insurance, and financial risks?
6. For what other purposes might I use the money spent or committed for this purchase?
7. What is the total cost of this product (cash price, deferred price, interest, shipping charges, and so on)?

Once you have made a decision that you will purchase the good or service, you need to determine whether to pay cash or use credit. Even though you may have the cash available, you should not automatically pay cash for all purchases. If you do, your cash reserves will dwindle, or you may have to do without many conveniences you could have now with wise use of credit. Figure 20-2 shows a comparison of various options available for buying a refrigerator, with positive and negative consequences.

Comparison shopping will allow you to determine whether you are getting the best quality for the price you are paying. The same brand often sells at considerably different prices at different retailers, depending on the seller's markups. By shopping various retail outlets you may be able to save money. In addition, many stores

Figure 20-2   *Cash or Credit Purchase?*

Item	Cash	Credit
Refrigerator		
Price	$800 + $15 delivery charge	$50/month ($900 total) + $15 delivery charge
Total cost	$815	$915
Substitute Used refrigerator		
Price	$400 + $15 delivery charge	$30/month for 15 months + $15 delivery charge
Total cost	$415	$465
Considerations	Ties up cash; cannot make other purchases. No monthly payments. Reduces savings balance. No interest charges.	Allows for budgeting; ties up future income. Can make other purchases. Establishes credit. Interest charged.

Resource Management

offer sale prices at various times of the year or at regular intervals. Before making a major purchase, ask if and when the merchandise will be placed on sale.

Take advantage of store policies that will refund part of your purchase price if the item you bought goes on sale within the next two weeks or month. This policy, together with a liberal return policy, should greatly affect your choice of merchants. For example, a store that allows you to return a gift or other purchase within a reasonable period of time (a month or more) is much better than a store that will not accept returns or give refunds.

The fact that you are paying a high price does not necessarily mean you are getting the best quality merchandise. It pays to be aware of what is good quality and what you should expect from the merchandise. The nonprofit Consumers Union tests the quality of many products and compares different brands. It publishes the results in its *Consumer Reports* print and online magazine. You can also find product reviews in specialty magazines and Web sites. For example, *Backpacker* magazine reviews outdoor equipment. However, keep in mind that reviews by for-profit organizations could be influenced by the manufacturers who advertise in the magazine or Web site. Especially for major purchases, check reviews in several sources before making your choice.

Marketing Strategies that Influence Spending

Numerous marketing strategies lure us into stores to buy goods and services. Many of these strategies are subtle, and we are often unaware of their impact on our buying patterns.

+PROS and CONS

When does the gathering and use of information about individuals constitute an invasion of privacy? This includes data gathered from mail orders, telephone records, credit card purchases, banking and Internet transactions, and numerous other electronic activities that occur daily. Most major companies do keep databases of information about their customers. These businesses profile their customers and target new customers with similar traits.

Think Critically: Do you object to information being gathered about your personal buying habits? If so, why? Do you feel that consumers should have control over how personal information about them is collected and used? Do you think that new privacy protection laws are needed to regulate the use of information in the computer age?

Advertising

The primary goal of all advertising is to create within the consumer the desire to purchase a product or service. Some advertising is false and misleading; other advertising is informational and valuable.

Advertising appears in variety of media (billboards, television, radio, Internet, newspapers, magazines, leaflets, balloons, and t-shirts), all carefully coordinated to reach specific consumer groups. Advertising agencies create colorful and attractive campaigns. They hire well-known athletes and role models, compose catchy jingles, develop slogans and trademarks, design colorful logos, and choose mascots to identify their products. There are three basic types of advertising: product, company, and industry.

1. *Product Advertising.* Advertising intended to convince consumers to buy a specific good or service is called **product advertising.** Advertisers often repeat the product name several times during commercials to help consumers remember it. Famous athletes, actors, authors, or other personalities are often hired to use the product. Testimonials from people who have used the product, giveaways, promotional gimmicks, and other clever and catchy methods are used to persuade consumers to purchase products and services. Advertisements are carefully planned to appeal to certain types of consumers. A **target market** is the specific consumer group to which the advertisements are designed to appeal. Television advertisers consider the day of the week, time of day, and type of program when placing their product ads. Products advertised during football games differ from products advertised during daytime television because the target markets are different.

2. *Company Advertising.* Advertising intended to promote the image of a store, company, or retail chain is known as **company advertising.** This type of advertising usually does not mention specific products or prices. Instead, it emphasizes the overall quality and reliability of the company and its products. For example, a company ad might feature company-sponsored environmental or community projects. A store ad might talk about the company's friendly employees, its wide selection of products or services, or its claim that you can find everything you want in one place. These advertisements are designed to promote a favorable attitude toward the company so that you develop a loyalty to the store and shop there frequently.

3. *Industry Advertising.* Advertising intended to promote a general product group without regard to where these products are purchased is called **industry advertising.** For example, the dairy industry emphasizes the nutritional value of milk and other natural dairy products. Consequently, the whole dairy industry benefits when people drink more milk and eat more dairy products. Often, industry advertisements stress concern about energy conservation, environmental protection, and the search for new alternative forms of fuels. General health and safety advertisements are often presented in industry advertising campaigns, such as ads by the tobacco industry that discourage teen smoking.

Pricing

The price of merchandise depends on several factors. Supply and demand determine what will be produced and the general price range. The cost of raw materials and labor, competitive pressures, and the seller's need to make a reasonable profit are some of the factors that determine the price of a product. But there is more to pricing than adding up the production costs and including a profit. Retailers understand the psychological aspects of selling goods and services and use pricing devices to persuade consumers to buy. For example, if buyers believe they are getting a bargain or think they are paying a lower price than they really are, they are more inclined to buy the product or service. **Odd-number pricing** is the practice of setting prices at uneven amounts rather than whole dollars to make them seem lower. For example, the price tag might read 99 cents instead of $1.00. Because the price is under a dollar, it seems lower. Consumers perceive a price of $5.98 to be significantly lower than $6.00. As a result, they are more likely to buy the product at $5.98 than at $6.00.

Discounts or low unit prices are often available for buying in large sizes or quantities. However, you cannot assume that because you are buying the large economy size you are actually paying less per ounce than if you bought a small size. Compare unit prices on all sizes.

Sales

Stores advertise end-of-month sales, anniversary sales, clearance sales, inventory sales, holiday sales, pre-season sales, and so on. They may mark down merchandise substantially, slightly, or not at all. In order to be sure that you are actually saving money by buying sale items, you must practice comparative shopping and know the usual prices. When an advertisement states that everything in the store is marked down, check carefully for items that only appear to be marked down in price.

A **loss leader** is an item of merchandise marked down to an unusually low price, sometimes below the store's cost. The store may actually lose money on every sale of this item because the cost of producing the item is higher than the retail price. However, they use the loss leader to get customers into the store in the hope that they will buy other products as well. Profits from the sale of other items are expected to make up for the loss sustained on the loss leader. There is nothing illegal or unethical about a loss leader as long as the product advertised is available to the customer on demand. A customer who buys only loss leaders is called a **cherry picker.** Retailers rely on customers to buy other products to make up for the loss on loss leaders, so they are not fond of cherry pickers.

How can you ensure that you are actually saving money by buying sale items?

Promotional Techniques

To lure customers into their stores, retailers may use promotional techniques, such as displays, contests and games, frequent-buyer cards, coupons, packaging, sampling, and micromarketing.

1. *Displays.* Retail stores often use window displays and special racks of new items to entice customers. Products are arranged attractively, and the promotion may carry a theme centered on the nearest holiday—Halloween, Thanksgiving, or Christmas, for example. Color schemes, decorations, music, and special effects often set off the products being offered in a way that will attract attention.

2. *Contests and Games.* Grocery stores, department stores, fast-food restaurants, and other retail stores that depend on repeat customers often use contests and games to bring cus-

tomers into the store. Individual product packages, such as cereal boxes, may contain game cards. The possibility of winning something or getting something for nothing appeals to many people. Large and small prizes are offered with the intention of getting customers to come back and buy more so they can get more game cards, have more chances to win, and receive some of the minor prizes. Careful reading of the rules on the game card or other token reveals the customer's chances of winning. Usually, the chances of winning a major prize are small.

3. *Coupons. Manufacturer coupons* offer cents off on specifically described products from a specific manufacturer and may be redeemed wherever the product is sold. *Store coupons* offer discounts on specific products, usually for a short period of time, and only at a specific store. Manufacturer and store coupons may be inside or outside the package, in newspapers or magazines, on a store shelf, or even online. Coupons may not be redeemed for cash but do reduce the price of the product when purchased, encouraging customers to buy this product over a competitor's. Stores that accept manufacturer coupons return the coupons to the manufacturer for a refund of the amount given to the customer.

When using coupons, read the fine print. Some coupons may restrict the days or hours when they may be used or the locations where they are accepted. In addition, some coupons may not be applied in combination with other discounts.

4. *Frequent-Buyer Cards.* Some stores use frequent-buyer cards that they punch with each purchase. Customers who accumulate enough punches can redeem the cards for merchandise. Frequent-buyer cards are used to build customer loyalty and repeat business for future purchases.

5. *Packaging.* Packages do more than just protect the product inside. They are also promotional tools. Manufacturers design packaging to appeal to the eye as well as provide the necessary consumer information. Distinctively designed packages attract the customer's attention away from competitive products. Company logos, brightly colored designs, pictures of people happily using the product, and other

attention-getters may appear on product boxes. Packaging emphasizes special features, such as "sugar free," "no preservatives," "new and improved," and many others. Manufacturers know that the package must be attractive because it plays such an important role in inducing purchases. Size and shape of packages are significant. Containers that appear to hold more of the product or are reusable as storage devices also attract consumers. Boxes that contain a game or prize inside will say so prominently on the outside of the box. Coupons may be included inside or on the package.

6. *Sampling.* Many companies promote their products through sampling. Small sample-size free packages of a product may be sent directly to households, included with newspapers delivered to consumers' homes, or distributed within a store or shopping center. When a new product is first introduced into the marketplace, sampling enables potential customers to try the new product. Some companies advertise in magazines and newspapers, with offers for free samples by mail.

7. *Micromarketing.* Many companies buy information about consumers in order to target promotions to those who are most likely to buy their products. Information about a person's lifestyle, marital status, family, age, and buying habits is known as *psychographics.* Micromarketers gather this information from previous purchases using credit cards or checks, public information, and other sources that are provided by government, the post office, banks, and credit bureaus. Internet stores can also discover your preferences by electronically tracking your progress around the site. The product pages you view give the store a sense of the kinds of products that interest you. The purpose of gathering this kind of information is to target you with promotions for specific products and services that will likely interest you.

While mass marketing is designed to reach millions at once through television ads, coupons, and other techniques, **micromarketing** is a marketing strategy designed to target specific people or small groups with products that they are likely to want. For example, when a couple has their first child, they are likely to receive advertisements, samples, and coupons for baby products. The birth record of the child is public information, and micromarketers gather it to find out who is most likely to want baby products. Targeted promotions make marketing more efficient. Rather than pay the cost of mailing samples of baby products to everyone, baby-product manufacturers can send samples only to consumers with babies.

Check Your Understanding

Review Terms

1. custom
2. economy
3. product advertising
4. target market
5. company advertising
6. industry advertising
7. odd-number pricing
8. loss leader
9. cherry picker
10. micromarketing

Review Concepts

1. How do social pressures affect your buying habits?
2. Why do companies use micromarketing?

PERSONAL PERSPECTIVE

Micromarketing, Internet-Style

If you have ever purchased a product from an online retailer, then you have registered with the site and provided some information about yourself. The next time you visit, the site may present you with suggestions for products. The products may be companions to your previous purchase or products similar to items you are currently browsing at the site. How does the Web site know who you are and what you like?

When you register with an online retailer—and sometimes even when you don't—the site places a cookie, or small data file, on your computer. The next time you visit the site, the cookie sends the stored information about you back to the site. This way, the site can recognize its returning customer. As you travel around the site, the cookie keeps track of the product pages you visit. The online retailer is building a database of your preferences. This is micromarketing, Internet-style. The advertising targets you, a target market of one customer. This custom tailoring benefits you in that the ads you see really might interest you. It benefits the retailer by increasing the chances of making another sale to you.

With your e-mail address provided in your registration, the retailer can also send you advertising by e-mail. By knowing your product interests, the retailer can inform you of special offers on related products.

Internet micromarketing has its dark side—privacy concerns. The same technology that allows legitimate retailers to personalize their site for you can also be used by hackers to steal information from you. Also, reputable sites have privacy policies that promise to protect your information. But what happens to your data if the company goes out of business? Some companies sell their customer databases to other companies. Consumers don't have much control over the distribution of their personal information gathered online.

Think Critically

1. Suppose you bought a music CD at an online music store. The next time you visited, the site popped up a list of similar music CDs for your consideration, including some at a special low price. Is this kind of service worth the possible loss of privacy to you? Explain.
2. Would you like to receive e-mail advertising? How is this kind of advertising like or unlike advertising delivered by U.S. mail?

20.1 Making Better Decisions

- The decision-making process typically involves six steps: define the problem, obtain accurate information, compare alternatives, select an alternative, take action, and reevaluate. Following this process will help you make rational, rather than emotional, decisions.
- Basic survival needs include food, clothing, and shelter. Everything else is a "want" rather than a "need."
- Beyond the basics, your wants are shaped by such factors as your values, personal preferences, income, and leisure time.
- Collective or societal values that affect spending habits include the need for legal protection, employment, progress (buying the latest innovations), maintaining or improving the quality of the environment, and providing public goods and services.

20.2 Spending Habits

- Personal factors that influence individual spending habits include personal resources (time, energy, skills, and credit); position in life (age, marital status, and employment status); customs, religion, and background; and values and goals.
- Factors outside yourself that affect your spending habits include the financial health of the economy, advances in technology, the environment, and social pressures.
- When planning major purchases—those that tie up future income—you should make sure you want the product for rational rather than emotional reasons. Then take the time to research the product through reviews and price comparisons before buying.

- Advertising seeks to create a desire to purchase goods and services.
- Product advertising promotes a specific product to its target market (people who are likely to buy it).
- Company advertising promotes a company image and seeks to instill a positive attitude about the company.
- Industry advertising promotes a general product group, such as milk or meat, to benefit all sellers in that industry.
- Marketers price products to induce people to buy their products over a competitor's. Consumers perceive prices stated in uneven amounts (odd-number pricing) as lower than they really are. Loss leaders are products priced very low, often below cost, to lure customers to the store, hoping to then sell them other products at a profit.
- Promotional techniques to increase spending include displays in the store, contests and games, coupons, frequent-buyer cards, attractive packaging, sampling, and micromarketing.

Review Terms

Directions: Can you find the definition for each of the following terms used in Chapter 20?

basic needs
cherry picker
collective values
company advertising
custom
economy
industry advertising
innovations
loss leader

micromarketing
odd-number pricing
product advertising
target market
values

1. Ingredients necessary for maintaining physical life.
2. Things that are important to society as a whole; all citizens share in their benefit and in their cost.
3. Merchandise marked down to a very low price, often below the store's cost.
4. The practice of setting prices at uneven amounts rather than whole dollars to make them seem lower.
5. New ideas, methods, or devices that bring about changes in a society's way of life.
6. A long-established practice that takes on the force of an unwritten law.
7. All activities related to production and distribution of goods and services in a geographic area.
8. Advertising that attempts to convince consumers to buy a specific good or service.
9. Advertising intended to promote the image of a store, company, or retail chain.
10. The specific consumer group to whom an advertisement is designed to appeal.
11. Advertising that attempts to sell a general product group without regard to where these products are purchased.
12. A person who buys only the store's loss leaders.
13. The principles by which a person lives.
14. A marketing strategy designed to target specific people or small groups with products that they are likely to want.

Review Facts and Ideas

1. List and describe the six steps in the decision-making process.
2. How can the Internet help you comparison shop?
3. What is the difference between basic needs and wants?
4. Why is it important to distinguish between wants and needs when defining the problem in a buying decision?
5. What are some personal factors that influence a person's or a family's spending patterns?
6. How do your values affect your use of money?
7. What are some outside factors that determine a person's or family's spending patterns?
8. For major purchases, why should you check reviews from more than one source before making a decision?
9. List six different advertising media. Which are mass media?
10. Why do companies use odd-number pricing?
11. Why aren't retailers fond of cherry pickers?
12. On what theme do promotional displays often center?
13. What is the purpose of frequent-buyer cards?
14. What are two functions of a product's package?
15. What is the purpose of micromarketing?

1. Using the steps in the decision-making process, make a decision that will satisfy your need for a CD player.

2. Use key words to search the Internet for a price comparison site. Go to one of the sites you find. Then request a price comparison for a product you are interested in. What range of prices did the search engine find for the same product? What other features does the price comparison site offer to help you research and select products?

3. How do your spending patterns differ from those of your parents? What things do you buy that your parents also purchase? Can you trace any of these purchases to a strong family custom, background, or religion?

4. How are you or the members of your family affected when interest rates are very high? Do you benefit, or are you hurt? How? Can you think of anyone who is affected in the opposite way from you? Why is this so?

5. What community-centered and national environmental concerns do you have? What can you do as a single concerned citizen to help preserve the quality of the environment?

6. Spend an evening viewing television. List the jingles, key words, and slogans used in each commercial. How many commercials can you automatically sing along with? Also list the celebrities you saw in the ads and the products they promoted. Why do you think each celebrity was chosen for that particular product?

7. Log onto the Internet. What advertisements appear on your home page? Do they seem targeted to you? Next, surf around a well-known online store. What products are advertised on each page you visit? Why do you think the retailer chose to advertise those particular products in those places?

8. Look around at some different types of Internet advertising. What kinds of things can advertisers do with their ads online that they cannot do in a print magazine? Do you think Internet advertising is as effective at getting customers to buy as advertising on television? Why or why not?

Solve Problems

1. Think of a major purchase that you would like to make if you could. Then follow the steps in the decision-making process up to the point of taking action. Write a description of what you did at each step. Include cost and feature comparisons where appropriate. What specific model and brand would you buy? Why?

2. Watch a television program for one hour anytime during the day. Determine the program's target audience (teenagers, children, homemakers, sports fans, families, adults). Pay close attention to all commercials shown during the hour. Write your answers to the following questions on a separate piece of paper.
   a. List all the commercials. Categorize them as either product, company, or industry advertising. (Public-service advertisements and political campaigns are industry advertisements.)
   b. Rate each commercial as good, fair, or poor, depending upon how well it is directed to the television program's target audience.
   c. Rate each commercial according to tastefulness (either good taste or poor taste). Do you find it offensive, degrading, insulting? Explain why you liked or disliked the commercial.
   d. Which ads were most effective? Why?

3. Bring to class an advertising insert from a newspaper. It should be from a department store, local discount store, or grocery store. Write your answers to these questions on a separate piece of paper:
   a. How many individual advertisements show odd-number pricing?
   b. How many mention how much money the buyer will save or what the regular price is?

c. How many contained coupons or references to coupons?

d. Which ones mentioned frequent-buyer cards, games, or special incentives?

e. Is the insert attractively presented? Rate each ad for attractiveness and readability.

f. Identify any loss leaders.

Attach the advertising insert to your answers. On the insert, write comments next to the items to identify them as examples of loss leaders, odd-number pricing, and so on.

4. Describe a store display built around the theme of the most recent major holiday. Describe colors used, products displayed, product arrangement, location in the store, and other aspects. Were there any actual price reductions?

5. List any stores in your area that use one or more of the following promotional techniques. Beside each store name, describe the specific techniques used.

a. Contests and games

b. Frequent-buyer cards

c. Coupons

d. Sampling

e. Other

6. Find an appealing advertisement on the Internet and click on it. Then answer the following questions:

a. What product or service is the advertiser selling?

b. How does the advertiser's site set-up help you learn more about the product or service?

c. How can you order the product or service?

d. Did the company give you a way to contact it for additional information?

e. Would you buy this product or service? Why or why not?

For related activities and links, point your browser to
www.mypf.swep.com

Chapter 21

Renting a Residence

dormitory
efficiency apartment
security deposit
fee

landlord
tenant
lease
eviction

Up Front

Ichiro was finishing his sophomore year in college, and at age 20, he was able to make housing choices. During his first two years, he had lived in university housing.

"We have lots of important decisions to make," he told his roommate. "We could stay right here in the dorm, but that may not be our best bet. Living off-campus has advantages, but there are also some variables that we haven't been concerned about living here. For example, we'll have to pay separate utility bills, and we'll need transportation to get to class. Parking is limited on campus, too. To afford to rent a house, we'd have to take in a few more people. But this is also pretty exciting, and I'm looking forward to the change."

Housing Decisions

Goals

★ Describe the various housing rental alternatives, including commuting to school or work from home, living on campus, apartments, duplexes, and houses.

★ Discuss potential living arrangements and decisions related to moving choices.

Housing Alternatives

When you complete high school and reach the age of adulthood, you will face important decisions. One of the first will be where to live. If you will be attending a college that is close by, you may want to live at your parents' home and commute to campus each day. Many students and young adults choose to continue living with their parents for a short time because the lower costs help them save money toward getting a place of their own. Even when parents charge a monthly rent or other amount to help defray costs, it is usually less expensive to commute than to move out on your own.

Once you reach the age of adulthood, what are some different housing alternatives open to you?

COMMUNICATION CONNECTION

Would you consider living with your family after you finish high school? Write a one-page report on what you see as the advantages and disadvantages of this living arrangement. Would your parents agree with you?

On-Campus Housing

Many college students prefer to live on campus. A **dormitory** is an on-campus building that contains many small rooms that colleges rent to students. The rooms usually contain beds, dressers, closets, and study areas. Typically, you would have a roommate, or for an extra charge, you might be able to have your own private room. Most dormitories have centrally located lounges for watching television and facilities for doing laundry. Dormitories provide a convenient location, plus eating facilities, with the meals included in the cost. Although individual rooms are small, with limited space for living and studying, the cost per school term may be less than for other housing alternatives.

Many colleges have sororities and fraternities that provide on-campus housing. To live in one of their buildings, you would have to become a member in a process called *pledging*. Typically, sororities and fraternities seek new members with goals, abilities, and ideals similar to those of the organization. For example, some require a certain grade point average. Others look for an interest in community service.

Housing cooperatives are also available on many larger campuses. When you live in a cooperative, you get a room similar to one in a dormitory. But the difference is in your responsibilities. In addition to keeping your room clean and usable, you share in cooking, cleaning, and maintaining the building. In exchange, your monthly rent is less because you help provide services for yourself and the group.

Major advantages of on-campus housing include closeness to classes and campus activities, access to campus resources such as a library and health center, and a feeling of being a part of campus life. On the other hand, students pay a flat fee for housing and meals, often a term or semester in advance, and do not have the opportunity to budget their resources.

Apartments

If you don't attend college, or you don't want to live in a dormitory, then your first residence away from home will likely be an apartment. At this stage of your life, your resources will probably be tight. The rent amount is usually based on the size and quality of the apartment and facilities provided, as well as distance to downtown jobs, college campuses, and shopping centers. You can find apartments in your chosen area in brochures, newspaper ads, and online.

An **efficiency apartment,** or *studio apartment*, is an apartment with one large room that serves as the kitchen, living room, and bedroom, plus a bathroom. Efficiencies have less living space than other apartments, but they are the least expensive. Larger apartments with separate living and dining areas are available in a variety of floor plans, including two-story models, called *townhouses.*

Apartments are usually located in multi-unit buildings in which the number of units may be as few as two or as many as several hundred. Facilities provided may include a laundry room, storage area, swimming pool, tennis courts, and clubhouse. In addition, all or part of the utilities (heat, light, and garbage service) may be included in the rent payment.

Apartments provide independence and flexibility but also require responsibility and good judgment. Most apartment buildings have rules that make close living more enjoyable for all, such as no pets, no music or noise after 11 p.m., and restricted hours for use of some facilities, such as a pool.

Duplexes

As you learned in Chapter 14, a *duplex* is a building with two separate living quarters. Usually both living areas of the house are exactly the same, but there are separate entrances for each. Duplexes usually offer more space than apartments and more privacy, with only one close neighbor. They may include a garage or carport, private laundry facilities, and other privileges and responsibilities similar to a house. For example, an apartment renter is not expected to perform maintenance activities; a duplex renter, however, may be expected to mow the grass and maintain the landscaping surrounding the unit.

Condominiums

As you recall from Chapter 14, a *condominium* is an individually owned unit in an apartment-style complex with shared ownership of common areas. The condominium owner, upon purchase of a unit, becomes a member of the homeowners' association, which is responsible for the property management. Each owner pays a monthly fee to cover the cost of maintaining the common areas and the outside portion of the units. The individual owners are responsible for maintaining the interior of the units. Common areas may include a variety of athletic and recreational facilities. If you are renting a condominium, you will have the same responsibilities for upkeep and maintenance as the owner.

Rental houses are private and offer many attractive features. Unfortunately, they are often considerably more expensive to rent than apartments. You are paying for neighborhood living, garage space, often more living area, privacy, and the other comforts of home ownership. But you are also likely to find many of the same restrictions as with all other rentals, such as no pets allowed. Because rented houses are investment properties that people buy and sell, the property may be shown to prospective new owners while you are living there. You may be asked to move if a new owner is purchasing it for private use rather than as a rental.

Living Arrangements

Choosing a roommate can be difficult. Do you have friends with whom you would enjoy living? Just because you like each other doesn't mean that you can successfully live together. Your living habits may be very different. Be sure you are compatible with your potential roommate before you move in together. Discuss possible areas of disagreement that may cause trouble if not settled in advance. Some questions that you should answer for each other before making a commitment to share living quarters are listed below:

1. Do you smoke or drink? How do you feel about others who do?
2. Do you like a clean living area at all times, or are you easy-going and casual about your environment?
3. Do you have steady employment or another source of income to ensure that you can be depended on to pay your share of the common expenses?
4. What are some of your goals? Do you want to continue your education, work full-time, travel?
5. What are your leisure activities? What activities will you share with (or impose on) your roommate?
6. What type of transportation do you and your roommate have? What is the approximate cost? Will you share expenses? If so, how will you divide them?

You might want to consider having more than one roommate. The more personalities involved, however, the more difficult it becomes to have problem-free relationships. Matching similar personality types will increase the chances for a successful living arrangement.

The more you know about each potential roommate, the better you will be able to get along and work out problems. It is a good idea to get to know each person before moving in together. Spend time with each other at school, after school, in the evenings, and on weekends participating in group activities. In this way, you can see what interests you have in common, how each of you interacts with the others and in groups, and what personality traits are strongest. It is not necessary that roommates be completely alike in order to get along. However, they do need to be aware of, and be able to accept, each other's qualities and differences.

Roommates may decide to split the rent equally or unequally, depending on their own personal wishes. However, such agreements don't have any impact on the landlord. If one tenant can't pay a share of the rent in a particular month, or simply moves out, the other tenant(s) must still pay the full rent.

Where to Live

The decision of where to live will depend largely on finances. For students attending college and choosing on-campus housing, many of the decisions discussed in this chapter will be predetermined. Off-campus housing involves more planning. Those who will not attend college or who choose an off-campus residence must begin their housing plan with a solid financial analysis: What is a realistic amount to pay for rent? You must determine how much you can comfortably pay. Then you can begin shopping for the best housing plan to meet your needs. Here are some considerations to think about as you decide where to live:

1. *Deposits and fees.* A **security deposit** is a refundable amount

On what factors does the decision of where to live depend?

paid in advance to protect the owner against damage or non-payment. If you take care of the property and pay your rent on time, you should get the security deposit back when you move. Utility companies (such as the power company) may require you to make a security deposit when you first open an account. A **fee,** on the other hand, is a non-refundable charge for a service. For example, the owner may charge a cleaning fee to cover the cost of making the apartment clean and sanitary for the next renter.

2. *Length of time you plan to live in the residence.*
3. *Distance from work or school.*
4. *Distance from laundry, shopping facilities, and other frequently used services.*
5. *Costs of maintenance you are expected to perform.*

Most financial experts advise allotting 30 percent of your total budget for housing. At first, you may need a roommate to share costs. Later, you may be able financially to carry the burden of living alone.

What to Take

On-campus residences are usually furnished. However, you can find the other types of rental residences furnished or unfurnished. *Furnished* means that the basics are provided—bed and dresser; sofa, chairs, and lamps; dining table and chairs; and essential appliances. An *unfurnished* rental residence may or may not include basic kitchen appliances such as stove and refrigerator. Usually the fewer the items furnished, the lower the rent. If you have enough furnishings or can acquire the essentials for an unfurnished residence, you can save a considerable amount in rent.

You can buy or rent home or apartment furnishings. Compare purchase and rental payments carefully before you make a decision. Many companies rent furniture with an option to buy. For example, at the end of the rental period, you would have the option to buy the furniture at a price reduced by the portion of each rental payment made during that time. However, rent-to-own options can be very expensive. Be sure to compute total costs and compare them to other financing options for purchasing furniture.

Basic household and personal items necessary for setting up housekeeping include the following:

1. Towels, sheets, tablecloths, and cleaning cloths
2. Cleaning supplies (including mops, brooms, buckets, vacuum cleaner, detergent, and cleansers)

3. Personal items (including shampoo, cosmetics, soap, lotions, medicines, and other personal hygiene items)
4. Clothing, shoes, and other apparel
5. Dishes, silverware, pots, and pans
6. Lamps, clothes hangers, clocks, radio, television, plants, and other decorations

Carpeting is usually provided, but you may need to supply such items as throw rugs, draperies, a shower curtain, and mirrors. You or your roommates may be able to contribute some of these items. Others you may decide to buy jointly. Make a list of things to be purchased jointly. Each roommate should have available his or her share of the expenses prior to making the purchases. If you buy some things jointly and one of you decides to move, you must then divide the purchases. Before you move in together, you and your roommates should agree on who will get what joint items when you dissolve the living arrangement. To avoid arguments later, keep a written record of these agreements.

Planning Your Move

Begin planning your move several months in advance. Others who have experienced a similar move can help you with advice and contributions of household items. Here are some ways to prepare:

1. Set aside money in savings to cover cleaning deposits, first and last months' rent, fees, and initial expenses and

Why is it wise to plan your move several months in advance?

purchases. You may need $1,500 or more. If you have a pet, you may have to pay an additional security deposit or monthly fee.

2. Have a steady and reliable source of income with which you can pay the obligations you agree to pay, such as rent, utility bills, and shared expenses.

3. Accumulate over time what you need to live independently, such as clothing, towels, sheets and other bed items, small appliances, and dishes to minimize the items you need to buy when you move.

4. Plan the move with your career goals in mind. If your goal is to finish college, then your plan should work in harmony with that goal and help you achieve it. For example, if you are planning to go to college in September and live on campus, it would probably not be wise to go out on your own for the three summer months. The expenses would be too high, and you would be better off saving your money to help meet college expenses.

5. Make arrangements for transporting furnishings. Professional movers can be expensive and must be reserved in advance. If you instead enlist friends to help you move, you may need to rent a truck that you reserve in advance. Also, plan to provide refreshments or a meal for your friends if the move will take several hours.

A good way to organize your preparations is to make a household needs inventory, such as the one shown in Figure 21-1. Decide with your roommates what you will need and check off each item as you fulfill the need.

Group Financial Decisions

All roommates are responsible for meeting the obligations they agree upon. For example, each person must pay his or her share of the rent, so that the total rent is paid on time. You will probably share utilities equally, as well as garbage service, cable TV, Internet access charges, monthly telephone charges, and group activity expenses. Long-distance telephone calls and cell phone charges should be paid for individually. But expenses such as gasoline or groceries might be divided according to percentage of use. Laundry services usually are an individual expense.

Group budgeting allows for the careful allocation of expenses, so that each person pays his or her share. The budget should be prepared and put into writing following a good discussion. Figure 21-2 is an example of a group budget.

Household Needs Inventory Figure 21-1

What Is Needed	Date Needed	Cost	Date Completed
1. Dishes/towels	October 1	$100	_____
2. First and last months' rent	October 1	$1,400	_____
3. Security deposit	October 1	$100	_____
4. Moving-in fees	October 1	$250	_____
5. Car (share of expenses)	September 1	$150	_____
6. Job (part-time)	August 1		_____
7. Prepare household budget	September 1		_____
8. Plan with roommates	June 1		_____
9. Plan with parents	May 1		_____

Group Budget Figure 21-2

Expense	Monthly Cost	Robin's Share	Carmen's Share	Kendra's Share
Rent	$900	$300	$300	$300
Utilities (average)	150	50	50	50
Cable TV and Internet access	45	15	15	15
Gasoline/insurance /repairs	120	40	40	40
Groceries	600	200	200	200
Household supplies	90	30	30	30
TOTALS	$1,905	$635	$635	$635

As one method of paying these expenses, each person could have a separate account for individual expenses, and the group could have a joint account from which shared expenses are paid. You and your roommates should decide how much each person must deposit into the joint account by a certain date each month. Then you can decide who will write checks from the joint account to pay for rent, utilities, and other expenses incurred throughout the month. Individual roommates should be responsible for paying their own individual expenses on time.

Any plan for taking care of expenses should be agreed upon by all roommates so that everyone is satisfied. Put your agreements in writing so that no misunderstandings occur.

Moving Costs

Moving costs include the time and money spent in careful packing, storing, transporting, loading and unloading, and unpacking. Professional movers charge according to the amount you have to move, the distance to your new residence, and whether or not you want them to do the packing. You can save a lot of money by doing your own packing.

You can save even more by renting a truck or trailer and using your own labor for loading, driving, and unloading. If you are just moving across town, the rental will likely be cheaper if you can return the vehicle to the place where you rented it. However, for a longer move, you can rent a truck or trailer one way and return it to the rental agency's branch in the new city. One-way rental fees are usually a flat rate, plus mileage and gasoline, and a refundable security deposit. The rates vary, so compare before renting.

Installation Charges

When you move into a new residence, you will pay some installation charges. These may include charges for installing a telephone and cable TV and for turning on the electricity and other utilities. Many utility companies charge a security deposit that is refundable after a year or two, when you have proved your ability to pay your bills.

Other companies, such as the telephone company, charge a one-time fee that is not refundable. The installation charge is added to your first bill. Then monthly service rates vary according to the kinds of services you select. For example, you will pay more for services such as call-waiting or caller ID. You will need to buy your own telephone and other attachments, such as caller ID or a messaging machine.

Check Your Understanding

Review Terms

1. dormitory
2. efficiency apartment
3. security deposit
4. fee

Review Concepts

1. The decision of where to live will depend largely on what?
2. What questions should you and your potential roommate ask each other before deciding to live together?

PERSONAL PERSPECTIVE

Affordable Housing

The availability of affordable housing for low-income families is a problem in the U.S. Several organizations are mobilizing citizens to help. One such group, Housing America, is trying to eliminate homelessness by pressing legislators for federal funds for housing. At its Web site, www.housingamerica.net, the group lists a number of ways that students can join in the effort.

Another group, Habitat for Humanity, is a nonprofit, nondenominational Christian organization that builds affordable houses for low-income families in the United States and around the world. Many young people volunteer to work side-by-side with those in need to build these houses. Through volunteer labor and tax-deductible donations, Habitat builds and rehabilitates simple, decent houses and sells them at no profit and with no-interest loans to families who would not otherwise be able to buy a home. To learn more about the group's efforts and ways you can participate, visit its Web site at www.habitat.org.

Homelessness is a social problem in this country that joint efforts of citizens should be able to solve. Many people believe that a safe and comfortable place to live is a requirement for human dignity and that people must be given every opportunity to participate fully in society. Having a place to live is just the beginning, but it helps people make that first step toward self-reliance and responsibility.

You can make a difference. Consider volunteering in an activity of your choice to help others in your community or elsewhere. If you volunteer with a group, you could gain valuable skills as well as the satisfaction of helping people in need and working with others to accomplish a goal. Communities offer many opportunities to get involved in helping others, from serving meals at a homeless shelter to gathering donations for a local free-food store.

Think Critically

1. What programs are available in your community to help alleviate homelessness?
2. What other services do volunteer organizations provide in your community? Which of these activities most interest you? Why?

Goals

★ List the advantages and disadvantages of renting a place to live.
★ Describe the elements of a rental application, rental inventory, and lease.
★ Discuss landlord and tenant responsibilities.

Advantages of Renting

A **landlord** is the owner of rental property. A **tenant** is the person who rents property from a landlord. Because renting offers many advantages, it is a popular choice, especially among young people just getting started on their own. Some of the advantages renters enjoy are as follows:

1. *Mobility.* Many people prefer to rent because of the ease and speed with which they can move when a good job opportunity comes along elsewhere. If you are unsure about whether or not you will stay in the same location for a long period, then renting a residence is wise.

2. *Convenience.* Many landlords provide a number of conveniences for their tenants. For example, rental properties often have laundry and recreational facilities. Also, rental units are often conveniently located near major shopping areas, downtown, or business centers.

3. *Minimal Responsibilities.* Renting usually relieves you of many of the responsibilities of home ownership. The landlord bears most responsibility for repairs, maintenance of the grounds, and property management.

4. *Social Life.* Apartments located in multi-unit buildings offer the opportunity to meet others and socialize informally. When living in a rental complex, you are not isolated, without neighbors and other people nearby. Also, recreational facilities at many large complexes provide opportunities to socialize regularly.

5. *Lower Living Expenses.* Apartment rent is usually lower than the cost of buying a house. But another important factor in lowering individual living expenses is sharing expenses with roommates.

Disadvantages of Renting

Anyone who has lived in an apartment or other rental property can list several disadvantages. Some frequently mentioned disadvantages of renting are as follows:

1. *Noise.* Residents of apartments, duplexes, or condominiums share common walls with neighbors above, below, or beside them. Consequently, music, conversations, and other activities of neighbors can be overheard. Strange hours or unusual habits of neighbors can be very irritating.

2. *Lack of Privacy.* Because conversations and other activities can be overheard through common walls, tenants often feel that their neighbors know too much about their private lives. Problems associated with shared facilities—laundry and recreation, for example—also become annoying to some tenants.

3. *Small Quarters.* The typical apartment is smaller than some other housing alternatives. Five hundred to 1,000 square feet of living space is average for an apartment. A house may have 1,200 or more square feet of living space.

4. *Lack of Storage Area.* The small size of many apartments means less cabinet and closet space. Also, few rental properties offer more than a small amount of additional storage space for rarely used items.

5. *Lack of Parking.* Many rental properties do not provide garages or off-street parking, especially in city centers. Tenants' cars are subjected to the hazards of the weather and those associated with parking on busy streets. In complexes that provide parking lots, visitor parking is often very limited.

Rental Agreements

Whenever you rent a place to live, you will have to fill out an application similar to the one shown in Figure 21-3. The purpose of the application is to allow the landlord to check your employment (income), previous rental experience, credit rating, and so on. The landlord does this type of checking to assure that you are a good risk—that you will likely pay your rent and be a good tenant. The landlord may refuse to rent you property because of your past rental history, employment record, or credit rating. Rental may not be denied, however, solely on the basis of race, religion, national origin, sex, or marital status. Some states have passed laws to prohibit denial of rental to tenants with small children.

RENTAL APPLICATION

Date _____

Section 1. Personal Information

Applicant:
Name _____
Current Address_____

_____
Phone_____
Landlord _____
Landlord's Phone_____
Previous Address _____

_____
Previous Landlord _____
Landlord's Phone_____

Co-Applicant:
Name _____
Current Address_____

_____
Phone _____
Landlord _____
Landlord's Phone_____
Previous Address _____

_____
Previous Landlord_____
Landlord's Phone_____

Section 2. Employment

Employer _____
Address_____

_____
Phone_____
Monthly take-home pay $_____
Years employed at this job _____

Employer _____
Address_____

_____
Phone_____
Monthly take-home pay $_____
Years employed at this job _____

Section 3. Credit

Bank _____
___ Checking ___ Savings/Investment

Companies through which you have credit
cards or charge accounts:

_____
_____
_____

Bank _____
___ Checking ___ Savings/Investment

Companies through which you have credit
cards or charge accounts:

_____
_____
_____

Section 4. Personal References

Name _____
Phone_____
Relationship to applicant_____

Name_____
Phone_____
Relationship to applicant_____

I hereby swear that the above information is true and complete. I understand that incomplete or inaccurate information on this application may result in denial and/or eviction.

Applicant Signature:
_____ *Date:* _____

Co-Applicant Signature:
_____ *Date:* _____

Leases and Month-to-Month Agreements

Basically there are two types of rental agreements: leases and month-to-month tenancy agreements. A **lease** is a written agreement that allows a tenant to use property for a specified time period and rent. You may sign a lease for six months, one year, two years, or any period agreed upon. The landlord cannot raise the rent until the lease expires, except as agreed upon in the lease. But if you decide to move before the lease expires, you are still responsible for the remaining rent payments. At least 30 days prior to the end of your lease, the landlord should inform you of any rent increase. If you do not wish to stay longer than the time of your lease, you must notify the landlord in writing in advance, as specified in the lease. Often leases require 30-days' notice prior to departure. Figure 21-4 is an example of a lease agreement.

If you rent month-to-month, you can leave anytime, as long as you give 30-days' notice. The agreement does not bind you to pay rent for a period of time longer than a month, as a lease does. However, renting by the month also does not establish the rent amount for more than a month. The landlord can raise the rent anytime or ask you to leave anytime. Still, the ease of moving in and out is an advantage of renting month-to-month. If your plans are very uncertain and you need maximum flexibility, then month-to-month rental may be a good option for you.

Both a lease and a month-to-month rental agreement will include provisions for deposits and their return, termination of rental, rent payments, tenant and landlord responsibilities, and various other matters. If you do not understand any part of the agreement, ask the landlord to explain. If the answer is not satisfactory, get a legal interpretation or refuse to sign the agreement and go elsewhere. Both a lease and a month-to-month rental agreement are legally binding documents when you have

RESIDENTIAL LEASE AGREEMENT
AND SECURITY DEPOSIT RECEIPT

THIS INDENTURE, made this <u>29th</u> day of <u>October</u> , 20 <u>- -</u> , between

<u>Brendan Martin</u> , hereinafter designated the Lessor

or Landlord, and <u>Teresa Thomas</u> , hereinafter designated the Lessee,

WITNESSETH: That the said Lessor/Landlord does by these presents lease and demise the residence

situated at <u>614 Dundas Street</u> in <u>Cincinnati</u> City,

<u>Hamilton</u> County, <u>Ohio</u> State,

of which the real estate is described as follows:

614 Dundas Street, Cincinnati, Ohio,

upon the following terms and conditions:

1. **Term:** The premises are leased for a term of <u>one (1)</u> years, commencing the <u>1st</u> day of <u>November</u> , 20 <u>- -</u> , and terminating the <u>31st</u> day of <u>October</u> , 20 <u>- -</u> .

2. **Rent:** The Lessee shall pay rent in the amount of $ <u>$600.00</u> per month for the above premises on the <u>1st</u> day of each month in advance to Landlord.

3. **Utilities:** Lessee shall pay for service and utilities supplied to the premises, except <u>None</u> which will be furnished by Landlord.

4. **Sublet:** The Lessee agrees not to sublet said premises nor assign this agreement nor any part thereof without the prior written consent of Landlord.

5. **Inspection of Premises:** Lessee agrees that he has made inspection of the premises and accepts the condition of the premises in its present state, and that there are no repairs, changes, or modifications to said premises to be made by the Landlord other than as listed herein.

6. **Lessee Agrees:**
   (1) To keep said premises in a clean and sanitary condition;
   (2) To properly dispose of rubbish, garbage, and waste in a clean and sanitary manner at reasonable and regular intervals and to assume all costs of extermination and fumigation for infestation caused by Lessee;
   (3) To properly use and operate all electrical, gas, heating, plumbing facilities, fixtures and appliances;
   (4) to not intentionally or negligently destroy, deface, damage, impair, or remove any part of the premises, their appurtenances, facilities, equipment, furniture, furnishings, and appliances, nor to permit any member of his family, invitee, licensee or other person acting under his control to do so;
   (5) Not to permit a nuisance or common waste.

7. **Maintenance of Premises:** Lessee agrees to mow and water the grass and lawn, and keep the grass, lawn, flowers, and shrubbery thereon in good order and condition, and to keep the sidewalk surrounding said premises free and clear of all obstructions; to replace in a neat and workmanlike manner all glass and doors broken during occupancy thereof; to use due precaution against freezing of water or waste pipes and stoppage of same in and about said premises and that in case water or waste pipes are frozen or become clogged by reason of neglect of Lessee, the Lessee shall repair the same at his own expense as well as all damage caused thereby.

8. **Alterations:** Lessee agrees not to make alterations or do or cause to be done any painting or wallpapering to said premises without the prior written consent of Landlord.

9. **Use of Premises:** Lessee shall not use said premises for any purpose other than that of a residence and shall not use said premises or any part thereof for any illegal purpose. Lessee agrees to conform to municipal, county and state codes, statutes, ordinances, and regulations concerning the use and occupation of said premises.

10. **Pets and Animals:** Lessee shall not maintain any pets or animals upon the premises without the prior written consent of Landlord.

11. **Access:** Landlord shall have the right to place and maintain "for rent" signs in a conspicuous place on said premises for thirty days prior to the vacation of said premises. Landlord reserves the right of access to the premises for the purpose of:
    (a) Inspection;
    (b) Repairs, alterations or improvements;
    (c) To supply services; or
    (d) To exhibit or display the premises to prospective or actual purchasers, mortgagees, tenants, workmen, or contractors. Access shall be at reasonable times except in case of emergency or abandonment.

12. **Surrender of Premises:** In the event of default in payment of any installation of rent or at the expiration of said term of this lease, Lessee will quit and surrender the said premises to Landlord.

13. **Security Deposit:** The Lessee has deposited the sum of $ <u>600.00</u> , receipt of which is hereby acknowledged, which sum shall be deposited by Landlord in a trust account with <u>Citizens</u> bank; savings and loan association, or licensed escrow, <u>Cincinnati</u> branch, whose address is <u>201 Main Street, Cincinnati, Ohio</u>
All or a portion of such deposit may be retained by Landlord and a refund of any portion of such deposit is conditioned as follows:
    (1) Lessee shall fully perform obligations hereunder and those pursuant to Chapter 207, Laws of 1973, 1st Ex Session or as may be subsequently amended.
    (2) Lessee shall occupy said premises for <u>one (1)</u> months or longer from date hereof.
    (3) Lessee shall clean and restore said residence and return the same to Landlord in its initial condition, except for reasonable wear and tear, upon the termination of this tenancy and vacation of apartment.
    (4) Lessee shall have remedied or repaired any damage to apartment premises;
    (5) Lessee shall surrender to Landlord the keys to premises;
Any refund from security deposit, as by itemized statement shown to be due to Lessee, shall be returned to Lessee within fourteen (14) days after termination of this tenancy and vacation of the premises.

IN WITNESS WHEREOF, the Lessee has hereunto set his hand and seal the day and year first above written.

/s/ *Brendan Martin*	/s/ *Teresa Thomas*
LANDLORD	LESSEE
610 Dundas Street	
Cincinnati, Ohio	
ADDRESS	

(Acknowledgment)

signed them. Therefore, it is very important that you fully understand the agreement before signing.

Rental Inventory

If you reside in a rental property, you are expected to leave it as you found it. Normal wear and tear is expected and accepted. However, anything broken or misplaced is not acceptable. Therefore, to assure that you are not accused of such acts as breaking, damaging, or taking furnishings, prepare an inventory of the premises at the time you move in. The inventory should list and describe the conditions of the property. Note such things as broken windows, missing window screens, holes in walls, torn carpeting, plumbing problems, and appliance damage or problems. You and your landlord should tour the property together to take the inventory, so that you both agree on its contents. Then you or the landlord should make a copy for each of you. When you move out, you and your landlord should once again take an inventory. The comparison between this inventory and the initial one will often determine whether or not you get your security deposit back. Figure 21-5 shows an inventory and condition report that can be used in a variety of rental situations.

Landlord/Tenant Responsibilities

Although most states have passed landlord/tenant laws, there are no national laws. However, landlord/tenant laws for residential rental units generally include similarly worded landlord and tenant obligations.

Landlord Obligations

Housing laws in most states require that landlords provide a dwelling that is habitable (livable) at all times. A dwelling is considered habitable if the following conditions are met:

1. The exterior (including roof, walls, doors, and windows) is weatherproof and waterproof.
2. Floors, walls, ceilings, stairs, and railings are in good repair.
3. Elevators, halls, and stairwells meet fire and safety regulations. (Smoke detectors are required in each unit in most

INVENTORY AND CONDITION REPORT

Use this report to record the contents and condition of your unit when you move in and before moving out. If you mark anything as being either dirty or damaged, describe it fully on an additional sheet. Use the blank before each item to indicate how many there are. Ask the landlord to sign your copy.

Living Room

		Dirty Yes*	No	Damaged Yes*	No
___ Couch	1	☐	☐	☐	☐
___ Chair	2	☐	☐	☐	☐
___ End table	3	☐	☐	☐	☐
___ Easy chair	4	☐	☐	☐	☐
___ Floor lamp	5	☐	☐	☐	☐
___ Table lamp	6	☐	☐	☐	☐
___ Coffee table	7	☐	☐	☐	☐
___ Light fixture	8	☐	☐	☐	☐
___ Rug or carpet	9	☐	☐	☐	☐
___ Floor	10	☐	☐	☐	☐
___ Walls	11	☐	☐	☐	☐
___ Ceiling	12	☐	☐	☐	☐

Bedroom

		Dirty Yes*	No	Damaged Yes*	No
___ Bed frame(s)	13	☐	☐	☐	☐
___ Headboard(s)	14	☐	☐	☐	☐
___ Mattress	15	☐	☐	☐	☐
___ Mattress cover	16	☐	☐	☐	☐
___ Bed springs	17	☐	☐	☐	☐
___ Dresser	18	☐	☐	☐	☐
___ Nightstand	19	☐	☐	☐	☐
___ Drapes or curtains	20	☐	☐	☐	☐
___ Mirror	21	☐	☐	☐	☐
___ Light fixture	22	☐	☐	☐	☐
___ Rug or carpet	23	☐	☐	☐	☐
___ Floor	24	☐	☐	☐	☐
___ Walls	25	☐	☐	☐	☐
___ Ceiling	26	☐	☐	☐	☐

Bedroom

		Dirty Yes*	No	Damaged Yes*	No
___ Bed frame(s)	27	☐	☐	☐	☐
___ Headboard(s)	28	☐	☐	☐	☐
___ Mattress	29	☐	☐	☐	☐
___ Mattress cover	30	☐	☐	☐	☐
___ Bed springs	31	☐	☐	☐	☐
___ Dresser	32	☐	☐	☐	☐
___ Nightstand	33	☐	☐	☐	☐
___ Drapes or curtains	34	☐	☐	☐	☐
___ Mirror	35	☐	☐	☐	☐
___ Light fixture	36	☐	☐	☐	☐
___ Rug or carpet	37	☐	☐	☐	☐
___ Floor	38	☐	☐	☐	☐
___ Walls	39	☐	☐	☐	☐
___ Ceiling	40	☐	☐	☐	☐

Kitchen

		Dirty Yes*	No	Damaged Yes*	No
___ Working stove	41	☐	☐	☐	☐
___ Working oven	42	☐	☐	☐	☐
___ Oven racks	43	☐	☐	☐	☐
___ Broiler pan	44	☐	☐	☐	☐
___ Working refrigerator	45	☐	☐	☐	☐
___ Ice trays	46	☐	☐	☐	☐
___ Working sink	47	☐	☐	☐	☐
___ Working garbage disposal	48	☐	☐	☐	☐
___ Counter tops	49	☐	☐	☐	☐
___ Range hood w/working fan	50	☐	☐	☐	☐
___ Working dishwasher	51	☐	☐	☐	☐
___ Hot and cold running water	52	☐	☐	☐	☐
___ Drawers	53	☐	☐	☐	☐
___ Dinette table	54	☐	☐	☐	☐
___ Dinette chairs	55	☐	☐	☐	☐
___ Light fixture	56	☐	☐	☐	☐
___ Floor	57	☐	☐	☐	☐
___ Walls	58	☐	☐	☐	☐
___ Ceiling	59	☐	☐	☐	☐

Bathroom

		Dirty Yes*	No	Damaged Yes*	No
___ Towel racks	60	☐	☐	☐	☐
___ Tissue holder	61	☐	☐	☐	☐
___ Mirror	62	☐	☐	☐	☐
___ Medicine cabinet	63	☐	☐	☐	☐
___ Counter top	64	☐	☐	☐	☐
___ Working sink	65	☐	☐	☐	☐
___ Working tub	66	☐	☐	☐	☐
___ Working shower	67	☐	☐	☐	☐
___ Working toilet	68	☐	☐	☐	☐
___ Toilet seat	69	☐	☐	☐	☐
___ Shower curtain	70	☐	☐	☐	☐
___ Cabinet	71	☐	☐	☐	☐
___ Light fixture	72	☐	☐	☐	☐
___ Hot and cold running water	73	☐	☐	☐	☐
___ Floor	74	☐	☐	☐	☐
___ Walls	75	☐	☐	☐	☐
___ Ceiling	76	☐	☐	☐	☐

Miscellaneous

		Dirty Yes*	No	Damaged Yes*	No
___ Door key	77	☐	☐	☐	☐
___ Windows	78	☐	☐	☐	☐
___ Window screens	79	☐	☐	☐	☐
___ Mailbox	80	☐	☐	☐	☐
___ Mailbox key	81	☐	☐	☐	☐
___ Thermostat	82	☐	☐	☐	☐
___ Other	83	☐	☐	☐	☐
___	84	☐	☐	☐	☐

Do all the windows work?.............................
Does the heat work properly?........................

_____ Tenant

_____ Witness

_____ Date

_____ Landlord

_____ Date

*Describe fully on an additional sheet.

states. Tenants are responsible for testing the alarms, replacing batteries, and reporting any defects.)

4. Adequate locks are provided for all outside doors, working latches are provided for all windows, and exits meet fire and safety regulations.
5. Plumbing facilities comply with local and state laws and are in good working condition.
6. Water supply provided is adequate.
7. Lighting, wiring, heating, air conditioning, and appliances are in good condition and comply with local and state building and safety codes.
8. Buildings and grounds are clean and sanitary; garbage receptacles are adequate. (Tenants may be responsible for garbage removal charges.)

States typically require landlords to provide advance notice (usually 24 hours) before entering a rental unit. In most states, without advance notice, a landlord or manager may enter rented premises while a tenant is living there only in an emergency, such as a fire, or when the tenant gives permission.

Tenant Obligations

Tenant obligations usually are stated specifically in the lease or month-to-month agreement. If they are not stated, the following obligations and responsibilities are implied:

1. To read, understand, and abide by the terms of any lease or month-to-month agreement.
2. To pay the rent on or before the due date. Failure to make a rent payment as stated in the rental agreement may result in late fees, termination of the agreement, or eviction. **Eviction** is the legal process of removing a tenant from rental property.
3. To give 30- to 60-days' notice of intent to move. This notice will prevent the loss of security deposits and allow the landlord time to rent the unit before you move.
4. To keep the premises in good, clean condition and to prevent unnecessary wear and tear or damage to the unit.

5. To use a dwelling unit only for the purposes for which it is intended. For example, you should treat appliances and other furnishings in a reasonable manner. If the landlord pays for utilities, you should use them in a reasonable manner.

6. To allow the landlord access to the living unit to make repairs or improvements.

7. To obey the rules of the apartment complex or other community living area covering such things as quiet hours, use of recreational facilities, use of laundry facilities, and parking regulations.

What are some obligations owed by tenants to their landlords?

✓Check Your Understanding

Review Terms
1. landlord
2. tenant
3. lease
4. eviction

Review Concepts
1. How is a lease different from a month-to-month rental agreement?
2. Explain the purpose of a rental inventory prepared when you first move into rental property and when you move out.

21.1 Housing Decisions

- Living at your parents' home and commuting to school or work will help you save money toward a place of your own but does not offer the advantages of living on your own.
- On-campus housing options include dormitories, fraternity or sorority houses, and housing cooperatives.
- Apartments are living spaces in multi-unit buildings. Generally, the more facilities and conveniences an apartment offers, the higher the rent.
- Duplexes, condominiums, and rental houses offer more space than apartments, but they are usually more expensive and have more responsibilities, such as maintenance of lawns and property.
- To live together successfully, you and your roommates must have compatible living habits and work out individual and joint responsibilities in advance.
- When deciding where to live, consider deposits and fees, length of time you plan to live there, distance from work or school, nearby shopping and services, and the costs of maintenance.
- Prepare to move by planning what you need and accumulating these items over time. Arrange to transport your furnishings and set aside money to cover deposits, fees, and moving expenses.
- Professional movers charge according to amount to be moved, distance, and extent of packing services desired. Renting a vehicle and moving yourself is less expensive but labor-intensive.
- When you move in, you will have to pay installation charges to have utilities installed or turned on.

21.2 The Rental Process

- Advantages of renting include mobility (ease of changing residence), convenience to shopping and work, minimal responsibilities for maintenance, opportunity for social interaction, and lower expenses than most other choices.
- Disadvantages of renting include noise from close neighbors, lack of privacy, small living space, lack of storage, and scarce parking.
- Rental applications are similar to credit applications, and you must prove that you are a good risk as a tenant.
- If you lease, you agree to rent the space for a specified time and rent. During this time the landlord cannot raise the rent, but you must pay for the entire term if you move out early. If you rent month-to-month, you are not obligated to pay for an extended period of time, but the landlord can raise the rent at any time.
- Landlords are responsible for providing a safe and habitable place for tenants to live.
- Tenants are responsible for paying rent on time, obeying the rules, and taking reasonable care of the property.

Review Terms

Directions: Can you find the definition for each of the following terms used in Chapter 21?

dormitory
efficiency apartment
eviction
fee
landlord
lease

security deposit
tenant

1. The legal process of removing a tenant from rental property.
2. A non-refundable charge for a service.
3. A refundable amount paid in advance to protect the owner against damage or non-payment.
4. Person who rents property from a landlord.
5. On-campus building that contains small rooms that colleges rent to students.
6. The owner of rental property.
7. A written agreement that allows a tenant to use property for a specified time period and rent.
8. An apartment with one large room that serves as the kitchen, living room, and bedroom, plus a bathroom.

Review Facts and Ideas

1. If you go to college, what are some advantages of living on campus?
2. How do landlords protect themselves against damage tenants do to the property?
3. What kinds of responsibilities should roommates share jointly?
4. List four advantages of renting a residence.
5. List four disadvantages of renting a residence.
6. What is the purpose of a rental application?
7. How does a lease differ from a month-to-month rental agreement?
8. Why should you take an inventory of your rental unit and have the landlord sign it before you move in?
9. List several conditions a landlord must meet in order to make rental property habitable.
10. List several tenant obligations when renting.

APPLY YOUR KNOWLEDGE

1. Ask two people separately to answer the questions below. Based on the answers, determine if the three of you would be a compatible living group.
   a. Do you smoke or drink? How do you feel about people who do?
   b. Are you a clean, fussy housekeeper or easygoing, casual, and relaxed about your surroundings? How often do you clean?
   c. Do you work steadily, part-time or full-time? How would you pay your share of the rent and other shared expenses?
   d. What are some of your goals regarding college, your job, or recreation?

e. What do you like to do in your spare time? What are your group activities? your individual activities?

f. What type of transportation do you have or plan to have? Would you be interested in sharing transportation costs?

2. What possessions have you accumulated that you would need in order to set up housekeeping in an apartment?

3. What basics would you have to acquire in order to live independently? Which of these would you have to buy and which could you borrow to save money?

4. Make a list of things you should do before moving out on your own.

5. In order to move your possessions from your present home to a new residence, what types of transportation are available to you? What is the best and least expensive for you?

Solve Problems

1. Prepare a report comparing the rental prices and availability of apartments, duplexes, condominiums, and houses in your area. To compare prices, living conditions must be comparable; you must compare two-bedroom unfurnished apartments to two-bedroom unfurnished duplexes, and so forth. Also, note how many are presently available in each category, the high and low prices, and the average rental prices. (Hint: You can look up this information on the Internet. Your local newspaper's classified section will probably be available online.)

2. Select a large city in another state. Search the Internet for apartments to rent in that city. Hint: Include the city name as well as "rent" and "apartment" as key words in your search engine. Select a moderately priced apartment there and print out or write down the description of it. Be sure to note the rent. Then find a similar apartment in a smaller town. What is the rent for this apartment? What can you conclude about the cost of living between these two locations, based on apartment rents?

3. Using the community resources in your area, find out the installation deposits and fees for the following services:
    a. Telephone
    b. Electricity

c. Cable TV

d. Water or garbage services

Are any of these fees partially or fully refundable? If so, under what conditions?

4. Find out the rates or prices for the following telephone services in your area:

a. Standard phone

b. Pager

c. Voice messaging

d. Caller ID

e. Wireless communications

f. Call forwarding

g. Call waiting

h. Unlisted telephone number

i. Additional phone jack installed

For related activities and links, point your browser to
www.mypf.swep.com

Chapter 22

Buying a Home

Up Front

Blake and Cheri have been married for five years, and they have managed to save money toward buying their own home.

"I think we have enough down-payment money saved to buy a home with four bedrooms, though we really need only two bedrooms right now," Blake said to his wife.

"I'm not sure we have as large a down payment as you think," Cheri said. "We'll have to pay other costs as well, such as closing costs and moving expenses."

"Okay," Blake agreed. "Let's start out with a smaller house that meets our needs and has potential for improvement. We can sell and move to another house when we start our family. By then we'll have built up some equity."

Goals

★ Discuss the financial and quality-of-life advantages of home ownership.

★ Describe the costs and responsibilities that accompany home ownership.

Advantages of Home Ownership

At some point in your life, you will probably have to decide whether to buy a house or continue to rent. Because the purchase of a home may be the most expensive decision you ever make, you should carefully weigh the advantages, costs, and responsibilities. Although many single people own their own homes, marriage and family usually create the greatest need for home ownership. The need for room to expand, hobbies, and recreation for children is often the main reason that families buy a home.

Home ownership offers financial advantages, such as tax savings and an investment that usually grows in value over time. But owning a home is more than a financial decision. Your own home also offers advantages that improve your quality of life. These personal advantages are important factors in your decision to buy a home.

Equity Increases

In Chapter 12, you learned that the market value of a stock is the price for which it is bought and sold on the market. Similarly, the **market value** of a home is the highest price that the property will bring on the market. In other words, it is the price at which the property could be bought and sold on the market. Real estate agents and professional appraisers from a bank can *appraise* or estimate the market value of your home by comparing it to similar homes that have sold recently. The typical price for which these similar homes sold is a good estimate of the current market value of your home. Real estate agents appraise homes to help the owners establish a selling price. Banks appraise homes to determine how much they can safely loan to the buyers.

The market value of homes tends to increase or *appreciate* over time. For example, if you buy a home for $100,000, and two years later you could sell it for $110,000, then your property has appreciated by $10,000. Appreciation is one way that your equity in your home increases. **Equity** is the difference between the market value of property and the amount owed on it.

Your equity also increases because each loan payment you make decreases your debt. When you sell your home years later, the increased market value and the lower remaining debt owed will result in greater equity. Equity turns to cash when you sell the home. For example, if you purchase a home valued at $150,000 and have a loan of $120,000, your initial equity is $30,000. Suppose that when you decide to sell, the market value has increased to $170,000 and your loan debt is down to $100,000. Your equity would be the $170,000 selling price minus $100,000 owed, or $70,000. The cash you receive from the sale would be the $70,000 equity minus selling expenses. The Math Minute shows the step-by-step calculations in determining the current equity in a home.

Tax Savings

The interest you pay on your home loan, along with the property taxes, are tax deductible. These deductions lower the cost of home ownership. Because of these tax savings, owning real estate is a *tax shelter*. Renters cannot deduct any part of their rent payments from their income taxes. Even though your equity in your home may be increasing each year, you do not pay tax on it until you sell your home, and even then you can avoid taxes on the gains.

Quality-of-Life Advantages

What kinds of quality-of-life advantages do homeowners enjoy?

Home ownership offers privacy and personal freedom not available to renters. In your own home you make all the decisions and have free use of all facilities. Owning a home also provides a feeling of security and independence. Knowing that the home is yours to do with as you wish and when you wish can be very

Resource Management

satisfying. You also get a sense of stability and belonging to your community. You have "put down roots," so you care about what happens in your neighborhood.

Computing Current Equity in a Home

Suppose you bought a home for $200,000. Your lender required a 20 percent down payment. Therefore, your down payment amount was:

$$\$200,000 \times .2 = \$40,000$$

Your initial loan amount (ignoring other costs) was:

$$\$200,000 - \$40,000 = \$160,000$$

Now let's say that you have been making payments on your house for two years, reducing your debt by $8,000. Therefore, you now owe $160,000 - $8,000 = $152,000.

Your house has been appreciating at 5 percent per year for two years. As a result, the current market value is:

$$\$200,000 \times .05 = \$10,000$$
$$\$200,000 + \$10,000 = \$210,000 \text{ after year 1}$$
$$\$210,000 \times .05 = \$10,500$$
$$\$210,000 + \$10,500 = \$220,500 \text{ after year 2}$$

Your equity is now:

$$\$220,500 \text{ market value} - \$152,000 \text{ remaining debt} = \$68,500$$

Problem: Eugene and Shawna bought a house two years ago for $175,000. They put 15 percent down. Their payments over the last two years reduced their debt by $6,000. Houses in their area have been appreciating at 4 percent per year. Find the following:

1. The amount of their down payment.
2. The amount of their initial loan.
3. The amount of their current debt.
4. The current market value.
5. Their current equity.

Solution:

1. Down payment = $26,250
2. Initial loan = $148,750
3. Current debt = $142,750
4. Current market value = $189,280
5. Current equity = $46,530

Costs and Responsibilities of Home Ownership

Home ownership carries significant costs and responsibilities. Before deciding to buy a home, you must make sure that you can financially handle the costs and that you are personally ready to accept the responsibilities.

Generally, older homes may be in more established neighborhoods, offer more character, and have lower property tax rates. Owners, however, shouldn't mind maintaining their home and making some repairs. Newer homes tend to use more modern architecture and systems, are usually easier to maintain, and may be more energy-efficient. People who buy new homes often don't want to worry initially about upkeep and repairs.

Down Payment

Most conventional (not government-backed) loans require a 10 to 30 percent down payment. For example, if you are purchasing a home for $150,000, you will need $15,000 (10 percent) to $45,000 (30 percent) for the down payment. For many people, saving enough money for the down payment takes a number of years.

Mortgage

Home buyers usually borrow the rest of the purchase price, after the down payment, from a bank or other financial institution. As you learned in Chapter 14, a loan to purchase real estate is called a *mortgage.* Payments on a mortgage are made over an extended period—for example, 15 or 30 years. The larger your down payment, the lower your monthly mortgage payments. Property taxes and the cost of property insurance are often included with the mortgage payments.

Closing

The **closing costs,** also referred to as *settlement costs,* are the expenses incurred in transferring ownership from buyer to seller in a real estate transaction. Closing costs may add another $3,000 to $5,000 to the purchase of your home. The purchaser usually pays for a title search to make sure the seller is the legal owner and that no one else has claims on the property. The purchaser may also pay for a personal credit report, loan fees, assumption fees (to take over someone else's mortgage), fees for preparing the paperwork, recording fees, some portion of taxes and interest owed, and property insurance.

Property Taxes

The real estate property tax is a major source of funding for local governments. Homeowners pay property taxes based on the assessed value of land and buildings. A local taxing authority determines the assessed value of your property, usually a percentage of the market value. A home worth $100,000 might have an assessed value of $90,000 (or 90 percent of its market value). If the property tax rate is $24 per thousand of assessed value, you will pay 90 times $24, or $2,160 a year in property taxes. Your annual property taxes are tax deductible.

Once you have purchased a house, what kinds of financial obligations can you expect?

Insurance

A homeowner must have property insurance covering the structure as well as the contents of a home. A more detailed explanation of homeowners insurance is presented in Chapter 26.

Utilities

Because most homes are larger than apartments or other rental units, the utility bills are usually larger. The homeowner pays for all utilities and garbage services, whereas a renter may pay for some but not all of these services. In addition, when repairs are needed to water or sewer lines, the homeowner is fully responsible for the costs.

Maintenance and Repairs

As a homeowner, you will be responsible for maintenance and repairs inside and outside your home. Before you choose to buy, make sure you are willing to spend the time and money needed to keep your home in good condition.

Ongoing maintenance includes such tasks as painting, mowing, landscaping, shoveling snow, and fixing things that break or wear out from normal use. You would incur not only the costs but also the responsibility for doing these tasks or arranging to have them done.

In addition to ongoing maintenance, you will occasionally have to make very expensive repairs or improvements to your home. For example, a roof lasts only about 15 years. The furnace and water heater will also need replacing in about that length of time. You must save to cover these future major expenses.

NET NOTES

At its Web site, www.hud.gov, the Department of Housing and Urban Development provides a "homebuyer's kit" that is especially helpful for first-time homebuyers. Included are commonly asked questions about home buying; mortgage tips and calculators; advice on choosing a real estate agent; information on appraisals and inspections; settlement and closing suggestions; and moving pointers.

✓ Check Your Understanding

Review Terms
1. market value (real estate)
2. equity
3. closing costs

Review Concepts
1. Why do people choose to buy a house rather than rent it?
2. What responsibilities go with home ownership?

The Home-Buying Process

Goals

★ Describe the steps in the home-buying process, from selecting a home to buy through taking possession of it.
★ Discuss how to obtain financing and the events that occur at closing.

Finding and Selecting a Home

In buying a home, you should consider such factors as location, accessibility, nearness to employment, type and quality of construction, cost and effort of maintenance, and personal likes and dislikes. Before starting your search, make a list of the features you want your home and neighborhood to have and the price range you can afford. Prioritize the list according to each feature's importance to you. No house will meet all your desires. You will have to make trade-offs. Therefore, you should have a clear understanding of what you want most before you begin to look.

Working with a Real Estate Agent

Before selecting a home to buy, look at many houses. You can look by yourself or work with a real estate agent, who is trained to know the market, help you find the right home, and assist you with the purchase, financing, and closing.

Real estate agents earn a commission for their work. The commission is a percentage of the sale price, usually around 5 percent to 7 percent. The seller pays the commission, and the agents working for the buyer and seller split it. As the purchaser, you do not pay the agent's commission. However, be aware that because the seller pays the commission, the agents representing both the buyer and the seller really work for the seller. The more you spend for the home, the more money your agent earns.

Career Links

Real estate agents have a thorough knowledge of the real estate market in their community. They know which neighborhoods are best suited to fit their clients' needs and budgets. Agents also act as middlemen in price negotiations between buyers and sellers. Real estate agents must have a high school degree, be 18 years old, and pass a written test, which includes questions on basic real estate transactions and laws. Agents must have a license, which is renewed every two years. Maturity, tact, trustworthiness, and enthusiasm for the job are required in order to motivate prospective customers.

For more information, refer to the *Occupational Outlook Handbook* at www.bls.gov or search the Internet using such key words as "careers," "jobs," and "real estate."

You can find homes for sale in the newspaper classified ads, including those that the owners are selling themselves, without a real estate agent. A big advantage of having an agent, however, is to gain access to the multiple listings. The **Multiple Listing Service (MLS)** is a real estate marketing service in which agents from many real estate agencies pool their home listings and agree to share commissions on the sales. Home sellers contract with a particular agency to have their homes listed. Agents from all participating real estate agencies can then show all properties in the listings to their potential buyers. Sellers gain wide exposure for their property. Buyers can sift through the large pool of property descriptions to select those they want to visit.

In some locations, the complete MLS is available to everyone online. In other locations, only real estate agencies that pay a subscription fee have access to the complete listings. In most places, individual agencies post some of their listings on their Web site for anyone to see. Listings include detailed descriptions of the homes, including number of rooms, total square footage, special features such as a fireplace and garage, and amount of land included. Most listings also include photographs of the homes. Some online listings include virtual tours in which you can see a video presentation that goes from room to room. When viewing properties online, you have the advantage of being able to compare prices while viewing numerous homes without having to be there in person.

After you have narrowed your choices to a small number of homes that are in your price range and match your buying needs

PERSONAL PERSPECTIVE

Finding the Right Real Estate Agent

If you decide to list your home with a real estate agent, first ask your friends and relatives for recommendations. They may offer names of agents who did a good job for them. Then contact agents from several companies for a listing presentation. You want to find an agent that you feel comfortable with and that knows the market in your area well. Here are some questions to ask:

1. Are you licensed?
2. How long have you been working as a real estate agent?
3. How long have you worked in this area?
4. About how many homes have you sold recently?
5. For about how many of these sales did you find the buyers?
6. What services will you provide for me as your client?
7. Do you subscribe to the Multiple Listing Service?
8. How will you market my home? Will you hold open houses? How many?
9. At what price should I list my home? Please show me the prices for which comparable homes actually sold recently to support your assessment.
10. What commission percentage will you charge?

Keep in mind that an agent's commission is negotiable. The agent will not likely tell you so, but he or she may be willing to come down on the commission in order to make the sale. As part of negotiating with a prospective buyer, consider negotiating the agent's commission as well.

Reject any agent who is not licensed. Also reject any whose company is not a member of the local Multiple Listing Service. A listing in the MLS is a major benefit that a real estate agent can provide that you cannot get on your own. The MLS exposes your home listing to many buyers, increasing your chances for making the sale.

Think Critically

1. Ask a real estate agent to explain an agent's responsibilities to buyers and sellers in a real estate transaction.
2. Why is it important for your agent to know the market in your area?

fairly well, you should visit the homes with your agent. Take notes, both pro and con, on the features of each house and neighborhood. Do not make a decision on the spot. After touring your list of finalists, use the decision-making process to make your final selection.

Visit as many houses as it takes to find the one you want. On average, homebuyers see 15 houses before choosing one.

Making an Offer

To let the homeowner know of your interest in buying the home and the price you are willing to pay, you sign an agreement called an offer. An **offer** is a formal document that expresses interest in entering into a contract with someone else. A real estate offer explains the terms of the purchase, including the price you are offering, the down payment, the mortgage amount, and the dates when you will close the deal and take possession. You will have to include earnest money with your offer. **Earnest money** is a portion of the purchase price that the buyer deposits as evidence of good faith to show that the purchase offer is serious. This money is set aside in an account until the transaction is completed.

Earnest money protects the seller in case you fail to meet the terms of the agreement. If you and the seller have agreed on the transaction, the seller will take the house off the market until the deal is completed. During that time, the house cannot be sold to anyone else. If you then back out of the deal, you will likely forfeit your earnest money to the seller. One way to avoid losing your money is to make your offer *contingent* (dependent) on obtaining financing and the property passing an inspection. That way, if you do not qualify for a mortgage on this property, or an inspection reveals major flaws in the house, you will not have violated the contract and you will get your earnest money back.

The seller may or may not accept your initial offer. When the seller agrees to your offer exactly as stated, you have an acceptance. An **acceptance** is a formal agreement to the terms of an offer, forming a contract between the parties. You may withdraw your offer only until the seller accepts it. Once accepted, the offer is a contract.

If the seller wants to change any part of the offer, he or she makes a **counteroffer,** or an offer in response to another offer. For example, if you offered to buy at a lower price than the seller was willing to accept, the seller may make a counteroffer with a different price. Often a buyer's initial offer is lower than the price for which the house is listed. The seller then counteroffers a price below the initial listing but higher than the buyer's first offer. Buyer and seller negotiate until they either agree on a mutually acceptable selling price or decide not to make the transaction. You have the choice of accepting or rejecting each counteroffer.

Obtaining Financing

After you have come to an agreement with the seller, you will have to arrange for your loan. To finance your purchase, you must have funds for a down payment and closing costs, meet certain requirements of your lending institution, and select the type of mortgage you want.

Down Payment Sources

The most common sources of down payment money are personal savings and informal loans from parents or relatives. Most lending institutions will not allow mortgage applicants to formally borrow their down payment. In other words, you must invest a substantial amount of your own cash in the property. Because the down payment can be $5,000 to $10,000 or more, many first-time home buyers have difficulty saving the money and must "borrow" it informally from parents or relatives.

Qualifying for a Mortgage

To qualify for a mortgage, you must complete an extensive loan application. The financial institution will check your credit history and references. You must prove to the lender that you are capable of meeting the monthly payment. The lender will look for evidence that you can meet your current bills. The lender will also look at the type and amount of your current debts, the amount and source of your income, and your creditworthiness. Generally, the lender will judge that you can handle monthly mortgage payments that do not exceed 30 to 40 percent of your take-home pay.

The lender will also appraise the house you intend to buy. Since the house is the collateral for the loan, the lender must be assured that it is worth enough to cover the loan. If you default, the lender will have to repossess and sell the house to recover the loan amount.

Types of Mortgages

What are the two basic types of mortgages?

There are two basic types of mortgages: fixed-rate mortgages and adjustable-rate mortgages. A **fixed-rate mortgage** is a mortgage on which the interest rate does not change during the term of the loan. An **adjustable-rate mortgage (ARM)** is a mortgage for which the interest rate changes in response to the movement of interest rates in the economy as a whole.

The rate for an ARM usually starts lower than the current rates for a fixed-rate mortgage. The lender then adjusts the ARM rate based on the ups and downs of the economy. The lender may decrease the ARM's rate, but usually the rate goes up. For example, at a given time, fixed-rate loans may be offered at 8 percent. This rate would remain unchanged for the 30-year term of the loan. At the same time, adjustable-rate mortgages may be offered at 5 percent. The trade-off for this low initial rate is its variability. The lender may raise the rate over time to 10 or 12 percent as interest rates go up in the economy. Most adjustable-rate mortgages specify maximum rate increases (such as 2 or 3 percent a year) and ceilings (such as a top of 12 percent) to which the interest rate can rise.

Taking Title to Property

After you and the seller have reached an agreement, and you have arranged your financing, the next step is the *closing*. At this meeting, title to the property will be transferred to you. The **title** is a legal document that establishes ownership. The **deed** is a legal document that transfers title of real property from one party to another.

Before you take ownership, you will want to make sure that the title is *clear*—that is, free of any liens. A **lien** is a financial claim on property. For example, if the previous owner used the home as collateral for a loan other than the mortgage, then

What is the difference between the title and the deed?

that lender has a financial claim or lien. This claim must be paid before ownership of the property can be transferred. To ensure a clear title, you should order a *title search*. For a fee, a title insurance company will search public records and issue a report. If the company discovers that the title is clear, it will issue you a title insurance policy that protects you from any claims arising from a defective title. Most lenders require that the borrower buy title insurance.

Before the closing, the lending institution prepares the loan papers. If any problems arise, the lender will notify you and the seller. For example, some deeds may carry restrictions that limit the kind of building that can be erected and the use of the property. Inspections, such as termite examinations, must be carried out. Any repairs required by the terms of the sale must be completed.

When all these procedures are completed, you and the seller will be notified of the closing date. In this meeting, you and the seller sign the papers and pay all related closing costs, such as those shown in Figure 22-1 on page 632. If you have a real estate agent, the agent will attend the meeting with you and help you through the process. At the closing, the home becomes yours.

Figure 22-1 *Typical Closing Costs*

REAL ESTATE CLOSING COSTS

Type of Cost	Typical Amount	Who Pays
Credit Report (on buyer)	$50	Buyer
Property Appraisal Fee	$300 to $500	Buyer
Pest/Damage Inspection	$150 to $300	Buyer
Electrical/Plumbing/Water Inspection Report	$150 to $300	Buyer
Mortgage Loan Fee	Varies	Buyer
Mortgage Loan Assumption Fee	Varies	Buyer
Document Preparation (Escrow Closing Fee)	$150 to $750 depending on selling price of property	Buyer and Seller
Notary Fees and Filing Fees	$25 to $100	Buyer and Seller
Title Search; Title Insurance	$300 to $750 depending on selling price of property	Seller
Survey	$250 to $750	Seller
Real Estate Sales Commission	A percentage of price of home, from 5% to 7% of sale price	Seller
Attorney's Fees	Varies	Buyer and Seller
Interest and Taxes Owed	Varies	Buyer and Seller
Transfer Taxes and Fees	Varies	Seller

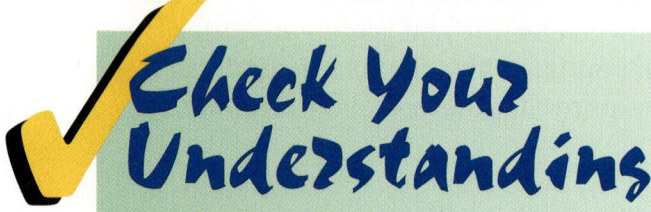

Check Your Understanding

Review Terms
1. Multiple Listing Service (MLS)
2. offer
3. earnest money
4. acceptance
5. counteroffer
6. fixed-rate mortgage
7. adjustable-rate mortgage (ARM)
8. title
9. deed
10. lien

Review Concepts
1. What are the advantages of the Multiple Listing Service?
2. What is the difference between a fixed-rate loan and an ARM?

22.1 Why Buy a Home?

- Home ownership has financial advantages, such as increasing equity and tax savings from deductible mortgage interest and property taxes.
- Homeownership also has quality-of-life advantages, such as privacy, freedom, and a sense of belonging to a community.
- Home ownership involves costs, such as a down payment, mortgage payments, closing costs, property taxes, and property insurance.
- As a homeowner, you are responsible for ongoing repairs and maintenance plus any major expenses required to keep your home in good condition.

22.2 The Home-Buying Process

- Before starting your house search, prioritize a list of the features you want in your home and neighborhood and determine the price range you can afford.
- Real estate agents are trained to know the market, help you find the right home, and assist you with the purchase, financing, and closing. Their commission is a percentage of the sale price, paid by the seller.
- Search the multiple listings for homes that meet your criteria. Once you have narrowed your choices, visit these homes and note their good and bad points. Then use the decision-making process to make your final selection.
- Make an offer on your selected home and put up earnest money. The seller may accept your offer or make a counteroffer. Once you have agreed on a price and terms of the sale, the offer becomes a contract.

- To obtaining financing, you have to fill out an application and meet the lender's requirements. You can get a fixed-rate or an adjustable-rate mortgage.
- At the closing, you will sign papers and money will exchange hands. At the end of the meeting, title will be transferred to you, and the house will be yours.

Review Terms

Directions: Can you find the definition for each of the following terms used in Chapter 22?

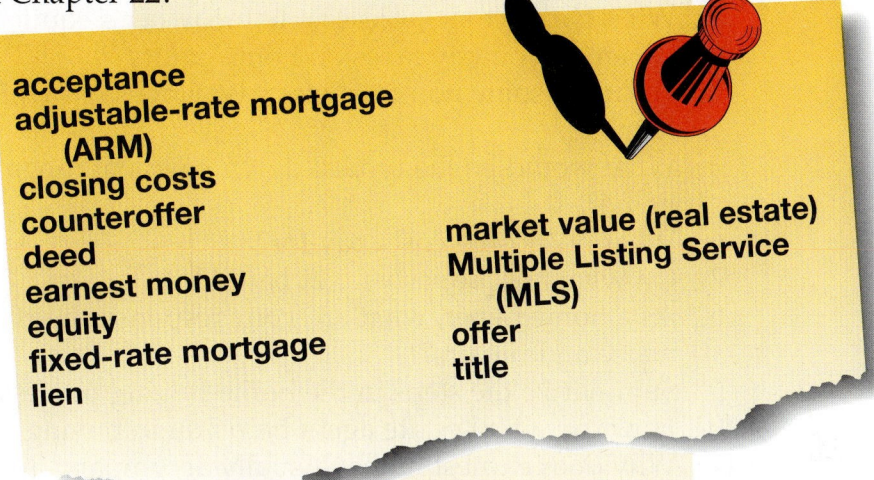

acceptance
adjustable-rate mortgage
    (ARM)
closing costs
counteroffer
deed
earnest money
equity
fixed-rate mortgage
lien

market value (real estate)
Multiple Listing Service
    (MLS)
offer
title

1. A legal document that establishes ownership.
2. The expenses incurred in transferring ownership from buyer to seller in a real estate transaction.
3. A real estate marketing service in which agents from many real estate agencies pool their home listings and agree to share commissions on the sales.
4. The highest price that a property will bring on the market.
5. A mortgage on which the interest rate does not change during the term of the loan.
6. A formal agreement to the terms of an offer, forming a contract between the parties.
7. A legal document that transfers title of real property from one party to another.
8. A formal document that expresses interest in entering into a contract with someone else.
9. The difference between the market value of property and the amount owed on it.
10. An offer in response to another offer.
11. A portion of the purchase price that the buyer deposits as evidence of good faith to show that the purchase offer is serious.
12. A financial claim on property.
13. A mortgage for which the interest rate changes in response to the movement of interest rates in the economy as a whole.

1. What are some financial advantages of owning your home?
2. What two factors increase a homeowner's equity?
3. When do you pay taxes on home equity?
4. What are some non-financial advantages of owning your home?
5. What would be the typical down payment range on a $100,000 home?
6. What do closing costs pay for?
7. On what are property taxes based?
8. As a homeowner, what are your responsibilities for maintenance and repairs?
9. Summarize the steps in the home-buying process.
10. How can a real estate agent help you in buying a home?
11. Why does earnest money usually accompany an offer?
12. Describe the negotiation process between the buyer and seller of a home.
13. Why are the initial interest rates offered for ARMs usually less than the rates offered for fixed-rate loans?
14. What is the purpose of a title search and title insurance?

1. Go to the library or search the Internet to find out the annual rate that houses are appreciating in your area. If you bought a house for $150,000 now, how much would it be worth a year from now, at the current rate of appreciation?

2. With your instructor's permission, arrange to visit a real estate agent at work. Discuss with the agent the process of purchasing a house, including the steps, length of time, and costs involved. Ask the agent to show you what the multiple listings look like. If possible, ask the agent if you can go along when the agent shows a house to a prospective buyer. Write a brief paper summarizing what you have learned.

3. Search the Internet for the multiple listings in your area. If you cannot gain access without a subscription, go to the Web site of a large real estate agency that operates in your area. Write a 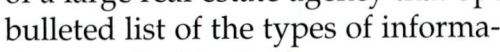 bulleted list of the types of information supplied in the house listings. Look at the listings for several houses in your neighborhood. Write a brief summary of the kinds of houses available near you, including their price range, house styles, internal features, and amount of land included.

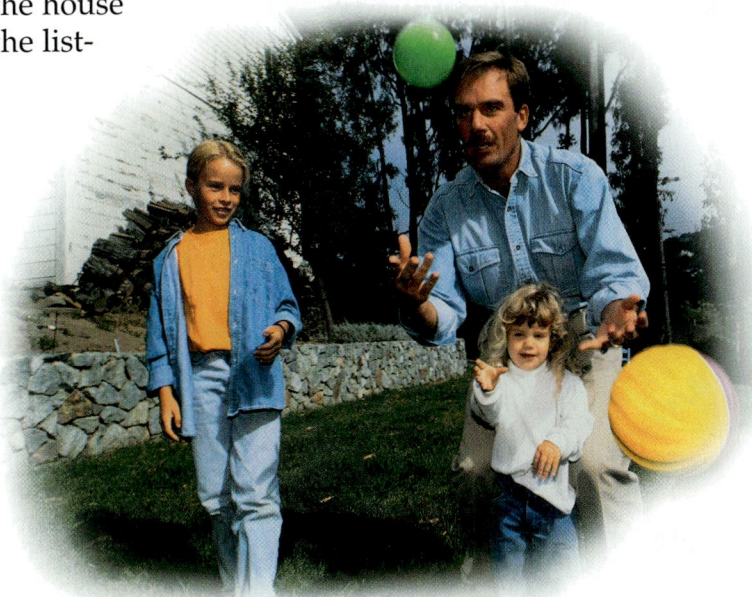

4. With your instructor's permission, visit a title insurance company in your area and ask people there what they do, how they gather information, and how they are able to insure titles. Briefly summarize your notes in one page or less.

5. Obtain the home mortgage rates from a local bank, savings and loan association, credit union, and, if possible, online lenders. Compare these rates and such terms as the down payment, loan costs (points), loan length, and maximum amount available to determine which of them offers the best financing rates.

6. You might ask, "Why should I go to the expense of hiring someone to sell my property for me?" Because of the complexities of real estate ownership today, it is often wise and less expensive in the long run to engage the services of a professional real estate agent. Find out through research or an interview with one or more real estate agents at least five services that a professional can provide in selling your home.

Solve Problems

1. If you buy a house for $125,000, how much down payment will you have to make if the lender requires a down payment of (a) 10 percent, (b) 15 percent, (c) 20 percent, (d) 25 percent?

2. You bought your home last year for $130,000. You made a down payment of 20 percent. Through your mortgage payments, you have reduced your debt by $2,000. The annual appreciation rate for homes in your area has averaged 3 percent.
   a. What was the amount of your down payment?
   b. What was your initial loan amount?
   c. How much do you owe now?
   d. What is the current market value of your home?
   e. What is your equity in the home now?

3. Suppose your local taxing authority requires you to pay property taxes at the rate of $16 per thousand. Your house is assessed at $210,000. How much property tax will you owe each year?

4. Make a list of the features you want in a home. Be sure to include features of the location where you would like to live as well as features of the house and property. Then prioritize your list in order of importance to you. Select a moderate price

range for homes in your area. Then search the newspaper classified ads or online listings for houses in that price range that meet your criteria. Clip or print out the listings for three houses that you would like to tour if you were in the market for a home. Which of your criteria do these houses meet and which do they not meet?

5. Using just the closing costs specifically stated in Figure 22-1, what range of costs should the buyer expect to pay (minimum and maximum)? What range of costs should the seller expect to pay? Assume that the house sold for $180,000.

6. Use your Loan Planner Tool to solve this problem. To buy the home you want, you will have to borrow $100,000 at 7 percent interest for 30 years (or 360 monthly payments). What will your monthly payment be?

PLANNING TOOLS

For related activities and links, point your browser to
www.mypf.swep.com

Chapter 23

Buying and Caring for a Vehicle

Terms to Know

pre-approval
vehicle identification
   number (VIN)
vehicle emission test
sticker price
low-balling
high-balling

dealer add-ons
lemon
oxidize
polishing compound
abrasives
upholstery

Up Front

Hee-Jan works part-time and attends school full time. He lives at home with his parents, and his take-home pay is over $600 a month.

"I'm ready to buy a car," he told his parents. "It says here in the paper that with just $100 down, I can finance the purchase of a brand-new car. I'd have to make 60 payments of $350 each. I make nearly twice that much each month, so I can afford the car. How can I get the best deal?"

Buying a Vehicle

Goals

★ Describe the process of buying a new or used car, including selection, financing, and wise buying practices.

★ Explain automobile leasing costs, processes, advantages, and disadvantages.

★ Discuss consumer protection available for new- and used-car buyers.

Steps in the Car-Buying Process

What is your dream car? You might long to drive a small, red sports car—a convertible with two seats, a floor shift, and a high-powered engine. Unfortunately, for most people this type of car is not very practical. The high purchase price of the car is only one factor. You must also consider the cost of insurance, licensing and registration, gas, maintenance, and repairs.

Identify Your Needs and Wants

Buying a car starts with identifying your needs (not just your wants). What do you need to do with your car? Will you drive a lot of miles? If so, then good gas mileage should be a major factor in your buying decision. Do you plan to haul a lot of people or gear? Will you take the car off-road? What features would you like to have if you could afford them? After you have made your list of wants and needs, prioritize them. You may have to trade off some of the wants for a lower price.

Determine What You Can Afford

Before you start shopping for a car, determine how much you can afford to spend. One general guideline is that you can afford monthly payments of no more than 20 percent of the money you have left after paying all your regular monthly expenses, such as rent, utilities, credit card payments, etc. Also figure into your budget the costs of maintaining your car and putting gas in it.

Identify and Research Your Choices

Why is it important to research your car choices?

Select several types of cars that would meet your needs. In the library or online, research the features of each possibility. Print and online magazines such as *Consumer Reports, Edmund's New Car Prices,* and *Car and Driver* offer an abundance of information on different car models. Look for articles about performance, repair records, safety records, gas mileage, and prices.

Compare the features of the models you are considering against your list of wants and needs. Note the pros and cons for each car model. Use your list and price range to narrow your choices to just a few that best fit you. When comparing prices, be sure to compare models with the same options.

Decide Whether to Buy New or Used

A primary decision is whether to buy a new car or a used one. Cost is a major factor in this decision. A new car is much more expensive than the same model bought used. Can you afford the high price of a new car? Also, a new car loses much of its market value as soon as you drive it off the lot. A car can lose as much as 20 percent of its value in its first year. By buying a well-maintained used car, you can get more car for your money.

On the other hand, a used car is likely to need more repairs. Even if you have a mechanic check the car's overall health before you buy, a used car is still a bit of an unknown, especially if you are buying from an individual rather than a dealer. You could be buying someone else's problems. A dealer may offer a warranty that you would not get from an individual, but a dealer will typically charge more for the used car.

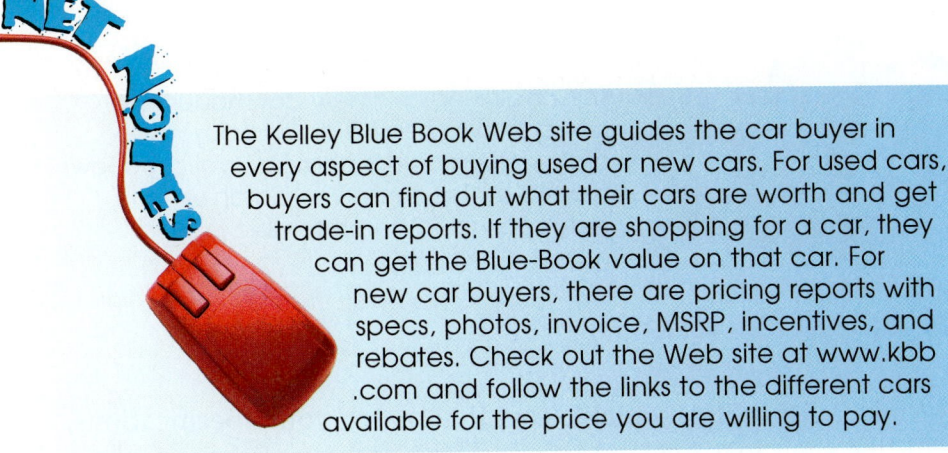

Get Credit Pre-Approval

Find out how much money you will be qualified to borrow *before* visiting car dealers. This process is called **pre-approval.** Pre-approval separates financing from the process of negotiating the price of the car. You may or may not actually take the loan from the financial institution that pre-approved you, but at least you will know how much you can spend before you shop for a car.

To get pre-approved, visit your credit union or bank and fill out an application. Based on the information you supply on the application, the loan officer will determine how much the institution would be willing to lend you. The loan officer will then give you a form stating this pre-approved amount. Typically, the pre-approval will expire in 30 or 60 days, after which you must reapply if you want the loan.

Search for Available Vehicles

Search your newspaper's classified ads and the Internet for cars available in your local area from dealers and from individual sellers. Many areas offer a free print publication, such as *Auto Trader*, dedicated to used-vehicle listings. If your area has such a publication, you can probably find it in the lobby of car parts stores and various other neighborhood stores and restaurants. Many Web sites, such as http://autotrader.com, www.autobytel.com, www.edmunds.com, and http://carpoint.msn.com, allow you to search electronically for specific models, both new and used. Most will even get price quotes for you.

Make a list of the available cars that match your specifications, including their features and prices. These are your finalists—the cars that you think are worth your time to investigate further.

Test Drive Each Vehicle

Sometimes descriptions are quite different from the actual car. Test drive the vehicles of interest to you. Compare ride, handling, braking, features, and cost. Try all the features to see how well they work. Play the radio to judge the sound, but then turn it off so that you can hear the sounds of the car as you drive. Is the engine quiet? Especially when evaluating used cars, listen for noises that might indicate a problem. When you accelerate, look for dark smoke from the exhaust. This is a sign that the car is burning oil, which would require an expensive repair. Look for rust and mismatched paint that might mean the car has been in an accident.

Take your time. Never be in a hurry when shopping for a car. Some salespeople will try to pressure you into buying right away. Resist that temptation. You will enhance your bargaining position with patience and knowledge of the car you are planning to purchase. Experts recommend never purchasing a vehicle on your first visit to a dealership, and before buying, check the dealer's reputation. A call to the Better Business Bureau will give you valuable information about the number and types of complaints consumers have made about this dealer.

Check the History of a Used Vehicle

You can learn the history of any used vehicle if you have its **vehicle identification number (VIN).** Each car has a unique VIN that identifies it. This number is available on car documents and on the dashboard in front of the driver, and is visible through the front windshield.

Get the VIN from the used car you are considering, and enter it into the online search tool at Carfax (www.carfax.com) or call 1-888-4CARFAX. The initial report is free. A detailed history costs approximately $15–$20. This full report provides information such as whether the car has been in a serious accident, how many times the car has been sold, and the mileage readings each time it was sold, so that you can check for odometer rollbacks.

Get the Vehicle Checked Mechanically

After the used vehicle has passed the VIN check and you've decided you'd like to buy it, have it checked out by a mechanic to make sure it is sound. You'll want to know whether the engine is in good shape; a compression test can tell you if a head gasket is about to go out. You'll also want to be sure the transmission is okay. If the car passes these two critical tests, then ask for a complete check to see what might need to be done and how much the repairs would cost. For example, you'll want to know if the car needs a tune-up, how much longer the brakes will last, whether it needs new tires, and so on. A vehicle inspection typically costs around $150. Be sure to ask how much the inspection will cost before you have the vehicle checked.

Many states require vehicles to pass a **vehicle emission test,** which is a test to verify that a vehicle meets the minimum clean-air standards. The fee for the test is usually only $10 to $25. However, repairs needed to meet the test requirements may cost an additional $150 or more. Before deciding to buy a car, ask the seller for the record showing that it passed the most recent vehicle emission test. If the seller cannot produce the record, ask the seller to have the vehicle tested before you buy.

Determine a Fair Price

Decide what price you feel is fair before you make any offer for a car. Kelley Blue Book publishes a popular pricing guide for all models and years. You can find the publication in the library or online at www.kbb.com. By looking up the model and year of the car you are considering, you can find an estimated fair price for it. You can also get a feel for a fair price by checking other ads for cars of the same model and year to see what other sellers are charging.

For a new car, the **sticker price** or *manufacturer's suggested retail price (MSRP)* is the price shown on the tag in the car's window. A fair price for a new car usually lies somewhere between the sticker price and the price the dealer paid for it (the *invoice price*). Many car-buying Web sites, such as www.edmunds.com and http://carpoint.msn.com, can tell you the dealer's invoice price. According to the Automobile Association of America (AAA), the dealer's invoice is approximately 90 percent of sticker for compact and subcompact cars. It is approximately 84 to 87 percent of sticker for luxury cars. Depending on the car's popularity and the number currently on the market, a fair price is likely to be 3 to 6 percent above invoice. Arm yourself with this knowledge before making an offer.

Negotiate the Price

Make up your mind that you will not be pressured into paying more than you feel is fair. Stick to facts and don't reveal emotions to sellers. For example, don't make statements like, "This car is just what I want." This type of information can weaken your bargaining position. Make your initial offer lower than your top price. Then be prepared to negotiate.

To prevent confusion in determining the true price of the new car, negotiate the price of the new car separately from the price for your trade-in. After you have settled on a fair price for the new car, ask how much the dealer will give you for your old car. If the dealer does not offer an amount close to the trade-in value quoted for your car in the Kelley Blue Book, then plan to sell your old car yourself rather than trade it in. Selling the car yourself is a hassle, but you will likely get more money for it that way.

What are some tips in successfully negotiating the price of the car?

PERSONAL PERSPECTIVE

How to Sell a Used Car

If you sell your old car yourself, here are some steps that will help you make a quicker sale:

1. Wash and polish the outside, vacuum and clean the inside, and shampoo the upholstery. Check fluid levels and tire pressure, and make certain all lights are functioning. A car that appears well-cared-for will bring a higher price.
2. Set a reasonable price. Check a recent National Automobile Dealers Association (NADA) or Kelley Blue Book in print or online for estimates of fair market value. Check the classified ads in your newspaper to be sure this price is within the range advertised by other people selling the same model and year as your car.
3. Advertise your vehicle in local newspapers. Weekend ads are usually most effective. If possible, also advertise in a used-car listing publication in print and online.
4. Present the truth to prospective buyers—what's good about the car as well as its weaknesses. Disclose the last time you had a tune-up, and allow prospective buyers to check maintenance records.
5. Go along when the potential buyer test-drives your car. Give the buyer a chance to think and evaluate your car. Observe any inspections performed by a mechanic.
6. Always ask for cash or a cashier's check in payment. Remove the license plates if they cannot be transferred.
7. Make sure that you have the title, registration, and other documents that are required to sell the car. Meet the buyer at the motor vehicles division and transfer title when you receive the cash or cashier's check. Never let a new owner drive away with a car that is still in your name.
8. Notify your insurance company immediately that you have sold the car. During the time you are attempting to sell your car, be sure to maintain at least the minimum coverage (usually liability) required in your state.

Think Critically

1. Why should you tell the truth about your car?
2. Why should you go along on a potential buyer's test drive?
3. Why should you insist on cash or a cashier's check in payment for your car?

If you are uncomfortable negotiating the price of a vehicle, you may wish to use the services of a professional. Through your automobile club, a wholesale membership such as Costco, your credit union, or an online car-buying service, you can get a price that is based on cost to the dealer. Once you know exactly what car you want, the service will locate the car, negotiate the price, and arrange for its delivery. This service may not be free, but it can potentially save you thousands of dollars.

Dealer Negotiating Techniques

If you do your own negotiating, you should be aware of common dealer negotiating practices. For example, the salesperson might say that he or she needs approval from a supervisor. The salesperson leaves you for several minutes and then returns to say your low offer just isn't acceptable. Be polite but don't be intimidated. If the price you are discussing is still below the maximum you set for yourself as the fair price, then make a counteroffer that is a little higher but still no higher than your top price. Walk away from the deal if you feel you are being pressured or the dealer won't come down to a price you feel is fair.

Two deceptive, but not illegal, bargaining techniques are low-balling and high-balling. **Low-balling** is an unrealistically low price offered by the dealer for the buyer's old car as part of the new-car deal. After the customer vigorously protests the low offer, the salesperson pretends to be talked into a better trade-in allowance and thus a sale. **High-balling** is an unrealistically high price offered by the dealer for the buyer's old car as part of the new-car deal. The customer agrees to the buy the new car, based on the high trade-in price offered. However, at the last moment, usually just before the sales agreement is signed, the salesperson remembers that all contracts must be cleared through a higher authority. The salesperson disappears for a few minutes and then reappears with the following news: "My boss won't allow that much for your trade-in." At that point, the salesperson indicates the trade-in would be "good" on a more expensive car or the same car with more options.

Dealer Add-Ons

After you have agreed on the price, the dealer may try to increase the purchase price by the use of **dealer add-ons**—high-priced, high-profit dealer services that add little or no value. For example, dealer preparation is nothing more than cleaning the car and checking the air in the tires and the oil in the engine. These services should be provided without extra charge. Other common dealer add-ons include protective wax or polish, rust-proofing, and extended warranties. Rarely are these special services worth the cost. Just say no!

Financing Your Car

The best way to buy a car is with cash. You'll get the best deals that way. Unfortunately, most people don't have enough money to buy a car for cash. Therefore, you will probably have to get a loan.

Financial Institutions

Banks, credit unions, and even insurance companies offer vehicle loans for 36, 48, or 60 months. Longer terms mean lower monthly payments but higher total interest paid because you are using the money for a longer period of time. In many cases, your local credit union will offer the best car loan. Often, a credit union will finance more of your purchase (requiring less of your own cash), have lower interest rates, and require smaller monthly payments. Compare rates and terms from several financial institutions before selecting a loan.

Car Dealers

Most new car dealers offer financing. On particular models and at particular times of the year, they may offer you better terms than those available from other sources. These special deals are sponsored by the manufacturers or their financing agencies to stimulate sales or to promote a particular model. GMAC (General Motors Acceptance Corporation) is an example of a finance company that makes loans on cars through dealerships. Ford, Chrysler, and most other manufacturers offer similar programs. You would make your payments to the finance company—not the dealer. You will have to qualify for the credit just as if you were applying for credit at a financial institution. Use caution with this type of financing. Don't allow a special promotional loan rate to influence you to buy a more expensive car.

Leasing a Car

Rather than purchasing a new car, you might consider leasing. A car lease is similar to an apartment lease. It is a written agreement that allows you to use the property (in this case, a car) for a specified time period and monthly payment. You do not own the car. You are simply renting its use. However, at the end of the lease period, you usually have an option to buy the car for the price specified in the lease agreement. For example, you may lease a car for two years. At the end of two years, you can turn it in and lease a new one, or you can buy the car. The selling price specified in the lease is based on the expected value of the car at the end of the two-year lease term.

Because interest on car loans is no longer tax deductible, auto leasing is more popular than ever. Individuals can afford to lease a more expensive car than they could buy on credit. In 2000, one third of all cars and trucks were leased rather than sold. The reason is that many people cannot afford the big price tag on new cars. Leasing provides an alternative—no large down payment or trade-in to worry about. Just drive away for a set monthly payment! On the other hand, remember that after making all of the payments, you still own nothing.

Consumer Protection for Car Buyers

As you learned in Chapter 8, a *warranty* is a written statement about a product's qualities or performance that the seller assures the buyer are true. A warranty clearly states what the manufacturer will do if the product does not perform as it should. A new car warranty provides a buyer with some assurance of quality. Car warranties vary in the time and mileage of the protection they offer and in the parts they cover. The main aspects of a warranty are the coverage of basic parts against manufacturer's defects; the power train coverage for the engine, transmission, and drive train; and the corrosion warranty that usually applies to holes due to rust, not to surface rust.

Sometimes, however, being aware of warranty provisions is not enough. Some cars have so many problems (or such hard-to-fix problems) that warranty coverage is of little comfort to their owners. As a result of consumer frustration, many states have enacted lemon laws.

Lemon Laws

Even the most careful purchases can turn out to be lemons. A **lemon** is a car with substantial defects that the manufacturer has been unable to fix after repeated attempts. Because some vehicles just seem to lead from one repair to another, many states have lemon laws. According to most state laws, you have a lemon if, in the first year of ownership or 12,000 miles, (a) you've taken the car into the dealer for four unsuccessful attempts to repair the same substantial defect or (b) your car has been out of service for a total of at least 30 days. Lemon laws allow you to get a new car or your money back. Unfortunately, this protection is not automatic. You need to have good documentation and be prepared for a long process. A proceeding called arbitration and a possible lawsuit may be necessary to enforce your state's law. Figure 23-1 indicates what to do if you have a lemon.

What to Do If You Have a Lemon   **Figure 23-1**

Here are some things you can do to protect yourself in the event you end up with a lemon:

1. When you take the car in for repair, give the dealer a written list of problems. Make sure these problems are in the dealer's repair records. Keep copies of each list and the repair receipts you are given.

2. Any time you are returning to have the same item repaired, point it out to the dealer. Make the dealer aware that the problem is continuing and not new. Again, keep copies of each list and their attempted repairs.

3. If your car qualifies as a lemon, tell the car dealer. Bring copies of your records. If the dealer is not responsive, contact the manufacturer's zone office. Talk to the consumer relations office, or go all the way to their national headquarters if necessary. Follow up the conversation with a letter and copies of your records. Be sure you keep your own copy of the letter and the original documentation.

4. If the defect is serious and the car is dangerous to drive, file for arbitration immediately. Make sure you fill out all necessary forms. State the problem clearly and, once again, provide copies of your documentation.

5. Demand a quick hearing date. Remind the arbitrators that under Section 703 of the Magnuson-Moss Warranty Act you are entitled to an arbitration decision within forty days of filing.

6. You are under no obligation to accept a prolonged hearing. You can demand that the arbitration panel meet and make a decision.

7. If you are not satisfied with the arbitrator's decision or the process, you might want to contact a lawyer who specializes in lemon-law cases. The Center for Auto Safety in Washington, D.C., may be able to help you.

The FTC Used-Car Rule

People who buy a used car must be concerned about whether it has some hidden defects or potentially expensive repairs ahead. The Federal Trade Commission "Used-Car Rule" is designed to protect used-car buyers. This rule does not guarantee that the car has no problems. However, it does require used-car dealers to inform consumers ahead of purchase about who will be responsible for paying for certain repairs if they occur after the sale.

The rule requires dealers to place a sticker, called the "Buyer's Guide," on all used cars they offer. Figure 23-2 illustrates this sticker. If the "As is" box is checked, the buyer must pay all repair costs. If the "Warranty" box is checked, the dealer will pay to repair the items listed as under warranty for the specified period of time. Cars bought from a private seller do not carry a warranty. While you may save money by buying directly from the previous owner, you cannot expect the previous owner to make repairs or stand by the condition of the vehicle. For this reason, a pre-purchase mechanical check is crucial when buying from an individual or with an "as is" sticker.

Check Your Understanding

Review Terms
1. pre-approval
2. vehicle identification number (VIN)
3. vehicle emission test
4. sticker price
5. low-balling
6. high-balling
7. dealer add-ons
8. lemon

Review Concepts
1. Why should you not play the radio the whole time you are test driving a car?
2. Why is it important to know the dealer invoice price before making an offer on a new car?

BUYERS GUIDE

IMPORTANT: Spoken promises are difficult to enforce. Ask the dealer to put all promises in writing. Keep this form.

Chrysler | New Yorker | 1993 | A0A085C147961
VEHICLE MAKE | **MODEL** | **YEAR** | **VIN NUMBER**

T6204B
DEALER STOCK NUMBER (Optional)

WARRANTIES FOR THIS VEHICLE:

☒ AS IS – NO WARRANTY

YOU WILL PAY ALL COSTS FOR ANY REPAIRS. The dealer assumes no responsibility for any repairs regardless of any oral statements about the vehicle.

☐ WARRANTY

☐ **FULL** ☐ **LIMITED WARRANTY. The dealer will pay ___% of the labor and ___% of the parts for the covered systems that fail during the warranty period. Ask the dealer for a copy of the warranty document for a full explanation of warranty coverage, exclusions, and the dealer's repair obligations. Under state law, "implied warranties" may give you even more rights.**

SYSTEMS COVERED: **DURATION:**

_____   _____
_____   _____
_____   _____
_____   _____

☒ **SERVICE CONTRACT. A service contract is available at an extra charge on this vehicle. Ask for details as to coverage, deductible, price, and exclusions. If you buy a service contract within 90 days of the time of sale, state law "implied warranties" may give you additional rights.**

PRE PURCHASE INSPECTION: ASK THE DEALER IF YOU MAY HAVE THIS VEHICLE INSPECTED BY YOUR MECHANIC EITHER ON OR OFF THE LOT.

SEE THE BACK OF THIS FORM for important additional information, including a list of some major defects that may occur in used motor vehicles.

Maintaining Your Vehicle

★ List the costs of owning and operating a car, from depreciation, gas, and taxes to the cost of accessories.
★ Describe methods for extending the life of your car and maintaining its resale value.

Cost of Operating a Car

What kinds of costs are involved in operating a car?

Most people spend more of their income on a car and related expenses than on any other item except housing and food. The initial outlay for the vehicle (down payment, taxes, title registration, and other fees) plus ongoing loan and insurance payments are just part of the cost of ownership. Costs associated with operating your car add considerably to the overall cost of ownership.

Gas and Oil

The cost of gasoline depends on the fuel-efficiency of your car's engine and the number of miles you drive. More-powerful engines often require more fuel to run than less-powerful engines. Gasoline and oil are variable operating expenses. This means that your cost varies with the number of miles you drive and with the constantly fluctuating price of gas.

In an effort to improve gas mileage and reduce air pollution from exhaust fumes, car manufacturers are starting to introduce hybrid vehicles. These cars combine a gasoline engine with an electric motor. They can currently get as much as 68 miles per gallon and 700 miles on a tank of gas.

Depreciation

As you learned in Chapter 14, *depreciation* is a decline in the value of property due to normal wear and tear. As a car ages, the number of miles driven increases, the physical condition begins to deteriorate, and mechanical difficulties arise. Also, styles and consumer tastes change over time. All these factors usually cause cars to lose market value. However, not all cars depreciate. Very old vehicles in excellent condition may *appreciate,* or increase in value, if people value them as collectors' items.

Depreciation is the single greatest cost of owning a car. The cost of gasoline comes second. In most cases, the age of a car is the most important factor in determining its resale or trade-in value. Other factors include mileage, mechanical condition, brand or style popularity, size, and color. A car will retain more of its value over time if it is well-maintained and has fewer miles on it at the time of sale. Especially-popular models depreciate more slowly than other models.

Registration and Title

All states charge a fee to register a car title. As you learned in the last chapter, a *title* is a legal document that establishes ownership. A car title lists the legal owner (usually the lending institution) and the registered owner (you). You must pay title fees and sales taxes only at the time you buy the car. However, you must pay a license car tag fee each year.

Maintenance and Repairs

The owner's manual will tell you what services your car needs and how often. Typically, you can expect to change the oil every few thousand miles, have a major engine tune-up every 20,000 to 30,000 miles, and perform other maintenance at scheduled intervals. Car systems that you should monitor and maintain include emissions control, air-conditioning, brakes, and transmission.

You also should plan for unscheduled repairs. Such things as flat tires, broken belts, and leaky hoses happen from time to time, and the repairs can be costly. Saving money for car repairs should be part of your monthly budget. As your car gets older, repair costs will increase. You should expect to replace relatively inexpensive parts such as fan belts, hoses, the battery, and the muffler, but also plan for occasional expensive repairs such as replacing the alternator. You will also need new tires at some point. Tires can cost from $50 to $200 apiece.

Career Links

Automotive technicians inspect, maintain, and repair cars and light trucks. New automotive technology requires workers who can use computerized shop equipment and work with electronic components. Technicians should complete a formal training program after graduating from high school. Various automobile manufacturers sponsor certification or degree programs, with internships at dealers. Good reading, math, and computer skills are needed in order to stay current with technology.

For more information, refer to the *Occupational Outlook Handbook* at www.bls.gov or search the Internet using such key words as "careers," "jobs," and "automobiles."

Accessories

Many people choose to add certain features to make their vehicles safer, more functional and attractive, or more efficient. These items include snow tires, floor mats, seat covers, wheel covers, striping and paint features, alarm systems, and sound systems. In some cases, these costs will add to the value of the vehicle; in other cases, they will subtract from it.

Extending the Life of Your Car

Because a car is expensive, you will get your best value (cost versus benefit) if you take care of your investment. By performing routine maintenance, taking care of the interior and exterior, and practicing good driving habits, you can keep your car running well and looking good.

Maintain Fluid Levels

Most newer cars can run 7,000 or more miles between oil changes. But changing oil more frequently can add years of life to a car. Oil lubricates the moving parts of the engine and keeps it clean. Oil must be changed to eliminate accumulated dirt and sludge. Your

ENGINE OIL GRADES AND VISCOSITY

All engine oils are not the same. There are various service grades, depending on additives that are mixed in.

Service Grade

Service SF is the highest grade of engine oil for gasoline-powered vehicles. If you drive a late model car, the owner's manual will specify service grade, or may simply say "heavy duty." Service SF will work in these cars.

Viscosity

Oil thickness requirements vary with temperature ranges in your area. Viscosity is indicated by the letters "SAE." The higher the number, the thicker the oil. For example, SAE 40 means the oil is thicker than SAE 30. If your area has great variations in temperature, you will likely want a multigrade oil for changes in temperature.

Multigrade oil is marked with two numbers, such as 10W-40. In this example, the 10 applies to cold weather and the 40 applies to hot weather. If, for example, the rating is 5W-30, then the car needs more viscosity to get started, and then evens out once it is warm. Usually a 10W-30 or 10W-40 can be used year-round.

individual driving habits will dictate how often you should change the oil. For example, the frequent starting and stopping of city driving wear oil out sooner than do long expressway trips.

Experts advise changing oil every 3,000 miles, or every three months, whichever comes first, for city driving. You should replace the oil filter when you change the oil. The filter helps clean the oil circulating through the engine. Lubrication, oil change, and oil filter replacement (called "lube, oil, and filter") should cost from $18 to $30, depending on the size of the engine. Figure 23-3 points out differences in engine oil and helps you decide which one is right for your vehicle.

You should also regularly check and maintain the proper fluid levels for your transmission, power-steering, and brakes. These car functions must have fluid to work properly.

Perform Routine Maintenance

Don't wait for trouble before checking fluid levels and inspecting belts, hoses, and tire pressure. Most car owners find that by replacing parts periodically, they can avoid major problems. These ongoing routine checks and fixes should cost $100 to $250 a year but will save you major repairs in the long run. The owner's manual will tell you mileage or time intervals for certain servicing.

Keep Your Car in a Garage

If possible, keep your car in a garage. A car kept in the garage at night, and when its owner is at home, is safe from theft and vandalism. It is also protected from the weather, which can damage or destroy its finish and even affect its mechanical condition. Low temperatures, for example, affect almost every component. The engine is harder to start, and the battery is weaker. Thus the starter has to work harder, and the charging system is stressed.

Preserve the Exterior

It's important to keep your car clean. When water sits on the surface of metal, it can cause rust. Cleaning off road grime occasionally will protect your car's shiny finish. Apply protective wax to guard your paint from the damaging rays of the sun and from snow-melting chemicals spread on streets in cold climates. If you live near the coast, car wax is essential for protecting your car from the salty air.

Wax your car twice a year—before the cold and rainy winter and before the hot and dry summer. Once your car has begun to **oxidize** (permanently lose its color and shine because of chemical reaction with the air), it is

Why is it important to keep your car clean?

very difficult to restore the original gloss. In most cases, a car with oxidized paint must be repainted to restore its shine. A **polishing compound** is a substance that can smooth out surface scratches, scuffs, and stains. Polishing compounds, often called cleaners and pre-waxes, can be tricky to use. They often contain **abrasives,** which are coarse materials that scour or rub away a surface. Used gently, an abrasive can remove the top layer of paint. An abrasive will expose the shiny paint underneath. But rubbed too vigorously or too often, an abrasive will strip the paint right down to the primer.

Just as important as washing and waxing is repairing dents and paint chips before rust has a chance to take hold. You can get a small amount of vehicle paint that matches your car's color from a dealer that sells your make of car. When something nicks your paint, such as a rock that hits your car when you drive, you should touch up the ding. First clean the area with mild soap and dry it. Then apply the touch-up paint in very small amounts.

Preserve the Interior

The condition of the inside of your car is also very important for good resale value. Your car's **upholstery** is the seat-covering material. Generally, cloth upholstery is more durable than vinyl. Although spills and dirt are more difficult to clean off of cloth upholstery, vinyl can crack and tear when it gets too hot or cold and can be punctured by sharp objects. Leather upholstery holds up best, but it is more expensive and requires regular cleaning and lubricating to keep it soft.

Floor mats will protect the carpeting and are a good investment. You can cover the interior of your trunk with an old blanket to protect it. Avoid eating messy foods in the car and vacuum frequently to keep your car's interior in good condition. Products are available to rub on vinyl dashboards and plastic interior surfaces to protect them from fading and cracking from exposure to the sun's rays. If you must park your car in the sun for long periods of time, you might consider covering the inside of your windshield with an inexpensive cardboard shade made for the purpose.

Follow Wise Driving Habits

Good driving habits can keep your car running efficiently for years. New cars have a "break-in period." You will need to drive differently during this period than later in your car's life.

When the car is new:

1. Don't drive for long stretches at a constant speed. Vary speed as driving conditions permit.
2. During the first thousand miles, drive progressively faster, accelerating gradually.
3. Avoid fast starts, sudden stops, sharp turns, and rapid gear changes to help your brakes get broken in.
4. Drive at moderate speeds and around town, avoiding long trips so your tires can get adjusted. You may need additional wheel balancing and front-end alignment.

For all cars:

1. Don't race a cold engine. Give it 10 to 15 seconds to warm up to allow the oil to start circulating. Then drive off gently as soon as the engine is running smoothly.
2. Keep coolants in your car's radiator during hot weather and antifreezes in it during very cold weather.
3. When driving a car with a manual transmission, shift deliberately, pausing as you move through the neutral position.
4. Don't shift into a forward gear when your car is rolling backward, or vice versa.
5. When stopped in traffic, hold the car in place with the brakes rather than engaging the clutch, to avoid excessive wear on the clutch.
6. Don't turn the steering wheel when the car is motionless. This strains the front-end components. Turn the wheel only when the car is moving.
7. Keep the windshield and back window free of ice, using a scraper rather than your wiper blades. Running wipers over a dry surface can scratch the glass and tear the blades.
8. Glance at gauges and warning lights as you drive. When your car signals you to stop or to get something checked, do it right away. For example, if the oil pressure gauge or warning light shows, it could mean your engine is about to self-destruct. When your engine shows it's too hot, turn off the air-conditioner and drive slower. If overheating is severe, pull over and stop the engine quickly. Open the hood, but do not unscrew the radiator cap.
9. Finally, always wear your seat belt. It can save your life!

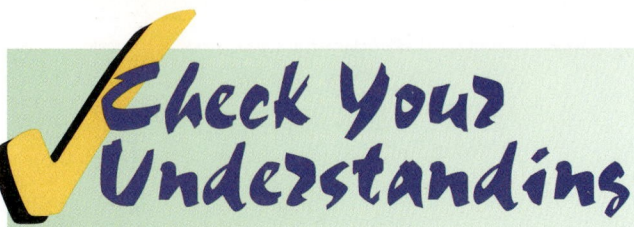

Check Your Understanding

Review Terms
1. oxidize
2. polishing compound
3. abrasives
4. upholstery

Review Concepts
1. Why do cars usually depreciate? What might cause a particular car to appreciate?
2. Why should you avoid turning the steering wheel while the car is not in motion?

23.1 Buying a Vehicle

- Buying a car starts with identifying your needs, not just your wants, and prioritizing your list. Then determine what you can afford. In general, your payments should be no more than 20 percent of the money left over after you pay all other expenses.
- Identify different models that would meet your needs. Research them, compare their features to your list, and narrow your choices to a few that best fit your criteria and price range.
- Decide whether to buy new or used. You can get more for your money with a good used car, but it may need more repairs and carries no warranty if you buy it from a private seller.
- Get a loan pre-approved. Then search for available vehicles in your chosen model. Test drive your top choices. Before buying a used car, check its history by looking up its VIN and have a mechanic check it.
- Determine a fair price before you make an offer. Kelley Blue Book provides estimated prices for used cars. For new cars, a fair price lies between the sticker price and the invoice price.
- Make your initial offer below your top price. Then negotiate, but do not allow the seller to pressure you into paying more than the price you feel is fair. Negotiate the price of a new car separately from the price of your trade-in. Resist dealer add-ons.
- Banks, credit unions, insurance companies, or the car dealer offer car loans. Compare rates and terms before selecting a loan.

- If you decide to lease a car, you are actually renting it, though you will likely have an option to buy at the end of the lease term.
- Lemon laws help consumers get a new car or their money back if the car they purchased has substantial, unfixable defects. The FTC Used-Car Rule requires dealers to display a sticker on their used cars, stating who is responsible for paying for certain repairs.

23.2 Maintaining Your Vehicle

- Costs of operating a vehicle include the down payment, title registration, sales taxes, loan and insurance payments, and annual license fees.
- The amount you spend for gasoline will depend on the fuel efficiency of your engine, the number of miles you drive, and the constantly fluctuating gas prices.
- Most vehicles depreciate, or decline in value, as they get older, wear out, and go out of style. Some vehicles can appreciate if people value them as collectors' items.
- Perform regular maintenance, such as oil changes and tune-ups, according to the schedule in your owner's manual.
- Protect your vehicle's exterior by cleaning, waxing, touching-up paint chips, and keeping it in a garage, if possible.
- Protect your vehicle's interior by vacuuming, applying protective products to vinyl and leather surfaces, and buying protective coverings such as floor mats.
- During the break-in period on a new car, vary your speed, accelerate gradually, and drive at moderate speeds.
- Wise driving habits include allowing the vehicle to warm up, keeping coolants and fluid levels up, acting on early warning signs announced by gauges and noises, and wearing your seat belt.

Review Terms

Directions: Can you find the definition for each of the following terms used in Chapter 23?

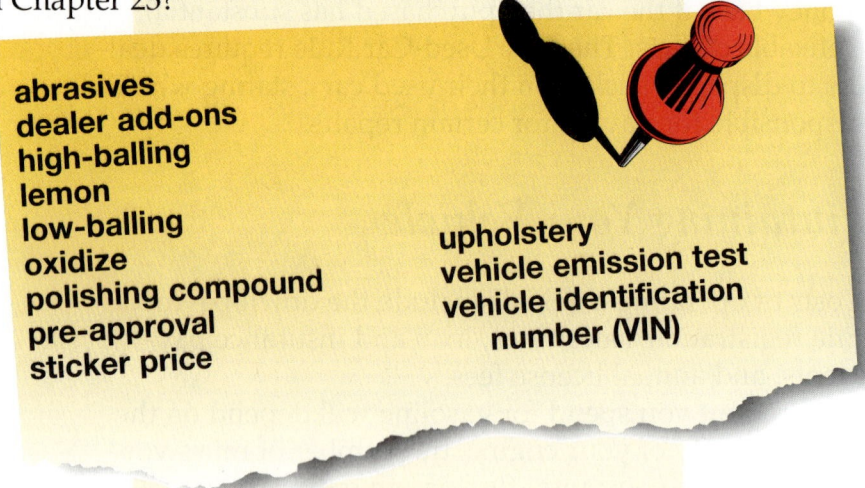

abrasives
dealer add-ons
high-balling
lemon
low-balling
oxidize
polishing compound
pre-approval
sticker price

upholstery
vehicle emission test
vehicle identification number (VIN)

1. A car with substantial defects that the manufacturer has been unable to fix after repeated attempts.
2. A deceptive negotiating technique in which a car dealer offers an unrealistically low price for the buyer's old car as part of the new-car deal.
3. A deceptive negotiating technique in which a car dealer offers an unrealistically high price for the buyer's old car as part of the new-car deal.
4. The process of qualifying for a loan before you begin looking for a car.
5. A number unique to a car that serves to identify it.
6. High-priced, high-profit dealer services that add little of value to your car purchase.
7. A test to verify that a vehicle meets the minimum clean air standards.
8. A substance that can smooth out surface scratches, scuffs, and stains.
9. Coarse materials that scour or rub away a surface.
10. Seat-covering material.
11. The price shown on the tag in a new car's window.
12. Permanently lose color and shine because of chemical reaction with the air.

1. What is the first step in the car-buying process?
2. How can you determine how much you can afford to spend for a car?
3. What are some sources of information about cars—their safety, repair record, reliability, and so on?
4. What are the advantages and disadvantages of buying a used car?
5. What should you do to evaluate a car during a test drive?
6. How can you find out if the mileage shown on a used car's odometer has been rolled back?
7. What should you do to assure that the used car you are considering is mechanically sound?
8. How can you determine a fair price for a new or used car?
9. How is leasing different from buying a car?
10. What are some costs of operating a car?
11. What are some factors that cause a car to depreciate?
12. What are some steps you can take to extend the life of your car?
13. Why is it important to change the oil regularly?
14. List three things you can do to protect your car's interior.
15. Explain five wise driving strategies.

APPLY YOUR KNOWLEDGE

1. Make a list of car dealerships in your area. Divide into groups. Each group should visit one dealer. Collect brochures on various car models and look at sticker prices. As a group, report your findings—characteristics of the cars in the dealer's product line, price ranges, how you were treated, and so on.
2. Choose a car topic that you would like to learn more about, such as which is the best car stereo or which motor oil works

best for a particular kind of car. Find articles about this topic in current issues of *Consumer Reports* and *Car and Driver* magazine in print or online. Write a one-page summary of your findings.

3. Choose a particular model of used car. Find listings for this model for sale in your area, using an Internet car-buying site or your newspaper's classified ads in print or online. Write a paragraph about the cars you found. How many are for sale? What are their years and prices? What options did they include? How did the prices offered by dealers compare to those of private sellers?

4. Find a car loan calculator online at a popular car-buying Web site, such as Edmunds (www.edmunds.com) or Carpoint (http://carpoint.msn.com). Often you will find such a calculator on the "advice" page. If you have a job, put in your salary and other financial information required by the calculator. How much car does the calculator say you can afford? Next, locate your dream car at the site. How much does it cost? Insert different salaries into the calculator until you find the amount you would have to make to afford this car. What would your monthly salary have to be?

5. Visit Kelley Blue Book at www.kbb.com and look up the trade-in value of your car or your family's car. This is the estimated amount a dealer would give you for your car in trade for a new one. Now look up the used-car retail price for the same car. This is an estimate of a fair price that a buyer could expect to pay for the car. Now subtract the two figures. What is the difference? What does this number represent?

6. Talk to a loan officer about the process of pre-approval for a car loan. Ask to see application forms and discuss qualifications. Based on the information gathered, prepare a summary of income requirements for an auto loan. For example, what monthly income would it take to be able to afford a particular model of Ford? What would the monthly payments be?

7. In groups, prepare a list of options that you feel are very important to have in a car. Then research the price of each of these options. For example, if you choose a CD player as vital, then what would it cost to add this feature to the base price of a car? You will find prices for these items in consumer magazines in your library or at online car-buying sites, or visit dealerships and study the sticker prices on cars of your choice. Are the prices of options different for different car models?

8. Research vehicle leasing in your area. Begin by looking in the Yellow Pages to find several companies that offer lease pro-

grams. Call or visit them to get information on how leasing works, the costs, and the benefits. If possible, talk to a person who leases a vehicle, or who has leased one, to write a list of advantages and disadvantages of leasing.

9. Prepare a budget that lists potential costs a car owner may face. Ask someone who has owned a car for a long time to help you complete the list. For example, in computing the year's depreciation, check the classified ads to see what that year and model of car is selling for. Deduct this from the purchase price of the car and divide by the years of age. Keep in mind that a vehicle depreciates more in the first few years than it does later. Determine a total cost and summarize in a paragraph your findings about the costs of operating a vehicle.

10. Call your state motor vehicles division or visit a local office and get information about registration and license fees in your state. You may have to wait in line to get the information, or you may be able to locate pamphlets that explain these costs. While you are there, pick up a copy of the driver's manual and other information about your state's vehicle laws.

11. Borrow an owner's manual and read through it. In the section that discusses regular maintenance schedules, find out how often the oil needs to be changed, how often a major tune-up is required, and what things must be checked, repaired, or replaced at regular intervals. Based on this information, prepare a cost summary for a year of regular maintenance.

12. Research different types of waxes and cleaning compounds that you might use on a vehicle. Compare their features— what they will do and the costs, together with possible hazards. Estimate the cost of keeping a car clean, waxed, and touched up for a year.

13. For a week, observe drivers as you are riding to and from school or at other times of the day. Keep a list of things drivers do to avoid injuries and accidents. Also keep a list of things drivers do that could potentially cause harm to themselves and others. Write a summary of what you have learned.

Solve Problems

1. Your friend Marsha is considering buying a small older car. She works part-time after school and on holidays. In the summer, she makes good wages but is saving for a college

education. She visits a local dealer who suggests that buying an older car is not a good idea. The dealer points out that the car may break down, will likely cost a lot to maintain, and wouldn't be dependable. Do you agree? What advice would you give Marsha?

2. Your friend Denzel has decided to buy a car. Because he is working at a regular job, he thinks he can afford a new car. He isn't sure how much money he can afford to pay for monthly car payments, and he doesn't know how much of a down payment he might need to make. How would you advise him to get started in the car-buying process?

3. To buy the new car Denzel selected, he would need a loan for $20,000. The dealer would finance the loan at 9.5 percent, and Denzel's payments would be $420 a month. Use your Loan Planner Tool to calculate how many payments Denzel would have to make to pay off the loan. How many years would he be paying for the car?

PLANNING TOOLS

4. Jack Stein has already purchased two cars. He is ready to buy a third car but frankly, he tells you, the experience is so negative that he's putting it off for as long as possible. When you talk to him, you discover that the problem lies in the buying process itself. When Jack gets into a dealership, he feels pressured. He then buys something that he later regrets. What advice can you give him to have a more positive experience?

5. Consuela Chavez just purchased a new car. Now she faces a decision: Should she add to the cost of her purchase with undercoating and rust protection, a polish shine application, and a three-year extended warranty? Altogether, these items will add almost $1,000 to the price of the car. She's concerned because the dealer told her that these will add to the life of the car, and she plans to keep it for a long time. What is your advice?

6. You are buying a new car and are considering whether to trade in your old vehicle. The dealer tells you that you are paying $1,500 less on the new car because of your trade-in. But you find that in reality you would get a $1,500 reduction in price for having no trade-in and for paying cash. Discuss the pro's and con's of trading in your car versus selling it yourself.

7. Your friend Kendra has a car that has been fixed four times for the same problem—a faulty starter. Advise her about lemon laws.

8. You are looking at a vehicle for possible purchase. A sticker on the window called the "Buyer's Guide" says this vehicle is sold strictly "As Is." What does this mean?

Resource Management

9. Your friend Brett is excited about buying his first car. He is paying cash for the car. This purchase will deplete his savings, but he has a part-time job that pays $100 a week. Explain to him the costs of operating a car.

10. Yami Okihiro just purchased a new car. He plans to drive the car at least 100,000 miles and then get as much money as he can for it. What advice can you give him about extending the life of the car and improving its resale value?

For related activities and links, point your browser to
www.mypf.swep.com

Chapter 24

Family Decisions

Terms to Know

wedding party
civil ceremony
itinerary
reservation
travel agency
overbook

dissolution of
   marriage
property settlement
   agreement
alimony
cremation

Up Front

Lionel and Keisha have announced their engagement and plans to be married. They both have large families and want a formal wedding with all the trimmings.

"By waiting a year, we'll be able to plan this wedding thoroughly, and we'll both be finished with college," Lionel said to Keisha. "It also gives us time to save money, since we can't expect our parents to pay for the type of wedding we'd like to have."

"You're right," replied Keisha. "There are a million details, and I'd like to enjoy this period of time. I think a year is just the right amount of time between the announcement and the wedding. We also need to plan the honeymoon. Do you want to hike in the mountains or relax on the beach?"

Goals

★ Describe the steps, costs, and planning involved in getting married.
★ Discuss important family living decisions and why financial goals are important.
★ Outline the steps needed to plan a successful vacation.

Marriage and Commitment

Statistics show that people are waiting until later to get married and start families, and that more people than ever are choosing to remain single. For those who choose to have a long and committed relationship, the process can be vastly rewarding and surprisingly complex.

Assuming that a couple has the legal capacity to get married (age 18 in most states), many honest discussions about goals and values should precede the decision to legalize their commitment. For example, if one person feels that having children is a vital part of the couple's lives together while the other does not want children, this difference could present an insurmountable obstacle. It's also important to discuss issues such as working, political and religious beliefs, where to live, roles (such as who pays the bills), hobbies, vacations, and living styles (from perfectionist to slob).

Engagement

When a couple decides to commit to a life together, they become engaged, or formally pledged to each other. An engagement or commitment ring, a symbol of this pledge, can cost between a few hundred and a few thousand dollars, depending on the style, size, and kind of stone and setting selected.

Why is it important to take time to plan a wedding?

An engagement period of six months to a year allows the couple time to prepare for the wedding, make plans for the future, and set joint goals. Once the couple announces their engagement to friends and family, they are ready to begin carefully planning the many steps to ensure a smooth and memorable wedding.

In 1998, the median age for first marriages in the United States was 26 for males and 25 for females.

Premarital Counseling

Some religions require pre-wedding counseling sessions. The couple meets with a member of the clergy or designated counselor, together and separately, to discuss issues that will be vital to the success of the marriage and later family life. There may be a predetermined number of sessions, or the number of sessions may vary according to how well prepared for marriage the counselor or cleric thinks the couple is. Topics most often discussed include money and budgeting, the meaning of the marriage commitment, in-laws and other potential problems, and religious aspects of marriage that are unique to each faith. The counseling sessions should be planned early, well before making final preparations for the wedding.

Ceremony Plans and Costs

Planning for the wedding ceremony should begin at least six months in advance. Figure 24-1 is a bride's budget worksheet, which shows the many preparations to consider. (A groom may use a similar worksheet, covering expenses he can expect to incur.) This worksheet should be completed in rough-draft form as the wedding plans progress. The cost of each item will vary according to style, quantity, and preferences. As costs begin to add up, the bride and groom may decide to adjust their preferences to reduce some of the expenses.

A number of print magazines and Web sites offer helpful information for planning a wedding. At www.brideandgroom.com and www.modernbride.com, you can find the latest ideas on making

Bride's Budget Worksheet   **Figure 24-1**

Engagement Party

Invitations . . . . $ _____
Food . . . . _____
Beverages . . . . _____
Music . . . . _____
Rental fees . . . . _____
Decorations . . . . _____
Professional services . . . . _____
Gratuities . . . . _____

Total . . . . $ _____

Stationery

Invitations . . . . $ _____
Announcements . . . . _____
At-home cards . . . . _____
Personal stationery . . . . . _____
Stamps . . . . _____

Total . . . . $ _____

Clothing

Wedding dress . . . . $ _____
Headpiece/veil . . . . _____
Shoes . . . . _____
Accessories . . . . _____
Personal trousseau . . . . . _____

Total . . . . $ _____

*Denotes expenses usually
shared by both families

Bridesmaids' Luncheon

Invitations and
   place cards . . . . $ _____
Food . . . . _____
Beverages . . . . _____
Rental fees . . . . _____
Decorations . . . . _____
Professional services . . . . _____
*Gratuities . . . . _____

Total . . . . $ _____

Photographs

Engagement portrait . . . . $ _____
Wedding portrait . . . . . . _____
Formal photos . . . . _____
Reprints . . . . _____

Total . . . . $ _____

Wedding Ceremony

Sanctuary rental . . . . $ _____
Music . . . . _____
Decorations . . . . _____
Flowers for attendants . . . _____
Aisle runner . . . . _____
Transportation
   to/from ceremony . . . . _____
*Gratuities . . . . _____
Miscellaneous . . . . _____

Total . . . . $ _____

Reception

Hall rental . . . . $ _____
Decorations . . . . _____
Music . . . . _____
Food . . . . _____
Beverages . . . . _____
Wedding cake . . . . _____
Favors . . . . _____
Professional services . . . . _____
*Gratuities . . . . _____

Total . . . . $ _____

Other

Bridal consultant fees . . . $ _____
Accommodations for
   out-of-town
   attendants . . . . _____
*Security guard . . . . _____
Sound recording of
   ceremony . . . . _____
*Insurance for
   wedding gifts . . . . _____
Bride's blood test
   (if required) . . . . _____
Groom's ring . . . . _____
Gift for groom . . . . _____
Gift for attendants . . . . . _____
Special effects . . . . _____
Other fees . . . . _____
   _____
   _____
   _____

Total . . . . $ _____

GRAND TOTAL . . . . $ _____

the wedding memorable and seamless. The site www
.Click4Weddings.com offers checklists and a budget worksheet
to help you plan your wedding. At www.AmericanBride.com,
brides can register to receive special offers and information about
all types of products and services, from engraved invitations to
caterers.

The bride and groom and each set of parents should prepare guest lists and then combine them. The number of guests and the size of the wedding party will determine the number of invitations needed, size of the church, cost of the reception, and so forth. The **wedding party** consists of the people who are active participants in the wedding ceremony: the bride and groom, best man, maid or matron of honor, bridesmaids, ushers, flower girl, and so on.

In the past, wedding expenses were paid by the bride's family. This custom is changing. Now, the couple is paying for more of the expenses, along with the groom's family, who usually pays for items such as the rehearsal dinner or reception or maybe splits the expenses with the bride's family.

Typically, the following expenses belong solely to the groom:

1. Bride's ring(s)
2. Marriage license
3. Wedding gift for the bride
4. Gifts for the best man, groomsmen, and ring bearer
5. The bride's bouquet and going-away corsage, corsages for mothers and grandmothers, and boutonnieres for the men in the wedding party
6. Cleric's or judge's fee
7. Bachelor dinner (unless given and paid for by the best man)
8. Lodging (if necessary) for out-of-town groomsmen
9. Groom's special clothing, including clothing for rehearsal dinner, wedding, and honeymoon
10. Delivery of wedding presents to new home

The bride and groom usually plan the wedding jointly, giving much consideration to cost. The size of the wedding, the time of day, the location, and the formality of the bride's dress are what determine the style of the wedding. A *formal wedding* may be held in the daytime or in the evening, and all guests and participants wear formal attire (which, for evening, includes long gowns and tuxedos). A *semiformal wedding* usually is held during the afternoon or early evening, with less formal wear required of guests. While the wedding party may still dress as formally or informally as they choose, guests generally wear suits and dresses normally chosen for special occasions. An *informal wedding* may be held outside, in a church, or almost anywhere. No special clothing is required for the wedding party or for the guests.

Some couples prefer a **civil ceremony**, which is a wedding performed by a public official, such as a judge or justice-of-the-peace, rather than a member of the clergy. This is a quick, inexpensive ceremony and requires the presence of two witnesses in most states.

The Honeymoon

Immediately following the wedding reception, the newly married couple usually takes a honeymoon trip. Most couples plan a trip out of town. Resorts and places that provide different types of entertainment are popular. Honeymoons may be inexpensive car trips, elaborate cruises, or flights to exotic islands. A honeymoon may last from several days to several weeks and cost several thousand dollars. A couple generally plans the honeymoon together, carefully considering preferences and sharing costs involved.

Family Financial Decisions

When people live together in a committed relationship, they form a new family unit. The family should make major decisions together, based on each person's needs and wants. Ideally, decisions regarding goals, the budget, and division of responsibilities must be open to discussion at all times.

Family Goals

Couples should examine their needs and priorities and set goals for the future together. Short-term goals involve decisions about the near term, such as where to live for now, whether both partners will work, what major purchases to make this year and next, and what leisure activities they will participate in, jointly and separately. Intermediate goals are goals the couple wants to pursue in the next five to ten years: whether they want children, where the couple will live in the foreseeable future, and whether either partner should consider a career change. Long-term goals are goals for the distant future. They include decisions about children's education (savings and investments), special events, and retirement.

To guide your financial decision making, keep the following in mind:

1. Financial goals should be realistic and based on your income and life situation. An annual vacation in the Caribbean would not be realistic on a modest income.
2. Financial goals should be listed in specific measurable terms. The goal of "accumulating $10,000 in a mutual fund within five years" is a clearer goal than "saving money for future expenses."

3. Your financial goals should specify the action you plan to take and should serve as the basis for various financial activities.

As you learned in Chapter 8, a *financial plan* is an orderly program for spending, saving, and investing the money you earn. It summarizes your current financial situation, analyzes your financial needs, and suggests a direction for your financial activities. You can create this document yourself or use the assistance of a professional financial planner.

The Family Budget

In Chapter 8, you learned the steps in creating a budget. You can follow these same steps in creating a budget for your family. But unlike an individual budget, a family budget should consider the needs and goals of every family member in allocating resources. Since family resources are limited, family members cannot have everything they want. They will have to negotiate with each other and make compromises to prepare a plan that works best for the family as a whole.

A family budget allocates spending, saving, borrowing, and investing of the family's pooled resources to meet future goals. Joint decisions are often difficult because more people are involved in the decision making. Nevertheless, family budgeting is an essential part of a successful marriage. Continually communicate with the other members of your household about financial goals and the financial activities needed to attain them.

Dividing Responsibilities

Maintaining a household entails many ongoing responsibilities, many of them financial. Couples should agree on how to arrange their family finances. For example, a couple may choose to have individual as well as joint checking accounts. If the family has only one checking account, managing the account will be easier if only one person writes the checks. Otherwise, accidental overdrawing can easily result.

Many couples choose to have individual checking accounts, and each partner is responsible for part of the income and part of the bills. For example, the couple may decide that one partner will pay utilities, groceries and household expenses, and the car payment, and the other will pay the rent, entertainment expenses, insurance premiums, and miscellaneous expenses. Then each partner is responsible for balancing his or her checking account each month and meeting his or her part of the budget.

Couples must divide other ongoing household tasks as well. Perhaps one partner might take charge of preparing tax returns and doing the family grocery shopping. The other partner might take responsibility for making vacation arrangements, planning social engagements, and arranging to have home repairs done. Housecleaning can be less distasteful if partners do the tasks they like best and share equally the tasks that neither likes to do. By agreeing on how to divide up household responsibilities, both partners can do their fair share and avoid the resentment that may result from an unequal division of labor.

AROUND THE GLOBE

Some 95 percent of all marriages in India are arranged, even among those in the educated middle class. Many Indians believe that arranged marriages are more successful than marriages in Europe and the U.S. They assert that romantic love does not necessarily lead to a good marriage and that real love comes from a properly arranged union between two individuals and their families.

Think Critically: How might family decision making be different in India from the way it is in Western societies?

Vacation Planning

Vacations are an important part of life. Well-planned vacations maximize the time available for fun.

Why should you plan vacations ahead of time?

Kind of Vacation

Apply the decision-making process to help you choose a vacation. First, define the problem: What does your family want most from a vacation—relaxation, excitement, travel, adventure, special events, visiting relatives, or a combination? Based on these goals for the vacation and the time and

Figure 24-2 *Vacation Analysis*

VACATION ANALYSIS

$299 or less	$300 – $1,000 to spend	More than $1,000
Camping	Car trip	Car or plane trip
Visiting relatives	Sports (skiing, other adventure)	Tours/group travel
Sports events	Amusement parks	Varied entertainment options
Three days or less	Three to five days	Five days or more

money available, identify your alternatives, as shown in Figure 24-2. Then gather information about each alternative, weigh the pros and cons of each, and make a final decision.

The more money available, the longer and more expensive the vacation can be. Your choices may be different from those listed in Figure 24-2. Each family should select the type of vacation that best matches its goals and budget. Having a successful vacation depends on selecting the trip that will best satisfy family members, saving the money to spend on it, and planning it carefully.

Itineraries

If you plan your vacation activities ahead of time, then you can use your vacation time to do them rather than waste time finding hotels, figuring out transportation, and other practical details. Start your planning by writing out what will happen, when, at what cost, and what needs to be done. An **itinerary** is a detailed schedule of events, times, and places. You can make your own for the entire trip, listing each day's activities, as shown in Figure 24-3. Build in flexibility, however. Bad weather or unexpected problems may require you to change your plans on the fly. Plan a few alternative activities that you can do if you need to make a change.

You may want to list on your itinerary the time it takes to do certain activities, distances to get to and from activities, methods of transportation, and special notes, such as "bring camera." When designing your itinerary, be sure to leave enough time to do the planned activities in comfort and relaxation. Check on seasonal adjustments that may change operating days, fees, and opening or closing times. Before going on vacation, leave a copy of your itinerary with a neighbor or friend in case of emergency.

ITINERARY

Date	Time	Activity
Monday	8:00 A.M.	Arrive at airport (Flight 739 leaves at 9:05 A.M.).
	10:00 A.M.	Arrive at Los Angeles airport. Take hotel shuttle service; arrive at hotel by 10:45 A.M.
	12:00 noon	Lunch at hotel restaurant.
	1:30 P.M.	Disneyland for remainder of day. Dinner at Disneyland.
Tuesday	8:00 A.M.	Breakfast at Howard Johnson's.
	9:00 A.M.	Knott's Berry Farm (20 minute ride by tour bus). Spend day there; eat lunch there.
	7:00 P.M.	Leave Knott's Berry Farm; go to dinner at Bob's Big Boy.
	8:00 P.M.	Return to hotel.
Wednesday	8:00 A.M.	Breakfast at Pancake House.
	9:00 A.M.	Universal Studios. Tour begins at 10:00 A.M., lasts until noon.
	12:00 noon	Lunch at nearby restaurant. Catch tour bus at 1:30 P.M. to return to hotel.

Reservations

Make reservations whenever possible. A **reservation** is an advance commitment to receive a service at a specified later date. A room reservation guarantees that a hotel or motel room will be waiting for you when you arrive. Hotels and motels may be booked up, or full, well in advance of your vacation date. Therefore, make reservations early; a month or more before your vacation is not too soon. You can make reservations for airlines, buses, trains, boats, and car rentals. You can get airline boarding passes and seat assignments a few days before your trip. Confirm your flight reservations at least 24 hours before you leave, because flights are often canceled or changed at the last minute.

You may choose to use a **travel agency,** which is a business that arranges transportation, accommodations, and itineraries for customers. The agent can make plane and hotel reservations for you, and can help you plan the whole trip if you like. Agents get their fee from the airlines and hotels you book. However, if you

PERSONAL PERSPECTIVE

Online Travel Planning

Have you ever considered doing all of your travel planning online? The Net offers a number of travel-planning sites; and while there are some risks, the savings can be substantial.

At some Web sites, you can do fare searches, check seat availability, book flights, and even book cruises, car rentals, and hotel rooms. For example, www.cheaptickets.com offers discount fares and rates on reservations, once you register online. You will need to give personal information including your credit card number to use this service.

At www.priceline.com, you can check the availability of flights that are inexpensive and underbooked because they are often scheduled at less desirable flight times—after 10 P.M. or before 8 A.M. Using this Web site you can also get substantial discounts on flights to "hot destinations." The downside is that you must be able to take the openings on short notice, and this requires flexibility in travel plans.

Another popular site, www.travel.com, offers special advisories, airport locations and gate locations, ATM locations, embassy locations, flight information, and weather reports. This type of information can be very important when traveling to foreign countries or when time between flights is extremely tight.

Many sites, such as www.travel-for-less.com, provide discount airfares and discount cruises. This type of site offers tickets on an auction basis. You bid on the tickets that are available, and the airline or cruiseline will take the highest bid.

Internet research when planning trips can save you both time and money. Even if you book your tickets by telephone, you can still benefit from the information and search-and-compare features of the Internet.

Think Critically

1. What distant vacation destination appeals to you most? Use the Internet to find the best airfare and motel rate for this destination.
2. What is the downside of using the Internet to make reservations and pay for flights?

want itinerary planning, you will likely have to pay a fee for the service.

You can book your flights and accommodations online by going to the Web sites of specific airlines, hotels, car rental agencies, and entertainment centers, or make all the reservations through a full-service travel site such as Expedia (www.expedia.com) or Travelocity (www.travelocity.com). If you enter your travel times and preferences at a full-service site, the search tool will present you a list of available flights that meet your criteria. You can even have them listed in order of price. You can select a flight and pay for it online with your credit card number.

Flights today are often ticketless. You receive a reservation number when you book your flight. At the airport, you check in and receive your boarding pass. Ticketless flying protects you from lost or stolen tickets, which would cost you $50 or more to have replaced.

Plan to arrive at the airport at least an hour before your flight's departure time. This gives you time to check in, which can be very time consuming when lines are long. Often, airlines **overbook** flights, which means that they sell more reservations than they can fulfill. Airlines overbook flights because some people do not show up for a scheduled flight, and the airlines make more money if their flights are full. If more people show up for the flight than the plane can accommodate, the airline will ask people who are not in a hurry to give up their seats voluntarily in exchange for a future free ticket and a later flight. Passengers bumped against their will are usually entitled to compensation, often in the form of cash, a coupon, or a free flight. By arriving early to check in, you can decrease your risk of an overbooking problem.

By signing up for an airline's free frequent-flyer program, you can earn credit toward a free ticket. You receive credit for miles traveled each time you fly with that airline. You can also receive a specified number of frequent-flyer miles for staying at a participating hotel, renting from a participating car rental agency, booking online, or whatever the airline defines in its program. After you accumulate enough miles, you earn a free flight, though the airlines will limit your flight options.

At-Home Preparations

Before leaving on your vacation, you should take care of a few things at home. Ask a neighbor to pick up your newspaper, or call the paper to stop delivery if the vacation is longer than a few days.

Fill out a form at the post office to have your mail held there rather than delivered. By stopping these deliveries, you avoid a buildup of mail and newspapers that may tip off burglars that you are away from home.

Arrange for someone to feed your pets, care for your plants, mow the lawn, and do other household duties that cannot wait for your return. Use an automatic timer for lights so that they come on in the evening and go off a few hours later, giving the appearance that you are home. Lock all doors and windows and close the curtains. It is also a good idea to ask a neighbor to keep an eye on things while you are away. Finally, alert the local police, so that an officer can check the security of your home while you are on vacation.

Last-Minute Details

Plan your packing so that you have everything you need, but don't overpack. Remember, you have to carry that heavy suitcase from place to place. Make a list of things you will need, such as cameras, special clothing, and personal items. Take only what you need in the smallest possible containers. Be sure to pack enough clothing to last the entire vacation without laundering (unless it is a very long vacation). Close all bottles and other containers tightly to avoid leaks. Do not forget prescriptions or other medications you might need.

You may wish to take major credit cards. However, leave at home in a safe place all the cards you do not need. Take enough cash to pay the expenses that require cash only; charge other expenses on a bank card. Because of the availability of ATMs across the country and around the world, you can obtain cash easily while on vacation.

Be sure that all appliances are turned off before you leave home. As a precaution, do not use any appliances the morning of your departure. In the excitement of preparing to leave, you could easily forget to turn off or unplug them. A last check before leaving will reassure you that you have left nothing on.

✓ Check Your Understanding

Review Terms

1. wedding party
2. civil ceremony
3. itinerary
4. reservation
5. travel agency
6. overbook

Review Concepts

1. Why is it important to have at least six months' time between engagement and the wedding?
2. What is an advantage of booking a flight online through a full-service travel site?

Goals

★ Describe the steps and costs in a divorce.
★ Discuss preparations for death, life's final plans.

Divorce

In all but a few states, a *divorce* is now called a **dissolution of marriage,** which means that irreconcilable differences have led to the breakdown of the marriage. Furthermore, one partner does not have to prove fault by the other partner to be granted a divorce. If one partner wants the marriage to be dissolved, it can be done. The only time fault is considered is when the issue of child custody arises.

Cost of Divorce

Expenses involved in divorce are high. They may include attorneys' fees (one attorney for each party), court costs and filing fees, child support and alimony, division of property, expenses for a child-custody hearing, and settlement costs. The more issues there are to settle, the higher the attorneys' fees will be.

Often the divorcing couple can agree outside of court and enter into a **property settlement agreement.** This is a document specifying the division of assets agreed to by both parties and entered in court for the judge's approval. The more that the divorcing couple can settle outside of court, the less the divorce proceedings will cost.

In divorce, the law assumes that both parents are responsible for supporting the children to the best of their ability. The *custodial parent,* or

What is the value in a divorcing couple settling issues outside of court?

the parent with whom the children will live, fulfills most support obligations by taking care of the children every day. In most cases, the parent who is not granted custody will be required to pay *child support*—monthly payments to the custodial parent to help provide food, clothing, and shelter for the children. The amount of the payments will depend on the income of both parents and their ability to pay. Sometimes both parents share custody, and the children live part of the year with each parent.

Alimony is money paid by one former spouse to support the other. The money may be paid as one lump sum or monthly payments, usually for a set number of years, until the former spouse can become self-supporting. Alimony is awarded in some cases when one spouse has been dependent on the other for a number of years and has little means of self-support. Child support and alimony are at the discretion of the judge and become binding on the parties under the divorce decree. Amounts of child support and alimony can be modified only by another court order.

Steps in Divorce

Dissolving a marriage is often a lengthy and unpleasant matter. One party goes to an attorney, and the attorney prepares the documents, which are filed with the court. The other party is served with copies of the papers, called Petition for Dissolution of Marriage, and given a short time to appear (file papers) if there is a disagreement with the proposals set forth in the petition. The petition sets forth how the first party proposes to divide property and award custody, amounts desired for any child support, visitation rights, and so on. If the second party fails to appear (defaults), then the first party is awarded whatever is asked in the petition. In most cases, the second party does appear, and a court date is set to decide the issues that cannot be settled between the parties.

Often it takes many months, even a year or more, for the case to be heard in court. Consequently, a hearing will be held to establish temporary custody, child support, visitation rights of the non-custodial parent, and other matters. Many of the temporary provisions tend to become permanent. Often both parties agree in writing to property settlement and other matters prior to the court date. When the judge approves the agreement, it is entered as part of the *decree*, which is a final statement of the dissolution decisions. A decree is final and binding on both parties until modified by the court.

If the parties cannot agree on a settlement, the case then goes to court. There is no jury in divorce cases. Both parties present their cases. In child-custody cases, witnesses may be called to determine which parent would be the better custodial parent. The judge's decision is based entirely on the best interests of the children. All other matters—property, alimony, amount of child support, visitation rights—are also decided in court. Once the decree is entered, the court usually imposes a waiting period before either party may remarry.

Death: A Final Plan

Aging and death are parts of living and need planning to make the process easier for loved ones left behind. All adults should prepare for death, not just people who are about to die.

Survivors' Benefits

Why should all adults plan their final arrangements and expenses?

The surviving spouse and children are usually provided with some kind of death benefits. Survivors need to check to see what benefits have accrued through the years.

Life insurance benefits are not taxable to the recipients. Benefits from a life insurance policy can be obtained by mailing a copy of the death certificate, the original life insurance policy, and a claim form to the life insurance company. (Life insurance is described in detail in Chapter 27.)

The Veterans Administration pays a benefit to survivors of

veterans. The benefit may include a grave marker, funeral services, and cash of $400 or more, depending on type and length of service and branch of armed forces. Children of veterans may also be entitled to scholarships and educational grant benefits. The Social Security Administration also pays a nominal (currently $255) death benefit to estates of people who were receiving social security benefits.

Many employer pension plans pay lump-sum or monthly benefits to widows and families. Employer-paid benefits may not be automatic, and the widow(er) may have to apply to receive these benefits.

Last Expenses

The costs involved when a person dies can range from a few hundred dollars to many thousands. These expenses include final medical and hospital charges, funeral expenses and casket, and burial. By preparing instructions and making provisions for these costs in advance, you spare survivors the emotional decision-making process at a time of vulnerability. Survivors who are grieving the loss of a loved one are often unprepared to make the many decisions involved in planning a funeral and burial. At such an emotional time, a family may incur elaborate final expenses that they or the estate cannot afford.

Funerals

The cost of a funeral can range from $2,500 to $10,000 or more, depending on type of casket and burial. Typical funeral charges include moving the body (to funeral home, church or synagogue, and cemetery); embalming and preparation for public viewing; casket; use of facilities; funeral staff fees; hearse; family limousine; pallbearers' car; flower car; escort to cemetery; obituary (newspaper death notice); clergy fees; printed memorial folders, memorial book, and thank-you cards; death certificate; and all necessary permits. The cost of a burial plot and marker are additional expenses.

Many funeral homes have prearranged plans available at guaranteed costs. Payments made in advance for the funeral are placed in trust and earn interest. You should be able to get a full refund if you cancel the plan. Look over any "pre-need" or prepayment plan you consider. It may lock you into using the services of a particular funeral home at uncertain future prices. If you move away or the home goes out of business, you may have trouble getting your money back.

Cremation

Cremation is a process of reducing a body to ashes in a high-temperature oven. The ashes are placed in an urn. The urn is presented to the family for safekeeping or burial. Cremation is a less expensive alternative to embalming and "cosmetizing" the body for public viewing. When a body is not cremated within a certain time span, usually two days, it must be embalmed or otherwise prepared for burial. Cremation, like immediate burial without a funeral, permits the survivors to hold a memorial service at any time or place, without having the body present. This procedure is less expensive and may be more comfortable for families and other mourners.

COMMUNICATION
CONNECTION

Select an older adult, such as a parent, grandparent, or friend, with whom you feel comfortable speaking. Ask the person if he or she has made any plans covering last expenses, such as funeral arrangements. Discuss why the person has or hasn't made such plans. Then write a one-page report, covering your conversation. Did the discussion change your mind about any such arrangements you might make?

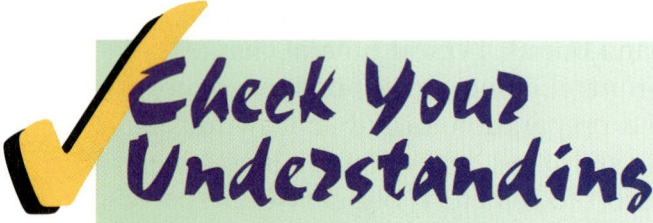

Check Your Understanding

Review Terms
1. dissolution of marriage
2. property settlement agreement
3. alimony
4. cremation

Review Concepts
1. What is the particular circumstance that causes the court to consider "fault" in a divorce proceeding?
2. What are some costs involved in a funeral?

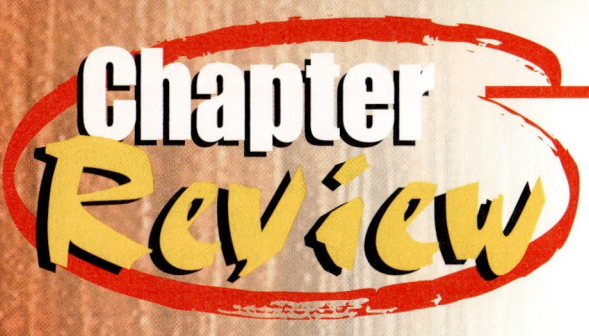

24.1 Family Plans and Goals

- The marriage commitment generally begins with an engagement, or pledge to go through life together. This marks the time to begin planning the marriage ceremony, honeymoon, and living arrangements.
- Some religions require premarital counseling to discuss topics that will help couples prepare for a successful marriage.
- Wedding ceremonies can be very expensive and plans can be very detailed and time-consuming. Your wedding can be formal, semiformal, or informal, or you can choose a civil ceremony.
- Family financial decisions should be based on common family goals and a family budget that is established by and agreed to by all family members.
- Families should divide up household responsibilities so that all family members do their fair share.
- Vacation planning is based on time and money available, along with interests of all family members.
- Plan your itinerary and make reservations ahead of time, so that you can relax and enjoy your vacation time. You can gather vacation information, compare prices, and make most reservations online.
- Make arrangements for the proper care and maintenance of your home, mail, pets, and other responsibilities while you are away.

24.2 Dealing with Life's Uncertainties

- In most states, divorce laws are no-fault, which means irreconcilable differences have caused the breakdown of the marriage.
- Divorce can be expensive, especially when attorney's fees and court costs are involved. The former spouses must decide how to divide property and which parent will have custody of any children and which will pay child support. If they cannot agree, the court will decide.
- Steps in getting a divorce include filing a petition, agreeing to a property settlement, attending a court hearing, and obtaining a divorce decree.
- Death is part of life, and all adults must prepare to make the process easier for their loved ones left behind.
- Families are often eligible for survivors' benefits from life insurance policies, veterans' or social security benefits, or employer pension plans.
- Last expenses include the costs of hospital and medical care, a funeral, possibly cremation, and burial.

Review Terms

Directions: Can you find the definition for each of the following terms used in Chapter 24?

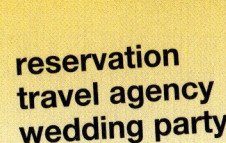

alimony
civil ceremony
cremation
dissolution of marriage
itinerary
overbook
property settlement
  agreement

reservation
travel agency
wedding party

1. An advance commitment to receive a service at a specified later date.
2. The people who are active participants in the wedding ceremony.
3. A detailed list of events, times, and places planned for a trip.
4. To sell more reservations than can be fulfilled.
5. Another term for divorce, meaning irreconcilable differences have led to the breakdown of the marriage.
6. A document specifying the division of assets agreed to by both parties in a divorce.
7. Money paid by one former spouse to support the other.
8. The process of reducing a body to ashes in a high-temperature oven.
9. A business that arranges transportation, accommodations, and itineraries for customers.
10. A wedding performed by a public official, such as a judge or justice-of-the-peace, rather than a member of the clergy.

Review Facts and Ideas

1. What is the purpose of premarital counseling?
2. How long before the wedding should a couple begin making preparations?
3. List some expenses that are traditionally handled by the bride and her family.
4. List some expenses that are traditionally handled by the groom and his family.
5. What are the differences among a formal wedding, a semiformal wedding, an informal wedding, and a civil ceremony?
6. What are some household responsibilities that families should divide among family members?
7. How can your family go about choosing a family vacation?
8. What types of things should you list on your vacation itinerary?
9. Why should you build flexibility into your itinerary?
10. How can the Internet help you with your vacation plans?
11. How can frequent-flyer programs benefit you, and how do you earn credit toward the benefit?
12. List some preparations that you need to make before leaving on vacation. Include preparations designed to keep burglars from realizing that you are gone.
13. What are some of the costs involved in getting a divorce?
14. What are the steps in getting a divorce?
15. What types of survivors' benefits are available when a person dies?
16. What are some costs of death and burial?

1. Describe a wedding that you have attended in the last year or two (include wedding party, dress, flowers, reception, and so on).
2. Describe the wedding you would choose for yourself, including setting, type of ceremony, wedding party, total cost, number of guests, honeymoon plans, and so on.
3. Use three Web sites to obtain information about wedding costs and planning. List the site addresses and summarize the kinds of assistance they provide to couples who are planning to get married.
4. How does a family's budget differ from an individual's budget?
5. Design a three-day itinerary for a trip to a resort area within about 1,000 miles of where you live. Include all necessary information. Use the Internet to determine prices and availability of transportation, accommodations, and entertainment tickets.

Solve Problems

1. Write a report describing different engagement ring options:
   a. Diamond solitaire with matching bands. Compare costs of different sizes of diamonds.
   b. Gold and silver bands. Compare quality, width, and costs.
   c. Costs of stones other than diamonds: rubies, emeralds, and sapphires. Compare different sizes of each.
   d. Financing plans available.
2. Ramon Velez and Lucia Cintron will be married in a month. Both are working now and plan to work at least five years before having children. They have asked for your opinion on how they should divide household duties, because both of them work eight hours a day, five days a week. Devise a plan for dividing financial responsibilities, including checkbook balancing and financial planning, along with non-financial duties.
3. You and a friend have decided to take a trip. For each of the following situations, describe a trip you would take and list all of the costs that would be involved in each trip.
   a. You each have $75 to contribute and could get away for a three-day weekend. You have one car that does not need maintenance or repairs.

b. You each have $500 to spend and could get away for three to five days.

c. You each have $1,500 to spend and could be away for 10 days.

4. What types of divorce/dissolution laws are in effect in your state? Are they no-fault or fault laws? What are the waiting periods? Describe the procedures for dissolution. [Hint: This information is probably available online through your state government Web site.]

5. Divide into groups. With the instructor's permission, each group should arrange to visit a local funeral home. Ask someone there to walk you through preparations for a funeral, including the costs and decisions you would have to make. Each group should present an oral report to the class.

For related activities and links, point your browser to
www.mypf.swep.com

Unit *five*

PROJECT

Managing Your Resources

Project

5

Unit 5 presented personal decision making (Chapter 20), renting or buying a home (Chapters 21 and 22), owning a car (Chapters 23), and family decisions (Chapter 24). This project will extend your knowledge into related areas.

Personal Decision Making

There are many ways the unwary consumer can be "taken to the cleaners." Home improvement, car purchases, and other major expenses are common ways to take advantage of unsuspecting people whose objective is to take good care of their property, to extend its life, and to build its value. Let's look at some situations you may face in the future.

Don't Call Me, I'll Call You

When people knock on your door to sell you goods or services, be sure to go slowly, ask questions, and check them out before you buy. A typical home improvement fraud would work like this: Someone knocks on your door and compliments you on your well-maintained yard. The person notices that your trees are wilting or that your roof could use cleaning. The person assures you that he or she is qualified to perform the work and could do the job more quickly and cheaply than a large company. But because the company is small, he or she will need payment up front to buy materials and cover expenses. After getting your money, the person may never do the work or may do such a poor job that you would have been better off without it. Even worse, the person could do damage to your property that would require further expense. Figure U5-1, on page 698, shows a list of things you should and should not do when confronted with this type of pitch.

Promises, Promises

An "unconditional, lifetime, money-back guarantee" is only as good as the person or company that offers the guarantee. When the

697

Unit Five Project

When you are solicited at home:

1. Don't sign today. Any agreement that is worthwhile can wait until you have time to think about it.

2. Don't give cash. When you give a check, you may have the option of stopping payment. But you must act quickly. It is better to avoid giving cash or check until you have had time to reconsider. Many states have laws (called "green river laws") that allow you three business days after a purchase over $25 with a check or credit card to change your mind and revoke the transaction.

3. Check it out. Ask the Better Business Bureau or your state attorney general's office for consumer complaints about the individual or company. Are they authorized to do business in your state? Are there consumer complaints on file against them?

4. Compare prices. Compare the prices for labor and materials with other sources. This may take several days but is worth it.

5. Don't hurry. If you didn't originate the sale, don't allow others to "create demand" for a product. Don't allow others to talk you into something you don't want.

6. When in doubt, don't. Make this your motto. As the saying goes, "If something seems too good to be true, it probably is." Get all the information you need, then evaluate it carefully. If you still have doubts, wait.

company goes out of business, the guarantee goes with it. Another common guarantee says, "Good as long as you own this car." The dealer offering this guarantee is counting on the fact that you won't keep the car more than a few years. When things start to go wrong, you will no longer be the owner.

All That Glitters

This investment scheme capitalizes on your desire to get rich quick, coupled with an attraction to beautiful and rare objects (from gold to diamonds). There are thousands of counterfeit Krugerrands (gold coins) circulated across the nation. Investors have no idea they are fake until they try to sell them. By then the seller has vanished. Gold-painted lead also appears to be the real thing—gold bullion. Investors who pay up front, before true value is verified, get stuck with worthless lead. Junk gems are passed off as valuable rubies, sapphires, emeralds, and diamonds. These "phenomenal bargains" are no bargain. They are advertised as rough stones that need polishing, but they are junk. When you purchase these items by mail, you may have little recourse.

Complete Worksheet 1 (Before You Buy: Ripoffs and Warning Signals) in the *Student Activity Guide* to analyze situations involving good consumer decision making. (This worksheet also appears on page 705 of this project.)

Mortgage Loans

First-time homebuyers need to know the anticipated monthly payment when they purchase a house. The monthly payment will depend on the type of mortgage: fixed rate or variable rate.

Computing the Payment Amount

Clearly, the largest cost of homeownership (whether the home is new or previously owned) is the house payment. The total payment is based on the (a) amount of the loan, (b) interest rate charged, and (c) length of time to repay the loan. As you learned in Chapter 22, the interest rate on a *fixed-rate mortgage* remains constant over the life of the loan. Under a fixed-rate mortgage, a $50,000 loan at 8 percent spread over 15 or 30 years would result in the following payment:

	30-Year Loan	15-Year Loan
Monthly payment:		
Principal and interest	$366.85	$477.68
Property taxes (based on assessed value of $70,000 and tax rate of $15 per thousand)	87.50	87.50
Fire insurance premium	10.00	10.00
Total monthly payment	$464.35	$575.18

Note, however, that while monthly payments are higher on the 15-year loan, your total interest would be lower over the life of the loan. For example, under the 30-year plan, you would repay $132,066 ($366.85 × 360 payments); under the 15-year plan, you would repay $85,982 ($477.68 × 180 payments). [12 payments per year × 30 years = 360. 12 payments per year × 15 years = 180.] This is a savings of $46,084!

The interest rate on an *adjustable rate mortgage (ARM)* starts low but changes as the loan progresses. For example, for the first three or five years, the rate may be several percentage points below a similar fixed-rate loan. After that initial time period, the lender can raise the rate as much as two or three percentage points a year, with a cap or maximum rate that can be charged. Typically, when fixed mortgage rates are 8 percent, an ARM might start at 5 percent for three years but increase to as much as 12 percent, if interest rates continue to rise. This type of loan is ideal for someone who plans to move frequently and can sell the house and move when it is time for a mortgage rate increase.

Loan Fees

When financial institutions loan money to homebuyers, they charge *loan fees* that pay the costs of setting up the loan. Loan fees may range from $100 to $2,500 or more, depending on the loan. In most cases, if the loan does not go through for some reason, the borrower forfeits the loan fees.

Mortgage lenders often charge *points,* or finance charges that the borrower must pay at the beginning of the loan. One point is 1 percent of the loan amount. For a $50,000 loan, if the point rate is 3, then the borrower will have to pay a 3 percent fee, or $1,500 ($50,000 × 3% = $1,500).

Mortgage Payment Amount

The chart on page 701 provides a simple way to estimate what your mortgage payment amount would be. The higher the rate of interest you are paying on the mortgage, the higher your monthly payment will be. To estimate your monthly mortgage payment (for principal and interest only), complete these steps:

1. In the chart, find your mortgage interest rate in the first column.
2. Run your finger across that row until you reach the column for the length of your loan. This number is your monthly mortgage payment factor. For example, for a 7 percent, 30-year mortgage, the factor is $6.64.
3. Multiply this factor by the number of thousands in the mortgage principal. For example, in $50,000, there are 50 thousands. Multiply $6.64 times 50. Your monthly payment for a $50,000 loan at 7 percent for 30 years would be $332.

Monthly Mortgage Payment Factors (per $1,000 of loan amount)	Loan Rate	30 Yrs.	25 Yrs.	20 Yrs.	15 Yrs.
	6.0%	5.94	6.40	7.16	8.40
	6.5%	6.29	6.73	7.46	8.69
	7.0%	6.64	7.06	7.76	8.98
	7.5%	6.99	7.39	8.06	9.27
	8.0%	7.34	7.72	8.36	9.56
	8.5%	7.69	8.05	8.68	9.85
	9.0%	8.05	8.39	9.00	10.14
	9.5%	8.41	8.74	9.32	10.44
	10.0%	8.78	9.09	9.65	10.75

Complete Worksheet 2 (Computing Mortgage Payments) in the *Student Activity Guide* to determine estimated mortgage payments for different mortgage rates and amounts. (This worksheet also appears on page 705 of this project.)

Housing Option: Building a Home

When you decide to build a new home rather than buy an existing one, you hire a builder and the process begins. First, you must choose house plans for the size and style of the house you want. Often the builder has real estate lots for sale, and you must select a lot from the builder's inventory. In other cases, you may own a vacant lot or purchase a lot and contract with the builder for only the house itself.

The first cost of building a house is the *architect's fee* for drawing up the house plans. Based upon your desires and what you can afford, the architect prepares a house plan. The architect's fee ranges from $1,000 to $2,500 or more, depending on house size and value. The more complicated the floor plans, the higher the fee. Floor plans can take several weeks, or in some cases, the builder already has several floor plans from which you can choose. While choosing among pre-existing plans limits your choices, you would not have to pay an architect's fee.

Once you and the builder (often called a *building contractor*) agree upon the house specifications and the price, the builder will have a building contract drawn. It specifies what is to be done, what materials are to be used, and a timetable for completion. You would probably have to make a large down payment so that the builder can purchase materials. Your loan will generally be approved only after the house is completed. Therefore, the builder may provide a *construction loan* that finances construction and is paid off when the house is completed. While you do not pay for the construction loan, the interest costs on the loan are a part of the builder's costs of operation and are included in the price of the house.

Any changes in the original plans will increase your costs. For example, as the house is being built, you may want an improvement, such as a bay window or a slightly larger room. Such a change requires a separate agreement to account for the added costs of this construction.

Building a new home will likely take six months to a year from the time you first begin to negotiate with the builder. Along the way there are decisions to make, such as color of carpeting, type of tile or countertop, and choices of paint or wallpaper. You can make your selections within a prescribed price range. If a selection exceeds the agreed-upon allotment, you pay the added charge.

The government requires inspections for new construction at regular intervals for electricity, plumbing, and so on. While the builder is responsible for these charges (as a part of the total price), delays can result when construction must wait for inspectors to arrive. Closing costs are similar to those for buying a previously owned home, except that the builder replaces the seller. At closing, all subcontractors (companies working for the contractor, such as plumbers and electricians) and all expenses of construction would be paid.

The experience of buying a new home can be very rewarding, because you can see the house in its various stages of construction and make small changes along the way. But it can also be frustrating because of time delays due to weather, inspections, or shortage of materials.

Complete Worksheet 3 (Building Your Dream Home) in the *Student Activity Guide* to get an idea of the type of house you would like to build. (This worksheet also appears on page 706 of this project.)

Auto Repair Ripoffs

Overcharging and needless repairs cost motorists billions of dollars each year, according to the U.S. Department of Transportation. This agency has concluded that at least 50 cents of every dollar spent for auto repairs is unnecessary due to inflated prices or needless work!

Some states require repair shops to give written estimates. The final bill cannot be increased by more than 10 percent without your authorization. Many states require that the repair shop return defective or worn-out parts to you rather than discard them. This practice allows you to examine the damaged, worn-out, or defective part that has been replaced.

You should be wary when allowing others to check your car's engine, tires, belts, fluid levels, and the like. For example, you go in for an oil change and the mechanic reports that you should replace your water pump, hoses, valve covers, and other parts. These repairs may be needed, or maybe not. If the mechanic finds a number of problems, or one very expensive problem, be suspicious. Ask for evidence of the problem. Get a second opinion before having major repairs done. Dishonest mechanics find work that doesn't need to be done, add inflated time (labor) charges and parts to a bill, and remove parts in good condition and replace them with used or rebuilt parts.

Figure U5-2, on page 704, shows a list of tips from New York City's Department of Consumer Affairs to help you know what to do when you experience car trouble. Complete Worksheet 4 (Ripoffs and Warning Signals) in the *Student Activity Guide* about suspicious situations related to car repairs. (This worksheet also appears on page 707 of this project.)

Tips from New York City's Department of Consumer Affairs

- Look for a reliable mechanic before you are faced with an emergency. Ask friends for references.

- If you suspect your car needs repairs, have it checked before it becomes a big repair.

- For large repairs, get two estimates and compare the charges. Let the shops know you are comparison shopping.

- List all symptoms so you won't forget anything when you are talking to a mechanic. Give a copy of the list to the mechanic and keep a copy for yourself. Make sure all of the symptoms are taken care of before you accept the work for full payment.

- Don't authorize work unless you understand what is being done. Add-on work that does not apply to the reason for your repair should be suspect.

- Don't tell a mechanic to "get this car in good running order." This is a blanket opportunity for them to do anything whether or not it is essential.

- Don't sign a repair order unless you understand what is being done to your car. Question each line item.

- Keep itemized bills. Good records will help you in the event work is not satisfactory. Mechanics should stand behind their work. Be able to tell the mechanic, "I had this fuel pump replaced by you two months ago. It should be working." Have the documentation with you to prove it.

- If you suspect you are being overcharged, ask to see the supplier's parts price list.

- Find out which local and state government agencies have jurisdiction over auto-repair complaints. Use the agency if necessary to get satisfaction.

WORKSHEET 1

Before You Buy: Ripoffs and Warning Signals

BEFORE YOU BUY. . .

Directions: Analyze the following situations and determine what might be wrong.

Situation 1. You receive a tantalizing offer in the mail. There's a new development being constructed at your favorite mountain skiing area. You have failed on several occasions to get reservations in the area, so you are excited at the prospect of having a place of your own. The invitation spells out what the new development will look like—buildings, ski lifts, and other amenities. At the bottom it invites you to an informational meeting. You must attend the meeting to be considered for this opportunity. You are asked to bring your checkbook or credit card. Free food will be provided and prizes will be given.

Situation 2. You receive a telephone call that offers you free products for answering a few simple questions. All you have to do is give them your name, social security number, address, and other personal information, and they will send you free samples of merchandise that you use or would like to try based on your lifestyle.

Situation 3. You see an ad in the classified pages where a desperate investor is seeking to unload his collection of rare baseball cards and comic books at lower-than-market prices. He needs the money right away and will sell to the highest bidder. You call to get the address, and when you show up, there are several others there who are interested in the merchandise and are bidding on it.

WORKSHEET 2

Computing Mortgage Payments

Directions: Compute the following estimated mortgage amounts, using the chart supplied on page 701.

What is your estimated mortgage payment for:

30-year mortgage		25-year mortgage		15-year mortgage	
1. $50,000	8%	2. $70,000	6%	3. $80,000	7.5%
4. $100,000	6%	5. $100,000	7%	6. $100,000	8%
7. $150,000	7.5%	8. $150,000	9%	9. $150,000	10%

WORKSHEET 3

Building Your Dream Home

Directions: Answer the following questions and complete the research suggested to specify your dream home. Be sure to list your sources of information.

1. What style of house do you prefer? (two-story, ranch, Victorian, Tudor, and so on)

2. Attach a picture of a house that closely resembles the home of your dreams.

3. Prepare a floor plan that details the rooms and configuration, along with windows, doors, and so on.

4. What is the total square footage of your home?

   How many bedrooms?

   Bathrooms?

   Describe the kitchen and eating area(s).

   Describe the general layout of the house, starting at the front door and ending at the back door or on the second floor.

5. Describe the lot and landscaping, including lot size and shape.

6. Describe the block—what part of town, city or country, the neighborhood or region.

7. Based on today's costs of building real estate, what would it cost to build this house? (Hint: You need to consult the newspaper ads that describe similar new properties or interview a builder or other reliable source.)

8. Prepare a report of your findings, including a cover page, drawings or exhibits, narrative of information, and list of sources of information.

WORKSHEET 4

Ripoffs and Warning Signals (Your Car)

Directions: Read each of the following statements that could be a potential ripoff. Write the warning signal (a point that makes you uncomfortable) and what you would do about it.

1. Your car is making pinging noises every time you accelerate to pass another car or go up a hill. You stop by a service station and while your car is being filled with gas, you casually ask what could be wrong. The attendant replies that he would be happy to take a look at it when he gets off work, and that he could probably fix it in his spare time. Repairs could cost as little as $50 or as much as $250.

2. You are on vacation and driving the family car. You had it tuned up before you left, and your tires are fairly new. Along the way, you stop for gas. While checking the oil, the attendant notices that one of your hoses is loose. He fixes it (no charge) but then sees that you have an oil leak. He offers to make the repair within an hour for $100 plus parts.

3. You take your car in for its regular tune-up and maintenance. You take a list of things that need to be done. An hour later, you receive a telephone call and are asked to authorize extra repairs that total $500. These repairs are not related to the tune-up or regular maintenance. But when the car is up on the rack, the mechanic sees that the work needs to be done.

Unit *six*

Risk Management

Chapters

25 *Introduction to Risk Management*

26 *Property and Liability Insurance*

27 *Health and Life Insurance*

Project: Managing Personal Risks

Unit 6 begins with a discussion of risk—what it is and how individuals manage it, usually through insurance. In Chapter 25, you will examine different types of risks along with a strategy to manage those risks.

In Chapter 26, you will learn the specifics of property insurance—how to protect your residence and personal possessions and how to protect yourself from liability as a result of your negligence or errors in judgment.

In Chapter 27, you will learn about rising health costs and the need for health insurance. Finally, you will learn about life insurance: who needs it, how it works, and the types available.

Chapter 25

Introduction to Risk Management

Terms to Know

risk (insurance)
insurance
insurer
policy
premium
policyholder
indemnification

probability
personal risks
property risks
liability risks
pure risk
speculative risk
insurable interest

risk management
risk avoidance
risk reduction
risk assumption

Up Front

Ann was visiting with her financial planner and discussing plans for purchases and investments in the future. Her planner asked about Ann's current insurance coverage.

"I have basic insurance on my car," she answered, "but I don't really know whether it's adequate or too much. I hear a lot about life insurance, but I haven't bought a policy. At this point in my life, I can't afford a lot of money going for payments. Still, I don't want to take chances that could drain my savings. What do you mean by risk management? Is that the same thing as insurance?"

Lesson 25.1 — What Is Insurance?

Goals

★ Explain the concept of insurance: what it is and how it works.
★ Define basic insurance terminology and types of risk.

Spreading the Risk

Chapter 11 described *risk* as the chance of financial loss from a decline in an investment's value. In terms of insurance, **risk** is the chance of financial loss from perils to people or property. Perils to people include declining health, injury, and death. Perils to property include damage or loss from fire, vandalism, car accidents, and theft, among many others. All of these perils can result in sizable costs. **Insurance** is a method for spreading individual risk among a large group of people to make losses more affordable for all. There are many types of insurance, including life, health, homeowners, and automobile. They all provide one important thing: relief from fear of severe financial loss due to events beyond your control.

Here's an example of how insurance works. Suppose your textbook for this class costs $40. If you lose it, you will have to pay that amount to replace it. An average of 10 out of every 100 textbooks (or 1 out of every 10) are lost each school year. Based on this statistic, the expected losses in a class of 30 students would come to 3 books, at a total cost of $120 (3 × $40). The class could establish an insurance company to help lower the cost of these expected losses to individual students. Every student would contribute $4 to the company. The total of $120 collected would be used to replace the books. The cost to each student would be relatively low ($4), and no one student would have to pay the full $40.

An insurance company, or **insurer,** is a business that agrees to pay the cost of potential future losses in exchange for regular fee payments. When people buy insurance, they join a risk-sharing group (the insurer) by purchasing a written insurance contract (a **policy**). Under the policy, the insurer agrees to assume an identified risk for a fee (the **premium**), usually paid at regular intervals by the owner of the policy (the **policyholder**). The insurer collects insurance premiums from policyholders under the assumption that only a few policyholders will have financial losses at any given time. To make a profit, the insurer must collect more in premiums than it pays out for losses and operating expenses. In years when a major disaster occurs, such as a hurricane, flood, or earthquake, an insurer may pay out more in benefits than it receives in premiums.

Insurance is not meant to enrich—only to compensate for actual losses incurred. This principle is called indemnification. **Indemnification** means putting the policyholder back in the same financial condition he or she was in before the loss occurred. **Probability** is the mathematics of chance and the root of indemnification. Every event can be described in terms of probability or likelihood that something will happen.

Insurers set premiums based on statistical probability. In other words, they estimate the likelihood of potential losses. They gather and analyze large amounts of historical data to determine how many of a particular loss occurred, on average, in a population over a given time period. From this analysis they can predict approximately how many such losses to expect among their policyholders over a similar future time period, such as a year. For example, in a sample of 100,000 drivers under the age of 18, an insurer can predict approximately how many will have accidents in a given year. The higher the probability of a loss occurring, the higher the premium for insuring against it. Remember that insurers deal in averages. They cannot predict which individuals will suffer losses.

Insurance Terminology

To understand all types of insurance, let's begin with some basic vocabulary. In addition to the terms defined above, here are some typical words that relate to insurance:

1. *Actuarial table*—a table of premium rates based on ages and life expectancies.
2. *Actuary*—a specialist in insurance calculations and statistics.
3. *Beneficiary*—a person named on an insurance policy to receive the benefits from the policy.
4. *Benefits*—sums of money to be paid for specific types of losses under the terms of an insurance policy.
5. *Cash value*—the amount of money payable to a policyholder upon discontinuation of a life insurance policy.
6. *Claim*—a policyholder's request for reimbursement for a loss under the terms of an insurance policy.
7. *Coverage*—protection provided by the terms of an insurance policy.
8. *Deductible*—the specified amount of a loss that the policyholder pays before the insurer is obligated to pay anything. The insurance company pays only the amount in excess of the deductible.
9. *Exclusions*—specified losses that the insurance policy does not cover.
10. *Face amount*—the amount stated in a life insurance policy to be paid upon death.
11. *Grace period*—the additional time after the premium due date that the insurer allows the policyholder to make the payment without penalty (usually 30 days).
12. *Hazard*—a condition that creates or increases the likelihood of some loss. For example, lightning can create a fire and defective house wiring can increase the likelihood of a fire.

13. *Insurance agent*—a professional insurance salesperson who acts for the insurer in negotiating, servicing, or writing an insurance policy.
14. *Insured*—the person or company protected against loss (not always the owner of the policy).
15. *Loss*—an unexpected reduction in value of the insured's property caused by a covered peril; the basis of a valid claim for reimbursement under the terms of an insurance policy.
16. *Peril*—an event whose occurrence can cause a loss; people buy policies for protection against such perils as a fire, storm, explosion, accident, or robbery.
17. *Proof of loss*—the written verification of the amount of a loss that must be provided by the insured to the insurer before a claim can be settled.
18. *Standard policy*—the contract form that has been adopted by many insurers, approved by state insurance divisions, or prescribed by law (modifications are made to suit the needs of the individual).
19. *Unearned premium*—the portion of a paid premium that the insurer has not yet earned because the policy term has not ended. The unearned premium is returned to the policy-holder when a policy is canceled.

How is an insurable risk defined?

Insurable Risks

You face risks every day. From the moment you get out of bed, you take chances. You could slip and fall; you could have an accident in the kitchen. You could have your stereo stolen or injure another person or property while driving your car. Insurance gives you financial protection from the losses associated with these types of risks. To be *insurable*, the risk must have the potential to result in serious financial loss not under the control of the insured.

There are three major insurable risks: personal, property, and liability. You should consider each of these risks as you make plans to protect your financial interests. Figure 25-1 gives examples of common risks and ways to protect yourself from their occurrence or to reduce their impact on you financially.

Figure 25-1

Risks	Causes (Perils)	Ways to Protect Yourself
1. Losing job (income)	Poor economy Company's financial condition Job-skills obsolescence	Learn new skills; make yourself more valuable
2. Illness or injury	On-the-job accident Chronic health condition or handicap	Health insurance Disability insurance Retraining programs
3. Death of wage earner	Dangerous activities including sports or job; illness	Life insurance Get training/lessons Take safety precautions
4. Liability for others' injuries	Careless driving Hazard at home/place of work	Liability insurance Signs, warnings, supervised uses
5. Loss of property to theft	Vehicle stolen Robbery	Locks/security devices Park in well-lit and secure places

Personal Risks

Personal risks are the chances of loss involving your income and standard of living. You can protect yourself from personal risks by buying life, health, and disability insurance. Besides protecting yourself, insurance against personal risks protects others who are depending on your income to provide food, clothing, shelter, and the comforts of life. As you will learn in Chapter 27, this type of insurance can be very expensive. You will be faced with many choices in coverage, costs, and potential benefits.

Long-term care insurance is designed to cover the costs of certain nursing-home expenses not covered by Medicare. Long-term care insurance is of special importance to women. Women are much more likely than men to need nursing home care. It is estimated that the majority of women (and only one third of men) reaching the age of 60 will need nursing-home care before they die.

Property Risks

The chances of loss or harm to personal or real property are called **property risks.** For example, your home, car, or other possessions could be damaged or destroyed by fire, theft, wind, rain, accident, and other hazards. To protect from such losses, you purchase property insurance. As you will learn in Chapter 26, insurance for your home and your car requires many decisions that will affect premiums and coverage.

Liability Risks

Liability risks are the chances of loss that may occur when your errors or inappropriate actions result in bodily injury to someone else or damage to someone else's property. For example, you could accidentally cause injury or damage to others or their property by your conduct while driving a car. Or a person could fall because of your home's crumbling front steps and break an arm. Liability insurance will protect you when others sue you for injuring them or damaging their property.

✓ Check Your Understanding

Review Terms
1. risk (insurance)
2. insurance
3. insurer
4. policy
5. premium
6. policyholder
7. indemnification
8 probability
9. personal risks
10. property risks
11. liability risks

Review Concepts
1. What is the purpose of insurance?
2. Explain the concept of an insurable risk.

Risk Management

Lesson 25.2 — Risk Management

Goals

★ List the steps and discuss the risk-management process.
★ Explain how to create a risk-management plan.
★ Discuss ways to reduce the costs of insurance.

Risk-Management Process

Personal, property, and liability risks are all types of pure risk. A **pure risk** is a chance of loss with no chance for gain. Because pure risks are accidental and result in loss (not gain), they are generally insurable. In contrast, a **speculative risk** is a risk that may result in either gain or loss. When you buy stock, you could either make or lose money. Because speculative risks are not accidental and may result in gain or loss, they are uninsurable.

In order for you to buy insurance, the risk must be insurable and you must have an insurable interest to protect. An **insurable interest** is any financial interest in life or property such that, if the life or property were lost or harmed, the insured would suffer financially. For example, you cannot buy insurance on someone else's house. Unless you own the house, you would not suffer a financial loss if it burned down. However, if you depend on your spouse's income to live, then you have an insurable interest in your spouse and can buy insurance on his or her life.

While you cannot eliminate risk, you can manage it so that a loss does not become financially devastating. **Risk management** is an organized strategy for controlling financial loss from pure risks. As shown in Figure 25-2 on page 718, the risk-management process involves three steps: (1) identify risks of loss, (2) assess the seriousness of their financial impact, and (3) select the best ways to handle the risks.

Risk management is more than buying insurance for every possible peril that could occur. Some risks are not serious enough to insure. Others are better handled by taking steps to avoid the risk or reduce the chances that the risk will occur.

Step 1: Identify Risks of Loss

Ask yourself what types of financial risks you take when you drive a car, own a house, or plan a party. As you will see in subsequent

Figure 25-2

Risk-Management Process

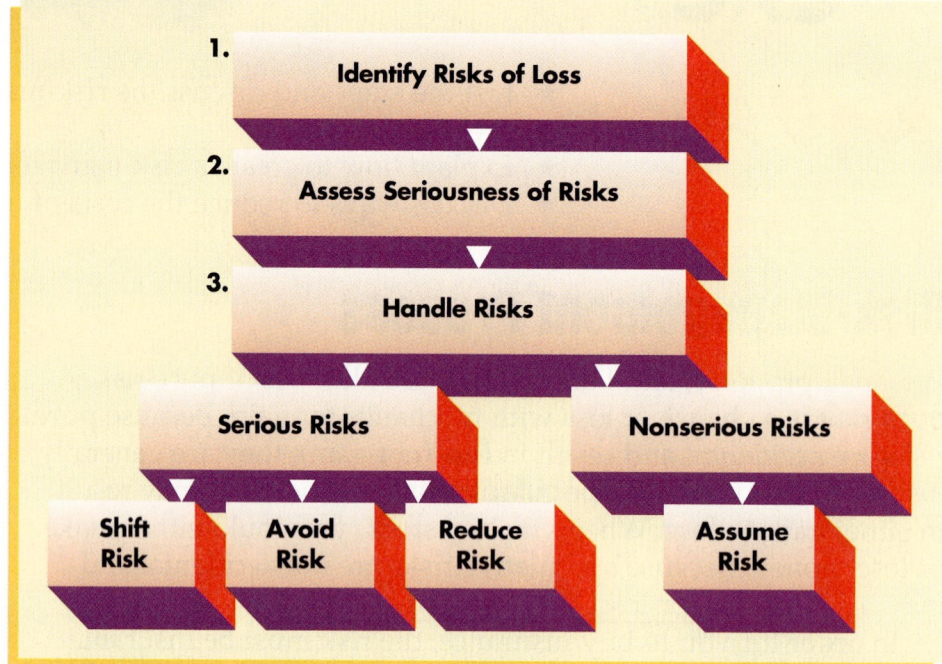

chapters, many potential losses could occur. Even though they may not happen as a result of your error or fault, you still can be responsible for damages to others and to property.

Step 2: Assess Seriousness of Risks

Human activities and the ownership of property reflect a certain amount of risk. Some risks are high priority because they could have serious financial consequences. For example, when driving your car, you could destroy the property of others, injure others, or even kill someone. Because potential losses are very great, driving is a high-priority risk. Other types of risk may have a relatively low financial consequence or may have only a very small chance of occurring. These types of risk are therefore of a lower priority.

Crashes involving young drivers typically are single-vehicle crashes, primarily run-off-the-road crashes, that involve driver error and/or speeding. They often occur when other young people are in the vehicle with the young driver, so teenagers are disproportionately involved in crashes as passengers as well as drivers.

Step 3: Handle Risks

There are four risk-management techniques: avoid, reduce, assume, or shift. A good risk-management program uses a combination of these strategies to balance risks, costs of insurance, and potential losses.

To *avoid* risk, called **risk avoidance,** you would eliminate the chance for loss by never doing the activity that could result in the loss. For example, instead of having a party at your house, you could decide to reserve a section of a restaurant. Or instead of buying a house, you could decide to rent.

To *reduce* risk, called **risk reduction,** you would take measures to lessen the frequency or severity of losses that may occur. For example, you may put studded snow tires on your car, install fire alarms or sprinklers in your home, or insist that seat belts be used in your car. All these steps would lessen the financial risk of potential losses.

To *shift* or *transfer* risk, you buy insurance to cover financial losses caused by destructive or damaging events. Insurance provides protection against many risks of financial uncertainty and unexpected losses. Most Americans acquire protection against risk such as fire, theft, injury, illness, and old age.

What are some means by which risks can be reduced?

To *assume* risk, called **risk assumption,** you would establish a monetary fund to cover the cost of a loss. In effect, you would be self-insuring. This strategy can reduce the cost of insurance. In some cases the cost of insuring against a particular risk may be too great, or the probability that the risk will occur may be too low to justify paying an insurance premium.

Based on the nature and seriousness of the risks you identified, you should select the risk-management techniques that best handle each risk. For example, you just purchased a car. Because driving a car is a serious risk, you buy auto insurance to shift some of the risk. (It's also required in most states.) You like bungee-jumping, but since engaging in this activity would make your health insurance premium extremely high, you decide to avoid the risk and not do the activity. You know that your old house will probably

 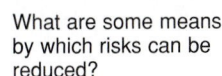

need major repairs soon. You decide to assume this risk by starting a home-maintenance fund and contributing regularly to it.

Making a Risk-Management Plan

Everyone faces risks and the potential losses they bring. Some people choose to do nothing—but this is in fact a choice. When you allow events to control your life, they also drain your finances in unpredictable and expensive ways. To avoid possible financial disaster, create a risk-management plan, listing the risks you identified, your assessment of their financial impact, and the techniques that you plan to use to manage each risk.

Figure 25-3 outlines a risk-management plan that a young person might develop. As you progress through different life stages, your priorities will change, and you will need to adjust your plan accordingly. For example, life insurance may become a higher priority when you have children who depend on your income. You can use the model presented as Figure 25-3 for developing a risk-management plan for any stage in life.

Insurance is an important part of any risk-management plan. In general, financial advisers say that a basic insurance program should help reduce or alleviate the following:

1. Potential loss of income due to the premature death, illness, accident, or unemployment of a wage earner.
2. Potential loss of income and extra expense resulting from the illness, disability, or death of a spouse or other family member.
3. Potential loss of real or personal property due to fire, theft, or other hazards.

Risk	Seriousness of Financial Impact	Method for Handling
1. Auto accidents	High	Collision and liability insurance Reduce risk—driver's education class
2. Theft or damage to personal property in apartment	Medium	Renter's insurance Reduce risk—add bolt lock to door
3. Theft or damage to personal property at work or in my car	Medium	Renter's/homeowner's standard policy Floater policy (for higher priced items) Reduce risk—alarm in vehicle; keep items locked and out of sight
4. Injury to apartment visitors	Medium	Renter's insurance Low probability of occurring—assume risk above renter's insurance coverage
5. Personal illness and sports injuries	High	Health insurance Avoid some risk—stop bungee-jumping Reduce some risk—wear a helmet for mountain biking Reduce risk—get special training
6. Vision and dental needs	Low	Assume risk—contribute $10 a month to a fund to pay for new glasses and dental work, when needed (self-insure).
7. Income protection	Medium/low (depending on life situation)	Life insurance (to protect dependents) Disability insurance (to provide income if I can't work) Insurance to make minimum payments when I am unemployed

4. Potential loss of income, savings, and property resulting from personal liability (injuring a person or damaging the property of others).

For each risk that you will face, you can determine ways that you can reduce, avoid, or assume part of the risk yourself. However, when a risk is significant and can have drastic consequences, then purchasing insurance is a good idea. In Chapters 26 and 27, you will learn more about specific types of insurance. As you consider an insurance plan, you should also think about the practices discussed below, which will help you save on insurance costs.

Increase Deductibles

A deductible is the specified amount of a loss that you must pay. The insurer's obligation to pay begins only after you have paid your full deductible. Generally, the higher the deductible, the lower the insurance premium. For example, premiums for a policy with a $100 deductible will be considerably higher than for a policy with a $500 deductible. To reduce your premiums, you can accept a higher deductible.

Purchase Group Insurance

The premiums for group plans are usually considerably lower than for an individual plan, especially for health insurance. If group plans are available to you through your job, credit union, a social or professional organization, or other similar group, you will likely save money by enrolling in them.

Consider Payment Options

How you pay premiums can save you considerable money over a short period of time. Monthly payments usually contain an extra charge, while semiannual payments do not. Typically, premiums are paid annually or semiannually. Agreeing to have your premiums automatically deducted from your checking account or paying electronically may also reduce your costs. Always compare payment options and weigh the differences in costs.

Look for Discount Opportunities

Many insurance companies offer discounts to policyholders for special conditions. For example, non-smokers can get lower premiums on fire and health insurance. Taking driver's education and getting good grades can reduce automobile insurance costs for teenagers. Having more than one vehicle or more than one insurance policy with a company can allow multiple policy discounts. You should also check your credit union and other professional or social groups to see if discounts are available.

Comparison Shop

Like many other things you buy, it pays to shop around for insurance. The variety of available insurance products makes it possible to tailor a plan to fit your needs.

Risk Management

Get quotes from several different insurers, and be sure to give each one the same information so you can compare exact coverage and costs. When getting cost estimates for many types of insurance, you need to know what your property is worth. In addition, maintaining a good driving record is important when getting price quotes for automobile insurance. It's also important to know exactly what coverage you need—and don't need—before talking to insurers.

Shop around for the best insurer. When evaluating insurers, remember that the most reputable companies provide good coverage at reasonable prices. The financial strength of the company may be a major factor in keeping down insurance costs for consumers. You can find ratings for different insurers in print and online publications of the A.M. Best Company and Standard & Poor's.

Ask people you know for recommendations about insurers they have used. Check with your state insurance commissioner to see what companies are legally doing business in the state, and which companies have had complaints filed against them. You can access your state insurance commissioner at your state government Web site.

Check Your Understanding

Review Terms
1. pure risk
2. speculative risk
3. insurable interest
4. risk management
5. risk avoidance
6. risk reduction
7. risk assumption

Review Concepts
1. What is a "pure risk"?
2. How can changing your deductible reduce your insurance premium?

PERSONAL PERSPECTIVE

Choosing an Insurance Agent

The agent you choose can be as important as the insurance company and coverage you select. The insurance agent is an important person because he or she explains your options and helps you plan for your insurance needs. The agent should:

1. Be available to you locally. You should be able to reach the agent by telephone and have a personal visit every few years to keep your insurance needs current.
2. Give you full-service counseling for all your insurance needs, including advice about when you do *not* need insurance.
3. Not exert pressure on you or try to sell you coverage or policies that are not appropriate. He or she should also inform you of when to reduce coverage (when property values decrease) and when to drop coverage.
4. Be professional, knowledgeable, and up-to-date about insurance. In addition, the agent should be able to explain to you, in language you can understand, exactly what is covered and what is not, and how policies work.
5. Be willing and able to answer your questions and keep you informed as to company changes and laws that affect you and your insurance policies.

You can buy directly from an insurance company, or you can buy through an insurance agency. An *insurance agency* represents many different insurance companies and can match you with the company and policy that meets your needs. An insurance agent may work directly for a particular insurer or be independent (and work for an agency). It is not unusual for a relationship with an insurance agent to extend over 20 or 30 years.

Think Critically

1. What are some advantages of working with an independent insurance agent?
2. Would you consider buying insurance from an out-of-state company if the premiums were considerably less but the company would not have any local agents? Why or why not?
3. Describe the kind of person you would like to have as your insurance agent.

Summary

25.1 What Is Insurance?

- Insurance is a method of spreading an individual's risk among a large group, so that no one in the group must endure the full cost of a devastating loss.
- Insurers sell insurance policies to policyholders in exchange for regular premium payments. Insurers make a profit by collecting more in premiums than they pay out in losses and operating expenses.
- Insurance is based on the principal of indemnification, meaning that the goal is to return the policyholder to the same financial condition as before the loss occurred. Insurance is not meant to enrich the policyholder.
- Insurers analyze historical data to help them predict how many losses to expect among their policyholders over a given time period. They base their premium amounts on these statistical averages, but they cannot predict which individuals will suffer losses.
- To be insurable, a risk must have the potential to result in serious financial loss not under the control of the insured. Insurable risks include personal risks (life and health), property risks (home and car), and liability risks (to protect income and assets).

25.2 Risk Management

- In order for you to buy insurance, the risk must be insurable and you must have an insurable interest to protect. You have an insurable interest in a life or property if its loss or damage would cause you financial harm.
- Risk management is an organized strategy for controlling financial loss from pure, not speculative, risks.
- The risk-management process begins with identifying risks, then assessing their financial impact, and finally devising a plan to handle them.
- Buying insurance is not the only option for managing risk. You might choose to assume risks that are not financially serious enough to insure. You might decide to handle other risks by taking steps to avoid them or reduce the chances that they will occur.
- Based on your assessment of the nature and seriousness of the risks you identified, you should select the best risk-management techniques for handling each one, and combine these into a plan.
- To reduce insurance costs, you can increase deductibles, buy group plans, change payment options, take advantage of discounts, and comparison shop.

Review Terms

Directions: Can you find the definition for each of the following terms used in Chapter 25?

indemnification
insurable interest
insurance
insurer
liability risks
personal risks
policy
policyholder
premium
probability
property risks

pure risk
risk (insurance)
risk assumption
risk avoidance
risk management
risk reduction
speculative risk

1. A method of spreading individual risk among a large group of people to make losses more affordable for all.
2. The chances of loss involving your income and standard of living.
3. A chance of loss with no chance for gain.
4. An organized strategy for controlling financial loss from pure risks.
5. The risk-management technique that involves taking measures to lessen the frequency or severity of losses.
6. The mathematics of chance; the likelihood that something will happen.
7. The chance of financial loss from perils to people or property.
8. The chances of loss or harm to personal property or real estate.
9. The chances of loss that may occur when your errors or inappropriate actions result in bodily injury to someone else or damage to someone else's property.
10. A risk that may result in either gain or loss.
11. The risk-management technique of eliminating the chance for loss by never doing the activity that could result in the loss.
12. The risk-management technique of establishing a monetary fund to cover the cost of a loss.
13. Putting the insured back in the same financial condition as before the loss occurred.
14. Any financial interest in life or property such that, if the life or property were lost or harmed, the insured would suffer financially.

15. A business that agrees to pay the cost of potential future losses in exchange for regular fee payments.
16. A written insurance contract.
17. A fee usually paid at regular intervals to an insurer for an insurance policy.
18. The person who owns an insurance policy.

Review Facts and Ideas

1. Why do people buy insurance?
2. Explain how insurance works.
3. How do insurers make a profit?
4. Explain the concepts of probability and indemnification.
5. How do insurers decide how much to charge in premiums?
6. Define the words *deductible, peril, and loss*.
7. List the three major types of insurable risks.
8. What type of risk is not insurable?
9. Why can't you buy insurance on your neighbor's house?
10. Explain the three-step risk-management process.
11. Explain the concepts of risk avoidance, risk reduction, risk assumption, and risk transfer.
12. What should you include in a risk-management plan?
13. How can you reduce your insurance costs?
14. What qualities should you consider in selecting an insurance agent?

1. Prepare a list of insurers in your area. Include the types of insurance sold by each company. For each insurance agency, list the insurance companies represented. (Hint: The Yellow Pages of your telephone directory should have all these listed under "Insurance.")

2. Based on Figure 25-1, list any current or anticipated risks you or your family faces or will face in the near future. You might include risks for recreation and travel opportunities, injuries on the job, and so on.

3. Based on your personal situation, analyze your current personal, property, and liability risks. Then assume that you are now 10 years older. Based on being where you would like to be and doing what your current goals dictate, analyze your personal, property, and liability risks for this stage in your life.

4. Using Figure 25-2 as a guide, identify your most significant risks and the perils that cause them. Then list ways that you can protect yourself by either reducing the financial impact of the risk or reducing its chances of occurring.

5. Visit your state insurance commissioner online. Download and print the complaint form if one is available, and write a paragraph about what recourse you may have when you feel an insurer is treating you unfairly.

6. Visit Standard & Poor's online at www.standardandpoors .com, and follow the links to ratings for insurance companies. Look up the financial strength ratings for particular insurance companies until you find two with different ratings. Then search the site for the meaning of these ratings. Which company did Standard & Poor's judge to be financially stronger? How did the two ratings differ?

7. Using Figure 25-3 as a guide, prepare a risk-management plan for yourself. You may need assistance from parents to determine your current insurance coverage. As an alternative, interview a person at a different life stage and ask for advice on an appropriate risk-management plan.

Solve Problems

1. Doris and Andrew are planning to get married next summer. They don't own a car and plan to rent an apartment. They intend to have children in the next few years. What advice can you give them about risk and risk management? When should they consider purchasing insurance?

2. Your cousin Tameka has decided to take up snow skiing. She has asked you how she can avoid paying for high medical bills if she gets injured. Currently, she is under her parents' group health insurance policy, but her parents have informed her that she will be responsible for all costs of learning to ski, including any costs not paid by insurance. How can she maximize her opportunities while minimizing her risks and costs?

3. A neighbor has asked for your advice regarding insurance. She is single, owns her own car, and works full time. She is buying a home and has student loans and other debts to pay. She would like to know what risks she is facing and what she might do about them. Help her identify and assess her risks, and develop a plan to manage them, based on her situation.

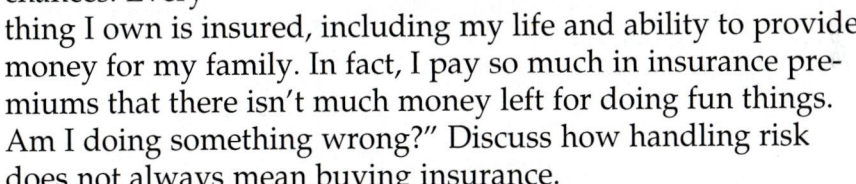

4. Carlos Montoya made this statement: "I don't take any chances. Everything I own is insured, including my life and ability to provide money for my family. In fact, I pay so much in insurance premiums that there isn't much money left for doing fun things. Am I doing something wrong?" Discuss how handling risk does not always mean buying insurance.

5. Sue Watanabe is single and under age 25. She just started her first full-time job with group health insurance. She has a car. She has had no accidents or traffic tickets. She has an apartment that contains furnishings and personal belongings. Prepare a list of the risks she may face. What types of insurance coverage may she need?

6. Interview an insurance agent. Find out what an agent can do to help you purchase various types of protection.

For related activities and links, point your browser to
www.mypf.swep.com

Chapter 26
Property and Liability Insurance

Up Front

Barry attends college full time and shares a rented house with two housemates.

"As renters, we have to insure our personal possessions, and we're responsible for what happens on the property, even though we're only renting," he told his housemates. "We need to talk to an agent about renter's insurance to protect us in case of theft, fire, or freezing pipes. The good news is that we won't have to pay very much—less than $100 a year."

Goals

★ Explain why renters and homeowners need property insurance.

★ Describe fire, theft, and other forms of property insurance and types of policies.

Renter's Insurance

If you rent your residence, you don't have to worry about insuring the building. That is the landlord's responsibility. However, if your apartment burned down, you could still suffer a significant financial loss. Your personal possessions that you keep in your rented home are your responsibility to protect—not the landlord's. You are also responsible for personal injuries that occur inside your home.

A **renter's policy** is insurance that protects renters from property and liability risks. A renter's policy will protect your personal possessions inside the rental property from loss due to fire, smoke, and other types of damage such as water or moisture, freezing, or heat. For example, if you rent an apartment and there is a fire in the building, your personal property (couch, chairs, bed, clothing, and so on) may suffer damage. A renter's policy will cover the costs of repairing or replacing damaged or destroyed property.

If someone is injured while in your rented home, you may be *liable*, or legally obligated to pay the expenses that result from the injury. Your renter's policy will pay for medical costs incurred by your guests. A renter's policy will also protect your personal possessions while they are in your car or at work. If you have particularly valuable possessions at your home, in storage, or with you as you travel, you might have to buy special coverage for the items. For example, a standard renter's or homeowner's policy often does not cover a notebook computer. Tell your insurance agent about your most valuable possessions to find out if you need extra coverage.

Homeowner's Insurance

A **homeowner's policy** is insurance that protects property owners from property and liability risks. It is similar to renter's insurance, except that it includes coverage for the building as well as personal possessions inside the building. All homeowner's policies cover property owners' losses from these three types of risks:

1. Hazards such as fire, water, wind, and smoke that may physically damage the house or its contents.
2. Criminal activity, such as robbery, burglary, arson, and vandalism.
3. Liability—the legal responsibility to pay the cost of another person's losses or injuries. Doing something careless, such as improperly supervising a swimming pool or not removing items from a staircase, may be classified as negligence in a lawsuit.

Homeowner's policies may be very basic or very broad in their coverage. Figure 26-1 lists common types of homeowner's policies, together with the coverage each provides. *Package policies* that include several types of coverage in a single contract usually carry a lower premium than you would pay for each coverage separately.

Federally-backed flood insurance is available in communities that enforce regulations to reduce flood losses. If you have a flood insurance policy, you can be reimbursed for all your covered losses. In contrast, federal disaster assistance is often a loan, repayable in full with interest.

HO-1	Basic Coverage	Fire, lightning, windstorm, hail, explosion, riot, civil commotion, aircraft, nonowned vehicles, smoke, vandalism, malicious mischief, theft, and glass breakage. Limits apply, such as $500 or 5 percent of policy value, whichever is less.
HO-2	Broad Form	Broader list of perils; broader definitions; still has restrictions and limits, such as fire from fireplaces being excluded; limit of $1,000 or 10 percent of policy value, whichever is less.
HO-3	Special Form	All-risk coverage on dwelling itself; a loss not specifically excluded (such as flood) is covered.
HO-4	Renter's	Insuring personal property on a broad-form basis with advantages of homeowner's policy (such as special coverage in event of flood or water damage).
HO-5	Comprehensive	Most comprehensive policy available; dwelling and contents are covered on all-risk basis.
HO-6	Condominium Owner's	HO-4 coverage for condominium owners (wording is adjusted to fit legal status of condominium owner).
HO-7	Older Homes	Meets special needs of owners of older buildings that have been remodeled and would have high replacement costs (actual cash value basis rather than replacement cost basis).

How Much Coverage Do You Need?

Generally, people insure the contents of their house for at least half the value of the building. For example, a building insured for $150,000 is likely to have contents covered for $50,000 to $100,000. This includes all types of personal possessions, from furniture and furnishings to clothing, appliances, utensils, artwork, and other personal property.

To be sure you are reimbursed for all damaged or destroyed property, you should complete a household inventory, as shown in Figure 26-2 on page 736. This inventory is similar to the personal

Figure 26-2 *Household Inventory*

HOUSEHOLD INVENTORY

Room	Type of Property	Replacement Cost	Receipt/Proof
Kitchen	Appliances:		
	Stove/oven	$ 600	Wards, 7/98
	Microwave	400	Penneys, 9/97
	Toaster	25	Gift
	Mixer/blender	125	Shaleys, 1/99
	Bread maker	250	K-Mart, 6/99
	Cabinets and contents:		
	Dishes	500	
	Pots and pans	500	
	Silverware	800	Oneida, 2/96
	Clock on wall	100	Gift
	Table and chairs	1,200	Dixons, 5/99
	Curtains	500	Wards, 8/98
Family Room	Bookcase, books	2,000	
	Couch and chair	1,000	Dixons, 2/99
	End tables/lamps	800	Dixons, 2/99
	Television	1,000	Mel's, 3/00
	Stereo	1,200	Mel's, 3/00
	Paintings	700	Dixons, 2/99
Bedroom	Antique bedroom set	5,000	Appraisal
	Clothing	2,000	
	Jewelry	500	
	Picture/mirrors	800	Dixons, 2/99
Garage	Lawn mower	900	Swath's, 3/98
	Garden tools	300	
	Camping equipment	800	Mel's, 3/00
	Bicycles	1,800	Jon's, 3/00
Utility Room	Washer/dryer	1,200	Sears, 3/99
	Cleaning supplies	100	

property inventory you prepared in Chapter 8, except that a home-owner's inventory usually needs to be more comprehensive. Your household inventory should include documentation that shows proof of ownership and value. Some people keep receipts and take pictures or a home video. Keep this documentation in a safe place (such as a safe deposit box). Most insurance agents provide household inventory forms to their customers. However, some things are not covered by property insurance. Figure 26-3 lists items that generally are excluded (not covered).

Items Typically Excluded from Homeowner's Policies

Figure 26-3

Items Not Covered by Most Homeowner's Insurance Policies:

- Articles insured separately (floater) such as jewelry, collections, and portable computers

- Animals, birds, fish, and other pets

- Motorized land vehicles (licensed for use), except for lawn mowers and things used on the property exclusively

- Stereos, radios, CBs, cellular phones, or CD players in vehicles

- Aircraft and parts of aircraft

- Property of renters, boarders, and other tenants (unless they are related to the owner and not paying rent)

- Business property in storage, such as samples

- Business property pertaining to a business that is conducted at the residence (separate insurance is required)

- Business property away from the residence

Avoid overinsuring property—that is, buying more insurance than is necessary to cover the value. An insurer will pay no more than the actual replacement value of the home. For example, if your home valued at $150,000 with contents worth $75,000 were totally destroyed, the insurer would pay no more than $225,000 ($150,000 + $75,000). If you owned a $300,000 homeowner's policy, you would still receive reimbursement of no more than $225,000. The principle of indemnity, a legal doctrine, limits recovery under an insurance policy to the lesser of the actual cash value of a loss or the amount that will restore the insured to his or her position prior to the loss.

Claims adjustors, also known as *insurance adjustors,* determine the value of the property destroyed or damaged by a covered hazard. In addition, insurers employ *insurance investigators* who look for evidence of destroyed or damaged property. They also look into cases where people try to claim damages that did not occur. Fraudulent insurance claims can result in criminal charges, fines, or both.

An **endorsement** is a written amendment to an insurance policy. Policyholders often use endorsements to add coverages to their policy for an additional premium. For example, you can add flood or earthquake insurance as an endorsement to your homeowner's policy. Coverage added to the existing policy by endorsement is often called *extended coverage*. Instead of adding coverages to existing policies, some homeowners save money by purchasing a more comprehensive form of homeowner's policy.

Most property insurance policies contain a **co-insurance clause**, a provision requiring policyholders to insure their building for a stated percentage of its replacement value in order to receive full reimbursement for a loss. The percentage is usually at least 80 percent. Insurers do not require 100 percent coverage because even if your property is completely destroyed, the land and the building foundation will probably still be usable. If you do not meet the co-insurance minimum coverage, then you will receive less than the full amount of the damages.

MATH MINUTE

Calculating Insurance Reimbursement for a Loss

The co-insurance clause in a homeowner's policy requires that you buy coverage equal to a stated percentage of the property's replacement value in order to receive full reimbursement for a loss. For example, an 80 percent co-insurance clause would require the following coverage on a $150,000 house:

$150,000 × .8 = $120,000 coverage required

Many homeowners believe they can save money by underinsuring. Say the owners of the home in our example decide to buy only $100,000 of insurance instead of the required $120,000, thinking that $100,000 will cover most losses. Then they have a fire that results in a loss valued at $50,000. They think their $100,000 policy will cover the loss. But that isn't the case. Because they did not meet the $120,000 requirement, the insurer will reimburse based on the percentage of coverage they do have:

$100,000/$120,000 = .833 or 83⅓%

To determine the reimbursement, the insurer will multiply the value of the loss by this percentage:

$50,000 × .833 = $41,650

Thus, for a $50,000 loss, the homeowners will receive only $41,650, or 83⅓% of the loss.

Problem: Jerry bought a house for $200,000. His co-insurance requirement is 85 percent. Jerry bought insurance for $120,000 to save money on insurance premiums. Last month, a storm caused $50,000 damage to his house. How much will the insurer reimburse?

Solution:
$200,000 × .85 = $170,000 required coverage
$120,000/$170,000 = .7059, or 70.59%
$50,000 × .7059 = $35,295 reimbursement Jerry will receive

Physical Damage Coverage

Hazards such as fire, wind, water, and smoke may damage or destroy your home, or cause you to temporarily lose use of it. The main component of homeowner's insurance is protection against financial loss due to damage or destruction to a house or other structures. Detached structures on the property, such as a garage or shed, as well as trees, plants, shrubs, and fences are also included in the coverage. If damage from a covered hazard prevents you from using your property while it is being repaired or replaced, your homeowner's policy will pay for temporary housing for a limited time (usually six months or less).

Theft and Vandalism Coverage

Theft and vandalism coverage protects your personal belongings against loss from criminal activity, such as robbery and criminal damaging. It covers your property when it is in your home or with you when you are away from home. Common types of homeowner's and renter's policies include this coverage.

COMMUNICATION CONNECTION

Make a list of all the items in your school locker, backpack, handbag, or the like. How difficult or costly would it be to replace these items if they were stolen? Can you place a replacement cost on each item? What about items of "sentimental" value?

A **personal property floater** is insurance coverage for the insured's moveable property wherever it may be located. People often buy it to protect specific items of high value, such as jewelry, coin and stamp collections, fine art, musical instruments, and the like. A standard homeowner's policy has limits on coverage of personal property. For example, your policy may pay up to $1,000 for computers and related technology, $5,000 for jewelry, and $1,000 for collections. If, in fact, you have personal property worth more than these minimum amounts, you can protect it with a floater.

A floater protects property without regard to its location at the time of loss. If you have a floater to cover your jewelry, then you would receive compensation if your jewelry were stolen from your motel room while you were on vacation. Rates for floater policies

Why might someone take out a personal property floater?

are reasonable. For example, a ring worth $7,500 could be insured for about $80 a year. A floater requires a detailed description of the item and periodic appraisals to verify its current value.

Liability Coverage

Liability coverage is insurance to protect against claims for bodily injury to another person or damage to another person's property. For instance, if a guest in your home slips and falls, you may be held liable for medical expenses for a broken leg or other injuries. If you own a dog, you are responsible for acts of the dog. If the dog bites someone, you are covered for the medical expenses of treating the injury. If your child hits a baseball through a neighbor's window, you are covered for the physical damage caused.

Lawsuits can be very expensive, so all homeowners and landlords should carry liability insurance. Most common homeowner's and renter's policies include liability coverage. Homeowners are responsible for acts occurring on their property, even acts involving *uninvited* people, such as door-to-door solicitors or delivery people. In most cases, homeowners will not be held liable for damages by a trespasser (unlawful intruder) unless they set a trap with the intent to harm the trespasser.

An **attractive nuisance** is a dangerous place, condition, or object that is particularly attractive to children, such as a swimming pool. If a child sneaks into a private pool without permission and is hurt, the homeowner will be held liable for the child's injuries. The owner is usually responsible, even if he or she takes steps to prevent entry into the pool.

Shopping Online for Insurance

Most large insurers have Web sites where you can get information about the policies and premiums they offer. To compare the offerings of many companies, the Internet is a good resource. Searching on the keyword "insurance" will lead you to many consumer-oriented sites, such as InsuranceMachine.com, NetQuote.com, and Insure.com. At these sites you can get insurance quotes for all types of insurance policies, along with a wealth of information to help you evaluate insurance options.

✓ Check Your Understanding

Review Terms
1. renter's policy
2. homeowner's policy
3. endorsement
4. co-insurance clause
5. personal property floater
6. liability coverage
7. attractive nuisance

Review Concepts
1. Why do renters need insurance?
2. Why is it important not to overinsure your property?

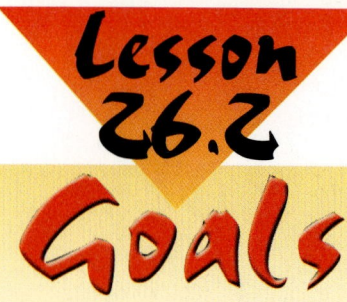

Automobile and Umbrella Insurance

Goals

★ Discuss common types of automobile insurance coverage and what each coverage is designed to protect.

★ Explain the concept of liability insurance as it relates to an umbrella policy.

Automobile Insurance

All states have financial responsibility laws. These laws are intended to keep off the highways those drivers who cannot pay for the property damage or injuries they might cause. Most states require minimum automobile insurance for registration of a motor vehicle.

Automobile insurance provides protection to owners and operators of motor vehicles. It covers costs of damage to the vehicle, its owner, and any passengers. It also covers costs of repairs to other vehicles, medical expenses of occupants in other vehicles involved in an accident, and property damage (shrubs, trees, and fences) caused by vehicle operation. Standard policies also cover theft. Each year at least 1 car in 50 is stolen. Many are found later, but most of them are damaged or stripped of parts.

Cost of Automobile Insurance

Automobile insurance is expensive. Premiums are based on a number of factors, such as:

1. Model, style, and age of car
2. Driver classification (age, sex, marital status, driving record)
3. Location (city, county) of driver and car
4. Distances driven
5. Purpose of driving (such as work)
6. Age and sex of other regular drivers of the car

Premium discounts are available for certain conditions, such as more than one vehicle insured with the same company, driver's education training, and good grades in high school (usually a B average or better).

Your driving record includes the number and type of traffic tickets, called *infractions,* along with your accident record. Arrests for more serious traffic offenses, called *misdemeanors,* will increase your insurance premiums. An infraction might be a parking ticket, failure to come to a complete stop at a stop sign, or an improper left-hand turn. Misdemeanors include speeding, driving without a license, or reckless driving. Very serious traffic violations, such as drunk driving, hit and run, or leaving the scene of an accident, are *felonies* in many states. All these events not only increase your insurance premium but remain a part of your driving record for at least three years. In many states, when drivers receive three or more tickets in a 12-month period, they are required to take a driver's safety course.

Except for vintage (antique) cars, older cars require less insurance than newer cars, because older cars are worth less. New and expensive cars cost more to insure because they are worth more and would therefore be more expensive to repair or replace.

As you learned in Chapter 25, insurers base their premiums on statistical probabilities calculated from historical data. From their analyses, insurers have determined that some classes of drivers have a higher probability of getting into accidents than others. For example, young single drivers are statistically more likely to be involved in an accident than are married drivers over 25. As a result, insurers charge higher premiums to young single drivers.

NET NOTES

Teen drivers have the highest crash risk of any age group. Per mile traveled, they have the highest involvement rates in all types of crashes, from those involving only property damage to those that are fatal. The Web site www.carsafety.org, which is co-sponsored by the Insurance Institute for Highway Safety, provides detailed statistics about the problem. Also included are stories of teenagers involved in car accidents, along with practical tips on what teens and their parents can do to promote safe driving.

Similar statistics cause insurers to charge higher premiums on sports cars than on family cars and on young male drivers than on their female counterparts. Certain geographic locations have had higher accident rates than others over the years. As a result, insurers charge higher rates to drivers in these hazardous areas.

The farther you drive on a regular basis (such as to work), the higher your insurance premiums. Who will be driving, primarily and occasionally, will also be a factor in determining cost. Adding a teenage driver to an existing policy will increase premiums. Another important consideration is the number of claims filed.

When you file too many claims, your premiums increase. Also, when you are in an accident that is your fault, and your insurance company has to pay money to another person, you are likely to see a *surcharge*, or increased premium for one to three years.

Types of Automobile Insurance Coverage

There are five basic types of automobile insurance: liability, collision, comprehensive, personal injury protection (PIP), and uninsured/underinsured motorist. All types of insurance purchased in a single policy are known as *full coverage*. Figure 26-4 shows a comparison of coverages for automobile insurance.

Liability Coverage

Most states require all drivers to carry liability insurance. The purpose of liability coverage in auto insurance is the same as in homeowner's insurance: it protects the insured against claims for bodily injury to another person or damage to another person's property. It pays nothing toward the insured's own losses, either personal injury or damage to the vehicle. However, if an accident is legally not your fault, the other driver's liability coverage will pay for

Figure 26-4 *Automobile Coverage*

AUTOMOBILE INSURANCE

	Who Is Protected:	
	Policyholder	Other Persons
Liability coverage:		
Personal injuries	No	Yes
Property damage	No	Yes
Collision coverage:		
Damage to insured vehicle	Yes	No
No-fault provision	Yes	No
Comprehensive coverage:		
Damage to insured vehicle	Yes	No
Personal injury protection:		
Medical payments	Yes	Yes
Pedestrian coverage	Yes	No
Uninsured/underinsured motorist coverage:		
Bodily injury	Yes	Yes

damages to your car. If the accident is your fault and all you have is liability coverage, your insurance will not pay for the damages to your car.

Liability insurance coverage is usually described using a series of numbers, such as 100/300/50. These numbers mean that the insurer will pay up to $100,000 for injury to one person, $300,000 total for all people, and $50,000 for property damage in an accident. Premiums charged for liability insurance vary according to the amount of coverage.

Collision Coverage

Collision coverage is automobile insurance that protects your own car against damage from accidents or vehicle overturning. This coverage will pay for the damage to your car in the event you are at fault and the other driver's liability insurance does not have to pay. Most collision coverage has a deductible. For example, you may pay the first $100 or $500 (as specified by your policy) for repairs, and the insurer pays the rest. Because many minor traffic accidents involve damage that costs less than many deductibles, it is wise to have a larger deductible and pay lower premiums. In other words, paying the first $250 for each accident might be less expensive than having a $50 deductible and paying higher premiums.

What is the difference between collision coverage and comprehensive coverage?

Comprehensive Coverage

Damage to your car from causes other than collision or vehicle overturning is covered by **comprehensive coverage.** The causes might be fire, theft, tornado, hail, water, falling objects, natural disasters, and acts of vandalism. For example, if your car is scratched while parked in a mall lot, your comprehensive insurance pays for the damage. Usually, there is a very small or no deductible for comprehensive coverage.

DID YOU KNOW

It may not be cost-effective to have collision or comprehensive coverage on cars worth less than $1,000 because any claim you make would not substantially exceed annual cost and deductible amounts.

Personal Injury Protection (PIP)

Also known as *medical coverage insurance*, **personal injury protection (PIP)** is automobile insurance that pays for medical, hospital, and funeral costs of the insured and his or her family and passengers, regardless of fault. If the insured is injured as a pedestrian or bicyclist, this insurance will pay the medical costs. To reduce costs for this kind of insurance, buy a car with airbags, antilock brakes, and other safety devices that lower the risk of injury.

Uninsured/Underinsured Motorist Coverage

Uninsured/underinsured motorist coverage is automobile insurance that pays for your injuries when the other driver is legally liable but unable to pay. In other words, if the other driver is legally at fault for the accident but has no insurance or insurance that is insufficient to cover the costs, your insurer will pay your medical costs. This coverage also protects you as a pedestrian if you are hit by an uninsured vehicle.

No-Fault Insurance

Many states have passed *no-fault insurance laws*. These laws set up a system of compensation for auto accidents that does not require a legal determination of who was at fault. **No-fault insurance** is automobile insurance in which drivers involved in an accident receive reimbursement for their medical and repair expenses from their own insurer.

The basic idea behind no-fault insurance is to avoid the years of legal battling required to settle a case and determine fault. Even then, drivers with no assets and no insurance will not be able to fix the other driver's car or pay for damages resulting from their negligence. It was also hoped that by reducing the number of lawsuits, more money could go to injured people and get to them faster.

Assigned-Risk Policies

If you have an accident that costs your insurer large sums of money for property damage, injuries, or liability settlements, the insurer may cancel your insurance. The number of traffic citations and fines on your record may also cause your insurer to cancel your policy. If so, you may not be able to find another insurer willing to insure you.

Every state has an *assigned-risk pool* that consists of people who are unable to obtain automobile insurance. The state assigns these people to different insurers in the state. The insurers must then provide coverage. However, the insurance would cost you several times the normal rate for insurance premiums until you were able to establish a good driving record.

Umbrella Liability Insurance

As you learned in the previous two sections, renters and home-owners need liability insurance to protect them from claims of others who may be injured on their property, and liability insurance is required in most states as minimum automobile coverage. People who maintain minimum liability coverage on their automobile and residence can also purchase an umbrella liability policy to pick up where the other coverage left off. **Umbrella liability insurance,** also called a *personal catastrophe policy,* supplements your basic auto and property liability coverage by expanding reimbursement limits and including some risks that were excluded in the basic coverage.

Umbrella liability insurance would generally pay up to $1 million or $2 million for any accidental injuries caused to another person while you are driving, for an accident that occurred on your property, or in the course of your employment. This type of policy protects you from extraordinary losses, which are extremely high claims because of unusual circumstances. For example, you may be involved in an automobile accident in which a person receives a permanent injury. Medical costs may exceed $500,000 with additional costs for many years to come. As long as you carry minimum liability requirements on your automobile insurance, the umbrella policy would cover the rest.

Check Your Understanding

Review Terms
1. collision coverage
2. comprehensive coverage
3. personal injury protection (PIP)
4. uninsured/underinsured motorist coverage
5. no-fault insurance
6. umbrella liability insurance

Review Concepts
1. Why do young, single drivers generally pay higher automobile insurance premiums than do married drivers over 25?
2. What is the purpose of no-fault insurance laws?

PERSONAL PERSPECTIVE

Understanding an Insurance Policy

Many people find insurance policies difficult to read and understand. Consumers complain to state insurance commissioners that they do not know enough about insurance to know whether they are getting a good deal or a ripoff.

Most insurance policies contain a number of standard parts, including the declaration, the insuring agreement, the conditions, the exclusions, and endorsements.

1. *The Declaration.* This piece of paper is attached to the policy itself. It declares the property that is being insured, the dollar amounts of coverage and deductibles, and other basic information that applies specifically to one person's insurance policy. The declaration is different for every insurance policy.

2. *The Insuring Agreement.* This section sets forth who the insured is and what coverages are specifically included in the policy. Footnotes explain the abbreviations used.

3. *The Conditions.* This section explains the duties of the insured and of the insurer. For example, it is the insured's responsibility to pay premiums on time and to meet conditions that were agreed upon in the setting of premiums. The insurer will collect premiums, process claims, and pay the cost of damages as agreed.

4. *The Exclusions.* This section describes all circumstances that will not be covered. For example, intentional acts are not accidents and therefore may be excluded from coverage. Certain perils, property, and types of losses may also be specifically excluded, such as acts of war or civil disobedience.

5. *The Endorsements.* Any modification or addition to the insurance agreement is included as an endorsement. An endorsement can either add a coverage or delete a coverage. Endorsements can be added at a later date and serve to modify the original agreement.

Your best protection is to read and understand all this information prior to signing and agreeing to pay the premiums. You should also compare insurers and policies, not merely premiums, before choosing coverage and insurers.

Think Critically

1. Why do you think the declaration is different for every policy?
2. Why do you think some situations are excluded from coverage?
3. For what kinds of things might a policyholder use endorsements?

26.1 Property Insurance

- Renter's insurance protects your possessions at home, in the car, and at work from fire, theft, and other perils. It also pays medical costs if someone is injured in your rented home.
- Homeowner's insurance includes property and liability protections similar to renter's insurance, with the addition of coverage for the building itself. It protects homeowners from three risks: physical damage from natural perils, losses resulting from theft or vandalism, and liability.
- Insurers will reimburse no more than the replacement value, so overinsuring will result in higher premiums with no increase in benefits.
- The co-insurance clause in most homeowner's policies requires you to insure your building for a stated percentage of its replacement value to receive full reimbursement for a loss. If you do not meet this requirement, you will receive a reduced reimbursement based on the percentage of coverage you do have.
- Renters and homeowners can buy a personal property floater to cover particularly valuable moveable property, such as jewelry, that generally is not covered sufficiently by basic policies.
- Liability coverage in a homeowner's or renter's policy covers you in the event someone is injured in your residence or on property for which you are responsible.
- You can shop for insurance online at insurers' Web sites, or compare quotes from many insurers at consumer-oriented insurance search sites.

26.2 Automobile and Umbrella Insurance

- All states require minimum liability insurance coverage for owners and operators of motor vehicles.
- Premiums for automobile insurance vary according to factors such as type of car, driving record, coverage desired, deductibles, and other discounts or surcharges. Insurers also charge more to drivers in categories that statistics reveal as having a higher probability of getting into accidents.
- Liability automobile coverage protects other people who may be injured or have property damage as a result of your negligence.
- Collision automobile coverage repairs damage to your own vehicle when you are at fault in an accident.
- Comprehensive automobile coverage protects your vehicle from non-collision losses, such as from theft, storms, and falling objects.
- Uninsured/underinsured motorist coverage protects you in the event the other driver, who is at fault, is uninsured or does not have enough insurance.
- No-fault insurance laws require insurers to pay the losses of their own insureds rather than requiring the at-fault driver's insurer to pay.
- People who own basic liability coverage on their car and home can buy umbrella liability insurance to expand the reimbursement limits and include coverage for risks otherwise excluded.

Review Terms

Directions: Can you find the definition for each of the following terms used in Chapter 26?

attractive nuisance
co-insurance clause
collision coverage
comprehensive coverage
endorsement
homeowner's policy
liability coverage
no-fault insurance
personal injury protection (PIP)

personal property floater
renter's policy
umbrella liability insurance
uninsured/underinsured motorist coverage

1. Insurance coverage for the insured's moveable property wherever it may be located.
2. An insurance policy provision requiring policyholders to insure their building for a stated percentage of its replacement value in order to receive full reimbursement for a loss.
3. Insurance to protect against claims for bodily injury to another person or damage to another person's property.
4. Automobile insurance in which drivers involved in an accident receive reimbursement for their medical and repair expenses from their own insurer.
5. Automobile insurance that pays for medical, hospital, and funeral costs of the insured and passengers involved in an accident, regardless of fault.
6. Insurance that supplements basic auto and property liability coverage by expanding reimbursement limits and including some risks that were excluded in the basic coverage.
7. Insurance that protects renters from property and liability risks.
8. Insurance that protects property owners from property and liability risks.
9. A written amendment to an insurance policy.
10. A dangerous place, condition, or object particularly attractive to children.
11. Automobile insurance that protects the insured's own car against damages from accidents or vehicle overturning.
12. Automobile insurance that protects the insured's own car against damages from causes other than collision or vehicle overturning.
13. Automobile insurance that pays for the insured's injuries when the other driver is legally liable but unable to pay.

1. Explain the differences between a renter's policy and a home-owner's policy.
2. All homeowner's policies cover property owners' losses from what three types of risks?
3. As a general guideline, how much coverage should you buy for the contents of your house?
4. What are some items typically excluded from property insurance?
5. What do insurance adjustors and insurance investigators do?
6. What kind of coverage should you buy to insure your expensive guitar collection?
7. Explain the concept of co-insurance.
8. Give several examples of an attractive nuisance.
9. List several factors that affect the cost of automobile insurance.
10. How are infractions different from misdemeanors?
11. What is the purpose of automobile liability insurance?
12. Explain the difference between comprehensive physical damage coverage and collision coverage.
13. Why should a person carry uninsured/underinsured motorist protection?
14. Explain the concept of no-fault insurance.
15. What is the purpose of an assigned-risk pool?
16. Why might someone purchase an umbrella liability policy?

1. Prepare a household inventory, listing only the contents of your room or one room in your home. Follow Figure 26-2 as an example. Next to each item, record its approximate value, and indicate whether or not you have a receipt to prove its cost and a photo of each item.

2. Write a few paragraphs discussing the perils of overinsuring or underinsuring property. Be specific in the consequences that may result in either case. How can you be sure that you are insuring property for its appropriate replacement value? (Hint: Ask people who have property insurance how they determined value, such as the assessed valuation as provided on property tax rolls.)

3. Outline ways you can protect valuables from being stolen from your home or automobile. Research the cost of protection devices or services.

4. Get a price quote for full-coverage automobile insurance on the car of your choice. Determine ways to reduce premium costs through discounts or other methods. Write a paper reporting your results.

5. Visit your state government Web site and gather information to answer these questions: What type and how much liability coverage does your state require for drivers? How are financial responsibility laws enforced? For example, is vehicle insurance tied to vehicle registration? What are the fines or penalties if a driver is caught without insurance? You can get information on this subject from a driver's manual, or look in the library or online for relevant laws.

6. Visit the Web sites of two insurers and list the features of each insurer's basic automobile policy. How are their coverages alike or different? If possible, get a price quote from both companies for their auto policy. Which do you think provides the best coverage for your premium dollar? Why?

7. Interview an insurance agent about the need for umbrella liability insurance in your state. Ask questions about coverage availability, maximum policy limits, and premium costs. Also ask about exclusions. What situations would not be covered by the policy?

Solve Problems

1. Your friend Kwan is renting an apartment. She has nice furniture that she inherited from her grandparents. One day while you are having lunch, she mentions to you that last year the pipes burst in her apartment building and she was lucky that her valuable furnishings were not damaged. You ask if she has renter's insurance, and she says no. The landlord has insurance. How would you advise her?

2. As a first-time house buyer, your friend Tim is considering what type of insurance to buy. Describe the types of insurance that Tim might consider. (Refer to Figure 26-1.)

3. Your friend Carlota owns a home that has a value of $180,000. Her insurance policy has an 80 percent co-insurance clause.

She has the property insured for $140,000. Later that year, a tree falls on her house during a storm, causing damages of $25,000. How much reimbursement will she be able to collect?

4. Your neighbor owns a particularly valuable collection of antique plates. She estimates their value at more than $10,000. When talking about the plates, you learn that she has home-owner's insurance but no personal property floater for the plates. Explain to her the reason for a floater.

5. Your friend Dario is complaining about the high cost of automobile insurance. He really would like to own his own car but, at age 19, he feels he can't afford the insurance premiums. Discuss with him ways he can reduce the amount of insurance premiums.

6. Benito Mendoza carried the following insurance on his car at the annual costs shown:

Comprehensive physical damage	$ 80
Property damage liability ($25,000)	70
Bodily injury liability (100/200)	175
Collision ($250 deductible)	150
Total Premium	$475

As a result of an accident in which Benito was negligent, the driver of the other car was awarded $9,800 for injuries to himself and $2,100 in damages to his car. Benito's auto was damaged at a cost of $820. His medical bills were $135.

a. How much did the insurer have to pay in claims as a result of the accident?

b. What is the maximum the policy would pay for injuries to the other driver?

c. Provided the premiums stayed the same, how many years' premiums would be required to equal the total paid by the insurer as a result of this one accident?

For related activities and links, point your browser to
www.mypf.swep.com

Chapter 27

Health and Life Insurance

health insurance
group health insurance
COBRA
coordination of
    benefits
preferred provider
    organization (PPO)

health maintenance
    organization
    (HMO)
Medicare
Medicaid
disability insurance
life insurance

incontestable clause
rider
term life insurance
permanent life
    insurance
cash value

Up Front

Elena wasn't feeling well and was sure it was strep throat. She had had it before and knew the symptoms.

"I need a doctor's appointment," she told her friend. "I'm insured under my mother's policy at work. I have an insurance card that allows me to see the doctor, but I have to pay a $15 co-payment at the time I go to the clinic. The doctor will give me a test called a 'lab culture' to be sure that I have strep. I'll have to pay 20 percent of the cost of that test. Then I'll get a prescription, and I have a $10 co-payment for that. Even with insurance, this illness will cost me $50 plus another $75 for time lost from work. Healthcare sure is expensive!"

Goals

★ Describe group and individual health insurance plans.
★ Discuss common types of health insurance coverage and plans.
★ Explain Medicare and Medicaid coverage available to those who qualify.

Group and Individual Health Plans

The cost of medical care, from office visits to hospital charges and laboratory tests, has escalated dramatically. People with no health insurance provided through employment often cannot afford individual policies. Millions of Americans do not receive proper medical care because they have no insurance. Many states have implemented healthcare reform to meet the needs of vast numbers of uninsured people. Also, rising premiums have forced employers who provide health insurance for their employees to search for ways to control costs. Many are requiring employees to pay a larger share of the cost.

Health insurance is a plan for sharing the risk of high medical costs resulting from injury or illness. Like other forms of insurance, health insurance reduces risk by spreading it among many people. Persons buy policies by paying a regular premium. In exchange, the insurer promises to pay medical expenses for the treatments covered by the policy.

Group Policies

The most common type of health insurance is **group health insurance.** This is health insurance issued to a group, such as an employer or trade association, to cover individuals in the group and sometimes their dependents. All

How has the rising cost of healthcare affected Americans?

those insured have the same coverage and pay a set premium. Because a group represents a large portion of potential business for an insurer, a group can usually negotiate better coverage and lower premiums than individuals can get on their own.

Some groups pay the premiums as a benefit to their members. More commonly, however, as in the case of employer and employee, the two share the premium costs. Group plans make up over 70 percent of all health insurance issued. The insurer may not cancel the insurance of any group member unless the person leaves the group or the group plan itself is terminated.

The *Consolidated Omnibus Reconciliation Act*, or **COBRA,** adopted in 1985, allows people who leave employment to continue their health insurance under the company plan for a limited period of time (usually 18 months). During this period, former employees pay premiums individually for the same group coverage they had while employed. The purpose of this law is to give former employees time to obtain other insurance, either on their own or through a new employer.

The *Health Insurance Portability and Accountability Act of 1996 (HIPAA)* limits the pre-existing conditions that group plans may exclude. It also makes it illegal for an insurer to deny coverage based on health status, though it does not limit the amount the insurer may charge for coverage. The purpose of the law is to increase your ability to obtain insurance when you start a new job and lower your chances of losing your current health insurance.

If a family has more than one group insurance plan, the insurers will share the costs of a claim. **Coordination of benefits** is a group health insurance provision that specifies how the insurers will share the cost when more than one policy covers a claim. This provision assures that reimbursement will not exceed 100 percent of allowable expenses. For example, if a couple has two policies— one through the husband's employer and one through the wife's employer—then one policy may pay 80 percent of the medical expenses and the other the remaining 20 percent. The couple would not be reimbursed for more than 100 percent of the expenses incurred.

Individual Policies

People can also buy individual health insurance policies. The premiums are usually high. Unlike group plans, most individual policies require a physical exam, and insurers may refuse to cover individuals with health problems. Moreover, individuals may have to wait a certain length of time (usually 90 days) before coverage begins. Members of group plans receive immediate coverage.

Most states require insurers to make some type of individual policy available for purchase by people who do not have group policies. States have high-risk insurance pools whereby people with pre-existing conditions (such as diabetes) can buy insurance. Unfortunately, the premiums are very high and placement on a waiting list can exclude people from coverage when they need it.

Sometimes medical costs can exceed the limits of a standard health policy. To protect against this risk, people can buy *supplemental health insurance*. This type of policy is designed to pay high deductibles and co-payments as well as medical fees that are higher than the insured's standard policy allows. For example, a standard plan may pay up to $350 a day for a hospital room, but the actual charges may come to $400 per day. A supplemental policy would pay the difference of $50 per day.

Types of Health Insurance Coverage

Standard health insurance policies typically cover basic health (medical, hospital, and surgical), major medical, dental, and vision needs. The main purpose of these kinds of coverage is to protect consumers from doctor and hospital bills that could ruin them financially. Figure 27-1 on page 760 summarizes common health insurance coverages.

Basic Health Insurance

Basic health coverage includes medical, hospital, and surgical costs. Medical coverage helps pay for physician care that does not involve surgery. This type of coverage pays for office visits and routine services, such as X rays and laboratory tests. Hospital coverage pays hospital bills for room, board, and drugs. Surgical coverage pays for part or all of a surgeon's fees for an operation. Usually the insurance covers only necessary (not cosmetic or elective) surgery and excludes some types of surgery.

Major Medical Expense Insurance

Major medical coverage provides protection against the catastrophic expenses of a serious injury or illness. Coverage is beyond

Figure 27-1 *Health Insurance Coverages*

What a Typical Health Insurance Plan Provides:

1. Basic coverage for hospital and doctor bills; co-payments of $10 to $20 per visit or 80 percent of reasonable charges. Elective and cosmetic surgery typically are not covered.

2. Cost of prescriptions, with a co-payment of $10 to $15 applied to generics; additional cost for brand-name drugs.

3. Pre-approved hospital stay coverage, including coverage of customary medical services. Second opinions required and paid for by insurance.

4. Yearly deductibles per person and per family, with a stop-loss protection depending on plan limits. These range from $1,000 to $5,000 or more.

5. Pre-existing conditions may be excluded for up to 90 days. After that, full benefits apply.

6. A $1 million to $5 million maximum coverage for major medical expenses.

7. Coverage available, at extra cost, for dental and vision care, with yearly maximum benefits and exclusions for work such as braces, dental implants, or corrective vision laser surgery.

Why is major medical coverage so important?

basic health insurance and typically extends to a maximum of $1 million or more. For example, when a patient is admitted to the hospital for a bone marrow transplant, organ transplant, or some other major type of surgery, the cost can be $500,000 or more.

The major medical coverage often has a *co-insurance provision* requiring the insured to pay some portion (often 20 percent) of all bills. However, a *stop-loss provision* would generally provide that after the insured has paid some specified amount, such as $1,000, in deductibles and co-insurance payments, the insurer would fully pay the rest.

Dental and Vision Insurance

Many group plans also provide dental and vision coverage. Most dental plans have low deductibles and co-insurance requirements of 20 percent or more. They also state upper limits, such as $1,500 per year per person, and cover only certain types of services, such as exams, X rays, and fillings. Insurers often pay for some services, such as crowns or bridges, at a much lower rate (such as 50 percent).

In some cases, insurers cover only certain types of services. For example, the cost of an amalgam filling (metal) is far less than a porcelain filling. Most dental policies will pay only for amalgams except when the filling is in the front teeth. If you want a porcelain filling for a back tooth, you would have to pay the cost difference. For instance, if your dentist charges $130 for a porcelain filling, and your insurance allows only $75, then insurance will pay 80 percent and you must pay 20 percent of the $75. In addition, you must pay the $55 difference between dentist's fee and the allowable amount.

MATH MINUTE

Calculating Costs of Services Not Fully Paid by Insurance

George decided to have a porcelain crown rather than a gold crown. His dental insurance will pay 80 percent of the cost of a gold crown. The policy sets the allowable amount for a gold crown at $600. George's dentist billed his insurer for $800, the cost of the porcelain crown. How much will insurance pay? How much does George have to pay?

First, compute how much insurance will pay on the gold crown:

$600 × .8 = $480 will be paid by insurance

Then subtract the amount paid by insurance from the total for the porcelain crown:

$800 − 480 = $320 due from George

Problem: Maria is considering having special dental work done for a total of $1,200. Her dental insurance policy sets $1,000 as the allowable amount for the procedure and covers the procedure at 90 percent. How much will insurance pay? How much will Maria have to pay?

Solution:

The insurer will pay $900 ($1,000 × .9).

Maria must pay $300 ($1,200 − 900).

Vision insurance often pays for exams for eye disease as well as for prescription adjustments and lenses. Policies usually cover an eye examination on a regular basis—once every year or two—and the purchase of single-vision corrective lenses. Some policies offer limited coverage for prescription sunglasses and contact lenses.

Private Health Plans

Employee health plans are grouped into two categories: unmanaged and managed. *Unmanaged (traditional fee-for-service) plans* allow employees to choose any doctor and to be reimbursed for usually 80 percent of the expenses incurred after a deductible. Deductibles often range from $50 to $250 per patient, or $450 per family. This plan is the most expensive of all because there is less strict control on costs or services.

Managed-care plans rely on a network of contracts with health-care providers. To receive maximum reimbursement, employees covered by a managed-care plan must select doctors who belong to the network. The policy requires employees to obtain pre-approval for any surgery or hospital admission and two or three doctors' opinions before allowing a major procedure to be done. The insurer exercises significant control over the types of services provided and the maximum benefits allowed for those services. Preferred provider organizations and health maintenance organizations are the two most common types of managed-care plans.

Insurance plans vary. Before choosing a plan, decide what is most important to you. Remember that the most important service to be covered is hospitalization. If you are not covered for hospital care, then one sickness could cost you thousands of dollars.

A **preferred provider organization (PPO)** is a group of health-care providers (doctors and hospitals, for example) who band together to provide health services for set fees. Patients must choose doctors from an approved list. There are limits on types of services that can be provided and fees that can be charged. Patients usually must pay a *co-payment,* or an amount in addition to premiums. The co-payment is a set amount, typically $5 to $25, per office visit or per prescription.

A **health maintenance organization (HMO)** is a group plan offering prepaid medical care to its members. An HMO often has its own facilities and usually provides a full range of medical services. Patients must choose doctors on the HMO staff, including one doctor to be their *primary-care physician (PCP),* or main provider. To see a specialist, patients must get a referral from their

PCP first. Otherwise, the insurance will not cover the visit to the specialist. In this way, the PCP acts as a "gatekeeper."

An advantage of belonging to an HMO is that preventive care, such as routine physical exams, is generally covered. The idea of an HMO is to encourage people to come in for treatment before a minor ailment becomes a major problem. The HMO patient often pays no deductible or co-payment. HMOs that are *capitated* (meaning "per person") receive a fixed monthly premium for each patient, regardless of whether or not the patient seeks medical care. Thus, while an HMO plan is generally less expensive for employees, people sometimes feel that their choices of doctors and treatment options are limited.

Healthfinder® serves as a gateway consumer health information Web site, developed by the United States Department of Health and Human Services. Among the site's many offerings is a section for teenagers. Subjects include hot topics (such as athletics, eating disorders, and car safety); smart choices (for example, information on tattoooing and body piercing); and special interests (employment and babysitter's training). Check out the site at www.healthfinder.gov/justforyou/teens.

Hybrid plans are also available today. They strongly resemble an HMO, but they allow you to choose your own doctor or allow you to go to specialists without seeing your primary-care physician first. Many people prefer these plans because they have more choice and control over medical services.

Self-Insurance Plans

Some larger employers (with usually 100 employees or more) may elect to self-insure. Rather than contract with an insurer, a company will collect insurance premiums from employees to pay medical benefits as needed. Based on mathematical probability, the plan works on the assumption that only a small number of employees will need extensive healthcare in a given period of time. If medical costs exceed money in the plan, then the company pays the difference. Often self-insured companies contract with insurers to process claims made against the company's insurance plan.

Medicare and Medicaid

Medicare is government-sponsored health insurance for people currently age 65 or older. For people born after 1960, the age for full benefits is 67. Medicare is funded by employee payroll deductions (currently 1.45 percent of all money earned). Coverage is paid through the Social Security Administration. Like other plans, there are maximum benefits, exclusions, and other requirements. Retired people pay a monthly premium for Medicare insurance. For an additional premium, people can buy *Medigap* insurance (a supplemental private insurance policy) to pay the deductibles and co-payments not covered by Medicare.

Medicaid is government-sponsored health insurance for people with low incomes and limited resources. This program is designed to help families who live in poverty and are unable to afford private health insurance or medical care. Like Medicare, there are limitations and exclusions.

Check Your Understanding

Review Terms
1. health insurance
2. group health insurance
3. COBRA
4. coordination of benefits
5. preferred provider organization (PPO)
6. health maintenance organization (HMO)
7. Medicare
8. Medicaid

Review Concepts
1. Why is group insurance generally less expensive than individual policies?
2. What is the purpose of COBRA?

PERSONAL PERSPECTIVE

Alternative Medicine

Alternative medicine is the use of nontraditional treatments such as naturopathy, acupuncture, and biofeedback. Many health insurance plans today allow members to use these services in addition to or in place of more conventional therapies.

Naturopathy is the use of natural medicines and procedures to remove toxins (poisons) from the body. Naturopaths suggest ways to build immunity by taking natural supplements. Naturopathy's goal is to promote or restore health by support of the individual's self-healing process. Because these remedies do not involve licensed physicians, they remain controversial.

Acupuncture is the use of needles inserted into the body at specific points to relieve pain. It is a Chinese medicine but is used around the world to treat conditions from bipolar disorder to boosting anesthesia.

Biofeedback is a form of treatment that helps patients gain some control over internal body functions. It is based on the idea that the mind and the body are linked and that the mind can control the body. Patients are hooked up to monitoring devices that provided feedback to them on bodily functions such as heart rate and blood pressure. Patients can then practice techniques that favorably affect these functions. For example, they can use relaxation techniques to lower blood pressure.

If you are going to use a form of alternative medicine, be sure to read about it and understand the methods and products and how they work with the human body.

Think Critically

1. Do you take vitamins? Why or why not?
2. Do you believe there is a mind/body connection that can help you stay healthy? Explain.

Disability and Life Insurance

Goals
★ Discuss different types of disability insurance.
★ Describe the characteristics of different life insurance plans.

Disability Insurance

Disability insurance is an insurance plan that makes regular payments (usually monthly) to replace income lost when illness or injury prevents the insured from working. This type of insurance is frequently referred to as *income protection* because coverage compensates workers for loss of income resulting from serious illness or injury. Generally there are two types of disability insurance: short-term and long-term. Short-term disability insurance provides benefits for up to two years. For periods over two years and up to retirement, people need long-term disability insurance.

Of all types of insurance, disability insurance is the most overlooked. People think nothing can happen to them that will interrupt their earning power. Unfortunately, recovery from an accident or an illness can extend for weeks or even months. Yet while you are disabled (unable to perform your job), your regular living expenses go on.

Why is disability insurance the most overlooked type of insurance?

Disability coverage requires a *waiting period*. Benefits don't begin the day you become disabled. The waiting period may be from 30 to 180 days. (The longer the waiting period, the lower the premium.) During this time, you would likely be on sick leave from work and would be collecting regular pay. Disability benefits begin after the waiting period and end as soon as you can return to work.

The maximum *duration of benefits* under most disability policies would be until age 65 or early retirement if you qualify. A few policies pay benefits for life if you become permanently disabled. In addition, the maximum amount you can collect is usually 50 to 75 percent of your regular pay. (The lesser the percentage, the lower the premium.)

Guaranteed renewability of coverage will protect you against cancellation if your health declines. Without this provision, an insurer could refuse to renew your insurance. The premium for renewability is higher, but the coverage may be worth the extra cost.

Before purchasing an individual disability insurance policy, remember that you may already have this insurance, such as from your employer and social security. In addition, you may also be eligible for income protection from the Veterans Administration (if you served in the military), civil service disability income (if you worked for the government), state welfare benefits, automobile insurance disability benefits, and many other potential sources, depending on your situation.

Group Disability Insurance

Group disability insurance plans are generally the least expensive option. In many cases, the employer pays for part or all of the plan. However, the insurance is good only as long as you work for the employer. When you leave, you lose all policy rights.

Social Security Disability Insurance

Most workers in the United States participate in the social security program. As you learned in Chapter 5, social security is more than retirement income. Social security is OASDI (old age, survivors, and disability insurance) as well as HI (health insurance—Medicare). Because you have social security taxes deducted from your paycheck, you are entitled to disability payments from social security in the event you become disabled and cannot work. To qualify, you will have to prove the extent of your disability, fill out forms, and have medical exams as required by the Social Security Administration. Workers are considered disabled if they have a physical or mental condition that prevents them from doing any gainful work, and the condition is expected to last for at least 12 months or result in death. Your benefits are determined by your pay and by the number of years you have been covered under social security.

Workers' Compensation Insurance

You learned in Chapter 5 that workers' compensation is insurance that covers your expenses if your injury or illness resulted from your job. If you are partially or totally permanently disabled, workers' compensation will pay monthly benefits. This insurance also carries a death benefit. It provides a burial payment and an allowance for living expenses for survivors of people killed on the job. Like social security benefits, these benefits are determined by your earnings and your work history.

Life Insurance

Life insurance is insurance that provides funds to the beneficiaries when the insured dies. Consider the financial needs that a family will face after the death of a wage earner—and how much income will be needed to pay the ongoing expenses of daily living. The purpose of life insurance, then, is to protect others who depend on you as a source of income. Figure 27-2 shows a list of purposes that life insurance can fulfill. As you can see from the list, and will learn about below, some types of life insurance provide savings as well as death benefits.

Like all types of insurance, life insurance is based on risk sharing and probability. To predict the probability of death at different ages, insurers use *mortality tables*. These are based on statistics gathered about life expectancy and death rates among various types of people. Insurers set premiums based on these tables. For example, older people have a higher probability of dying while the policy is in effect than do younger people. As a result, insurers generally charge older people higher premiums. Other factors enter the calculation as well. For example, people who smoke tend to die sooner than people who don't, and premiums reflect this. Someone with a serious health problem, such as heart disease, may not be able to buy life insurance at all.

Why are younger people generally charged lower life insurance premiums?

Purposes of Life Insurance **Figure 27-2**

Why You Should Purchase Life Insurance:

- to pay off a home mortgage and other debts at the time of death

- to provide lump-sum payment to children when they reach a specified age

- to provide an education or income for children

- to make charitable bequests after death

- to provide for retirement income

- to accumulate savings

- to make estate and inheritance tax payments

- to take care of children's needs as they are growing up

- to provide cash value that can be borrowed

To obtain life insurance, you will have to supply a detailed medical history. You may be required to have a medical examination, especially for large policies.

You may be able to buy inexpensive group life insurance through your employer. A *group life insurance plan* insures a large number of people under the terms of a single policy without a medical examination. Employers often provide group life insurance as an employee benefit. However, when you leave your job, you cannot take the coverage with you.

Life insurance may be important even for those who are not the primary wage earner in the family, to help cover the financial burden of childcare, funeral expenses, or any other unforeseen costs that can arise.

Provisions of Life Insurance Policies

An important provision in every life insurance policy is the right to name your beneficiary. As you learned in Chapter 25, *beneficiaries* are the people named in an insurance policy to receive the benefits of the policy. The beneficiaries of a life insurance policy will receive the amount specified in the policy at the death of the insured. Beneficiaries can be anyone, but married couples often name each other or their children as beneficiaries. If the children are minors, parents may name a trustee to handle the money on behalf of the children.

An **incontestable clause** is a provision of a life or health insurance policy that once the policy has been in effect for a stated period of time (usually two years), the insurer may no longer question items on the application in order to deny coverage. After the specified period, the insurer cannot dispute the policy's validity during the lifetime of the insured for any reason, including fraud. A reason for this provision is that the beneficiaries should not be made to suffer because of acts of the insured.

A life insurance **rider** is a small insurance policy that modifies the coverage of the main policy. A rider usually adds or excludes various coverages or alters benefits. Insurers offer many riders, and the costs can add up. Be sure you need the extra coverage before agreeing to the added premium.

Guaranteed insurability riders give you the right to buy a new policy or additional coverage without showing evidence of good health. Many insurers offer *accidental death* riders. In the case of accidental death, some riders allow *double indemnity*. This means that the beneficiary is paid twice the face amount of the insurance. For your beneficiaries to collect this benefit, you would have to die within a certain time after the injury (and death must be directly related to the injury), and death must occur before you reach age 60 or 65. A *waiver of premium* rider allows you to stop paying premiums and keep your coverage in force if you become disabled and cannot work. This rider usually does not kick in until you've been disabled at least six months.

Types of Life Insurance

There are two main types of life insurance: temporary and permanent. Temporary life insurance lasts for a specified period and contains no savings or cash value. Permanent insurance, however, lasts for life. It also includes a residual or cash value and is therefore a form of savings plan.

Temporary Life Insurance

The most common form of temporary life insurance is term insurance. **Term life insurance** is a life insurance policy that remains in effect for a specified period of time. If the insured survives beyond that time, coverage ceases with no remaining value. Term policies are sometimes called "pure" insurance because they have value only if the covered risk occurs (death) while the policy is in effect. They have no savings component, as permanent life policies do. Parents often buy 15- or 20-year term policies to protect their children in case the parents should die while the children are still young. By the time the term policy ends, the children will be grown and out on their own, so the parents no longer need the policy.

Term insurance policies can have additional features, such as optional conversion to a permanent life policy. Additional features generally raise premiums, however, and beyond a certain age, term insurance may not be renewable. The main advantage of term insurance is its low cost.

With *decreasing term insurance,* the amount of coverage decreases each year while the premium remains the same. A 20-year decreasing term policy decreases in coverage each year until the value reaches zero at the end of 20 years. If the insured dies during the first year of the policy, it pays the full benefit (let's say $100,000). If the insured dies during the second year, death benefits decrease to, say, $95,000. So, the coverage of the policy decreases by a specified amount each year. In contrast, the death benefit on *level term insurance* remains constant from beginning to end.

Renewable term insurance gives the policyholder the right to renew each year, without having to pass a physical exam. Premiums increase with each renewal because the policyholder is older (and the risk of death greater), but the death benefits remain the same.

Another type of temporary life insurance is *credit life* or some version of it, such as mortgage life insurance. Credit life insurance will repay a debt should the borrower die before doing so. You can obtain this type of coverage from the lender. However, in most cases it would be cheaper to buy term insurance.

Permanent Life Insurance

Permanent life insurance is life insurance that remains in effect for the insured's lifetime and builds a cash value. **Cash value** is the savings accumulated in a permanent life insurance policy that you would receive if you canceled your policy. You could also borrow using your policy's cash value as collateral. If you do not repay the loan, the policy will repay it out of the death benefit when you die. Four common types of permanent life policies are straight life, limited-pay life, universal life, and variable life.

Straight life (also known as *whole* or *ordinary life*) is a policy for which you pay premiums throughout your life, and the policy pays a stated sum at death to your beneficiary. The amount of your premium depends primarily on the age at which you purchase the policy. The premiums are high enough to pay for the death benefit plus contribute to the policy's cash value.

Limited-pay life is a policy on which premiums are limited to a specific number of years (such as 20 years) or until age 65. At the end of the payment period, the policy is considered "paid up." However, you remain insured for life, and the company will pay the face value of the policy at your death.

Like all permanent life policies, *universal life* combines a savings plan with a death benefit. However, unlike the others, the premium and death benefit on a universal life policy are not fixed. The policyholder can choose to change the death benefit and the amount or timing of premiums during the life of the policy. Thus, the face value of the policy can be reduced or raised without

Risk Management

rewriting the policy. The interest rate earned on the cash value varies with short-term rates in the economy.

Variable life combines a death benefit with investment options. Variable life policyholders pay fixed regular premiums. The insurer invests part of the premiums in securities chosen by the policyholder. Policyholders designate what portion of the net premium (the amount left over after paying for the death benefits) is to be invested in stocks, bonds, or short-term money market instruments. Both the death benefit and the cash value rise (or fall) with the investment results. While a minimum death benefit is guaranteed, there is no guaranteed cash value.

Check Your Understanding

Review Terms
1. disability insurance
2. life insurance
3. incontestable clause
4. rider
5. term life insurance
6. permanent life insurance
7. cash value

Review Concepts
1. Why do insurers use mortality tables?
2. How is universal life insurance different from other permanent life policies?

27.1 Health Insurance

- Health insurance protects you from large medical bills due to injury or illness.
- Group health insurance provides broad coverage at lower rates than do individual policies, because a large group has more negotiating power with insurers than does an individual.
- COBRA allows people who leave their jobs to keep the company health insurance for a limited time.
- HIPAA limits the pre-existing conditions that group plans may exclude and makes it illegal for insurers to deny coverage based on health status, but does not limit what insurers can charge.
- People without a group plan can buy individual health insurance, but they may have to pass a physical exam and would pay high premiums.
- Standard health insurance includes basic medical services, major medical for serious conditions, and often basic dental and vision services. Optional supplemental health insurance covers deductibles and co-payments as well as costs that exceed the limits of a standard policy.
- Private health plans are either unmanaged or managed. Managed-care plans contract with a network of health-care providers, and patients must choose providers from the network and obtain pre-approval before having surgery.
- PPOs and HMOs are managed-care plans. PPOs are a group of healthcare providers who band together to offer services. Patients pay a co-payment for each service. HMOs are prepaid medical care from a group of providers. To see a specialist, HMO patients must get a referral from their primary-care physician.

- Medicare and Medicaid are government-sponsored health plans. Medicare covers people age 65 or older. Medicaid covers people with low incomes and limited resources.

27.2 Disability and Life Insurance

- Disability insurance replaces your income if you are injured or ill and cannot work.
- Social security offers disability insurance for workers who become disabled and cannot work for at least 12 months.
- Workers' compensation covers workers who are injured or killed on the job.
- Life insurance provides funds to beneficiaries when the insured dies.
- Insurers set life insurance premiums based on life expectancy and death rates among various types of people, as compiled in mortality tables.
- Life policies can be either temporary or permanent. Term life insurance is temporary. It remains in effect for a specified period of time. If the insured survives beyond that time, coverage ceases with no remaining value. Permanent life insurance remains in effect for the insured's lifetime and has a savings component (cash value) as well as a death benefit.
- Common types of permanent life policies are straight life, limited-pay life, universal life, and variable life. For straight life, you pay premiums throughout your life, and the policy pays a stated sum to your beneficiary when you die. Limited-pay life requires premiums for a stated number of years, but the policy remains in force for life. Universal life does not have a fixed premium or death benefit, and earnings on the cash value vary with interest rates in the economy. Variable life combines a death benefit with investment options.

Review Terms

Directions: Can you find the definition for each of the following terms used in Chapter 27?

cash value
COBRA
coordination of benefits
disability insurance
group health insurance
health insurance
health maintenance
    organization (HMO)
incontestable clause
life insurance

Medicaid
Medicare
permanent life insurance
preferred provider organi-
    zation (PPO)
rider
term life insurance

1. A group health insurance provision that specifies how the insurers will share the cost when more than one policy covers a claim.
2. An insurance plan that makes regular payments to replace income lost when illness or injury prevents the insured from working.
3. A small insurance policy that modifies the coverage of the main policy.
4. A plan for sharing the risk of high medical costs resulting from injury or illness.
5. Insurance that provides funds to the beneficiaries when the insured dies.
6. A provision of a life or health insurance policy that once the policy has been in effect for a stated period of time, the insurer may no longer question items on the application in order to deny coverage.
7. Government-sponsored health insurance for people currently age 65 or older.
8. Health insurance issued to a group, such as an employer or trade association, to cover individuals in the group and sometimes their dependents.
9. A group of healthcare providers who band together to provide health services for set fees.
10. Life insurance that remains in effect for the insured's lifetime and builds a cash value.
11. A group health insurance plan offering prepaid medical care to its members.
12. The savings accumulated in a permanent life insurance policy that you would receive if you canceled your policy.
13. Law that allows people who leave employment to continue their health insurance under the company plan for a limited period of time.

14. Government-sponsored health insurance for people with low incomes and limited resources.
15. A life insurance policy that remains in effect for a specified period of time, after which coverage ceases with no remaining value.

Review Facts and Ideas

1. What are many employers doing to help control their costs for providing health insurance for their employees?
2. Why do group health insurance plans usually have better coverage and lower premiums than individual plans?
3. What does HIPAA do and not do to help people obtain health insurance?
4. What is supplemental health insurance? Who should buy it?
5. What does basic health insurance cover?
6. What does major medical insurance cover?
7. How is a managed-care plan different from an unmanaged health insurance plan?
8. What is the difference between an HMO and a PPO?
9. In what way does a primary-care physician in an HMO act as a gatekeeper?
10. How is Medicare different from Medicaid?
11. What is the purpose of disability insurance?
12. Name and describe at least four sources of disability insurance.
13. Why would a person need life insurance?
14. How is permanent life insurance different from term life insurance?
15. Identify and describe three types of term insurance.
16. What is credit life insurance?
17. Identify and describe four types of permanent life insurance.

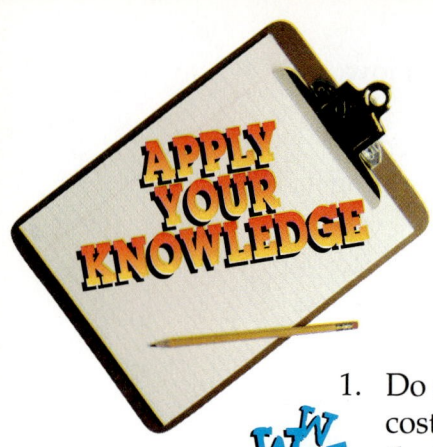

1. Do a mini-research project gathering information about the costs of healthcare in the last decade. Magazines, newspapers, the Internet, and books report the costs and trends. Write a paper describing what has been happening and who is to blame. (You will note that various sources blame each other.) Make your own determination based upon your findings.

2. Interview a person who has recently had surgery or been in the hospital for several days or longer. Ask this person about the type of services provided and the approximate cost per day of those services. Ask him or her how much of the cost was paid by insurance and how much (percentage or dollar amount) he or she will have to pay. Write a report on your findings.

3. Obtain a brochure describing the benefits of a group health insurance plan. If you don't know someone who belongs to this type of plan, your local library and the Internet will have information about group plans. Write a paper summarizing your findings—types of coverages, deductibles, co-payments, exclusions, and so on.

4. Search the Internet for information on Medicare. A good place to start is the government site for Medicare at www.medicare .gov. Find out what types of medical/hospital/surgical and major medical coverages it provides and how much of these costs the patients must pay. Then look into Medigap insurance. Based on your findings, do you feel that Medigap insurance is a good value for a person on Medicare?

5. Prepare an analysis of your disability needs, assuming that you are working full-time, are married, and have one child. Pick a career that you would like to have and use a realistic amount of income for a beginning worker (with 1 to 3 years of experience).

6. Examine the list of life insurance needs shown in Figure 27-2. Can you add anything to this list? Can you delete anything? Prepare a list of life insurance needs based on your personal situation as you imagine it will be in 10 years.

Solve Problems

1. Your friend is considering two career opportunities—one in which she would be an independent contractor and have no benefits provided, and one in which she would work as an employee of a company and have full health insurance as well as other benefits. Explain to her the importance of having health insurance and how her options for insurance might differ, depending on which of the two career choices she makes.

2. A young couple is a dual-income family. Both have full medical coverage provided through their employers. They figure that this "double coverage" will pay off if they get injured or become ill because they can claim benefits twice. Explain to them the concept of coordination of benefits for group health insurance policies such as theirs.

3. Your cousin is working but cannot afford to buy an individual health insurance policy. His employer does not provide a group plan. Explain to him the importance of major medical coverage.

4. Your friend Darnell is working full time at two jobs in order to make house payments and buy a new car. His wife Kara is working nights so she can care for the children during the day. Darnell can purchase both short-term and long-term disability insurance for a small premium ($10 a month) through his employer's group insurance plan. Explain to them the importance of disability insurance.

5. As a young, unmarried person, you are contemplating college next year and the pursuit of a professional degree that will take six years or more to complete. A neighbor sells life insurance and wants you to buy a universal life policy with a $100,000 face value. Explain to him what type of policy, if any, you would consider purchasing.

6. You and your spouse are in your mid-twenties. You are expecting your first child. Both of you are presently working. You hope to buy your first house in the next few years. Discuss your need for life insurance and the type of life insurance you would purchase now and five years from now.

For related activities and links, point your browser to
www.mypf.swep.com

Unit *six*
PROJECT

Managing Personal Risks

Project 6

In this project, you will apply risk and insurance concepts. You will also do some further exploring and assessing of your insurance needs and plans for the future. You'll learn how to compute the true cost of insurance, how to file an insurance claim, what to do if you have an accident, what you can do to reduce health insurance costs, how to use mortality tables, and how to build a good lifetime insurance plan.

The True Cost of Insurance

When people buy insurance, they usually feel that it is money spent for protection against the risks of financial uncertainty and unexpected losses. The alternative—being uninsured—represents large and undefined risks that can leave you feeling uncomfortable. Since the alternative of not being insured is often unacceptable, most people are covered by some type of insurance most of their lives.

Let's look at automobile insurance first. Your full-coverage policy might offer these coverages and annual costs:

Liability coverage, 100/300/50	$560
Collision coverage, $50 deductible	180
Comprehensive coverage, $50 deductible	90
Personal injury protection	80
Uninsured/underinsured motorist	60
Towing	15
Total annual cost	$985

If you make monthly payments, they might include an additional $2.50 per month (to cover the costs of monthly billing), adding an extra $30 to your yearly insurance costs. To avoid this extra cost, you can pay semiannually or have automatic monthly deductions from your checking account.

If you were willing to increase the deductibles, your savings could be considerable. Let's assume that a $250 collision deductible would reduce the cost of the coverage in our example by $50 a year. Over a five-year period, your total insurance costs would be:

Full coverage, $50 deductible:
$985 × 5 = $4,925

Full coverage, $250 deductible:
$935 × 5 = $4,675
Savings: $250

In five years, you would have saved enough in premiums to pay a $250 loss, should it occur. Check your options for saving on insurance premiums. Calculate the savings over time, and decide whether you would likely save more in premium reductions than you would likely pay out in losses.

You can also lower your premiums by reducing the limits of liability coverage from 100/300/50 to your state's minimum. This method of sharing the risk will save premium dollars, but you risk greater loss if you are at fault in an accident.

Figure U6-1 illustrates another way to save on premiums. In this case you would decide when it would be wise to save by reducing or dropping collision coverage on your car.

Let's now compute the cost of a whole life insurance policy and compare the results to the purchase of term insurance. To do this, we must use the time value of money concept—the fact that money will grow over time because it is earning interest.

Suppose you are age 25 and purchased a $100,000 face value whole life policy. The annual premium for this policy is $250. The policy will pay a guaranteed rate of 6 percent (on the policy's cash value) after the first year. At the end of the first year, there is no cash value. The entire premium is used to cover commissions and policy costs. After the first year, a portion of the premium covers the cost of insurance and the rest is deposited in a savings plan. The amount deposited accumulates as cash value.

In the example below, the death benefit remains at $100,000 over a five-year period. During this time, the cost of insurance rises slightly each year, leaving a smaller amount of the premium for savings. Assuming the 6 percent rate holds, the cash value of the policy after five years would be $626.28. (See the table that follows.)

Year	Premium	Insurance Cost	Savings Plan Deposit	+	Interest	Cash Value at Beg. Year
1	$250.00	$100.00	$0			$0
2	250.00	102.00	148	+	0	148
3	250.00	104.00	146	+	$8.88	302.88*
4	250.00	106.00	144	+	18.17	465.05
5	250.00	108.00	142	+	19.23	626.28
Totals	$1,250.00	$520.00	$580		$46.28	$626.28

*Assume the full premium is paid at the beginning of each year. To compute the interest earned at the end of Year 2, multiply $148 by 6 percent. Then add the deposits of $148 and $146 to interest earned of $8.88 to derive the Year 3 cash balance of $302.88.

As an alternative, you could purchase a term life insurance policy instead of whole life insurance. The term premiums are as fol-

Determining When to Reduce or Drop Collision Insurance

Figure U6-1

Assuming the annual cost of collision insurance is $180.

The car is new. → Keep collision coverage.

The car is 5 years old.
→ Car is worth $3,000 or more. → Keep collision coverage.
→ Car is worth less than $3,000. → Reduce collision coverage.

The car is older than 5 years.
→ Car is antique or has collector's value. → Keep collision coverage.
→ Car is worth $1,000 or less. → Drop collsion coverage.

Once a car is worth less than $3,000 in value, look closely at the need for collision coverage. You might soon pay more in premiums than the car is worth.

lows: $100 (Year 1), $102 (Year 2), $103 (Year 3), $104 (Year 4), and $106 (Year 5). The difference between the whole life premium and the term premium is deposited at the beginning of each year in a 6 percent savings account. (Assume, of course, that $150 is invested in Year 1; $148, Year 2; $146, Year 3; $144, Year 4; $142, Year 5.) With whole life insurance, the cash value is $626.28. The accumulated value of the savings account at the end of five years would be $873.79. The difference is $247.51. (See the table that follows.) In this case, you can achieve a higher savings balance through buying term insurance and saving on your own.

Year	Beginning Balance	Deposit	Interest	Ending Balance
1	$ 0	$150	$ 9.00	$159.00
2	159.00	148	18.42	325.42
3	325.42	146	28.29	499.71
4	499.71	144	38.62	682.33
5	682.33	142	49.46	873.79**

**The total saved at the end of five years is $873.79.

Complete Worksheet 1 in the *Student Activity Guide* to compute the future value of savings between different life insurance policies. (This worksheet also appears on page 790 of this project.)

How to File a Claim

When you have sustained a loss, such as fire damage to your home, you must file a claim. In order to receive compensation for the insured property, you must be organized and prepared before you file the claim. First, you should know your policy and its coverages, limitations, and exclusions.

You should keep receipts and other documentation of value. If you own any antiques, collectibles, or other items for which you have no receipt, you should have the items appraised so that you will have a certificate of authenticated value. Such an appraisal may cost you $50 or more, but it will save you considerable time when filing a claim.

If property is stolen, you should call the police and fill out a report. Without evidence of a break-in or a police report as documentation, the insurance company has no way of knowing whether or not the incident took place. Remember, you must take ordinary precautions against break-in and theft. If, for example, you leave your car unlocked, the insurer may not pay benefits for stolen property. You should have good notes about what was taken, any witnesses, time of day, what you observed, and so on.

If property is damaged, you will need to get repair estimates—usually more than one. Contact your insurer right away, and have documentation and notes ready. The insurance adjustor will take your report and ask you questions. It's important to be clear and accurate when supplying information. You must also take reasonable precautions to avoid further damage. For example, if a storm creates a hole in your roof, you must cover the hole as soon as possible with plastic or some other protective covering to avoid rain damage to your home's contents. If you do not act quickly to protect your property, the insurer may not pay for the extra damage.

Figure U6-2 is a sample claim form that your insurer would require you to complete to report damage to property you have insured under a homeowner's policy. Fill out Worksheet 2 in the *Student Activity Guide* based on the hypothetical information provided. (This worksheet also appears on page 791 of this project.)

Claim No. _____

Name of Insured _____

Address _____

_____ Phone _____

Policy No. _____ Agent _____

Describe what happened: _____

_____

_____

_____

Was a police report filed? _____ Case No. _____
(Attach copy)

Police officer taking report _____

Were there any witnesses?_____ List their names and addresses:

_____

_____

Description of property damaged _____
Value of property_____
Date purchased _____ Purchase price _____
Where purchased_____ Receipt?_____

Where is property now located (for inspection)? _____

_____

_____   _____
Date   Signature of Insured

What to Do If You Have an Automobile Accident

Sooner or later, it is likely to happen to you. Either as a driver or as a passenger, you may be involved in an automobile accident. Most accidents are the result of human error. The higher the speed, the higher the likelihood of a serious injury and damage to property.

If you are involved in an accident, there are several things you must do. Figure U6-3, on page 786, lists standard procedures to follow. Your state may have additional things you should do, or not do, following an accident. You will find this information in your state's driver's manual or a similar publication from the motor vehicles division or licensing department. You should be familiar with this information before an accident occurs.

If you are involved in a motor vehicle accident, standard requirements are as follows:

1. Stop your vehicle, turn off the ignition, and remain at the scene of the accident. If feasible, pull your car to the side of the road so you won't impede traffic.

2. Get the names and addresses of other drivers, passengers, and witnesses. Make notes of what happened, including time of day, weather conditions, roadway location, signal lights, and so on. Write down vehicle license numbers.

3. Fill out the necessary accident report forms within the time requirements in your state (usually 3 days). Give a copy of the report to your insurance company. Also obtain a copy of the police report, if any.

4. Provide assistance to persons who are injured; seek medical help if needed. Stay at the scene of the accident until all needed information is exchanged and all involved parties leave the scene.

5. Always have your insurance and vehicle registration information with you. Get insurance and vehicle registration information from the other driver; copy it from the documentation rather than taking it down orally.

6. Know the laws of your state. There may be additional requirements where you live.

Your state has accident reporting forms; get one and fill it out for a fictional situation. In most cases, you have only three days (72 hours) to fill out an accident report once you are in an accident.

How to Reduce Health Care Costs

Whether you have health insurance or not, it's important to minimize health care costs. The best way to avoid high medical costs is to stay well. Corporations across America are realizing the importance of "wellness" programs in an attempt to keep their employees healthy. Here are some fundamental ways you can stay healthy:

1. Eat a balanced diet and keep your weight within reasonable limits.
2. Avoid smoking.
3. Don't drink to excess.
4. Get sufficient rest and relaxation.
5. Drive carefully; avoid and reduce risks where possible.

When you do visit doctors and use health care services, there are additional ways to minimize your costs and your insurer's costs. Figure U6-4 lists some methods of reducing health care costs and maximizing the benefit from services that you can use.

Complete Worksheet 3 in the *Student Activity Guide* to answer questions about your responsibilities in helping to reduce health care costs. (This worksheet also appears on page 792 of this project.)

How to Cut Health Care Costs   **Figure U6-4**

When you are the patient, whether or not insurance is involved, you can maximize your health care dollars by:

1. Knowing your insurance coverage, limitations, and exclusions.

2. Taking insurance information with you when visiting a hospital or doctor's office and when picking up prescriptions.

3. Taking a list of questions with you to the doctor. Take notes so you will remember specific answers.

4. Giving your doctor information needed to make correct diagnoses. Write down symptoms, relevant past history, what you have done or taken so far, and related information.

5. Asking the doctor about short- and long-term side effects of prescriptions. Read prescription directions and information supplied by a pharmacist and/or the manufacturer.

6. Getting second (and third) opinions for any type of surgery or medication with serious risks or potential for side effects.

7. Predetermining fees and services that will be provided for treatments, surgeries, and lab work. Exclude tests or costs that you can cover in less expensive ways. For example, you can go to a local clinic and have a cholesterol test for $5 to $10. At a doctor's office, it can cost you five to ten times that amount.

8. Using generic medicines.

9. Being cautious and asking lots of questions. Remember: You are in charge of your health care and the doctor is assisting you, not the other way around! Take charge of your own life, nutrition, and lifestyle and know what it takes to stay healthy and strong.

Life Expectancy and Mortality Tables

In a current edition of an almanac, you will find both life expectancy tables and mortality tables. For example, a person born in 2000 was expected to live 76.0 years if a man or 80.8 years if a woman. For a person who was 45 in 2000, life expectancy was another 34.8 years for men or 42.0 years for women.

Another table shows life expectancies over time. For example, in 1920, the average life span was 54.1 years (53.6 for men and 54.6 for women). By 1970, the average life span had risen to 70.8 (67.1 for men and 74.7 for women).

Life expectancy and mortality tables are used by insurance actuaries in setting life insurance premiums. A mortality table matches age with a mortality rate and sets a premium accordingly. Figure U6-5 is part of a mortality table from the American Council of Life Insurance.

Figure U6-5 *Mortality Table (partial)*

Age	Deaths per 1,000	Life Expectancy (Years)
25	1.11	59
30	2.33	48
40	3.21	37
45	4.58	33
50	5.86	28
55	8.44	21
60	12.88	18
65	17.22	15
70	26.10	13

Building a Personal Insurance Plan

As you make choices about the type and amount of insurance you will buy, keep the following guidelines in mind. They can save you money, time, and energy as you build your personal insurance plan:

1. To avoid billing fees, have premiums deducted automatically from your checking account, or pay them quarterly or semiannually.
2. Be sure to read the policy carefully. If you discover a clause you do not understand, call your agent immediately for clarification.
3. Review policies regularly to see if the coverage meets your needs. As your family situation changes, you might wish to modify your life insurance coverage. As your car gets older, you should consider dropping collision insurance.
4. Consider carefully the outcome of switching insurers or changing policies. If you do, be sure you are approved for the new insurance—and that it is correct as represented—before dropping your old insurance.
5. Get to know your insurance agent. Use his or her expertise. Ask lots of questions and be sure you understand all coverages, limitations, exclusions, and so on. Discuss your changing needs and get his or her recommendations, but make your own decisions.
6. Don't hold onto policies or companies for sentimental reasons. Be a wise comparison shopper. When you are certain you can do better with another company, and have taken proper precautions, move forward to secure a new policy.
7. Don't keep overlapping policies with the hope of making a quick profit off insurance claims. Group policies require coordination of benefits. Private policies that overlap coverage in a group policy can be very expensive.
8. Use deductibles wisely! By paying the first part of an expense yourself, you can save a bundle on insurance rates.
9. Keep your insurance up-to-date. Pay premiums promptly and take advantage of any discounts available. Ask regularly about what new discounts, such as for nonsmokers, are available to reduce premiums.

Complete Worksheet 4 in the *Student Activity Guide* to review what you have learned about preparing a personal insurance plan. (This worksheet also appears on page 793 of this project.)

WORKSHEET 1

Computing Future Value

Assume that you purchased a whole life policy for $100,000 and your premiums were $300 a year, with $150 covering insurance and $150 directed to your savings plan. The insurance cost increases by $3 every year. You are guaranteed 5 percent interest on your savings for the first five years, but will not earn interest until the end of the second year.

Required:

1. Prepare a table that lists how much total premium you will have paid in five years, total insurance cost for five years, and the balance in your savings portion at the end of five years for the whole life policy. (See page 782.)

2. How much would you have had in savings if you had bought a term policy for $150/year (for 5 years) and put the remainder in a savings account at your bank with interest compounding at the rate of 4 percent a year?

WORKSHEET 2
Insurance Claim Form

Directions: Fill out the claim form below based on the following information. The insured is Mary B. Ownbey, who lives at 845 Oak Street, Wellington, Ohio 45887. Her phone number is (202) 555-0180. Her policy number is KN338-44-2281, and her agent is G. Smiley. Her home was broken into sometime between 8 p.m. and 2 a.m. (Friday evening) while she was away. The kitchen was vandalized (spray paint on the walls and eggs thrown on the floor); the carpeting in the dining room was stained as well. A police report was filed (Case 95-2288) by Officer K. Bridges. There were no witnesses. The walls in the kitchen must be scraped and painted; the carpeting must be cleaned or replaced if the stain cannot be removed. The value of the damage is estimated at $500. The house was painted last year ($100 for the kitchen walls); the carpet was new a year ago ($2,000 for the damaged carpeting). Both were purchased at Excel Interiors and she has a receipt. The property is located in the home at the above address. Use today's date.

Claim No. _____

Name of Insured _____

Address _____

_____ Phone _____

Policy No. _____ Agent _____

Describe what happened: _____

_____

_____

_____

Was a police report filed? _____ Case No. _____
(Attach copy)

Police officer taking report _____

Were there any witnesses? _____ List their names and addresses:

_____

_____

Description of property damaged _____

Value of property _____

Date purchased _____ Purchase price _____

Where purchased _____ Receipt? _____

Where is property now located (for inspection)? _____

_____

_____   _____
Date   Signature of Insured

WORKSHEET 3

Reducing Health Care Costs

Directions: Answer the following questions about ways you can reduce health care costs.

1. Do you eat well-balanced meals and exercise regularly?

2. Do you get sufficient rest and relaxation?

3. Do you know your health insurance coverages, limitations, and exclusions?

4. Do you use generic prescriptions where possible? (Generic drugs are less expensive versions of brand-name drugs. Because there is no advertising or other expenses of mass marketing, the cost is lower.)

5. Do you shop around for the best prices in (a) dental work, (b) vision care and glasses, (c) prescriptions, (d) charges for office visits, and (e) supplies, vitamins, and other health care purchases?

6. List some things you and your family can do to reduce health care costs.

7. Explain why it is important to ask questions when you visit your doctor.

WORKSHEET 4
Your Personal Insurance Plan

1. Explain the purpose of each of the following types of insurance.

   a. Homeowner's insurance:

   b. Automobile insurance:

   c. Liability insurance:

   d. Health insurance:

   e. Disability insurance:

   f. Life insurance:

2. Based on your current situation, what types of insurance do you currently purchase?

   a. Homeowner's insurance:

   b. Automobile insurance:

   c. Liability insurance:

   d. Health insurance:

   e. Disability insurance:

   f. Life insurance:

3. How do you anticipate your need for each of these insurance coverages will change in the next five years?

   a. Homeowner's insurance:

   b. Automobile insurance:

   c. Liability insurance:

   d. Health insurance:

   e. Disability insurance:

   f. Life insurance:

4. List several guidelines for building a plan for purchasing all types of insurance.

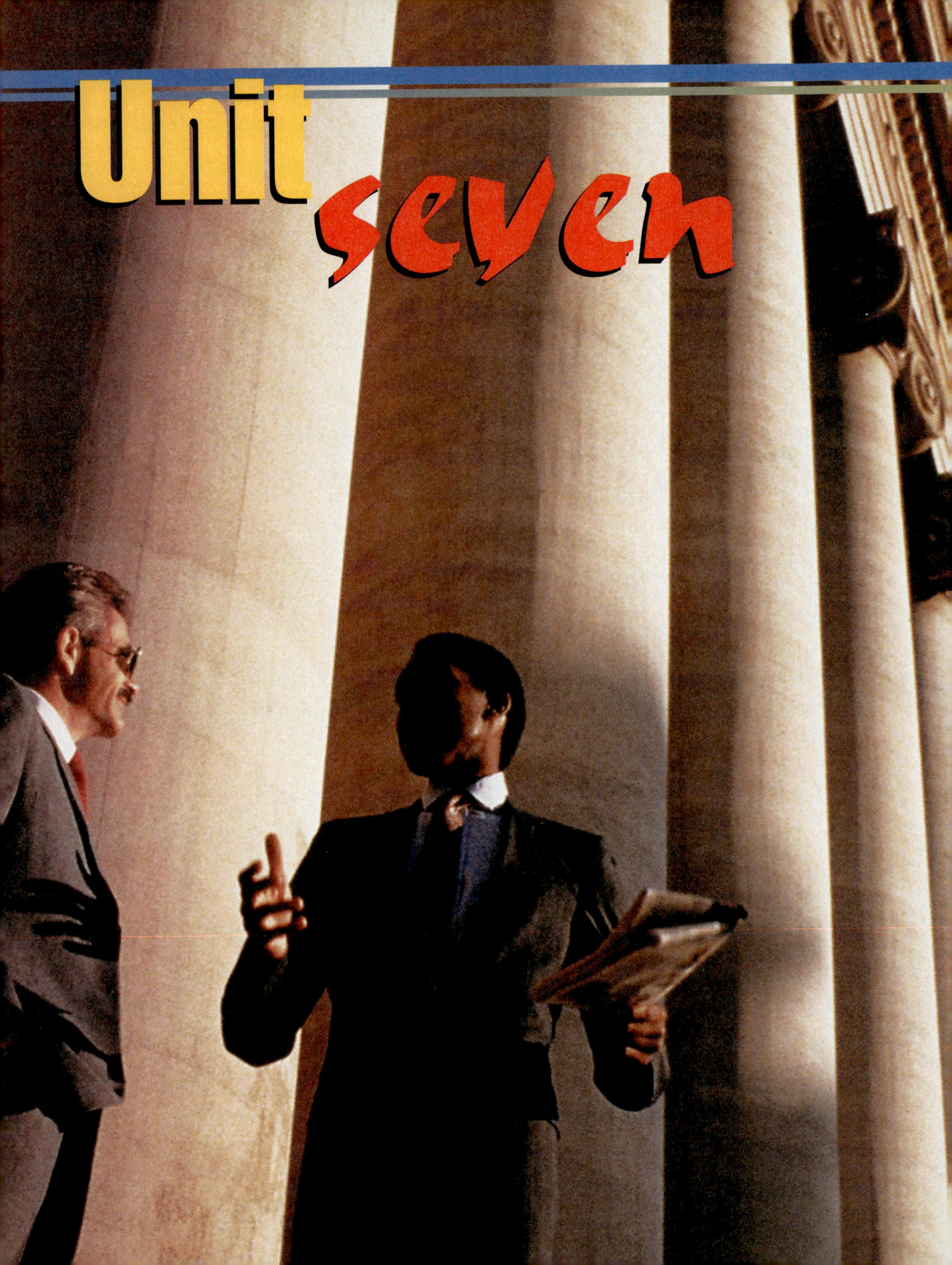

Unit *seven*

Consumer Rights and Responsibilities

Unit 7 focuses on the role of consumers in determining what is produced and sold. In Chapter 28, you will examine the market economy in which you live. You will explore wise buying practices and discover both your rights and your responsibilities.

In Chapter 29, you will take a look at federal laws and agencies that have been formed to help protect you. In Chapter 30, you will find out about the legal system of the United States. You'll learn about how a trial happens—the personnel, the process, and the results. You will also discover other methods of reaching redress, from negotiating to small-claims courts and governmental assistance.

Chapter 28

Role of Consumers in a Free Enterprise System

Terms to Know

free enterprise	equilibrium price	bait and switch
producers	competition	referral sale
consumers	monopoly	fake sale
scarcity	price-fixing	low-balling
supply	purchasing power	pyramid schemes
demand	transfer payments	redress

Up Front

Marjolein is a full-time student. She does side jobs to earn money during the school year and works full-time in the summer.

"I don't have a lot of money," she told her best friend, "so I have to spend carefully. There are just so many things I'd like to have. Yesterday, I saw an ad on TV about a hammock that would be perfect for my room. It really looks comfortable, and I could use it outside, too. I'm not sure whether it's a good buy or not. How can I find out about products like this one?"

Goals

★ Discuss the basic characteristics of the marketplace.
★ List and describe the three basic components of a free enterprise system.

Characteristics of the Marketplace

In the United States, we live in a free enterprise system. **Free enterprise,** also called a *market economy* or *capitalism,* is an economic system in which producers and consumers are free to engage in business transactions with minimal government interference. Both producers and consumers play an active role in the operation of the system. **Producers** are the manufacturers or makers of goods and services for sale. **Consumers** are the buyers and users of goods and services. Everyone is a consumer because everyone must consume at least some goods and services produced by others in order to live. Many consumers are also producers—that is, they provide goods and services for others to consume.

Scarcity

In any economy, consumers' wants are unlimited. However, the resources for producing the products to satisfy these wants are limited. This basic economic problem is called **scarcity.** A country's economic system determines what products its businesses will produce with its limited resources. In our free enterprise system,

Why is every person a consumer?

consumers play a key role in determining what businesses will produce. Consumers' purchasing decisions act as votes. When consumers buy a particular product, they are casting their dollar votes for that product. After the "votes" are counted, producers know what consumers want. To make a profit, producers must provide goods and services that consumers will buy.

DID YOU KNOW

The idea that consumer choices determine what goods and services are produced is called "consumer sovereignty." "Sovereignty" means to be in charge of something. This idea was proposed more than 200 years ago by British economist Adam Smith.

As an individual consumer, your resources are limited as well. You must decide what to buy with your limited money to achieve the greatest satisfaction or *utility*. As you make your individual buying decisions, other consumers are doing the same. Together, your spending decisions and those of other consumers determine which products will succeed and which will fail and leave the market. Producers want to maximize their profits. Therefore, they will heed these cues from the marketplace and produce more of the products that are selling and less of those that aren't.

Supply and Demand

A free enterprise system determines what goods and services businesses will produce, in what quantities, and at what prices through the interaction of supply and demand. **Supply** is the quantity of goods and services that producers are willing and able to provide. **Demand** is the willingness and ability of consumers to purchase goods and services at certain prices. You, along with other consumers, create demand for a product with your purchasing "votes."

Generally, if enough consumers demand a product (are willing and able to buy it at a certain price), producers will make it. The system works like this:

1. Increased demand creates a situation in which the supply of the product is not sufficient to satisfy all consumers who want to buy it. As a result, producers can raise their prices.

2. The high prices bring large profits to the producers.
3. Large profits prompt current producers to make more of the product and attract other producers to start providing the product, increasing the supply.
4. Supply then exceeds demand, and consumers can pick and choose. In order to entice consumers to buy their product instead of their competitors', producers reduce their prices.
5. Reducing prices, in turn, lowers profits, and producers begin to produce less.
6. Eventually, the product reaches the **equilibrium price.** This is the price at which the quantity supplied equals the quantity demanded of the product. At this price, there is just enough of the product available for all consumers who want to buy it.

Consumer Power

Consumers have the ultimate power in a free enterprise system. Consumers determine what is produced and at what price. Collectively, consumer buying decisions direct the production of goods and services. When consumers purchase a good or service, they are casting dollar votes for its continued production. If consumers refuse to buy a good or service, the price will drop. When the good or service still does not sell, producers will no longer provide it. Producers will supply only those goods and services that people want and are able to buy. Thus, in our free enterprise system, consumers actually exercise the power to determine what will be produced and at what price.

AROUND THE GLOBE

Various protest organizations have been conducting boycotts against China because of its occupation, since 1950, of Tibet. Consumers are encouraged not to purchase products made in China. Boycott supporters believe that this economic pressure against Chinese exports will persuade the country's government to change its political policies.

Think Critically: Do you believe that consumer boycotts are effective? Would you participate in a consumer boycott?

Producer Power

Producers also have power in a free enterprise system, because they can employ various techniques to influence consumer buying decisions. They use advertising and other marketing strategies, such as those discussed in Chapter 20, to induce consumers to want products. *Advertising* is the communication of product information through mass media to the consumer to increase the demand for a good or service. It can be informative and give important facts about the quality and features of goods and services. It can also be false and misleading and, unfortunately, damaging to the consumer's personal financial situation. To manage your personal finances successfully, you must understand the role of advertising and other marketing strategies in our economic system and become a careful consumer.

Parts of a Free Enterprise System

Three basic conditions must exist for a free enterprise economy to function smoothly: (1) competition, (2) purchasing power, and (3) informed consumers. If one of these conditions is missing or not functioning properly, the system begins to fail. The free enterprise system gains strength when each part of this triangle functions properly. Figure 28-1 illustrates the interplay of the three parts.

Figure 28-1 *Free Enterprise System*

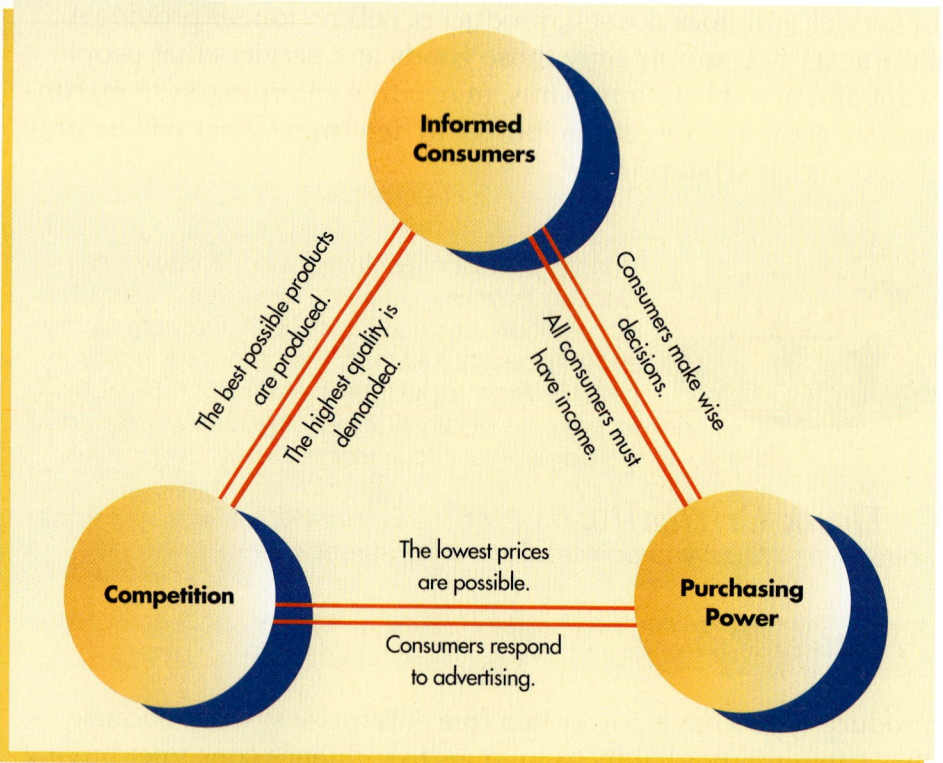

Consumer Rights and Responsibilities

Competition

In order for prices to rise and fall with changes in supply and demand, competition must exist. **Competition** is the rivalry among sellers in the same market to win customers. It occurs when there is more than one seller of a good or service. All businesses selling the same or similar products must compete for the same customers. A **monopoly** is a market with many buyers but only one seller. Without competition, the one seller has no incentive to improve quality or lower prices. However, when a market has many sellers, the competition results in improved quality and lower prices.

+PROS and CONS

In a global economy, products and services are available from around the world. And what you purchase will determine who will have jobs—and who won't. Many persons think that if you don't buy American-produced products, American workers will suffer. However, if you as a consumer buy a product that is not the best and the cheapest, you are not using your purchasing power wisely.

Think Critically: Do you buy American products first? Why or why not? Do you agree that consumers have the right to purchase the best value, regardless of who makes the product? Why or why not?

Illegal business practices can reduce competition and result in higher prices. **Price-fixing** is an illegal agreement among competitors to sell a good or service for a set price. There is no real competition because prices have been predetermined, or fixed. Because price-fixing prevents the forces of supply and demand from determining prices freely in the marketplace, it impedes free enterprise, and the government has made it illegal.

Purchasing Power

For free enterprise to operate, citizens must have the ability to buy. In the United States, most adults have income from their jobs that they can spend on goods and services. However, the purchasing power of the dollar goes up or down with the economy. **Purchasing power** is the value of money, measured in the amount of goods and services that it can buy.

In a period of *inflation*, when prices are generally rising in the economy, purchasing power decreases. For example, if the price of a soft drink rises from $1.25 to $1.50, then your income won't buy as many soft drinks. Your purchasing power has decreased. Purchasing power also declines during periods of *recession*, when production, employment, and income are declining. People who lose their jobs or have their wages reduced cannot buy as many goods. The result is an overall loss of purchasing power in the economy.

The government also shifts purchasing power among citizens by making transfer payments. **Transfer payments** are government grants to some citizens paid with money collected from other citizens. Welfare, social security, and veterans benefits are all transfer payments. So are food stamps and housing assistance.

Informed Consumers

A free enterprise system must have informed consumers who know their rights and responsibilities in the marketplace. When consumers make wise decisions, the system works to weed out inferior products and keep prices at acceptable levels. When consumers do not act in a responsible manner, prices increase.

Check Your Understanding

Review Terms
1. free enterprise
2. producers
3. consumers
4. scarcity
5. supply
6. demand
7. equilibrium price
8. competition
9. monopoly
10. price-fixing
11. purchasing power
12. transfer payments

Review Concepts
1. What group, as a whole, has the ultimate power to determine what will be produced and at what prices in a free enterprise system?
2. What happens when supply of a product exceeds demand?

Consumer Problems

Goals

★ Describe deceptive practices used to defraud consumers and explain how consumers can protect themselves.
★ Discuss how to be a responsible consumer by shopping wisely, staying informed, and seeking redress when you have a consumer problem.

Fraudulent and Deceptive Marketing Practices

The marketplace is full of deceptive and misleading ways for suppliers to increase demand for a product. These ways induce consumers to buy goods and services of inferior quality or things they do not really need or want. In many cases, little can be done once the consumer has been duped into making a purchase. Dishonest sellers quickly disappear or deny wrongdoing. Therefore, consumers must educate themselves to recognize a potential fraud before they become victims. Prevention is still the best safeguard against financial misfortune.

In 2000, the top complaints about consumer fraud included the following: (1) identity theft; (2) Internet services and computer complaints; (3) prizes, sweepstakes, and lotteries; (4) Internet auctions; and (5) advance-fee loan and credit protection/repair.

Bait and Switch

Bait and switch is an illegal sales technique in which a seller advertises a product with the intention of persuading consumers to buy a more expensive product. The "bait" is the bargain product that gets customers into the store. When they arrive to purchase the advertised product, however, the salesperson then switches their interest to a more expensive product. In some cases, the bait is a poor-quality product that is placed next to high-quality merchandise. The poor-quality bait is advertised to be of better quality than it is, giving customers the idea that they are really getting a bargain. In other cases, when customers ask for the bait merchandise, they are told that it has been sold out, but that comparable merchandise is available—for more money.

To avoid the bait-and-switch trap, educate yourself about products and prices. When a product is advertised at a special price, find out its quality and regular price. Shop around before making major purchases.

Referral Sales

A **referral sale** is a promise of a money rebate, prize, or discount in exchange for providing names of friends as prospective customers. Such promises are illegal if the seller does not actually give the rebate, prize, or discount. Delaying payment pending a sale, presentation, or other event is also illegal.

Referral sales techniques provide the seller with names, addresses, and telephone numbers of prospects. The seller hopes the people on the referral list will buy because their friend gave the seller their names. Most likely, your friends won't appreciate being harassed to buy products they don't want, so resist the temptation.

Fake Sales

Probably the most common of all consumer frauds is the **fake sale**. A merchant advertises a big sale but keeps the items at regular price or makes the price tags look like a price reduction when there actually is none. Often the merchant increases the prices just prior to the sale and alters the price tags to show the so-called markdowns. The only way consumers can protect themselves from fake sales is to know products and prices and to plan purchases. Just because a flashy sign shouts "SUPER SAVINGS" does not mean that prices have been reduced. Only product and price knowledge can help you distinguish a real bargain from a fake sale.

Low-Balling

In Chapter 23, you learned that car dealers sometimes *low-ball*, or offer an unrealistically low price for a trade-in as part of negotiating a new-car deal. Repair shops also use this deceptive practice. In

Role of Consumers in a Free Enterprise System

this context, **low-balling** is advertising a service at an unusually low price to lure customers, and then attempting to persuade them that they need additional services. For example, when repairers dismantle appliances, they discover other "necessary" repairs. If the consumers refuse the offer of additional repairs, the repairers then charge an extra fee for reassembly.

Another form of low-balling is applying pressure, either bluntly or subtly, to convince car owners that their cars need additional work for safe operation. For example, a repair shop may offer a special on brake relining. But when the mechanics inspect the brakes, they find several other "necessary" repairs. Customers may wind up with a front-end alignment, wheel balancing, or other repairs that are not really as urgent as they are led to believe.

To protect yourself from this type of low-balling, state that you want no repairs other than those agreed upon unless the repair shop informs you of the additional cost ahead of time and you choose to authorize the extra repairs. You should not pay for unauthorized work. Before having major work done, get a second opinion. Discuss major car repairs with someone you trust who knows about the mechanical aspects of cars.

Pyramid Schemes

Pyramid schemes are illegal multilevel marketing plans that promise distributors commissions from their own sales and those of other distributors they recruit. A cash investment of some kind is usually required to become a distributor. The pyramid consists of managers at the top and a lot of middle and lower distributors arranging parties, recruiting new distributors, and selling products to friends and acquaintances. The managers at the top make big profits by selling the products to the distributors below them in the pyramid—not to the general public. However, most distributors lower in the pyramid never make a profit or recover their initial investment. Instead, they are left with a lot of low-quality products that their friends won't buy.

The best defense against pyramid sales schemes is to remember that you cannot expect to make big profits without hard work. Before committing to such a plan, investigate it. Talk to people who have purchased the products; check with local consumer protection agencies; think it through. What is the company's track record? Does the company have evidence to back up its claims? Who will buy this product? Will your commission depend on recruiting other distributors? Be skeptical if the company requires you to buy a "starter kit" of sales brochures and product inventory.

Pigeon Drop

The term *pigeon drop* refers to any method used by experienced con artists to convince vulnerable people to invest in phony investments, swampland real estate, or other swindles. The pigeon is the unsuspecting consumer. Con artists often target trusting people who know little of such scams but do have a source of money. For example, senior citizens become the targets of fast-talking "financial experts." The con artist may ask them to deposit their savings in an investment fund. These funds are then to be loaned out at high interest rates. The con artist promises the victims monthly payments for the use of their money. In some cases the trusted adviser immediately disappears with the money. In other cases the swindler maintains an outwardly healthy business and pays dividends to the victims until it is no longer advantageous to do so. Then the swindler disappears with the investments. By maintaining a supposedly legitimate business for a period of time, the swindler can gain additional victims—friends eager to get in on the deal at the recommendation of the original victims.

The best protection against this type of swindle is the local Better Business Bureau. The Bureau is equipped to investigate questionable schemes, so-called investment experts, and unsound businesses. If someone approaches you with a suspicious deal, insist upon seeing credentials, annual financial reports, and proof of past dealings. Trust in and trade only with established firms with a proven track record. Deposit your money only in financial institutions that are insured by the government.

Fraudulent Representation

Telephone or door-to-door sales made by people who claim to represent well-known and reputable companies are another type of swindle. Consumers buy products and then learn that the products have been rebuilt or stolen, or are inferior merchandise with the reputable name on it. In some cases the product is worthless or unusable. One such scam is the sale of discount coupons to be used in numerous restaurants and businesses. When the buyers present the coupons for a discount or free merchandise, they discover that the merchant has not authorized the coupon.

Before buying from someone claiming to represent a major company, check with the company to verify the person's identity. Don't feel compelled to buy a product demonstrated to you. The local Better Business Bureau will have a record of salespeople who repeatedly engage in questionable practices.

Health and Medical Product Frauds

A common type of swindle involves deceptive advertising for expensive "miracle" pills, creams, and devices to enhance the consumer's health and beauty. The ads are designed to appeal to the typical consumer's desire to be healthy and attractive. Usually, deceptive health and medical advertisements carry endorsements and pictures of people who have found success using the product. Magazines, newspapers, Web sites, and flashy tabloids often carry these advertisements. The manufacturers ask you to mail money to a post office box to receive the miracle product. Often you pay your money but never receive the product. If you do receive the product, it is totally ineffective.

Infomercials

An *infomercial* is a lengthy paid commercial TV advertisement that includes testimonials, product demonstrations, and presentation of product features. These programs usually last 15 to 30 minutes and target people with specific needs that are usually emotional—from weight loss to hair growth. While the product may be reputable, there is no guarantee, and claims about results may be greatly exaggerated. With infomercials, it is important to find out before you buy whether the business is reputable and the product works. Be cautious about giving credit card numbers over the telephone. Don't expect that because something "worked" for the paid actors describing the product on television that you will receive the same results.

Internet Fraud

When you are online, you will be bombarded by advertisements, from banners to e-mails. Some of these are legitimate; others are not. On the Internet, fraudulent businesses can appear genuine. Don't assume that a professional-looking Web site means that the company is legitimate. You may order and pay for goods and never receive them. When you give credit card numbers and other personal information to these scam artists, you can be a victim of theft—of your money and even your identity. When shopping online, it is safest to stick to businesses you know.

Telemarketing Fraud

There are approximately 140,000 telemarketing firms operating in the U.S. According to AARP, over 10 percent of these (10,000) are fraudulent, and the FBI estimates that consumers lose over $40 billion each year to criminal telemarketers.

What kinds of telemarketing fraud might you experience?

One warning sign is the offer of a "free" prize if you pay shipping and handling. A truly free prize never requires that you pay a fee. Foreign lotteries are illegal, and sweepstakes requiring you to pay any money are not legitimate. Fake charities frequently ask for money around holidays and after disasters. Fraudulent telemarketers will ask you to courier money to them or give a credit card number to claim your prize. Unsolicited calls from people who know a lot about you should ring an alarm. Promises of big prizes, wonderful vacations, and no-risk investments usually turn out to be fraud. They collect the tax, fees, delivery charges, and other "costs" from you, and that's the last you ever hear.

Being a Responsible Consumer

Learning to identify various deceptive marketing tactics is the first step toward consumer responsibility. Prevention is your best protection. After you have been swindled, it is difficult to undo the financial damage. To protect yourself, be alert for the warning signs of a scam. Educate yourself on products and prices, and seek redress when necessary.

Identify Deceptive Practices

When you hear unrealistic claims, be suspicious. Watch for warning signals in claims or offers made through advertising and by salespeople. Figure 28-2 on page 810 lists common warning signals of possible deception that should catch your attention.

Figure 28-2 *Warning Signals*

WARNING SIGNALS
Watch Out When You Hear This:

1. You can get something for nothing.

2. You will receive a free gift if you reply now.

3. You or your home has been specially selected.

4. You can make high earnings with no exierence or little effort.

5. You have been selected to complete an advertising questionnaire.

6. You may attend a demonstration with no obligation to buy.

7. If you don't decide now, you will lose a golden opportunity.

8. You may buy a high-quality product for an incredibly low price.

9. To receive a product or service, you must first send money.

10. To receive your prize, you must supply your credit card or checking account number.

Shop Smart, Including Online

Our economy produces a large assortment of products from which to choose. Many products are complex, and the methods used to sell them are sometimes misleading. Internet shopping has added new dangers as well as helpful shopping tools. To make wise buying decisions, follow these recommendations:

1. *Be aware of prices.* Know regular or "list" prices of common items. Terms often used in advertising, such as "manufacturer's list price" and "suggested retail price," and phrases such as "comparable value," "important value," or "value $40, you pay only $35," attract your attention, but the prices actually may not be reduced.

2. *Shop at several stores. Comparative shopping* means comparing quality, price, and guarantees for the same products at several different stores. Use online price-comparison search tools to help you find the best deal.

3. *Understand sale terminology. Sale* means that goods are being offered for sale but not necessarily at reduced prices. *Clearance* means that the merchant wants to clear out all the advertised merchandise but not necessarily at a reduced price. *Liquidation* means that the merchant wants to sell immediately to turn the inventory into cash. Again, prices may not be reduced.

4. *Avoid impulse buying.* Take a list with you when you shop, and buy only what is on the list. Watch for displays of merchandise that attract your attention but are expensive and unnecessary. When shopping online, don't let an attractive Web site or the ease of entering a credit card number lure you into buying something you don't need.

5. *Plan your purchases.* Thoroughly research major purchases before making your choice. Read online and printed product information and comparative reviews. Do not make major purchases during periods of emotional stress, during a time of loneliness or frustration, or at any time when your judgment is impaired.

6. *Compute unit prices.* Unit pricing is the cost for one unit of an item sold in packages of more than one unit. For example, to compare the price of a 15-ounce box with the price of a 24-ounce box, divide the total price of each box by the number of ounces in it. The result is the price per ounce of each box. The lowest unit price for products of comparable quality is the best buy.

MATH MINUTE

Computing Unit Prices

Which is better: 24 ounces for $2.59 or 15 ounces for $1.89? To determine which is better, you'll need to know the cost per unit. To compute cost per unit, divide the total cost by total units:

$2.59/24 ounces = 10.8 cents per ounce
$1.89/15 ounces = 12.6 cents per ounce

In this case, the 24-ounce container is the better buy.

Problem: Which is better, 3 for $.89 or 6 for $1.99?

Solution:

$.89/3 = 29.7 cents each
$1.99/6 = 33.2 cents each

Thus, 3 for $.89 is the better buy.

7. *Read labels.* Know ingredients and what they mean. For example, a shirt that is 100 percent cotton may shrink, or if it is a dress shirt, it will probably have to be pressed each time you wear it. A product that says, "Dry Clean Only" will be more expensive to maintain.

8. *Check containers carefully.* Be sure packages have not been opened or damaged. Occasionally harmful substances have been injected into products. Report any suspicious openings in packages to the store manager.

9. *Read contracts.* Read and understand contracts and agreements before signing.
10. *Keep receipts and warranties.* Print out warranty statements and sales receipts from online purchases. For all major purchases, keep receipts along with warranties, guarantees, or other written promises for possible enforcement later.
11. *Compute total cost.* Check the total cost of an item, including supplementary items (such as batteries), delivery charges, finance charges, and other add-on costs. In some cases, the base price may be lower than for similar products, but once you add up all the related charges, you will find that the total cost exceeds other choices.
12. *Ask for references.* Ask for references from company representatives to be sure they really do represent the company. Call the company to check.
13. *Be loyal.* Patronize online and bricks-and-mortar businesses that have good reputations and have served you well in the past. Tell others when you have a good experience, and ask others for recommendations of doctors, accountants, repair shops, and other service businesses.
14. *Check up on businesses.* Check for valid certifications, licenses, bonding, and endorsements. Use your local Better Business Bureau and state records divisions to be sure you are getting service from qualified and reputable professionals.
15. *Wait a day for major purchases.* Always wait at least 24 hours before making a major purchase. Be sure that you would not be making the purchase on impulse and that you were not coerced into wanting the item. Many people change their minds after a "cooling-off" period before making a major buying decision.

Stay Informed

You are responsible for educating yourself about products and services before you buy. To protect yourself, actively seek consumer information in the following ways:

1. Become familiar with sources of information on goods and services, such as *Consumer Reports,* consumer-oriented Web sites, and local agencies.
2. Read warranties and guarantees. Ask questions so that you can fully understand performance claims. Get written guarantees and warranties whenever possible.

PERSONAL PERSPECTIVE

Your Mouse Tracks on the Web

When you explore different Web sites, be aware that you are not always anonymous. Some sites can immediately determine certain information about you when you visit that site, such as the type of computer system you use, the company you use to access the Internet, and the last site you visited. You can find out what information your computer automatically transmits by visiting the Center for Democracy and Technology's privacy demonstration at http://snoop.cdt.org/.

At some Web sites you must log in, register, and/or give them information about yourself. This information is saved and often shared with others. These *mouse tracks* enable others to determine whether you are a potential customer and what types of interests you have.

Some Web sites electronically record information about your visit to their site by depositing a piece of information called a *cookie* onto your computer. Once a cookie is saved on your computer, that Web site can keep track of information about your visit, such as which parts of the site you visit. This helps site operators determine the most popular areas of their site and it helps them improve what they offer. Cookies also allow for more efficiency when revisiting a site because:

- Your preferences for visiting certain areas of the site are stored in your cookie file. The next time you return, the section you like best may already be displayed for you.
- You may be alerted to new areas of interest based on sites you have previously visited.
- Your past activity may be recorded in the cookie file so the site knows what you like, and thus offer you products and services tailored to your interests.

Some versions of browser software can be set to notify you before a Web site places a cookie on your computer. Then you can choose to accept or reject the cookie. Some browsers will allow you to deactivate a cookie. You can also delete cookie files, but you would then lose the customizing offered by the sites.

Think Critically

1. What Web sites do you visit regularly? What information have you given them about yourself?
2. How could you benefit from having cookies on your computer?

3. Read and understand care instructions before using a product.
4. Analyze advertisements about products before buying.
5. Know the protections offered by consumer protection laws, and know how to seek a remedy to consumer problems.
6. Inform appropriate consumer protection agencies of fraudulent or unsafe performance of products and services. Do not hesitate to make your dissatisfaction known to help others avoid the problem and to prompt producers to improve their product or service.
7. Report wants, likes, and dislikes as well as suggested improvements and complaints to retailers and manufacturers.

Seek Redress

When you have a complaint or need to solve a problem about a product or service, you have a right to seek redress. **Redress** is a remedy to a problem. When you have a consumer problem, you have a right to expect the business to work with you to resolve the problem. The remedy might be your money back, a repair, or some other compensation. Here are some suggestions for filing a complaint and resolving problems.

First, take the product back to the store where you bought it. Calmly explain the problem to a salesperson there. If necessary, talk to a manager. If you bought the item online, then talk to a customer service representative on the phone. Explain the specifics about the problem and give evidence. Retain all warranties, sales receipts, and related material. If necessary, provide photocopies of necessary information to explain and support your position. Be firm but not angry. Say that you are dissatisfied and explain why. Indicate the type of adjustment you want: refund, repair, replacement, or other action. Many consumer problems can be resolved simply by discussing them reasonably with the retailer.

If you are not satisfied with the manager's remedy, then put your complaint in writing to the store's owner or headquarters. If you do not receive satisfaction, write to the manufacturer or distributor and state your complaint. In any written correspondence, describe your previous interactions with store personnel and explain why you are dissatisfied with the result. Be specific. Send photocopies of evidence, such as sales receipts, warranties, or anything else that will help you support your position. Be firm and again state the type of adjustment you want. Specify a reasonable time limit in which to resolve the problem.

If you are still dissatisfied with the result, file a complaint with the appropriate government agency for consumer protection. There may be more than one private or public agency to assist you in solving the problem.

A last resort is to seek legal recourse. For claims involving relatively small sums (usually a maximum between $2,000 and $5,000, as specified by the state), small-claims court offers a much faster process than a full court procedure. It is also less expensive because attorneys are not required. You must pay a filing fee of usually less than $100 and appear on the assigned court date. Small-claims courts are discussed in detail in Chapter 30.

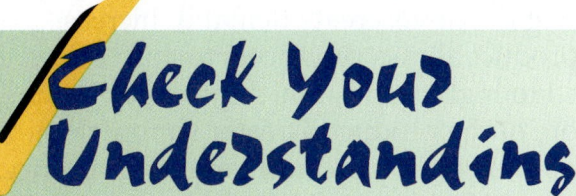

Check Your Understanding

Review Terms
1. bait and switch
2. referral sale
3. fake sale
4. low-balling
5. pyramid schemes
6. redress

Review Concepts
1. What makes a sale a "fake sale"?
2. What is the first step toward consumer responsibility?

Summary

28.1 Our Free Enterprise System

- All economies face the problem of scarcity, because consumer wants are unlimited but resources to satisfy these wants are limited. A country's economic system determines what the limited resources will be used to produce.
- In a free enterprise system, consumers determine what products will be produced and at what prices. When consumers buy a product, they are casting their dollar votes for that product. The spending decisions of all consumers together tell producers what they want. To make a profit, producers must provide the goods and services consumers will buy.
- The interaction of supply and demand determine what will be produced, in what quantities, and at what prices. Consumer buying decisions create demand. Increased demand for a product allows producers to raise prices. High prices lead to high profits, which prompt producers to make more of the product. Greater supply then gives consumers choices, so producers must lower prices to compete. High profits disappear, and producers begin to make less. Eventually, the product reaches an equilibrium price at which quantity supplied equals quantity demanded.
- Producers have the power to influence buying decisions through advertising and other marketing strategies.
- To function smoothly, a free enterprise economy needs competition, purchasing power, and informed consumers.
- Competition among sellers to win customers leads to better quality products and lower prices. Illegal price-fixing reduces competition and results in higher prices.

- Consumer purchasing power rises and falls with economic conditions. Inflation and recession reduce consumer purchasing power. Government transfer payments shift purchasing power from some citizens to others.

28.2 Consumer Problems

- Bait-and-switch schemes lure customers into the store with advertised bargains. Then salespeople try to switch customers to a more expensive product.
- Referral sales can cost you friendships by putting your friends on unwanted solicitation lists.
- Fake sales make customers think prices have been reduced when they really haven't been.
- Low-balling repair shops offer a repair at a low price, and then discover several other "necessary" services while performing the repair.
- Pyramid schemes depend on recruiting multiple levels of distributors. Managers at the top of the pyramid make big profits by selling products to the distributors below them. The lower distributors usually make no profit because they cannot sell the low-quality products to the public.
- Pigeon drops lure trusting people into making phony investments with promises of extraordinary returns.
- Some telephone and door-to-door salespeople sell inferior products, claiming to represent a reputable company.
- Health and medical product frauds involve millions of dollars of worthless products with promises of enhanced beauty and health.
- Infomercials are lengthy TV ads with emotional appeals that often do not meet expectations.
- Internet ads bombard surfers. Most are legitimate, but some are frauds. A professional-looking Web site can lead consumers to believe that the business is legitimate when it is not.
- To be a responsible consumer, learn to identify deceptive practices, follow wise buying habits, stay informed, and seek redress for consumer problems.

Review Terms

Directions: Can you find the definition for each of the following terms used in Chapter 28?

bait and switch
competition
consumers
demand
equilibrium price
fake sale
free enterprise
low-balling
monopoly
price-fixing
producers

purchasing power
pyramid schemes
redress
referral sale
scarcity
supply
transfer payments

1. A remedy to a problem.
2. Illegal multilevel marketing plans that promise distributors commissions from their own sales and those of other distributors they recruit.
3. Advertising a service at an unusually low price to lure customers, and then attempting to persuade them that they need additional services.
4. An advertised "big sale" that really offers merchandise at regular prices.
5. A promise of a money rebate, prize, or discount in exchange for providing names of friends as prospective customers.
6. A market with many buyers but only one seller.
7. An illegal sales technique in which a seller advertises a product with the intention of persuading consumers to buy a more expensive product.
8. Government grants to some citizens paid with money collected from other citizens.
9. The value of money, measured in the amount of goods and services that it can buy.
10. The rivalry among producers in the same market to win customers.
11. Willingness and ability of consumers to purchase goods and services at certain prices.
12. The quantity of goods and services that producers are willing and able to provide.
13. An economic system in which producers and consumers are free to engage in business transactions with minimal government interference.
14. The buyers and users of goods and services.

Consumer Rights and Responsibilities

15. Manufacturers or makers of goods and services for sale.
16. The basic economic problem of unlimited consumer wants but limited resources to satisfy those wants.
17. The price at which the quantity supplied equals the quantity demanded of a product.
18. An illegal agreement among competitors to sell a good or service for a set price.

Review Facts and Ideas

1. The United States operates under what economic system?
2. What causes the basic economic problem of scarcity?
3. As the supply of a product increases, what happens to the price?
4. Why do producers heed the cues of the marketplace?
5. How do consumers have the power to determine what is produced and at what price?
6. What power do producers have in a free enterprise system?
7. What are the three basic conditions that must exist in a free enterprise system?
8. How does competition affect prices and product quality?
9. What economic conditions cause purchasing power to decrease?
10. How can you protect yourself from bait-and-switch tactics?
11. Why do people at the top in a pyramid scheme make big profits while those lower in the pyramid do not?
12. List five warning signals that alert consumers to the possibility of deceptive marketing practices.
13. What are some wise buying practices that can help you shop smart?
14. What are some ways that you can stay informed in the marketplace?
15. What procedures should you follow to seek redress for a consumer problem?
16. Under what circumstances should you consider using a small-claims court to resolve a consumer complaint?

APPLY YOUR KNOWLEDGE

1. Give an example of a new product that has succeeded and one that has failed because of consumers' influence.

2. Watch one hour of television in the early evening and record the number and types of commercials. What do the advertisements tell you about products and their target consumers? Make a chart on a piece of paper listing each commercial and describing it as shown in the following example:

Time of Commercial	Product Advertised	Length of Commercial	Product Information Featured
7 P.M.	Toothpaste (NewBrite)	30 seconds	New flavor; old also available

3. Cut two product advertisements out of different magazines. Select ads that seem very different from each other in their appeal. Describe the consumers that you think each ad is targeting. How does each ad try to influence its target consumers to buy the product?

4. How is the market price of a good or service affected by:
   a. An increase in demand?
   b. A decrease in demand?
   c. An increase in supply?
   d. A decrease in supply?

5. Search through magazines, newspapers, and other sources for advertisements. Collect and bring to class ads that offer the following:
   a. Something for nothing
   b. Bonus for early reply
   c. Offers of gifts and prizes
   d. Guarantees

6. Visit the Web site of a well-known business and check its prices and variety of products available online. Answer the following questions:
   a. Does the site show pictures of the items offered for sale?
   b. Are you able to readily determine the full price, including shipping and other charges?
   c. When can you expect to receive the goods ordered?
   d. What are your payment options?

e. What types of personal information do you have to supply?

f. Does the site offer secure ordering (look for the closed-lock icon at checkout)?

g. What is the return policy?

h. Does the business have a privacy policy?

Solve Problems

1. Compute unit prices for the following pairs and determine which of the two is the better deal:

   a. 3 for 98 cents or 8 for $2.99

   b. 4 for $1.00 or 12 for $3.39

   c. 24 oz. for $1.98 or 36 oz. for $2.49

   d. 2 lbs. for $2.19 or 5 lbs. for $5.89

2. Copy the ingredients from the labels of the following products:

   a. Pain pills

   b. Breakfast cereal

   c. Liquid cleaning product

   d. Bug spray

   Do any of the labels carry warnings? What types of precautions are suggested?

3. Read the warranty or guarantee for a household product that your family has purchased. What does the manufacturer agree to do? What exceptions are stated? What actions does the manufacturer state it will not agree to do?

4. Visit *Consumer Reports* online or obtain an issue from your library, and answer the following questions:

   a. Who publishes the magazine?

   b. Who advertises in the magazine?

   c. How are products tested and compared for quality?

   Select a tested product and summarize three key findings that would most influence your buying decision.

5. Assume that you bought a new hair dryer at a local department store last week. Write a letter of complaint because the hair dryer makes a strange rattling noise. Give factual information concerning the dryer and request a refund or other adjustment.

For related activities and links, point your browser to
www.mypf.swep.com

Chapter 29
Consumer Protection

Terms to Know

flammability
recall
generic drugs
childproof devices

care labels
fraud
consumer advocate

Up Front

McKenzie bought a computer at an online auction Web site. She gave her credit card number and expiration date, along with her name and home address for shipping.

"I think you can get a pretty good deal when you buy online," she told her instructor, "but at the same time, I worry about giving personal information to a company that I don't know. When I checked with the Better Business Bureau online, I learned that this company meets its criteria and that there are no complaints filed against it. That makes me feel a little better."

Laws to Protect Consumers

Goals

★ Describe your rights as set forth in the Consumer Bill of Rights.

★ Describe the protections provided by major federal consumer protection laws.

The Consumer Bill of Rights

For many years the consumer's position in the marketplace was characterized by the phrase "buyer beware." The consumer had little protection against unfair business practices. Since 1960, however, Congress has passed a number of major consumer-protection laws. One of the most important steps in the direction of consumer protection was the adoption of the Consumer Bill of Rights. This was proposed by President John F. Kennedy during his 1962 State of the Union Address, and later was expanded by Presidents Richard Nixon and Gerald Ford. It outlines the following consumer rights:

1. The right to safety: protection against products that are hazardous to life or health.
2. The right to be informed: protection against fraudulent, deceitful, or grossly misleading practices and assurance of receiving facts necessary to make informed choices.
3. The right to choose: access to a variety of quality products and services offered at competitive prices.
4. The right to be heard: assurance of representation of consumer interests in formulating government policy and of fair and prompt treatment in enforcement of the laws.
5. The right to redress (remedy): assurance that buyers have ways to register their dissatisfaction and to receive appropriate compensation for valid complaints.
6. The right to consumer education: assurance that consumers have the necessary assistance to plan and use their resources to their maximum potential.

Federal Consumer Protection Laws

Since 1930s, Congress has passed many laws to protect consumers from unsafe products and unfair or deceptive business practices. These laws help ensure that consumers get quality goods and services for their hard-earned dollars. We may be on the verge of another wave of consumer legislation as Congress considers consumer privacy rights in the Information Age.

Food, Drug, and Cosmetic Act of 1938

What are the advantages and disadvantages of the FDA's testing of drugs?

The Food, Drug, and Cosmetic Act of 1938 requires that foods be safe, pure, and wholesome; that drugs and medical devices be safe and effective; and that cosmetics be safe. The law also requires truthful labeling on these products. The weight or volume of the contents and name and address of the manufacturer must be on the label. The law prohibits use of containers that are misleading because of size, thickness, or false bottoms.

The FDA approves drugs before they can be sold. Requirements for salability include years of research, testing, and proof of effectiveness and safety. While this process takes time and slows down the availability of drugs to consumers, it assures them that products meet standards of safety, purity, and usefulness.

Wool Products Labeling Act of 1939

The Wool Products Labeling Act of 1939 requires proper labeling of the amount and kind of wool contained in all products made of wool, except carpeting and upholstery. Percentages of new, reused, or reprocessed wool and other fibers, care of the product, and the identity of the manufacturer must be shown on the labels of products containing 5 percent or more wool.

Flammable Fabrics Act of 1953

The Flammable Fabrics Act enabled the Consumer Product Safety Commission to set flammability standards for clothing, children's sleepwear, carpets, rugs, and mattresses. **Flammability** is the capacity for catching on fire. The law prohibits the selling of wearing apparel made of easily ignited material. The flammability standard for children's sleepwear requires that the garment will not catch fire when exposed to a match or small fire. The flame-retardant finish must last for 50 washings and dryings. Proper care instructions to protect sleepwear from agents or treatments known to cause deterioration of the flame-retardant finish must be on all labels.

Meat Inspection Laws

The Poultry Products Inspection Act of 1957 requires poultry to be inspected for harmful contaminants. Passed in 1967, the Wholesome Meat Act updated the Meat Inspection Act of 1906 and provided for stricter standards for slaughtering facilities of red-meat animals. Both of these acts protect consumers in the purchase of chicken and beef by standardizing inspection procedures.

Hazardous Substances Labeling Act of 1960

The Hazardous Substances Labeling Act, passed in 1960, requires that warning labels appear on all household products that are potentially dangerous to the consumer. In most cases, products found to be unacceptably hazardous must be recalled. A **recall** is a request for consumers to return a defective product to the manufacturer. The manufacturer will either refund the consumers' money or fix the product so that it is no longer hazardous. Before producing more of the product, the manufacturer will fix the flaw in its design.

Kefauver-Harris Drug Amendment of 1962

As a result of the Kefauver-Harris Drug Amendment of 1962, drug manufacturers are required to file notices of all new drugs, which must be tested for safety and effectiveness before being sold to consumers. This amendment also provides for the manufacture and sale of generic drugs. **Generic drugs** are medications with the same composition as the equivalent brand-name drugs, but they are generally less expensive. National brand names are usually more expensive than generic products because of the added costs of development, advertising, and marketing. To compensate drug companies for the costs of developing new drugs, the law offers the developing companies patent protection. Patents give the companies the sole right to sell their new drugs for a certain number of years before other companies may produce and sell the generic equivalents.

Cigarette Labeling and Advertising Act of 1965

The Cigarette Labeling and Advertising Act of 1965 requires warning labels of possible health hazards from smoking. Today these warning labels are even more specific. For example, original labels read: "Warning—Cigarette smoking may be hazardous to your health." Current labels read: "Surgeon General's Warning: Quitting smoking now greatly reduces serious risks to your health."

National Traffic and Motor Vehicle Safety Act of 1966

The National Traffic and Motor Vehicle Safety Act of 1966 established national safety standards for automobiles and for new and used tires. The National Highway Traffic Safety Administration of the Department of Transportation is charged with supporting and enforcing provisions of the act. Its responsibilities include increasing public awareness of the need for safety devices, testing for safety, and inspecting vehicles for proper safety equipment.

Child Protection and Toy Safety Act of 1966

As a precaution against accidents to children, the Child Protection and Toy Safety Act was passed in 1966. This act bans the sale of toys and children's articles containing hazardous substances and those that pose electrical, mechanical, or thermal dangers. These products can be inspected and removed from the marketplace.

The act requires special labeling for children's products, along with devices that make potentially dangerous products childproof. **Childproof devices** are devices designed to resist tampering by young children. For example, childproof caps on medications are designed so that children cannot open them.

Fair Packaging and Labeling Act of 1966

The Fair Packaging and Labeling Act requires product labels to contain accurate names, quantities, and weights. The labeling rules apply to all types of consumer products, such as groceries, cosmetics, cleaners, and chemicals. It is the responsibility of the consumer to compare weights and sizes of products available—a much easier job when good, standard information is available for comparison.

Permanent Care Labeling Rule of 1972

What is the value of having care labels in clothing?

Effective since 1972, the care labeling rule specifies that clothing and fabrics must be labeled permanently with laundering and care instructions. Labels must give instructions sufficient to maintain a garment's original character. By carefully reading the labels on garments you purchase, you can estimate how much time or money will be required to maintain the garment. **Care labels** give instructions for cleaning, wash and dry temperature, and other care needed to preserve the product. The labels must stay attached and be easy to read for the life of the garment.

Toy Safety Act/Generic Drug Act (1984)

The Toy Safety Act of 1984 permits the Consumer Product Safety Commission to quickly recall toys and other articles intended for use by children that might present a substantial risk of injury. Similarly, the Generic Drug Act of 1984 speeds up the Food and Drug Administration approval process of generic versions of drugs whose patents have expired. These two laws attempt to protect the consumer more quickly than in the past by reducing roadblocks that would slow down safety recalls or keep drug prices high for consumers.

Children's Online Privacy Protection Act of 1998

The Children's Online Privacy Act applies to the online collection of personal information from children under 13. Rules spell out what a Web site operator must include in a privacy policy, when and how to seek verifiable consent from a parent, and what responsibilities an operator has to protect children's privacy and safety online.

In many Latin American countries, consumer protection is a new concept. Frequently, companies convicted of wrongdoing get away with minimal penalties, and monetary judgments are capped by law. However, this situation is beginning to change. For example, Venezuela's Consumer Institute was among the first groups to spot structural flaws in the Ford Explorer, as well as defects in the Firestone tires on the vehicles. It has also organized workshops around the country to educate consumers about their rights.

Think Critically: Why are consumer protection laws and organizations so critical in warning consumers and helping them get redress? What responsibility does each consumer have in this process?

Check Your Understanding

Review Terms
1. flammability
2. recall
3. generic drugs
4. childproof devices
5. care labels

Review Concepts
1. What are some ways that consumer laws protect you as a consumer?
2. Why should the online safety of young children be a consumer concern?

Lesson 29.2 Agencies to Protect Consumers

Goals

★ Identify national sources of consumer information and assistance.
★ List and describe state and local agencies and private organizations that provide consumer assistance and information.
★ Explain how to contact public officials to express opinions.

Sources of Consumer Protection

When you need assistance with a consumer problem, numerous federal, state, local, and private organizations are available to help you. These sources also offer an abundance of helpful consumer information at their Web sites. You can even file a consumer complaint online.

Federal Agencies

Numerous federal government agencies provide information of interest to consumers. Some of these agencies handle consumer complaints, and others direct complaints to agencies or sources that address consumer issues.

Department of Agriculture

Within the Department of Agriculture (USDA), there are a number of agencies that exist to meet various consumer needs. The Agricultural Marketing Service inspects food to ensure wholesomeness and truthful labeling, develops official grade standards, and provides grading services. For example, eggs must meet specific standards to be classified as extra large, jumbo, large, medium, or small. The Food and Nutrition Service provides food assistance programs, such as the food stamp and school lunch programs, and information on diets, nutrition, and menu preparation. The Cooperative Extension Services provides consumer education materials (pamphlets and booklets) on such topics as budgeting, money management, food preparation and storage, gardening, credit counseling, and many more. Most of the materials are free. You can find the USDA online at www.usda.gov/.

National Institute of Standards and Technology

The National Institute of Standards and Technology (NIST) (www.nist.gov) is an agency within the Department of Commerce. Its mission is to promote economic growth by working with industry to develop and apply technology, measurements, and standards. NIST sponsors the *Malcolm Baldrige National Quality Award* given each year to U.S. businesses that achieve high standards of quality in their business practices.

NIST serves an important purpose for consumers. It sets uniform standards of weights and measures. NIST is the reason that you don't have to shop with a tape measure, scale, or other measuring device to make sure you get what you pay for. NIST sponsors a network of state and local agencies that set performance standards for measuring devices used to determine the costs and amounts of products sold to consumers. For example, agencies of the NIST network would determine the amount of error that is acceptable for a gas pump or grocer's scale and establishes testing procedures for enforcing the standards.

Food and Drug Administration

One of the many agencies within the Department of Health and Human Services (www.os.dhhs.gov/) is the Food and Drug Administration (FDA) (www.fda.gov/). The FDA enforces laws and regulations preventing distribution of mislabeled foods, drugs, cosmetics, and medical devices. The FDA does the following:

1. Requires testing and approval of all new drugs.
2. Tests new and existing products for health and safety standards.
3. Provides standards and guidelines for poisonous substances.
4. Controls the standards for identification, quality, and volume of food containers.
5. Establishes guidelines for labels and proper identification of product contents, ingredients, nutrients, and directions for use.
6. Investigates complaints.
7. Conducts research and issues reports, guidelines, and warnings about substances found to be dangerous or potentially hazardous to health.

Consumer Product Safety Commission

The Consumer Product Safety Commission (CPSC) (www.cpsc.gov/) protects consumers from unreasonable risk of injury or death from potentially hazardous consumer products. The commission enforces standards for consumer products, bans products that are too dangerous, arranges recalls, and researches potential product hazards.

What government agency protects consumers from hazardous products?

Federal Communications Commission

The Federal Communications Commission (FCC) (www.fcc.gov/) regulates interstate and international communications by radio, television, wire, satellite, and cable. The FCC's Consumer Information Bureau (www.fcc.gov/cib/) is the consumer's one-stop source of information, forms, applications, complaints, and current issues before the FCC.

Federal Trade Commission

The Federal Trade Commission (FTC) regulates unfair methods of competition, false or deceptive advertising, deceptive product labeling, inaccurate or obsolete information on credit reports, and concealment of the true cost of credit. The FTC is also the federal clearinghouse for complaints of identity theft. The FTC refers victims to the appropriate agencies for action.

NET NOTES

The Federal Trade Commission's Web site provides consumer protection information. The area dedicated to e-commerce and the Internet offers tips on how to protect your privacy online; Net-based business opportunities; "dot cons"; unsolicited e-mail; shopping safely online; and many other related topics. Check out this valuable site at www.ftc.gov/ftc/consumer.htm.

United States Postal Inspection Service

The United States Postal Inspection Service (USPSIS) (www.usps.gov/websites/depart/inspect) is a federal law enforcement agency that investigates consumer problems pertaining to illegal use of the mail. The USPSIS enforces postal laws, protecting consumers from dangerous articles, contraband, fraud, pornography, and identity theft involving the mail. Through its Consumer Protection Program, USPSIS resolves unsatisfactory mail-order transactions, even in cases where no fraud has occurred. **Fraud** is the intentional misrepresentation of information with the intent to deceive or mislead.

Federal Aviation Administration

The Federal Aviation Administration (FAA) (www.faa.gov/) is an agency of the U.S. Department of Transportation. It controls air traffic and certifies aircraft, airports, pilots, and other personnel. The FAA writes and enforces air safety regulations and air traffic procedures.

Securities and Exchange Commission

The main purpose of the Securities and Exchange Commission (SEC) (www.sec.gov) is to protect investors and maintain the integrity of the securities markets. The SEC requires companies to disclose certain financial and other information, so that investors can research investment options before buying. The SEC also oversees stock exchanges, brokers, and investment advisors to protect investors in their dealings with securities professionals. SEC's Office of Investor Education and Assistance serves investors who complain to the SEC about investment fraud or the mishandling of their investments by securities professionals.

State and Local Assistance

Most states have a consumer protection agency, or the state attorney general may handle consumer affairs. Many county and city governments have set up consumer protection agencies or offices. Consumer leagues and public-interest research groups are also active at the state and local levels, with newsletters, pamphlets, handbooks, and Web sites on current consumer issues.

At the local level, consumers have access to legal aid societies, newspaper and broadcast action reporters, and consumer representatives on local utility or licensing boards. Independent consumer groups focusing on specific issues, such as food prices, may operate on the local level as well.

Private Organizations

The Better Business Bureau (BBB) (www.bbb.org) serves as a clearinghouse of information about local businesses. Complaints against local businesses may be filed with the BBB. The merchants are given an opportunity to respond to the complaint; if they do not, the Better Business Bureau may advise consumers to seek another form of redress. You can request reports regarding the nature of complaints filed against local merchants from the BBB in your area, or look up reports on specific merchants at the BBB Web site.

The BBB is not the only guardian of consumer interests in the business community. For example, the Major Appliance Consumer Action Panel (MACAP) is comprised of representatives of the home appliance industry and provides assistance in resolving or minimizing consumer problems in the purchase and use of home appliances. The automobile and furniture industries, all of which produce goods that represent significant investments for buyers, have voluntary consumer-action panels.

Consumers may also seek the support of a **consumer advocate**—a person who actively promotes consumer causes. Ralph Nader is the best-known consumer advocate. When Ralph Nader finds, through research and investigation, that an injustice or dangerous condition exists, he pursues it in behalf of all consumers. Ralph Nader may file lawsuits against companies to force them to meet safety standards, correct inequitable situations, or properly inform consumers of dangers in the use of their products.

The National Consumers League (NCL) operates the National Fraud Information Center, established in 1992 to combat fraud. In 1996, the Internet Fraud Watch was created. You can find out more about your rights and remedies at www.fraud.org. Trained counselors will help you identify danger signs of fraud as well as help law enforcement agencies get information quickly so they can respond quickly. These services are free.

The Federal Consumer Information Center (FCIC) (www.pueblo.gsa.gov) of the U.S. General Services Administration was created in 1970 to assist federal agencies in the development, promotion, and distribution of practical consumer publications. You can order free, or at very low cost, brochures on topics from how to apply for a passport to *The Consumer's Almanac.* You can order publications by mail, toll-free number, fax, or Internet.

Other consumer organizations help guide consumers in the marketplace. One such organization is Consumers Union. A not-for-profit organization, Consumers Union has the largest consumer testing facility in the world. Through its monthly magazine, *Consumer Reports,* Consumers Union gives test results and product ratings. To assure that all ratings are unbiased, Consumers Union buys all products it tests and accepts no advertising. *Consumer Reports* also prints articles dealing with insurance, credit, and other items of consumer interest. An annual buying guide is also published by Consumers Union. For a subscription fee, you can access all Consumers Union product reports online at www.consumerreports.org.

Public Officials

National elected officials include the president and the vice president of the United States, serving four-year terms; United States senators, serving six-year terms; and the members of the United States House of Representatives, serving two-year terms. Governors of states usually are elected to four-year terms. Other state elected officials include the secretary of state, state treasurer, and state attorney general; superintendent of public instruction; labor commissioner; and state senators and representatives.

Each court (federal, state, and local) has at least one judge, and several clerks of the court assist in filing and information gathering. County elected officials include the county administrator, district attorney, sheriff, and tax assessor, plus a number of commissioners. Other elected local officials include the mayor, city council members, and city manager. These officials are available at county and city office buildings and meet regularly or are available to the public by appointment. The phone book lists various officials separately by state and by county, with each department listed alphabetically.

If you wish to communicate with a public official about a consumer issue, there are several ways to do so:

1. *In Person.* You can make an appointment during regular office hours as well as at meetings of government bodies, which are generally open to the public (except for executive sessions). Almost all hearings offer citizens the opportunity to speak.
2. *By Phone.* Brief calls at reasonable hours are generally effective. Your state may supply toll-free numbers for contacting public officials.
3. *By E-mail.* Legislators receive e-mail correspondence from their constituents (people who live in the areas they represent). You can get e-mail addresses of senators and representatives from your state government Web site links.
4. *By Letter.* An effective letter written to the appropriate representative states clearly the purpose of the letter, identifies the bill by proper name and number, refers to only one issue, and arrives while the issue is current. Give reasons for your position and avoid emotionalism. Ask for specific relief—what you want the public official to do.

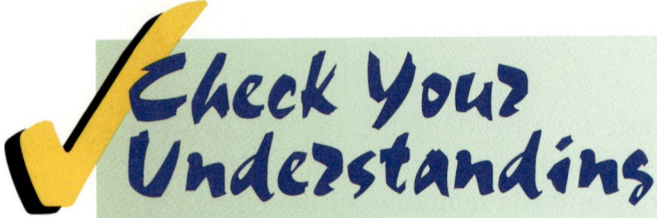

Check Your Understanding

Review Terms
1. fraud
2. consumer advocate

Review Concepts
1. What is the purpose of the CPSC?
2. Which government agency protects stock market investors?

PERSONAL PERSPECTIVE

Identity Theft: Protecting Yourself

Skilled identity thieves can rob you of your identity despite your best efforts at managing your personal information. For example:

1. Stolen wallets and purses containing identification cards, bank cards, and credit cards are used by thieves to call your credit card issuer and change the mailing address on your accounts. They run up charges and you don't get the bill, so you don't know what's happening until the debt gets large. Or, they use your identification to make more false identification, have checks printed, and make purchases with your debit card.

2. Mail can be stolen from your mailbox or your garbage. These documents can be used to have fake checks made up based on your bank account information. Or, new bank accounts based on your identity can be opened, with bad checks written on the accounts.

3. By posing as a landlord or employer, thieves can fraudulently get a copy of your credit report. Then they open accounts and borrow large sums of money, or buy cars and make other large purchases.

To minimize your risk, here are some things you can do:

- Do not give out personal information unless you have initiated the contact and know whom you are dealing with.
- Give your social security number only when absolutely necessary (when you will be receiving money). Don't carry your social security card.
- Pay attention to billing cycles; follow up when bills are late.
- Guard your mail from theft. Use post office collection boxes for outgoing mail; promptly remove mail when it arrives or get a post office box.
- Minimize the number of accounts you have and cards you carry.
- Keep items with personal information in a safe place; shred copies you are discarding.
- Order a copy of your credit report every year; be sure it is accurate.

For more information on identity theft and what to do if it happens to you, call toll free 1-877-IDTHEFT, or visit www.consumer.gov/idtheft online.

Think Critically

1. If someone stole your wallet or purse, what could the person do with the contents?
2. What should you do if your wallet or purse is lost or stolen?
3. Why should you memorize your social security number?

29.1 Laws to Protect Consumers

- The Consumer Bill of Rights outlines the basic rights that consumers should expect to have in the marketplace. These rights have led to laws that protect consumer rights.
- Some laws (such as the Food, Drug, and Cosmetic Act; Flammable Fabrics Act; meat inspection laws; and National Traffic and Motor Vehicle Safety Act) set standards for product purity and safety.
- Many consumer laws (including the Wool Products Labeling Act, Hazardous Substances Labeling Act, Cigarette Labeling and Advertising Act, Fair Packaging and Labeling Act, and Permanent Care Labeling Rule) set requirements for complete and truthful information on product labels.
- Several consumer laws (such as the Child Protection and Toy Safety Act, the Toy Safety Act of 1984, and the Children's Online Privacy Protection Act) are designed to protect children from harm.

29.2 Agencies to Protect Consumers

- The Department of Agriculture inspects and grades food.
- The Food and Drug Administration approves new drugs, tests products for safety, and sets labeling guidelines.
- The Consumer Product Safety Commission enforces product standards and bans or recalls hazardous products.
- The Federal Communications Commission regulates communications by radio, television, wire, satellite, and cable.

- The Federal Trade Commission regulates unfair methods of competition, false or deceptive advertising, deceptive product labeling, inaccurate or obsolete information on credit reports, and concealment of the true cost of credit.
- The U.S. Postal Inspection Service investigates consumer problems pertaining to illegal use of the mail.
- The Securities and Exchange Commission requires businesses to disclose certain information for investors to evaluate and oversees the securities markets.
- Private organizations, such as the Better Business Bureau, can assist consumers with incidents of unethical and illegal practices.
- The National Consumers League operates a national fraud information center that can be reached online.
- Public officials can be reached in person (by appointment), by phone (toll-free state numbers), by e-mail, or by letter.

Review Terms

Directions: Can you find the definition for each of the following terms used in Chapter 29?

care labels
childproof devices
consumer advocate
flammability

fraud
generic drugs
recall

1. Medications with the same composition as the equivalent brand-name drugs but that are generally less expensive.
2. A request for consumers to return a defective product to the manufacturer for repair or a refund.
3. A person who actively promotes consumer causes.
4. Labels on clothing that give instructions for cleaning, wash and dry temperature, and other care needed to preserve the product.
5. The capacity for catching on fire.
6. The intentional misrepresentation of information with the intent to deceive or mislead.
7. Devices designed to resist tampering by young children.

Review Facts and Ideas

1. What consumer protection action did President Kennedy propose in 1962?
2. What six consumer rights are listed in the Consumer Bill of Rights?
3. What was the purpose of the Food, Drug, and Cosmetic Act of 1938?
4. How long must a flame-retardant finish last in children's sleepwear as provided by the Flammable Fabrics Act of 1953?
5. How do patents encourage drug companies to develop new drugs?
6. What are some responsibilities of the National Highway Safety Administration?
7. What was the major purpose of the Permanent Care Labeling Rule of 1972?
8. What agency sets the standard for accuracy that your grocer's scale must meet?
9. What agency tests all new drugs that companies produce for sale in the marketplace?
10. Which agency can ban dangerous products and arrange recalls?
11. What types of communications, in addition to radio and television, are controlled by the FCC?
12. Which agency regulates false or deceptive advertising?
13. If you have a complaint about an unethical stockbroker, which agency should you contact?
14. What do the letters BBB stand for?
15. What should you include in a letter of complaint to an elected official?

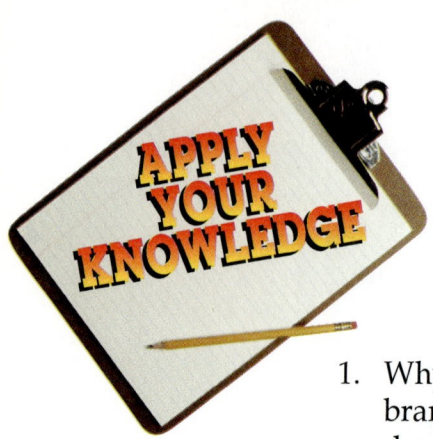

1. Why should you consider buying generic products rather than brand-name products? What do you think would happen if drug development companies did not receive patent protection for a number of years before other companies could sell generic equivalents?

2. Select any garment from your closet. Read the care label. What kinds of information are on the label?

3. Cut the labels from three or four food products, such as soup, cereal, snacks, and processed foods. List the different types of information—such as quantity per serving, ingredients, and vitamin and mineral content—you find on the label. Are there ingredients you do not recognize? Is the nutritional value what you expected?

4. Go to the Better Business Bureau Web site at www.bbb.org, and look up the reports on two local companies. Write a brief summary of the kinds of information the reports give about companies.

5. Visit www.fraud.org online and answer the following questions: What services are available to consumers who have complaints? What is the process of registering a complaint?

6. Visit the Federal Consumer Information Center at www.pueblo.gsa.gov and locate a news article that interests you. Write a bulleted list of the most important consumer information facts you found in the article.

Solve Problems

1. List your state and local sources that can provide assistance with a consumer complaint.

2. Consult the *Consumer Reports Buying Guide* for the current year. Summarize the key points of three product reports that interest you.

3. Your local library contains much information about consumer problems and assistance. Visit the library and list in outline form what types of information are available for consumers.

4. Attend a public hearing on a local issue—land use or zoning, for example—and write a report on who was present, what was discussed, and the conclusion reached. Hearings are held in city hall or county buildings and are open to the public for testimony and input.

5. Check your local newspaper for public notices of hearings by local government groups. List hearings that are scheduled. Which hearings are on issues affecting consumers? How would consumers be affected in each case? Attend a hearing and prepare a report on it.

6. Check recent issues of the newspapers, news magazines, or online news sources for reports of proposed laws and regulations. Choose an issue that concerns you and investigate it. Prepare an e-mail message to the appropriate official with your comments on the proposed law or regulation.

For related activities and links, point your browser to
www.mypf.swep.com

Chapter 30

Dispute Resolution

Terms to Know

court
jurisdiction
trial court
appellate court
civil court
criminal court
statute of limitations
plaintiff

defendant
counterclaim
depositions
judgment
class-action lawsuit
alternate dispute
   resolution (ADR)
mediation

voluntary
   arbitration
binding
   arbitration

Up Front

Jeri wanted to paint her apartment. The landlord promised to pay for the paint if she provided the labor. Jeri painted the apartment, as agreed, but when she asked the landlord for reimbursement, he refused.

"I've tried everything," she told her sister. "I talked to him nicely and referred to our verbal agreement. He said that he never made such an agreement, and I have nothing in writing to prove it. Then when I moved out of the apartment, he refused to refund my deposit. He said that I painted the apartment without authorization, so he was entitled to keep my deposit. Together the paint and the deposit total $900! What can I do to get my money back?"

Goals

★ Describe the organization of the legal system in the United States at federal, state, and local levels.

★ Explain the legal procedures involved from the time a complaint is filed until the court enters a judgment.

Structure of the Legal System

The legal system in the United States is based on common law. *Common law* is a system of laws based on decisions made in court cases. These decisions set legal *precedents,* serving as models for deciding similar cases in the future. At the base of our common law legal system are the courts. A **court** is a person or group of people whose task it is to hear and decide matters according to the law.

There are many types of courts—federal, state, and local. Each court is empowered to decide certain types or classes of cases. This power is called **jurisdiction,** which is the legal authority to hear and decide a case. A court may have original or appellate jurisdiction, or both. The court of original jurisdiction, or the first court to hear a case, is the **trial court.** An **appellate court** has appellate jurisdiction, or the authority to review the judgment of a lower court.

Courts are also classified in terms of the nature of their jurisdiction. A **civil court** has the authority to hear non-criminal cases. Civil courts typically settle matters for individuals, such as divorce or estate settlement after someone dies, or between individuals and businesses, such as contract or copyright violations and consumer complaints. Civil courts also settle disputes against a branch of the government. A **criminal court** hears cases involving punishable offenses against society. In a criminal case, the government, representing all the people, prosecutes the alleged wrongdoer.

The losing parties may appeal the decision of a civil or criminal court if they believe the court made an error in applying the law. Then an appellate court will review the decision.

Court Personnel

Our federal and state court systems require many people in order to operate efficiently. Some people are employees of the court. Others are called to serve temporarily on a jury.

Judge

The judge is the presiding officer in the court and is either elected or appointed. Attorneys are usually selected by the parties in the dispute, but are sometimes selected by the judge to present the case to the court.

Clerk

The clerk of the court enters cases on the court calendar; keeps an accurate record of the proceedings; accepts, labels, and provides safekeeping for all items of evidence; administers the oath to witnesses and jurors; and sometimes approves bail bonds and computes the costs involved.

Reporter

The court reporter keeps a word-by-word record of the trial, usually through the use of a special recording machine. These trial records are available to each attorney and are used for appeals.

Bailiff

Deputy sheriffs serve as sergeants-at-arms during court proceedings. Bailiffs maintain order in the courtroom at the instruction of the judge.

Jury

The *jury* is a body of citizens sworn by a court to hear the facts submitted during a trial and to render a verdict. A trial jury consists of not more than 12 people. A juror must be of legal age, a resident of the county, and able to see and hear. Jurors are chosen from a list of local citizens—usually from tax or voter rolls or from motor vehicle registration records.

The Federal Court System

The authority of federal courts comes directly from the United States Constitution and the laws enacted by Congress. The federal courts hear matters that concern the nation as a whole. These matters pertain to constitutional rights, civil rights, interstate commerce, patents and copyrights, federal taxes, currency, and foreign relations. Other matters, such as non-federal crimes, contract disputes, and divorces, are left to the states in which they occur. The federal courts may hear a dispute between citizens of two different states, but only if it involves $75,000 or more.

The United States Supreme Court

The Supreme Court is the top court of the federal court system and is located in Washington, D.C. The Supreme Court is the only federal court expressly established by the Constitution. Appeals from federal appellate courts and from state supreme courts that pertain to federal issues are heard by the Supreme Court. The Supreme Court chooses which cases it will hear. The Court sets its own *docket*, or schedule of cases, dates, and times for issues to be heard. Only cases of the greatest importance and national consequence are accepted. Thousands of actions are appealed every year, but the Supreme Court accepts only a small percentage of them.

All oral arguments at the Supreme Court are open to the public, but seating is limited and on a first-come, first-seated basis. Visitors must go through a security checkpoint as they enter the courtroom. Note taking is not permitted. Sunglasses, display buttons, and inappropriate clothing may not be worn.

What kinds of cases are heard by the U.S. Supreme Court?

There are nine Supreme Court justices, including a chief justice. The president appoints the justices to their positions for life. No federal judge may be dismissed or impeached for any reason other than gross misconduct.

Courts of Appeal

The United States is divided into 12 judicial circuits. Each circuit has a court of appeals. Each appellate court has from five to nine judges, who review final decisions of the district courts. The decisions of the courts of appeal are final in most cases.

District Trial Courts

The United States is divided into 90 federal districts, with a court assigned to each. Each district covers a state or a portion of a state. Consequently, some states may be home to more than one federal district court, while other states contain none. (These states are part of a federal district whose court is in a different state.) Each district court is a trial court, also divided into civil or criminal divisions. District courts are staffed by judges who hear cases individually, not as a panel.

Some issues are always considered federal issues, such as bankruptcy and crimes involving interstate commerce. For example, hijacking, kidnapping, bank robbery, and counterfeiting are all federal crimes and would be prosecuted in federal courts. Any criminal sentenced for a federal crime would be sent to a federal prison or penitentiary.

Special Federal Courts

Congress established special courts to hear only particular kinds of cases. These special federal courts include the Court of Claims, Customs Court, Court of International Trade, Tax Court, Court of Military Appeals, and the territorial courts. If you wanted to sue the United States, you would file a claim in a U.S. district or special federal court.

The state court systems handle the greatest share of legal matters, because the Constitution sets limits on the federal system. The Tenth Amendment to the Constitution grants each state the sovereign power to enact and enforce state laws.

A state's laws are contained in its constitution and enacted by its own legislature. These laws are binding upon the citizens of the state and must not violate the U.S. Constitution. Each state has the power to run its own court system to decide issues that involve state laws. Each state establishes its own set of court procedures, determines court names, divides areas of responsibility among the various courts, and sets limits of authority among the state courts. Some issues are tried exclusively in state trial courts, such as divorce, probate, and adoption.

State Supreme Courts

In most states the highest court is the state supreme court, sometimes called the court of final appeal. Ordinarily, the state supreme court has appellate jurisdiction. The decision of a state supreme court is final, except in cases involving the federal Constitution, laws, and treaties. In many states, there are appellate courts and one supreme court.

District and Circuit Courts

General trial courts, often called state district courts, circuit courts, or superior courts, decide matters beyond local courts. These courts hear civil cases involving large sums of money, criminal matters with major penalties, and cases that are appealed from local courts whose decisions are questionable. Judges at this level are usually appointed by the state governor, although some may be elected for terms of four to six years. Decisions from district courts may be reviewed by the highest state court.

County and City Courts

The lowest state courts are found at the city or county level. These courts may also be called municipal or justice courts. Courts at this level have authority limited by geographic boundaries. Civil and criminal cases are heard at the local level. However, civil cases must be for small amounts only. At the local level, disputes usually are heard and decided by judges, not by juries. In very small areas, a judge may be called a justice of the peace, who is an appointed, part-time official. Justices of the peace in other areas are elected officials. Special courts at the local level may be called police courts, traffic courts, small-claims courts, and justice-of-the-peace courts.

Court Proceedings

Filing a lawsuit involves many steps, costs, and outcomes. You would need an attorney who would advise you of your chances of winning your case, explain the laws pertaining to your case, and tell you what you need to do to prepare for trial. The services of a competent attorney can cost $200 an hour or more. Some attorneys will work on a *contingency-fee* basis, which means they receive fees only if you win the case. Your state bar association can supply names of attorneys who specialize in the area of your complaint. Your attorney will appear in court on your behalf and represent your interests.

Career Links

Paralegals help lawyers prepare for closings, hearings, trials, and meetings. They organize files, draft agreements, and coordinate law office activities. They may work in wide areas of the law or may specialize. Many paralegals use computers in their work to search or index materials. Employers usually require formal paralegal training obtained through associate or bachelor's degree programs or through a certification program. Paralegals need to have good research and investigative skills, along with computer applications knowledge

For more information, refer to the *Occupational Outlook Handbook* at www.bls.gov or search the Internet using such key words as "careers," "jobs," and "paralegal."

All states have a **statute of limitations,** which is a legally defined time limit in which a lawsuit may be filed for various complaints. For example, in many states personal injury lawsuits must be filed within two years from the date of the injury. A lawsuit filed after the two-year limit will be dismissed.

Generally, a lawsuit involves the following steps:

1. Someone files a complaint, worded in a legally acceptable format called a *pleading*.
2. The person at whom the lawsuit is aimed is *served,* or receives notice of the suit.

3. The attorneys for both parties gather information in a period called *discovery*.
4. A trial takes place and the court makes a decision.
5. The losing party may appeal the decision to a higher court.

Plaintiff Files Complaint

The person who begins a lawsuit by filing a complaint is the **plaintiff.** The plaintiff discusses the facts of the case with an attorney. The attorney considers the matter, conducts extensive research on similar cases, and advises the client of the prospect of winning the lawsuit. If the client (plaintiff) wishes to pursue the matter, the attorney draws up the necessary papers, which the plaintiff signs. The attorney begins the action by filing the complaint with the clerk of the appropriate court. Usually the plaintiff must pay a filing fee. Generally, the complaint consists of a description of the offending acts and a request for relief.

Defendant Is Served

A certified copy of the complaint is served or presented to the defendant named in the lawsuit. The **defendant** is the person against whom the lawsuit is filed. The local sheriff's department or a private company may be used to serve the defendant. Because the officials must present the papers to the defendant personally, the serving process may take several days. The defendant then has a specified amount of time in which to *appear* (file a response to the complaint). The defendant must decide whether to default (not answer and automatically lose) or answer the complaint. If the defendant does not answer, the plaintiff will win the case by *default judgment*.

The defendant usually discusses the case with an attorney. Then the defendant's attorney prepares and files an answer to the complaint. The defendant may choose to file a counterclaim. A **counterclaim** is a defendant's assertion that the plaintiff is at fault and should pay damages to the defendant.

Discovery

After the defendant's attorney has filed an answer to the complaint with the appropriate court, a formal investigation called *discovery* begins. During the discovery period before trial, attorneys gather information, talk to witnesses, prepare legal arguments, take depositions, hire investigators, examine reports, and negotiate with the opposing party. The purposes of discovery are (1) to preserve evidence, (2) to eliminate surprise, and (3) to lead to settlement.

Depositions are sworn statements of witnesses taken before court appearances and recorded in writing or on videotape to preserve the memory of the issues. Many cases are settled before going to trial because both parties realize the risk involved in a trial and because information gathered by both sides is both known and shared. If the opposing parties can reach a settlement, they sign a formal agreement and the case is dropped.

Trial Takes Place

After discovery and when the parties cannot reach agreement, a trial date is set. Defendants may be entitled to a jury trial (if they could go to jail), and often juries are provided, but the right is not automatic. If there is a jury trial, the first step is choosing a jury. Citizens have a duty to serve on a jury when called by the court. The court identifies a pool of potential jurors from voting records or motor vehicle registration records. Attorneys for both sides select jurors from the pool and may *challenge* jurors (have them dismissed) if they believe the jurors are biased. Once the jury is seated, the trial begins.

The trial starts with opening statements from both sides. The plaintiff then presents evidence and witnesses, followed by the defendant. Both sides attempt to prove their claims. Both sides also attempt to discredit evidence and witnesses presented by the other side. Then the attorneys make closing arguments, and the judge instructs the jury on relevant points of law. The jury *deliberates*, or carefully considers the arguments of both sides. Then the jury reaches a decision, and the jury *foreman* (chosen leader) announces it to the court.

In deciding civil cases, one side must simply prove its position by a *preponderance*, or superiority, of the evidence. In other words, one side convinces the jury that its side is more believable. This is sometimes called "clear and con-

During a trial, what role do the plaintiff and the defendant play?

Consumer Rights and Responsibilities

vincing evidence." In deciding criminal cases, however, prosecutors must prove their case *beyond a reasonable doubt.* The defense attorneys must prove reasonable doubt of the guilt of the accused; they do not have to prove innocence.

The Court Enters a Judgment

Based on the decision of the jury or the judge, called the *verdict,* the court enters a judgment. A **judgment** is the final court ruling that resolves the key issues and establishes the rights and obligations of each party. In a criminal case, the judgment is the ruling of the defendant's guilt or innocence, and the consequences of guilt. In a civil case, the judgment typically establishes an amount that the losing party must pay.

The losing party has a limited time in which to appeal. A case heard in a state district court may be appealed to a circuit court. After the circuit court, the case may go to the state appeals court, and then to the state supreme court. Any matters involving national interests may be appealed to the United States Supreme Court, which may or may not choose to hear the case.

In a civil lawsuit, the losing party often must pay the costs of filing papers with the court, the cost of having the sheriff or other officers of the court take official action, fees paid to witnesses, jury fees, and the cost of printing the record of the trial. Sometimes the losing party must also pay the winner's attorney's fee.

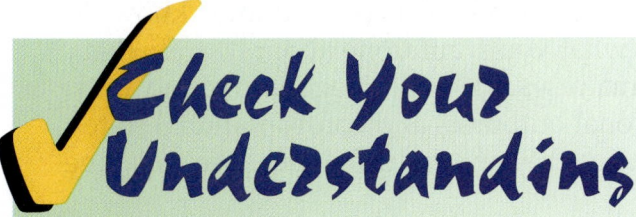

Check Your Understanding

Review Terms
1. court
2. jurisdiction
3. trial court
4. appellate court
5. civil court
6. criminal court
7. statute of limitations
8. plaintiff
9. defendant
10. counterclaim
11. depositions
12. judgment

Review Concepts
1. What is common law?
2. Who serves on a jury?

Goals

★ Define remedies available to consumers other than individual lawsuits.
★ Explain alternative dispute resolution (ADR) options.

Self-Help Remedies

Lawsuits are lengthy, expensive, and emotionally draining. If you have a consumer problem, pursue a settlement yourself before deciding to sue. Negotiating and withholding payment are two self-help techniques that can resolve many consumer problems.

Negotiating

Negotiating is the process of finding a solution that is acceptable to both sides. The buyer must be willing to give up some things in return for the seller's changing his or her position. In most cases, when consumers complain and want some type of settlement, the seller is willing to discuss the issues to reach some type of agreement to maintain the goodwill of the customer.

Negotiating requires tactful give-and-take. You must know the specifics of the problem, what you want done about it, and what you are willing to do to make a settlement. Negotiate calmly and reasonably. Avoid emotional outbursts and confrontational statements. These only create hostility and reduce the chances of agreeing on a remedy.

COMMUNICATION CONNECTION

Assume that you purchased a CD from a local retailer, using cash. When you put it into your player, the CD will not play. You want to return the CD, but unfortunately you didn't keep the receipt from the merchant. Role-play this situation with a classmate. What are you willing to accept or do in order to achieve a settlement?

If you buy a defective product, first seek an agreeable remedy with the merchant before pursuing legal remedies. Negotiated settlements are often much less expensive and easier to achieve than legal remedies. They are also less stressful than pursuing lawsuits. Begin the negotiation soon after the problem occurs. If you wait too long, you may lose your opportunity for an agreeable settlement.

Withholding Payment

As a consumer, you can withhold payment in a purchase dispute. However, you must put your complaint in writing right away and explain the reason why you are withholding payment on the disputed amount. The law requires the seller to respond to your complaint within a reasonable time limit. You should pay all other amounts due as agreed. Your credit should not be damaged if you follow the proper procedures for questioning credit charges.

When you buy merchandise with credit, you have more leverage than if you pay cash. You can instruct the credit card company to withhold payment to the merchant. If you follow the credit card company's procedure for disputing a payment, the company will help you resolve the problem with the merchant.

Small-Claims Court

If the amount is relatively small, you might consider small-claims court. The matter will be heard quickly, but the decision is final. You must represent yourself—no attorneys are allowed—and there is no jury. A judge decides the matter. Most states set a maximum amount of $2,000 to $5,000 in damages that can be recovered in a small-claims court.

Small-claims courts are easy to use. You can get an instruction sheet from your county courthouse that explains how to file a small claim. You must know the name and address of the person with whom you have a problem. You must know the amount in contention and make a short statement of why you are entitled to the money.

Once you file your claim, the court will serve a copy of it to the defendant. The defendant has 10 days to appear. If the defendant contests (disagrees with) the claim, the court sets a hearing date.

Why might you want to resort to small-claims court rather than a jury trial?

The hearing lasts about a half hour. You present your side of the case; the defendant does the same. You may bring in written statements or evidence as well as witnesses. You should summarize your position on one page and present it to the judge.

No record is made of the small-claims court hearing. It cannot be appealed. The judge's decision is final. The benefit of taking your dispute to small-claims court is financial: you pay no attorneys' fees. Court filing fees are small; $50 to $150 is common. The case is heard in a few weeks at most, giving you speedy relief. If the defendant does not appear, you win by default. The judge proclaims a judgment, and the losing party is required to pay damages.

It is important in a small-claims court hearing that you be organized, calm, and specific about your complaint. If you are asking for $500 in damages, you must be prepared to show why you deserve that sum. The judge will ask questions of you and the defendant. Usually the judge will make an immediate decision or will take a 15-minute break and return with the decision.

Class-Action Lawsuits

A **class-action lawsuit** is a legal action in which a large number of people with similar complaints against the same defendant join together to sue. Often class-action lawsuits involve products that injured many people, and the defendant is the product's manufacturer. Sometimes employees join together to sue their employer for discrimination affecting all of them. In a class-action suit, a person sues another person or a company on behalf of himself or herself and all others in the same situation. If the plaintiffs win, they split the judgment.

In some cases, you can convince a consumer protection group to file a lawsuit on your behalf. For example, the American Civil

Liberties Union (ACLU) files lawsuits to protect the rights of groups of citizens. The ACLU collects money from donations to pay the costs involved in filing lawsuits. Many individuals cannot afford to pursue legal remedies without the help of such groups because of the expense involved.

Governmental Assistance

In addition to the sources of consumer assistance listed in Chapter 29, you may wish to seek help from a government agency to stop some objectionable practice and get your money back. In many cases, the cost to you is small, while the benefit to all consumers is great. Government agencies that can assist you with a consumer complaint include the sources shown in Figure 30-1.

Sources of Government Assistance **Figure 30-1**

Automobiles	National Highway Traffic Safety Administration
Collection, Credit	State Consumer Protection Division (at your state capitol)
Drugs/Foods	Food and Drug Administration
Household	Consumer Product Safety Commission
Investment Fraud	Federal Trade Commission Securities and Exchange Commission
Medical/Dental	State Board of Medical Examiners State Department of Commerce State Board of Dental Examiners State Health Division State Board of Pharmacy
Medicare	Social Security Administration
Misrepresentation/Fraud	State Consumer Protection Division Local District Attorney Local or State Better Business Bureau
Transportation	Interstate Commerce Commission
Warranties	Federal Trade Commission

Alternate Dispute Resolution

Alternate dispute resolution (ADR) is a general term covering several methods of settling disputes without using the court system. It can mean negotiations (described earlier), mediation, or several forms of arbitration.

When the parties cannot reach a negotiated settlement themselves, the next step to take without involving a court is mediation. **Mediation** is a dispute resolution method in which an independent third person (a *mediator*) helps the parties come to their own solution. Mediation has no formal rules for how to proceed. The mediator listens to both sides and helps both sides sort out what is important and what they would be willing to give up to get it. The mediator has no power to impose a settlement. He or she just facilitates the negotiations between the disputing parties. Typically, the mediator charges a fee that the two parties split.

Another form of ADR is arbitration. *Arbitration* is similar to mediation, in that an independent third person, called an *arbitrator*, helps resolve the dispute. But unlike mediation, arbitration does use some rules of procedure, though they are less formal than court procedures. There are two common types of arbitration: voluntary and binding. In **voluntary arbitration,** an independent third person listens to both sides and makes a recommendation but cannot impose it. Both parties are free to accept or reject it. With **binding arbitration,** the independent third person has the power to impose a decision that both parties must accept. The parties agree before arbitration begins that they will accept the decision as final. Like mediation, the arbitrator charges a fee for this service. The two parties choose the arbitrator, who is usually a professional with expertise in the subject matter and often has a legal background.

The Yellow Pages of your telephone book has listings for mediation and arbitration services. You can also find many such resources online. Figure 30-2 lists some dispute resolution resources that you can contact.

DID YOU KNOW

The alternative dispute resolution process can be used in various settings. For example, some high schools use peer mediation programs. Selected students are trained to serve as neutral third parties to mediate disputes among their fellow students. Peer mediators are respected because they honor the problem-solving process as well as honor their peers in the dispute by the way they conduct the mediation session.

Consumer Rights and Responsibilities

Arbitration	The American Arbitration Association (headquarters) 140 W. 51st Street New York, NY 10020 Call: 212-484-4000 Has offices in 25 cities (see your local telephone book).
Bar Referral	The American Bar Association can give the name and address of the nearest dispute resolution center. Write: American Bar Association's Special Committee on Alternative Dispute Resolution 1800 M Street NW Washington, D.C. 20036 Call: 202-331-2258 You will receive a list of 200 centers for $10.
Business Disputes	For free publications for businesses on saving money on legal disputes through use of a panel of dispute resolves, write: Center for Public Resources 680 Fifth Avenue New York, NY 10019 Call: 202-541-9830
Divorce Mediation	Divorce Mediation Research Project 1720 Emerson Street Denver, CO 80218 Send $10 to receive a partial list of mediators who specialize in divorce. Endispute Suite 803 11 Dupont Circle NW Washington, D.C. 20036 Call: 202-232-5368 Offices also in Chicago, Los Angeles, and San Francisco. West Coast affiliate: Judicial Arbitration & Mediation Service P.O. Box 10333 Santa Ana, CA 92711 Call: 714-972-1616
Lawyer Tips	For tips on dealing with lawyers, write: HALT Americans for Legal Reform Suite 309 201 Massachusetts Avenue NE Washington, D.C. 20002 Call: 202-546-4558

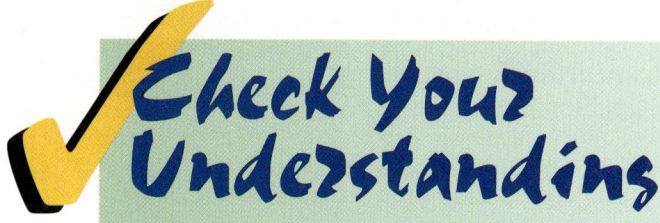

Check Your Understanding

Review Terms

1. class-action lawsuit
2. alternate dispute resolution (ADR)
3. mediation
4. voluntary arbitration
5. binding arbitration

Review Concepts

1. Why might you choose small-claims court over filing a lawsuit in regular court?
2. How is arbitration different from mediation?

PERSONAL PERSPECTIVE

Resolving Disputes for E-Consumers

When you buy products online, you are taking a risk. If something goes wrong, you can't return the product to a physical store and talk to the manager. Online dispute resolution services include the ability to file a complaint, insurance provided through seal owners (that guarantee sites), and online dispute resolution.

If you buy from a business that displays a seal of approval, such as Square Trade (www.squaretrade.com), Webtrust (www.webtrust.org), or TRUSTe (www.truste.org), you can also find assistance in resolving disputes at these Web sites. These companies will keep track of complaints, alert members of problems, and monitor to see that disputes are resolved satisfactorily and within a reasonable period of time.

At the Better Business Bureau (www.BBBonline.com), consumers can file complaints and view complaints filed by others, as well as see which companies have complaints filed against them. For complete alternate dispute resolution services similar to those in the traditional brick-and-mortar world, you can go to official ADR sites, such as Cyber Settle (www.cybersettle.com). These Web sites offer arbitration for those who wish to use the service.

To file a complaint, go to the appropriate Web site and complete forms that explain the issue. The online merchant responds, and both of you can continue a dialog until all issues are "on the table." This service is often called *hosted message board negotiation,* and it is a free process for consumers.

You do have avenues for redress when shopping on the Internet. Still, it is wise to shop carefully online and buy only from known merchants. You might also want to consider using a service such as Tradenable (www.tradenable.com), which allows you to pay for online purchases into an escrow account. When you receive the goods and judge them to be satisfactory, the escrow account pays the online merchant. There is a small fee for this service.

Think Critically

1. Have you purchased something online that was poor quality or wasn't what you ordered? How did you resolve the problem?
2. In what ways is online shopping riskier than shopping in a physical store?
3. What can you do to reduce the risk of shopping online?

Summary

30.1 The Legal System

- The U.S. legal system is based on common law, or decisions made in court cases that serve as models for deciding similar future cases.
- Each federal, state, and local court has a particular jurisdiction, or authority to handle certain types of cases. Trial courts have original jurisdiction, or the authority to hear cases first. Appellate courts have appellate jurisdiction, or the authority to review the decisions of lower courts.
- Civil courts hear non-criminal cases, such as divorce and consumer complaints. Criminal courts hear cases involving punishable offenses against society. Losing parties in civil or criminal cases can appeal if they believe the lower court made an error in applying the law.
- The judge, clerk, reporter, and bailiff are court employees. The jury is a group of citizens selected to hear cases for a short time.
- The federal court system consists of district trial courts, circuit courts of appeal, and the United States Supreme Court. Federal courts deal with matters concerning the nation as a whole.
- State court systems vary according to state but typically include trial courts, appellate courts, and a state supreme court. State courts handle the majority of legal matters.
- Court proceedings begin when a plaintiff files a complaint. The defendant must respond within a prescribed time period. A period of discovery, or formal investigation, then follows. When the disputing parties do not agree to settle, the case goes to trial.

- The attorneys select jurors from the pool of citizens called by the court. The two sides present their cases. After closing statements by both sides, the judge instructs the jury on relevant laws. The jury deliberates and reaches a verdict.

30.2 *Other Ways to Seek Redress*

- Consumers can resolve most disputes themselves, without outside help, through negotiating or withholding payment until they reach an agreement.
- Small-claims court is a faster and less expensive way to settle disputes over amounts below the legal maximum set by the state. It requires no attorney and small filing fees, but the decision of the judge is final.
- A class-action lawsuit is a legal action in which a large number of people with similar complaints against the same defendant join together to sue. Often these suits involve products that injured many people.
- Alternative dispute resolution means settling disputes without using the court system. Mediation and arbitration are the two most common types.
- Mediation is a dispute resolution method in which an independent third person (a mediator) helps the parties come to their own solution. It has no formal rules of procedure, and the parties are not required to accept the settlement.
- Arbitration also uses an independent third person (an arbitrator), but it has some rules of procedure. In voluntary arbitration, the arbitrator makes a recommendation that the parties are free to accept or reject. In binding arbitration, the parties must accept the arbitrator's decision.

Review Terms

Directions: Can you find the definition for each of the following terms used in Chapter 30?

alternate dispute resolution (ADR)
appellate court
binding arbitration
civil court
class-action lawsuit
counterclaim
court
criminal court
defendant
depositions
judgment

jurisdiction
mediation
plaintiff
statute of limitations
trial court
voluntary arbitration

1. A general term covering several methods of settling a dispute without using the court system.
2. A person or group of people whose task it is to hear and decide matters according to the law.
3. A court that hears cases involving punishable offenses against society.
4. A court that hears non-criminal cases.
5. The legal authority to hear and decide a case.
6. A dispute resolution method in which an independent third person has the power to impose a decision that both parties must accept.
7. A dispute resolution method in which an independent third person helps the parties come to their own solution.
8. The first court to hear a case.
9. The person who initiates a lawsuit by filing a complaint.
10. A court that has the authority to review the judgment of a lower court.
11. A legally defined time limit in which a lawsuit may be filed for various complaints.
12. The person against whom a lawsuit is filed.
13. Sworn statements of witnesses taken before court appearances and recorded in writing or on videotape to preserve the memory of the issues.
14. A defendant's assertion that the plaintiff is at fault and should pay damages to the defendant.

Consumer Rights and Responsibilities

15. The final court ruling that resolves the key issues and establishes the rights and obligations of each party.
16. A dispute resolution method in which an independent third person listens to both sides and makes a recommendation but cannot impose it.
17. A legal action in which a large number of people with similar complaints against the same defendant join together to sue.

Review Facts and Ideas

1. How do court decisions affect other cases in a common law system?
2. Describe the types of matters that each of these courts hears:
   a. Trial court
   b. Appellate court
   c. Civil court
   d. Criminal court
3. On what basis may the losing party in a case appeal the decision?
4. List and briefly describe the officers of the court.
5. What is a jury and how is it selected?
6. What is the highest court of the federal court system?
7. How many federal court districts are in the United States?
8. List several "special" courts in the federal system.
9. What are the lowest state courts? Give two examples.
10. What are the steps in a lawsuit?
11. What happens during discovery?
12. What are some ways you can settle consumer problems without outside help?
13. How is a class-action lawsuit different from an individual lawsuit?
14. What are the advantages of alternate dispute resolution (ADR)?

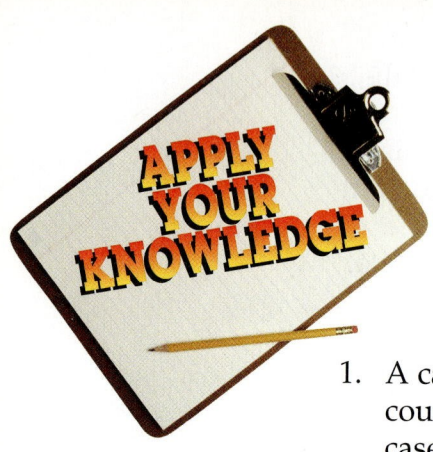

1. A case that involves a dispute in a city is filed with the circuit court of a county in the same state. After a trial court hears the case, where can it be appealed?

2. A plaintiff files a lawsuit. Explain what happens until a court renders a judgment. What happens if the losing party thinks the court made a legal error in the case?

3. As a store customer, you are dissatisfied with a product purchased. Explain the self-help remedies and actions to consider in resolving the dispute.

4. Small-claims courts were set up to give the ordinary person "a say in court" for small matters otherwise not worth taking to court. Why are small-claims courts easy to use and, in some cases, more advantageous than a formal court proceeding?

5. Use the Internet to investigate government agencies that can assist you with consumer complaints. What type of complaint is each agency responsible for? Think of a past consumer complaint you or a member of your family has had. Which agency would you choose for help with this consumer problem?

6. Search the Internet for information about mediators or arbitrators. Write a one-page report on what they do, how they do it, and how consumers can employ their services.

Solve Problems

1. Visit your local law library located at the county courthouse, a public university, or at a law school if there is one in your area. List five types of references available. Look up the statute of limitations for filing lawsuits in your state and tell how long you have to file actions in the following situations:
   a. Wrongful death or injury
   b. Real property infringement
   c. Civil action where you are the injured party in a contract

Also in your law library, you will find books that summarize cases tried and decided in your state. Find a case that interests you and summarize the issues involved, the court's decision, and your reactions.

2. Spend a half-day at a local county courthouse. Make arrangements to observe a case being tried. Generally, you will not be allowed to leave the room until the court adjourns, nor will you be allowed to enter while court is in session. You may observe a civil or criminal case. Write a report on what you observe.

3. Examine a lawsuit that has been filed. You can look at records of cases that have been filed in your county, although you will not be given copies free of charge. Read through each case and make notes about the plaintiff, the defendant, the issue at hand, what the plaintiff was asking, and how the matter was resolved.

4. Work in groups to determine the appropriate legal remedy for each of the following situations.

a. The plaintiff was driving his vehicle in a northerly direction when the defendant ran a stop sign going in an easterly direction and did severe damage to the plaintiff's vehicle, including personal injuries to the plaintiff.

b. A person has paid money to a telemarketer for a product that was promised but never received. The caller said the product was high quality and that the company was a non-profit organization to benefit disabled veterans.

c. A local restaurant served food that caused people who ate there on a particular night to get sick. No one died, but several people were very sick for several days, causing medical bills amounting to several thousand dollars. When the cause of the illness was detected, the restaurant was required to make needed changes, and then it was allowed to reopen for business.

For related activities and links, point your browser to
www.mypf.swep.com

Unit *seven*

PROJECT

Exploring Ethical Issues

Project

7

Ethics is the study of what is morally good and bad, right and wrong. We seek to learn what makes actions right or wrong. As you will discover, deciding the difference can be a more complex process than it might seem at first.

In this section, you will analyze situations involving ethics in the marketplace, in the workplace, and on the Internet. You will be asked to answer critical-thinking questions on each case. Please record your answers in the space provided on the worksheets in the *Student Activity Guide*. In analyzing each case, you must (1) identify the problem, (2) apply relevant knowledge to the solution of the problem, and (3) draw a conclusion or reach a decision based on careful analysis of the problem. People base ethical decisions on their personal values and principles, which they develop through individual life experiences. Therefore, since everyone has different experiences, decisions about each case will probably vary.

CASE 1

Cutting It Close

Lashondra wanted to earn extra money over the summer, so she decided to start a lawn-mowing business in her neighborhood. To advertise her business, she composed a flyer to put in her neighbors' mailboxes. On the flyer she listed her services: mowing, trimming, and blowing grass clippings off the driveway and sidewalk when she finished. She offered all of these services for one low price.

Several neighbors wanted her service. In fact, more asked than she had time to serve. Not wanting to pass up the opportunity to earn so much money, Lashondra agreed to do the lawns of all who asked. She figured she would find some way to mow them all. Since she was dealing with neighbors, she did not offer any written contracts. They just agreed verbally.

For three weeks, Lashondra worked very hard but still could not finish all the lawns she had agreed to mow. She realized, though, that if she didn't trim the lawns, she could mow one additional lawn each weekend, so that's what she decided to do. Lashondra reasoned that her mower could cut grass very close to trees and walls, so the trimming didn't really seem necessary. She was giving her customers a very low price, so it was a good deal even without the trimming. Besides, she could now satisfy more customers who otherwise would have to mow their own lawns or take the time to find someone else to do them.

1. Since Lashondra and her neighbors did not sign a written contract, is Lashondra obligated to do the services she listed on her flyer? Why or why not?

2. Lashondra is 16, so she is a minor. How does this fact affect her legal and ethical obligations to her neighbors?

3. Do you agree with Lashondra's reasons for not trimming? Why or why not?

4. Are the benefits she is offering her neighbors worth giving up the trimming service to obtain?

5. If you were in Lashondra's situation, what would you do? Why?

CASE 2

I'm Anonymous

Shuet works full time and lives in an apartment with two roommates. He has met many people online, and he uses several screen names. He visits chat rooms and reads personal ads frequently, and sometimes responds to them. He never uses correct information because he wants to feel safe from anyone finding out who he really is. On several occasions, Shuet made arrangements to meet someone, but often he did not show up as agreed.

As a joke, Shuet sometimes sends insulting or vaguely threatening messages to co-workers he doesn't like. He enjoys hearing them talk about the messages at work. He doesn't mean them any real harm, so the messages don't hurt anybody. And because he's anonymous, he doesn't take any risks.

1. Do you think Shuet is acting appropriately on the Internet? Why or why not?

2. Have you ever acted in similar ways toward people on the Internet? Explain.

3. How would you feel if you received an insulting or threatening e-mail from an anonymous sender?

4. What suggestions would you make to Shuet about behaving appropriately and staying safe on the Internet?

CASE 3

Something for Nothing

Jared and Kayla work together for a fast-food restaurant. They are both good workers and have been employed for over a year. Each Christmas the company they work for has a big party for all employees. Gifts are given away to employees with outstanding service during the year.

Jared and Kayla's manager has worked for the company for over ten years. She discovered a way to falsify information in the computer to her advantage. She gets more than her fair share of gifts while others in the company do not get as much. Jared and Kayla accidentally discovered this scam. The manager encouraged Jared and Kayla to participate in the scheme.

"You two can get more gifts if you participate. If you try to turn me in, I'll have both of you fired," she said.

1. What is the ethical problem involved in this situation?

2. What are Jared and Kayla's options?

3. What would you do if you were in this situation? Why?

4. How might this case be an example of employee stealing in the workplace?

CASE 4

It's a Good Deal

When Roberto flew to see his relatives last year, he was able to earn enough air miles for a free ticket. The frequent flyer club rules are clear: The ticket is non-transferable.

Roberto bought a ticket for a flight across the country, but later discovered he couldn't go. A friend of his was planning a similar trip, so Roberto offered him the ticket for $100—much cheaper than the cost of a full fare.

When Roberto's friend tried to use the ticket on his return flight, the agent discovered that the ticket belonged to someone else. The airline refused to allow him on the plane without his paying the full price. When he told Roberto about the problem, Roberto said it wasn't his concern.

1. Discuss the pros and cons of Roberto's dilemma.

2. What's wrong with the owner of a ticket giving or selling it to someone else?

3. Would you participate in this type of a deal? Why or why not?

CASE 5

Nobody Got Hurt

Loriann bought a new dress to wear for a special occasion. During the course of the evening, she spilled some juice on the dress and was unable to remove all of the stain. The stain was small and not really visible at first glance.

The next day, Loriann decided that she would probably never wear the dress again. Anyway, the dress didn't fit as well as she would have liked, so she decided to get her money back. That afternoon she returned the dress to the store. She claimed the dress was a gift that she didn't like. The store gave her credit for the dress, and Loriann bought something else.

When asked how she could do something like that, Loriann replied, "Why not? Nobody got hurt."

1. Was there anything wrong with what Loriann did? Did anybody get hurt? Who?

2. Why do some stores have lenient return policies? Why do some stores have "no return" policies?

3. What would you do if you worked in the store and knew what Loriann had done?

4. Discuss the ethical principles involved in this case.

Appendix A

1040EZ Tax Tables

These tax tables are provided for taxpayers to compute the amount of income tax liability they owe for the tax year. The 1040EZ tax tables are included with the instructions for preparing Form 1040EZ. After you file your first income tax return, these tables will be mailed to you each year from the IRS to assist you in preparing your tax return. The first year you must file a tax return, you can obtain the instructions and tax tables online, at a post office, state department of revenue office, or federal tax office in your area, or you can write or call the IRS to have them mailed to you. The tables are simple and easy to use once you compute your taxable income.

Section 5—Tax Table

For persons with taxable income
of less than $50,000

Example. Mr. Brown is single. His taxable income on line 6 of Form 1040EZ is $23,250. First, he finds the $23,250-23,300 income line. Next, he finds the "Single" column and reads down the column. The amount shown where the income line and filing status column meet → is $3,644. This is the tax amount he must enter on line 10 of Form 1040EZ.

At least	But less than	Single	Married filing jointly
			Your tax is—
23,200	23,250	3,630	3,484
23,250	23,300	(3,644)	3,491
23,300	23,350	3,658	3,499
23,350	23,400	3,672	3,506

If Form 1040EZ, line 6, is —		And you are —		If Form 1040EZ, line 6, is —		And you are —		If Form 1040EZ, line 6, is —		And you are —		If Form 1040EZ, line 6 —		And you are —	
At least	But less than	Single	Married filing jointly	At least	But less than	Single	Married filing jointly	At least	But less than	Single	Married filing jointly	At least	But less than	Single	Married filing jointly
		Your tax is—				**Your tax is—**				**Your tax is—**				**Your tax is—**	
$0	$5	$0	$0	1,500	1,525	227	227	**3,000**				**6,000**			
5	15	2	2	1,525	1,550	231	231	3,000	3,050	454	454	6,000	6,050	904	904
15	25	3	3	1,550	1,575	234	234	3,050	3,100	461	461	6,050	6,100	911	911
25	50	6	6	1,575	1,600	238	238	3,100	3,150	469	469	6,100	6,150	919	919
50	75	9	9					3,150	3,200	476	476	6,150	6,200	926	926
75	100	13	13	1,600	1,625	242	242	3,200	3,250	484	484	6,200	6,250	934	934
				1,625	1,650	246	246	3,250	3,300	491	491	6,250	6,300	941	941
100	125	17	17	1,650	1,675	249	249	3,300	3,350	499	499	6,300	6,350	949	949
125	150	21	21	1,675	1,700	253	253	3,350	3,400	506	506	6,350	6,400	956	956
150	175	24	24					3,400	3,450	514	514	6,400	6,450	964	964
175	200	28	28	1,700	1,725	257	257	3,450	3,500	521	521	6,450	6,500	971	971
				1,725	1,750	261	261	3,500	3,550	529	529	6,500	6,550	979	979
200	225	32	32	1,750	1,775	264	264	3,550	3,600	536	536	6,550	6,600	986	986
225	250	36	36	1,775	1,800	268	268	3,600	3,650	544	544	6,600	6,650	994	994
250	275	39	39					3,650	3,700	551	551	6,650	6,700	1,001	1,001
275	300	43	43	1,800	1,825	272	272	3,700	3,750	559	559	6,700	6,750	1,009	1,009
				1,825	1,850	276	276	3,750	3,800	566	566	6,750	6,800	1,016	1,016
300	325	47	47	1,850	1,875	279	279	3,800	3,850	574	574	6,800	6,850	1,024	1,024
325	350	51	51	1,875	1,900	283	283	3,850	3,900	581	581	6,850	6,900	1,031	1,031
350	375	54	54					3,900	3,950	589	589	6,900	6,950	1,039	1,039
375	400	58	58	1,900	1,925	287	287	3,950	4,000	596	596	6,950	7,000	1,046	1,046
				1,925	1,950	291	291	**4,000**				**7,000**			
400	425	62	62	1,950	1,975	294	294	4,000	4,050	604	604	7,000	7,050	1,054	1,054
425	450	66	66	1,975	2,000	298	298	4,050	4,100	611	611	7,050	7,100	1,061	1,061
450	475	69	69	**2,000**				4,100	4,150	619	619	7,100	7,150	1,069	1,069
475	500	73	73	2,000	2,025	302	302	4,150	4,200	626	626	7,150	7,200	1,076	1,076
				2,025	2,050	306	306	4,200	4,250	634	634	7,200	7,250	1,084	1,084
500	525	77	77	2,050	2,075	309	309	4,250	4,300	641	641	7,250	7,300	1,091	1,091
525	550	81	81	2,075	2,100	313	313	4,300	4,350	649	649	7,300	7,350	1,099	1,099
550	575	84	84	2,100	2,125	317	317	4,350	4,400	656	656	7,350	7,400	1,106	1,106
575	600	88	88	2,125	2,150	321	321	4,400	4,450	664	664	7,400	7,450	1,114	1,114
600	625	92	92	2,150	2,175	324	324	4,450	4,500	671	671	7,450	7,500	1,121	1,121
625	650	96	96	2,175	2,200	328	328	4,500	4,550	679	679	7,500	7,550	1,129	1,129
650	675	99	99	2,200	2,225	332	332	4,550	4,600	686	686	7,550	7,600	1,136	1,136
675	700	103	103	2,225	2,250	336	336	4,600	4,650	694	694	7,600	7,650	1,144	1,144
700	725	107	107	2,250	2,275	339	339	4,650	4,700	701	701	7,650	7,700	1,151	1,151
725	750	111	111	2,275	2,300	343	343	4,700	4,750	709	709	7,700	7,750	1,159	1,159
750	775	114	114	2,300	2,325	347	347	4,750	4,800	716	716	7,750	7,800	1,166	1,166
775	800	118	118	2,325	2,350	351	351	4,800	4,850	724	724	7,800	7,850	1,174	1,174
800	825	122	122	2,350	2,375	354	354	4,850	4,900	731	731	7,850	7,900	1,181	1,181
825	850	126	126	2,375	2,400	358	358	4,900	4,950	739	739	7,900	7,950	1,189	1,189
850	875	129	129	2,400	2,425	362	362	4,950	5,000	746	746	7,950	8,000	1,196	1,196
875	900	133	133	2,425	2,450	366	366	**5,000**				**8,000**			
900	925	137	137	2,450	2,475	369	369	5,000	5,050	754	754	8,000	8,050	1,204	1,204
925	950	141	141	2,475	2,500	373	373	5,050	5,100	761	761	8,050	8,100	1,211	1,211
950	975	144	144	2,500	2,525	377	377	5,100	5,150	769	769	8,100	8,150	1,219	1,219
975	1,000	148	148	2,525	2,550	381	381	5,150	5,200	776	776	8,150	8,200	1,226	1,226
1,000				2,550	2,575	384	384	5,200	5,250	784	784	8,200	8,250	1,234	1,234
1,000	1,025	152	152	2,575	2,600	388	388	5,250	5,300	791	791	8,250	8,300	1,241	1,241
1,025	1,050	156	156	2,600	2,625	392	392	5,300	5,350	799	799	8,300	8,350	1,249	1,249
1,050	1,075	159	159	2,625	2,650	396	396	5,350	5,400	806	806	8,350	8,400	1,256	1,256
1,075	1,100	163	163	2,650	2,675	399	399	5,400	5,450	814	814	8,400	8,450	1,264	1,264
1,100	1,125	167	167	2,675	2,700	403	403	5,450	5,500	821	821	8,450	8,500	1,271	1,271
1,125	1,150	171	171	2,700	2,725	407	407	5,500	5,550	829	829	8,500	8,550	1,279	1,279
1,150	1,175	174	174	2,725	2,750	411	411	5,550	5,600	836	836	8,550	8,600	1,286	1,286
1,175	1,200	178	178	2,750	2,775	414	414	5,600	5,650	844	844	8,600	8,650	1,294	1,294
1,200	1,225	182	182	2,775	2,800	418	418	5,650	5,700	851	851	8,650	8,700	1,301	1,301
1,225	1,250	186	186	2,800	2,825	422	422	5,700	5,750	859	859	8,700	8,750	1,309	1,309
1,250	1,275	189	189	2,825	2,850	426	426	5,750	5,800	866	866	8,750	8,800	1,316	1,316
1,275	1,300	193	193	2,850	2,875	429	429	5,800	5,850	874	874	8,800	8,850	1,324	1,324
1,300	1,325	197	197	2,875	2,900	433	433	5,850	5,900	881	881	8,850	8,900	1,331	1,331
1,325	1,350	201	201	2,900	2,925	437	437	5,900	5,950	889	889	8,900	8,950	1,339	1,339
1,350	1,375	204	204	2,925	2,950	441	441	5,950	6,000	896	896	8,950	9,000	1,346	1,346
1,375	1,400	208	208	2,950	2,975	444	444								
1,400	1,425	212	212	2,975	3,000	448	448								
1,425	1,450	216	216												
1,450	1,475	219	219												
1,475	1,500	223	223												

Continued on next page

Columns for each block: **If Form 1040EZ, line 6, is — At least / But less than** and **And you are — Single / Married filing jointly. Your tax is—**

9,000

At least	But less than	Single	Married filing jointly
9,000	9,050	1,354	1,354
9,050	9,100	1,361	1,361
9,100	9,150	1,369	1,369
9,150	9,200	1,376	1,376
9,200	9,250	1,384	1,384
9,250	9,300	1,391	1,391
9,300	9,350	1,399	1,399
9,350	9,400	1,406	1,406
9,400	9,450	1,414	1,414
9,450	9,500	1,421	1,421
9,500	9,550	1,429	1,429
9,550	9,600	1,436	1,436
9,600	9,650	1,444	1,444
9,650	9,700	1,451	1,451
9,700	9,750	1,459	1,459
9,750	9,800	1,466	1,466
9,800	9,850	1,474	1,474
9,850	9,900	1,481	1,481
9,900	9,950	1,489	1,489
9,950	10,000	1,496	1,496

10,000

At least	But less than	Single	Married filing jointly
10,000	10,050	1,504	1,504
10,050	10,100	1,511	1,511
10,100	10,150	1,519	1,519
10,150	10,200	1,526	1,526
10,200	10,250	1,534	1,534
10,250	10,300	1,541	1,541
10,300	10,350	1,549	1,549
10,350	10,400	1,556	1,556
10,400	10,450	1,564	1,564
10,450	10,500	1,571	1,571
10,500	10,550	1,579	1,579
10,550	10,600	1,586	1,586
10,600	10,650	1,594	1,594
10,650	10,700	1,601	1,601
10,700	10,750	1,609	1,609
10,750	10,800	1,616	1,616
10,800	10,850	1,624	1,624
10,850	10,900	1,631	1,631
10,900	10,950	1,639	1,639
10,950	11,000	1,646	1,646

11,000

At least	But less than	Single	Married filing jointly
11,000	11,050	1,654	1,654
11,050	11,100	1,661	1,661
11,100	11,150	1,669	1,669
11,150	11,200	1,676	1,676
11,200	11,250	1,684	1,684
11,250	11,300	1,691	1,691
11,300	11,350	1,699	1,699
11,350	11,400	1,706	1,706
11,400	11,450	1,714	1,714
11,450	11,500	1,721	1,721
11,500	11,550	1,729	1,729
11,550	11,600	1,736	1,736
11,600	11,650	1,744	1,744
11,650	11,700	1,751	1,751
11,700	11,750	1,759	1,759
11,750	11,800	1,766	1,766
11,800	11,850	1,774	1,774
11,850	11,900	1,781	1,781
11,900	11,950	1,789	1,789
11,950	12,000	1,796	1,796

12,000

At least	But less than	Single	Married filing jointly
12,000	12,050	1,804	1,804
12,050	12,100	1,811	1,811
12,100	12,150	1,819	1,819
12,150	12,200	1,826	1,826
12,200	12,250	1,834	1,834
12,250	12,300	1,841	1,841
12,300	12,350	1,849	1,849
12,350	12,400	1,856	1,856
12,400	12,450	1,864	1,864
12,450	12,500	1,871	1,871
12,500	12,550	1,879	1,879
12,550	12,600	1,886	1,886
12,600	12,650	1,894	1,894
12,650	12,700	1,901	1,901
12,700	12,750	1,909	1,909
12,750	12,800	1,916	1,916
12,800	12,850	1,924	1,924
12,850	12,900	1,931	1,931
12,900	12,950	1,939	1,939
12,950	13,000	1,946	1,946

13,000

At least	But less than	Single	Married filing jointly
13,000	13,050	1,954	1,954
13,050	13,100	1,961	1,961
13,100	13,150	1,969	1,969
13,150	13,200	1,976	1,976
13,200	13,250	1,984	1,984
13,250	13,300	1,991	1,991
13,300	13,350	1,999	1,999
13,350	13,400	2,006	2,006
13,400	13,450	2,014	2,014
13,450	13,500	2,021	2,021
13,500	13,550	2,029	2,029
13,550	13,600	2,036	2,036
13,600	13,650	2,044	2,044
13,650	13,700	2,051	2,051
13,700	13,750	2,059	2,059
13,750	13,800	2,066	2,066
13,800	13,850	2,074	2,074
13,850	13,900	2,081	2,081
13,900	13,950	2,089	2,089
13,950	14,000	2,096	2,096

14,000

At least	But less than	Single	Married filing jointly
14,000	14,050	2,104	2,104
14,050	14,100	2,111	2,111
14,100	14,150	2,119	2,119
14,150	14,200	2,126	2,126
14,200	14,250	2,134	2,134
14,250	14,300	2,141	2,141
14,300	14,350	2,149	2,149
14,350	14,400	2,156	2,156
14,400	14,450	2,164	2,164
14,450	14,500	2,171	2,171
14,500	14,550	2,179	2,179
14,550	14,600	2,186	2,186
14,600	14,650	2,194	2,194
14,650	14,700	2,201	2,201
14,700	14,750	2,209	2,209
14,750	14,800	2,216	2,216
14,800	14,850	2,224	2,224
14,850	14,900	2,231	2,231
14,900	14,950	2,239	2,239
14,950	15,000	2,246	2,246

15,000

At least	But less than	Single	Married filing jointly
15,000	15,050	2,254	2,254
15,050	15,100	2,261	2,261
15,100	15,150	2,269	2,269
15,150	15,200	2,276	2,276
15,200	15,250	2,284	2,284
15,250	15,300	2,291	2,291
15,300	15,350	2,299	2,299
15,350	15,400	2,306	2,306
15,400	15,450	2,314	2,314
15,450	15,500	2,321	2,321
15,500	15,550	2,329	2,329
15,550	15,600	2,336	2,336
15,600	15,650	2,344	2,344
15,650	15,700	2,351	2,351
15,700	15,750	2,359	2,359
15,750	15,800	2,366	2,366
15,800	15,850	2,374	2,374
15,850	15,900	2,381	2,381
15,900	15,950	2,389	2,389
15,950	16,000	2,396	2,396

16,000

At least	But less than	Single	Married filing jointly
16,000	16,050	2,404	2,404
16,050	16,100	2,411	2,411
16,100	16,150	2,419	2,419
16,150	16,200	2,426	2,426
16,200	16,250	2,434	2,434
16,250	16,300	2,441	2,441
16,300	16,350	2,449	2,449
16,350	16,400	2,456	2,456
16,400	16,450	2,464	2,464
16,450	16,500	2,471	2,471
16,500	16,550	2,479	2,479
16,550	16,600	2,486	2,486
16,600	16,650	2,494	2,494
16,650	16,700	2,501	2,501
16,700	16,750	2,509	2,509
16,750	16,800	2,516	2,516
16,800	16,850	2,524	2,524
16,850	16,900	2,531	2,531
16,900	16,950	2,539	2,539
16,950	17,000	2,546	2,546

17,000

At least	But less than	Single	Married filing jointly
17,000	17,050	2,554	2,554
17,050	17,100	2,561	2,561
17,100	17,150	2,569	2,569
17,150	17,200	2,576	2,576
17,200	17,250	2,584	2,584
17,250	17,300	2,591	2,591
17,300	17,350	2,599	2,599
17,350	17,400	2,606	2,606
17,400	17,450	2,614	2,614
17,450	17,500	2,621	2,621
17,500	17,550	2,629	2,629
17,550	17,600	2,636	2,636
17,600	17,650	2,644	2,644
17,650	17,700	2,651	2,651
17,700	17,750	2,659	2,659
17,750	17,800	2,666	2,666
17,800	17,850	2,674	2,674
17,850	17,900	2,681	2,681
17,900	17,950	2,689	2,689
17,950	18,000	2,696	2,696

18,000

At least	But less than	Single	Married filing jointly
18,000	18,050	2,704	2,704
18,050	18,100	2,711	2,711
18,100	18,150	2,719	2,719
18,150	18,200	2,726	2,726
18,200	18,250	2,734	2,734
18,250	18,300	2,741	2,741
18,300	18,350	2,749	2,749
18,350	18,400	2,756	2,756
18,400	18,450	2,764	2,764
18,450	18,500	2,771	2,771
18,500	18,550	2,779	2,779
18,550	18,600	2,786	2,786
18,600	18,650	2,794	2,794
18,650	18,700	2,801	2,801
18,700	18,750	2,809	2,809
18,750	18,800	2,816	2,816
18,800	18,850	2,824	2,824
18,850	18,900	2,831	2,831
18,900	18,950	2,839	2,839
18,950	19,000	2,846	2,846

19,000

At least	But less than	Single	Married filing jointly
19,000	19,050	2,854	2,854
19,050	19,100	2,861	2,861
19,100	19,150	2,869	2,869
19,150	19,200	2,876	2,876
19,200	19,250	2,884	2,884
19,250	19,300	2,891	2,891
19,300	19,350	2,899	2,899
19,350	19,400	2,906	2,906
19,400	19,450	2,914	2,914
19,450	19,500	2,921	2,921
19,500	19,550	2,929	2,929
19,550	19,600	2,936	2,936
19,600	19,650	2,944	2,944
19,650	19,700	2,951	2,951
19,700	19,750	2,959	2,959
19,750	19,800	2,966	2,966
19,800	19,850	2,974	2,974
19,850	19,900	2,981	2,981
19,900	19,950	2,989	2,989
19,950	20,000	2,996	2,996

20,000

At least	But less than	Single	Married filing jointly
20,000	20,050	3,004	3,004
20,050	20,100	3,011	3,011
20,100	20,150	3,019	3,019
20,150	20,200	3,026	3,026
20,200	20,250	3,034	3,034
20,250	20,300	3,041	3,041
20,300	20,350	3,049	3,049
20,350	20,400	3,056	3,056
20,400	20,450	3,064	3,064
20,450	20,500	3,071	3,071
20,500	20,550	3,079	3,079
20,550	20,600	3,086	3,086
20,600	20,650	3,094	3,094
20,650	20,700	3,101	3,101
20,700	20,750	3,109	3,109
20,750	20,800	3,116	3,116
20,800	20,850	3,124	3,124
20,850	20,900	3,131	3,131
20,900	20,950	3,139	3,139
20,950	21,000	3,146	3,146

Continued on next page

21,000

If Form 1040EZ, line 6, is —		And you are —	
At least	But less than	Single	Married filing jointly
		Your tax is—	
21,000	21,050	3,154	3,154
21,050	21,100	3,161	3,161
21,100	21,150	3,169	3,169
21,150	21,200	3,176	3,176
21,200	21,250	3,184	3,184
21,250	21,300	3,191	3,191
21,300	21,350	3,199	3,199
21,350	21,400	3,206	3,206
21,400	21,450	3,214	3,214
21,450	21,500	3,221	3,221
21,500	21,550	3,229	3,229
21,550	21,600	3,236	3,236
21,600	21,650	3,244	3,244
21,650	21,700	3,251	3,251
21,700	21,750	3,259	3,259
21,750	21,800	3,266	3,266
21,800	21,850	3,274	3,274
21,850	21,900	3,281	3,281
21,900	21,950	3,289	3,289
21,950	22,000	3,296	3,296

22,000

At least	But less than	Single	Married filing jointly
22,000	22,050	3,304	3,304
22,050	22,100	3,311	3,311
22,100	22,150	3,322	3,319
22,150	22,200	3,336	3,326
22,200	22,250	3,350	3,334
22,250	22,300	3,364	3,341
22,300	22,350	3,378	3,349
22,350	22,400	3,392	3,356
22,400	22,450	3,406	3,364
22,450	22,500	3,420	3,371
22,500	22,550	3,434	3,379
22,550	22,600	3,448	3,386
22,600	22,650	3,462	3,394
22,650	22,700	3,476	3,401
22,700	22,750	3,490	3,409
22,750	22,800	3,504	3,416
22,800	22,850	3,518	3,424
22,850	22,900	3,532	3,431
22,900	22,950	3,546	3,439
22,950	23,000	3,560	3,446

23,000

At least	But less than	Single	Married filing jointly
23,000	23,050	3,574	3,454
23,050	23,100	3,588	3,461
23,100	23,150	3,602	3,469
23,150	23,200	3,616	3,476
23,200	23,250	3,630	3,484
23,250	23,300	3,644	3,491
23,300	23,350	3,658	3,499
23,350	23,400	3,672	3,506
23,400	23,450	3,686	3,514
23,450	23,500	3,700	3,521
23,500	23,550	3,714	3,529
23,550	23,600	3,728	3,536
23,600	23,650	3,742	3,544
23,650	23,700	3,756	3,551
23,700	23,750	3,770	3,559
23,750	23,800	3,784	3,566
23,800	23,850	3,798	3,574
23,850	23,900	3,812	3,581
23,900	23,950	3,826	3,589
23,950	24,000	3,840	3,596

24,000

At least	But less than	Single	Married filing jointly
24,000	24,050	3,854	3,604
24,050	24,100	3,868	3,611
24,100	24,150	3,882	3,619
24,150	24,200	3,896	3,626
24,200	24,250	3,910	3,634
24,250	24,300	3,924	3,641
24,300	24,350	3,938	3,649
24,350	24,400	3,952	3,656
24,400	24,450	3,966	3,664
24,450	24,500	3,980	3,671
24,500	24,550	3,994	3,679
24,550	24,600	4,008	3,686
24,600	24,650	4,022	3,694
24,650	24,700	4,036	3,701
24,700	24,750	4,050	3,709
24,750	24,800	4,064	3,716
24,800	24,850	4,078	3,724
24,850	24,900	4,092	3,731
24,900	24,950	4,106	3,739
24,950	25,000	4,120	3,746

25,000

At least	But less than	Single	Married filing jointly
25,000	25,050	4,134	3,754
25,050	25,100	4,148	3,761
25,100	25,150	4,162	3,769
25,150	25,200	4,176	3,776
25,200	25,250	4,190	3,784
25,250	25,300	4,204	3,791
25,300	25,350	4,218	3,799
25,350	25,400	4,232	3,806
25,400	25,450	4,246	3,814
25,450	25,500	4,260	3,821
25,500	25,550	4,274	3,829
25,550	25,600	4,288	3,836
25,600	25,650	4,302	3,844
25,650	25,700	4,316	3,851
25,700	25,750	4,330	3,859
25,750	25,800	4,344	3,866
25,800	25,850	4,358	3,874
25,850	25,900	4,372	3,881
25,900	25,950	4,386	3,889
25,950	26,000	4,400	3,896

26,000

At least	But less than	Single	Married filing jointly
26,000	26,050	4,414	3,904
26,050	26,100	4,428	3,911
26,100	26,150	4,442	3,919
26,150	26,200	4,456	3,926
26,200	26,250	4,470	3,934
26,250	26,300	4,484	3,941
26,300	26,350	4,498	3,949
26,350	26,400	4,512	3,956
26,400	26,450	4,526	3,964
26,450	26,500	4,540	3,971
26,500	26,550	4,554	3,979
26,550	26,600	4,568	3,986
26,600	26,650	4,582	3,994
26,650	26,700	4,596	4,001
26,700	26,750	4,610	4,009
26,750	26,800	4,624	4,016
26,800	26,850	4,638	4,024
26,850	26,900	4,652	4,031
26,900	26,950	4,666	4,039
26,950	27,000	4,680	4,046

27,000

At least	But less than	Single	Married filing jointly
27,000	27,050	4,694	4,054
27,050	27,100	4,708	4,061
27,100	27,150	4,722	4,069
27,150	27,200	4,736	4,076
27,200	27,250	4,750	4,084
27,250	27,300	4,764	4,091
27,300	27,350	4,778	4,099
27,350	27,400	4,792	4,106
27,400	27,450	4,806	4,114
27,450	27,500	4,820	4,121
27,500	27,550	4,834	4,129
27,550	27,600	4,848	4,136
27,600	27,650	4,862	4,144
27,650	27,700	4,876	4,151
27,700	27,750	4,890	4,159
27,750	27,800	4,904	4,166
27,800	27,850	4,918	4,174
27,850	27,900	4,932	4,181
27,900	27,950	4,946	4,189
27,950	28,000	4,960	4,196

28,000

At least	But less than	Single	Married filing jointly
28,000	28,050	4,974	4,204
28,050	28,100	4,988	4,211
28,100	28,150	5,002	4,219
28,150	28,200	5,016	4,226
28,200	28,250	5,030	4,234
28,250	28,300	5,044	4,241
28,300	28,350	5,058	4,249
28,350	28,400	5,072	4,256
28,400	28,450	5,086	4,264
28,450	28,500	5,100	4,271
28,500	28,550	5,114	4,279
28,550	28,600	5,128	4,286
28,600	28,650	5,142	4,294
28,650	28,700	5,156	4,301
28,700	28,750	5,170	4,309
28,750	28,800	5,184	4,316
28,800	28,850	5,198	4,324
28,850	28,900	5,212	4,331
28,900	28,950	5,226	4,339
28,950	29,000	5,240	4,346

29,000

At least	But less than	Single	Married filing jointly
29,000	29,050	5,254	4,354
29,050	29,100	5,268	4,361
29,100	29,150	5,282	4,369
29,150	29,200	5,296	4,376
29,200	29,250	5,310	4,384
29,250	29,300	5,324	4,391
29,300	29,350	5,338	4,399
29,350	29,400	5,352	4,406
29,400	29,450	5,366	4,414
29,450	29,500	5,380	4,421
29,500	29,550	5,394	4,429
29,550	29,600	5,408	4,436
29,600	29,650	5,422	4,444
29,650	29,700	5,436	4,451
29,700	29,750	5,450	4,459
29,750	29,800	5,464	4,466
29,800	29,850	5,478	4,474
29,850	29,900	5,492	4,481
29,900	29,950	5,506	4,489
29,950	30,000	5,520	4,496

30,000

At least	But less than	Single	Married filing jointly
30,000	30,050	5,534	4,504
30,050	30,100	5,548	4,511
30,100	30,150	5,562	4,519
30,150	30,200	5,576	4,526
30,200	30,250	5,590	4,534
30,250	30,300	5,604	4,541
30,300	30,350	5,618	4,549
30,350	30,400	5,632	4,556
30,400	30,450	5,646	4,564
30,450	30,500	5,660	4,571
30,500	30,550	5,674	4,579
30,550	30,600	5,688	4,586
30,600	30,650	5,702	4,594
30,650	30,700	5,716	4,601
30,700	30,750	5,730	4,609
30,750	30,800	5,744	4,616
30,800	30,850	5,758	4,624
30,850	30,900	5,772	4,631
30,900	30,950	5,786	4,639
30,950	31,000	5,800	4,646

31,000

At least	But less than	Single	Married filing jointly
31,000	31,050	5,814	4,654
31,050	31,100	5,828	4,661
31,100	31,150	5,842	4,669
31,150	31,200	5,856	4,676
31,200	31,250	5,870	4,684
31,250	31,300	5,884	4,691
31,300	31,350	5,898	4,699
31,350	31,400	5,912	4,706
31,400	31,450	5,926	4,714
31,450	31,500	5,940	4,721
31,500	31,550	5,954	4,729
31,550	31,600	5,968	4,736
31,600	31,650	5,982	4,744
31,650	31,700	5,996	4,751
31,700	31,750	6,010	4,759
31,750	31,800	6,024	4,766
31,800	31,850	6,038	4,774
31,850	31,900	6,052	4,781
31,900	31,950	6,066	4,789
31,950	32,000	6,080	4,796

32,000

At least	But less than	Single	Married filing jointly
32,000	32,050	6,094	4,804
32,050	32,100	6,108	4,811
32,100	32,150	6,122	4,819
32,150	32,200	6,136	4,826
32,200	32,250	6,150	4,834
32,250	32,300	6,164	4,841
32,300	32,350	6,178	4,849
32,350	32,400	6,192	4,856
32,400	32,450	6,206	4,864
32,450	32,500	6,220	4,871
32,500	32,550	6,234	4,879
32,550	32,600	6,248	4,886
32,600	32,650	6,262	4,894
32,650	32,700	6,276	4,901
32,700	32,750	6,290	4,909
32,750	32,800	6,304	4,916
32,800	32,850	6,318	4,924
32,850	32,900	6,332	4,931
32,900	32,950	6,346	4,939
32,950	33,000	6,360	4,946

Continued on next page

20-- 1040EZ Tax Table —Continued

If Form 1040EZ, line 6, is —		And you are —	
At least	But less than	Single	Married filing jointly
		Your tax is—	

33,000

At least	But less than	Single	Married filing jointly
33,000	33,050	6,374	4,954
33,050	33,100	6,388	4,961
33,100	33,150	6,402	4,969
33,150	33,200	6,416	4,976
33,200	33,250	6,430	4,984
33,250	33,300	6,444	4,991
33,300	33,350	6,458	4,999
33,350	33,400	6,472	5,006
33,400	33,450	6,486	5,014
33,450	33,500	6,500	5,021
33,500	33,550	6,514	5,029
33,550	33,600	6,528	5,036
33,600	33,650	6,542	5,044
33,650	33,700	6,556	5,051
33,700	33,750	6,570	5,059
33,750	33,800	6,584	5,066
33,800	33,850	6,598	5,074
33,850	33,900	6,612	5,081
33,900	33,950	6,626	5,089
33,950	34,000	6,640	5,096

34,000

At least	But less than	Single	Married filing jointly
34,000	34,050	6,654	5,104
34,050	34,100	6,668	5,111
34,100	34,150	6,682	5,119
34,150	34,200	6,696	5,126
34,200	34,250	6,710	5,134
34,250	34,300	6,724	5,141
34,300	34,350	6,738	5,149
34,350	34,400	6,752	5,156
34,400	34,450	6,766	5,164
34,450	34,500	6,780	5,171
34,500	34,550	6,794	5,179
34,550	34,600	6,808	5,186
34,600	34,650	6,822	5,194
34,650	34,700	6,836	5,201
34,700	34,750	6,850	5,209
34,750	34,800	6,864	5,216
34,800	34,850	6,878	5,224
34,850	34,900	6,892	5,231
34,900	34,950	6,906	5,239
34,950	35,000	6,920	5,246

35,000

At least	But less than	Single	Married filing jointly
35,000	35,050	6,934	5,254
35,050	35,100	6,948	5,261
35,100	35,150	6,962	5,269
35,150	35,200	6,976	5,276
35,200	35,250	6,990	5,284
35,250	35,300	7,004	5,291
35,300	35,350	7,018	5,299
35,350	35,400	7,032	5,306
35,400	35,450	7,046	5,314
35,450	35,500	7,060	5,321
35,500	35,550	7,074	5,329
35,550	35,600	7,088	5,336
35,600	35,650	7,102	5,344
35,650	35,700	7,116	5,351
35,700	35,750	7,130	5,359
35,750	35,800	7,144	5,366
35,800	35,850	7,158	5,374
35,850	35,900	7,172	5,381
35,900	35,950	7,186	5,389
35,950	36,000	7,200	5,396

36,000

At least	But less than	Single	Married filing jointly
36,000	36,050	7,214	5,404
36,050	36,100	7,228	5,411
36,100	36,150	7,242	5,419
36,150	36,200	7,256	5,426
36,200	36,250	7,270	5,434
36,250	36,300	7,284	5,441
36,300	36,350	7,298	5,449
36,350	36,400	7,312	5,456
36,400	36,450	7,326	5,464
36,450	36,500	7,340	5,471
36,500	36,550	7,354	5,479
36,550	36,600	7,368	5,486
36,600	36,650	7,382	5,494
36,650	36,700	7,396	5,501
36,700	36,750	7,410	5,509
36,750	36,800	7,424	5,516
36,800	36,850	7,438	5,524
36,850	36,900	7,452	5,531
36,900	36,950	7,466	5,542
36,950	37,000	7,480	5,556

37,000

At least	But less than	Single	Married filing jointly
37,000	37,050	7,494	5,570
37,050	37,100	7,508	5,584
37,100	37,150	7,522	5,598
37,150	37,200	7,536	5,612
37,200	37,250	7,550	5,626
37,250	37,300	7,564	5,640
37,300	37,350	7,578	5,654
37,350	37,400	7,592	5,668
37,400	37,450	7,606	5,682
37,450	37,500	7,620	5,696
37,500	37,550	7,634	5,710
37,550	37,600	7,648	5,724
37,600	37,650	7,662	5,738
37,650	37,700	7,676	5,752
37,700	37,750	7,690	5,766
37,750	37,800	7,704	5,780
37,800	37,850	7,718	5,794
37,850	37,900	7,732	5,808
37,900	37,950	7,746	5,822
37,950	38,000	7,760	5,836

38,000

At least	But less than	Single	Married filing jointly
38,000	38,050	7,774	5,850
38,050	38,100	7,788	5,864
38,100	38,150	7,802	5,878
38,150	38,200	7,816	5,892
38,200	38,250	7,830	5,906
38,250	38,300	7,844	5,920
38,300	38,350	7,858	5,934
38,350	38,400	7,872	5,948
38,400	38,450	7,886	5,962
38,450	38,500	7,900	5,976
38,500	38,550	7,914	5,990
38,550	38,600	7,928	6,004
38,600	38,650	7,942	6,018
38,650	38,700	7,956	6,032
38,700	38,750	7,970	6,046
38,750	38,800	7,984	6,060
38,800	38,850	7,998	6,074
38,850	38,900	8,012	6,088
38,900	38,950	8,026	6,102
38,950	39,000	8,040	6,116

39,000

At least	But less than	Single	Married filing jointly
39,000	39,050	8,054	6,130
39,050	39,100	8,068	6,144
39,100	39,150	8,082	6,158
39,150	39,200	8,096	6,172
39,200	39,250	8,110	6,186
39,250	39,300	8,124	6,200
39,300	39,350	8,138	6,214
39,350	39,400	8,152	6,228
39,400	39,450	8,166	6,242
39,450	39,500	8,180	6,256
39,500	39,550	8,194	6,270
39,550	39,600	8,208	6,284
39,600	39,650	8,222	6,298
39,650	39,700	8,236	6,312
39,700	39,750	8,250	6,326
39,750	39,800	8,264	6,340
39,800	39,850	8,278	6,354
39,850	39,900	8,292	6,368
39,900	39,950	8,306	6,382
39,950	40,000	8,320	6,396

40,000

At least	But less than	Single	Married filing jointly
40,000	40,050	8,334	6,410
40,050	40,100	8,348	6,424
40,100	40,150	8,362	6,438
40,150	40,200	8,376	6,452
40,200	40,250	8,390	6,466
40,250	40,300	8,404	6,480
40,300	40,350	8,418	6,494
40,350	40,400	8,432	6,508
40,400	40,450	8,446	6,522
40,450	40,500	8,460	6,536
40,500	40,550	8,474	6,550
40,550	40,600	8,488	6,564
40,600	40,650	8,502	6,578
40,650	40,700	8,516	6,592
40,700	40,750	8,530	6,606
40,750	40,800	8,544	6,620
40,800	40,850	8,558	6,634
40,850	40,900	8,572	6,648
40,900	40,950	8,586	6,662
40,950	41,000	8,600	6,676

41,000

At least	But less than	Single	Married filing jointly
41,000	41,050	8,614	6,690
41,050	41,100	8,628	6,704
41,100	41,150	8,642	6,718
41,150	41,200	8,656	6,732
41,200	41,250	8,670	6,746
41,250	41,300	8,684	6,760
41,300	41,350	8,698	6,774
41,350	41,400	8,712	6,788
41,400	41,450	8,726	6,802
41,450	41,500	8,740	6,816
41,500	41,550	8,754	6,830
41,550	41,600	8,768	6,844
41,600	41,650	8,782	6,858
41,650	41,700	8,796	6,872
41,700	41,750	8,810	6,886
41,750	41,800	8,824	6,900
41,800	41,850	8,838	6,914
41,850	41,900	8,852	6,928
41,900	41,950	8,866	6,942
41,950	42,000	8,880	6,956

42,000

At least	But less than	Single	Married filing jointly
42,000	42,050	8,894	6,970
42,050	42,100	8,908	6,984
42,100	42,150	8,922	6,998
42,150	42,200	8,936	7,012
42,200	42,250	8,950	7,026
42,250	42,300	8,964	7,040
42,300	42,350	8,978	7,054
42,350	42,400	8,992	7,068
42,400	42,450	9,006	7,082
42,450	42,500	9,020	7,096
42,500	42,550	9,034	7,110
42,550	42,600	9,048	7,124
42,600	42,650	9,062	7,138
42,650	42,700	9,076	7,152
42,700	42,750	9,090	7,166
42,750	42,800	9,104	7,180
42,800	42,850	9,118	7,194
42,850	42,900	9,132	7,208
42,900	42,950	9,146	7,222
42,950	43,000	9,160	7,236

43,000

At least	But less than	Single	Married filing jointly
43,000	43,050	9,174	7,250
43,050	43,100	9,188	7,264
43,100	43,150	9,202	7,278
43,150	43,200	9,216	7,292
43,200	43,250	9,230	7,306
43,250	43,300	9,244	7,320
43,300	43,350	9,258	7,334
43,350	43,400	9,272	7,348
43,400	43,450	9,286	7,362
43,450	43,500	9,300	7,376
43,500	43,550	9,314	7,390
43,550	43,600	9,328	7,404
43,600	43,650	9,342	7,418
43,650	43,700	9,356	7,432
43,700	43,750	9,370	7,446
43,750	43,800	9,384	7,460
43,800	43,850	9,398	7,474
43,850	43,900	9,412	7,488
43,900	43,950	9,426	7,502
43,950	44,000	9,440	7,516

44,000

At least	But less than	Single	Married filing jointly
44,000	44,050	9,454	7,530
44,050	44,100	9,468	7,544
44,100	44,150	9,482	7,558
44,150	44,200	9,496	7,572
44,200	44,250	9,510	7,586
44,250	44,300	9,524	7,600
44,300	44,350	9,538	7,614
44,350	44,400	9,552	7,628
44,400	44,450	9,566	7,642
44,450	44,500	9,580	7,656
44,500	44,550	9,594	7,670
44,550	44,600	9,608	7,684
44,600	44,650	9,622	7,698
44,650	44,700	9,636	7,712
44,700	44,750	9,650	7,726
44,750	44,800	9,664	7,740
44,800	44,850	9,678	7,754
44,850	44,900	9,692	7,768
44,900	44,950	9,706	7,782
44,950	45,000	9,720	7,796

Continued on next page

If Form 1040EZ, line 6, is —		And you are —		If Form 1040EZ, line 6, is —		And you are —	
At least	But less than	Single	Married filing jointly	At least	But less than	Single	Married filing jointly
		Your tax is—				Your tax is—	

45,000				**48,000**			
45,000	45,050	9,734	7,810	48,000	48,050	10,574	8,650
45,050	45,100	9,748	7,824	48,050	48,100	10,588	8,664
45,100	45,150	9,762	7,838	48,100	48,150	10,602	8,678
45,150	45,200	9,776	7,852	48,150	48,200	10,616	8,692
45,200	45,250	9,790	7,866	48,200	48,250	10,630	8,706
45,250	45,300	9,804	7,880	48,250	48,300	10,644	8,720
45,300	45,350	9,818	7,894	48,300	48,350	10,658	8,734
45,350	45,400	9,832	7,908	48,350	48,400	10,672	8,748
45,400	45,450	9,846	7,922	48,400	48,450	10,686	8,762
45,450	45,500	9,860	7,936	48,450	48,500	10,700	8,776
45,500	45,550	9,874	7,950	48,500	48,550	10,714	8,790
45,550	45,600	9,888	7,964	48,550	48,600	10,728	8,804
45,600	45,650	9,902	7,978	48,600	48,650	10,742	8,818
45,650	45,700	9,916	7,992	48,650	48,700	10,756	8,832
45,700	45,750	9,930	8,006	48,700	48,750	10,770	8,846
45,750	45,800	9,944	8,020	48,750	48,800	10,784	8,860
45,800	45,850	9,958	8,034	48,800	48,850	10,798	8,874
45,850	45,900	9,972	8,048	48,850	48,900	10,812	8,888
45,900	45,950	9,986	8,062	48,900	48,950	10,826	8,902
45,950	46,000	10,000	8,076	48,950	49,000	10,840	8,916

46,000				**49,000**			
46,000	46,050	10,014	8,090	49,000	49,050	10,854	8,930
46,050	46,100	10,028	8,104	49,050	49,100	10,868	8,944
46,100	46,150	10,042	8,118	49,100	49,150	10,882	8,958
46,150	46,200	10,056	8,132	49,150	49,200	10,896	8,972
46,200	46,250	10,070	8,146	49,200	49,250	10,910	8,986
46,250	46,300	10,084	8,160	49,250	49,300	10,924	9,000
46,300	46,350	10,098	8,174	49,300	49,350	10,938	9,014
46,350	46,400	10,112	8,188	49,350	49,400	10,952	9,028
46,400	46,450	10,126	8,202	49,400	49,450	10,966	9,042
46,450	46,500	10,140	8,216	49,450	49,500	10,980	9,056
46,500	46,550	10,154	8,230	49,500	49,550	10,994	9,070
46,550	46,600	10,168	8,244	49,550	49,600	11,008	9,084
46,600	46,650	10,182	8,258	49,600	49,650	11,022	9,098
46,650	46,700	10,196	8,272	49,650	49,700	11,036	9,112
46,700	46,750	10,210	8,286	49,700	49,750	11,050	9,126
46,750	46,800	10,224	8,300	49,750	49,800	11,064	9,140
46,800	46,850	10,238	8,314	49,800	49,850	11,078	9,154
46,850	46,900	10,252	8,328	49,850	49,900	11,092	9,168
46,900	46,950	10,266	8,342	49,900	49,950	11,106	9,182
46,950	47,000	10,280	8,356	49,950	50,000	11,120	9,196

47,000			
47,000	47,050	10,294	8,370
47,050	47,100	10,308	8,384
47,100	47,150	10,322	8,398
47,150	47,200	10,336	8,412
47,200	47,250	10,350	8,426
47,250	47,300	10,364	8,440
47,300	47,350	10,378	8,454
47,350	47,400	10,392	8,468
47,400	47,450	10,406	8,482
47,450	47,500	10,420	8,496
47,500	47,550	10,434	8,510
47,550	47,600	10,448	8,524
47,600	47,650	10,462	8,538
47,650	47,700	10,476	8,552
47,700	47,750	10,490	8,566
47,750	47,800	10,504	8,580
47,800	47,850	10,518	8,594
47,850	47,900	10,532	8,608
47,900	47,950	10,546	8,622
47,950	48,000	10,560	8,636

$50,000 or over— use Form 1040

Appendix B

1040A Tax Tables

These tax tables are provided for taxpayers to compute the amount of income tax liability they owe for the tax year. The 1040A tax tables are included with the instructions for preparing Form 1040A. After you file your first income tax return, these tables will be mailed to you each year from the IRS to assist you in preparing your tax return. The first year you must file a tax return, you can obtain the instructions and tax tables online, at a post office, state department of revenue office, or federal tax office in your area, or you can write or call the IRS to have them mailed to you. The tables are simple and easy to use once you compute your taxable income.

Section 5—Tax Table

For persons with taxable incomes of less than $50,000

Example. Mr. and Mrs. Green are filing a joint return. Their taxable income on line 25 of Form 1040A is $23,250. First, they find the $23,250-23,300 income line. Next, they find the column for married filing jointly and read down the column. The amount shown where the income line and filing status column meet is $3,491. This is the tax amount they must enter on line 26 of Form 1040A.

At least	But less than	Single	Married filing jointly *	Married filing sepa-rately	Head of a house-hold
			Your tax is—		
23,200	23,250	3,630	3,484	4,105	3,484
23,250	23,300	3,644	(3,491)	4,119	3,491
23,300	23,350	3,658	3,499	4,133	3,499
23,350	23,400	3,672	3,506	4,147	3,506

If Form 1040A, line 25, is — At least	But less than	Single	Married filing jointly *	Married filing sepa-rately	Head of a house-hold
			Your tax is—		
$0	$5	$0	$0	$0	$0
5	15	2	2	2	2
15	25	3	3	3	3
25	50	6	6	6	6
50	75	9	9	9	9
75	100	13	13	13	13
100	125	17	17	17	17
125	150	21	21	21	21
150	175	24	24	24	24
175	200	28	28	28	28
200	225	32	32	32	32
225	250	36	36	36	36
250	275	39	39	39	39
275	300	43	43	43	43
300	325	47	47	47	47
325	350	51	51	51	51
350	375	54	54	54	54
375	400	58	58	58	58
400	425	62	62	62	62
425	450	66	66	66	66
450	475	69	69	69	69
475	500	73	73	73	73
500	525	77	77	77	77
525	550	81	81	81	81
550	575	84	84	84	84
575	600	88	88	88	88
600	625	92	92	92	92
625	650	96	96	96	96
650	675	99	99	99	99
675	700	103	103	103	103
700	725	107	107	107	107
725	750	111	111	111	111
750	775	114	114	114	114
775	800	118	118	118	118
800	825	122	122	122	122
825	850	126	126	126	126
850	875	129	129	129	129
875	900	133	133	133	133
900	925	137	137	137	137
925	950	141	141	141	141
950	975	144	144	144	144
975	1,000	148	148	148	148

1,000

At least	But less than	Single	Married filing jointly *	Married filing sepa-rately	Head of a house-hold
1,000	1,025	152	152	152	152
1,025	1,050	156	156	156	156
1,050	1,075	159	159	159	159
1,075	1,100	163	163	163	163
1,100	1,125	167	167	167	167
1,125	1,150	171	171	171	171
1,150	1,175	174	174	174	174
1,175	1,200	178	178	178	178
1,200	1,225	182	182	182	182
1,225	1,250	186	186	186	186
1,250	1,275	189	189	189	189
1,275	1,300	193	193	193	193

If Form 1040A, line 25, is — At least	But less than	Single	Married filing jointly *	Married filing sepa-rately	Head of a house-hold
			Your tax is—		
1,300	1,325	197	197	197	197
1,325	1,350	201	201	201	201
1,350	1,375	204	204	204	204
1,375	1,400	208	208	208	208
1,400	1,425	212	212	212	212
1,425	1,450	216	216	216	216
1,450	1,475	219	219	219	219
1,475	1,500	223	223	223	223
1,500	1,525	227	227	227	227
1,525	1,550	231	231	231	231
1,550	1,575	234	234	234	234
1,575	1,600	238	238	238	238
1,600	1,625	242	242	242	242
1,625	1,650	246	246	246	246
1,650	1,675	249	249	249	249
1,675	1,700	253	253	253	253
1,700	1,725	257	257	257	257
1,725	1,750	261	261	261	261
1,750	1,775	264	264	264	264
1,775	1,800	268	268	268	268
1,800	1,825	272	272	272	272
1,825	1,850	276	276	276	276
1,850	1,875	279	279	279	279
1,875	1,900	283	283	283	283
1,900	1,925	287	287	287	287
1,925	1,950	291	291	291	291
1,950	1,975	294	294	294	294
1,975	2,000	298	298	298	298

2,000

At least	But less than	Single	Married filing jointly *	Married filing sepa-rately	Head of a house-hold
2,000	2,025	302	302	302	302
2,025	2,050	306	306	306	306
2,050	2,075	309	309	309	309
2,075	2,100	313	313	313	313
2,100	2,125	317	317	317	317
2,125	2,150	321	321	321	321
2,150	2,175	324	324	324	324
2,175	2,200	328	328	328	328
2,200	2,225	332	332	332	332
2,225	2,250	336	336	336	336
2,250	2,275	339	339	339	339
2,275	2,300	343	343	343	343
2,300	2,325	347	347	347	347
2,325	2,350	351	351	351	351
2,350	2,375	354	354	354	354
2,375	2,400	358	358	358	358
2,400	2,425	362	362	362	362
2,425	2,450	366	366	366	366
2,450	2,475	369	369	369	369
2,475	2,500	373	373	373	373
2,500	2,525	377	377	377	377
2,525	2,550	381	381	381	381
2,550	2,575	384	384	384	384
2,575	2,600	388	388	388	388
2,600	2,625	392	392	392	392
2,625	2,650	396	396	396	396
2,650	2,675	399	399	399	399
2,675	2,700	403	403	403	403

If Form 1040A, line 25, is — At least	But less than	Single	Married filing jointly *	Married filing sepa-rately	Head of a house-hold
			Your tax is—		
2,700	2,725	407	407	407	407
2,725	2,750	411	411	411	411
2,750	2,775	414	414	414	414
2,775	2,800	418	418	418	418
2,800	2,825	422	422	422	422
2,825	2,850	426	426	426	426
2,850	2,875	429	429	429	429
2,875	2,900	433	433	433	433
2,900	2,925	437	437	437	437
2,925	2,950	441	441	441	441
2,950	2,975	444	444	444	444
2,975	3,000	448	448	448	448

3,000

At least	But less than	Single	Married filing jointly *	Married filing sepa-rately	Head of a house-hold
3,000	3,050	454	454	454	454
3,050	3,100	461	461	461	461
3,100	3,150	469	469	469	469
3,150	3,200	476	476	476	476
3,200	3,250	484	484	484	484
3,250	3,300	491	491	491	491
3,300	3,350	499	499	499	499
3,350	3,400	506	506	506	506
3,400	3,450	514	514	514	514
3,450	3,500	521	521	521	521
3,500	3,550	529	529	529	529
3,550	3,600	536	536	536	536
3,600	3,650	544	544	544	544
3,650	3,700	551	551	551	551
3,700	3,750	559	559	559	559
3,750	3,800	566	566	566	566
3,800	3,850	574	574	574	574
3,850	3,900	581	581	581	581
3,900	3,950	589	589	589	589
3,950	4,000	596	596	596	596

4,000

At least	But less than	Single	Married filing jointly *	Married filing sepa-rately	Head of a house-hold
4,000	4,050	604	604	604	604
4,050	4,100	611	611	611	611
4,100	4,150	619	619	619	619
4,150	4,200	626	626	626	626
4,200	4,250	634	634	634	634
4,250	4,300	641	641	641	641
4,300	4,350	649	649	649	649
4,350	4,400	656	656	656	656
4,400	4,450	664	664	664	664
4,450	4,500	671	671	671	671
4,500	4,550	679	679	679	679
4,550	4,600	686	686	686	686
4,600	4,650	694	694	694	694
4,650	4,700	701	701	701	701
4,700	4,750	709	709	709	709
4,750	4,800	716	716	716	716
4,800	4,850	724	724	724	724
4,850	4,900	731	731	731	731
4,900	4,950	739	739	739	739
4,950	5,000	746	746	746	746

Continued on next page

* This column must also be used by a qualifying widow(er).

If Form 1040A, line 25, is —		And you are —				If Form 1040A, line 25, is —		And you are —				If Form 1040A, line 25, is —		And you are —			
At least	But less than	Single	Married filing jointly *	Married filing sepa- rately	Head of a house- hold	At least	But less than	Single	Married filing jointly *	Married filing sepa- rately	Head of a house- hold	At least	But less than	Single	Married filing jointly *	Married filing sepa- rately	Head of a house- hold
		Your tax is—						Your tax is—						Your tax is—			
5,000						**8,000**						**11,000**					
5,000	5,050	754	754	754	754	8,000	8,050	1,204	1,204	1,204	1,204	11,000	11,050	1,654	1,654	1,654	1,654
5,050	5,100	761	761	761	761	8,050	8,100	1,211	1,211	1,211	1,211	11,050	11,100	1,661	1,661	1,661	1,661
5,100	5,150	769	769	769	769	8,100	8,150	1,219	1,219	1,219	1,219	11,100	11,150	1,669	1,669	1,669	1,669
5,150	5,200	776	776	776	776	8,150	8,200	1,226	1,226	1,226	1,226	11,150	11,200	1,676	1,676	1,676	1,676
5,200	5,250	784	784	784	784	8,200	8,250	1,234	1,234	1,234	1,234	11,200	11,250	1,684	1,684	1,684	1,684
5,250	5,300	791	791	791	791	8,250	8,300	1,241	1,241	1,241	1,241	11,250	11,300	1,691	1,691	1,691	1,691
5,300	5,350	799	799	799	799	8,300	8,350	1,249	1,249	1,249	1,249	11,300	11,350	1,699	1,699	1,699	1,699
5,350	5,400	806	806	806	806	8,350	8,400	1,256	1,256	1,256	1,256	11,350	11,400	1,706	1,706	1,706	1,706
5,400	5,450	814	814	814	814	8,400	8,450	1,264	1,264	1,264	1,264	11,400	11,450	1,714	1,714	1,714	1,714
5,450	5,500	821	821	821	821	8,450	8,500	1,271	1,271	1,271	1,271	11,450	11,500	1,721	1,721	1,721	1,721
5,500	5,550	829	829	829	829	8,500	8,550	1,279	1,279	1,279	1,279	11,500	11,550	1,729	1,729	1,729	1,729
5,550	5,600	836	836	836	836	8,550	8,600	1,286	1,286	1,286	1,286	11,550	11,600	1,736	1,736	1,736	1,736
5,600	5,650	844	844	844	844	8,600	8,650	1,294	1,294	1,294	1,294	11,600	11,650	1,744	1,744	1,744	1,744
5,650	5,700	851	851	851	851	8,650	8,700	1,301	1,301	1,301	1,301	11,650	11,700	1,751	1,751	1,751	1,751
5,700	5,750	859	859	859	859	8,700	8,750	1,309	1,309	1,309	1,309	11,700	11,750	1,759	1,759	1,759	1,759
5,750	5,800	866	866	866	866	8,750	8,800	1,316	1,316	1,316	1,316	11,750	11,800	1,766	1,766	1,766	1,766
5,800	5,850	874	874	874	874	8,800	8,850	1,324	1,324	1,324	1,324	11,800	11,850	1,774	1,774	1,774	1,774
5,850	5,900	881	881	881	881	8,850	8,900	1,331	1,331	1,331	1,331	11,850	11,900	1,781	1,781	1,781	1,781
5,900	5,950	889	889	889	889	8,900	8,950	1,339	1,339	1,339	1,339	11,900	11,950	1,789	1,789	1,789	1,789
5,950	6,000	896	896	896	896	8,950	9,000	1,346	1,346	1,346	1,346	11,950	12,000	1,796	1,796	1,796	1,796
6,000						**9,000**						**12,000**					
6,000	6,050	904	904	904	904	9,000	9,050	1,354	1,354	1,354	1,354	12,000	12,050	1,804	1,804	1,804	1,804
6,050	6,100	911	911	911	911	9,050	9,100	1,361	1,361	1,361	1,361	12,050	12,100	1,811	1,811	1,811	1,811
6,100	6,150	919	919	919	919	9,100	9,150	1,369	1,369	1,369	1,369	12,100	12,150	1,819	1,819	1,819	1,819
6,150	6,200	926	926	926	926	9,150	9,200	1,376	1,376	1,376	1,376	12,150	12,200	1,826	1,826	1,826	1,826
6,200	6,250	934	934	934	934	9,200	9,250	1,384	1,384	1,384	1,384	12,200	12,250	1,834	1,834	1,834	1,834
6,250	6,300	941	941	941	941	9,250	9,300	1,391	1,391	1,391	1,391	12,250	12,300	1,841	1,841	1,841	1,841
6,300	6,350	949	949	949	949	9,300	9,350	1,399	1,399	1,399	1,399	12,300	12,350	1,849	1,849	1,849	1,849
6,350	6,400	956	956	956	956	9,350	9,400	1,406	1,406	1,406	1,406	12,350	12,400	1,856	1,856	1,856	1,856
6,400	6,450	964	964	964	964	9,400	9,450	1,414	1,414	1,414	1,414	12,400	12,450	1,864	1,864	1,864	1,864
6,450	6,500	971	971	971	971	9,450	9,500	1,421	1,421	1,421	1,421	12,450	12,500	1,871	1,871	1,871	1,871
6,500	6,550	979	979	979	979	9,500	9,550	1,429	1,429	1,429	1,429	12,500	12,550	1,879	1,879	1,879	1,879
6,550	6,600	986	986	986	986	9,550	9,600	1,436	1,436	1,436	1,436	12,550	12,600	1,886	1,886	1,886	1,886
6,600	6,650	994	994	994	994	9,600	9,650	1,444	1,444	1,444	1,444	12,600	12,650	1,894	1,894	1,894	1,894
6,650	6,700	1,001	1,001	1,001	1,001	9,650	9,700	1,451	1,451	1,451	1,451	12,650	12,700	1,901	1,901	1,901	1,901
6,700	6,750	1,009	1,009	1,009	1,009	9,700	9,750	1,459	1,459	1,459	1,459	12,700	12,750	1,909	1,909	1,909	1,909
6,750	6,800	1,016	1,016	1,016	1,016	9,750	9,800	1,466	1,466	1,466	1,466	12,750	12,800	1,916	1,916	1,916	1,916
6,800	6,850	1,024	1,024	1,024	1,024	9,800	9,850	1,474	1,474	1,474	1,474	12,800	12,850	1,924	1,924	1,924	1,924
6,850	6,900	1,031	1,031	1,031	1,031	9,850	9,900	1,481	1,481	1,481	1,481	12,850	12,900	1,931	1,931	1,931	1,931
6,900	6,950	1,039	1,039	1,039	1,039	9,900	9,950	1,489	1,489	1,489	1,489	12,900	12,950	1,939	1,939	1,939	1,939
6,950	7,000	1,046	1,046	1,046	1,046	9,950	10,000	1,496	1,496	1,496	1,496	12,950	13,000	1,946	1,946	1,946	1,946
7,000						**10,000**						**13,000**					
7,000	7,050	1,054	1,054	1,054	1,054	10,000	10,050	1,504	1,504	1,504	1,504	13,000	13,050	1,954	1,954	1,954	1,954
7,050	7,100	1,061	1,061	1,061	1,061	10,050	10,100	1,511	1,511	1,511	1,511	13,050	13,100	1,961	1,961	1,961	1,961
7,100	7,150	1,069	1,069	1,069	1,069	10,100	10,150	1,519	1,519	1,519	1,519	13,100	13,150	1,969	1,969	1,969	1,969
7,150	7,200	1,076	1,076	1,076	1,076	10,150	10,200	1,526	1,526	1,526	1,526	13,150	13,200	1,976	1,976	1,976	1,976
7,200	7,250	1,084	1,084	1,084	1,084	10,200	10,250	1,534	1,534	1,534	1,534	13,200	13,250	1,984	1,984	1,984	1,984
7,250	7,300	1,091	1,091	1,091	1,091	10,250	10,300	1,541	1,541	1,541	1,541	13,250	13,300	1,991	1,991	1,991	1,991
7,300	7,350	1,099	1,099	1,099	1,099	10,300	10,350	1,549	1,549	1,549	1,549	13,300	13,350	1,999	1,999	1,999	1,999
7,350	7,400	1,106	1,106	1,106	1,106	10,350	10,400	1,556	1,556	1,556	1,556	13,350	13,400	2,006	2,006	2,006	2,006
7,400	7,450	1,114	1,114	1,114	1,114	10,400	10,450	1,564	1,564	1,564	1,564	13,400	13,450	2,014	2,014	2,014	2,014
7,450	7,500	1,121	1,121	1,121	1,121	10,450	10,500	1,571	1,571	1,571	1,571	13,450	13,500	2,021	2,021	2,021	2,021
7,500	7,550	1,129	1,129	1,129	1,129	10,500	10,550	1,579	1,579	1,579	1,579	13,500	13,550	2,029	2,029	2,029	2,029
7,550	7,600	1,136	1,136	1,136	1,136	10,550	10,600	1,586	1,586	1,586	1,586	13,550	13,600	2,036	2,036	2,036	2,036
7,600	7,650	1,144	1,144	1,144	1,144	10,600	10,650	1,594	1,594	1,594	1,594	13,600	13,650	2,044	2,044	2,044	2,044
7,650	7,700	1,151	1,151	1,151	1,151	10,650	10,700	1,601	1,601	1,601	1,601	13,650	13,700	2,051	2,051	2,051	2,051
7,700	7,750	1,159	1,159	1,159	1,159	10,700	10,750	1,609	1,609	1,609	1,609	13,700	13,750	2,059	2,059	2,059	2,059
7,750	7,800	1,166	1,166	1,166	1,166	10,750	10,800	1,616	1,616	1,616	1,616	13,750	13,800	2,066	2,066	2,066	2,066
7,800	7,850	1,174	1,174	1,174	1,174	10,800	10,850	1,624	1,624	1,624	1,624	13,800	13,850	2,074	2,074	2,074	2,074
7,850	7,900	1,181	1,181	1,181	1,181	10,850	10,900	1,631	1,631	1,631	1,631	13,850	13,900	2,081	2,081	2,081	2,081
7,900	7,950	1,189	1,189	1,189	1,189	10,900	10,950	1,639	1,639	1,639	1,639	13,900	13,950	2,089	2,089	2,089	2,089
7,950	8,000	1,196	1,196	1,196	1,196	10,950	11,000	1,646	1,646	1,646	1,646	13,950	14,000	2,096	2,096	2,096	2,096

* This column must also be used by a qualifying widow(er).

Continued on next page

14,000

If Form 1040A, line 25, is — At least	But less than	Single	Married filing jointly *	Married filing separately	Head of a house-hold
14,000	14,050	2,104	2,104	2,104	2,104
14,050	14,100	2,111	2,111	2,111	2,111
14,100	14,150	2,119	2,119	2,119	2,119
14,150	14,200	2,126	2,126	2,126	2,126
14,200	14,250	2,134	2,134	2,134	2,134
14,250	14,300	2,141	2,141	2,141	2,141
14,300	14,350	2,149	2,149	2,149	2,149
14,350	14,400	2,156	2,156	2,156	2,156
14,400	14,450	2,164	2,164	2,164	2,164
14,450	14,500	2,171	2,171	2,171	2,171
14,500	14,550	2,179	2,179	2,179	2,179
14,550	14,600	2,186	2,186	2,186	2,186
14,600	14,650	2,194	2,194	2,194	2,194
14,650	14,700	2,201	2,201	2,201	2,201
14,700	14,750	2,209	2,209	2,209	2,209
14,750	14,800	2,216	2,216	2,216	2,216
14,800	14,850	2,224	2,224	2,224	2,224
14,850	14,900	2,231	2,231	2,231	2,231
14,900	14,950	2,239	2,239	2,239	2,239
14,950	15,000	2,246	2,246	2,246	2,246

15,000

At least	But less than	Single	Married filing jointly *	Married filing separately	Head of a house-hold
15,000	15,050	2,254	2,254	2,254	2,254
15,050	15,100	2,261	2,261	2,261	2,261
15,100	15,150	2,269	2,269	2,269	2,269
15,150	15,200	2,276	2,276	2,276	2,276
15,200	15,250	2,284	2,284	2,284	2,284
15,250	15,300	2,291	2,291	2,291	2,291
15,300	15,350	2,299	2,299	2,299	2,299
15,350	15,400	2,306	2,306	2,306	2,306
15,400	15,450	2,314	2,314	2,314	2,314
15,450	15,500	2,321	2,321	2,321	2,321
15,500	15,550	2,329	2,329	2,329	2,329
15,550	15,600	2,336	2,336	2,336	2,336
15,600	15,650	2,344	2,344	2,344	2,344
15,650	15,700	2,351	2,351	2,351	2,351
15,700	15,750	2,359	2,359	2,359	2,359
15,750	15,800	2,366	2,366	2,366	2,366
15,800	15,850	2,374	2,374	2,374	2,374
15,850	15,900	2,381	2,381	2,381	2,381
15,900	15,950	2,389	2,389	2,389	2,389
15,950	16,000	2,396	2,396	2,396	2,396

16,000

At least	But less than	Single	Married filing jointly *	Married filing separately	Head of a house-hold
16,000	16,050	2,404	2,404	2,404	2,404
16,050	16,100	2,411	2,411	2,411	2,411
16,100	16,150	2,419	2,419	2,419	2,419
16,150	16,200	2,426	2,426	2,426	2,426
16,200	16,250	2,434	2,434	2,434	2,434
16,250	16,300	2,441	2,441	2,441	2,441
16,300	16,350	2,449	2,449	2,449	2,449
16,350	16,400	2,456	2,456	2,456	2,456
16,400	16,450	2,464	2,464	2,464	2,464
16,450	16,500	2,471	2,471	2,471	2,471
16,500	16,550	2,479	2,479	2,479	2,479
16,550	16,600	2,486	2,486	2,486	2,486
16,600	16,650	2,494	2,494	2,494	2,494
16,650	16,700	2,501	2,501	2,501	2,501
16,700	16,750	2,509	2,509	2,509	2,509
16,750	16,800	2,516	2,516	2,516	2,516
16,800	16,850	2,524	2,524	2,524	2,524
16,850	16,900	2,531	2,531	2,531	2,531
16,900	16,950	2,539	2,539	2,539	2,539
16,950	17,000	2,546	2,546	2,546	2,546

17,000

At least	But less than	Single	Married filing jointly *	Married filing separately	Head of a house-hold
17,000	17,050	2,554	2,554	2,554	2,554
17,050	17,100	2,561	2,561	2,561	2,561
17,100	17,150	2,569	2,569	2,569	2,569
17,150	17,200	2,576	2,576	2,576	2,576
17,200	17,250	2,584	2,584	2,584	2,584
17,250	17,300	2,591	2,591	2,591	2,591
17,300	17,350	2,599	2,599	2,599	2,599
17,350	17,400	2,606	2,606	2,606	2,606
17,400	17,450	2,614	2,614	2,614	2,614
17,450	17,500	2,621	2,621	2,621	2,621
17,500	17,550	2,629	2,629	2,629	2,629
17,550	17,600	2,636	2,636	2,636	2,636
17,600	17,650	2,644	2,644	2,644	2,644
17,650	17,700	2,651	2,651	2,651	2,651
17,700	17,750	2,659	2,659	2,659	2,659
17,750	17,800	2,666	2,666	2,666	2,666
17,800	17,850	2,674	2,674	2,674	2,674
17,850	17,900	2,681	2,681	2,681	2,681
17,900	17,950	2,689	2,689	2,689	2,689
17,950	18,000	2,696	2,696	2,696	2,696

18,000

At least	But less than	Single	Married filing jointly *	Married filing separately	Head of a house-hold
18,000	18,050	2,704	2,704	2,704	2,704
18,050	18,100	2,711	2,711	2,711	2,711
18,100	18,150	2,719	2,719	2,719	2,719
18,150	18,200	2,726	2,726	2,726	2,726
18,200	18,250	2,734	2,734	2,734	2,734
18,250	18,300	2,741	2,741	2,741	2,741
18,300	18,350	2,749	2,749	2,749	2,749
18,350	18,400	2,756	2,756	2,756	2,756
18,400	18,450	2,764	2,764	2,764	2,764
18,450	18,500	2,771	2,771	2,775	2,771
18,500	18,550	2,779	2,779	2,789	2,779
18,550	18,600	2,786	2,786	2,803	2,786
18,600	18,650	2,794	2,794	2,817	2,794
18,650	18,700	2,801	2,801	2,831	2,801
18,700	18,750	2,809	2,809	2,845	2,809
18,750	18,800	2,816	2,816	2,859	2,816
18,800	18,850	2,824	2,824	2,873	2,824
18,850	18,900	2,831	2,831	2,887	2,831
18,900	18,950	2,839	2,839	2,901	2,839
18,950	19,000	2,846	2,846	2,915	2,846

19,000

At least	But less than	Single	Married filing jointly *	Married filing separately	Head of a house-hold
19,000	19,050	2,854	2,854	2,929	2,854
19,050	19,100	2,861	2,861	2,943	2,861
19,100	19,150	2,869	2,869	2,957	2,869
19,150	19,200	2,876	2,876	2,971	2,876
19,200	19,250	2,884	2,884	2,985	2,884
19,250	19,300	2,891	2,891	2,999	2,891
19,300	19,350	2,899	2,899	3,013	2,899
19,350	19,400	2,906	2,906	3,027	2,906
19,400	19,450	2,914	2,914	3,041	2,914
19,450	19,500	2,921	2,921	3,055	2,921
19,500	19,550	2,929	2,929	3,069	2,929
19,550	19,600	2,936	2,936	3,083	2,936
19,600	19,650	2,944	2,944	3,097	2,944
19,650	19,700	2,951	2,951	3,111	2,951
19,700	19,750	2,959	2,959	3,125	2,959
19,750	19,800	2,966	2,966	3,139	2,966
19,800	19,850	2,974	2,974	3,153	2,974
19,850	19,900	2,981	2,981	3,167	2,981
19,900	19,950	2,989	2,989	3,181	2,989
19,950	20,000	2,996	2,996	3,195	2,996

20,000

At least	But less than	Single	Married filing jointly *	Married filing separately	Head of a house-hold
20,000	20,050	3,004	3,004	3,209	3,004
20,050	20,100	3,011	3,011	3,223	3,011
20,100	20,150	3,019	3,019	3,237	3,019
20,150	20,200	3,026	3,026	3,251	3,026
20,200	20,250	3,034	3,034	3,265	3,034
20,250	20,300	3,041	3,041	3,279	3,041
20,300	20,350	3,049	3,049	3,293	3,049
20,350	20,400	3,056	3,056	3,307	3,056
20,400	20,450	3,064	3,064	3,321	3,064
20,450	20,500	3,071	3,071	3,335	3,071
20,500	20,550	3,079	3,079	3,349	3,079
20,550	20,600	3,086	3,086	3,363	3,086
20,600	20,650	3,094	3,094	3,377	3,094
20,650	20,700	3,101	3,101	3,391	3,101
20,700	20,750	3,109	3,109	3,405	3,109
20,750	20,800	3,116	3,116	3,419	3,116
20,800	20,850	3,124	3,124	3,433	3,124
20,850	20,900	3,131	3,131	3,447	3,131
20,900	20,950	3,139	3,139	3,461	3,139
20,950	21,000	3,146	3,146	3,475	3,146

21,000

At least	But less than	Single	Married filing jointly *	Married filing separately	Head of a house-hold
21,000	21,050	3,154	3,154	3,489	3,154
21,050	21,100	3,161	3,161	3,503	3,161
21,100	21,150	3,169	3,169	3,517	3,169
21,150	21,200	3,176	3,176	3,531	3,176
21,200	21,250	3,184	3,184	3,545	3,184
21,250	21,300	3,191	3,191	3,559	3,191
21,300	21,350	3,199	3,199	3,573	3,199
21,350	21,400	3,206	3,206	3,587	3,206
21,400	21,450	3,214	3,214	3,601	3,214
21,450	21,500	3,221	3,221	3,615	3,221
21,500	21,550	3,229	3,229	3,629	3,229
21,550	21,600	3,236	3,236	3,643	3,236
21,600	21,650	3,244	3,244	3,657	3,244
21,650	21,700	3,251	3,251	3,671	3,251
21,700	21,750	3,259	3,259	3,685	3,259
21,750	21,800	3,266	3,266	3,699	3,266
21,800	21,850	3,274	3,274	3,713	3,274
21,850	21,900	3,281	3,281	3,727	3,281
21,900	21,950	3,289	3,289	3,741	3,289
21,950	22,000	3,296	3,296	3,755	3,296

22,000

At least	But less than	Single	Married filing jointly *	Married filing separately	Head of a house-hold
22,000	22,050	3,304	3,304	3,769	3,304
22,050	22,100	3,311	3,311	3,783	3,311
22,100	22,150	3,322	3,319	3,797	3,319
22,150	22,200	3,336	3,326	3,811	3,326
22,200	22,250	3,350	3,334	3,825	3,334
22,250	22,300	3,364	3,341	3,839	3,341
22,300	22,350	3,378	3,349	3,853	3,349
22,350	22,400	3,392	3,356	3,867	3,356
22,400	22,450	3,406	3,364	3,881	3,364
22,450	22,500	3,420	3,371	3,895	3,371
22,500	22,550	3,434	3,379	3,909	3,379
22,550	22,600	3,448	3,386	3,923	3,386
22,600	22,650	3,462	3,394	3,937	3,394
22,650	22,700	3,476	3,401	3,951	3,401
22,700	22,750	3,490	3,409	3,965	3,409
22,750	22,800	3,504	3,416	3,979	3,416
22,800	22,850	3,518	3,424	3,993	3,424
22,850	22,900	3,532	3,431	4,007	3,431
22,900	22,950	3,546	3,439	4,021	3,439
22,950	23,000	3,560	3,446	4,035	3,446

* This column must also be used by a qualifying widow(er).

Continued on next page

If Form 1040A, line 25, is —		And you are —				If Form 1040A, line 25, is —		And you are —				If Form 1040A, line 25, is —		And you are —			
At least	But less than	Single	Married filing jointly *	Married filing separately	Head of a household	At least	But less than	Single	Married filing jointly *	Married filing separately	Head of a household	At least	But less than	Single	Married filing jointly *	Married filing separately	Head of a household
		Your tax is—						Your tax is—						Your tax is—			
23,000						**26,000**						**29,000**					
23,000	23,050	3,574	3,454	4,049	3,454	26,000	26,050	4,414	3,904	4,889	3,904	29,000	29,050	5,254	4,354	5,729	4,354
23,050	23,100	3,588	3,461	4,063	3,461	26,050	26,100	4,428	3,911	4,903	3,911	29,050	29,100	5,268	4,361	5,743	4,361
23,100	23,150	3,602	3,469	4,077	3,469	26,100	26,150	4,442	3,919	4,917	3,919	29,100	29,150	5,282	4,369	5,757	4,369
23,150	23,200	3,616	3,476	4,091	3,476	26,150	26,200	4,456	3,926	4,931	3,926	29,150	29,200	5,296	4,376	5,771	4,376
23,200	23,250	3,630	3,484	4,105	3,484	26,200	26,250	4,470	3,934	4,945	3,934	29,200	29,250	5,310	4,384	5,785	4,384
23,250	23,300	3,644	3,491	4,119	3,491	26,250	26,300	4,484	3,941	4,959	3,941	29,250	29,300	5,324	4,391	5,799	4,391
23,300	23,350	3,658	3,499	4,133	3,499	26,300	26,350	4,498	3,949	4,973	3,949	29,300	29,350	5,338	4,399	5,813	4,399
23,350	23,400	3,672	3,506	4,147	3,506	26,350	26,400	4,512	3,956	4,987	3,956	29,350	29,400	5,352	4,406	5,827	4,406
23,400	23,450	3,686	3,514	4,161	3,514	26,400	26,450	4,526	3,964	5,001	3,964	29,400	29,450	5,366	4,414	5,841	4,414
23,450	23,500	3,700	3,521	4,175	3,521	26,450	26,500	4,540	3,971	5,015	3,971	29,450	29,500	5,380	4,421	5,855	4,421
23,500	23,550	3,714	3,529	4,189	3,529	26,500	26,550	4,554	3,979	5,029	3,979	29,500	29,550	5,394	4,429	5,869	4,429
23,550	23,600	3,728	3,536	4,203	3,536	26,550	26,600	4,568	3,986	5,043	3,986	29,550	29,600	5,408	4,436	5,883	4,436
23,600	23,650	3,742	3,544	4,217	3,544	26,600	26,650	4,582	3,994	5,057	3,994	29,600	29,650	5,422	4,444	5,897	4,447
23,650	23,700	3,756	3,551	4,231	3,551	26,650	26,700	4,596	4,001	5,071	4,001	29,650	29,700	5,436	4,451	5,911	4,461
23,700	23,750	3,770	3,559	4,245	3,559	26,700	26,750	4,610	4,009	5,085	4,009	29,700	29,750	5,450	4,459	5,925	4,475
23,750	23,800	3,784	3,566	4,259	3,566	26,750	26,800	4,624	4,016	5,099	4,016	29,750	29,800	5,464	4,466	5,939	4,489
23,800	23,850	3,798	3,574	4,273	3,574	26,800	26,850	4,638	4,024	5,113	4,024	29,800	29,850	5,478	4,474	5,953	4,503
23,850	23,900	3,812	3,581	4,287	3,581	26,850	26,900	4,652	4,031	5,127	4,031	29,850	29,900	5,492	4,481	5,967	4,517
23,900	23,950	3,826	3,589	4,301	3,589	26,900	26,950	4,666	4,039	5,141	4,039	29,900	29,950	5,506	4,489	5,981	4,531
23,950	24,000	3,840	3,596	4,315	3,596	26,950	27,000	4,680	4,046	5,155	4,046	29,950	30,000	5,520	4,496	5,995	4,545
24,000						**27,000**						**30,000**					
24,000	24,050	3,854	3,604	4,329	3,604	27,000	27,050	4,694	4,054	5,169	4,054	30,000	30,050	5,534	4,504	6,009	4,559
24,050	24,100	3,868	3,611	4,343	3,611	27,050	27,100	4,708	4,061	5,183	4,061	30,050	30,100	5,548	4,511	6,023	4,573
24,100	24,150	3,882	3,619	4,357	3,619	27,100	27,150	4,722	4,069	5,197	4,069	30,100	30,150	5,562	4,519	6,037	4,587
24,150	24,200	3,896	3,626	4,371	3,626	27,150	27,200	4,736	4,076	5,211	4,076	30,150	30,200	5,576	4,526	6,051	4,601
24,200	24,250	3,910	3,634	4,385	3,634	27,200	27,250	4,750	4,084	5,225	4,084	30,200	30,250	5,590	4,534	6,065	4,615
24,250	24,300	3,924	3,641	4,399	3,641	27,250	27,300	4,764	4,091	5,239	4,091	30,250	30,300	5,604	4,541	6,079	4,629
24,300	24,350	3,938	3,649	4,413	3,649	27,300	27,350	4,778	4,099	5,253	4,099	30,300	30,350	5,618	4,549	6,093	4,643
24,350	24,400	3,952	3,656	4,427	3,656	27,350	27,400	4,792	4,106	5,267	4,106	30,350	30,400	5,632	4,556	6,107	4,657
24,400	24,450	3,966	3,664	4,441	3,664	27,400	27,450	4,806	4,114	5,281	4,114	30,400	30,450	5,646	4,564	6,121	4,671
24,450	24,500	3,980	3,671	4,455	3,671	27,450	27,500	4,820	4,121	5,295	4,121	30,450	30,500	5,660	4,571	6,135	4,685
24,500	24,550	3,994	3,679	4,469	3,679	27,500	27,550	4,834	4,129	5,309	4,129	30,500	30,550	5,674	4,579	6,149	4,699
24,550	24,600	4,008	3,686	4,483	3,686	27,550	27,600	4,848	4,136	5,323	4,136	30,550	30,600	5,688	4,586	6,163	4,713
24,600	24,650	4,022	3,694	4,497	3,694	27,600	27,650	4,862	4,144	5,337	4,144	30,600	30,650	5,702	4,594	6,177	4,727
24,650	24,700	4,036	3,701	4,511	3,701	27,650	27,700	4,876	4,151	5,351	4,151	30,650	30,700	5,716	4,601	6,191	4,741
24,700	24,750	4,050	3,709	4,525	3,709	27,700	27,750	4,890	4,159	5,365	4,159	30,700	30,750	5,730	4,609	6,205	4,755
24,750	24,800	4,064	3,716	4,539	3,716	27,750	27,800	4,904	4,166	5,379	4,166	30,750	30,800	5,744	4,616	6,219	4,769
24,800	24,850	4,078	3,724	4,553	3,724	27,800	27,850	4,918	4,174	5,393	4,174	30,800	30,850	5,758	4,624	6,233	4,783
24,850	24,900	4,092	3,731	4,567	3,731	27,850	27,900	4,932	4,181	5,407	4,181	30,850	30,900	5,772	4,631	6,247	4,797
24,900	24,950	4,106	3,739	4,581	3,739	27,900	27,950	4,946	4,189	5,421	4,189	30,900	30,950	5,786	4,639	6,261	4,811
24,950	25,000	4,120	3,746	4,595	3,746	27,950	28,000	4,960	4,196	5,435	4,196	30,950	31,000	5,800	4,646	6,275	4,825
25,000						**28,000**						**31,000**					
25,000	25,050	4,134	3,754	4,609	3,754	28,000	28,050	4,974	4,204	5,449	4,204	31,000	31,050	5,814	4,654	6,289	4,839
25,050	25,100	4,148	3,761	4,623	3,761	28,050	28,100	4,988	4,211	5,463	4,211	31,050	31,100	5,828	4,661	6,303	4,853
25,100	25,150	4,162	3,769	4,637	3,769	28,100	28,150	5,002	4,219	5,477	4,219	31,100	31,150	5,842	4,669	6,317	4,867
25,150	25,200	4,176	3,776	4,651	3,776	28,150	28,200	5,016	4,226	5,491	4,226	31,150	31,200	5,856	4,676	6,331	4,881
25,200	25,250	4,190	3,784	4,665	3,784	28,200	28,250	5,030	4,234	5,505	4,234	31,200	31,250	5,870	4,684	6,345	4,895
25,250	25,300	4,204	3,791	4,679	3,791	28,250	28,300	5,044	4,241	5,519	4,241	31,250	31,300	5,884	4,691	6,359	4,909
25,300	25,350	4,218	3,799	4,693	3,799	28,300	28,350	5,058	4,249	5,533	4,249	31,300	31,350	5,898	4,699	6,373	4,923
25,350	25,400	4,232	3,806	4,707	3,806	28,350	28,400	5,072	4,256	5,547	4,256	31,350	31,400	5,912	4,706	6,387	4,937
25,400	25,450	4,246	3,814	4,721	3,814	28,400	28,450	5,086	4,264	5,561	4,264	31,400	31,450	5,926	4,714	6,401	4,951
25,450	25,500	4,260	3,821	4,735	3,821	28,450	28,500	5,100	4,271	5,575	4,271	31,450	31,500	5,940	4,721	6,415	4,965
25,500	25,550	4,274	3,829	4,749	3,829	28,500	28,550	5,114	4,279	5,589	4,279	31,500	31,550	5,954	4,729	6,429	4,979
25,550	25,600	4,288	3,836	4,763	3,836	28,550	28,600	5,128	4,286	5,603	4,286	31,550	31,600	5,968	4,736	6,443	4,993
25,600	25,650	4,302	3,844	4,777	3,844	28,600	28,650	5,142	4,294	5,617	4,294	31,600	31,650	5,982	4,744	6,457	5,007
25,650	25,700	4,316	3,851	4,791	3,851	28,650	28,700	5,156	4,301	5,631	4,301	31,650	31,700	5,996	4,751	6,471	5,021
25,700	25,750	4,330	3,859	4,805	3,859	28,700	28,750	5,170	4,309	5,645	4,309	31,700	31,750	6,010	4,759	6,485	5,035
25,750	25,800	4,344	3,866	4,819	3,866	28,750	28,800	5,184	4,316	5,659	4,316	31,750	31,800	6,024	4,766	6,499	5,049
25,800	25,850	4,358	3,874	4,833	3,874	28,800	28,850	5,198	4,324	5,673	4,324	31,800	31,850	6,038	4,774	6,513	5,063
25,850	25,900	4,372	3,881	4,847	3,881	28,850	28,900	5,212	4,331	5,687	4,331	31,850	31,900	6,052	4,781	6,527	5,077
25,900	25,950	4,386	3,889	4,861	3,889	28,900	28,950	5,226	4,339	5,701	4,339	31,900	31,950	6,066	4,789	6,541	5,091
25,950	26,000	4,400	3,896	4,875	3,896	28,950	29,000	5,240	4,346	5,715	4,346	31,950	32,000	6,080	4,796	6,555	5,105

* This column must also be used by a qualifying widow(er).

Continued on next page

If Form 1040A, line 25, is —		And you are —				If Form 1040A, line 25, is —		And you are —				If Form 1040A, line 25, is —		And you are —			
At least	But less than	Single	Married filing jointly *	Married filing sepa-rately	Head of a house-hold	At least	But less than	Single	Married filing jointly *	Married filing sepa-rately	Head of a house-hold	At least	But less than	Single	Married filing jointly *	Married filing sepa-rately	Head of a house-hold
		Your tax is—						Your tax is—						Your tax is—			
32,000						**35,000**						**38,000**					
32,000	32,050	6,094	4,804	6,569	5,119	35,000	35,050	6,934	5,254	7,409	5,959	38,000	38,050	7,774	5,850	8,249	6,799
32,050	32,100	6,108	4,811	6,583	5,133	35,050	35,100	6,948	5,261	7,423	5,973	38,050	38,100	7,788	5,864	8,263	6,813
32,100	32,150	6,122	4,819	6,597	5,147	35,100	35,150	6,962	5,269	7,437	5,987	38,100	38,150	7,802	5,878	8,277	6,827
32,150	32,200	6,136	4,826	6,611	5,161	35,150	35,200	6,976	5,276	7,451	6,001	38,150	38,200	7,816	5,892	8,291	6,841
32,200	32,250	6,150	4,834	6,625	5,175	35,200	35,250	6,990	5,284	7,465	6,015	38,200	38,250	7,830	5,906	8,305	6,855
32,250	32,300	6,164	4,841	6,639	5,189	35,250	35,300	7,004	5,291	7,479	6,029	38,250	38,300	7,844	5,920	8,319	6,869
32,300	32,350	6,178	4,849	6,653	5,203	35,300	35,350	7,018	5,299	7,493	6,043	38,300	38,350	7,858	5,934	8,333	6,883
32,350	32,400	6,192	4,856	6,667	5,217	35,350	35,400	7,032	5,306	7,507	6,057	38,350	38,400	7,872	5,948	8,347	6,897
32,400	32,450	6,206	4,864	6,681	5,231	35,400	35,450	7,046	5,314	7,521	6,071	38,400	38,450	7,886	5,962	8,361	6,911
32,450	32,500	6,220	4,871	6,695	5,245	35,450	35,500	7,060	5,321	7,535	6,085	38,450	38,500	7,900	5,976	8,375	6,925
32,500	32,550	6,234	4,879	6,709	5,259	35,500	35,550	7,074	5,329	7,549	6,099	38,500	38,550	7,914	5,990	8,389	6,939
32,550	32,600	6,248	4,886	6,723	5,273	35,550	35,600	7,088	5,336	7,563	6,113	38,550	38,600	7,928	6,004	8,403	6,953
32,600	32,650	6,262	4,894	6,737	5,287	35,600	35,650	7,102	5,344	7,577	6,127	38,600	38,650	7,942	6,018	8,417	6,967
32,650	32,700	6,276	4,901	6,751	5,301	35,650	35,700	7,116	5,351	7,591	6,141	38,650	38,700	7,956	6,032	8,431	6,981
32,700	32,750	6,290	4,909	6,765	5,315	35,700	35,750	7,130	5,359	7,605	6,155	38,700	38,750	7,970	6,046	8,445	6,995
32,750	32,800	6,304	4,916	6,779	5,329	35,750	35,800	7,144	5,366	7,619	6,169	38,750	38,800	7,984	6,060	8,459	7,009
32,800	32,850	6,318	4,924	6,793	5,343	35,800	35,850	7,158	5,374	7,633	6,183	38,800	38,850	7,998	6,074	8,473	7,023
32,850	32,900	6,332	4,931	6,807	5,357	35,850	35,900	7,172	5,381	7,647	6,197	38,850	38,900	8,012	6,088	8,487	7,037
32,900	32,950	6,346	4,939	6,821	5,371	35,900	35,950	7,186	5,389	7,661	6,211	38,900	38,950	8,026	6,102	8,501	7,051
32,950	33,000	6,360	4,946	6,835	5,385	35,950	36,000	7,200	5,396	7,675	6,225	38,950	39,000	8,040	6,116	8,515	7,065
33,000						**36,000**						**39,000**					
33,000	33,050	6,374	4,954	6,849	5,399	36,000	36,050	7,214	5,404	7,689	6,239	39,000	39,050	8,054	6,130	8,529	7,079
33,050	33,100	6,388	4,961	6,863	5,413	36,050	36,100	7,228	5,411	7,703	6,253	39,050	39,100	8,068	6,144	8,543	7,093
33,100	33,150	6,402	4,969	6,877	5,427	36,100	36,150	7,242	5,419	7,717	6,267	39,100	39,150	8,082	6,158	8,557	7,107
33,150	33,200	6,416	4,976	6,891	5,441	36,150	36,200	7,256	5,426	7,731	6,281	39,150	39,200	8,096	6,172	8,571	7,121
33,200	33,250	6,430	4,984	6,905	5,455	36,200	36,250	7,270	5,434	7,745	6,295	39,200	39,250	8,110	6,186	8,585	7,135
33,250	33,300	6,444	4,991	6,919	5,469	36,250	36,300	7,284	5,441	7,759	6,309	39,250	39,300	8,124	6,200	8,599	7,149
33,300	33,350	6,458	4,999	6,933	5,483	36,300	36,350	7,298	5,449	7,773	6,323	39,300	39,350	8,138	6,214	8,613	7,163
33,350	33,400	6,472	5,006	6,947	5,497	36,350	36,400	7,312	5,456	7,787	6,337	39,350	39,400	8,152	6,228	8,627	7,177
33,400	33,450	6,486	5,014	6,961	5,511	36,400	36,450	7,326	5,464	7,801	6,351	39,400	39,450	8,166	6,242	8,641	7,191
33,450	33,500	6,500	5,021	6,975	5,525	36,450	36,500	7,340	5,471	7,815	6,365	39,450	39,500	8,180	6,256	8,655	7,205
33,500	33,550	6,514	5,029	6,989	5,539	36,500	36,550	7,354	5,479	7,829	6,379	39,500	39,550	8,194	6,270	8,669	7,219
33,550	33,600	6,528	5,036	7,003	5,553	36,550	36,600	7,368	5,486	7,843	6,393	39,550	39,600	8,208	6,284	8,683	7,233
33,600	33,650	6,542	5,044	7,017	5,567	36,600	36,650	7,382	5,494	7,857	6,407	39,600	39,650	8,222	6,298	8,697	7,247
33,650	33,700	6,556	5,051	7,031	5,581	36,650	36,700	7,396	5,501	7,871	6,421	39,650	39,700	8,236	6,312	8,711	7,261
33,700	33,750	6,570	5,059	7,045	5,595	36,700	36,750	7,410	5,509	7,885	6,435	39,700	39,750	8,250	6,326	8,725	7,275
33,750	33,800	6,584	5,066	7,059	5,609	36,750	36,800	7,424	5,516	7,899	6,449	39,750	39,800	8,264	6,340	8,739	7,289
33,800	33,850	6,598	5,074	7,073	5,623	36,800	36,850	7,438	5,524	7,913	6,463	39,800	39,850	8,278	6,354	8,753	7,303
33,850	33,900	6,612	5,081	7,087	5,637	36,850	36,900	7,452	5,531	7,927	6,477	39,850	39,900	8,292	6,368	8,767	7,317
33,900	33,950	6,626	5,089	7,101	5,651	36,900	36,950	7,466	5,542	7,941	6,491	39,900	39,950	8,306	6,382	8,781	7,331
33,950	34,000	6,640	5,096	7,115	5,665	36,950	37,000	7,480	5,556	7,955	6,505	39,950	40,000	8,320	6,396	8,795	7,345
34,000						**37,000**						**40,000**					
34,000	34,050	6,654	5,104	7,129	5,679	37,000	37,050	7,494	5,570	7,969	6,519	40,000	40,050	8,334	6,410	8,809	7,359
34,050	34,100	6,668	5,111	7,143	5,693	37,050	37,100	7,508	5,584	7,983	6,533	40,050	40,100	8,348	6,424	8,823	7,373
34,100	34,150	6,682	5,119	7,157	5,707	37,100	37,150	7,522	5,598	7,997	6,547	40,100	40,150	8,362	6,438	8,837	7,387
34,150	34,200	6,696	5,126	7,171	5,721	37,150	37,200	7,536	5,612	8,011	6,561	40,150	40,200	8,376	6,452	8,851	7,401
34,200	34,250	6,710	5,134	7,185	5,735	37,200	37,250	7,550	5,626	8,025	6,575	40,200	40,250	8,390	6,466	8,865	7,415
34,250	34,300	6,724	5,141	7,199	5,749	37,250	37,300	7,564	5,640	8,039	6,589	40,250	40,300	8,404	6,480	8,879	7,429
34,300	34,350	6,738	5,149	7,213	5,763	37,300	37,350	7,578	5,654	8,053	6,603	40,300	40,350	8,418	6,494	8,893	7,443
34,350	34,400	6,752	5,156	7,227	5,777	37,350	37,400	7,592	5,668	8,067	6,617	40,350	40,400	8,432	6,508	8,907	7,457
34,400	34,450	6,766	5,164	7,241	5,791	37,400	37,450	7,606	5,682	8,081	6,631	40,400	40,450	8,446	6,522	8,921	7,471
34,450	34,500	6,780	5,171	7,255	5,805	37,450	37,500	7,620	5,696	8,095	6,645	40,450	40,500	8,460	6,536	8,935	7,485
34,500	34,550	6,794	5,179	7,269	5,819	37,500	37,550	7,634	5,710	8,109	6,659	40,500	40,550	8,474	6,550	8,949	7,499
34,550	34,600	6,808	5,186	7,283	5,833	37,550	37,600	7,648	5,724	8,123	6,673	40,550	40,600	8,488	6,564	8,963	7,513
34,600	34,650	6,822	5,194	7,297	5,847	37,600	37,650	7,662	5,738	8,137	6,687	40,600	40,650	8,502	6,578	8,977	7,527
34,650	34,700	6,836	5,201	7,311	5,861	37,650	37,700	7,676	5,752	8,151	6,701	40,650	40,700	8,516	6,592	8,991	7,541
34,700	34,750	6,850	5,209	7,325	5,875	37,700	37,750	7,690	5,766	8,165	6,715	40,700	40,750	8,530	6,606	9,005	7,555
34,750	34,800	6,864	5,216	7,339	5,889	37,750	37,800	7,704	5,780	8,179	6,729	40,750	40,800	8,544	6,620	9,019	7,569
34,800	34,850	6,878	5,224	7,353	5,903	37,800	37,850	7,718	5,794	8,193	6,743	40,800	40,850	8,558	6,634	9,033	7,583
34,850	34,900	6,892	5,231	7,367	5,917	37,850	37,900	7,732	5,808	8,207	6,757	40,850	40,900	8,572	6,648	9,047	7,597
34,900	34,950	6,906	5,239	7,381	5,931	37,900	37,950	7,746	5,822	8,221	6,771	40,900	40,950	8,586	6,662	9,061	7,611
34,950	35,000	6,920	5,246	7,395	5,945	37,950	38,000	7,760	5,836	8,235	6,785	40,950	41,000	8,600	6,676	9,075	7,625

* This column must also be used by a qualifying widow(er).

Continued on next page

20-- Tax Table—Continued

Columns for each section: **At least** | **But less than** | **Single** | **Married filing jointly *** | **Married filing separately** | **Head of a household** — "If Form 1040A, line 25, is —" / "And you are —" / "Your tax is—"

41,000

At least	But less than	Single	Married filing jointly *	Married filing separately	Head of a household
41,000	41,050	8,614	6,690	9,089	7,639
41,050	41,100	8,628	6,704	9,103	7,653
41,100	41,150	8,642	6,718	9,117	7,667
41,150	41,200	8,656	6,732	9,131	7,681
41,200	41,250	8,670	6,746	9,145	7,695
41,250	41,300	8,684	6,760	9,159	7,709
41,300	41,350	8,698	6,774	9,173	7,723
41,350	41,400	8,712	6,788	9,187	7,737
41,400	41,450	8,726	6,802	9,201	7,751
41,450	41,500	8,740	6,816	9,215	7,765
41,500	41,550	8,754	6,830	9,229	7,779
41,550	41,600	8,768	6,844	9,243	7,793
41,600	41,650	8,782	6,858	9,257	7,807
41,650	41,700	8,796	6,872	9,271	7,821
41,700	41,750	8,810	6,886	9,285	7,835
41,750	41,800	8,824	6,900	9,299	7,849
41,800	41,850	8,838	6,914	9,313	7,863
41,850	41,900	8,852	6,928	9,327	7,877
41,900	41,950	8,866	6,942	9,341	7,891
41,950	42,000	8,880	6,956	9,355	7,905

42,000

At least	But less than	Single	Married filing jointly *	Married filing separately	Head of a household
42,000	42,050	8,894	6,970	9,369	7,919
42,050	42,100	8,908	6,984	9,383	7,933
42,100	42,150	8,922	6,998	9,397	7,947
42,150	42,200	8,936	7,012	9,411	7,961
42,200	42,250	8,950	7,026	9,425	7,975
42,250	42,300	8,964	7,040	9,439	7,989
42,300	42,350	8,978	7,054	9,453	8,003
42,350	42,400	8,992	7,068	9,467	8,017
42,400	42,450	9,006	7,082	9,481	8,031
42,450	42,500	9,020	7,096	9,495	8,045
42,500	42,550	9,034	7,110	9,509	8,059
42,550	42,600	9,048	7,124	9,523	8,073
42,600	42,650	9,062	7,138	9,537	8,087
42,650	42,700	9,076	7,152	9,551	8,101
42,700	42,750	9,090	7,166	9,565	8,115
42,750	42,800	9,104	7,180	9,579	8,129
42,800	42,850	9,118	7,194	9,593	8,143
42,850	42,900	9,132	7,208	9,607	8,157
42,900	42,950	9,146	7,222	9,621	8,171
42,950	43,000	9,160	7,236	9,635	8,185

43,000

At least	But less than	Single	Married filing jointly *	Married filing separately	Head of a household
43,000	43,050	9,174	7,250	9,649	8,199
43,050	43,100	9,188	7,264	9,663	8,213
43,100	43,150	9,202	7,278	9,677	8,227
43,150	43,200	9,216	7,292	9,691	8,241
43,200	43,250	9,230	7,306	9,705	8,255
43,250	43,300	9,244	7,320	9,719	8,269
43,300	43,350	9,258	7,334	9,733	8,283
43,350	43,400	9,272	7,348	9,747	8,297
43,400	43,450	9,286	7,362	9,761	8,311
43,450	43,500	9,300	7,376	9,775	8,325
43,500	43,550	9,314	7,390	9,789	8,339
43,550	43,600	9,328	7,404	9,803	8,353
43,600	43,650	9,342	7,418	9,817	8,367
43,650	43,700	9,356	7,432	9,831	8,381
43,700	43,750	9,370	7,446	9,845	8,395
43,750	43,800	9,384	7,460	9,859	8,409
43,800	43,850	9,398	7,474	9,873	8,423
43,850	43,900	9,412	7,488	9,887	8,437
43,900	43,950	9,426	7,502	9,901	8,451
43,950	44,000	9,440	7,516	9,915	8,465

44,000

At least	But less than	Single	Married filing jointly *	Married filing separately	Head of a household
44,000	44,050	9,454	7,530	9,929	8,479
44,050	44,100	9,468	7,544	9,943	8,493
44,100	44,150	9,482	7,558	9,957	8,507
44,150	44,200	9,496	7,572	9,971	8,521
44,200	44,250	9,510	7,586	9,985	8,535
44,250	44,300	9,524	7,600	9,999	8,549
44,300	44,350	9,538	7,614	10,013	8,563
44,350	44,400	9,552	7,628	10,027	8,577
44,400	44,450	9,566	7,642	10,041	8,591
44,450	44,500	9,580	7,656	10,055	8,605
44,500	44,550	9,594	7,670	10,069	8,619
44,550	44,600	9,608	7,684	10,083	8,633
44,600	44,650	9,622	7,698	10,098	8,647
44,650	44,700	9,636	7,712	10,114	8,661
44,700	44,750	9,650	7,726	10,129	8,675
44,750	44,800	9,664	7,740	10,145	8,689
44,800	44,850	9,678	7,754	10,160	8,703
44,850	44,900	9,692	7,768	10,176	8,717
44,900	44,950	9,706	7,782	10,191	8,731
44,950	45,000	9,720	7,796	10,207	8,745

45,000

At least	But less than	Single	Married filing jointly *	Married filing separately	Head of a household
45,000	45,050	9,734	7,810	10,222	8,759
45,050	45,100	9,748	7,824	10,238	8,773
45,100	45,150	9,762	7,838	10,253	8,787
45,150	45,200	9,776	7,852	10,269	8,801
45,200	45,250	9,790	7,866	10,284	8,815
45,250	45,300	9,804	7,880	10,300	8,829
45,300	45,350	9,818	7,894	10,315	8,843
45,350	45,400	9,832	7,908	10,331	8,857
45,400	45,450	9,846	7,922	10,346	8,871
45,450	45,500	9,860	7,936	10,362	8,885
45,500	45,550	9,874	7,950	10,377	8,899
45,550	45,600	9,888	7,964	10,393	8,913
45,600	45,650	9,902	7,978	10,408	8,927
45,650	45,700	9,916	7,992	10,424	8,941
45,700	45,750	9,930	8,006	10,439	8,955
45,750	45,800	9,944	8,020	10,455	8,969
45,800	45,850	9,958	8,034	10,470	8,983
45,850	45,900	9,972	8,048	10,486	8,997
45,900	45,950	9,986	8,062	10,501	9,011
45,950	46,000	10,000	8,076	10,517	9,025

46,000

At least	But less than	Single	Married filing jointly *	Married filing separately	Head of a household
46,000	46,050	10,014	8,090	10,532	9,039
46,050	46,100	10,028	8,104	10,548	9,053
46,100	46,150	10,042	8,118	10,563	9,067
46,150	46,200	10,056	8,132	10,579	9,081
46,200	46,250	10,070	8,146	10,594	9,095
46,250	46,300	10,084	8,160	10,610	9,109
46,300	46,350	10,098	8,174	10,625	9,123
46,350	46,400	10,112	8,188	10,641	9,137
46,400	46,450	10,126	8,202	10,656	9,151
46,450	46,500	10,140	8,216	10,672	9,165
46,500	46,550	10,154	8,230	10,687	9,179
46,550	46,600	10,168	8,244	10,703	9,193
46,600	46,650	10,182	8,258	10,718	9,207
46,650	46,700	10,196	8,272	10,734	9,221
46,700	46,750	10,210	8,286	10,749	9,235
46,750	46,800	10,224	8,300	10,765	9,249
46,800	46,850	10,238	8,314	10,780	9,263
46,850	46,900	10,252	8,328	10,796	9,277
46,900	46,950	10,266	8,342	10,811	9,291
46,950	47,000	10,280	8,356	10,827	9,305

47,000

At least	But less than	Single	Married filing jointly *	Married filing separately	Head of a household
47,000	47,050	10,294	8,370	10,842	9,319
47,050	47,100	10,308	8,384	10,858	9,333
47,100	47,150	10,322	8,398	10,873	9,347
47,150	47,200	10,336	8,412	10,889	9,361
47,200	47,250	10,350	8,426	10,904	9,375
47,250	47,300	10,364	8,440	10,920	9,389
47,300	47,350	10,378	8,454	10,935	9,403
47,350	47,400	10,392	8,468	10,951	9,417
47,400	47,450	10,406	8,482	10,966	9,431
47,450	47,500	10,420	8,496	10,982	9,445
47,500	47,550	10,434	8,510	10,997	9,459
47,550	47,600	10,448	8,525	11,013	9,473
47,600	47,650	10,462	8,538	11,028	9,487
47,650	47,700	10,476	8,552	11,044	9,501
47,700	47,750	10,490	8,566	11,059	9,515
47,750	47,800	10,504	8,580	11,075	9,529
47,800	47,850	10,518	8,594	11,090	9,543
47,850	47,900	10,532	8,608	11,106	9,557
47,900	47,950	10,546	8,622	11,121	9,571
47,950	48,000	10,560	8,636	11,137	9,585

48,000

At least	But less than	Single	Married filing jointly *	Married filing separately	Head of a household
48,000	48,050	10,574	8,650	11,152	9,599
48,050	48,100	10,588	8,664	11,168	9,613
48,100	48,150	10,602	8,678	11,183	9,627
48,150	48,200	10,616	8,692	11,199	9,641
48,200	48,250	10,630	8,706	11,214	9,655
48,250	48,300	10,644	8,720	11,230	9,669
48,300	48,350	10,658	8,734	11,245	9,683
48,350	48,400	10,672	8,748	11,261	9,697
48,400	48,450	10,686	8,762	11,276	9,711
48,450	48,500	10,700	8,776	11,292	9,725
48,500	48,550	10,714	8,790	11,307	9,739
48,550	48,600	10,728	8,804	11,323	9,753
48,600	48,650	10,742	8,818	11,338	9,767
48,650	48,700	10,756	8,832	11,354	9,781
48,700	48,750	10,770	8,846	11,369	9,795
48,750	48,800	10,784	8,860	11,385	9,809
48,800	48,850	10,798	8,874	11,400	9,823
48,850	48,900	10,812	8,888	11,416	9,837
48,900	48,950	10,826	8,902	11,431	9,851
48,950	49,000	10,840	8,916	11,447	9,865

49,000

At least	But less than	Single	Married filing jointly *	Married filing separately	Head of a household
49,000	49,050	10,854	8,930	11,462	9,879
49,050	49,100	10,868	8,944	11,478	9,893
49,100	49,150	10,882	8,958	11,493	9,907
49,150	49,200	10,896	8,972	11,509	9,921
49,200	49,250	10,910	8,986	11,524	9,935
49,250	49,300	10,924	9,000	11,540	9,949
49,300	49,350	10,938	9,014	11,555	9,963
49,350	49,400	10,952	9,028	11,571	9,977
49,400	49,450	10,966	9,042	11,586	9,991
49,450	49,500	10,980	9,056	11,602	10,005
49,500	49,550	10,994	9,070	11,617	10,019
49,550	49,600	11,008	9,084	11,633	10,033
49,600	49,650	11,022	9,098	11,648	10,047
49,650	49,700	11,036	9,112	11,664	10,061
49,700	49,750	11,050	9,126	11,679	10,075
49,750	49,800	11,064	9,140	11,695	10,089
49,800	49,850	11,078	9,154	11,710	10,103
49,850	49,900	11,092	9,168	11,726	10,117
49,900	49,950	11,106	9,182	11,741	10,131
49,950	50,000	11,120	9,196	11,757	10,145

* This column must also be used by a qualifying widow(er).

50,000 or over — use Form 1040

Photo Credits

Units 1–7 Opening Pages © 2001 PhotoDisc

Chapter 1 3, 6, 10, 11, 14, 16, 23 © 2001 PhotoDisc

Chapter 2 25, 26, 28, 35, 39, 41, 45, 46 © 2001 PhotoDisc

Chapter 3 49, 58, 60, 63, 64, 67 © 2001 PhotoDisc

Chapter 4 77, 81, 85, 89, 96, 97, 99, 103 © 2001 PhotoDisc

Chapter 5 107, 115, 118, 120, 122, 124, 126, 130 © 2001 PhotoDisc

Unit 1 Project 136, 138 © 2001 PhotoDisc

Chapter 6 145, 154, 157, 160, 163, 164, 166, 171 © 2001 PhotoDisc

Chapter 7 174, 177, 181, 205 © 2001 PhotoDisc; 188: Netscape Communicator browser window © 2001 Netscape Communications Corporation. Used with permission. Netscape Communications has not authorized, sponsored, endorsed, or approved this publication and is not responsible for its content.

Chapter 8 207, 209, 211, 218, 225, 229, 234 © 2001 PhotoDisc

Chapter 9 238, 242, 255, 256, 258, 261, 263, 267 © 2001 PhotoDisc

Unit 2 Project 271 © 2001 PhotoDisc

Chapter 10 279, 284, 286, 288, 289, 294, 297, 298, 301 © 2001 PhotoDisc

Chapter 11 303, 307, 312, 320, 322, 323, 325, 329 © 2001 PhotoDisc

Chapter 12 331, 334, 338, 340, 348, 352, 357 © 2001 PhotoDisc

Chapter 13 359, 364, 368, 371, 374, 379 © 2001 PhotoDisc

Chapter 14 382, 387, 391, 397, 399, 405, 407 © 2001 PhotoDisc

Chapter 15 409, 413, 419, 421, 422, 427, 429, 434, 435, 436, 437 © 2001 PhotoDisc

Chapter 16 456, 460, 461, 466, 470, 477 © 2001 PhotoDisc

Chapter 17 480, 484, 490, 495, 496, 498, 500, 501, 502, 503 © 2001 PhotoDisc

Chapter 18 505, 509, 511, 521, 525, 527, 528 © 2001 PhotoDisc

Chapter 19 531, 535, 541, 546, 551 © 2001 PhotoDisc

Chapter 20 563, 568, 570, 572, 578, 581, 584, 586 © 2001 PhotoDisc

Chapter 21 591, 595, 597, 601, 611, 613, 617 © 2001 PhotoDisc

Chapter 22 620, 623, 630, 631, 634, 636, 637, 639 © 2001 PhotoDisc

Chapter 23 642, 646, 654, 658, 661, 669 © 2001 PhotoDisc

Chapter 24 671, 677, 683, 684, 686, 690, 692, 693, 694, 695 © 2001 PhotoDisc

Unit 5 Project 703 © 2001 PhotoDisc

Chapter 25 712, 714, 719, 726, 728, 729, 730, 731 © 2001 PhotoDisc

Chapter 26 734, 740, 741, 745, 750, 752, 753, 754, 755 © 2001 PhotoDisc

Chapter 27 757, 760, 766, 769 © 2001 PhotoDisc

Chapter 28 797, 802, 803, 809, 814 © 2001 PhotoDisc

Chapter 29 824, 827, 831, 836, 839, 843 © 2001 PhotoDisc

Chapter 30 848, 852, 856, 860 © 2001 PhotoDisc

Unit 7 Project 869 © 2001 PhotoDisc

Glossary

A

Abrasives. Cleaning agents in car polishing compounds that contain strong chemicals or are coarse and can cause surface damage. (p. 659)

Acceptance. A formal agreement to the terms of an offer, forming a contract between the parties. (p. 628)

Adjustable rate mortgage (ARM). A mortgage in which the interest rate changes in response to the movement of interest rates in the economy as a whole. (p. 630)

Adjusted gross income. Income minus allowable exclusions (such as IRAs and alimony). (p. 183)

Advanced degrees. Degrees earned through specialized, intensive post-baccalaureate programs. (p. 13)

Age Discrimination in Employment Act. Law that prohibits discrimination in employment decisions against people age 40 and over. (p. 115)

Agency bond. A bond issued by a federal agency, such as the Federal Home Loan Mortgage Corporation. (p. 365)

Alimony. Money paid by one former spouse to support the other. (p. 685)

Allowances. A number that reduces the amount of tax withheld from your paycheck. (p. 105)

Alternate dispute resolution (ADR). A general term covering several methods of settling disputes without using the court system. (p. 858)

Americans with Disabilities Act. Law that prohibits discrimination on the basis of physical or mental disabilities. (p. 115)

Annual percentage rate (APR). The cost of credit, expressed as a yearly percentage. (p. 464)

Annual percentage yield (APY). The actual interest rate an account pays per year, with compounding included. (p. 282)

Annual report. A summary of a corporation's financial results for the year and prospects for the future. (p. 314)

Annuity. A contract sold by an insurance company that provides the investor with a series of regular payments, usually after retirement. (p. 319)

Appellate court. A court having appellate jurisdiction (ability to hear a case that has been appealed from a trial court where it was first heard and decided). (p. 845)

Aptitude. A natural physical or mental ability that permits you to do certain tasks well. (p. 27)

Assets. Items of value that a person owns. (p. 212)

Attractive nuisance. A dangerous place, condition, or object that is particularly attractive to children. (p. 740)

Audit. The examination of your tax returns by the Internal Revenue Service. (p. 177)

B

Back-end load. A sales charge paid when you sell an investment. (p. 386)

Bait and switch. An illegal sales technique in which a seller advertises a product with the intention of persuading consumers to buy a more expensive product. (p. 804)

Balanced fund. A mutual fund that invests in a mixture of stocks and bonds to minimize risk. (p. 383)

Bankruptcy. A legal process that relieves debtors of the responsibility of paying their debts or protects them while they try to repay. (p. 534)

Basic needs. The ingredients necessary for maintaining physical life, including food, clothing, water, and shelter. (p. 567)

Bear market. A market characterized by falling prices and investor pessimism. (p. 341)

Benefits. Sick pay, vacation time, and other company-provided supplements to income. (pp. 6, 152)

Binding arbitration. When an independent third person has the power to impose a decision that both parties in a dispute must accept. (p. 858)

Blank endorsement. The signature of the payee written on the back of the check exactly as it appears on the front of the check. (p. 248)

Blue chip stocks. Stocks of large, well-established corporations with a solid record of profitability. (p. 334)

Body (of a letter). The message section of a letter, containing attention, interest, desire, and action. (p. 53)

Bond fund. A mutual fund that invests in bonds to try to achieve stable income with minimal risk. (p. 384)

Bonds. Debt obligations of corporations or governments. (p. 317)

Budget. A spending and saving plan based on your expected income and expenses. (p. 208)

Bull market. A prolonged period of rising stock prices and a general feeling of investor optimism. (p. 341)

C

Callable bond. A bond that the issuer has the right to pay off before its maturity date. (p. 360)

Canceled check. A check that the bank has processed. (p. 237)

Capacity. The ability to repay a loan from present income. (p. 482)

Capital. Property possessed that is worth more than debts owed. (p. 458)

Capital gain. An increase in the value of stock above the price initially paid for it. (p. 331)

Care labels. Labels found on clothing and other products that give instructions for cleaning, wash and dry temperature, and other care needed to preserve the product. (p. 827)

Cash value. The savings accumulated in a permanent life insurance policy that you would receive if you canceled your policy. (p. 772)

Cashier's check. A check written by a bank on its own funds. (p. 254)

Certificate of deposit (CD). A deposit that earns a fixed interest rate for a specified length of time. (p. 288)

Certified check. A personal check that the bank guarantees to be good. (p. 253)

Chapter 7 bankruptcy. A liquidation form of bankruptcy for individuals that wipes out most debts in exchange for giving up most assets. (p. 536)

Chapter 11 bankruptcy. A reorganization form of bankruptcy for businesses that allows them to continue operating under court supervision as they repay their restructured debts. (p. 536)

Chapter 13 bankruptcy. The wage earner's plan of bankruptcy, wherein debtors keep their property and repay a portion of their debts over a period of time under a court-enforced plan. (p. 537)

Character. A trait of creditworthiness indicating a responsible attitude toward living up to agreements. (p. 482)

Check. A written order to a bank to pay the stated amount to the person or business (payee) named on it. (p. 237)

Checkbook register. A record of deposits to and withdrawals from a checking account. (p. 244)

Cherry picker. A customer who buys only loss leaders. (p. 578)

Child support. Money paid to a former spouse for support of dependent children. (p. 182)

Childproof devices. Devices designed to resist tampering by young children. (p. 826)

Civil ceremony. A wedding performed by a public official rather than a member of the clergy. (p. 674)

Civil court. A court with the authority to hear non-criminal cases. (p. 845)

Civil Rights Act of 1964. Prohibits discrimination in hiring, training, and promotion on the basis of race, color, gender, religion, or national origin. (p. 115)

Class-action lawsuit. A legal action in which a large number of people with similar complaints against the same defendant join together to sue. (p. 856)

Closed-end credit. A loan for a specific amount that must be repaid, in full, including all finance charges, by a stated due date. (p. 466)

Closing costs. Expenses incurred in transferring ownership from buyer to seller in a real estate transaction. (p. 622)

COBRA. Federal law that allows people who leave employment to continue their health insurance under the company plan for a limited period of time. (p. 758)

Codicil. A document that explains, adds, or deletes provisions in your existing will. (p. 413)

Co-insurance clause. A provision requiring policyholders to insure their building for a stated percentage of its replacement value in order to receive full reimbursement for a loss. (p. 738)

Collateral. Property pledged to a lender to assure repayment of a loan. (p. 458)

Collective bargaining. The process of negotiating the terms of employment for union members. (p. 161)

Collective values. What is important to society as a whole. (p. 569)

College placement center. Source of career counseling available at colleges or technical training institutes. (p. 14)

Collision coverage. Automobile insurance that will cover costs of repairing or replacing your own car, even if you are at fault. (p. 745)

Common stock. A type of stock that pays a variable dividend and gives the holder voting rights. (p. 332)

Company advertising. Advertising intended to promote the image of a store, company, or retail chain. (p. 576)

Competition. The rivalry among sellers in the same market to win customers. (p. 801)

Complimentary close. The appropriate phrase that courteously ends a business letter. (p. 53)

Compound interest. Interest computed on the original principal plus the accumulated interest. (p. 281)

Comprehensive coverage. Insurance that pays for damage to your car from events other than collision or vehicle overturning. (p. 745)

Compressed workweek. A work schedule that shrinks the days worked but contains the same total hours; for example, four days, 10 hours each, totaling a 40-hour week. (p. 159)

Condominium. Individually owned unit in an apartment-style complex with a shared ownership of common areas. (p. 391)

Consideration. Anything of value exchanged as part of a contract. (p. 217)

Consumer advocate. A person who actively promotes consumer causes. (p. 834)

Consumers. Buyers and users of goods and services. (p. 797)

Contacts. People you know who can help you get an interview for a job. (p. 35)

Contract. A legally enforceable agreement between two or more parties to do or not to do something. (p. 215)

Convertible bond. A corporate bond that can be exchanged, at the owner's option, for a specified number of shares of the corporation's common stock. (p. 361)

Coordination of benefits. A method of integrating the benefits payable under more than one health insurance plan so that the benefits received from all sources are limited to 100 percent of allowable medical expenses. (p. 758)

Co-signer. A person who promises in writing to repay a promissory note if the maker fails to do so. (p. 222)

Counterclaim. A defendant's assertion that the plaintiff is at fault and should pay damages to the defendant. (p. 851)

Counteroffer. In a real estate transaction, a revised offer from the seller that is then accepted or rejected. (p. 629)

Court. A person or group of people whose task it is to hear and decide matters according to the law. (p. 845)

Creative listening. The ability to hear new ideas that can help you develop a plan of action. (p. 79)

Credit. Money borrowed to buy something now, with the agreement to pay for it later. (p. 455)

Credit bureau. A company that gathers, stores, and sells credit information to business subscribers. (p. 479)

Credit history. The complete record of your credit performance. (p. 479)

Credit rating. A measure of credit-worthiness based on an analysis of a consumer's financial history. (p. 487)

Credit report. A written report issued by a credit bureau that contains relevant information about a person's credit history. (p. 480)

Cremation. A process of reducing a body to ashes in a high-temperature oven. (p. 688)

Criminal court. A court that hears cases involving punishable offenses against society. (p. 845)

Critical listening. A type of listening in which you differentiate fact from fiction. (p. 79)

Custom. A long-established practice that may be considered an unwritten law. (p. 571)

Cyclical stocks. Stocks that follow the business cycle of advances and declines in the economy. (p. 280)

D

Database. A computer program that organizes data for easy search and retrieval. (p. 227)

Dealer add-ons. High-priced, high-profit car dealer services that add little or no value. (p. 648)

Debenture. A corporate bond that is not backed by collateral but only by the general credit standing of the corporation. (p. 361)

Debt collector. A person or company hired by a creditor to collect the balance due on an account. (p. 495)

Debtor. One who owes money to another. (p. 534)

Deductions. 1. Amounts subtracted from gross pay. (p. 145) 2. Expenses the law allows the taxpayer to subtract from adjusted gross income. (p. 183)

Deed. A document that transfers title of real property from one party to another. (p. 631)

Defendant. The person against whom a lawsuit is filed. (p. 851)

Deferred billing. A service to charge customers whereby purchases are not billed to the customer until a later date. (p. 460)

Defined-benefit plan. A company-sponsored retirement plan that specifies retirement benefits, based on wages earned and years of service. (p. 425)

Defined-contribution plan. A company-sponsored retirement plan that specifies a minimum contribution but no promise of a particular benefit at retirement. (p. 425)

Demand. The willingness and ability of consumers to purchase goods and services at certain prices. (p. 798)

Demand deposit. An account that lets you demand portions of your deposited funds at will. (p. 237)

Deposit. A pledge, or down payment. A refundable payment made to secure an apartment. (p. 504)

Deposition. A written, sworn statement of a witness that can take the place of court testimony and serves to preserve evidence. (p. 852)

Depreciation. In real estate, the decline in value of property due to normal wear and tear. (p. 394)

Direct investment. Buying stock directly from a corporation. (p. 345)

Disability insurance. An insurance plan that makes regular payments to replace income lost when illness or injury prevents the insured from working. (p. 766)

Discharged debt. A debt that is no longer owed after declaration of bankruptcy. (p. 536)

Discount bonds. Bonds purchased at less than their maturity value. (p. 317)

Discretionary income. Money that is left over when the bills have been paid. (p. 281)

Discrimination. Treating people differently based on prejudice rather than individual merit. (p. 492)

Disposable income. The money you have left to spend or save after taxes have been paid. (p. 207)

Dissolution of marriage. When irreconcilable differences have led to the breakdown of a marriage. (p. 684)

Diversification. The spreading of risk among many types of investments. (p. 307)

Dividend reinvestment. Using dividends previously earned on stock to buy more shares. (p. 346)

Dividends. The part of the corporation's profits paid to stockholders. (p. 331)

Dormitory. An on-campus building that contains many small rooms that colleges rent to students. (p. 592)

Down payment. A part of the purchase price paid in cash up front, reducing the amount of a loan. (p. 517)

Downward communication. Communication that flows from higher to lower levels in an organization. (p. 82)

Duplex. A building with two separate living quarters. (p. 391)

E

E-mail. The transmission of messages using computers. (p. 83)

Earnest money. In real estate, a portion of the purchase price that the buyer deposits as evidence of good faith to show that the purchase offer is serious. (p. 628)

Earnings per share. A corporation's after-tax earnings divided by the number of shares of common stock outstanding. (p. 336)

Economy. All activities related to production and distribution of goods and services in a geographic area. (p. 572)

Efficiency apartment. An apartment with one large room that serves as the kitchen, living room, and bedroom, plus a bathroom. (p. 593)

Empathy. The ability to see others' points of view and understand their feelings. (p. 84)

Employee expenses. Costs paid by employees and not reimbursed by employers. (p. 9)

Employee services. Special perks or features offered to employees to enhance employment and motivate workers. (p. 153)

Employment application. A preprinted form that must be filled out when applying for employment. (p. 64)

Endorsement. A written amendment to an insurance policy. (p. 737)

Entrepreneur. One who organizes, manages, and assumes the risks of a business or enterprise. (p. 10)

Equal Pay Act. Law that prohibits unequal pay for men and women doing substantially similar work. (p. 115)

Equilibrium price. The price at which the quantity supplied equals the quantity demanded of the product. (p. 799)

Equity. Ownership interest in property; the difference between the market value of property and the amount owed on it. (p. 620)

Estate. All that a person owns, less debts owed, at the time of the person's death. (p. 412)

Estate planning. Preparing a plan for transferring property during one's lifetime and at one's death. (p. 412)

Estate tax. A tax levied by the federal government on property transferred from deceased people to their heirs. (p. 419)

Eviction. The legal process of removing a tenant from rental property. (p. 610)

Exempt status. A claim on Form W-4 that allows you to have no federal tax withheld from your paycheck. (p. 105)

Exempted property. The possessions that the bankrupt debtor is allowed to keep because they are considered necessary for survival. (p. 537)

Exemption. An allowance a taxpayer claims for each person dependent on the taxpayer's income. (p. 180)

Experience. Knowledge and skills gained from direct participation in a job. (p. 32)

F

Face value. The amount a bondholder will be repaid when the bond matures or is due. (p. 359)

Fair Labor Standards Act. Law that established a minimum wage and required hourly workers to be paid $1\frac{1}{2}$ times their hourly rate for overtime. (p. 114)

Fake sale. An advertised sale that represents regular-priced merchandise. (p. 805)

Family and Medical Leave Act. Law that allows employees to take up to 12 weeks of unpaid, job-protected leave in a 12-month period for family and medical reasons. (p. 115)

Family of funds. A variety of mutual funds covering a whole range of investment objectives. (p. 381)

Fee. A non-refundable charge for a service. (p. 596)

Finance charge. The interest you pay to use credit. (p. 458)

Financial advisers. Trained professional planners who give overall investment advice. (p. 314)

Financial plan. An orderly program for spending, saving, and investing the money you earn. (p. 207)

Fixed expenses. Costs you are obligated to pay at specific times, regardless of other events. (p. 209)

Fixed-rate loans. Loans for which the interest rate does not change (up or down) over the life of the loan. (p. 513)

Fixed-rate mortgage. A mortgage in which the interest rate remains constant over the life of the loan. (p. 630)

Flammability. The capacity of a product to catch on fire. (p. 825)

Flextime. Flexible schedules that allow employees to choose their working hours within defined limits. (p. 158)

Floating a check. The practice of writing a check on insufficient funds and hoping to make a deposit to cover the check before it is cashed. (p. 238)

Form W-2. A form that lists income earned during the year and all amounts withheld by the employer for taxes. (p. 110)

Form W-4. A form completed for income tax withholding purposes. (p. 92)

Fraud. The intentional misrepresentation of information with the intent to deceive or mislead. (p. 832)

Free enterprise. An economic system in which producers and consumers are free to engage in business transactions with minimal government interference. (p. 797)

Front-end load. A sales charge paid when you buy an investment and sometimes when dividends are reinvested as well. (p. 386)

Futures. Contracts to buy and sell commodities or stocks for a specified price on a specified date in the future. (p. 321)

G

General obligation bond. A municipal bond backed by the power of the issuing state or local government to levy taxes and borrow. (p. 364)

Generic drugs. Medications with the same composition as the equivalent brand-name drugs, but generally less expensive. (p. 826)

Gift tax. A tax levied on the person giving a gift to another person in excess of $10,000 in a year. (p. 420)

Global fund. A mutual fund that purchases international stocks and bonds as well as U.S. securities. (p. 384)

Goal. A desired end toward which efforts are directed. (p. 31)

Gross income. All taxable income received, including wages, tips, salaries, interest, dividends, unemployment compensation, alimony, and so forth. (p. 181)

Gross pay. The total pay before any deductions are subtracted. (p. 143)

Group health insurance. Health insurance issued to a group, to cover individuals in the group and sometimes their dependents. (p. 757)

Growth and income fund. A mutual fund whose investment goal is to earn returns from both dividends and capital gains. (p. 383)

Growth fund. A mutual fund whose investment goal is to buy stocks that will increase in value over time. (p. 383)

Growth stocks. Stocks in corporations that reinvest their profits into the business so that it can grow. (p. 333)

H

Health insurance. A plan for sharing the risk of financial loss resulting from an accident or illness. (p. 757)

Health Maintenance Organization (HMO). A group health insurance plan that offers prepaid medical care to its members. (p. 762)

Hearing. The process of perceiving sound. (p. 77)

Heirs. Persons who receive property from someone who has died. (p. 410)

High-balling. An excessively high offer for a trade-in vehicle. (p. 648)

Homeowner's policy. Insurance that protects property owners from property and liability risks. (p. 733)

Horizontal communication. Less formal communication among employees of equal rank. (p. 82)

Human relations. Getting along with others. (p. 84)

Hygiene factors. Job elements that dissatisfy when absent but do not add to satisfaction when present. (p. 95)

I

Identity. Who you are. (p. 25)

Incentive pay. Money offered to encourage employees to strive for higher levels of performance. (p. 152)

Income fund. A mutual fund whose investment goal is to buy securities that consistently pay good dividends. (p. 383)

Income stocks. Stocks that have a consistent history of paying high dividends. (p. 333)

Incontestable clause. A provision of a life or health insurance policy that once the policy has been in effect for a stated period of time, the insurer may no longer question items on the application in order to deny coverage. (p. 770)

Indemnification. Putting an insurance policyholder back in the same financial condition as before a loss occurred. (p. 712)

Index fund. A mutual fund that tries to match the performance of a particular securities index by investing in the companies included in that index. (p. 384)

Individual retirement account (IRA). A retirement plan that allows workers to set aside up to $2,000 per year in tax-deferred savings. (p. 422)

Industry advertising. Advertising intended to promote a general product group, without regard to where these products are purchased. (p. 577)

Inflation. A rise in the general level of prices. (p. 306)

Inheritance tax. A tax levied by a state against an heir who inherits property from a decedent. (p. 419)

Initiative. A quality that allows you to do things on your own, without being told to. (p. 118)

Innovations. New ideas, methods, or devices that bring about change. (p. 569)

Insurable interest. Financial interest in life or property such that, if the life or property were lost or harmed, the insured would suffer financially. (p. 717)

Insurance. A method for spreading individual risk among a large group of people to make losses more affordable for all. (p. 711)

Insurer. A business that agrees to pay the cost of potential future losses in exchange for regular fee payments. (p. 711)

Interest. Money paid for the use of money; earnings on a savings account. (p. 281)

Interests. The things you like to do. (p. 27)

Investing. The use of savings to earn a financial return. (p. 304)

Investment-grade bond. Highly rated bonds that are considered safe because the issuers are stable and dependable. (p. 368)

Involuntary bankruptcy. A financial situation that occurs when creditors file a petition with the court, asking the court to declare a debtor unable to pay bills. (p. 535)

Itemize. To list allowable expenses on your tax return. (p. 183)

Itinerary. A detailed schedule of events, times, and places for a vacation or trip. (p. 678)

J

Job analysis. A procedure that lists the positive and negative attributes of a given career choice. (p. 6)

Job interview. A face-to-face meeting with a potential employer to discuss your job qualifications. (p. 66)

Job rotation. A job design in which employees are trained to do more than one specialized task. (p. 159)

Job sharing. A process in which two people share what was originally a full-time job, including salaries and benefits. (p. 159)

Judgment. The final court ruling that resolves key issues and establishes the rights and obligations of each party in a trial. (p. 853)

Junk bonds. A bond that has a low rating, or no rating at all. (p. 369)

Jurisdiction. The legal right and authority of a court to hear and decide a case. (p. 845)

K

Keogh plan. A tax-deferred retirement plan available to self-employed persons and their employees. (p. 423)

L

Labor union. A group of people who work in the same or similar occupations, organized for the benefit of all employees in these occupations. (p. 160)

Landlord. The owner of rental property. (p. 603)

Lease. A written agreement that allows a tenant to use property for a specified time period and rent. (p. 606)

Lemon. A car with substantial defects that the manufacturer has been unable to fix after repeated attempts. (p. 650)

Letter address. The part of a letter that shows the name and address of the person or company to whom you are writing. (p. 53)

Letter of application. A cover letter that introduces you to a potential employer and gives you the chance to sell your qualifications. (p. 49)

Letter of reference. A statement, in letter form, written by someone who can be relied upon to give a sincere report on your character, abilities, and experience. (p. 60)

Leverage. The use of borrowed money to buy securities. (p. 342)

Liabilities. Amounts of money that are owed to others. (p. 212)

Liability coverage. Insurance to protect against claims for bodily injury to another person or damage to another person's property. (p. 740)

Liability risks. The possibilities of loss due to errors or negligence. (p. 716)

Lien. A financial claim on property. (p. 631)

Life insurance. Insurance that provides funds to the beneficiaries when the insured dies. (p. 768)

Lifestyle. The way people choose to live their lives, based on the values they have chosen. (p. 26)

Line of credit. A pre-established amount that can be borrowed on demand with no collateral. (p. 459)

Liquidity. The ability of an asset to be converted into cash quickly without loss of value. (p. 287)

Listening. An active hearing process that requires mental concentration and effort. (p. 77)

Loan sharks. Unlicensed lenders who charge illegally high interest rates. (p. 469)

Lobbying. Supporting legislation and political action that is beneficial to a certain profession. (p. 164)

Locked in. The state of feeling trapped in a job because you cannot afford to take the cut in pay that may accompany starting over. (p. 34)

Loss leader. An item of merchandise marked down to an unusually low price, sometimes below cost, to attract customers into the store. (p. 578)

Low-balling. 1. Advertising one service, then adding others (repairs) that are not necessary or not expected. (p. 806) 2. An unrealistically low price offered by a dealer for a buyer's old car as part of a new-car deal. (p. 648)

M

Market value. 1. The price for which a stock is bought and sold in the marketplace. (p. 335) 2. The highest price that a property will bring on the market. (p. 619)

Marketable. A term describing work of a quality such that an employer can use or sell it. (p. 117)

Maturity date. The date on which an investment becomes due for payment. (p. 288)

Mediation. A dispute resolution method in which an independent third person helps the parties come to their own solution. (p. 858)

Medicaid. Government-sponsored health insurance for people with low incomes and limited resources. (p. 764)

Medicare. Government-sponsored health insurance for people currently age 65 or older. (p. 764)

Micromarketing. A strategy to target specific customers to meet their specific needs. (p. 580)

Minimum wage. The legally established lower limit on wages employers may pay. (p. 114)

Minors. Persons under the age of legal adulthood. (p. 110)

Money market account. A combination savings-investment plan in which money deposited is used to purchase safe, liquid securities. (p. 288)

Money market fund. A mutual fund that invests in safe, liquid securities, such as Treasury bills. (p. 384)

Monopoly. A market with many buyers but only one seller. (p. 801)

Mortgage. A loan to purchase real estate. (p. 394)

Mortgage bond. A corporate bond backed by specific assets as collateral to assure repayment of the debt. (p. 361)

Motivators. Job elements that increase job satisfaction. (p. 95)

Multiple Listing Service (MLS). A real estate marketing service composed of real estate offices that list and sell property, and share commissions on sales. (p. 626)

Municipal bond. A bond issued by state and local governments. (p. 364)

Mutual assent. Agreement to all terms of the contract by all parties to the contract. (p. 217)

Mutual fund. A large, professionally managed group of investments. (p. 319)

N

Negotiable instrument. An unconditional written promise to pay a specified sum of money upon demand of the holder. (p. 222)

Net pay. The amount left after all deductions have been taken out of your gross pay. (p. 146)

Net worth. The difference between your assets and your liabilities. (p. 212)

Networks. Communication lines established for people to talk to each other and share information. (p. 17)

No-fault insurance. Drivers involved in an accident collect medical expenses, lost wages, and related injury costs from their own insurance company, regardless of who is at fault. (p. 746)

No-load funds. Mutual funds that do not charge commissions because no salespeople are involved. (p. 386)

O

Odd-number pricing. The practice of setting prices at uneven amounts rather than whole dollars to make them seem lower. (p. 577)

Offer. A formal document that expresses interest in entering into a contract with someone else. (p. 628)

Open-ended credit. An agreement to lend the borrower an amount up to a stated limit and to allow borrowing up to that limit again, whenever the balance falls below the limit. (p. 463)

Option. The right, but not the obligation, to buy or sell a commodity or stock for a specified price within a specified time period. (p. 321)

Overbook. When an airline has sold tickets for more seats than are available. (p. 681)

Overdraft. A check written without sufficient money in an account to cover it. (p. 238)

Overtime. Hours worked over the regular hours in a workweek; usually more than 40 hours in a five-day period. (p. 143)

Oxidize. Permanently lose color and shine in the paint of a vehicle. (p. 658)

P

Par value. An assigned (and often arbitrary) dollar value that is printed on a stock certificate. (p. 335)

Participating preferred stock. A class of preferred stock that shares profits with common stock (beyond the guaranteed rate). (p. 278)

Participation certificate. An investment in a pool of mortgages that have been purchased by a government agency. (p. 393)

Pawnbroker. A legal business that makes high-interest loans based on the value of personal possessions pledged as collateral. (p. 469)

Penny stocks. Low-priced stocks of small companies that have no track record. (p. 322)

Permanent life insurance. Life insurance that remains in effect for the insured's lifetime and builds a cash value. (p. 772)

Personal injury protection. Automobile insurance coverage that pays for medical, hospital, and funeral costs of the insured and his or her family and passengers, regardless of fault. (p. 746)

Personal property floater. Insurance coverage for the insured's moveable property wherever it may be located; it protects property without regard to its location at the time of loss. (p. 739)

Personal risks. Possible losses involving income or standard of living. (p. 715)

Personality. Personal qualities and traits that make each person unique. (p. 28)

Plaintiff. The person who begins a lawsuit by filing a complaint. (p. 851)

Policy. A written insurance contract. (p. 711)

Policyholder. The person who owns, or holds, an insurance policy. (p. 711)

Polishing compound. A substance that is used to smooth out an automobile's surface scratches, scuffs, and stains. (p. 659)

Power of attorney. A legal document giving another person the power to act on your behalf. (p. 416)

Pre-approval. Finding out how much money you will be qualified to borrow before making a purchase. (p. 643)

Preferred Provider Organization (PPO). A group of healthcare providers who band together to provide health services for set fees. (p. 762)

Preferred stock. A type of stock that pays a fixed dividend and carries no voting rights. (p. 332)

Premium. The sum of money the policyholder agrees to pay to an insurance company periodically (monthly, quarterly, annually, or semiannually) for an insurance policy. (p. 711)

Price-fixing. An illegal agreement among competitors to sell a good or service for a set price. (p. 801)

Prime rate. The interest rate lenders offer their best commercial (business) customers. (p. 514)

Principal. 1. The total amount that is financed or borrowed and on which interest is computed. (p. 515) 2. The amount of money set aside by a saver that will earn interest. (p. 281)

Probability. The mathematics of chance; the chance of a loss occurring. (p. 712)

Producers. Manufacturers or makers of goods and services for sale. (p. 797)

Product advertising. Advertising intended to convince consumers to buy a specific good or service. (p. 576)

Productivity. The amount a worker produces per unit of time, such as an hour. (p. 94)

Professional organization. An organization of people in a particular occupation that requires considerable training and specialized skills. (p. 163)

Progressive taxes. Taxes that increase in proportion to income. (p. 173)

Promotion. The opportunity to advance, accept more responsibility, and work your way up in a company. (p. 8)

Property risks. The chances of loss or harm to personal or real property. (p. 716)

Property settlement agreement. A document specifying the division of property and assets agreed to by both parties to a divorce and entered into court for the judge's approval. (p. 684)

Proportional taxes. Taxes for which the tax rate remains constant, regardless of the amount on which the tax is imposed. (p. 174)

Prospectus. A legal document that offers securities or mutual fund shares for sale. (p. 386)

Proxy. A stockholder's written authorization to transfer voting rights to someone else, usually a company manager. (p. 332)

Purchasing power. The value of money, measured in the amount of goods and services that it can buy. (p. 801)

Pure risk. A chance of loss with no chance for gain. (p. 717)

Pyramid schemes. Illegal multilevel marketing plans that promise distributors commissions from their own sales and those of other distributors they recruit. (p. 806)

R

Reaffirmation. The agreement to repay discharged debts. (p. 538)

Real estate. Land and any buildings on it. (p. 390)

Real estate investment trust (REIT). A corporation that pools the money of many individuals to invest in real estate. (p. 393)

Rebate. A partial refund of an amount spent. (p. 512)

Recall. A request for consumers to return a defective product to the manufacturer, so the manufacturer can refund the consumer's money or fix the product. (p. 825)

Reconciliation. The monthly process of matching the bank's records with the checking account balance. (p. 246)

Redress. A remedy to a problem. (p. 814)

References. People over 18, not related to you, who have known you for at least one year and can report on your character and achievements. (p. 59)

Referral sale. A promise of a money rebate, prize, or discount in exchange for providing names of friends as prospective customers. (p. 805)

Regressive taxes. Taxes that decrease in proportion to increases in income. (p. 173)

Renter's policy. Insurance that protects renters from property and liability risks. (p. 733)

Reservation. An advance commitment that assures a traveler will receive a service. (p. 679)

Restrictive endorsement. An endorsement that restricts or limits the use of a check. (p. 249)

Resume. A summary of personal information, education, experience, additional qualifications, and references of a person seeking a job. (p. 55)

Retraining. Learning new and different skills in order to remain employable. (p. 13)

Return address. The part of a letter that shows the writer's street address, city, state, ZIP Code, and date of the letter. (p. 50)

Revenue. Money collected by the government from citizens and companies in the form of taxes. (p. 173)

Revenue bond. A municipal bond issued to raise money for a public-works project. (p. 364)

Reverse mortgage. An arrangement that allows a homeowner to receive monthly payments for a set period of time from a financial institution. When the house is sold, or the homeowner dies, the loan must be repaid. (p. 410)

Rider. A small insurance policy that modifies the coverage or the main policy. (p. 770)

Risk. 1. The chance that an investment's value will decrease. (p. 307) 2. The possibility of a loss from perils to people or property covered by insurance. (p. 711)

Risk assumption. Self-insuring; paying for losses personally. (p. 719)

Risk avoidance. Avoiding situations involving risk by never doing the activity that could result in the loss. (p. 719)

Risk management. An organized strategy for controlling financial loss from pure risks. (p. 717)

Risk reduction. Taking measures to lessen the frequency or severity of losses that may occur. (p. 719)

S

Salary. The amount of monthly or yearly pay. (p. 6)

Salutation. The letter greeting, using a person's name sometimes followed by a colon. (p. 53)

Scannable resume. A resume that has been designed for easy reading by a scanner and contains key words from the applicant's career field. (p. 59)

Scarcity. A basic economic problem in which consumers' wants are unlimited, but the resources for producing the products to satisfy these wants are limited. (p. 797)

Securities. Stocks and bonds issued by corporations or by the government. (p. 285)

Security deposit. A refundable amount paid in advance to protect the owner against damage or non-payment. (p. 595)

Self-actualization. A level at which workers meet their needs for accomplishment and satisfaction. (p. 94)

Self-assessment inventory. A listing of your strong and weak points and a plan of action. (p. 15)

Self-esteem. Feelings of self-worth about ourselves and our accomplishments. (p. 94)

Seniority. The policy that the last ones hired should be the first ones laid off. (p. 162)

Service credit. An agreement to have a service performed now and pay for it later. (p. 466)

Share account. A savings account at a credit union; the shares are ownership interest in the credit union. (p. 285)

Short selling. Selling stock borrowed from a broker that must be replaced at a later time. (p. 342)

Simple interest. Interest computed on the amount borrowed (or saved) only, without compounding. (p. 515)

Social Security Act. The first national social insurance program, which provides federal aid for the elderly and for disabled workers. (p. 113)

Social security number. A permanent work identification number issued to each citizen for purposes of identification on tax returns; used for record of earnings that have been taxed. (p. 106)

Special endorsement. An endorsement that transfers the right to cash the check to someone else. (p. 249)

Speculative risk. An event that may result in a loss or gain and is therefore uninsurable. (p. 717)

Spreadsheet. Computer software that organizes information into columns and rows and can perform calculations using the data. (p. 225)

Standard deduction. A stated amount that you may subtract from adjusted gross income instead of itemizing your deductions. (p. 183)

Statute of limitations. A legally defined time limit in which a lawsuit may be filed for various complaints. (p. 850)

Sticker price. The manufacturer's suggested retail price of a car, appearing on the car window. (p. 645)

Stock. A unit of ownership in a corporation. (p. 321)

Stock split. An increase in the number of outstanding shares of a company's stock. (p. 344)

Stockbroker. An employee of a brokerage firm, who buys and sells securities for investors. (p. 285)

Stockholders. Shareholders; owners of a corporation. (p. 331)

Stop payment order. A request that the bank not cash a specific check. (p. 256)

Strike. A job action whereby the members of a union refuse to work until an agreement is reached. (p. 162)

Subscriber. A business that pays a fee to a credit bureau and supplies information about its customer accounts. (p. 481)

Supply. The quantity of goods and services that producers are willing and able to manufacture. (p. 798)

Sympathetic listening. Technique of listening empathetically without offering advice. (p. 78)

T

Target market. A specific consumer group to which advertisements are directed. (p. 576)

Tax brackets. Income ranges on which tax rates apply. (p. 176)

Tax evasion. Willful failure to pay taxes. (p. 177)

Taxable income. The income on which you pay tax. (p. 183)

Technology. Improvements in work methods and equipment that increase productivity. (p. 3)

Tenant. One who rents property from a landlord. (p. 603)

Term life insurance. A life insurance policy that remains in effect for a specified period of time. (p. 771)

Thank-you letter. A follow-up tool used to remind the employer of your interest in the job, written after the job interview. (p. 69)

Title. A legal document that establishes ownership. (p. 631)

Transfer payments. Government grants to some citizens paid with money collected from other citizens. (p. 802)

Travel agency. A business that arranges transportation, accommodations, and itineraries for customers. (p. 679)

Trial court. The first court to hear a case or trial (a court of original jurisdiction). (p. 845)

Trust. A legal document in which an individual gives someone else control of property, for ultimate distribution to another person. (p. 416)

20/10 rule. Never borrow more each year than 20 percent of your yearly take-home pay, and never agree to monthly payments that are more than 10 percent of your monthly take-home pay. (p. 531)

U

Umbrella policy. Insurance that supplements basic auto and property liability coverage by expanding reimbursement limits and including some risks that were excluded in the basic coverage. (p. 747)

Unemployment insurance. Insurance that provides benefits to workers who lose their jobs through no fault of their own. (p. 113)

Uninsured/underinsured motorist coverage. Automobile insurance that pays for your injuries when the other driver is legally liable but unable to pay. (p. 746)

Unsecured debt. A loan that is not back by pledged assets. (p. 535)

Unused credit. The amount of credit above what you owe that you could charge, to a maximum amount. (p. 510)

Upgrading. Advancing to a higher level of skill. (p. 13)

Upholstery. Covering on seats, such as cloth, vinyl, or leather. (p. 659)

Upward communication. Communication that flows from lower to higher levels in an organization. (p. 83)

Usury laws. Laws setting maximum interest rates that lenders may charge. (p. 469)

V

Values. 1. The ideals in life that are important to you. (p. 26) 2. The principles by which a person lives. (p. 568)

Variable expenses. Expenses that change according to needs and short-term goals. (p. 211)

Vehicle emission test. A standard test required by large cities and urban areas to control pollution emitted from vehicles. (p. 645)

Vehicle identification number (VIN). A unique number that identifies an automobile. (p. 644)

Vested. Status of having worked long enough to have the right to at least a portion of the benefits you have accrued under an employer pension plan (within certain limits) even if you leave the employer before you retire. (p. 156)

Voluntary arbitration. When an independent third person listens to both sides in a dispute and makes a recommendation but cannot impose it. (p. 858)

Voluntary bankruptcy. A financial situation that occurs when a debtor files a petition with a federal court asking to be declared unable to meet his or her debts. (p. 536)

W

Warranty. A guarantee (usually written) from the manufacturer or distributor of a product that specifies the conditions under which the product can be returned, replaced, or repaired. (p. 223)

Wedding party. The active participants in a wedding ceremony—bride, groom, best man, maid of honor, and so on. (p. 674)

Will. A legal document that gives directions as to how the decedent wishes his or her property to pass upon death. (p. 412)

Work characteristics. Daily activities at work, such as indoor or outdoor work or working with people or alone. (p. 9)

Work history. A record of all jobs held and the length of time spent with each employer. (p. 38)

Workers' compensation. An insurance program that pays benefits to workers and their families for injury, illness, loss of income, or death that occurs as a result of a job or working conditions. (p. 114)

Z

Zero-coupon bond. A bond that is sold at a deep discount, makes no interest payments, and is redeemed for its face value at maturity. (p. 366)

Index